Over 4000 Films of Fear, Fright & Fantasy

THE **ANTHOLOGY** OF CINEMA: HORROR

SARAH M. MELLAND

Publisher: Ripe Melland Media
Miami, Florida, USA

ISBN: 978-1-969137-08-2

Table of Contents

History of Horror

Introduction

Horror has never been static. It is less a genre with fixed borders than a cultural shapeshifter: bending, mutating, and fusing itself with the anxieties of each age. From sacred myths carved into stone to today's prestige streaming releases, horror has survived because it adapts. Its monsters are not permanent; they are reflections, pressure valves, and warnings, whatever society most fears at the time. One century's vampire becomes another's serial killer, then another's alien parasite.

Rather than tracing horror decade by decade, this history follows its movements, because horror advances not in neat decades but in bursts of innovation, backlash, and re-invention. German Expressionism. Universal Monsters. Hammer Gothic. J-Horror. Torture porn. Social horror. Each movement carries echoes of the past while mutating into something new. The story of horror is the story of adaptation. How fear keeps rebranding itself.

Sacred Shadows: Ancient Myths and the Birth of Terror

Long before film, the roots of horror grew in oral traditions and sacred texts. Ancient myths teem with cannibal gods, vengeful spirits, and grotesque transformations. Egyptian hieroglyphics detail underworld monsters like Ammit devouring souls. Mesopotamian tablets spoke of Lilitu, a night demon who preyed on children. Greek tragedies stage madness, blood sacrifice and divine vengeance. These tales were both sacred ritual and cultural control: to terrify was to instruct. These stories reinforced moral order while giving shape to the chaos of death and the unknown.

In nearly every culture, horror first took the shape of myth. In Norse sagas, draugr rose from their graves to feast on the living, while the trickster Loki fathered monstrous children like the world-serpent Jörmungandr and the wolf Fenrir, destined to devour gods at Ragnarök. Celtic folklore imagined the banshee, whose wailing foretold death, and the dullahan, a headless rider carrying his skull under one arm. Aztec cosmology demanded rivers of blood to sustain the sun; deities like Huitzilopochtli and Tezcatlipoca thrived on sacrifice, their myths laced with decapitations and dismemberments. Mesoamerican tales also birthed the Camazotz, the bat-god of death, and the hungry tzitzimimeh, skeletal star demons who threatened to descend during eclipses.

In the ancient Near East, the Babylonian creation epic *Enuma Elish* describes Tiamat, a primordial sea-dragon carved apart by Marduk, her body split into the architecture of the world. Hebrew apocrypha warned of Lilith, the first

wife of Adam, cast out for rebellion and forever associated with infant mortality and sexual danger. In India's epics, rakshasas prowled as shape-shifting demons feeding on human flesh, while the goddess Kali wore a necklace of skulls and demanded blood to maintain cosmic order. Chinese ghost lore gave rise to the hungry ghosts, tormented spirits condemned by greed, and the jiangshi, hopping vampires that drained the life force from the living. Japanese tradition recorded oni (horned ogres), yurei (vengeful spirits of the wronged dead), and kuchisake-onna, the slit-mouthed woman who asks children if she is beautiful before cutting them to match.

From these myths came archetypes that never died: the vampire who feeds on innocence, the were-beast who loses control under cosmic cycles, the restless dead who return to punish the living. Horror's first texts were not novels but rituals and warnings, encoded in oral storytelling, hieroglyphics, runestones, and sacred drama. They reflected primal anxieties about famine, plague, childbirth, storms, and betrayal. To tell these stories was to try to master them. Horror, from the very beginning, was humanity's way of staring down death through imagination.

Medieval Horrors: Demons, Witches, and the Theatre of Damnation
(5th–15th centuries)

After the fall of Rome, horror was not merely entertainment, it was instruction. The medieval world was a place where life was short, disease was constant, and the boundary between natural and supernatural felt thin. Faith became the framework for terror, and the church wielded fear as both moral compass and social control.

Sacred terror

The Bible itself was filled with horrors: the Four Horsemen of the Apocalypse, rivers of blood, beasts with seven heads, and eternal torment in fire. Medieval preachers amplified these visions in sermons, painting graphic pictures of Hell to keep congregations obedient. The *Dies Irae* hymn warned of Judgment Day as a cosmic catastrophe where even kings would tremble. Fear of the afterlife was not metaphor but daily reality.

Demons and Witches

Bestiaries catalogued monstrous hybrids. Manticores, basilisks, cockatrices that blurred zoology with nightmare. Demonology texts described the torments awaiting sinners, and whispers of witchcraft crept into villages. By the late Middle Ages, fear of witches grew into obsession, setting the stage for centuries of persecution. The infamous *Malleus Maleficarum* (1487) would codify witch-hunting into a handbook of paranoia.

The Black Death

The plague (1347–1351) decimated Europe, killing nearly a third of the population. With rotting corpses in the streets

and entire villages erased, art and folklore absorbed the imagery of decay. The Danse Macabre (the Dance of Death) became a recurring motif in paintings, reminding rich and poor alike that no one escaped the grave. Skeletons, once abstract, now danced hand-in-hand with popes and peasants.

Theatre of Fear

Religious plays brought Hell to life before illiterate audiences. Mystery plays and morality plays staged demons dragging sinners into the pit, their costumes grotesque and terrifying. Pageant wagons rolled through towns with actors playing the damned, howling in flames. These early spectacles foreshadowed cinema's ability to shock through performance and illusion.

Global Echoes

Outside Europe, other cultures were staging their own horrors. In Japan, the Noh theatre (14th century onward) featured vengeful spirits and cursed masks. In Mesoamerica, rituals of sacrifice dramatized cosmic battles between gods and mortals. In the Islamic world, the *One Thousand and One Nights* wove stories of ghouls, jinn, and cursed places, embedding supernatural terror in popular imagination.

Archetypes Refined

From the medieval imagination came some of horror's most durable figures: the witch, the demon, the plague-bringer, the skeletal reaper. Horror was less about individual monsters than about cosmic punishment and collective fate. To terrify was still to instruct, but now it was also to control, to keep a world of chaos tethered to the promise of salvation.

By the Renaissance, terror began shifting from pulpit to page. As printing spread and humanism grew, horror stories no longer belonged only to the church. They became morality tales, cautionary legends, and finally Gothic novels. The next step in shaping horror's modern identity.

Sarah M. Melland

Renaissance Horrors: Witches, Tragedies, and the Stage of Blood
(15th–17th centuries)

As cultures evolved, horror shifted from oral myth to written page and staged performance. Medieval morality plays dramatized hellmouths and damnation, blending faith with fear. Renaissance tragedies spilled blood on stage to explore human ambition and madness. By the Enlightenment, horror became a literary experiment in psychology and science: a way of testing the limits of human imagination against the growing authority of reason.

Witchcraft and Paranoia

The witch became one of the central figures of Renaissance fear. Fueled by both superstition and institutional power, accusations of witchcraft swept across Europe. The publication of *Malleus Maleficarum* (1487) codified how to identify, interrogate, and punish supposed witches, blending theology with misogyny. Between the 15th and 17th centuries, tens of thousands of women were tried, tortured, and executed under the charge of consorting with the devil. Witches embodied anxieties about sexuality, fertility, and rebellion, and their persecution reflected the era's obsession with controlling both the natural and the female.

Salem and Transatlantic Echoes

While Europe was engulfed in centuries of witch hunts, the fear of sorcery crossed the Atlantic with the Puritans who settled in New England. In a society steeped in strict religious codes and obsessed with moral purity, whispers of witchcraft were magnified into collective hysteria.

The most infamous of these outbreaks was the Salem witch trials of 1692–1693 in Massachusetts. Sparked by the strange fits of several young girls, accusations spread rapidly through the community. Ordinary disputes over property, inheritance, and social standing were reframed as evidence of diabolic pacts. Nineteen people were executed by hanging, one man was pressed to death with stones, and over a hundred others were imprisoned on charges of witchcraft.

Salem was not an isolated event. Other New England towns: Hartford, Boston, and Stamford also held witchcraft trials, often echoing the patterns of accusation, confession, and execution that had already defined Europe's witch hunts. What made Salem uniquely chilling was the intensity of the collective panic in a small, tightly knit Puritan settlement, and the way its records preserved a blow-by-blow account of fear turning into judicial murder.

Comparing Old World and New World Witch Fears

- **Europe (15th–17th centuries):** The focus often rested on elaborate sabbats, nocturnal flights, shape-shifting, animal familiars, and orgiastic rites with the devil. Witches were imagined as part of a grand demonic conspiracy against Christendom. Trials in Germany, France, and Scotland frequently included confessions extracted under torture describing secret pacts, diabolic branding, or cannibalistic rituals.

- **New England (17th century):** The Puritans carried these beliefs but reframed them through their own social lens. Salem's anxieties centered less on mass sabbats and more on community breakdown. A bewitched neighbor represented not just a pact with the devil but a betrayal of the fragile social order. The New England witch was an intimate threat: a wife, mother, or servant who might undermine the household, the covenant, and the colony itself.

The legacy of Salem looms large in horror. The archetype of the New England witch: women gathering at night, consorting with the devil in the woods, signing dark books, and flying to sabbats became etched into cultural imagination. Later authors and filmmakers drew from this lore to create some of horror's most enduring symbols, from the chanting crones of *Macbeth* to the spectral presence of witches in films like *The Witch* (2015).

In Salem, the witch became more than a figure of folklore: she became a scapegoat, a way for a society under strain to externalize its fears. The trials illustrate how horror in history is not only told in stories but enacted in real life, with devastating consequences. They serve as both a cautionary tale about mass hysteria and a wellspring of imagery that horror continues to mine.

From the fires of European stakes to the gallows of Salem, witchcraft defined early modern horror as both spiritual terror and social paranoia. With the dawn of the 18th century, these fears would be reshaped into Gothic fiction. A new literary stage where witches, devils, and restless spirits stalked castles, crypts, and haunted landscapes.

Theatre of Tragedy and Revenge

As secular drama blossomed, the stage became a crucible for horror. Elizabethan and Jacobean playwrights drew blood across their boards:

- **William Shakespeare** conjured witches in *Macbeth* (1606), ghosts in *Hamlet* (1601), and psychological madness in *King Lear* (1606). His plays mingled supernatural dread with the frailties of ambition, guilt, and fate.
- *Christopher Marlowe's Doctor Faustus (1592)* dramatized the bargain with the devil, shaping the archetype of forbidden knowledge at terrible cost.
- **Revenge tragedies** such as Thomas Kyd's *The Spanish Tragedy* (1587) and John Webster's *The Duchess of Malfi* (1613) reveled in blood, poison, madness, and supernatural visitations, establishing a theatrical language of horror that echoed far beyond the playhouse.

This was horror not only as moral allegory but as entertainment, audiences cheered as kings went mad, lovers died, and ghosts rattled their chains.

Plague and Mortality

The specter of plague, which closed theatres and carved through cities, remained a cultural undertow. Death was omnipresent, and the Danse Macabre found new resonance in art, broadsheets, and ballads. The skeletal reaper became a universal emblem of fate, a figure that stalked both page and stage.

Printed Terror

The printing press, invented in the mid-15th century, gave horror a new medium. Chapbooks and pamphlets circulated lurid tales of murders, apparitions, and monstrous births. Ballads told of corpses walking from graves, demons tempting sinners, and signs of apocalypse. These stories were cheap, accessible, and ravenously consumed, transforming horror into popular culture.

Archetypes Refined

From the Renaissance, horror inherited the witch, the devil's bargain, the ghost of the restless dead, and the avenger driven to madness by blood and betrayal. These figures became fixtures not only of folklore but of literature, theatre, and eventually cinema.

By the 18th century, Gothic literature would channel these elements into sprawling castles, storm-lashed landscapes, and haunted minds. But it was the Renaissance that provided horror's dramatic stagecraft: witches chanting at cauldrons, ghosts demanding vengeance, scholars signing their souls away. The age of humanism still trembled at the supernatural, and that tension became the very fuel of modern horror.

The Gothic Eruption: Keystone Texts and Authors
(18th–19th centuries)

By the 18th century, horror escaped the pulpit and the scaffold, blooming into literature that fused medieval dread with Enlightenment anxieties. The Gothic imagination became a laboratory for fear: crumbling castles, ancestral curses, ghosts, forbidden desires, and monstrous creations. Horror here was not only about devils and witches but also about psychology, science, sexuality, and the fragility of empire. Gothic fiction created the scaffolding of modern horror, and the period produced a canon of texts and authors that defined its trajectory.

The Castle of Otranto (1764)

Horace Walpole's *The Castle of Otranto* is widely considered the first Gothic novel. Written as a "found manuscript," it introduced melodramatic doom, ancient curses, haunted castles, and supernatural apparitions. Walpole himself built a mock-Gothic mansion, Strawberry Hill, turning his fascination with medieval architecture into a literary aesthetic. The novel's success launched a wave of imitators and established the Gothic castle as the first true "haunted house" of literature.

Frankenstein and the Birth of Science Horror (1818)
Mary Shelley's *Frankenstein* fused Gothic atmosphere with modern anxieties about science. Written during the "Year Without a Summer" in 1816, when volcanic ash from Mount Tambora darkened European skies. Shelley's tale was born from a ghost-story contest at Lake Geneva, where she, Percy Bysshe Shelley, Lord Byron, and John Polidori challenged each other to write tales of terror. *Frankenstein* reflected Enlightenment tensions: the thrill of discovery versus the terror of overreach. Victor Frankenstein's stitched-together creature embodied fears of industrial progress, medical experimentation, and the cost of human hubris.

The Vampyre and the Aristocratic Predator (1819)
John Polidori's *The Vampyre*, published shortly after the same Geneva summer, crystallized the seductive undead. Unlike earlier folkloric vampires' grotesque, bloated, and rural, Polidori's vampire was aristocratic, elegant, and parasitic upon polite society. Modeled partly on Lord Byron, this new figure of charm and menace set the template for centuries of vampire fiction.

Carmilla and Forbidden Desire (1872)
Sheridan Le Fanu's *Carmilla* reimagined the vampire as feminine, sensual, and transgressive. The novella centered on an intimate relationship between two women, weaving eroticism into the supernatural. This fusion of sexuality and predation foreshadowed later queer readings of horror, while deepening the vampire mythos with themes of forbidden intimacy.

Dracula and the Empire in Decay (1897)
Bram Stoker's *Dracula* embodied the cultural anxieties of late Victorian England: fear of immigration, racial "contamination," female sexual independence, and disease. Count Dracula was an invader from the East, preying upon modern London, while Mina Harker's "New Woman" qualities made her both a threat and a savior. Written during a time of imperial uncertainty, *Dracula* gave horror a new monster for the modern age. A shape-shifter as much about politics and sexuality as blood.

Edgar Allan Poe and the Haunted Mind
Across the Atlantic, Edgar Allan Poe redefined horror as psychological descent. Tales like *The Tell-Tale Heart* (1843), *The Pit and the Pendulum* (1842), and *The Fall of the House of Usher* (1839) showed that the most terrifying monsters lived within the mind. Poe stripped horror of Gothic castles and placed it in chambers of paranoia, obsession, and decay. His claustrophobic settings, unreliable narrators, and fascination with premature burial gave American Gothic a uniquely inward turn that cinema later absorbed wholesale.

Penny Dreadfuls and the Democratization of Horror
While elite readers consumed Gothic novels, the working classes devoured cheap serialized tales. *Varney the Vampire* (1845–47), published as a penny dreadful, stretched to over a thousand pages of melodramatic horror, establishing tropes like fangs, nocturnal feeding, and the sympathetic monster. These lurid tales were considered lowbrow but expanded horror's audience dramatically, proving that fear sold across classes.

H. P. Lovecraft and Cosmic Dread
At the close of the 19th century, H. P. Lovecraft began laying the foundations of cosmic horror. Though his major works came in the early 20th century, Lovecraft drew upon the Gothic tradition of the unknown and enlarged it into a philosophy of insignificance before an uncaring universe. His vision of vast, indifferent powers dwarfed humanity, shifting horror away from castles and ghosts toward cosmic nihilism.

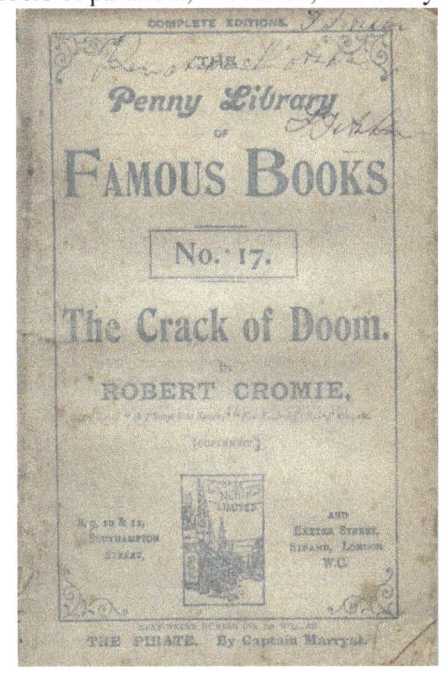

The Grand-Guignol (1897–1962): Horror as Spectacle

In Paris, the Grand-Guignol theatre specialized in graphic mutilations, staged executions, and gruesome realism. Actors used pig's blood, hidden bladders of stage gore, and sleight of hand to shock audiences. So visceral were its performances that doctors were hired to treat fainting spectators. The Grand-Guignol foreshadowed splatter cinema, turning horror into a bodily experience that blurred the line between shock and entertainment.

Catalysts and Gatekeepers

The printing press multiplied Gothic texts; circulating libraries spread them across Europe. Penny dreadfuls ensured horror's accessibility to the masses. Theatres provided communal immersion in supernatural dread, from Shakespeare's ghosts to Grand-Guignol bloodletting.

The Backlash

Critics condemned Gothic novels as immoral, indulgent, and sensational. The church attacked both Gothic literature and the Grand-Guignol as sinful spectacle. Yet scandal only drove sales and ticket lines higher. As in earlier eras, attempts to suppress horror only confirmed its power.

Craft Innovations

By the 19th century, horror had codified its symbols: haunted castles, labyrinthine corridors, storms, masks, forbidden manuscripts, damsels in peril, and villains torn between desire and damnation. These became the toolkit cinema would inherit.

By the time film technology emerged in the late 19th century, horror was already embedded in cultural DNA. From Walpole's castle to Shelley's laboratory, from Poe's chambers of madness to Stoker's vampire, the genre had prepared its stage. All that remained was for moving images to capture shadows and in Germany's Expressionist cinema, those shadows would finally move.

Silent Horrors & German Expressionism: Shadows That Learned to Move
(1900s–1920s)

By the dawn of the 20th century, horror had shifted from page and stage to the flickering screen. Early filmmakers, many of them magicians and illusionists, quickly realized that cinema was uniquely suited to conjuring ghosts, monsters, and nightmares. What literature described, film could now show. In the silence of darkened theaters, horror became both communal and hypnotic, a dream projected larger than life.

Early Cinematic Trickery

Georges Méliès, a stage magician, pioneered horror's first film illusions. Works like *The Haunted Castle* (1896) featured skeletons, devils, and disappearing phantoms through stop-motion and substitution cuts. Méliès treated cinema as a magic lantern of fear. playful but unsettling, turning the supernatural into spectacle. Across Europe and the United States, short films featuring ghosts, witches, and monsters flourished, often screened as novelties alongside travelogues and newsreels.

Expressionism and the War-Scarred Psyche

The horrors of World War I reshaped cinema. In Germany, filmmakers turned trauma into architecture. Expressionism warped sets into jagged lines, painted shadows onto walls, and bent perspective until the world itself looked insane. Horror here became the language of dread: a visual shorthand for instability, paranoia, and loss of control.

- *The Cabinet of Dr. Caligari* (1920) stands as the purest manifesto of Expressionism. Its twisted sets and unnatural shadows turned the screen into a psychological landscape. Caligari's story, a hypnotist commanding a somnambulist to kill, dramatized fears of authoritarian power and the fragility of free will. Audiences saw their postwar anxieties painted into every crooked frame.
- *Nosferatu* (1922), F. W. Murnau's unauthorized Dracula adaptation, gave horror its first great monster. Count Orlok was not just a vampire but a plague-bearer, his shadow stretching across walls like a disease of the mind. The film taught horror how to use shadow itself as character, a presence more terrifying than the creature it belonged to.

Together, these films showed that horror did not need dialogue. Shadows could think. Angles could lie. The set itself could go mad. Expressionism proved that horror was not simply about monsters on the screen, but about rendering the psychology of fear visible.

American Silent Horror
Meanwhile in Hollywood, Universal Studios began experimenting with Gothic archetypes. Lon Chaney, "The Man of a Thousand Faces," brought deformity and pathos to horror roles in *The Hunchback of Notre Dame* (1923) and *The Phantom of the Opera* (1925). His grotesque self-applied makeup, bulging eyes, distorted spines, gaping mouths, turned disability and disfigurement into icons of terror, while also humanizing the monster as tragic outsider.

Themes and Anxieties
Silent horror reflected its era's unease:
- Fear of authoritarian control (*Caligari*).
- Fear of disease and decay (*Nosferatu*).
- Fear of fractured identities and unstable psyches (*The Student of Prague*).
- Fear of the outsider, whether immigrant, monster, or disfigured figure (*Phantom of the Opera*).

These films made horror political and personal at once, using shadows and silence to mirror inner states of fear.

Craft Innovations
Expressionist horror introduced enduring cinematic techniques: extreme chiaroscuro lighting, exaggerated sets, subjective camerawork, and monsters framed as metaphors. The silent era proved that horror could be both visual poetry and social commentary.

The Backlash
Some critics dismissed horror films as vulgar or unhealthy for audiences, echoing the earlier disdain for Gothic novels and Grand-Guignol theatre. But international audiences flocked to them, and distributors quickly realized that fear traveled across borders better than almost any other emotion.

de Zurich, où Tzara animait les revues *Cabaret Voltaire* et *Dada* avant de venir

Un personnage typique du romantisme allemand : *L'étudiant de Prague (1926)*

14

Other Silent Landmarks
German Expressionism was the movement's beating heart, but other films broadened horror's reach:
- *The Phantom Carriage* (1921, Sweden) pioneered ghostly double exposures, staging Death himself as a spectral driver of a wagon collecting souls. It fused supernatural imagery with a moral warning, showing cinema's ability to blend allegory with dread.
- *The Golem: How He Came into the World* (1920, Germany) drew from Jewish folklore, telling of a clay protector brought to life by mysticism. It rooted horror in cultural myth and gave the genre one of its first monsters born from legend rather than literature.
- *The Hunchback of Notre Dame* (1923, U.S.) merged Gothic spectacle with tragic melodrama. Lon Chaney's grotesque makeup humanized deformity, casting the monster as both terrifying and sympathetic, a blueprint for Universal's future.

The Grammar of Fear
The Silent and Expressionist era codified horror's cinematic toolkit: shadows as menace, architecture as psychology, monsters as allegory. Every horror film that followed owes a debt to these silent phantoms.

By the late 1920s, horror had found its voice, literally. The coming of sound would add screams, whispers, and atmospheric scores to its arsenal. German Expressionism's distorted sets and American Gothic melodrama laid the foundation for the Universal monsters of the 1930s, where Dracula, Frankenstein, and the Wolf Man would become household names.

Classic Studio Horror: Monsters and Shadows
(1930s–1940s)

Synchronized sound transformed horror into full-bodied spectacle. The hiss of Dracula's accent, the clank of Frankenstein's lab, and the growl of the Wolf Man made terror audible. The 1930s gave rise to the Universal monster cycle, while the 1940s shifted toward psychological subtlety under Val Lewton at RKO. Between them, horror gained its first international icons and its first master of suggestion.

Horror moved from experimental trickery and shadowplay to codified franchises. Universal built a pantheon of monsters that became shorthand for the genre itself, while Lewton's RKO unit proved that silence, implication, and atmosphere could terrify as much as makeup and sets.

Universal Monsters: Gods and Monsters
Universal Pictures released a string of Gothic horrors that cemented the visual and thematic lexicon of the genre.
- *Dracula* (1931, Tod Browning) turned Bela Lugosi's aristocratic vampire into cinema's first Gothic icon. His measured cadence, Hungarian accent, and hypnotic stare were amplified by sound, making the vampire both exotic and terrifying.
- *Frankenstein* (1931, James Whale) gave the world Boris Karloff's tragic Monster, stitched together and misunderstood. Its lightning-charged lab became the definitive image of science unbound.
- *Bride of Frankenstein* (1935, Whale) pushed the Gothic into operatic excess: a mix of satire, camp, and blasphemy that scandalized the Church but elevated the Monster into a figure of pathos.
- *The Mummy* (1932, Karl Freund) reflected colonial anxieties, turning archaeology into a curse of the ancient world.
- *The Invisible Man* (1933, Whale) married science-fiction with horror, pioneering effects while dramatizing the madness of unchecked power.
- *The Wolf Man* (1941, George Waggner) gave modern shape to the werewolf myth, binding lycanthropy to fate, family, and inner rage.

Sequels like *Son of Frankenstein* (1939), *Dracula's Daughter* (1936), and crossover spectacles like *House of Dracula* (1945) built an interconnected "monster universe" decades before Marvel.

These films thrived partly because they were made before the Production Code crackdown of 1934. Censorship was looser, and directors smuggled in sexuality, violence, and subtext. *Dracula's Daughter* openly hinted at lesbian desire; *Bride of Frankenstein* was condemned for its mocking treatment of God. Universal's monsters embodied the Other in Depression-era America: anxieties about immigration, science without morality, and a world trembling at cultural change.

Other Currents: Kong and the First Global Shadows
While Universal dominated the Gothic screen, other traditions were quietly reshaping horror's future. In 1933, RKO released *King Kong*, a spectacle of stop-motion and sound that merged horror with adventure. Kong was not Gothic but mythic. A beast torn from his island and made spectacle in New York. Audiences gasped at the monster's size and realism, but beneath the thrills lay deeper anxieties: colonial conquest, technological hubris, and the fragility of civilization before nature's revenge. Kong showed that horror could be grand, spectacular, and commercially massive. A prototype for the creature features and disaster films to come.

Across the Pacific, Japan began adapting its own folkloric traditions to film. Kaidan: ghost stories drawn from kabuki theatre and Edo-period legends reached screens in works like *Ghost of Yotsuya* (1912, remade 1937). These tales of betrayal, vengeance, and cursed spirits mirrored Western Gothic in function, but not in form: their terrors were rooted in domestic tragedy, honor, and the supernatural's grip on everyday life. Films like Teinosuke Kinugasa's *A Page of Madness* (1926) further showed how psychological horror and experimental style could thrive outside Europe.

These parallel strands Kong's spectacle and Japan's spectral folklore remind us that by the 1930s horror was no longer confined to one cultural tradition. The seeds of a global genre were being planted, even if they would not fully bloom until after the war.

Body Horror Roots
Not all early 1930s horror was cloaked in Gothic capes and castles. Films like *Doctor X* (1932) and *Mystery of the Wax Museum* (1933) flirted with body horror before the term existed. Cannibalism, grisly medical experiments, and grotesque bodily transformation lurked beneath the surface. Though tame by modern standards, these films seeded an obsession with mutilated flesh and invasive science that would later explode in everything from *The Fly* (1958) to Cronenberg's cinema of the 1980s.

The Mad Scientist

If Dracula embodied foreign menace and the Wolf Man the beast within, the 1930s also gave rise to another enduring archetype: the mad scientist. These stories explored the perils of unchecked knowledge, where the laboratory replaced the haunted castle and the scalpel became as terrifying as the stake.

The trope reflected deep cultural unease about modernity. As technology accelerated in the interwar years: electricity, medicine, psychology, the figure of the scientist shifted from savior to transgressor. He was brilliant, arrogant, and willing to abandon ethics in the pursuit of discovery, unleashing horrors he could not control. Subcategories emerged early:

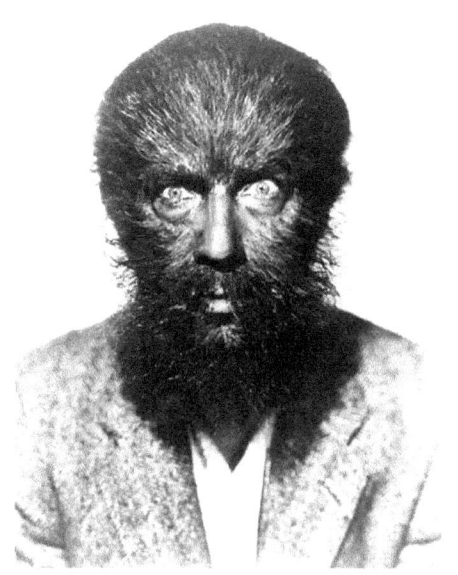

- **Creation-focused.** *Frankenstein* (1931) and *Bride of Frankenstein* (1935) set the template, where terror stemmed from the unnatural act of making life.
- **Obsession-focused.** In *The Invisible Man* (1933), the scientist himself was the danger, driven mad by his own formula. *Island of Lost Souls* (1932) showed Charles Laughton's Dr. Moreau remaking animals into humans, with his cruelty as frightening as his creations.
- **Mind-altering.** *Dr. Jekyll and Mr. Hyde* (1931) dramatized psychological transformation, turning scientific ambition inward into a metaphor for duality and repression.
- **Body horror precursors.** Films like *Doctor X* (1932) hinted at grotesque experimentation and mutilation, seeding later splatterpunk visions where science and gore entwined.

Though later decades would push the archetype into mutation, cybernetics, and splatterpunk extremes, the 1930s gave horror one of its most durable templates. The mad scientist was not just a villain, he was society's reflection of its own anxieties about progress, a reminder that the quest for knowledge could birth monsters more terrible than any myth.

Societal Transgression

From its earliest sound era, horror thrived on breaking social taboos. Where other genres affirmed morality or romance, horror made spectacle of what society repressed. Depravity, perversion, cannibalism, blasphemy, forbidden sexuality, these were not accidental flourishes but central provocations. Films like *Murders in the Rue Morgue* (1932) staged sadistic experiments; *Doctor X* (1932) reveled in grisly body modification; and *Dracula's Daughter* (1936) dared to suggest lesbian desire at a time when it was unspeakable.

These transgressions mattered because horror was never just entertainment. It was a pressure valve. By staging the forbidden: murder without remorse, science without conscience, sex without sanction, the genre exposed the cultural nerves society most wanted to keep hidden. And precisely because these subjects provoked scandal, horror drew crowds. Outrage was free advertising.

When the Production Code enforced morality, much of this explicitness had to retreat underground, transmuted into implication or metaphor. Yet the instinct remained. Horror has always carried society's repressed content, dragging it into the light whether through monsters, mad scientists, or suggestive shadows. In this sense, horror is not only about what terrifies, it is about what society forbids itself to admit.

The Production Code and Horror's Restraint

In 1934, Hollywood came under the strict enforcement of the Motion Picture Production Code, commonly called the Hays Code after Will H. Hays, the industry's chief censor. The Code had existed since 1930 but went largely unenforced during the early sound era. By mid-decade, however, pressure from church groups, state censors, and moral watchdogs forced studios to comply or risk boycotts and government regulation. The Code dictated what could and could not be shown on screen:

- Explicit sexuality, "perversion" (a catchall term that included queerness), and nudity were forbidden.
- Blasphemy, ridicule of religion, and sympathetic portrayals of the devil or witchcraft were restricted.
- Excessive violence, gore, and gruesome detail were prohibited.
- "Sympathy for crime" or stories where criminals went unpunished were banned.

For horror, this was a seismic shift. The early 1930s had thrived in what's now called the Pre-Code Era, when films like *Dracula's Daughter* (1936) could include lesbian undertones, and *Frankenstein* could openly challenge God. After enforcement began, those transgressions had to be implied rather than shown.

Filmmakers responded with creativity. James Whale leaned into camp and innuendo, smuggling subtext past censors. Val Lewton turned repression into a style, proving that shadows and suggestion could carry more dread than spectacle. The Code thus inadvertently pushed horror inward: monsters became metaphors, threats became whispers, and imagination filled the spaces that censorship left blank.

The Code lasted into the 1960s, and while it restrained explicitness, it also forced innovation. Horror would never again be just about what was on screen, it became equally about what audiences *thought* they saw.

Urban Paranoia, Noir Shadows and Val Newton

By the 1940s, Gothic spectacle had begun to feel excessive, and budgets shrank during wartime Enter Val Lewton, a literary producer at RKO, who redefined horror with psychological subtlety. Working with directors Jacques Tourneur, Robert Wise, and Mark Robson, he used shadows, silence, implication as weapons and repressed desire.

Cat People (1942) suggested its Serbian heroine might transform into a panther when aroused but showed almost nothing, relying on atmosphere and psychology. It turned an urban swimming pool into a site of terror, proving that horror could thrive in the ordinary spaces of city life. The monster was no longer a medieval relic or an exotic invader. It might be your lover, your coworker, your neighbor.

This psychological unease blurred into the aesthetics of film noir. The same years that gave us shadowy thrillers of crime and corruption also birthed horrors of repression and paranoia. In Lewton's cycle, the chiaroscuro lighting, alienated characters, and modern settings made horror and noir indistinguishable cousins. The genre was learning that the human psyche itself fractured, repressed, haunted by desire was as frightening as any stitched-together corpse.

I Walked with a Zombie (1943) reimagined *Jane Eyre* in the Caribbean, merging Gothic dread with colonial unease and voodoo ritual. *The Body Snatcher* (1945) dramatized grave robbing and medical ethics, with Karloff in one of his most chilling late-career roles.

Universal's makeup artist Jack Pierce gave faces to monsters; Whale gave them wit and irony. Sound technology itself was catalyst enough, transforming the experience of horror. The Production Code, enforced after 1934, forced a pivot from spectacle to implication. Lewton's tiny budgets at RKO paradoxically gave him freedom, allowing experimentation with mood and ambiguity.

Lewton's team innovated under censorship. Forbidden from showing gore or overt sexuality, they cultivated suggestion as terror. Lewton's method became legendary: "Lewton Bus" a sudden hiss of brakes interrupting silence in *Cat People* created the modern jump scare and remains a staple of horror craft today. His films gave horror a grammar of repression and imagination. They also illustrate how censorship forced creative innovation: when the Production Code forbade explicit sex or gore, suggestion became more frightening than spectacle.

Horror in Wartime: Silence, Shadows, and Restraint

The 1940s produced fewer horror films than the decades before and after, and the absence is telling. With the world at war, horror moved from screens to headlines. Real atrocities outstripped the Gothic imagination: concentration camps, blitzed cities, atomic fire. What horror could risk staging these terrors without seeming grotesque or disrespectful?

Studios turned their resources toward propaganda, musicals, and patriotic dramas. Horror was sidelined, not banned, but considered a luxury in a time of rationed film stock and war-bond drives. When it did appear, it often wore disguises: mysteries, thrillers, or psychological dramas with a spectral undertone. Val Lewton's cycle thrived in this climate precisely because it whispered rather than screamed.

There was also fear of repercussion. Monsters on screen risked offending when real soldiers were dying abroad. Too much darkness, too much violence, could be seen as unpatriotic or exploitative. The Production Code doubled this restraint, forcing filmmakers to veil sexuality, cruelty, and blasphemy. Thus, the war years became a period of shadows and suggestion, where horror survived in implication.

But silence is not absence. The restraint of the 1940s gave horror a new discipline. It proved that the genre did not need castles and capes to survive. It could adapt, hiding in shadows, waiting for the right moment to roar again. And when peace came, the world's nightmares had changed: radiation, paranoia, invasion. Horror was about to leave Europe's Gothic past behind and step into the atomic future.

Colonial Zombies: The Undead Before Romero

Long before George Romero redefined the zombie as a flesh-eating ghoul, the undead walked a different path on screen. In the 1930s and 40s, "zombie" meant not a cannibalistic corpse but a body robbed of will, animated through ritual and control.

White Zombie (1932), starring Bela Lugosi, was the first feature-length zombie film. Set in Haiti, it portrayed zombification as the theft of autonomy. Workers turned into mindless husks under a colonial overseer's command. The imagery drew directly from Western fears of voodoo and cultural otherness, playing into racist fantasies of exotic danger.

A decade later, Val Lewton's *I Walked with a Zombie* (1943) deepened the motif with atmosphere and ambiguity. Transplanting *Jane Eyre* into the Caribbean, it merged Gothic romance with voodoo ritual, using zombies as symbols of colonial exploitation and cultural repression. Lewton's film hinted that horror could be not just about monsters, but about history, politics, and the violence of empire.

These early zombies were not apocalyptic cannibals but colonized bodies. Metaphors for enslavement, control, and the fear of losing one's will. They planted a seed the genre would not fully reap until Romero's *Night of the Living Dead* (1968), when the zombie would shift from a colonial puppet to a global plague.

Psychological and Anthology Horror

The 1940s may have been a quieter decade for horror, but innovation persisted in unexpected corners. In Britain, *Dead of Night* (1945) pioneered the anthology format, weaving several uncanny tales together with a wraparound narrative. The most famous segment the ventriloquist's dummy that seems to possess a will of its own explored the uncanny valley of puppetry, doubling as a metaphor for fractured identity.

What distinguished *Dead of Night* was its turn inward. Where Universal relied on Gothic monsters and Lewton thrived in shadows, this film rooted horror in psychological dread: déjà vu, dream logic, and the sense that reality itself could splinter. Its influence would echo decades later in Amicus's anthology films, television shows like *The Twilight Zone*, and countless explorations of uncanny objects.

The Backlash

Catholic condemnation of *Bride of Frankenstein* for blasphemy, censor battles over queer subtext in *Dracula's Daughter*, and critics who dismissed Lewton's films as too quiet all show the genre under pressure. Yet backlash only expanded horror's cultural visibility.

Craft Innovations

Universal codified the *look* of Gothic horror: fog, castles, laboratories, stitched monsters, and exotic curses. Lewton codified its *subconscious grammar*: silences, shadows, suggestion, and the art of absence. Together, Universal and Lewton created two poles of classic horror: the baroque spectacle of monsters and the whispered dread of suggestion.

By the end of the 1940s, monsters had grown familiar enough to appear in comedy crossovers, while Lewton's whispered terrors pointed to psychological horror. Horror was poised to mutate again. With the atomic bomb and Cold War paranoia reshaping global fear, the monsters of the Gothic past would soon give way to the irradiated creatures and alien invaders of the Atomic Age.

Atomic Age & Paranoia Horror and the Global Gothic Revival
(1950s)

If Universal's monsters embodied Depression-era fears and Lewton's shadows whispered through wartime restraint, the 1950s confronted something far more immediate: the mushroom cloud. The detonation of nuclear bombs and the chill of the Cold War reshaped horror's imagination, shifting it from Gothic castles to deserts, laboratories, and suburban streets.

This was the decade when science itself became the new boogeyman. Radiation birthed colossal ants and spiders. Mutation blurred the line between human and beast. UFOs hovered above small towns, suggesting enemies could descend from the stars or already be among us. Films no longer asked audiences to fear vampires at their windows; they asked them to fear the skies, the soil, and their own government experiments.

Horror in the Atomic Age spoke in allegories of invasion, contamination, and annihilation. It reflected the unease of a world that had split the atom and seen the consequences, imagining futures where humanity's hubris or paranoia could erase civilization overnight.

Atomic Age & Paranoia Horror: Science as Boogeyman

The atomic bomb split not only atoms but also the imagination. The mushroom cloud became horror's new castle tower. In America and Japan alike, films wrestled with technology's fallout.

- *Them!* (1954, USA) unleashed irradiated ants across New Mexico, embodying fears of nuclear testing and unstoppable mutation.
- *Godzilla* (1954, Japan, Ishirō Honda) made the atomic metaphor explicit. Born of Hiroshima and Nagasaki's trauma, the monster was both dragon and mushroom cloud, a walking allegory of nuclear devastation.
- Alien invasion films like *Invasion of the Body Snatchers* (1956, USA) translated Cold War paranoia into metaphors of conformity, subversion, and loss of individuality.
- Creatures such as *The Blob* (1958, USA) and *The Fly* (1958, USA) fused adolescent fears of sex and contagion with the terrors of scientific experimentation.

In the 1950s, horror was less about ghosts than about modernity itself. Laboratories, deserts, and outer space replaced castles and graveyards. Science, once the promise of progress, became the source of dread.

Kaiju: Monsters Born of the Bomb

If the Gothic monster haunted castles and the Universal monster haunted laboratories, the Kaiju haunted the modern cityscape. In Japan, where the scars of Hiroshima and Nagasaki were fresh, horror took the shape of colossal "strange beasts" — kaiju — embodiments of nuclear trauma and nature's revenge.

The original *Godzilla* (1954, Ishirō Honda) emerged directly from atomic catastrophe. Awakened and mutated by nuclear testing, Godzilla was both monster and metaphor: a dragon-shaped mushroom cloud lumbering through Tokyo, unstoppable and indifferent. The film combined spectacle with grief, embedding horror in images of flattened cities, weeping mothers, and radiation-burned victims. Godzilla was not merely a creature feature; it was a national exorcism.

As the franchise continued, kaiju evolved from destroyers into protectors. Later Godzilla films, along with Mothra and Rodan, reframed the monsters as guardians of Earth against alien invaders and even more monstrous foes. The horror was diluted into fantasy adventure, but the subgenre still carried its roots: the idea that humanity's fate could hinge on forces far larger than itself.

In America, the kaiju idea morphed into pulpier forms. Films like *Them!* (1954), with its irradiated ants, or *Tarantula!* (1955), played atomic mutation for both terror and camp. Where Japanese kaiju conveyed trauma and national mourning, American giant-monster films often leaned into drive-in thrills, embodying Cold War anxieties with a more sensational gloss.

The kaiju concept has remained fertile ground for reinvention. *Cloverfield* (2008) reintroduced the giant monster through shaky found-footage immediacy, blending apocalypse with post-9/11 paranoia. *Shin Godzilla* (2016) returned to the original's allegorical power, turning Godzilla into a commentary on bureaucratic paralysis and disaster mismanagement in the wake of Fukushima.

Kaiju films carved out horror's most primal scale: fear not of fangs or shadows, but of enormity itself. They reflected the terror of a small humanity crushed beneath indifferent, catastrophic forces of its own making. While later installments blurred into action or camp, the subgenre's roots remain steeped in horror: the spectacle of devastation as metaphor for survival in an atomic world.

Alien Invasion & Paranoia Horror: The Enemy Among Us

If kaiju embodied humanity's terror before the bomb, alien invasion films dramatized Cold War paranoia. In the atomic age, the menace didn't always tower above cities sometimes it slipped quietly into them, indistinguishable from ordinary neighbors. Horror turned its gaze toward infiltration, mind control, and the fear of becoming something unrecognizable.

Invasion of the Body Snatchers (1956, Don Siegel) became the quintessential paranoia film. In a small California town, humans are replaced by emotionless duplicates grown in alien pods. To mid-century audiences, the metaphor was obvious: fears of communist infiltration, suburban conformity, or even the crushing blandness of postwar consumer culture. The film's horror lay not in spectacle but in recognition that one's spouse, child, or co-worker might look the same but no longer be human.

The Thing from Another World (1951) and *Invaders from Mars* (1953) imagined hostile extraterrestrials as metaphors for outside ideologies or foreign powers. Their timing coincided with McCarthyism, HUAC hearings, and the growing obsession with hidden enemies. Horror merged with propaganda, urging vigilance against what might lurk beyond (or within) the national border.

Not all invasion horror was solemn. *The Blob* (1958) wrapped paranoia in teen melodrama, with a gelatinous monster consuming a small town as local authorities refused to believe the youth who warned them. Beneath the pulpiness, it reflected a generational divide: adults complacent in authority, youth alert to the shapeless dread of the future.

Invasion and paranoia horror taught the genre how to weaponize suspicion. Unlike Gothic castles or laboratory sparks, these films set terror in suburban streets and small-town diners. The monster wasn't only "out there," it might already be sitting across the table. In a decade when ideological fear was omnipresent, horror mirrored the anxiety that the real enemy was not a giant beast but the familiar face gone suddenly strange.

Science-Horror & Mutation: The Laboratory Unleashed

If the Gothic warned against forbidden knowledge in candlelit towers, the atomic age reimagined the laboratory as the new haunted castle. Science-horror and mutation films turned microscopes and test tubes into instruments of dread, reflecting anxieties that unchecked experimentation might spawn monstrosities more terrifying than any myth.

The Fly (1958, Kurt Neumann) epitomized the era's fascination with hybrid horror. A brilliant scientist testing matter-transmission devices accidentally merges with a housefly, producing a grotesque hybrid of part man, part insect. The horror lay not only in the grotesque reveal of his insect head but in the tragedy of his slow disintegration, a metaphor for science's promise unraveling into nightmare.

American drive-in staples like *Tarantula!* (1955) and *Attack of the 50 Foot Woman* (1958) played radiation as mutation. Creatures grew enormous, humans transformed into giants, and scale itself became horror's weapon. These films fused pulp spectacle with genuine unease, dramatizing the fear that atomic testing might unleash mutations on an unimaginable scale.

Creature from the Black Lagoon (1954) offered a different twist: a prehistoric monster discovered during a scientific expedition in the Amazon. Both alluring and dangerous, the Gill-Man blurred the line between discovery and desecration. The film echoed anxieties about colonial intrusion, sexual predation, and the cost of penetrating nature's last mysteries.

Science-horror and mutation stories continued the lineage of the mad scientist but amplified it with atomic dread. Where Frankenstein's hubris created one monster, the atomic laboratory threatened to create legions. In these films, the line between progress and peril blurred: every new experiment carried the potential for catastrophe. Science was no longer savior, it was the new boogeyman, promising miracles and delivering abominations.

Eco-Horror: Nature's Revenge Begins

The atomic age didn't only birth giant monsters and cosmic dread, it also planted the seeds of eco-horror, where humanity's own interference with nature unleashed the terror. If science could awaken prehistoric beasts, it could also warp the natural order, turning the earth itself against us.

In *Them!* (1954), nuclear testing spawns ants the size of tanks, swarming across the desert and threatening civilization. The horror wasn't just the ants' size, it was the suggestion that nature, once disturbed, would respond with unimaginable force. *Tarantula!* (1955) pushed the idea further, with a giant spider born of experiments in growth serums, symbolizing both ecological imbalance and the arrogance of scientists who thought they could control life itself.

Unlike Gothic castles or alien pods, eco-horror grounded its fears in the environment audiences knew. The implication was chilling: human progress — bombs, pesticides, radiation — might trigger retaliation from the very world that sustained us. This "first wave" of eco-horror framed nature not as victim but as avenger, a theme that would resurface with even greater urgency in the 1970s as anxieties about pollution, overpopulation, and extinction grew.

Cosmic Horror: The Universe Indifferent

While giant monsters and atomic mutants ruled theaters, another, quieter strand of horror began to gestate in the 1950s, one less about spectacle and more about philosophy. Cosmic horror, inspired by H. P. Lovecraft's Cthulhu Mythos, suggested that the greatest terror was not claws or fangs but the revelation of our own insignificance. Humanity, these stories insisted, was fragile, ignorant, and irrelevant in a universe ruled by incomprehensible forces.

Lovecraft's "Great Old Ones" beings like Cthulhu or Yog-Sothoth embodied the idea that simply perceiving them could drive mortals insane. Films rarely attempted to visualize such entities directly, but the imagery of unfathomable creatures slumbering beneath oceans or stars influenced 1950s cinema deeply. The "thing in the ice" of

The Thing from Another World (1951) or the alien gods of pulp magazines carried his fingerprints.

Equally central was the trope of knowledge as poison. Ancient tomes, hidden scrolls, or unspeakable secrets could unravel sanity. Though films like *Quatermass and the Pit* (1958, UK, aka *Five Million Years to Earth*) came later, their DNA was Lovecraftian: archaeology revealing truths too great for human minds. The horror was not in the monster itself, but in the realization of what it meant for humanity's place in the cosmos.

Where others feared, some worshipped. Lovecraftian cults embodied the terror of people willingly embracing annihilation. In cinema, paranoid whispers of secret sects echo this theme, merging Cold War fears of infiltration with occult devotion. Horror shifted from monsters outside the gates to the possibility that our neighbors might already be in thrall to unspeakable gods.

Unlike kaiju or invasion films, cosmic horror rarely framed the apocalypse as battle. Instead, it was incidental: the awakening of something vast and indifferent. If Godzilla was Japan's mushroom cloud given form, cosmic horror asked what would happen if that mushroom cloud was just one idle gesture of a universe that did not even notice us.

Cosmic horror in the 1950s was not yet mainstream cinema, but its philosophy seeped into creature features, alien thrillers, and pulp science fiction. It expanded horror beyond the laboratory and battlefield into existential dread. The ultimate terror was not death at the hands of a monster, it was the revelation that life itself meant nothing against the indifferent void.

Post-Apocalyptic & Survival Horror: Imagining the End

By the end of the 1950s, horror began looking beyond the single monster or isolated invasion to something larger. The destruction of civilization itself. If kaiju embodied the bomb's immediate devastation, post-apocalyptic stories imagined what came after: a world of silence, radiation, and survival in the ruins.

On the Beach (1959, Stanley Kramer), though often classified as drama, carried horror's DNA. It depicted a world awaiting inevitable death from spreading radioactive fallout, with survivors in Australia facing extinction as calmly as possible. Its quiet tone made it more chilling than many creature features: horror not of monsters but of inevitability, a future poisoned by human hands.

Other films flirted with survivalist horror, imagining what humanity might become when systems failed. *Five* (1951) told of a handful of survivors after nuclear war, wrestling not only with hunger and exposure but with mistrust and prejudice. Horror here was social as much as environmental: the collapse of order revealing how fragile civilization truly was.

These early works planted the ideas that would bloom in the 1960s and 70s with films like *Planet of the Apes* (1968) and Romero's *Night of the Living Dead* (1968). They suggested that horror need not confine itself to a haunted house or one rampaging monster. The genre could engulf the entire planet, asking audiences to consider what it meant to live or die in the shadow of extinction.

Post-apocalyptic horror expanded the scale of fear. Instead of dramatizing one creature or one lab accident, it imagined a landscape where all of humanity could vanish. It forced audiences to confront the unthinkable: not just death, but the erasure of the species. In the Atomic Age, this was no fantasy. It was the logical conclusion of the mushroom cloud.

Catalysts and Gatekeepers

The atomic bomb was the ultimate catalyst, reshaping horror's scale and subject matter. In Japan, Godzilla embodied Hiroshima and Nagasaki's trauma, while in America the Cold War and McCarthyism fueled paranoia about infiltration and loss of individuality. Drive-in culture and cheap production also played a role: giant-monster films and alien thrillers could be made quickly and marketed easily to teen audiences.

Television and pulp magazines helped spread these stories, while distribution networks carried Godzilla across the Pacific, making kaiju a global language of horror. The cross-pollination between America's campier atomic creatures and Japan's national trauma made the 1950s the first truly international horror decade since the Gothic.

The Backlash

Critics often dismissed creature features and invasion films as juvenile pulp, drive-in fodder for teenagers rather than serious art. Religious and political voices worried about the moral decay of films that depicted blasphemous science or social paranoia. In Japan, some condemned Godzilla as exploitative of national tragedy. Yet, as with Gothic horror before it, backlash only increased fascination. The very things critics scorned: spectacle, allegory, sensationalism were what audiences embraced.

Craft Innovations

- **Kaiju** used miniature sets, suitmation, and widescale destruction to create spectacles of devastation.
- **Alien invasion films** weaponized paranoia, using suburban streets and small towns as stages for fear.
- **Science-horror** updated the mad scientist, replacing candlelit castles with atomic labs.
- **Eco-horror** planted early seeds of nature's revenge, showing radiation and meddling triggering catastrophe.
- **Cosmic horror** shifted the scale from planet to universe, introducing existential dread into pulp cinema.
- **Post-apocalyptic horror** expanded narrative scope, imagining the death of humanity itself.

By the close of the 1950s, horror had broken free of its Gothic past. The genre no longer belonged only to shadows and superstition but to science, paranoia, and the mushroom cloud. Horror became a mirror of modernity, reflecting both the promise and peril of human progress. Yet while America and Japan turned to radiation and aliens, Europe began charting its own path. In Britain, Hammer Films revived the Gothic in blood-soaked color, and in Italy, Mario Bava and later Argento would turn Catholic dread into psychedelic nightmares. Horror was about to go global, erotic, and operatic.

Hammer & Euro-Gothic Revival
(1957–1970s)

From Hammer's blood-drenched castles to Bava and Argento's color-saturated nightmares, Gothic horror resurrected itself in full spectacle during the mid-20th century. This was the era when horror became global, erotic, and painterly. Gothic decay reimagined for a world no longer content with shadows alone.

Hammer Horror: Blood in Technicolor

In 1957, Britain's Hammer Film Productions jolted Gothic back to life with *The Curse of Frankenstein* (1957). It was the first Gothic horror in color, shocking audiences with gore, cleavage, and a sadistic new edge. Peter Cushing's ruthless Baron and Christopher Lee's scarred Monster revitalized Shelley's myth for a postwar audience hungry for sensation.

One year later, *Horror of Dracula* (1958) gave Lee's Count feral sexuality: crimson lips, bloodshot eyes, and a physicality far from Lugosi's hypnotic aristocrat. Blood ran red, flesh was exposed, and Gothic horror became carnivalesque. Sequels multiplied (*The Satanic Rites of Dracula*, *Twins of Evil*), each re-energizing old myths with a lurid, transgressive charge.

Hammer's Gothic was Gothic without restraint: it scandalized the establishment, drew censorship battles, and made horror profitable again.

The Shock of Color: Horror's New Palette

When Hammer splashed crimson blood across the screen in *The Curse of Frankenstein* (1957), it wasn't just shocking, it was revolutionary. For decades, horror had lived in black and white, its atmosphere dependent on shadow, fog, and chiaroscuro. Color changed the grammar of fear. What color meant:

- **Blood as spectacle.** No longer black ink against grey skin, blood now gleamed red, visceral and undeniable. Horror could be bodily in a way expressionist shadows never allowed.
- **Eroticism and skin.** Flesh tones carried new weight. Hammer reveled in cleavage and pallor, playing Gothic sexuality for scandal and allure.

- **Atmosphere in saturation.** Technicolor allowed for lurid skies, deep emerald forests, and saturated castle interiors that turned Gothic into carnival. Color heightened unreality, making horror both more sensual and more surreal.

Color arrived at the same moment as loosening censorship in Britain and abroad. What could not be shown explicitly in the 1940s could now be smuggled in through spectacle: blood, eroticism, and blasphemy intensified by the palette itself. Audiences were scandalized, but they also came in droves. Horror's profitability was proven again.

Italy embraced color in operatic excess, with Mario Bava using it as brushstroke and atmosphere in *Black Sunday* (1960) and later Argento turning entire films into color-saturated nightmares (*Suspiria*, 1977). In America, Roger Corman's Poe cycle painted Gothic decay in lush, morbid tones. Japanese directors, too, would later use color to accentuate the surreal violence of kaidan and kaiju alike.

Where Expressionism gave horror its language of shadows, and Lewton its language of silence, Hammer gave it the language of color. Horror was no longer confined to black-and-white dread; it could be lurid, sensual, and painterly. Blood became art, flesh became symbol, and the palette itself became a tool of fear.

Roger Corman and the Poe Cycle

While Hammer drenched Gothic in crimson and Bava wrapped it in baroque shadows, America found its own revival through Roger Corman's Poe cycle at American International Pictures. Between 1960 and 1964, Corman adapted seven Edgar Allan Poe stories into lurid Technicolor spectacles, each anchored by Vincent Price as a decadent antihero.

House of Usher (1960) set the tone: a decaying mansion, ancestral curses, and Price's morbidly elegant presence. *The Pit and the Pendulum* (1961) pushed further with torture chambers and madness, while *The Masque of the Red Death* (1964) bathed plague and Satanic ritual in saturated reds and gothic excess. These films combined literary prestige with exploitation thrills, smuggling Poe's language of decay, guilt, and obsession into mainstream drive-ins.

What distinguished the Poe cycle was its balance of artistry and economy. Corman worked with tiny budgets, reusing sets and costumes, but transformed limitations into atmosphere: fog, colored gels, and Vincent Price's theatrical gravitas carried more weight than special effects. The cycle also foregrounded themes that resonated with the 1960s: plague as metaphor for social collapse, torture as political allegory, and decadent aristocracies crumbling under their own corruption.

The Poe films gave America its equivalent to Hammer's Gothic revival: a series that proved horror could be profitable, poetic, and popular. They also cemented Vincent Price as one of horror's defining icons, his voice and presence synonymous with Gothic doom.

Italian Gothic and the Birth of Giallo

Meanwhile in Italy, Gothic horror fused with Catholic dread and operatic artistry. Mario Bava became its architect. His *Black Sunday* (1960), with Barbara Steele's witch executed by an iron mask and resurrected centuries later, remains one of horror's most brutal and beautiful Gothic films at once medieval nightmare and modern shocker. His *The Whip and the Body* (1963) layered sadomasochistic desire and spectral revenge, making eroticism itself horrific.

From this baroque Gothic foundation, Giallo was born. The name comes from the yellow ("giallo") covers of pulp mystery novels popular in Italy since the 1920s, signaling lurid crime and sensational thrills. Giallo blended crime, thriller, and horror into something new: a subgenre defined by its masked, black-gloved killers, elaborate whodunit structures, and heightened, often surreal style.

Mario Bava again set the stage with *The Girl Who Knew Too Much* (1963), often cited as the first true Giallo film. He followed it with *Blood and Black Lace* (1964), where vibrant colors, disorienting camerawork, and fetishized violence announced the subgenre's distinctive grammar.

Dario Argento carried Giallo into its golden age. *The Bird with the Crystal Plumage* (1970) and *Deep Red* (1975) refined the form, combining brutal kills with complex mysteries and stylized excess. Argento then stretched Giallo into supernatural territory with *Suspiria* (1977), turning a ballet academy into a witches' coven bathed in neon blues and blood reds. Less narrative than nightmare, the film became a fever dream of color, sound, and sensation, an aesthetic assault that influenced global horror for decades.

Giallo shifted horror from story to spectacle. Where Gothic had once whispered in shadows, Giallo screamed in saturated color, baroque framing, and soundtracks that turned murder into opera. It was horror as sensation, where the experience of watching mattered as much as plot resolution. Its influence reached far beyond Italy, laying the stylistic groundwork for the American slasher boom of the late 1970s and 80s, from *Halloween* to *Friday the 13th*.

Occult Horror and the Satanic Panic

As Giallo painted nightmares in lurid style, another current of horror emerged one rooted not in knives or masks but in metaphysical dread. The late 1960s and 1970s became the age of the occult horror film, where devils, demons, and forbidden rituals dominated screens.

Roman Polanski's *Rosemary's Baby* (1968) signaled the shift. Set not in a Gothic castle but a Manhattan apartment, it told the story of a young woman manipulated into bearing the Antichrist. The film fused psychological unease with satanic conspiracy, making paranoia itself terrifying: the realization that one's neighbors, husband, and even doctors might be agents of evil.

William Friedkin's *The Exorcist* (1973) pushed further. Based on William Peter Blatty's novel, it turned Catholic ritual into a spectacle of terror. Possession, blasphemy, and the profane were staged with such intensity. Pea soup vomit, levitating bodies, obscenities shouted by a child that audiences fainted and rioted. It became one of the most profitable films of the decade, proving that horror could dominate the mainstream while scandalizing it.

The cycle continued with Richard Donner's *The Omen* (1976), where a diplomat discovers his adopted son is the Antichrist. Its imagery of cursed deaths and satanic prophecy tapped directly into 1970s anxieties about the breakdown of family and faith. Other films like *The Devil Rides Out* (1968, UK) and *The Sentinel* (1977, USA) deepened the genre's fixation on cults, demonic gateways, and the fragility of the soul.

The occult boom coincided with cultural upheavals: the decline of traditional religion, the rise of New Age spirituality, and the social turbulence of Vietnam, Watergate, and second-wave feminism. Horror became the stage where society wrestled with the fear that evil was no longer outside in monsters or foreign invaders, it was inside the home, the family, the body itself.

If Giallo reveled in color and sensation, occult horror borrowed its aesthetic force but redirected it toward metaphysics. The camera that once lingered on blood now lingered on ritual. The neon excess of *Suspiria* echoed in stained-glass windows and candlelit altars. Horror's stage expanded from the streets of Rome to the apartments of New York, but its message was the same: the familiar was no longer safe.

By the late 1970s, horror had fused spectacle with sacrilege. Murder mysteries and demonic possession were two sides of the same coin: both asked what happens when order collapses and chaos takes hold, whether through the hand of a black-gloved killer or the whisper of the Devil.

Cults and Conspiracies

Occult horror did not thrive on demons alone. Equally terrifying was the idea of ordinary people bound together in secret devotion to evil, hiding their rituals in plain sight. These films shifted fear from isolated monsters to entire communities. Neighbors, families, or villages conspiring under the veil of normalcy.

Polanski's *Rosemary's Baby* (1968) crystallized this fear, where every kindly neighbor was revealed as a Satanist, complicit in Rosemary's exploitation. Robin Hardy's *The Wicker Man* (1973, UK) pushed the theme into folk ritual: a police sergeant discovers an island community bound by pagan sacrifice, their conspiracy as polite as it is murderous. Even lesser-known works like *The Brotherhood of Satan* (1971) and *Race with the Devil* (1975) captured the paranoia that cults operated in the shadows of everyday life.

These stories resonated with a culture shaken by real-world upheavals. Charles Manson and his "family," the rise of new religious movements, and growing distrust of authority. The horror was not only that evil forces might exist, but that entire groups of people might willingly serve them, smiling as they prepared the altar.

In these films, horror became communal. The true terror lay not in a singular monster but in the crowd: an organized, believing, and complicit society where morality was inverted and ritual demanded blood. Cult horror bridged the stylish murders of Giallo with the metaphysical dread of the Satanic Panic, while laying the groundwork for Folk Horror's full flowering.

Folk Horror: Rituals in the Soil

While the Satanic Panic explored devils in the city and cults in the suburbs, another current of horror looked backward, to the fields, forests, and villages where old beliefs still lingered. Folk horror drew its power from folklore, rural traditions, and pagan rituals, staging terror not in laboratories or apartments but in landscapes haunted by history. The horror often came from outsiders stumbling upon communities where time moved differently, and where ritual demanded sacrifice.

Perhaps the most famous example is *The Wicker Man* (1973, UK). A devout police sergeant arrives on a remote island to investigate a missing girl, only to discover a pagan community united by ritual sacrifice. Its climax, the burning wicker effigy, epitomizes folk horror's collision of modern rationality and ancient, blood-soaked tradition. Decades later, Ari Aster's *Midsommar* (2019) reimagined the same dynamic, with American tourists lured into a Swedish commune where sunlight illuminated ritual dismemberment.

Some folk horror explored the persistence of curses, magic, and the land itself as a malignant force. *Blood on Satan's Claw* (1971, UK) showed rural England consumed by demonic corruption, while Robert Eggers' *The Witch* (2015) returned to Puritan New England to depict a family unraveling under isolation, superstition, and witchcraft. These tales suggested that history itself could cling like a shadow, with families and villages trapped by forces older than memory.

In America, folk horror often took a more brutal form: the "backwoods" or "hillbilly" subgenre. Films like *Deliverance* (1972) and later *The Texas Chain Saw Massacre* (1974) recast rural isolation as grotesque violence, with inbred families and feral traditions preying on urban outsiders. The horror here was less pagan ritual than social decay, a fear that civilization had left pockets of savagery festering within its own borders.

Beyond Europe and America, folk horror tapped into local mythologies. Southeast Asian cinema, for example, drew on spirits and curses unique to the region: the penanggalan of Malaysian folklore, a vampiric head with trailing organs dangling from the neck, or Thai films about forest ghosts and ancestral curses. These stories broadened folk horror into a global mode, showing how every culture carried its own rituals of unease.

Folk horror revealed that terror could live not only in science, Satan, or psychology but in the soil itself. It was a genre about community, ritual, and history pressing down on the present. Outsiders were rarely safe; to stumble into the wrong village, the wrong farmhouse, or the wrong forest clearing was to discover that the past was not dead, it was waiting, and it demanded blood.

The Global Gothic Revival

The Gothic revival wasn't confined to Britain's Hammer or Italy's Giallo. Across Europe and America, filmmakers reimagined Gothic tropes through local anxieties, bending them into folk ritual, erotic excess, and surreal experimentation:

- Roger Corman's Poe cycle (USA, 1960–64) — *House of Usher*, *The Masque of the Red Death* gave Vincent Price a gallery of decadent antiheroes, draped in morbidity and doomed desire.
- Belgium's *Daughters of Darkness* (1971) draped vampirism in aristocratic rot and queer desire, recasting the Gothic femme fatale as both alluring and fatal.
- Spain, under Franco's censorship, birthed hybrids of Catholic repression and Gothic imagery, where saints and sinners bled into nightmare.
- Britain produced folk-inflected Gothic such as *Blood on Satan's Claw* (1971), where rural England fell into demonic corruption, anticipating the broader folk-horror movement.
- France and Germany offered erotic, surreal hybrids, pushing Gothic into arthouse terrain where horror blurred into dream and delirium.

Together, these films signaled horror's internationalization. No longer confined to Hollywood or the Universal monsters, horror became polyglot: Catholic guilt, folk ritual, erotic decadence, and neon surrealism all filtered through Gothic decay.

Catalysts and Gatekeepers
Hammer thrived by exploiting gaps in censorship, testing limits of blood, sex, and blasphemy. Italian horror expanded through independent financing and the growing appetite for genre exports. Festivals and distribution networks carried films like *Black Sunday* and *Suspiria* across borders, while American drive-ins absorbed both Gothic excess and European imports. Horror had become a global trade, sustained by scandal and spectacle.

The Backlash
Censors targeted Hammer for indecency, condemning its cleavage and crimson gore. Giallo was dismissed as exploitative pulp, little more than "murder with style." Folk horror's pagan rituals were accused of blasphemy, while art-house surrealism was too often dismissed as obscenity or confusion. Yet, as with every wave before, backlash only amplified allure. Audiences came precisely because the films promised what mainstream cinema would not.

Craft Innovations
- **Hammer** codified blood, sex, and Gothic spectacle in color.
- **Giallo** fused horror with style saturated palettes, disorienting camerawork, and murder as aesthetic event.
- **Occult horror** merged metaphysics and shock, staging possession and satanic ritual with unprecedented realism.
- **Folk horror** drew terror from landscape and ritual, showing how communities and traditions could become monstrous.
- **Arthouse hybrids** blurred Gothic and surrealism, expanding horror into forms unthinkable in the 1930s.

By the 1970s, horror was global, erotic, and experimental. Gothic had been resurrected in blood and neon, while nuclear and alien anxieties still kept science at the center of fear. But new terrors were emerging. As social upheaval shook the late 1960s and early 70s, horror would turn its gaze inward once again toward possession, serial killers, and the monstrous within the family home.

New Hollywood & American Nightmares
(1960s–1970s)
By the 1960s, the glossy Gothic of Hammer and Corman could no longer contain the cracks in American culture. Vietnam, civil rights struggles, Watergate, and the erosion of trust in authority demanded a new horror language. Enter New Hollywood horror: raw, nihilistic, and grounded in everyday terrors.

Psycho and the Birth of the Modern Horror Film
Alfred Hitchcock detonated the genre with *Psycho* (1960, USA). What began as a story about a secretary's embezzlement swerved into the knife of Norman Bates, whose "Mother" persona killed with domestic intimacy. The shower scene's 78 edits in 45 seconds redefined cinematic violence suggestive yet shocking and Bernard Herrmann's shrieking violins became horror's anthem.[1] Hitchcock also demolished taboos: the first flushing toilet in American cinema, voyeurism as pathology, and the monster next door.

Released the same year, Michael Powell's *Peeping Tom* (1960, UK) followed a cameraman who murdered women while filming their final moments. Condemned as obscene, it destroyed Powell's career but decades later, critics recognized it as a prophetic meditation on cinema itself as an instrument of violence.[2]

Together, these films shifted horror inward: away from castles and monsters, into psychology, voyeurism, and repression.

Night of the Living Dead: Horror Goes for the Jugular
In 1968, George A. Romero's *Night of the Living Dead* (USA) dragged horror out of Gothic mansions and into a Pennsylvania farmhouse under siege. Shot in grainy black-and-white on a shoestring budget, it birthed the modern zombie and injected horror with political venom. Its Black protagonist (Duane Jones) survives the night only to be shot

---

[1] *Psycho*, dir. Alfred Hitchcock, Paramount Pictures, 1960.
[2] *Peeping Tom*, dir. Michael Powell, Anglo-Amalgamated, 1960.

by a white posse, a chilling echo of civil rights-era America. Romero claimed it was unintentional, but the timing made it an accidental manifesto.

Censors couldn't keep up: children were traumatized at Saturday matinees, watching corpses rise and devour flesh. The film's nihilism: the dead cannot be stopped. The survivors turn on each other ushering horror into the age of Vietnam and Kent State.[3]

Zombie Horror: The First Modern Wave

While zombies had shuffled through cinema before the 1960s, they were often depicted as voodoo thralls enslaved bodies robbed of will by sorcery (*White Zombie*, 1932). That changed forever in 1968, when George A. Romero's *Night of the Living Dead* dragged the dead out of folklore and into the modern world.

Romero's zombies were no longer passive slaves but flesh-eating ghouls, mindless consumers of human flesh whose very existence turned survival into siege warfare. His vision birthed the zombie apocalypse template: a small group of survivors barricaded in a farmhouse, struggling not only against the monsters outside but also their own paranoia and infighting inside.

The social commentary was unavoidable. Casting Duane Jones, a Black actor, as the film's protagonist gave *Night* a radical edge, especially in its ending where his character survives the night only to be killed by a white militia. Romero insisted it wasn't planned, but in 1968, amid civil rights upheaval and assassinations, the film became an accidental political manifesto.

The film's low budget and grainy black-and-white photography amplified its sense of realism. Audiences including children at Saturday matinees were stunned by its explicit cannibalism and nihilism. Critics attacked it as obscenity; fans embraced it as revelation. Horror had never felt so raw, so political, or so merciless.

Romero's sequels *Dawn of the Dead* (1978), set in a shopping mall, and *Day of the Dead* (1985) in a military bunker expanded the allegory, satirizing consumerism, militarism, and humanity's inability to cooperate in crisis. Other filmmakers followed suit, cementing the zombie as one of horror's most flexible metaphors.

The modern zombie was not just a monster but a mirror: a reflection of society's collapse, of mass conformity, of death made banal. With *Night of the Living Dead*, Romero didn't just create a subgenre, he opened a vein of horror that continues to bleed into every era, from the grindhouses of the 70s to today's global pandemics and streaming apocalypses.

The Texas Chain Saw Massacre: Rural Apocalypse

If *Psycho* cracked the suburban facade, Tobe Hooper's *The Texas Chain Saw Massacre* (1974, USA) ripped the heart out of the American pastoral. Inspired loosely by Wisconsin murderer Ed Gein, it trapped a van of young people in rural Texas, where Leatherface and his cannibal family turned slaughterhouse tools on human flesh. The sunbaked

cinematography suggested documentary realism; audiences swore they saw gore that wasn't actually there.

Released during the fallout of Vietnam and Watergate, *Chain Saw* reflected the sense that America itself was predatory, its heartland rotting. Leatherface wasn't supernatural, he was a working-class butcher in a mask of human skin, wielding a chainsaw as blue-collar weapon turned nightmare.[4]

New Hollywood horror was revolutionary because it removed the safety net. Happy endings dissolved. Monsters weren't in castles. They were in motels, in neighbors, in rural gas stations. Horror had become modern: psychological, political, and mercilessly real.

---

[3] Tony Williams, *The Cinema of George A. Romero* (London: Wallflower Press, 2003).
[4] *The Texas Chain Saw Massacre*, dir. Tobe Hooper, Bryanston Pictures, 1974.

Demonic Possession and the Satanic Panic

If zombies reflected political collapse, the late 1960s and 70s brought horror back to the metaphysical. Demonic possession, Satanic cults, and the Antichrist became dominant themes, mirroring a culture gripped by a crisis of faith. The counterculture challenged Christianity, New Age movements spread, and real-world events like the Manson murders made whispers of Satanism feel disturbingly plausible. Horror absorbed these fears and turned them into ritual.

Roman Polanski's *Rosemary's Baby* (1968) ignited the craze. Set in an ordinary New York apartment, the film

suggested that evil didn't need castles or cloaks, it lived in your neighbors, your doctor, even your husband. Its quiet dread and shocking climax, revealing Rosemary as the mother of the Antichrist, redefined horror as conspiracy, paranoia, and betrayal within the family home.

William Friedkin's *The Exorcist* (1973) detonated the genre. Its raw, realistic depiction of demonic possession from a child spewing obscenities to the visceral violence of Catholic exorcism horrified audiences, many of whom fainted or fled theaters. The film became one of the most profitable of all time, its cultural impact so vast that it redefined possession as a permanent subgenre of horror.

Richard Donner's *The Omen* (1976) carried the momentum. Here, evil took the form of Damien, a young boy destined to become the Antichrist. With its string of spectacular "accidental" deaths and its apocalyptic undertones, the film amplified anxieties about cursed children, broken families, and prophecies of doom.

The Satanic Panic cycle gave horror a new gravitas. These weren't simply movies about fear, they were cultural events that sparked debates about religion, morality, and the devil's place in modern life. If Gothic horror had once terrified audiences with superstition, the Satanic films of the 70s terrified them with faith itself, exposing cracks in the sacred and suggesting that evil was already here, working from within.

Natural Horror and the First Eco-Horror Wave

As possession films wrestled with the devil and zombies gnawed on society's collapse, another current of horror emerged from an older, primal fear: the terror of nature itself. Natural horror turned the ordinary animal or landscape into predator, suggesting that humanity's dominance was fragile and easily overturned.

Alfred Hitchcock's *The Birds* (1963) stands as the first landmark. Set in a small California town besieged by inexplicable bird attacks, it stripped away supernatural explanations. The horror was elemental, unmotivated, and relentless. Hitchcock showed that nature needed no reason to rebel, its silence and sudden violence were terrifying enough.

By the mid-70s, natural horror became blockbuster material. Steven Spielberg's *Jaws* (1975) terrified audiences with the spectacle of a great white shark turning summer leisure into blood-soaked panic. The film invented the summer blockbuster while also reinvigorating the idea that a single animal magnified by camera and sound design could paralyze entire communities.

From this root grew eco-horror, where nature's violence was explicitly linked to human recklessness. Radiation, pesticides, or pollution awakened beasts or warped the ecosystem. Films like *Frogs* (1972) and *Phase IV* (1974) suggested that animals might one day rise against humanity for its sins against the earth. The theme echoed anxieties about environmental collapse, overpopulation, and technological arrogance, foreshadowing the ecological nightmares of the 1970s and beyond.

Natural horror re-centered the genre in the environment audiences knew: oceans, skies, forests. Its terror wasn't ancient or metaphysical, it was immediate, tangible, and alive. When a shark fin sliced the water, or when birds blackened the sky, horror reminded viewers that humanity was not master but prey.

Splatter and Gore: The Carnival of Blood

If *Psycho* shocked with implication and *Night of the Living Dead* disturbed with nihilism, Herschell Gordon Lewis simply put the guts on screen. Known as the "Godfather of Gore," Lewis pioneered the splatter film in the early 1960s, a subgenre defined not by subtlety but by its relentless commitment to showing mutilation, dismemberment, and buckets of blood.

His *Blood Feast* (1963), often called the first true gore film, told the story of an Egyptian caterer murdering women to prepare a feast for his goddess. What mattered wasn't the plot, it was the imagery: hacked limbs, torn tongues, blood spilling in bright red. Audiences recoiled, critics dismissed it as trash, but the film made money and proved that gore could sell.

Lewis followed with *Two Thousand Maniacs!* (1964), in which a Southern town exacts grotesque vengeance on Northern tourists. The film reveled in bloody set-pieces, from dismemberment to rolling-barrel mutilations, combining exploitation shock value with a sly cultural jab at America's unresolved Civil War scars.

These films were cheaply made, poorly acted, and often laughed at yet they were revolutionary. For the first time, violence wasn't symbolic or implied. It was spectacle. Where Hitchcock's knife suggested a wound, Lewis showed it being carved.

Splatter films carved out space for gore as its own draw, creating a carnival-like atmosphere where audiences came to shriek, squirm, and gag. They were grindhouse attractions, dismissed by critics but devoured by cult audiences. More importantly, they paved the way for the rising tolerance of explicit horror. By the 1970s and 80s, Italian exploitation and American slashers would take Lewis's crude blueprint and refine it into operatic gore, making blood not just shocking but stylish.

Body Horror: The Flesh as Nightmare

While the seeds of body horror appeared in earlier films from *Doctor X* (1932) to *The Invisible Man* (1933), the subgenre came into full force in the 1960s and 70s, when directors began to confront the body itself as the site of horror. Instead of cloaked figures or external monsters, the terror came from within: the grotesque transformation, the parasitic invasion, the body betraying itself.

Eyes Without a Face (1960). Georges Franju's French masterpiece remains one of the most hauntingly beautiful examples. A brilliant surgeon kidnaps young women to graft their faces onto his disfigured daughter, blending medical obsession with fairy-tale nightmare. Its imagery of surgical violation: scalpel against flesh, masks hiding wounds was shocking for its time and became a touchstone for later explorations of bodily mutilation.

Japan and the grotesque. In Japan, filmmakers turned body horror into hallucinatory spectacle. Teruo Ishii's *Horrors of Malformed Men* (1969) fused surrealism, erotic grotesquerie, and the legacy of Edogawa Ranpo's pulp fiction into a fever dream of surgical mutilation and island experiments. The film was so disturbing it was banned for decades in Japan. Kinji Fukasaku's *Black Lizard* (1968), though more camp than horror, also trafficked in bodily transformation and obsession with perfection, showing how the Japanese avant-garde flirted with the aesthetics of mutilation and the uncanny. These films paralleled the rise of ero-guro ("erotic grotesque") culture, where art, horror, and taboo collided.

Cronenberg and the new flesh. By the mid-70s, Canadian director David Cronenberg pushed the subgenre into radical new territory. *Shivers* (1975) introduced parasitic organisms that turned humans into sex-driven, violent creatures, merging body horror with social commentary on repression, disease, and desire. His early works announced a career-long obsession with "the new flesh": a cinema of transformation where the body itself is unstable, fragile, and endlessly corruptible.

Body horror thrived in the 60s and 70s because it spoke to anxieties about medicine, sexuality, and modern science. As organ transplants, plastic surgery, new viruses, and sexual liberation captured public imagination, films revealed the flip side of progress: that the body was not sacred but malleable, vulnerable, and grotesque. In body horror, the monster is never far away, it's already under the skin.

Catalysts and Gatekeepers

Drive-ins, midnight screenings, and grindhouse theaters gave a home to films too raw for the mainstream. Independent financing allowed mavericks like George A. Romero and Tobe Hooper to bypass studio oversight, while exploitation producers like Herschell Gordon Lewis built entire careers on gore and shock. Meanwhile, the decline of the Production Code and the rise of the MPAA ratings system in 1968 opened the gates for violence, nudity, blasphemy, and taboo-breaking that would have been unthinkable a decade earlier.

The Vietnam War, the civil rights movement, and Watergate seeped into every frame: horror became the language of political disillusionment. Even animal attacks and eco-horror thrillers reflected growing environmental anxieties. The genre was no longer escapist, it was responding directly to the world audiences lived in.

The Backlash

The response was outrage. *Night of the Living Dead* was condemned as "a porn of violence" when children staggered out of Saturday matinees in shock. *The Texas Chain Saw Massacre* was banned in multiple countries for its disturbing tone, even though much of its gore was suggested rather than shown. Hitchcock was accused of corrupting cinema with *Psycho*. *The Exorcist* triggered fainting, vomiting, and protests outside theaters. Herschell Gordon Lewis's gore films were dismissed as trash. Yet every scandal only fed the flames. What critics deemed obscene, audiences consumed. What one generation tried to censor, the next enshrined as classic.

Craft Innovations

- *Psycho* pioneered the modern slasher template: voyeuristic killer, shocking mid-film death, and violence edited into rhythm.
- *Peeping Tom* revealed cinema itself as voyeuristic weapon, decades ahead of its time.
- *Night of the Living Dead* reinvented the zombie as flesh-eating ghoul, codifying the apocalypse template and embedding political allegory.
- *The Texas Chain Saw Massacre* stripped horror to documentary rawness: handheld camerawork, sunlit terror, and suggested gore more horrifying than explicit blood.
- *The Exorcist* and *The Omen* elevated demonic possession into cultural events, marrying horror with religious crisis.
- *The Birds* and *Jaws* proved nature itself could be monstrous, spawning the first eco-horror wave.

- Herschell Gordon Lewis's splatter films (*Blood Feast*, *Two Thousand Maniacs!*) pioneered gore as carnival spectacle, a grindhouse attraction.
- *Eyes Without a Face* and Cronenberg's *Shivers* planted body horror firmly in the genre, making the flesh itself unstable, corruptible, and terrifying.

By the mid-1970s, horror had been reborn as modern myth. Castles and barons gave way to killers with mother fixations, zombies in farmhouses, possessed children in suburban bedrooms, sharks off summer beaches, and cannibal families lurking in rural backroads. The genre no longer promised escape into fantasy, it dragged audiences into the anxieties of their own world: violence, madness, corruption, and systems breaking down.

And yet, just as horror reached its most nihilistic extremes, it discovered something new: spectacle. Gore, possession, and apocalypse sold tickets in record numbers, proving horror wasn't just shocking, it was profitable. The stage was set for the 1980s, when slashers, exploitation, and global video culture would take the raw innovations of New Hollywood and sharpen them into a booming industry of blood.

Slashers & Video Nasties
(Late 1970s–1980s)

If the 1960s and 70s were about breaking taboos, the late 70s and 80s distilled horror into formulas that were brutally efficient, endlessly imitated, and globally censored. Slashers dominated American screens. Cannibal and gore films shocked Europe. VHS tapes spread terror directly into homes. And the UK launched a censorship firestorm with the infamous Video Nasties panic. Horror had never been more visible or more vilified.

VHS: Blood in a Plastic Clamshell

Home video changed horror more than any single studio or director. With the rise of VHS in the late 1970s and 1980s, terror left the theater and moved into living rooms, dorms, and sleepovers. A new ecosystem formed around the cassette: mom-and-pop rental stores, lurid box art, unrated cuts, and a constant churn of titles designed to jump off the shelf.

VHS turned horror into a weekly ritual. You did not need a downtown cinema or a midnight screening. You needed a VCR and a rental card. Word of mouth traveled through aisles and school hallways. A hand-painted sleeve or a single outrageous still could sell a movie before anyone pressed play.

Tapes slipped through cracks that theatrical releases could not. In the United States, studios dodged harsh ratings by issuing unrated or "director's cut" cassettes. In the United Kingdom the panic over "video nasties" led to bans and seizures, which only increased demand. Blacklists created bootlegs, bootlegs created cults.

Horror was cheap to make and reliable to rent. A film could flop in theaters yet become a hit on tape, which kept sequel machines running. The shelf life of a title stretched for years, so masked killers and rubber monsters became brands. Franchises thrived because the rental market guaranteed a second and third chance to find fans.

Direct-to-video changed how horror felt. Effects were built to be paused and rewound. Stories front-loaded shocks to hook renters in the first ten minutes. Synth scores, claustrophobic interiors, and single-location shoots became a house style. Practical gore played bigger on a 27-inch screen when the camera stayed close.

Affordable camcorders created a parallel pipeline: shot-on-video slashers and backyard splatter that bypassed theaters entirely. Regional filmmakers found audiences far from Los Angeles, proving you could build a cult with tape duplication and a few outrageous set pieces.

VHS erased borders. Italian gore epics, Canadian body horror, and Japanese oddities all traveled on cassette. A film banned in one country could circulate in another, then boomerang back through fan trading. The cassette was both distributor and passport.

Horror learned to market itself through sleeves, taglines, and store-window standees. The cover became a promise: a mask, a blade, a creature mid-lunge. Even mediocre films could rent on the strength of their clamshell alone, which pushed designers and producers to cultivate instantly iconic images.

VHS democratized horror. It created the long tail that kept monsters alive between theatrical cycles, funded risks that studios would not take, and trained a generation to think of horror as a library rather than a one-night event. The cassette did not just distribute the slasher era. It made that era possible, then preserved it for endless rewatching.

The Invention of the Slasher

The slasher did not appear fully formed; it evolved out of fragments scattered across decades of cinema. By the late 1970s it solidified into a formula, but its roots stretched back to Hitchcock, giallo, and rural nightmares that redefined what horror could be.

Alfred Hitchcock detonated the genre with *Psycho*. Norman Bates brought horror out of Gothic castles and into the suburban motel. The infamous shower scene. Seventy-eight cuts in forty-five seconds turned violence into cinematic rhythm. Bates was boyish and monstrous at once, proof that the killer could be hidden in plain sight. *Psycho* gave slashers their voyeurism, their fractured killers, and the shock of killing off a protagonist midway through.

The same year, Michael Powell's *Peeping Tom* destroyed its director's career but planted another seed. Following a cameraman who murdered women while filming them, it made the act of watching itself predatory. This was the first true "killer's POV" film, a visual grammar that slashers would adopt wholesale.

In Italy, directors like Mario Bava and Dario Argento fused crime, horror, and eroticism. *The Girl Who Knew Too Much* (1963) and *Deep Red* (1975) perfected the template of the masked, black-gloved killer, elaborate murder set-pieces, and whodunit revelations. Slashers borrowed these wholesale: the fetishized weapon, the unmasking climax, the obsession with how a murder looked as much as what it meant.

Bob Clark's Canadian thriller set its killings in a sorority house at Christmas, weaving obscene phone calls, urban legends, and escalating deaths into a structure Carpenter would echo in *Halloween*. It made the holiday setting essential to the formula, ritualizing violence into a calendar event.

Tobe Hooper's nightmare of cannibal families and slaughterhouse imagery stripped horror to its bones. Its handheld camerawork, sunlit violence, and Leatherface's butcher's mask suggested not Gothic fantasy but America itself rotting from the inside. *Chain Saw* gave slashers their brutality, their rural isolation, and their documentary rawness.

The "golden age" of slashers stretched from *Halloween* (1978) through *Friday the 13th* (1980) and *A Nightmare on Elm Street* (1984). These films defined the genre's grammar: a group of teens isolated from authority, a masked killer picking them off one by one, and a "Final Girl" who survives through resilience or purity. The killers became icons: Michael Myers as faceless evil, Jason Voorhees as vengeance incarnate, Freddy Krueger as the dream-invading sadist.

Drawing from giallo, many slashers treated their killers as puzzles. *Terror Train* (1980) and *Prom Night* (1980) concealed the murderer's identity, forcing both characters and audiences to guess. The mask became both disguise and motif, turning revelation into climax. This tradition set the stage for *Scream* (1996), which merged whodunit logic with meta-commentary, reviving the slasher after its 80s peak.

Some of the most chilling slashers brought horror into the home. *When a Stranger Calls* (1979) exploited the urban legend of a babysitter terrorized by a caller inside the house. *Black Christmas* (1974) did the same with sorority sisters stalked in their own dormitory. These films struck a deeper nerve: horror as the violation of safety itself.

Slashers thrived on ritual. Holidays provided readymade calendars for bloodletting. *My Bloody Valentine* (1981), *April Fool's Day* (1986), and the endless *Halloween* sequels turned communal celebration into collective nightmare. The formula was simple: tie the killings to a day everyone recognized, and the film became an annual event.

By the 1990s, the formula had worn thin. But rather than abandon it, filmmakers turned the knife inward. *Scream* (1996) mocked, honored, and revitalized the slasher by making its characters aware of "the rules." Later, *The Cabin in the Woods* (2011) dissected not just the slasher but horror itself, staging its tropes as sacrificial ritual. Meta-slashers proved the subgenre was not dead, it had simply become self-aware.

Some slashers abandoned mystery and suspense in favor of pure spectacle. William Lustig's *Maniac* (1980) and Juan Piquer Simón's *Pieces* (1982) lingered on mutilation, making gore the main event. These films foreshadowed later "torture porn" cycles (*Saw*, *Hostel*), where the mechanics of pain became the story.

The slasher unified horror's past innovations into one endlessly repeatable machine: voyeurism from Hitchcock, ritual from folk horror, gore from exploitation, and suspense from giallo. It became horror's most commercial form, spawning franchises that outlived their creators and villains that became pop icons. For many audiences, the masked slasher is not just a subgenre but horror itself. The purest expression of fear, repetition, and catharsis.

Halloween and the Slasher Template

John Carpenter's *Halloween* (1978, USA) did not invent the slasher, but it crystallized it. With a shoestring budget of just $325,000, Carpenter transformed simplicity into terror. Michael Myers, introduced as a child who murders his sister and returns years later to stalk babysitters in Haddonfield, Illinois, embodied evil as faceless and motiveless. He was not a vampire, zombie, or ghost. He was a shape, an absence, a blank white mask drifting through suburban streets.

The film's craft was revolutionary. Carpenter's Steadicam prowls turned the audience into the killer's eyes, weaponizing the POV innovations of *Peeping Tom* and giallo. His minimalist synth score, built on just a few repeating notes, became a pulse of dread that haunted theaters for decades. And in Jamie Lee Curtis's Laurie Strode, horror found its archetypal Final Girl: resourceful, resilient, marked by vulnerability but never helpless. The formula clicked into place:

- A holiday setting (*Halloween night* as ritualized backdrop).
- A group of teen victims, distracted by sex, rebellion, or indifference.
- A masked killer, both everywhere and nowhere at once.
- An escalation of set-piece kills, each choreographed like a grim ritual.

Audiences responded with fervor. Grossing $60 million worldwide, *Halloween* became one of the most profitable independent films in history. But beyond its box office success, it proved that horror could thrive on austerity. Stripped of castles, monsters, or elaborate effects, the slasher distilled fear to its essence: the sense that someone is watching, and that the safe spaces of suburbia are not safe at all.

The imitators arrived instantly. Within two years, *Friday the 13th* would transplant the formula to summer camp, and by the mid-80s every holiday, prom, and birthday party seemed destined for blood. Carpenter hadn't just made a film, he had written a blueprint.

Friday the 13th and the Franchise Machine

If *Halloween* built the slasher blueprint, *Friday the 13th* (1980, USA) proved how profitable it could be to Xerox it. Sean S. Cunningham's film transplanted the formula to Camp Crystal Lake, a rural summer camp haunted by the death of a child years earlier. But the twist was audacious: the killer wasn't the rumored "Jason" at all, but his grieving mother, Pamela Voorhees, slicing through counselors as vengeance for her drowned son. The reveal tied horror to parental grief and repression, making violence the legacy of neglect.

The film's notoriety came not from its plot but its effects. Tom Savini's gore arrows through throats, axes to faces, decapitations pushed boundaries for American horror, each kill staged as grotesque spectacle. The shocking final image of Jason erupting from the lake, though originally intended as a one-off dream sequence, became a pop culture earthquake. Audiences demanded more.

By *Part II* (1981), Jason himself had stepped into the role of killer, first with a sackcloth mask, then in *Part III* (1982) with the hockey mask that became an icon of horror. That mask was more than costume, it was brand. The franchise machine was born.

Sequels arrived with metronomic regularity. Jason was resurrected as zombie, chained beneath lakes, dragged to Manhattan (*Jason Takes Manhattan*, 1989), and eventually launched into outer space (*Jason X*, 2001). Each installment reset the stage: a new group of teens, a familiar setting, and increasingly elaborate kills.

Friday the 13th revealed a new truth: horror could operate like sports or soap opera. Audiences didn't come for new stories; they came for the return of a familiar face or in Jason's case, a mask. The franchise model transformed the slasher into ritual, sequels into annual events, and killers into mascots of fear. Horror had become not just a genre, but an industry of repetition and reinvention.

A Nightmare on Elm Street: The Dream Slayer

By 1984, the slasher formula was beginning to calcify masked killers, teen victims, sequels multiplying with diminishing returns. Wes Craven detonated it with *A Nightmare on Elm Street* (1984, USA), a film that reimagined the killer not as a physical stalker but as an invader of dreams. Freddy Krueger was no longer bound by geography, doors, or even reality. Sleep itself became the trap, every bed a potential execution chamber.

Freddy's mythology deepened the horror. Once a child murderer burned alive by vengeful parents, he returned as a dream demon, wielding a glove tipped with blades. His kills were surreal tableaus: a teenager dragged across the ceiling, another swallowed by her own bed in a geyser of blood, phones sprouting tongues to lick their victims. Craven fused slasher rhythm with surrealist nightmare logic, making terror as much psychological as physical.

Unlike Michael Myers or Jason Voorhees, Freddy talked. His sardonic one-liners, grotesque humor, and sadistic playfulness made him perversely charismatic. This banter transformed him into both monster and entertainer, a duality that carried him beyond the horror audience into broader pop culture. By the late 80s, Freddy adorned lunchboxes, Halloween costumes, and MTV bumpers. He was as much a brand as a boogeyman.

The film also gave horror one of its most enduring heroines: Nancy Thompson (Heather Langenkamp), who turned Freddy's dream logic against him. Her ingenuity: booby-trapping her home, refusing to play victim elevated the Final Girl archetype from survivor to strategist.

Sequels proliferated almost immediately. *A Nightmare on Elm Street 3: Dream Warriors* (1987) weaponized dreamscapes into fantasy battlegrounds, while later entries veered into spectacle and camp. But Freddy's impact was undeniable. He revitalized the slasher, demonstrating that the formula could evolve, mutate, and tap into the primal vulnerability of sleep.

If Michael Myers was faceless dread and Jason Voorhees was brute inevitability, Freddy Krueger was the id: mocking, imaginative, and inescapable. Together, the three giants defined horror's 1980s pantheon, each embodying a different face of fear.

Italian Gore and the Cinema of Decay

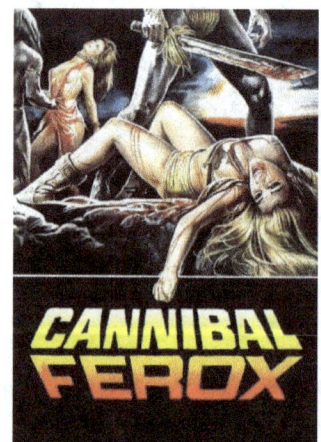

If America's slashers turned death into ritual, Italy turned it into art: grotesque, surreal, and drenched in blood. Italian gore cinema reveled in the spectacle of the body's destruction, not as allegory but as sensory assault.

Lucio Fulci became the architect of this movement. *Zombie* (1979) stunned audiences with its infamous shark-versus-zombie battle and its slow-motion eyeball impalement, an image that burned into horror history. *City of the Living Dead* (1980) featured intestine-pulling and head-drilling, while *The Beyond* (1981) collapsed narrative logic into a fever dream of rot, worms, and surreal cosmic dread. For Fulci, gore was not plot but atmosphere: a world literally decomposing before the viewer's eyes.

Dario Argento, meanwhile, took giallo's sleek stylization and fused it with crimson excess. *Tenebrae* (1982) staged murders as ballets of color and camera movement, its legendary Steadicam shot prowling around an entire house before descending into violence. For Argento, gore was choreography: murder as operatic set-piece.

Other directors like Umberto Lenzi (*Cannibal Ferox*, 1981) and Ruggero Deodato (*Cannibal Holocaust*, 1980) pushed gore into even more transgressive territory. Cannibal films blurred the line between fiction and documentary, so convincingly staged that Deodato was put on trial for obscenity and had to prove his actors were alive. These films became lightning rods for censorship battles across Europe, particularly during the UK's "Video Nasties" panic. Italian gore was baroque, brutal, and unapologetic. It turned gore into spectacle, not to terrify with restraint but to overwhelm with excess. Cinema as autopsy, nightmare as theater.

Splatterpunk and the American Gore Revolution

Across the Atlantic, a different current surged: splatterpunk. Less surreal than Fulci and Argento but just as transgressive, splatterpunk embraced gore with anarchic humor and DIY ingenuity.

Sam Raimi's *The Evil Dead* (1981) epitomized the movement. Shot with raw inventiveness on a shoestring budget, it turned a cabin in the woods into a carnival of dismemberment, whirling camerawork, and geysers of blood. Raimi fused terror with slapstick, laying the foundation for horror-comedy hybrids and proving gore could be as funny as it was horrifying.

Stuart Gordon's *Re-Animator* (1985) took H. P. Lovecraft's premise of resurrection and pushed it into outrageous excess: severed heads performing grotesque acts, corpses reanimated in spasms of violence. It was transgressive, yes, but also gleefully tongue-in-cheek, horror as grotesque parody of its own taboos.

Films like Frank Henenlotter's *Basket Case* (1982) and even early Peter Jackson efforts like *Bad Taste* (1987, New Zealand) carried the splatterpunk ethos: gore as rebellion, gore as punk performance art. These films thrived in grindhouses and VHS circulation, gaining cult status far outside the mainstream.

Where Italy treated gore as spectacle of decay, splatterpunk made it playful, outrageous, even satirical. It mocked authority, thumbed its nose at censorship, and embraced gore as excess for its own sake. Critics often dismissed it as juvenile, but fans recognized its inventiveness and anarchic spirit.

Splatterpunk was not simply about showing gore, it was about celebrating its impossibility, its absurdity, its gleeful violation of cinematic "taste." It was horror's punk rock: fast, loud, obscene, and impossible to ignore.

Video Nasties and Cannibal Savagery

If American slashers were a franchise machine and Italian gore was an art of decay, the exploitation wave of cannibal films and their censorship battles became horror's most notorious scandal.

Ruggero Deodato's *Cannibal Holocaust* (1980, Italy) is still whispered about as one of the most transgressive films ever made. Framed as a found-footage documentary, it followed Western filmmakers exploiting the Amazon only to be devoured by the tribes they mocked. Its depictions of sexual assault, mutilation, and ritual cannibalism were so extreme that Italian courts charged Deodato with obscenity and even murder. He had to produce his cast in court to prove they were still alive. Real animal killings added further controversy, cementing the film's reputation as both pioneering and indefensible.

Cannibal Holocaust was not alone. Umberto Lenzi's *Cannibal Ferox* (1981) and others in the cycle trafficked in the same blend of exoticism, violence, and taboo-breaking excess. These films were condemned as racist, exploitative, and depraved, but they were also fiercely watched, debated, and smuggled.

At the dawn of the VHS era, horror slipped past traditional gatekeepers. Suddenly, uncut tapes of films once confined to grindhouses could sit on the same shelves as family movies. In Britain, tabloids seized on the panic. Headlines warned of children renting films like *The Driller Killer* (1979), *The Evil Dead* (1981), and *Cannibal Holocaust* from corner shops.

The backlash culminated in the infamous "Video Nasties" list, a government crackdown that banned or prosecuted over seventy titles under the Obscene Publications Act. Tapes were seized, distributors prosecuted, and horror was painted as a corrupting threat to youth.

Yet as often happens in horror's history, censorship only increased allure. Banned tapes circulated as contraband, creating a black-market economy where forbidden films gained cult reputations precisely because they were outlawed. The label "Video Nasty" became a badge of honor. Fans hunted bootlegs. Directors wore the stigma as proof that their work had struck cultural nerves too raw to ignore.

The Video Nasties panic revealed horror's unique power to provoke moral outrage. It wasn't just about gore; it was about who controlled images, who defined morality, and how far art could go in reflecting human savagery. The hysteria proved that horror was not trivial exploitation but a cultural battleground, where questions of censorship, freedom, and violence collided.

In hindsight, the Nasties era defined the 1980s as much as the slashers did. Where Carpenter and Craven turned horror into global franchises, Deodato and his peers turned it into contraband. Together, they proved that horror could be mainstream and underground, legal and illegal, spectacle and scandal all at the same time.

The Franchise Firestorm

If the *Video Nasties* panic cast horror as contraband, the other half of the 1980s made it an industry. Slashers, once shocking, became serialized ritual. Killers returning year after year like clockwork.

After *Halloween, Friday the 13th*, and *A Nightmare on Elm Street* found box office gold, sequels flooded theaters. Jason Voorhees rose from the grave in one installment only to be resurrected in the next. Freddy Krueger evolved from sinister child killer to pop-culture icon, his quips and dreamscapes marketed almost as spectacle. Even Michael Myers, briefly retired after *Halloween II* (1981) and the anthology experiment of *Halloween III: Season of the Witch* (1982), was resurrected to reclaim his mask in *Halloween 4* (1988).

Each sequel promised little innovation but guaranteed ritual: a holiday release date, a recognizable villain, a new set of disposable teens. The repetition itself became the draw, transforming horror into the closest thing cinema had to a seasonal blood sport.

Horror icons crossed into toys, Halloween masks, and television spots. Freddy hosted MTV, Jason appeared on lunchboxes, and Chucky (*Child's Play*, 1988) added a doll to the pantheon of branded killers. Slashers were no longer just movies, they were mascots of fear, marketed as heavily as superheroes.

The franchise model bred escalation. Kills grew more elaborate, gore more outrageous, and premises more absurd. Jason ventured to Manhattan (*Friday the 13th Part VIII*, 1989). Freddy invaded video games (*A Nightmare on Elm Street Part 6*, 1991). Sequels became contests in one-upmanship, testing how far spectacle could be stretched before parody overtook fear.

This industrialization made horror one of the most profitable genres of the 1980s, but it also diluted its power. By the end of the decade, critics and even fans complained of fatigue. The mask had become merchandise, the monster routine. But even in decline, the franchises proved horror's resilience. What began as low-budget rebellion had become a Hollywood machine.

Body Horror and the New Flesh

If the slasher stripped horror to knives and masks, body horror went the opposite direction into the flesh itself. The 1980s, with its explosion of practical effects wizardry, became the decade when skin split, organs writhed, and the body betrayed its owner. Horror no longer lurked outside; it erupted from within.

David Cronenberg emerged as the prophet of this subgenre. His films treated the body as a site of invasion, corruption, and transformation. *Videodrome* (1983) envisioned television itself as a virus, with videotapes fusing into torsos and flesh sprouting grotesque orifices. The film declared "long live the new flesh," a mantra for an age when technology and biology were becoming indistinguishable.

In *The Fly* (1986), Cronenberg translated tragedy into mutation. Jeff Goldblum's scientist, fused with a housefly during an experiment, slowly deteriorates in front of his horrified lover. Fingernails peel, skin sloughs, organs liquefy. The grotesque was married to heartbreak, making the horror of decay profoundly human.

John Carpenter's *The Thing* (1982) was another landmark, pushing practical effects to unthinkable heights. Rob Bottin's creations turned the Antarctic outpost into a theater of monstrosity: dogs splitting open into tendrils, heads sprouting legs to scuttle across the floor, human bodies mutating mid-transformation. Beneath the spectacle lay Cold War anxieties: paranoia, infiltration, the fear that anyone could be "other."

Elsewhere, Stuart Gordon's *Re-Animator* (1985) blended Lovecraftian science with gleeful grotesquery. Severed heads reanimated into obscene parody, corpses jerked back to life in spasms of violence. Gordon's film reveled in the absurdity of resurrection. Horror pushed so far into excess, it circled back into black comedy.

Body horror was more than gore. It mirrored the fears of its age: the spread of AIDS, the rise of biotechnology, and cultural unease around sexuality and disease. The human body, once sacrosanct, became unstable. Liable to sprout, melt, or betray its owner at any moment.

In Cronenberg's words, the "new flesh" was both promise and curse. The body could evolve, but its evolution was monstrous. Horror had always punished transgression; now it revealed that simply existing in a body was transgression enough.

Supernatural and Demonic Horror

Even as masked killers and splatterpunk gore defined the decade's headlines, the supernatural refused to fade. In fact, the 1980s proved that ghosts, demons, and cosmic evil could thrive alongside slashers, feeding the same anxieties with different weapons.

If slashers made suburbia unsafe from the outside, supernatural horror suggested the threat was already inside the home. *The Changeling* (1980, Canada) offered a masterclass in atmosphere: a grieving composer alone in a mansion, haunted by whispers, thuds, and a spectral child. No gore was needed; the terror lay in the persistence of grief and memory.

Two years later, *Poltergeist* (1982, USA) blew the haunted house wide open. Produced by Steven Spielberg and directed by Tobe Hooper, it transplanted ghosts into a picture-perfect suburban development. The very dream of Reagan-era prosperity. When the television set became a portal for spirits and a child was dragged into another dimension, the message was clear: no space, however safe or modern, was immune to haunting.

Sam Raimi's *The Evil Dead* (1981) fused supernatural horror with the unruly energy of splatter. Its premise was simple: five friends in a cabin awaken ancient demons through a cursed book, but its execution was groundbreaking. Possessed bodies spewed fluids, limbs were hacked, and demons taunted their victims with obscene glee. It was demonic possession reframed as grindhouse nightmare, a fusion of occult dread and outrageous gore that birthed its own cult legacy.

John Carpenter's *Prince of Darkness* (1987) blended theology with quantum physics, imagining Satan not as a horned villain but as a swirling, liquid embodiment of cosmic evil unearthed in a Los Angeles church basement. Its visions of anti-God, transmission through mirrors, and apocalyptic prophecy gave possession horror a new scope, expanding it from exorcism to cosmic terror.

The 1980s had no shortage of occult thrillers, from lesser-known possession stories to films like *Hellraiser* (1987), which fused sadomasochistic demons with erotic horror, creating one of cinema's most enduring nightmare mythologies in Pinhead and his Cenobites. These films suggested that evil wasn't fading in an era of slashers, it was mutating, finding new ways to invade the mind, the home, and the flesh.

Supernatural horror in the 1980s didn't vanish beneath the slasher craze; it thrived alongside it. If slashers represented nihilism on the ground, the supernatural reminded audiences that the heavens and hells above them were just as terrifying, and just as eager to break through.

Erotic Horror

The loosening of censorship in the 1970s and 80s also opened the door for one of horror's most provocative hybrids: the fusion of sex and death. Erotic horror thrived on the recognition that desire itself could be terrifying that pleasure and annihilation were two sides of the same instinct.

In France, Jean Rollin created dreamlike, atmospheric vampire films that blurred the line between softcore eroticism and Gothic fantasy. Works like *The Nude Vampire* (1970) and *Fascination* (1979) featured languid pacing, ethereal women, and surreal imagery: coffins, castles, and female vampires whose intimacy was as threatening as their fangs. Rollin's cinema turned eroticism into ritual, suggesting that seduction and death were inseparable.

Tony Scott's *The Hunger*[5] (1983, UK/USA) brought erotic horror into the arthouse mainstream. Catherine Deneuve and David Bowie played ageless vampires whose beauty masked rot, while Susan Sarandon's seduction scene with Deneuve became iconic for its blending of sensuality, queerness, and predation. The film epitomized the 1980s: sleek, stylish, and obsessed with surfaces that concealed decay.

The most enduring erotic horror of the decade came from Clive Barker. *Hellraiser* (1987, UK) envisioned a puzzle box that opened gateways to the Cenobites, beings who blurred angelic and demonic, pain and pleasure. Hooks pierced flesh, leather-clad bodies promised ecstasy through torment, and sexuality became indistinguishable from mutilation. Barker's film was both transgressive and philosophical, interrogating the limits of sensation itself.

Beyond these high-profile works, erotic horror threaded through European exploitation and American B-cinema alike. Italian directors layered nudity and sex into Gothic and giallo hybrids, while vampire films everywhere leaned on seduction as their central metaphor. What unified them was the recognition that eroticism destabilized, it blurred consent, blurred identity, blurred life and death.

Erotic horror was not simply titillation. It revealed that sexuality itself could be monstrous, whether as seduction into vampirism, the bondage of Hell's demons, or the decay hidden beneath glamor. Horror had always punished desire, but in the 1980s it celebrated its terror, making lust itself into a haunted landscape.

Anthology Horror: Short Shocks, Long Shadows

The 1980s didn't just belong to masked killers and gore-soaked splatter. It also revived an older format: the anthology, where multiple short tales were stitched together by a unifying frame. These "horror mixtapes" gave filmmakers room to experiment with tone, pacing, and taboo in a way feature-length narratives often couldn't.

George A. Romero and Stephen King's *Creepshow* (1982) became the archetype. Styled after the EC Comics of the 1950s: *Tales from the Crypt*, *The Vault of Horror*, it presented lurid morality plays with comic-book transitions, garish colors, and gleeful gore. Each vignette carried a darkly ironic twist: cheaters buried alive, gluttons consumed by their excess, the dead clawing back for revenge. *Creepshow* was both a love letter to pulp and a proof-of-concept that horror could thrive in the short form.

The same year, *Twilight Zone: The Movie* (1983) carried anthology horror further into the mainstream. Drawing on Rod Serling's iconic television series, it updated the moral parables of midcentury sci-fi-horror with the spectacle of Hollywood budgets. Though uneven, it showed that anthology structure could hold blockbuster appeal, keeping alive the tradition of compact tales of terror.

Internationally, the format spread with films like *The Monster Club* (1981, UK), which mixed camp, folklore, and Gothic pastiche, while Japanese and European directors experimented with surreal short-form frights. The anthology model echoed across decades, resurfacing in later cult entries like *Necronomicon* (1993) and modern revivals like *The Mortuary Collection* (2020).

What anthologies revealed was horror's versatility. A single film could carry five different terrors, yet they shared one atmosphere of dread. They also embodied the VHS boom: short, punchy shocks perfect for late-night rental marathons. In an era of sequels and franchises, anthologies reminded audiences that horror's essence could be distilled into a single unforgettable scare.

Foreign Horror: A Global Language of Fear

The 1980s were not just an American bloodbath of slashers and sequels. Abroad, horror was mutating into forms as distinctive and transgressive as anything in Hollywood, proving the genre had become truly global.

In Italy, horror reached its goriest zenith. Lucio Fulci, nicknamed the "Godfather of Gore," drenched audiences in decay with *Zombie* (1979), *City of the Living Dead* (1980), and *The Beyond* (1981). His films reveled in eyeball piercings, rotting cadavers, and surreal nightmare logic. Dario Argento, already established by his giallo films, pushed into extremes with *Tenebrae* (1982) and *Phenomena* (1985), where color-saturated murder scenes became works of deranged art. Italian horror in this decade was lurid, stylish, and unapologetically visceral.

In Japan, directors revived kaidan, traditional ghost stories, but set them against modern anxieties. Early stirrings of urban curse narratives began appearing, foreshadowing the J-horror boom of the 1990s. Films like *Evil Dead Trap* (1988) blended slasher influences with surreal, curse-driven imagery, hinting at what would become *Ringu* and *Ju-On* a decade later.

Elsewhere in Europe, horror crossed into arthouse cinema. Andrzej Żuławski's *Possession* (1981, France/West Germany) blurred psychological breakdown with grotesque body horror, staging Isabelle Adjani's infamous subway convulsions and Sam Neill's marital disintegration against a backdrop of Cold War paranoia. The result was part domestic drama, part cosmic nightmare. A reminder that horror could also be art cinema at its most unhinged.

Spain and France produced their own hybrids, from occult thrillers to erotic vampire tales, while Mexico and Latin America drew on folklore and Catholic guilt. Across the world, filmmakers tapped into local fears: political oppression, colonial legacy, nuclear trauma and translated them into universal monsters.

By the 1980s, horror spoke a global language. Whether it was Fulci's worms crawling from corpses, Adjani screaming in Berlin tunnels, or Japanese curses creeping into the city, every culture found its own horrors yet all resonated with the same dread, the same fascination with what lies beyond control.

Horror-Comedy: Now on a Lighter Note

By the mid-80s, horror had grown self-aware and playful. After a decade of nihilistic slashers and relentless gore, audiences were ready to laugh at the same monsters that once kept them awake. Horror-comedy thrived because it struck that balance acknowledging the absurdity of the genre while still reveling in its creatures and chaos.

Gremlins (1984) set the tone. Joe Dante's film began as a whimsical Christmas story, then erupted into mayhem as tiny creatures trashed suburbia with slapstick carnage. Equal parts Spielbergian wonder and cartoonish menace, it proved that horror could be fun without losing its bite.

The Return of the Living Dead (1985) went further, punking up the zombie mythos. Its mohawked corpses moaned not for flesh but for "braaains," cementing a new pop-culture cliché. Self-aware, irreverent, and anarchic, it turned Romero's social allegory into midnight-movie satire, while still delivering gory shocks.

The Lost Boys (1987) fused vampires with teen rebellion and MTV swagger. Its leather-clad bloodsuckers rode motorcycles, blasted rock, and made vampirism feel both seductive and dangerous. It captured the decade's youth culture while poking fun at the Gothic tropes it borrowed.

Elsewhere, *Evil Dead II* (1987) transformed Sam Raimi's cabin-in-the-woods splatterfest into slapstick absurdity. Chainsaws, flying eyeballs, and Bruce Campbell's gurning face made horror itself the punchline.

Horror-comedy worked because the genre had become oversaturated. By laughing with the audience without abandoning the monsters, it kept horror fresh. These films didn't just spoof; they expanded the genre's emotional range. By the end of the decade, horror had proven it could make audiences scream and howl with laughter in the same breath.

Catalysts and Gatekeepers

The slasher boom thrived on low budgets, high returns, and the rise of the multiplex. VHS and home video exploded horror's reach, giving grindhouse films second lives in living rooms and dorms. Practical effects workshops led by maestros like Tom Savini, Rob Bottin, and Rick Baker became the new engines of horror, crafting spectacles of transformation and gore that critics dismissed but fans adored. Festivals, fanzines, and censorship boards alike gave horror visibility, ensuring it was both condemned and impossible to ignore.

The Backlash

The backlash was ferocious. Parents' groups lobbied for bans. Britain criminalized tapes in the *Video Nasties* panic. American critics decried slashers as sexist, juvenile, and nihilistic. *Silent Night, Deadly Night* (1984) was pulled from theaters after protests over Santa Claus as a killer. Yet outrage only amplified the genre's allure. By mid-decade, icons like Freddy, Jason, and Chucky had transcended the screen, appearing on lunchboxes, comics, and late-night talk shows. Horror was both reviled and embraced moral panic on one hand, pop culture juggernaut on the other.

Craft Innovations

- **Steadicam prowls** (*Halloween*) turned suburbia into a hunting ground.
- **Practical gore effects** (Savini, Bottin, Baker) raised the bar for visceral realism.
- **Slashers codified tropes**: the Final Girl, the masked killer, and the endless sequel machine.
- **Italian gore and splatter** pushed violence into surreal, artful extremes.
- **Cronenberg and Carpenter** made the body itself monstrous, fusing flesh with technology and paranoia.
- **Anthologies and horror-comedy** proved the genre could reinvent tone without losing its bite.

By the end of the 1980s, horror had reached saturation. Slashers clogged theaters, gore flooded VHS shelves, and censors fought a losing battle against the tidal wave of blood. The genre was at once formulaic and experimental, populist and avant-garde.

But fatigue was setting in. Sequels grew stale. Audiences, now jaded, sought something new. The 1990s would bring a reckoning. A wave of meta-commentary, irony, and reinvention that forced horror to look in the mirror and ask: *what's left to fear when the formula itself is the monster?*

New Hollywood Exhaustion and Global Shockwaves
(1990s–2000s)

The 1990s were a decade of transition for horror. Some of the 1980s' most prolific subgenres fizzled under sequel fatigue, while others reinvented themselves with self-aware energy. At the same time, international cinema took the spotlight, making horror more global than ever before. The era was defined by meta-storytelling, supernatural resurgence, and a new breed of realism powered by camcorders and digital culture.

Neo-Noir and Psychological Horror

The 1990s blurred horror with crime thriller and neo-noir aesthetics, producing some of the most acclaimed and unsettling films of the decade. Here, the monsters weren't vampires or masked killers, they were human beings, terrifying precisely because of their intelligence, precision, and proximity to the ordinary.

Jonathan Demme's *The Silence of the Lambs*[6] (1991, USA) marked a cultural watershed. It became only the third film in history to sweep the "Big Five" Academy Awards, proving horror could command prestige. At its center was Hannibal Lecter, played by Anthony Hopkins with unnerving calm. Lecter was a monster of manners: erudite, polite, and unspeakably violent. The film balanced psychological horror with procedural grit, embedding its terror in the cat-and-mouse dynamic between Lecter, FBI trainee Clarice Starling (Jodie Foster), and serial killer Buffalo Bill. Its cultural impact was seismic: horror was now not just pulp but Oscar material.

David Fincher's *Se7en* (1995, USA) dragged noir into hell. In a rain-drenched, unnamed city, detectives (Brad Pitt, Morgan Freeman) pursued a killer whose murders staged the seven deadly sins with operatic cruelty. Each crime scene was a tableau of grotesque allegory, culminating in a finale so bleak that it redefined Hollywood's limits on despair. "What's in the box?" became shorthand for the nihilism of the 90s, a decade increasingly preoccupied with systems collapsing and morality unraveling.

Other films contributed to this psychological turn: *Cape Fear* (1991, Martin Scorsese) reimagined the stalker as a primal force of revenge; *Jacob's Ladder* (1990) blurred war trauma and hallucination into a descent of surreal dread; *Kalifornia* (1993) and *Copycat* (1995) merged road movie with serial-killer anxiety. Together, they revealed how horror could infiltrate mainstream thrillers, reframing crime as existential terror.

Neo-noir and psychological horror thrived because they reflected the 1990s' anxieties: about urban decay, moral ambiguity, and the collapse of trust in institutions. The monster wasn't hiding in the woods or lurking in a Gothic ruin. He was in the next cellblock, the next tenement, the next suburban home.

Backlash & Legacy: Horror in Thriller's Shadow

The success of *The Silence of the Lambs* and *Se7en* elevated horror's imagery, but often at the expense of the word itself. Studios branded these films "psychological thrillers," distancing them from the stigma of horror, which critics still dismissed as lowbrow or exploitative. For much of the early 1990s, "thriller" became the safe label: marketable, respectable, awards-friendly while "horror" was pushed to the margins.

This left the genre in an odd limbo. On one hand, audiences craved serial killers, mystery structures, and gritty realism. On the other, the supernatural and slasher roots of horror felt passé, buried under sequels and clichés. The genre was profitable but identity-starved, fractured between the multiplex's "thrillers" and the video store's exploitation bins.

That identity crisis set the stage for Wes Craven's return. In 1996, *Scream* didn't just revive the slasher, it proudly reclaimed the word "horror," mocking and honoring its tropes in the same breath. After years of dilution, horror finally stepped out from under thriller's shadow to announce itself again, sharper and bloodier than ever.

Meta-Horror and the Teen Slasher Revival

By the early 1990s, the slasher was exhausted. Sequels had hollowed out the menace of Michael, Freddy, and Jason, leaving audiences immune to their repetition. The "Final Girl" had become predictable, the jump scares mechanical, and the villains camp icons rather than nightmares. Horror needed a fresh mask.

Wes Craven, who had already revolutionized the genre with *A Nightmare on Elm Street*, struck again with *Scream* (1996, USA). The film detonated the stale formula with a single innovation: self-awareness. Its teenagers had seen horror films, knew the "rules of survival," don't have sex, don't say "I'll be right back" and quoted them aloud, only to die by them anyway. The script, by Kevin Williamson, turned the genre inside out, making the audience complicit in its clichés while still delivering genuine suspense.

At its center was Sidney Prescott (Neve Campbell), a Final Girl who was neither naïve virgin nor passive victim. She was self-aware, resilient, and self-reflexive. A heroine forged in trauma who understood the tropes and survived by transcending them. In a decade defined by irony and postmodern detachment, *Scream* felt electric: a horror movie about horror movies, both parody and reinvention.

The Scream Effect: Teen Slashers Go Glossy

The massive success of *Scream* ($173 million worldwide on a $15 million budget) reanimated the slasher subgenre. Hollywood rushed to replicate its formula, packaging horror for a new generation of MTV-raised teens.

- *I Know What You Did Last Summer* (1997, USA) replaced the masked killer with a hook-wielding fisherman, spinning vengeance into a glossy mystery populated by television stars like Jennifer Love Hewitt and Sarah Michelle Gellar.
- *Urban Legend* (1998, USA) mined college campus myths for death scenes, from killers in the backseat of cars to poison-dosed soda, blending whodunit intrigue with teen horror sheen.
- *Valentine* (2001, USA) and *Cherry Falls* (2000, USA) pushed the aesthetic further, leaning on attractive casts and ironic setups.

These films shared common DNA: attractive ensembles, pop-soundtrack marketing, and the self-awareness that the audience was in on the game. Slashers were no longer grim morality tales about sex and punishment; they were pop-cultural mirrors, stylish and ironic.

Whodunit Revival

If *Scream* turned horror into a self-aware game, films like *Urban Legend* (1998, USA) and *Valentine* (2001, USA) leaned into the mystery element with straight-faced commitment. These slashers revived the structure of Agatha Christie-style whodunits: a closed circle of suspects, red herrings scattered across campus or suburban settings, and a climactic unmasking that revealed the killer's grudge.

Unlike the silent boogeymen of the 1980s, these killers had backstories tied to secrets and betrayals. A friend wronged, a holiday tragedy, a legend passed down. The violence was stylized, but the tension often came less from the gore than from the guessing game: *who among us is wearing the mask?* This return to mystery connected slashers back to their Giallo lineage, where black-gloved killers and elaborate motives made murder a puzzle as much as a spectacle.

Glossy Teen Horror

I Know What You Did Last Summer (1997, USA) exemplified the polished, star-driven approach that defined late 90s horror. Featuring a cast plucked from TV hits (*Party of Five*, *Buffy the Vampire Slayer*, *Dawson's Creek*), it sold horror with the same appeal as teen dramas. The killer was less supernatural archetype and more local bogeyman. A hook-wielding fisherman tied to the sins of the past.

These films emphasized style: slick cinematography, pop soundtracks, and poster-ready faces. They became events marketed as much for their casts as for their scares. This MTV-era horror was less about shadows and trauma and more about packaging. A glossy blend of thriller, soap opera, and slasher tradition.

While commercially successful, critics dismissed them as hollow imitations of *Scream*. But their popularity showed horror's adaptability: in the 90s, slashers could survive not by being scarier, but by being fashionable.

Backlash & Decline

By the turn of the millennium, meta-horror had eaten itself. What began as sharp self-awareness in *Scream* (1996) became formula by its third sequel (*Scream 3*, 2000), where in-jokes and celebrity cameos drowned out suspense. The irony that once felt fresh now played as smug.

Then came *Scary Movie* (2000), a parody so successful it grossed over $275 million worldwide. It lampooned *Scream* and *I Know What You Did Last Summer* with such blunt force that the joke of self-aware horror became impossible to play straight. What had been satire turned into spoof, and the genre's credibility suffered.

Meanwhile, diminishing returns hit hard. Teen slashers like *Urban Legends: Final Cut* (2000) and *Valentine* (2001) felt like reheated leftovers, predictable even to casual viewers. Critics accused the genre of being shallow, manufactured, and reliant on the same faces and beats. The slasher, once a site of transgression and fear, had become corporate product.

Audiences moved on. Box office momentum shifted to fresher terrors: imported ghost stories from Japan and Korea, gothic experiments from Spain, and the looming revolution of found footage. Horror's center of gravity was no longer suburban America, it was global, diffuse, and whispering in new, unfamiliar languages.

By the early 2000s, the American slasher had collapsed under its own self-reflection. To scare again, horror would have to shed irony and look outward to curses carried on videotapes, to ghosts rooted in cultural trauma, and to cinematic styles far from Hollywood's glossy sheen.

J-Horror: Ghosts in the Machine

While American horror of the late 90s winked at itself, Japan resurrected the ghost story with chilling restraint. Hideo Nakata's *Ringu* (1998, Japan) became the flashpoint. Its premise was simple but devastating: a cursed videotape kills its viewers in seven days. At the center was Sadako, a pale, long-haired figure whose image became instantly iconic. Her slow crawl out of a television set collapsed the boundary between media and reality, between viewer and viewed.

Unlike American slashers, J-horror did not rely on gore, quips, or excess. Its terrors were slow-burn and uncanny, drawn from centuries of Japanese ghost tradition: the *yūrei*, spirits of the wronged dead, marked by long hair, white funeral garb, and relentless grudges. These films built dread through silence, atmosphere, and sudden ruptures of the ordinary: a ringing phone, a dripping faucet, the hum of static.

The success of *Ringu* ignited a wave. Nakata followed with *Dark Water* (2002), where a haunted apartment mirrored urban alienation and maternal fear. Kiyoshi Kurosawa's *Pulse* (2001) used ghostly figures on the internet to explore isolation and the terror of a world becoming digitally fragmented. Takashi Shimizu's *Ju-On: The Grudge* (2002) fractured timelines and characters, suggesting that curses spread like viruses, beyond control or logic.

Hollywood quickly took notice. Gore Verbinski's remake of *The Ring* (2002, USA) translated Sadako into Samara and made $250 million worldwide, proving J-horror's global export power. Remakes of *Ju-On* (*The Grudge*, 2004), *Dark Water* (2005), and others followed. Even when diluted, the essence of J-horror: atmosphere over spectacle, trauma over villainy seeped into Western filmmaking.

Thematically, J-horror spoke to anxieties at the turn of the millennium: technology as a haunted conduit, the viral spread of trauma, the fragility of family bonds in urban modernity. Its ghosts were not monsters to be vanquished, but forces of inevitability. Grief, loneliness, and cultural memory taking shape on screen.

By the early 2000s, J-horror had reshaped the genre's global language. Where slashers shouted, Japan whispered and the whisper was far more terrifying.

Korea: Trauma and Family Horror

If J-horror gave the world viral curses and technological dread, South Korea responded with horror rooted in trauma, grief, and the disintegration of the family. Kim Jee-woon's *A Tale of Two Sisters* (2003, Korea) was the spark. Adapted from a Joseon-era folktale, it cloaked its twist ending in lush Gothic imagery: shadowy corridors, spectral mothers, and domestic spaces warped by repression. Beneath the scares was a portrait of grief, abuse, and memory itself as a haunting.

Korean horror in the 2000s leaned into extremes both emotional and stylistic. Park Chan-wook's *Thirst* (2009) reimagined vampirism as a Catholic crisis of faith and desire, mixing eroticism with gore. Na Hong-jin's *The Wailing* (2016) drew global attention for its fusion of shamanism, possession, and cosmic uncertainty. Korea's horror was operatic in its emotions, blending melodrama with folkloric unease.

Unlike Hollywood slashers or Japan's restrained ghosts, K-horror forced audiences to confront grief, guilt, and inherited trauma, making the personal and the familial inseparable from the supernatural.

Global Shockwaves: Beyond Hollywood

By the early 2000s, horror had gone truly global. Cheap distribution (VHS, DVD, and later the internet) carried films across continents, and the genre became a vessel for cultural trauma and historical memory.

In Spain, Guillermo del Toro's *The Devil's Backbone* (2001) placed a ghost child amid the ruins of the Spanish Civil War. Horror here was allegory: the real monster was history itself. His *Pan's Labyrinth* (2006) perfected this blend of horror and fantasy, winning Oscars while proving the genre's capacity for high art.

Meanwhile, Latin America exported bold visions. *Here Comes the Devil* (2012, Mexico) and *Tigers Are Not Afraid* (2017, Mexico) tied supernatural dread to the ongoing trauma of cartel violence. Argentina's *Terrified* (*Aterrados*, 2017) became a festival sensation for its inventive, nerve-wracking staging of paranormal terror. Uruguay's *The Silent House* (2010) impressed with its "single-take" real-time haunted house format. These films revealed how horror could localize trauma, refracting violence, poverty, and political instability through spectral imagery.

Europe, too, fed into this wave. Andrzej Żuławski's *Possession* (1981, France/West Germany), though earlier, lingered as a cult influence throughout the 90s and 2000s, with its unhinged mix of marital collapse, possession, and surreal monstrosity. Its legacy echoed in the arthouse-horror hybrids that surged in later decades, proving horror could be as experimental and avant-garde as any festival darling.

The 1990s–2000s marked horror's digital globalization. VHS tapes, DVDs, and eventually the internet allowed films like *Ringu* and *The Devil's Backbone* to leap borders instantly. Hollywood noticed, and remakes poured in (*The Ring*, *The Grudge*, *Dark Water*). At the same time, critics began taking horror seriously, granting it new legitimacy as allegory and art.

This global wave showed that horror was not just an American pastime or a Japanese export, it was a universal language of fear, each culture speaking in its own dialect, yet all resonating together. It laid the groundwork for the "prestige horror" of the 2010s, where trauma, allegory, and artistry became the genre's dominant grammar.

Body Horror and Surreal Experiments

Body horror did not end with Cronenberg's 1980s reign, it mutated. In the 1990s, the grotesque fused with allegory and surrealism, expanding beyond gore into metaphors of time, technology, and trauma.

Guillermo del Toro's *Cronos* (1993, Mexico) was a watershed moment. Its golden scarab-like device, granting immortality at the cost of vampiric thirst, corroded not just flesh but morality. Del Toro fused Gothic horror with Catholic symbolism and alchemical lore, establishing his signature blend of fantasy, body horror, and melancholy.

Elsewhere, filmmakers embraced the body as site of existential puzzle. Vincenzo Natali's *Cube* (1997, Canada) turned architecture itself into a killing machine, trapping strangers in a geometric nightmare where survival meant dismemberment and distrust. Paul W. S. Anderson's *Event Horizon* (1997, USA/UK) pushed sci-fi horror into cosmic territory: a spaceship opening a gateway to hell, revealing mutilated corpses and psychological breakdowns.

These films signaled a shift in body horror from viscera to vision. The grotesque was no longer only about splitting skin or mutating flesh, it became surreal, dreamlike, even philosophical. Horror asked not just "what if the body breaks?" but "what if reality itself is a trap, reshaping us into forms we can't comprehend?"

By the end of the 1990s, body horror had escaped its 80s ghetto of splatter and become a laboratory for ideas. Still gory, but also poetic, allegorical, and surreal.

Gothic Revival on a Grand Scale

Even as postmodern irony and minimalist dread defined much of 1990s horror, the decade also saw a return to Gothic excess on an operatic scale. Big studios poured budgets into ornate sets, sweeping romances, and elaborate costuming, proving that Gothic imagery remained a potent draw in the age of VHS and digital spectacle.

Ford Coppola's *Bram Stoker's Dracula* (1992, USA) was the crown jewel of this revival. With Gary Oldman's shapeshifting Count, Winona Ryder's tragic Mina, and Anthony Hopkins' frenzied Van Helsing, the film staged vampirism as both erotic romance and historical epic. Coppola embraced theatrical artifice: crimson-drenched costumes, matte-painted castles, and practical in-camera illusions evoked early cinema while elevating Gothic to operatic grandeur. Horror here was spectacle: lush, sensual, and baroque.

Tim Burton's *Sleepy Hollow* (1999, USA) closed the decade by turning Washington Irving's folktale into a macabre fairy tale. Johnny Depp's Ichabod Crane investigated a town cloaked in mist and blood, while Christopher Walken's Headless Horseman fused folklore with Burton's playful morbidity. The film blended digital effects with practical gore, capturing the genre's ability to feel both old and new at once.

This Gothic revival was not nostalgia but renewal. It proved that, even in an era dominated by slashers, irony, and found realism, the grand traditions of castles, curses, and doomed romance still had power. Horror's 20th century closed where it began: in the shadow of Gothic ruins, reimagined with 1990s extravagance.

As the millennium turned, Gothic castles and lavish studio spectacles gave way to stripped-down terror. Audiences no longer needed operatic grandeur to feel fear; they wanted immediacy, realism, and extremity. Technology made it possible: camcorders, the internet, and cheap digital editing fueled the rise of found footage, while loosening taboos about violence birthed torture horror and the so-called "New Extremity." If the 1990s flirted with self-awareness and global allegory, the 2000s demanded rawness. Horror that felt unfiltered, intimate, and impossible to look away from.

Torture, Found Footage & New Extremity
(2000s–2010s)

If the 1990s globalized horror, the 2000s tested how far audiences would go. Horror split into extremes: stripped-down realism through found footage, calculated cruelty in torture cinema, and a European movement that treated horror as philosophical extremity. Meanwhile, Hollywood leaned hard on remakes, zombies sprinted into the new millennium, and whispers of "elevated horror" began to stir.

Found Footage: Fear Becomes "Real"

3:04:56 AM

The Blair Witch Project (1999, USA) detonated the subgenre like a curse passed through modem static. Marketed with one of the first viral internet campaigns: faux missing posters, "real" websites, whispered rumors. Its grainy camcorder footage convinced many that what they saw might not be fiction at all. With a $60,000 budget and $248 million in returns, it proved horror didn't need castles or creatures, only the illusion of authenticity. In the 2000s, the style metastasized across borders:

- **Paranormal Activity (2007, USA)** — made for the same sum as a family sedan, it turned the suburban home into a surveillance nightmare. Its horror came not from gore but from stillness: a door creaking, a sheet shifting, a camera staring too long into the dark.
- **[REC] (2007, Spain)** — claustrophobic and relentless, it fused zombie infection with real-time reportage, trapping audiences in a quarantined apartment alongside a doomed TV crew.
- **Cloverfield (2008, USA)** — applied the handheld immediacy to kaiju spectacle, reframing the monster movie as panic captured by accident, one shaky angle at a time.

Found footage wasn't just a gimmick, it was a philosophy. It stripped away polish, denying audiences the comfort of cinematic distance. The camera became both witness and weapon, framing terror as if it had spilled raw into the world. Where Gothic had given us shadows, and slashers gave us masks, found footage gave us a mirror: what if horror was real, and you were holding the camera?

Analog Horror: Signals from the Past

Out of found footage's grainy camcorders grew a stranger cousin: analog horror. Less about handheld panic and more about corrupted memory, analog horror presents itself as lost broadcasts, government PSAs, or eerie VHS signals bleeding through the static of late-20th-century media.

The horror lies in distortion itself flickering emergency alerts, warped children's shows, cryptic logos that promise safety but drip menace. The low-fi textures evoke a collective memory of when television felt both authoritative and uncanny, the era when Cold War PSAs or local news interruptions could stop hearts.

Popularized on YouTube decades later, series like *Local 58* and *The Mandela Catalogue* embraced this uncanny grammar. Their "recovered tapes" aesthetic blurred nostalgia with paranoia, asking what nightmares might hide in dead air and corrupted signals.

Analog horror proved that the medium of horror could mutate again. Where found footage simulated authenticity, analog horror simulated memory itself: fragile, corrupted, and always one broadcast away from something unspeakable.

Saw and the Game of Pain

James Wan's *Saw* (2004, USA) turned a filthy, tiled bathroom into one of horror's most enduring arenas. Two men chained to pipes, a corpse on the floor, a tape recorder instructing them to mutilate or die, it was minimalist staging wrapped around maximalist dread. What seemed like a one-off indie became a billion-dollar franchise. Across sequels, John Kramer, the so-called "Jigsaw," evolved into a twisted moralist, punishing perceived sins through elaborate traps. Each contraption became both execution and sermon, pushing victims toward self-destruction under the guise of "choices."

The films married exploitation to morality play, their violence framed not as random but as punishment. Yet the effect was the same: buckets of blood and an annual October ritual where audiences gathered to see how the next trap would spring. The *Saw* franchise wasn't just horror, it was industrialized horror. Sequels churned out like clockwork, box office guaranteed by the promise of new contraptions in every film.

Hostel and Global Sadism

If *Saw* was the grim puzzle-box, Eli Roth's *Hostel* (2005, USA) reveled in unfiltered sadism. A trio of American backpackers, lured into a Slovakian torture factory, became metaphors for anxieties of the post-9/11 world: American vulnerability abroad, fear of foreign hostility, and the lurking suspicion that Western imperialism had earned karmic revenge. Where *Saw* suggested victims might "deserve" their punishment, *Hostel* displayed cruelty as commodity. The wealthy literally buying the right to mutilate human bodies.

The sequels twisted the gaze, sometimes granting women vengeance against the system, but the core remained: horror as spectacle of dehumanization. Critics dismissed it as "torture porn," but its box office returns proved audiences were compelled, even addicted, to its unflinching sadism.

The Devil's Rejects and the American Grindhouse

Rob Zombie added another flavor with *The Devil's Rejects* (2005, USA), a sun-bleached nightmare about a murderous family on the run. Less puzzle-driven than *Saw* and less global than *Hostel*, Zombie's film reimagined 1970s exploitation: sweaty, vulgar, relentless and pushed it into the mainstream. Sadism here was Americana: guns, grit, and cruelty on the open road.

Torture Porn: Label and Legacy

Critics coined "torture porn" as a dismissal, but the phrase stuck because it captured both the extremity and the allure. These films were less about monsters and more about the body itself: bound, pierced, punished. They reflected a decade steeped in images of war, terror, and Abu Ghraib, where real-world torture made the genre feel uncomfortably relevant.

For some, these films were empty excess; for others, they were the most honest reflection of a violent age. Either way, they carved a subgenre where suffering was both currency and philosophy.

The New French Extremity: Suffering as Philosophy

While American horror of the 2000s perfected the franchise (*Saw*, *Hostel*), French filmmakers pushed horror into an art-house abyss. Critics dubbed it the "New French Extremity," a movement where mutilation was not just spectacle but inquiry — suffering treated as philosophy, the body as a site of transcendence.

- **High Tension (2003, Alexandre Aja)** — A home invasion turned into a relentless gauntlet of brutality, capped by a twist that fractured identity and perception. Its shock value was not only the gore, but how it bent reality itself, forcing viewers to question what they'd just witnessed.
- **Inside (2007, Bustillo & Maury)** — Pregnancy became battlefield. A grieving woman, armed with scissors, stalks a soon-to-be mother in one of the most unrelenting visions of maternal horror ever filmed. It was sadistic, yes, but also symbolic: life and death, creation and violation, embodied in blood.
- **Martyrs (2008, Pascal Laugier)** — The apex of the movement. What begins as a revenge story spirals into imprisonment, torture, and transcendence. Its infamous flaying sequence wasn't mere gore but an existential gamble: can absolute suffering reveal the divine? For some, it was exploitation with French pretension. For others, it was the most terrifying meditation on faith and martyrdom ever committed to film.

Where American "torture porn" often reveled in sadism for spectacle, the French extremity insisted that pain *meant* something. It interrogated why we endure, why we watch, and what the human body and spirit might yield when pushed beyond annihilation. Horror was not just entertainment; it became an existential test.

Remake & Reboot Boom

By the early 2000s, Hollywood saw horror not as a playground for new ideas but as a library of proven brands waiting for bloodier reinvention. Nostalgia met the decade's appetite for visceral realism, and the result was a flood of remakes and reboots.

- **The Texas Chainsaw Massacre (2003, Marcus Nispel)** — Michael Bay's Platinum Dunes reimagined Hooper's 1974 nightmare with a slick, grimy sheen. Where the original thrived on suggestion, the remake leaned on sweat, screams, and explicit gore. It became a sleeper hit, proving old titles could be resurrected for a new generation.
- **Dawn of the Dead (2004, Zack Snyder)** — George Romero's critique of consumerism was reborn as a kinetic, action-horror spectacle. The zombies were fast, the violence relentless, and the nihilism intact. It marked Snyder's debut and showed that remakes could launch careers.
- **The Hills Have Eyes (2006, Alexandre Aja)** — Aja, fresh from *High Tension*, turned Craven's tale of cannibals in the desert into a blistering ordeal of blood and fire. It was part remake, part escalation taking the bones of the original and feeding them steroids.

These films were not reverent; they were confrontational. They amplified gore, sped up pacing, and embraced a nastier aesthetic in tune with post-9/11 anxieties. Studios saw dollar signs, and soon nearly every classic was on the block: *Halloween* (2007), *Friday the 13th* (2009), *A Nightmare on Elm Street* (2010).

The remake boom spoke to a broader industry fear: originality was risky, but familiarity sold. For audiences, it was a chance to revisit legends of the past, dressed in the grit of the present. For critics, it was often proof of creative bankruptcy. Yet love them or hate them, these remakes defined the 2000s. Horror wasn't just recycling, it was cannibalizing its own history.

Zombie Resurgence

By the early 2000s, the zombie had shuffled out of fashion, buried under decades of Romero imitations. But the new millennium dug it back up faster, meaner, and more versatile than ever.

- **28 Days Later (2002, Danny Boyle, UK)** cracked the subgenre wide open. Its "infected" weren't technically undead but rabid humans infected by a rage virus. Yet their speed, their ferocity, and the film's haunting images of an empty London felt apocalyptic in a way Romero never could have imagined. Shot on digital video, it was gritty, immediate, and raw. The zombie reborn for a world already anxious about pandemics and collapse.
- **Shaun of the Dead (2004, Edgar Wright, UK)** took the opposite approach, treating zombies with affection and parody. A romantic comedy with zombies ("a rom-zom-com," as Wright called it), it skewered genre clichés but also delivered one of the most beloved zombie films of all time. By laughing at the genre, it breathed new life into it, proving that the undead could be funny, tragic, and terrifying. Sometimes all in the same scene.
- **Dawn of the Dead (2004, Zack Snyder, USA)** turned Romero's slow-burn critique of consumerism into an adrenaline-fueled action horror spectacle. Fast zombies stormed shopping malls, and the film's relentless pace mirrored the acceleration of both cinema and society in the 21st century.

This resurgence was more than a stylistic update. Zombies became metaphors again for pandemics, terrorism, social collapse, or the inevitability of extinction. They were infinitely flexible: sprinting monsters, comedic foils, viral allegories. Whether played for satire or shock, the undead proved once again that no other monster adapts to the times quite like the zombie.

From Post-9/11 Outbreaks to Viral Curses

The zombie resurgence of the early 2000s carried unmistakable echoes of post-9/11 dread. *28 Days Later* opened on a deserted London that felt like ground zero after catastrophe, its sprinting infected embodying panic, terror cells, and a fear that chaos could erupt anywhere without warning. The *Dawn of the Dead* remake placed survival inside shopping malls turned bunkers, mirroring anxieties about consumer culture's fragility. Even *Shaun of the Dead*, with its pub-crawling satire, spoke to a society desperate to laugh at its own helplessness in the face of sudden disaster.

Yet horror was never confined by borders. As zombies embodied Western fears of attack and collapse, Japan conjured a different plague: curses that spread not through bites but through images. *Ringu's* VHS tape killed in seven days, turning technology itself into a carrier of doom. Where zombies dramatized explosive trauma, J-horror revealed a slower, viral contamination. Trauma that lingered, replicated, and seeped into every household. Together, they mapped a world where apocalypse could arrive as fast as a plane crash or as quietly as a whisper on tape.

The New Wave of J-Horror and Its Global Influence

If zombies embodied post-9/11 chaos in the West, Japan offered a quieter but no less devastating horror: curses that spread like viruses, indifferent to borders or logic. This was J-horror's golden export era, when the ghost story became globalized through technology.

Hideo Nakata's *Ringu* (1998) had already reshaped Japanese horror, but its American remake, *The Ring* (2002, USA), detonated internationally. Gore Verbinski's version translated Sadako into Samara, her waterlogged crawl from the television seared into pop culture. Suddenly, horror wasn't just about masked killers or gore, it was about images themselves as carriers of death. VHS tapes, television screens, later even cell phones: the very mediums of communication became conduits for dread.

Hot on its heels, *The Grudge* (2004, USA) brought Takashi Shimizu's *Ju-On* franchise into Hollywood, with Sarah Michelle Gellar navigating a haunted Tokyo apartment where curses lingered like contagions. The American box office proved what Japan had already known: these ghosts spoke to a global audience, articulating modern anxieties about trauma, technology, and inevitability.

But Japan was only the epicenter. Thailand's *Shutter* (2004) used photography as a medium of guilt, its spectral figures etched onto film like moral scars. South Korea's *A Tale of Two Sisters* (2003) wrapped Gothic repression in family melodrama, making the uncanny deeply intimate. Each culture translated ghostly tradition into a modern medium: cameras, screens, houses ensuring that horror felt both ancient and unnervingly contemporary.

What made J-horror and its imitators unique was their restraint. Violence was rare, gore minimal. Terror came from atmosphere, silence, and uncanny intrusion. The ghost was not a spectacle to be vanquished but a trauma that returned, inevitable and unresolved. Where slashers had rules, curses in J-horror had none, they could not be stopped, only endured.

By the mid-2000s, J-horror had reshaped the global marketplace. Hollywood's flood of remakes: *The Ring, The Grudge, Dark Water, Pulse* proved not just commercial appetite but a shift in horror's grammar. Horror was no longer only American. It was international, viral, and deeply psychological.

The Streaming Shift: Horror Without Borders

As J-horror's viral curses crawled across the globe, the method of horror's delivery changed just as radically as its content. VHS had given way to DVDs, and suddenly foreign films could circulate faster, subtitled or remade within months. By the mid-2000s, the arrival of Netflix. First as a DVD-by-mail service, then as an on-demand streaming platform cracked distribution wide open. Horror was no longer dependent on grindhouses, midnight screenings, or the luck of an international festival circuit. A cursed tape in Tokyo could terrify a family in Kansas weeks later.

Streaming also rewired audience behavior. Viewers could binge franchises in one sitting, revisit classics on demand, and discover obscure cult titles alongside glossy remakes. For horror, this democratization was revolutionary. Once-marginal subgenres of folk horror, Asian ghost stories, French extremity were suddenly accessible to anyone with a subscription. Global horror became not only visible but viral, laying the groundwork for the prestige boom of the 2010s. This democratization didn't just broaden access, it accelerated the genre's evolution, ensuring that the next great wave of horror would not only be international but inescapable.

Proto-Elevated Horror

Though the "elevated horror" label wouldn't dominate until the 2010s, its roots were already breaking through the soil in the mid-2000s. Amid slashers, remakes, and torture chambers, certain films reminded audiences that horror could still be poetic, layered, and hauntingly human.

Neil Marshall's *The Descent* (2005, UK) plunged a group of women into a cave system where creatures lurked, but the deeper terror was psychological: claustrophobia, betrayal, and the collapse of trust in the dark. Guillermo del Toro's *Pan's Labyrinth* (2006, Spain) blurred fairy tale and fascism, weaving war trauma and myth into a vision that won Oscars while refusing to let its horror soften. Tomas Alfredson's *Let the Right One In*[7] (2008, Sweden) reimagined the vampire not as predator but as lonely companion. A fragile, chilling exploration of childhood, intimacy, and violence.

These works proved that horror could transcend the grindhouse and the franchise machine. They were not ashamed of blood or monstrosity, but they folded those elements into allegory, emotion, and art-house sensibility. If the decade was defined by excess and extremity, these films suggested another path: horror as literature, as cinema, as myth reborn for a new age.

Horror-Comedy

On a lighter note, the 2000s reminded audiences that horror could grin while it gutted. The *Final Destination* franchise (2000–2011, USA) turned Death into a cosmic prankster, staging elaborate, ironic Rube Goldberg massacres that were as funny as they were terrifying. Every spilled coffee or loose screw became a setup for fate's punchline.

By the end of the decade, *Zombieland* (2009, USA) reimagined apocalypse as buddy comedy. Woody Harrelson and Jesse Eisenberg road-tripped through undead America with banter, Twinkies, and zombie kills scored to Metallica.

The film balanced gore with charm, satire with sincerity, proving that horror could be just as effective with laughs as with screams.

Humor and horror coexisted comfortably here, winking at a media-savvy audience already saturated with slashers and remakes. The message was clear: horror didn't have to choose between terror and parody. It could have both. Laughing with the genre while still delivering its monsters.

Catalysts and Gatekeepers

The 2000s thrived on two new engines: cheap technology and globalization. Camcorders and digital editing made *Blair Witch*, *Paranormal Activity*, and *[REC]* possible on shoestring budgets, while DVDs and the internet turned obscure imports into cult sensations overnight. Horror's distribution was no longer bound to theaters; it lived in living rooms, torrents, and viral campaigns. At the same time, special effects workshops kept pushing gore into the mainstream, from *Saw's* traps to *Hostel's* sadism. Festivals like Sundance, Sitges, and Toronto became launchpads for extremity, elevating once-underground visions into international talking points.

The Backlash

Critics decried "torture porn" as cynical and sadistic, accusing films like *Hostel* and *Saw* of reveling in cruelty. Censors in Europe battled the French New Extremity, just as parents in the U.S. protested unrated DVDs circulating among teens. Found footage was dismissed by some as lazy filmmaking, while remakes were scorned as creatively bankrupt. But backlash only fueled notoriety. Films banned, condemned, or mocked often found second lives as cult touchstones. Horror's resilience lay in its ability to weaponize controversy: every attempt to silence it only amplified its reach.

Craft Innovations
- Found footage made the camera itself complicit, pulling horror into "real time."
- Torture films turned morality into machinery, testing bodies as puzzles.
- French extremity forced audiences to confront suffering as philosophy, not just spectacle.
- Remakes fused nostalgia with brutality, proving old myths could be reborn.
- Zombies sprinted, vampires brooded, and ghosts spread like viruses. Monsters were remade for a new millennium.

By the end of the 2000s, horror had proven it could be anything: cheap, extreme, global, or ironic. But exhaustion set in. Sequels spun endlessly, gore became parody, and the found footage craze risked collapsing under its own shaky cams. Out of this fatigue rose a new demand. Horror that wasn't just shocking, but *meaningful*. The seeds planted by *Pan's Labyrinth*, *The Descent*, and *Let the Right One In* began to bloom. As the 2010s opened, horror was poised for a renaissance: the age of prestige and social horror, where terrors of race, class, gender, and trauma would claim the screen with both box-office power and critical acclaim.

Prestige & Social Horror
(2010s–Present)

By the 2010s, horror had completed its long march from grindhouse exploitation to the red carpet. No longer dismissed as lowbrow, it was rebranded as prestige horror or social horror. Films that blended arthouse aesthetics with allegorical bite. This wave didn't abandon fear; it elevated it, demanding critics and audiences alike take horror seriously.

Jordan Peele and the Language of Social Horror

The inflection point was Jordan Peele's *Get Out* (2017, USA), which detonated in culture like few horror films ever had. Framed as a horror-satire, it followed Chris, a Black man who slowly uncovers that his white girlfriend's liberal family is harvesting Black bodies for white consciousness transfers. The film used familiar tropes: the haunted house, the mad scientist, the hypnotist to expose systemic racism with a clarity and urgency horror had rarely attempted. Its symbols became instant cultural shorthand: the Sunken Place as a metaphor for silenced Black experience, the polite garden party as a slave auction in disguise. Peele won the Academy Award for Best Screenplay, and *Get Out* became proof that horror could be both terrifying and critically lauded.

Peele didn't stop there. *Us* (2019) literalized America's buried underclass through doppelgängers rising from the tunnels beneath our feet, while *Nope* (2022) reframed spectacle itself as a devouring monster, critiquing Hollywood's history of exploitation. Together, his films carved a new cinematic language where horror dissected race, class, media, and power with scalpel precision.

Social Horror as Movement

Jordan Peele's *Get Out* may have been the lightning strike, but it landed in a storm already gathering. The 2010s were marked by horror films that wore their allegories on the surface, no longer content to hide social critique under monsters or metaphors. This was horror as discourse, horror as op-ed, horror as mirror.

- **The Purge (2013, USA):** Introduced a night where all crime is legal, but beneath the pulp setup lay a furious allegory about wealth, inequality, and systemic violence. Each sequel sharpened its politics, moving from home invasion to outright class war.
- **Us (2019, USA):** Peele's doppelgänger allegory expanded beyond race into class, privilege, and collective guilt. America haunted not by outsiders, but by its own buried shadow-selves.
- **Candyman (2021, USA):** Nia DaCosta's continuation of Bernard Rose's 1992 classic reframed the urban legend through the lens of gentrification, systemic racism, and cycles of violence passed down like folklore.
- **His House (2020, UK):** Turned the haunted house into an allegory for displacement, survivor's guilt, and the trauma carried by refugees where the horror follows you across borders.

What defined this wave was self-awareness. Allegory had always been part of horror (*Night of the Living Dead*, *The Texas Chain Saw Massacre*), but these films weren't hiding their politics, they declared them. The scares came wrapped in urgent cultural critique.

Prestige Horror: Trauma, Faith, and Allegory

By the mid-2010s, horror wasn't just surviving, it was ascending. Indie studios like A24 and Neon rebranded the genre with arthouse aesthetics, slow-burn pacing, and allegories that critics could no longer dismiss. Though many filmmakers resisted the label, "elevated horror" became shorthand for films that fused atmosphere, psychology, and metaphor into nightmares as rich as any drama.

The Babadook (2014, Australia): Jennifer Kent reframed horror as the story of unprocessed grief. A widow and her troubled son are stalked by a top-hatted demon from a sinister children's book, but the true terror is mourning itself: the suffocating, unspeakable weight of trauma and maternal breakdown. Marketed as a monster movie, it became a cultural phenomenon, later embraced as an LGBTQ+ meme icon, its "closeted monster" status expanding its resonance far beyond its release.

The Witch (2015, USA): Robert Eggers plunged audiences into 17th-century New England, where a Puritan family exiled to the wilderness falls apart under paranoia, repression, and whispered witchcraft. Shot with obsessive historical detail and archaic dialogue, *The Witch* turned folk horror into allegory for faith, isolation, and the corrosive nature of dogma. The final embrace of satanic liberation "Wouldst thou like to live deliciously?" became one of the most quoted lines of the decade.

Hereditary (2018, USA): Ari Aster's operatic debut became the decade's defining shocker. Beginning as a family drama about grief, it descends into a spiral of demonic inheritance, cult conspiracies, and grotesque imagery: headless corpses, spectral rituals, and Toni Collette's unforgettable anguish. Critics hailed it as the modern *Exorcist*. Alongside *Midsommar* (2019), which staged pagan ritual as breakup therapy, Aster cemented A24 as the home of prestige horror where trauma itself was the monster.

Get Out (2017, USA): Jordan Peele detonated the genre by blending satire with allegory. A Black man meeting his white girlfriend's family uncovers a conspiracy of body theft and liberal racism, where assimilation becomes literal possession. Its images the Sunken Place, the silent auction entered the cultural lexicon, winning Peele an Oscar for Best Screenplay and proving horror could dominate both the box office and the awards circuit.

Saint Maud (2019, UK): Rose Glass turned religious zeal into psychological and corporeal terror. Maud, a devout palliative nurse, believes she communes with God while spiraling into self-destruction. Its final shot an ecstatic vision of divine rapture, instantly undercut by the reality of her burning body became one of the most haunting and unforgettable images of 21st-century horror.

This era also gave us *It Follows* (2014, USA), where sexual transmission became literalized as a stalking curse, tying horror to both intimacy and inevitability. Robert Eggers' *The Lighthouse* (2019, USA) stripped two men on a rock of sanity, blending folklore, surrealism, and black comedy into a hallucinatory chamber piece. And Alex Garland's *Men* (2022, UK) turned trauma into allegory, staging cycles of patriarchal violence in grotesque, body-horror loops.

Together, these films showed the elasticity of "prestige horror." Whether framed as folk parable, psychological allegory, or surreal nightmare, they confirmed that horror could move fluidly between art-house and multiplex, between allegory and viscera, while still commanding serious critical attention.

This wave wasn't about "classing up" horror so much as refusing to separate allegory from fear. Whether through grief (*The Babadook*, *Hereditary*), repression (*The Witch*), systemic racism (*Get Out*), or religious madness (*Saint Maud*), these films made horror a tool for cultural dissection. They didn't abandon monsters, they revealed that the monsters were us, our systems, and our histories.

Folk Horror Revival

By the 2010s, the long shadow of *The Wicker Man* (1973) stretched back across the genre. Rural isolation, ritual sacrifice, and pagan dread returned with new force, reframed for an era of global anxiety and personal grief. Where earlier folk horror often carried the anxieties of postwar Britain, the revival drew on themes of alienation, grief, and cultural dislocation. Outsiders encountering communities bound by rituals older and darker than modernity itself.

Midsommar (2019, Ari Aster, USA/Sweden): Aster inverted Gothic darkness by staging his tale in endless daylight. A grieving woman follows her boyfriend and friends to a remote Swedish commune, where sunlit rituals mask brutality. The horror came not from shadows but from the blinding brightness of communal ecstasy, grief and codependence transfigured into a sacrificial ceremony.

The Ritual (2017, David Bruckner, UK): In the Scandinavian wilderness, four friends mourn the death of one of their own while being stalked by a monstrous Norse deity. Blending grief with mythology, the film suggested that ancient gods still linger, demanding tribute in the most unforgiving landscapes.

Kill List (2011, Ben Wheatley, UK): Beginning as a bleak crime thriller about a hitman, the film pivots into folk horror as its protagonist stumbles into a pagan conspiracy. Its final act ritualistic, shocking, and ambiguous confirmed folk horror's power to mutate even familiar genres into nightmares of inevitability.

This revival wasn't confined to Europe. Films like *The Witch* (2015, USA) also fit into the folk horror framework, with Puritan paranoia and wilderness isolation birthing a satanic mythos. Internationally, folkloric horror tapped into local legends and rituals from Southeast Asian ghost traditions to Latin American tales of witchcraft and saints.

The resurgence of folk horror reflected broader cultural unease: distrust of modernity, nostalgia curdled into dread, and the return of communal rituals in an era otherwise marked by alienation. Its power lay in confronting audiences with landscapes where the past is never past, and where human sacrifice literal or metaphorical remains the cost of belonging.

Elevated Found Footage & Screenlife

By the 2010s, found footage had matured past shaky cams and surprise jump scares. Filmmakers began using the format as more than a gimmick, experimenting with narrative, character, and even digital life itself. Horror wasn't just about what was caught on camera anymore, it was about what the camera *meant*.

V/H/S (2012, USA): A horror anthology delivered through "discovered" tapes, each short pushing the found footage premise into different subgenres from haunted houses to demonic lovers. It proved the style could be modular, adaptable, and endlessly experimental.

Creep (2014, USA): Stripped to two actors and a handheld camera, Patrick Brice and Mark Duplass turned the format into an intimate psychological nightmare. Its horror came not from gore but from proximity: the unease of being trapped with someone whose friendliness masks obsession.

The Taking of Deborah Logan (2014, USA): Framed as a medical documentary on Alzheimer's, the film escalates from clinical realism into demonic possession. The merging of disease and supernatural horror showed how found footage could double as social commentary.

At the same time, a new variation emerged: *Screenlife*. These films unfolded entirely through webcams, chat windows, and digital interfaces, reflecting a world where identity, intimacy, and fear were increasingly mediated by screens.

Unfriended (2014, USA): A teenage Skype call turned séance, where a vengeful spirit haunts group chats and webcams. Its gimmick became its genius: every terror unfolded within the same computer screen audiences used daily.

Host (2020, UK): Shot during the COVID-19 lockdown, it trapped friends in a Zoom call that becomes a séance gone wrong. At under an hour, it distilled digital isolation and supernatural terror into one of the most effective pandemic-era films.

This evolution proved that found footage wasn't a fad but a *language*. One that could adapt to new technologies and anxieties. Whether through cursed tapes, handheld intimacy, or corrupted Skype calls, horror found new ways to mirror how we communicate, watch, and fear in the digital age.

Foreign Horror Rising

While Asian and European horror had been shaping the genre for decades, the 2010s marked the first time many of these films reached *mainstream* global audiences with critical acclaim. Streaming platforms and international festivals dissolved barriers of distribution, allowing works once confined to niche audiences to break through to the cultural center.

The Wailing (2016, South Korea): Na Hong-jin's masterpiece wove police procedural, folk horror, and occult dread into a sprawling tale of possession, suspicion, and paranoia. With its ambiguous ending and spiritual unease, it became a touchstone for horror that resists resolution.

Train to Busan (2016, South Korea): Yeon Sang-ho revitalized the zombie genre with breakneck pacing and unexpected emotional weight. Its moving train became a pressure cooker for social commentary on class, sacrifice, and survival, proving zombies still had bite in the 21st century.

Raw (2016, France/Belgium): Julia Ducournau's coming-of-age cannibal film fused body horror with feminist allegory. Its blend of intimacy, sexuality, and grotesquerie positioned it at the center of both controversy and acclaim, paving the way for Ducournau's Palme d'Or–winning *Titane* (2021).

Global horror no longer operated at the margins. These films weren't just festival darlings, they became widely streamed, passionately debated, and critically celebrated. The "foreign" qualifier began to dissolve: horror was now a *global language*, and the monsters of Seoul, Busan, and Brussels stood alongside those of Hollywood as equals.

Catalysts & Gatekeepers

The prestige boom of the 2010s wasn't born in a vacuum. Indie distributors like A24 and Neon packaged allegorical horror in arthouse wrapping, positioning it for critical acclaim. Streaming platforms (Netflix, Shudder, Amazon Prime) gave global distribution to films that once would have languished on the festival circuit. At the same time, horror fandom thrived online: memes, Reddit threads, and YouTube analysis turned films like *The Babadook*[8] or *Hereditary* into cultural events as much as cinematic ones.

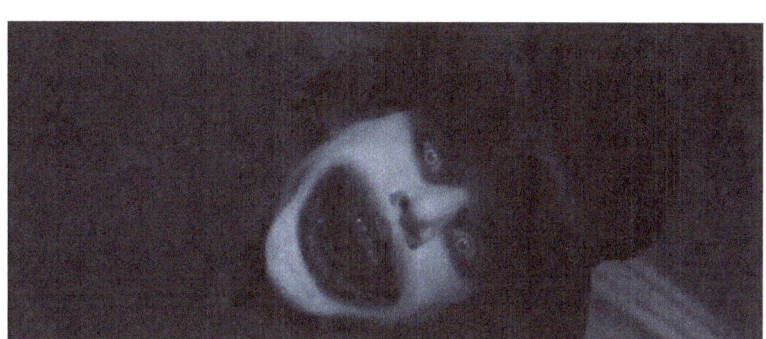

The Backlash

Prestige horror's seriousness sparked debate. Critics accused the "elevated" label of dismissing traditional horror, as if slashers and monster movies were somehow less worthy. Audiences sometimes rejected the slow-burn style (*The Witch* drew walkouts; *Hereditary* left crowds divided). Meanwhile, Hollywood still leaned on franchises (*The Conjuring*, *It*) to balance the arthouse with popcorn horror. The tension between "serious" and "fun" horror became one of the decade's defining conversations.

Craft Innovations

- Allegory became the genre's engine: grief, trauma, race, and faith folded into horror storytelling.
- Streaming made international horror accessible, expanding the canon in real time.
- Screenlife and digital horror (*Unfriended*, *Host*) reframed the haunted house as a haunted screen.
- Marketing relied on virality. Think *Hereditary*'s head-tilt poster or *It Follows*' enigmatic tagline.

By the late 2010s, horror's ecosystem shifted once again. Streaming platforms weren't just distribution pipelines, they became horror incubators, where films could bypass theaters and reach global audiences instantly. Netflix pushed *The Ritual* and *Veronica* to international recognition. Shudder carved out a niche for indie and experimental horror.

When the COVID-19 pandemic hit, the genre adapted with eerie speed. *Host* (2020), shot entirely on Zoom during lockdown, turned social isolation into a séance gone wrong. Screenlife horror mirrored our quarantined reality, while outbreak films like *Contagion* or zombie narratives suddenly felt documentary-adjacent. Horror proved itself the most responsive genre to cultural crisis. Once again, the mirror for our collective anxieties.

Streaming & Pandemic Horror
(2020s–Present)

The 2020s confirmed horror's ultimate truth: it mutates faster than any other genre. With theaters shuttered during the COVID-19 pandemic and audiences trapped at home, horror didn't just survive, it thrived. Streaming platforms, microbudgets, and digital-native forms turned isolation and technology into terror, proving once again that horror is the most adaptable genre alive.

---

[8] "babadook: in person" by AtomicPunk23 (https://www.flickr.com/photos/126763824@N06) licensed under CC BY 2.0.

Analog Horror & Screenlife

As audiences migrated online, horror followed them not just in subject matter, but in form. Two digital-native subgenres crystallized in the 2010s and exploded during the pandemic: screenlife and analog horror.

Screenlife told stories entirely through computer screens, webcams, and chat windows. *Unfriended* (2014) pioneered the format, but it was *Host* (2020, UK) that perfected it. Filmed during lockdown over Zoom, Rob Savage's pandemic séance gone wrong turned glitching laptops, frozen faces, and buffering screens into genuine terror. At just 57 minutes, it captured the uncanny isolation of quarantine better than any blockbuster could. Its success on Shudder proved streaming could make microbudget horror go global overnight.

Analog Horror, by contrast, looked backward into static, corrupted broadcasts, and grainy VHS aesthetics. YouTube series like *Local 58* and *The Mandela Catalogue* transformed dead air, emergency alerts, and signal degradation into creeping dread. What once looked like technical error became a new language of fear, exploiting the uncanny gap between familiar media and something very wrong lurking beneath it.

Together, screenlife and analog horror demonstrated that the medium itself could be the monster. Whether through the everyday intimacy of a laptop call or the haunted texture of obsolete technology, these forms made horror inseparable from the way audiences now consume it on screens, in fragments, and through endless digital feeds.

Skinamarink and the Liminal Turn

If *Host* was hyper-contemporary, Kyle Edward Ball's *Skinamarink* (2022, Canada) turned to memory. Grainy VHS textures, static shots of ceilings and hallways, and whispered fragments conjured the uncanny space of childhood nightmares. With almost no plot, it split audiences. Some walked out, others called it a revelation. On TikTok, clips spread like digital campfire tales, marking the rise of "liminal horror," where vibe and atmosphere mattered more than narrative.

The Outwaters and Cosmic Dread

Robbie Banfitch's *The Outwaters* (2023, USA) fused found footage with Lovecraftian terror. What began as a desert camping trip dissolved into time fractures, disembowelment, and surreal cosmic chaos. Chaotic and divisive, it became a festival-circuit cult item. Proof that the found footage ethos still had room to evolve.

TikTok, ARGs & Viral Horror

The 2020s didn't just change what horror looked like, it changed how it spread. Beyond theaters and streaming platforms, horror began thriving in a decentralized, digital-first landscape. Short-form virality, analog aesthetics, and participatory storytelling created new micro horrors that circulated not as films but as phenomena.

TikTok became the new campfire. Creepypastas once confined to forums mutated into viral clips, each only seconds long but capable of unsettling millions. Creators weaponized filters, sound distortions, and uncanny visual effects to bend reality in miniature. Algorithms rewarded fear: linger on a spooky video, and you were plunged into a rabbit hole of escalating horror, drip-fed by the app's code. Accounts like *Shortest Blockbusters* turned micro horror into an art form, proving a jump scare or uncanny glitch could be as effective in 15 seconds as in 90 minutes.

At the same time, analog horror, low-fi nightmares rendered through VHS fuzz and corrupted broadcasts exploded. The most iconic example was *The Backrooms*. What began as a single unsettling image of a yellow-walled office labyrinth posted to 4chan in 2018 morphed into an entire mythology. The idea of "noclipping" out of reality into endless liminal corridors resonated with digital culture's obsession with spaces that feel wrong.

On YouTube, 16-year-old Kane Parsons (Kane Pixels) expanded *The Backrooms* into a cinematic universe of eerie corporate experiments and lost footage, his 2022 shorts gaining millions of views. TikTok amplified the aesthetic, turning liminal horror into a movement. The viral success was so potent that A24 greenlit a feature film. Proof that an internet meme could leap into mainstream cinema.

Alternate Reality Games (ARGs) took immersion even further, scattering horror across platforms and blurring fiction with reality. Instead of passively watching, audiences became investigators decoding cryptic YouTube uploads, chasing hidden websites, piecing together Discord clues. Horror lived inside the internet itself, its glitches and fragmented posts turning the act of searching into part of the scare. These projects tapped into paranoia about conspiracies and online manipulation, making the audience complicit in their own unease.

Taken together, these micro horrors represent horror's latest evolution: not a single story but a network of constantly mutating tales. TikTok clips, ARG trails, and analog shorts circulate like digital folklore, reinterpreted and expanded by thousands of creators at once. Instead of a studio dictating canon, horror has become participatory, endlessly remixable, and algorithmically amplified.

In the 2020s, you don't just watch horror, you scroll into it, fall into it, share it. Fear doesn't premiere; it goes viral.

Elevated Horror Expands

If the 2010s proved horror could be arthouse, the 2020s confirmed it wasn't a trend but a new language of the genre. What began as experiments in grief and allegory became a fully developed mode of filmmaking: films that carried the visual polish of indie dramas but weaponized atmosphere, metaphor, and psychological depth to disturb audiences on deeper levels.

Where the 2010s often circled trauma and family collapse, the 2020s widened the canvas. Horror became a lens for aging, gender violence, social alienation, and the erosion of trust in technology itself.

- **Relic (2020, Australia):** A haunted house story that played less like Gothic fantasy and more like dementia made spatial. Rooms that shifted and collapsed as memory itself rotted.
- **The Night House (2020, USA):** Widowed grief became uncanny architecture, its mirror houses and doubling selves literalizing the disorientation of loss.
- **The Invisible Man (2020, USA):** Updating Universal's monster into a tale of coercive control and gaslighting, Leigh Whannell crafted one of the decade's first horror hits. A fusion of sci-fi premise and #MeToo anxieties.

Studios like A24 and Neon doubled down, turning horror into awards-season contenders and festival darlings. No longer an outlier, elevated horror became infrastructure: critics covered it seriously, audiences expected allegory alongside scares, and filmmakers used horror's elasticity to tackle subjects once reserved for high drama.

This wasn't just prestige for prestige's sake. It was expansion. An ongoing mutation that showed horror could be intimate (a single grieving family), societal (abuse and systemic control), or existential (memory as a haunted labyrinth). If the 2010s cracked the door open, the 2020s stepped through fully, proving horror could thrive as both mirror and metaphor without losing its power to terrify.

Post-Pandemic Horror

As elevated horror deepened its focus on grief, trauma, and allegory, the pandemic forced those themes into sharper relief. Lockdowns, contagion, and isolation weren't abstract metaphors anymore, they were lived experience. Horror responded immediately, mining the anxieties of quarantine and its aftermath.

- *Sick* (2022, USA) reframed slasher tropes through COVID-era paranoia, with isolation rules and social distancing woven into its kills.
- *In the Earth* (2021, UK) fused pandemic imagery with folk horror, as nature itself seemed infected and pagan rituals blurred with viral madness.
- *The Sadness* (2021, Taiwan) pushed contagion horror to its limit, imagining a virus that turned the infected into sadistic torturers, forcing audiences to confront the violence lurking beneath social collapse.

Pandemic horror thrived because it was both immediate and eternal. Illness, isolation, and paranoia have always been primal fears; the pandemic only magnified them. These films weren't escapist, they were mirrors, confronting audiences with the uncanny horror of their own recent past.

Queer Horror in the Spotlight

Where queerness had long been subtext, the 2020s made it central.

- *They/Them* (2022) confronted conversion therapy through slasher tropes.
- *Swallowed* (2022) blended queer romance with grotesque body horror.
- Netflix's *Fear Street Trilogy* (2021) tied its meta-slasher framework to a sapphic love story across centuries.

These films marked a shift from coded subtext toward explicit representation, situating queer identity within the core of horror storytelling.

Global Horror Ascendant

If earlier decades proved horror could travel, the 2020s confirmed it could dominate worldwide screens overnight. Streaming platforms erased the traditional barriers of distribution, allowing films rooted in deeply local folklore, politics, and anxieties to play simultaneously in living rooms across continents. What once might have been confined to regional markets became instant global talking points.

Taiwan's *Incantation* (2022) exemplified this shift. A cursed-footage film steeped in Buddhist and Taoist taboos, it spread virally on Netflix, terrifying audiences far outside its cultural origins. Argentina's *When Evil Lurks* (2023) brought rural grit and breakneck pacing to the demonic possession narrative, its vision of contagion and collapse earning global critical acclaim. In Russia, *Sputnik* (2020) fused Cold War paranoia with parasitic body horror, showing how national history could feed the monstrous. And *The Medium* (2021), a Thai–Korean co-production, presented shamanism and inherited spiritual power through a faux-documentary lens, blending regional ritual with modern genre conventions.

The cumulative effect was a polyglot horror landscape. Each film was fiercely specific to its cultural roots: rituals, politics, landscapes but their distribution and reception were global. Horror had finally become a lingua franca: a shared cinematic language where fear translated effortlessly across borders.

Extreme & Arthouse Hybrids

As the 2020s unfolded, horror didn't just diversify, it hardened into something sharper, stranger, and more confrontational. At the margins of mainstream cinema, filmmakers tested not only the boundaries of the genre but the patience and endurance of audiences themselves. These weren't popcorn scares; they were gauntlets, designed to provoke walkouts, viral discourse, and cult allegiance in equal measure.

Damien Leone's *Terrifier 2* (2022, USA) resurrected grindhouse brutality with shocking confidence. Clocking in at over two hours, it drenched audiences in sadistic, over-the-top gore, reviving the spirit of splatter cinema while escalating it to a carnival of excess. In stark contrast, Kyle Edward Ball's *Skinamarink* (2022, Canada) leaned into radical minimalism. Grainy VHS fuzz, static ceilings, and fragmented childhood dread turned experimental horror into a mainstream phenomenon, spreading like digital folklore through TikTok clips and midnight screenings. Julia Ducournau's *Titane* (2021, France), meanwhile, defied categorization altogether. Winner of the Palme d'Or, it fused car-crash surrealism, body horror, and tender family drama into a fever dream that blurred the line between arthouse and exploitation.

Together, these films marked horror's edgiest turn in decades. They asked not just what we fear, but how much we can withstand. Whether in grotesque spectacle, avant-garde abstraction, or surreal provocations that leave the genre's very definition in question. In pushing form and content to their limits, extreme and arthouse hybrids reminded audiences that horror is not always about comfort or catharsis. Sometimes, it's about confrontation.

Horror's Future

The 2020s have shown that horror is no longer bound by geography, budget, or even traditional screens. It slips across theaters, streaming platforms, TikTok loops, ARG labyrinths, and the avant-garde festival circuit with equal ease. Pandemic paranoia, digital folklore, and the rise of global voices have reshaped horror into a sprawling, many-headed creature part pop culture, part art cinema, part internet phenomenon.

What comes next may not resemble the Gothic castles of old or the slashers of the '80s, but the DNA is the same: fear mutates, and horror follows. Whether through AI-generated nightmares, immersive VR hauntings, or stories yet to be told from underrepresented cultures, the genre's adaptability ensures it never dies.

If there's one throughline across its history, it is this: horror thrives wherever the world feels unstable. And in an era defined by climate anxiety, political upheaval, and digital disorientation, horror is not just surviving, it is poised to reign.

A Note on Overlaps

Horror is a shape-shifter. Categories look clean on paper, but monsters bleed across borders. A ghost story can double as a psychological breakdown. A slasher might smuggle in social satire. And some films: *Carrie*, *Psycho*, *The Wicker Man* live in multiple shadows at once.

For clarity, each chapter places a film where its strongest current runs. That's why you might see certain titles surface again not in the main lists, but in pairing nights or as "essentials to revisit." When that happens, don't see it as a mistake. See it as an invitation: proof that horror resists neat shelves, refracting into different fears depending on the lens: supernatural, psychological, bodily, cultural.

As one critic put it: *"Horror isn't about labels, it's about intersections. Carrie isn't just supernatural or psychological. It's both. That's what makes it endure."*

Gothic Horror

Gothic horror is the architecture of dread: looming manors, mildewed corridors, shuttered windows that rattle when no wind blows, and secrets mortared into the walls. Born from late-18th and 19th-century fiction (think ruined lineages, grief-struck ghosts, cursed laboratories), it pairs atmosphere with obsessions: forbidden knowledge, sexual repression, inherited guilt, faith shaken by science, and the past refusing burial. Onscreen, the Gothic speaks in textures: candle flame on damp stone, staircases that narrow like a throat, portraits that watch as if memory itself had eyes. Its monsters are often tragic, less pure evil than cursed consequence; terror blooms not from jump scares but from the slow realization that the house knows what you've done.

Why People Are Drawn to Gothic Horror

Gothic endures because it is equal parts haunting and romantic. It seduces with spectacle: stormlight, lace, stained glass, brocade and bone while smuggling in psychological unease. The mode lets us wander through beautiful ruins and confront the desires we pretend are dead: lust, envy, the ache for immortality, the fear that bloodlines and mistakes outlive us. It's nostalgia braided to nightmare. Viewers are lured by the beauty, then trapped by the shadows that beauty casts.

Essentials

1. **The Uninvited** (1944) – helped establish the haunted house film as serious Gothic cinema rather than mere cheap thrills. Its use of atmosphere, layered family secrets, and a ghostly presence tied to unresolved trauma marked a shift toward psychological sophistication in supernatural horror.
2. **Dead of Night** (1945, UK) – A landmark British anthology that stitched together multiple uncanny tales within a single framing nightmare. Its chilling mix of ghost stories, psychological unease, and the iconic ventriloquist sequence set the standard for portmanteau horror and foreshadowed the recursive dread of modern anthology films.
3. **The Haunting** (1963) – Distilled Shirley Jackson's novel into one of the most unnerving ghost stories ever filmed. Robert Wise's inventive camerawork, distorted sound design, and psychological ambiguity turned Hill House into a living entity, leaving viewers unsure whether the terror is supernatural or born from the fragile mind of its protagonist.
4. **The Innocents** (1961, UK) – Distilled Henry James's *The Turn of the Screw* into a haunting study of repression and ambiguity. Its meticulous use of suggestion, atmosphere, and psychological tension leaves viewers uncertain whether the evil lies in the ghosts or in the governess's own unraveling mind.
5. **The Shining** (1980) – Redefined haunted space through Kubrick's icy precision, transforming a remote hotel into a labyrinth of madness and malevolence. Its fusion of supernatural menace with Jack Torrance's psychological unraveling created one of horror's most enduring studies of isolation, violence, and the collapse of family.

Deep Cuts

1. **A Page of Madness** (1926, Japan) – Stands as one of the earliest and most radical experiments in cinematic horror. Directed by Teinosuke Kinugasa, it abandons linear narrative for a fever-dream of fractured editing, distorted sets, and expressionist imagery inside a mental asylum. The film reflects not only the anguish of its characters but also Japan's avant-garde engagement with modernism, presenting madness as both a psychological state and a visual experience. Without intertitles to guide interpretation, it forces viewers into the same disoriented state as its inmates, making it a rare silent film that still feels unsettlingly modern. Its influence lingers in how horror depicts mental instability, less as a story to be told than as a state of perception to be endured.

2. **Mystery of the Wax Museum** (1933, USA) – An early Technicolor horror that blended macabre spectacle with crime-thriller energy. Its grotesque imagery of wax figures concealing death and its atmospheric use of color foreshadowed both the Gothic stylization of later horror and the gruesome appeal of Vincent Price's *House*

3. **Castle of Blood** (1964, Italy) – Embodies Italian Gothic at its most eerie, with baroque visuals, spectral seduction, and a fatalistic atmosphere. Its story of a journalist lured into a haunted castle for one night blurs the line between desire and doom, cementing its place as a cult classic of Euro-horror.

4. **The Changeling** (1980, Canada) – A masterclass in restrained supernatural horror, using mood, sound, and silence to evoke dread rather than spectacle. Its tale of grief entwined with a vengeful spirit set the template for the modern haunted house film's blend of tragedy and terror.

5. **The Others** (2001) – Revived the Gothic ghost story with quiet restraint, emphasizing atmosphere and psychological unease over spectacle. Its slow-building tension, reliance on suggestion, and devastating twist reasserted the power of ambiguity in modern supernatural horror.

Critical Essay

"Gothic Is Not Just Castles"

A common myth shrinks Gothic to a ruined pile on a cliff. In truth, Gothic is an emotional design: dread mapped onto place. A parlor, a hospital ward, a decaying theater, even a spacecraft can be Gothic if it channels isolation, repression, and the return of what was buried. The mode is psychological architecture walls that bend the way memory bends, corridors that lead back to the original wound.

Global Spotlight: Italy

Italy turned Gothic into operatic fever dream. Mid-century auteurs painted darkness in chiaroscuro and saturated color, staging curses like arias: velvet and violence, mirrors and mortification. Later stylists folded witchcraft, sadomasochistic romance, and labyrinthine mansions into a baroque grammar of fear. Italian Gothic proves the mode is not confined to foggy moors; it thrives wherever beauty and decay share a ceiling.

Defining Gothic

☐ **The House of the Devil (Le Manoir du Diable)** (1896, France) - A giant bat flies into a medieval castle room and suddenly transforms into Mephistopheles, or the Devil. The Devil then proceeds to torment two unsuspecting cavaliers who enter the room. He uses a series of illusions and magical spells to conjure and manipulate a series of bizarre creatures and phantoms, including a giant cauldron, skeletons, and ghosts. As a trick film from early cinema pioneer Georges Méliès, the movie's primary appeal came from its special effects. The film's use of substitution splices and other illusions was intended to create a sense of magic and amazement. The only official adaptation of *The House of the Devil* is *The Haunted Castle* (*Le Château hanté*), a 45-second remake also directed by Méliès.

- **OTHER MELIES FILMS**
  - ☐ **The Infernal Cauldron** (1902) - Two demons throw helpless captives into a boiling cauldron, and then try to summon forth their spirits.
  - ☐ **The Devil's Money Bags** (1902) - The setting of this fantastic scene represents the hall of an old chateau in which a miser has locked up seven large bags containing his wealth. Satan, who has made his way into the chateau, puts the seven bags in a strong box, and makes with his hands some cabalistic motions. The miser comes into the hall and is greatly astonished to find his fortune missing. He opens the coffer and immediately the bags leap out.
  - ☐ **The Black Imp** (1905) - Another Méliès creation, this film is known for its dark humor and impressive visual tricks, including a mischievous imp that causes chaos.

☐ **Bluebeard** (1901) – Based on the famous French folktale first published by Charles Perrault in 1697. A silent film directed by Georges Méliès.

• **ADAPTIONS:** Bluebeard is a French folktale of wealth, secrecy, and dread. A nobleman with a striking blue beard weds a young bride and grants her the keys to his vast estate, forbidding entry to a single locked chamber. Her curiosity draws her toward the one door she is told never to open, where the true horror of her husband's past lies waiting.

☐ **Bluebeard** (1912, France) - A French silent film directed by Camille de Morlhon.

☐ **Bluebeard** (1944) - In Paris, an artist hires portrait models, and after he finishes their portraits, he strangles them. The film was based on a script originally intended for Boris Karloff at Universal. It was later sold to PRC, a smaller studio, where Ulmer directed it. The film's controversial subject matter and low-budget production have been noted by critics.

☐ **Bluebeard** (1972) - A horror film starring Richard Burton, which is more directly based on the folktale.

☐ **Bluebeard** (2009, France) - A modern French adaptation that also explores the dark themes of the original story.

• **HENRI DÉSIRÉ LANDRU:** The serial killer known as the "Bluebeard of Gambais."

☐ **Landru, der Blaubart von Paris** (1923, Austria) - This Austrian silent film is likely the earliest on the subject.

☐ **Monsieur Verdoux** (1947) - This American black comedy was directed by and starred Charlie Chaplin as a bigamist wife-killer. Chaplin's character is directly inspired by Landru. Orson Welles initially conceived the story and intended to direct, but Chaplin bought the rights to write, direct, and star in it himself.

☐ **Bluebeard's Ten Honeymoons** (1960, UK) - British thriller loosely based on Landru's case. George Sanders stars as a modified version of the killer.

☐ **Landru** (1963, France) - Directed by Claude Chabrol, this French film tells the shocking true story with a satirical tone. Charles Denner plays the title role.

☐ **Desire Landru** (2005, France) - A French TV movie that closely examines Landru's life and crimes in a serious and measured way.

☐ **The Last Circus** (2010, Spain) - A wax figure of Landru appears in an amusement park's haunted house attraction in this Spanish film.

☐ **The House of Ghosts** (1906) - A short film that explores spooky themes with ghostly apparitions and supernatural events, establishing early horror tropes.

☐ **The Red Spectre** (1907, France) - A French film that showcases the supernatural with visual effects like apparitions and mystical transformations.

☐ **The Haunted Hotel** (1918, France) - This short French film is notable for its use of special effects, such as stop-motion animatiosn and forced perspective, to create a chilling atmosphere.

☐ **The Haunted Castle** (1921, Germany) - In the castle Vogeloed, a few aristocrats are awaiting baroness Safferstätt. But first count Oetsch invites himself. Everyone thinks he murdered his brother, baroness Safferstat's first husband, three years ago. So, he is rather undesirable. But Oetsch stays; arguing he is not the murderer and will find the real one... This film is directed by F.W. Murnau, one of his earlier works before his iconic *Nosferatu*.

• **OTHER F.W MURNAU HORRORS**

☐ **Der Januskopf** (1920, Germany) - A lost film, this was an unauthorized adaptation of Robert Louis Stevenson's *Strange Case of Dr. Jekyll and Mr. Hyde*. Conrad Veidt starred in the dual role.

☐ **Satanas** (1920, Germany) - Also a lost film, this movie featured a three-part narrative with the devil appearing at different points in history to tempt humans.

☐ **The Hunchback and the Dancer** (1920) - Another lost film, this psychological horror follows a hunchback who uses a magical poison to make a beautiful dancer fall in love with him.

☐ **Phantom** (1922, Germany) - Also made the following year, this film about obsession and doppelgängers continues some of the psychological and dark fantasy themes seen in *The Haunted Castle*, but not a horror.

☐ **Faust** (1926, Germany) - This fantasy horror film is an adaptation of the German legend of Faust. It tells the story of an alchemist who makes a deal with the devil, Mephisto, in exchange for youth and worldly desires. Based on the Christopher Marlowe's Doctor Faustus dramatization.

- **ADAPTIONS OF DOCTOR FAUSTUS**
Doctor Faustus is the legendary German scholar who, dissatisfied with earthly knowledge, wealth, and power, makes a pact with the Devil in exchange for supernatural abilities. The tale first appeared in 16th-century chapbooks and was immortalized in Christopher Marlowe's play *The Tragical History of Doctor Faustus* (c. 1604) and later in Goethe's monumental *Faust* (1808/1832). His story embodies the archetype of the overreacher, the intellectual who seeks forbidden knowledge and pays with his soul. The legacy of Faustus runs deep: he is a cautionary figure of Renaissance hubris, a prototype of the mad scientist, and a recurring symbol in literature, music, and film whenever human ambition collides with damnation.

    ☐ **Faust** (1910) - his entrancing story, drawn from the world-renowned tragedy of Goethe, opens in the mysterious working den of Dr. Faust, who, old and worn out with years of stern study, and on the verge of despair through longing for the pleasures of his bygone youth, all of which he has surrendered to his learning, thinks of resorting to in order to end the weariness of his declining days.

    ☐ **Doctor Faustus** (1967) - Co-directed by and starring Richard Burton, this British horror film is based on a stage production he had previously starred in. Elizabeth Taylor appeared in a silent role as Helen of Troy.

    ☐ **Doctor Faustus** (1982) - A West German film adaptation featuring Jon Finch in the title role.

    ☐ **Doctor Faustus** (2012) - This film is based on the 2012 stage production by the Royal Shakespeare Company.

    ☐ **Doctor Faustus** (2021) - A modern, low-budget British adaptation with a female Doctor Faustus, directed by and starring Mariana Lewis.

- **FILMS IMSPIRED BY THE FAUST LEGEND**

    ☐ **The Devil and Daniel Webster** (1941) - This classic film adaptation is based on a short story by Stephen Vincent Benét about a New England farmer who sells his soul to the devil.

    ☐ **Damn Yankees** (1958) - A musical comedy about a Washington Senators baseball fan who sells his soul to become a young, star slugger and lead his team to the pennant.

    ☐ **Bedazzled** (1967 and 2000) - Both the original British film and its American remake are comedic takes on the Faust legend, with a hopeless man selling his soul for seven wishes.

    ☐ **Phantom of the Paradise** (1974) - Brian De Palma's rock opera horror film is a Faustian tale about a rock composer who makes a pact to have his music produced, with tragic results.

- ☐ **Needful Things** (1993) - A mysterious new shop opens in a small town which always seems to stock the deepest desires of each shopper, with a price far heavier than expected. The horror is derived from a Faustian pact, where a mysterious shopkeeper exploits the deep-seated rivalries of a small town for his own demonic amusement. The film is a loose adaptation of Stephen King's novel of the same name.
- ☐ **The Devil's Advocate** (1997) - A supernatural thriller starring Keanu Reeves as a hotshot defense attorney who discovers his boss (Al Pacino) is Satan himself.
- ☐ **Faust** (2011) - Russian director Alexander Sokurov's film is a free interpretation of the Faust legend that won the Golden Lion at the Venice International Film Festival.
- ☐ **Sunrise: A Song of Two Humans** (1927) - This American film, considered one of Murnau's masterpieces, follows a husband who contemplates murdering his wife. It features a tense, suspenseful tone in its first half before shifting to a more optimistic story.
- ☐ **The Phantom Carriage** (1921, Sweden) – On New Year's Eve, the driver of a ghostly carriage forces a drunken man to reflect on his selfish, wasted life. Charlie Chaplin stated this was the best film ever made.
- ☐ **The Hunchback of Notre Dame** (1923) - In 15th-century Paris, the brother of the archdeacon plots with the gypsy king to foment a peasant revolt. Meanwhile, a freakish hunchback falls in love with a gypsy dancer. Based on the 1831 novel by Victor Hugo.

- • **ADAPTIONS**
- ☐ **The Hunchback of Notre Dame** (1939) - One of the most famous and acclaimed film versions, starring Charles Laughton as Quasimodo and Maureen O'Hara as Esmeralda. This remake solidified the story's place in cinematic history and remains a classic of Hollywood's golden age.
- ☐ **The Hunchback of Notre Dame** (1956, France/Italy) - A French-Italian co-production starring Anthony Quinn as Quasimodo and Gina Lollobrigida as Esmeralda. This is often considered one of the more faithful theatrical adaptations of the novel.
- ☐ **Notre Dame de Paris** (1998) - A highly successful French-language rock musical that has been performed in many countries.

- ☐ **Maciste in Hell** (1925, Italy) - The devil takes Maciste down to hell in an attempt to corrupt and ruin his morality. *Maciste in Hell* is one of many films featuring the Maciste character, a super-strong hero who first appeared in the 1914 film *Cabiria*. Over the course of dozens of films, Maciste travels through different historical settings.
  - • **ADAPTIONS AND INFLUECES**
    - ☐ **Maciste in Hell** (1962) - A remake produced during the *peplum* (sword-and-sandal) boom of the 1960s. The film, released internationally as *The Witch's Curse*, stars Kirk Morris as Maciste, who travels to 17th-century Scotland to combat a witch.
    - ☐ **The Mask of Satan** (1960) - The initial witch-burning sequence in *Maciste in Hell* has been compared to the opening of Mario Bava's classic gothic horror film.
- ☐ **A Page of Madness** (1926, Japan) - A man takes a job at an asylum with hopes of freeing his imprisoned wife. *A Page of Madness* was lost for over four decades before being rediscovered by the director in 1971. It was reissued in 1973 with a musical score, as the original narrative intertitles and *benshi* (silent film narrator) commentary were missing. There are no other official remakes or direct adaptations of the work.
  - • **THEMATIC AND STYLISTIC INFLUENCE**
    - ☐ **Pink Floyd: The Wall** (1982) - The surreal and disorienting visuals reflecting the protagonist's psychological breakdown bear a strong resemblance to the visual language of *A Page of Madness*.
    - ☐ **Perfect Blue** (1997) - Satoshi Kon's psychological horror anime explores the fractured psyche of a woman, with visuals that blur the line between reality and hallucination, much like Kinugasa's film.

- **Shutter Island** (2010) – Federal marshal trapped in psychological conspiracy. The setting of a mental asylum and the exploration of an unreliable narrator's grasp on reality are key elements shared with *A Page of Madness*
- **The Last Warning** (1929, Silent) – Based on the novel Backstage Phantom by Wadsworth Camp. A producer decides to reopen a theater, that had been closed five years previously when one of the actors was murdered during a performance, by staging a production of the same play with the remaining members of the original cast.
  - **ADAPTIONS**
    - **The House of Fear** (1939) - A detective goes undercover as a producer to investigate an actor's murder, which occurred during the performance of a play. The actor's body disappeared shortly after the crime, and his ghost is rumored to be haunting the theater.
- **The Mummy** (1932) - A resurrected Egyptian mummy searches Cairo for the girl he believes to be his long-lost princess.

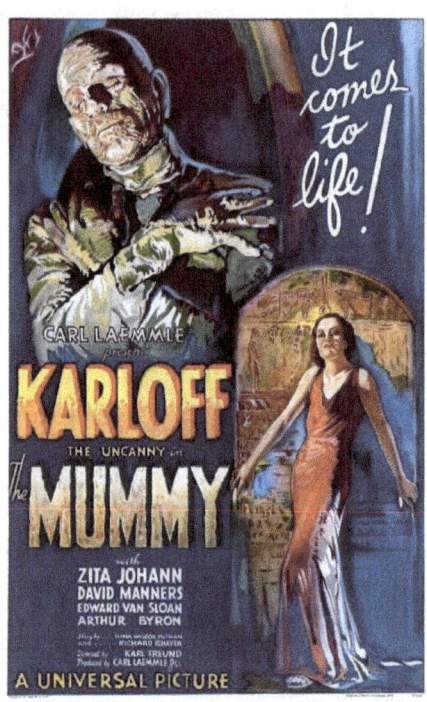

  - **KHARIS ADAPTIONS**
  - **The Mummy's Hand** (1940) - Archaeologists discover the lost tomb of Princess Ananka and the mummy Kharis, who was buried alive for trying to resurrect her. The High Priest Andoheb (George Zucco) uses the tana leaves to revive Kharis and commands him to kill anyone who desecrates the tomb.
  - **The Mummy's Tomb** (1942) - Thirty years after the events of the first film, Andoheb is revealed to have survived and is now elderly. He dispatches a new High Priest, Mehemet Bey (Turhan Bey), and the resurrected Kharis (now played by Lon Chaney Jr.) to the United States to kill the remaining members of the original expedition and their families.
  - **The Mummy's Ghost** (1944) - The mummies of Kharis and Princess Ananka are once again resurrected and taken to the US, where Ananka is reincarnated into a young woman of Egyptian descent named Amina (Ramsay Ames). The new High Priest, Yousef Bey (John Carradine), commands Kharis to kidnap Amina and bring her back to Egypt.
  - **The Mummy's Curse** (1944) - Beginning where the previous film ended, this installment inexplicably moves the swamp from Massachusetts to a bayou in Louisiana. Kharis and Ananka's bodies are recovered during a swamp drainage project, but they are revived and escape into the local community. Kharis begins to stalk the now-amnesiac Ananka, who has been taken in by the locals.

- **Mystery of the Wax Museum** (1933) - The disappearance of people and corpses leads a reporter to a wax museum and a sinister sculptor.
  - **ADAPTIONS & SIMILAR FILMS**
    - **The Man with Wax Faces** (1914, France) - A French film known for its dark themes and use of visual effects, it was an early example of horror cinema.
    - **House of Wax** (1953) - The story focuses on a disfigured wax sculptor, Vincent Price's character, who seeks to murder people and use their corpses as wax-coated displays in his museum.

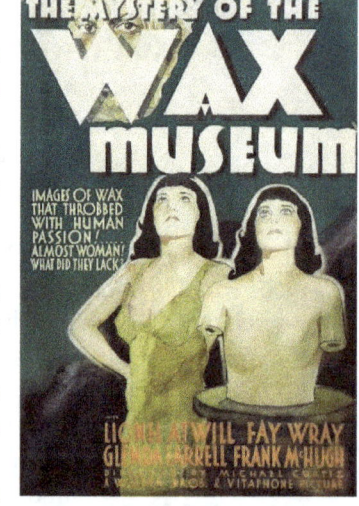

      - **COMPANION PIECE**
        - **The Mad Magician** (1954) - An illusionist becomes homicidal when his best kept magic secrets are stolen by his rival.
    - **House of Wax** (2005) - A group of college friends on a road trip are stalked and killed by insane twin brothers in a deserted town and their wax museum.
    - **Waxwork** (1988) – Teens trapped in horror wax museum exhibits. The 1988 film was partially inspired by the 1924 silent German film *Waxworks*. The concept of being trapped in the "pocket dimensions" of a wax museum also likely drew from classic horror traditions and anthology formats.

- **SEQUELS & INFLUENCE**
  - ☐ **Waxwork II: Lost in Time** (1992) – Dimension-hopping horror-comedy sequel.
  - ☐ **Waxworks** (1924) - A wax museum hires a writer to give the sculptures stories. The writer imagines himself and the museum owner's daughter in the stories.

☐ **The Black Cat** (1934) - Stranded honeymooners follow mad doctor to manor.
  - **INFLUENCES**
    - ☐ **The Shadow of the Cat** (1961) - A house cat sees her mistress murdered by two servants under orders from her husband, and becomes ferociously bent on revenge.

☐ **The Black Room** (1935) - Ignoring an ancient prophecy, evil brother Gregor seeks to maintain his feudal power on his Tyrolean estate by murdering and impersonating his benevolent younger twin.

☐ **The Hound of the Baskervilles** (1939) - A classic adaptation from 20th Century Fox, starring Basil Rathbone as Holmes and Nigel Bruce as Watson.

  - **ADAPTIONS**
    - ☐ **Der Hund von Baskerville** (1929 & 1937) - German film adaptations.
    - ☐ **The Hound of the Baskervilles** (1959) – Produced by Hammer Film Productions and the third most famous novel featuring Sherlock Holmes written by Sir Arthur Conan Doyle. When a nobleman is threatened by a family curse on his newly inherited estate, detective Sherlock Holmes is hired to investigate.
    - ☐ **The Hound of the Baskervilles** (1978) - A comedic parody starring Peter Cook and Dudley Moore.
  - **FULL RATHBONE/BRUCE SERIES**
    - ☐ **The Adventures of Sherlock Holmes** (1939) - The second and final film from Fox, featuring Holmes pitted against his archenemy, Professor Moriarty.
    - ☐ **Sherlock Holmes and the Voice of Terror** (1942) - The first Universal film, which updated the characters and set them in a contemporary World War II setting.
    - ☐ **Sherlock Holmes and the Secret Weapon** (1942) - Holmes and Watson must protect a bomb sight from falling into Nazi hands.
    - ☐ **Sherlock Holmes in Washington** (1943) - The duo travels to the U.S. capital to recover a secret document.
    - ☐ **Sherlock Holmes Faces Death** (1943) - A murder mystery is set at a convalescent home where Watson is volunteering.
    - ☐ **The Spider Woman** (1943) - Holmes investigates a series of bizarre murders he believes were committed by a female criminal mastermind.
    - ☐ **The Scarlet Claw** (1944) - Holmes travels to Canada and faces a monster legend that may have a human origin.
    - ☐ **The Pearl of Death** (1944) - The theft of a legendary pearl is linked to a series of gruesome murders.
      - **SEQUELS**
        - ☐ **House of Horrors** (1946) - An unsuccessful sculptor saves a madman (Rondo Hatton) named "The Creeper" from drowning. Seeing an opportunity for revenge, he tricks the psycho into murdering his critics.
        - ☐ **The Brute Man** (1946) - It is a prequel to *House of Horrors* and explores the backstory of Hatton's character.
    - ☐ **The House of Fear** (1945) - Sherlock Holmes investigates a series of deaths at a castle with each foretold by the delivery of orange pips to the victims.
    - ☐ **The Woman in Green** (1945) - Another encounter with a devious female killer, this time involving dismembered corpses.

- ☐ **Pursuit to Algiers** (1945) - Holmes and Watson are recruited to protect a prince on a cruise ship.
- ☐ **Terror by Night** (1946) - A jewel theft and murder take place on a train from London to Edinburgh.
- ☐ **Dressed to Kill** (1946) - In their final film, Holmes and Watson investigate a series of murders linked to a set of music boxes.

☐ **Rebecca** (1940) – A Gothic romance where the memory of the first Mrs. de Winter haunts the corridors of Manderley. Based on the Daphne du Maurier novel of the same name.
- • **ADAPTIONS**
  - ☐ **Kohraa** (1964, India) - Adaptation of *Rebecca*, drenched in Hindi gothic sensibilities.

☐ **Crimes at the Dark House** (1940) - A madman kills a man who has just inherited a large estate, then impersonates his victim to gain entrance to the estate so he can murder his enemies. Based on the Wilkie Collin's novel *The Woman in White*.
- • **ADAPTIONS OF THE NOVEL**
  - ☐ **The Woman in White** (1948) - This highly regarded American film stars Eleanor Parker, Alexis Smith, and Sydney Greenstreet.

☐ **I Walked with a Zombie** (1943) – Tropics meet Gothic dread in a tale of voodoo and spiritual unease. Inspired loosely by *Jane Eyre*. Lewton described it as "*Jane Eyre* with the West Indies."
- • **SIMILAR THEMES**
  - ☐ **Zombi Child** (2019) - A modern film that revisits the true story behind Haitian zombies, offering a more nuanced and historical exploration of the subject.

☐ **The Uninvited** (1944) – A haunted coastal estate, ghostly presences, and fraying sanity—one of the era's most delicate ghost stories. Based on the 1941 novel Uneasy Freehold by Dorothy Macardle
- • **SIMILAR THEMES**
  - ☐ **The Terror** (1963) - A young French soldier cut off from his unit is beguiled by a mysterious woman, whom he learns is the wife of the local Baron - and that she seemingly died twenty years earlier.
  - ☐ **The Legend of Hell House** (1973) – A haunted mansion tale with sexual repression and supernatural terror.

☐ **The Body Snatcher** (1945) – A macabre Gothic tale of grave robbing and vigilant superstition. It features a menacing performance by Boris Karloff. Produced by Val Lewton. Loosely based on the Robert Louis Stevenson short story of the same name. The story revolves around a doctor who hires a former student to provide fresh cadavers, leading to murder.

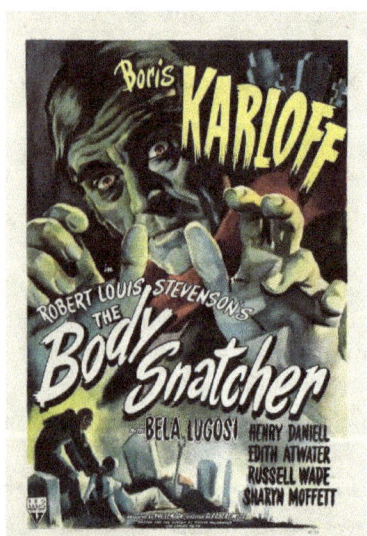

- • **MOVIES BASED ON BURKE & HARE:** Burke and Hare were 19th-century "resurrection men" in Edinburgh who turned to murder to supply cadavers to medical schools. Their case, killing at least 16 victims and selling the bodies to Dr. Robert Knox, crystallized cultural fears about science without ethics, making them folk-villains in horror history and precursors to the mad-scientist archetype itself.
- ☐ **The Greed of William Hart** (1948) - This film starred Tod Slaughter as a character based on William Hare. It was originally made as a more direct historical adaptation, but British censors insisted that all references to the real-life murderers be removed.
- ☐ **Corridors of Blood** (1958) - Dr. Thomas Bolton fights for the use of anesthetic in surgery and uses himself as a guinea pig, but soon finds himself addicted. The character of Dr. Bolton was very loosely inspired by the true story of Horace Wells, a dentist who experimented with anesthetics on himself. Additionally, the theme of graverobbing and body snatching was a popular trope in Victorian horror, with real-life cases like Burke and Hare being a common influence.
- ☐ **The Flesh and the Fiends** (1960) - A more explicit and gory adaptation starring Peter Cushing as Dr. Robert Knox and Donald Pleasence as William Hare. It is often considered one of the best Burke and Hare films.

- ☐ **Dr. Jekyll & Sister Hyde** (1971) - A Victorian scientist tests a serum that transforms him into a lascivious murderess. A Hammer film that depicts Burke and Hare as employees of Dr. Jekyll.
- ☐ **Burke & Hare** (1972) - A low-budget British horror-comedy version directed by Vernon Sewell.
- ☐ **The Doctors and the Devils** (1985) - Based on a screenplay by Welsh poet Dylan Thomas, this film changes the names of the main characters but keeps the events. Timothy Dalton stars as Dr. Rock, with Jonathan Pryce and Stephen Rea as the analogs for Burke and Hare.
- ☐ **I Sell the Dead** (2008) - A grave robber reflects on his life of crime. The film captures the feel of a vintage Hammer horror movie with its fog-laden graveyards, moody lighting, and period costumes, though on a much lower budget.
- ☐ **Burke & Hare** (2010) - A black comedy directed by John Landis, starring Simon Pegg as Burke and Andy Serkis as Hare. It focuses on the duo's murderous plot and their relationship with the competing medical schools in Edinburgh.

☐ **Dead of Night** (1945) - Architect Walter Craig senses impending doom as his half-remembered recurring dream turns into reality. The guests at the country house encourage him to stay as they take turns telling supernatural tales. The film's structure was influential in the way the "Amicus" horror films were made.

- • **RELATED FILMS**
    - ☐ **Magic** (1978) – Starring Sir Anthony Hopkins. A ventriloquist is at the mercy of his vicious dummy while he tries to renew a romance with his high school sweetheart.
    - ☐ **Trilogy of Terror** (1975) - This TV movie includes a segment where a Zuni fetish doll comes to life, leading to the "killer doll" concept becoming more mainstream.
    - ☐ **Pin** (1988) - Another psychological horror film that follows a deranged character who believes his anatomically correct dummy is alive.

☐ **The Beast with Five Fingers** (1946) - In a turn-of-the-century Renaissance Italian mansion, its tyrannical owner, a wheelchair-bound one-handed pianist with a strong belief in the occult is murdered. Based on the 1928 short story by William Fryer Harvey. The idea of a severed, animated hand has been revisited in other films such as the ones listed below and even *Evil Dead 2* and *The Addams Family*.

THE BEAST WITH FIVE FINGERS

WILLIAM FRYER HARVEY

- • **INFLUENCES**
    - ☐ **The Hands of Orlac** (1924) - A silent Austrian expressionist film where a concert pianist's mental state unravels after he learns his new hands were a murderer's.
    - ☐ **Mad Love** (1935) - An American film focusing on the obsessive surgeon who performed the hand transplant and his mad scheme to possess the pianist's wife.
    - ☐ **The Hands of Orlac** (1960) - A French-British co-production with a magician-hypnotist as the antagonist, where the pianist receives the same hand transplant and is blackmailed.
    - ☐ **Hands of a Stranger** (1962) - An American film where a doctor experiments with a hand transplant on an amnesiac man, creating a monster with a murderer's hands and impulses.
    - ☐ **The Hand** (1981) - Directed by Oliver Stone, this film stars Michael Caine as a cartoonist whose hand is severed in an accident. The hand then takes on a murderous life of its own.
    - ☐ **Body Parts** (1991) - After losing his arm in a car accident, a criminal psychologist has it replaced with a limb that belonged to a serial killer.
    - ☐ **Idle Hands** (1999) – A teenage slacker's right hand becomes possessed with murderous intent. Finn Wolfhard (*Stranger Things*) and Billy Bryk, who previously collaborated on the horror-comedy *Hell of a Summer*, are writing the screenplay for the "reimagining". They are also being considered to direct.
    - ☐ **The Hands of Roxana** (2012, France) - A French TV movie featuring a female protagonist who receives the same hand transplant and begins to be haunted by a murderer's tendencies.
    - ☐ **Talk to Me** (2022) - When a group of friends discover how to conjure spirits using an embalmed hand, they become hooked on the new thrill, until one of them goes too far and unleashes

terrifying supernatural forces. The Philippou brothers have indicated their new film, *Bring Her Back* (2025), is part of the *Talk to Me* cinematic universe. *Talk 2 Me* - A24 officially approved a sequel to the original film in August 2023.

- ☐ **The Strange Door** (1951) - In 17th-century France, the wealthy and sadistic Sire Alain de Maletroit (Charles Laughton) has nursed a deep grudge against his brother for 20 years. To enact his revenge, he holds his brother captive in a hidden dungeon within his manor and forces his niece, Blanche, to live in misery. Based on the short story "The Sire de Maletroit's Door" by Robert Louis Stevenson. Film historians have described *The Strange Door* as a "well-disguised remake" of Universal's 1935 film *The Raven*. Both films feature a villain who uses a torture chamber inspired by Edgar Allan Poe's writing.
  - • **RELATED FILMS**
    - ☐ **The Black Castle** (1952) - Man investigates the disappearance of two of his friends who were the guests of a sinister Austrian count. This Universal film, released a year later, is a similar Gothic melodrama also starring Boris Karloff. It is considered a companion piece to *The Strange Door*, as both represented Universal's brief return to Gothic horror before the sci-fi boom of the mid-50s.
- ☐ **The Haunted Strangler** (1958) - A researcher investigating a notorious serial killer who was hanged 20 years earlier seemingly becomes possessed by the long-dead strangler.
- ☐ **The Bat** (1959) - A crazed killer known as "The Bat" is on the loose in a mansion full of people. Based on the nove *The Circular Staircase* by Mary Roberts Rinehart.
  - • **OTHER ADAPTIONS**
    - ☐ **The Bat** (1926) - A masked criminal who dresses like a giant bat terrorizes the guests at an old house rented by a mystery writer.
    - ☐ **The Bat Whispers** (1930) - A master criminal terrorizes the occupants of an isolated country mansion.
- ☐ **The Haunting** (1963) – Robert Wise's adaptation of *The Haunting of Hill House*; subtle Gothic supernatural terror. Hill House has stood for about 90 years and appears haunted: its inhabitants have always met strange, tragic ends. Now Dr. John Markway has assembled a team of people who he thinks will prove whether or not the house is haunted. Based on the novel by Shirley Jackson.
  - • **ADAPTIONS & RELATED TV**
    - ☐ **The Haunting** (1999) – A flawed remake, but steeped in Gothic architecture and ghostly lore.
    - ☐ **The Haunting of Hill House** (2018) - Flashing between past and present, a fractured family confronts haunting memories of their old home and the terrifying events that drove them from it.
- ☐ **The Gorgon** (1964) - In the early twentieth century, a Gorgon takes human form and terrorizes a small European village by turning its citizens to stone. Peter Cushing and Christopher Lee made many films together for Hammer, often playing enemies. Their on-screen chemistry is a highlight of *The Gorgon*, as it was in classics like *Horror of Dracula* (1958) and *The Curse of Frankenstein* (1957).
  - • **SILMILAR HAMMER THEMES**
    - ☐ **The Curse of the Mummy's Tomb** (1964) - This was the double-bill pairing for *The Gorgon*'s American release, and both films are included together in home video collections.
    - ☐ **The Reptile** (1966) - This film also features a woman who transforms into a serpentine monster, another example of Hammer blending different genres with traditional horror.
- ☐ **The Crimson Cult (Curse of the Crimson Alter** (1968, UK) - Robert Manning visits the remote country house where his brother Peter was last

seen. While his host seems outwardly friendly and his niece more demonstrably so, Robert detects a feeling of menace in the air. Christopher Lee regarded this film as one of the worst in his entire career.

- **RELATED FILMS**
  - ☐ **The Sorcerers** (1967) - Also produced by Tigon, this film stars Boris Karloff and explores hypnosis and sinister psychological control.
  - ☐ **Blood on Satan's Claw** (1971) – Folk meets Gothic as rural England succumbs to demonic corruption.

☐ **The Curse of the Living Corpse** (1964) - Relatives gather in an old house for the reading of a will, but the "dead" man comes back to life and starts killing.

- **RELATED FILMS:**
  - ☐ **The Horror of Party Beach** (1964) - This low-budget monster movie was often released as a double feature with *Curse of the Living Corpse*, as they were produced by the same team.

☐ **Suspiria** (1977, Itally) – An American newcomer to a prestigious German ballet academy comes to realize that the school is a front for something sinister amid a series of grisly murders. **Memorable Quote:** "Magic is everywhere. You just have to be able to see it."

- **SEQUELS**
  - ☐ **Inferno** (1980, Italy) – Argento's dreamlike "Three Mothers" continuation. *See Video Nasties*
  - ☐ **The Mother of Tears** (2007) - The final and long-delayed entry in the trilogy, which explores the third witch, Mater Lachrymarum, the Mother of Tears.

☐ **The Others** (2001) – Nicole Kidman stars in a haunted manor story with one of modern Gothic's most devastating twists. A woman who lives in her darkened old family house with her two photosensitive children becomes convinced that the home is haunted.

- **HAUNTED HOUSE MYSTERIES**
  - ☐ **The Abandoned** (2006) - An adopted woman returns to her home country and the family home that she never knew and must face the mystery that lies there. The film is known for its slow-burn, atmospheric approach to a ghost story that blurs the line between supernatural horror and psychological terror.
  - ☐ **The Orphanage** (2007) – Spanish Gothic tale of grief and spectral children.
  - ☐ **The Silent House** (2010, Uruguay) – Real-time haunted house dread. A young woman becomes trapped inside a house and is unable to contact the outside world as mysterious forces haunt it. *The Silent House* was reportedly made for a budget of only $6,000.
    - **ADAPTIONS**
      - ☐ **Silent House** (2011) - The plot follows a similar premise to the original, focusing on a young woman who is trapped and terrorized inside a house.
  - ☐ **The House at the End of Time** (2013, Venezuela) - After being wrongly imprisoned for the mysterious, supernatural death of her husband and son, Dulce returns back to her old home to unravel the mystery that has haunted her for so long.
  - ☐ **Oculus** (2013) – A cursed mirror manipulates reality, turning family against itself.
  - ☐ **Marrowbone** (2017) - A young man and his three younger siblings, who have kept secret the death of their beloved mother in order to remain together, are plagued by a sinister presence in the sprawling manor in which they live.
  - ☐ **The Night House** (2020) – After her husband's unexpected death, a widow begins uncovering disturbing secrets about the home he built for her and a mysterious, haunting presence.
  - ☐ **Martyrs Lane** (2021) - Leah, 10, lives in a large vicarage, full of lost souls and the needy. In the day the house is bustling with people; at night it is dark, empty, a space for Leah's nightmares to creep into. A small, nightly visitor brings Leah comfort, but soon she will realize that her little visitor offers knowledge that might be very, very dangerous.
  - ☐ **Presence** (2024) - A family becomes convinced they are not alone after moving into their new home in the suburbs.

☐ **Crimson Peak** (2015) – Guillermo del Toro's lush, ghost-ridden mansion story combines romance, dread, and spectacular visuals.

Queen of Gothic Horror

Shirley Jackson

Shirley Jackson (1916–1965) was an American novelist and short story writer who made the ordinary terrifying. Living in small-town Vermont, she wrote about domestic spaces, social rituals, and women's inner lives then turned them uncanny. Jackson's horror lens wasn't cosmic like Lovecraft's but intimate: madness, repression, and the suffocating weight of conformity. Her fiction sits at the intersection of psychological unease and supernatural suggestion, where you're never sure if the haunting is external or born from the mind.

Signature Works (Curated)
- *The Lottery* (1948, short story) — A sunny village ritual ends in shocking sacrifice; one of the most controversial stories ever published in *The New Yorker*.
- *The Haunting of Hill House* (1959) — A group investigates a cursed mansion; subtle prose and psychological ambiguity make it the definitive haunted-house novel.
- *We Have Always Lived in the Castle* (1962) — A reclusive family is slowly unraveled by paranoia and townsfolk suspicion; gothic isolation meets psychological breakdown.

The Fingerprints
- Domestic unease: families, homes, and communities as sites of dread.
- Ambiguity: is it supernatural or psychological collapse?
- Female-centered horror: repression, madness, and agency within suffocating social roles.
- A deceptively simple style that builds dread through the mundane.

Legacy & Influence
Jackson is the mother of modern psychological horror. *The Lottery* shocked mid-century readers, sparking letters of outrage. *Hill House* shaped the haunted-house genre, influencing Stephen King (*The Shining*), Mike Flanagan (*The Haunting of Hill House* series), and Robert Eggers' focus on paranoia in isolation. Writers from Neil Gaiman to Joyce Carol Oates cite her as essential. Today, her blend of everyday dread and ambiguous haunting feels more modern than ever.

Pairing Night Watchlist
- *The Haunting* (1963, dir. Robert Wise) → Classic black-and-white ambiguity. Look for the way camera angles suggest the house itself is alive.
- *The Haunting of Hill House* (2018, Netflix) → Flanagan's reimagining; watch how grief and trauma refract through Jackson's DNA.
- *We Have Always Lived in the Castle* (2018) → A faithful, slow-burn adaptation of her claustrophobic gothic tale.

Quick Facts to Sound Smart
- When *The Lottery* was published in *The New Yorker*, readers canceled subscriptions en masse. One of the most infamous literary scandals of the 20th century.
- Stephen King has called *The Haunting of Hill House* "one of the finest horror novels of the late 20th century."
- Jackson's influence reached television: Shirley Crain, a character in Netflix's *Hill House*, is named in tribute.
- Her husband, critic Stanley Edgar Hyman, downplayed her genius during her lifetime, but posthumously, she's recognized as one of America's greatest horror writers.

Italian and 60s–70s Gothic

- ☐ **House of Usher** (1960) – Upon entering his fiancée's family mansion, a man discovers a savage family curse and fears that his future brother-in-law has entombed his bride-to-be prematurely. Another Corman-Poe, lush with color and crumbling mansions.
  - • **ROGER CORMAN'S POE**
    - ☐ **The Pit and the Pendulum** (1961) – In the sixteenth century, Francis Barnard travels to Spain to clarify the strange circumstances of his sister's death after she had married the son of a cruel Spanish Inquisitor. Roger Corman and Vincent Price adapt Poe into a claustrophobic nightmare of guilt and torture.
    - ☐ **The Premature Burial** (1962) - Based on Edgar Allan Poe's story about a cataleptic Englishman obsessed with the fear of being buried alive.
      - • **SIMILAR FILM**
        - ☐ **The Crime of Doctor Crespi** (1938) - A crazed scientist invents a serum that induces a catatonic state in whoever it is injected into. He uses the serum to paralyze his enemies, so that he can bury them alive.
    - ☐ **Tales of Terror** (1962) - Three tales of terror involve a grieving widower and the daughter he abandoned; a drunkard and his wife's black cat; and a hypnotist who prolongs the moment of a man's death.
    - ☐ **The Raven** (1963) – A Gothic parody starring Karloff, Price, and Peter Lorre in wizardly duels.
      - • **ADAPTIONS**
        - ☐ **The Raven** (1935) - A brilliant surgeon with a morbid obsession for instruments of torture grows dangerously obsessed with a young socialite whose life he's saved.
        - ☐ **The Raven** (2012) - This film is a fictionalized crime thriller starring John Cusack as Edgar Allan Poe. In the movie, Poe must team up with a detective to hunt a serial killer whose murders are inspired by the author's stories.
    - ☐ **The Haunted Palace** (1963) – Corman merges Poe with Lovecraft in a tale of ancient curses and sinister legacies.
    - ☐ **The Masque of the Red Death** (1964) – Price presides over plague, decadence, and satanic ritual.
      - • **ADAPTIONS**
        - ☐ **Masque of the Red Death** (1989, Larry Brand) - This was Corman's official, Roger Corman-produced remake. It starred Adrian Paul as Prince Prospero and Patrick Macnee.
        - ☐ **Masque of the Red Death** (1989, Alan Birkinshaw) - This was a rival, low-budget slasher version.
    - ☐ **The Tomb of Ligeia** (1964) – Gothic love and obsession, with Price tormented by spectral visions.
  - • **OTHER ADAPTIONS AND SIMILAR FILMS**
    - ☐ **The Fall of the House of Usher** (2023, Netflix Series) - Siblings Roderick and Madeline Usher

have built a pharmaceutical company into an empire of wealth, privilege and power; however, secrets come to light when the heirs to the Usher dynasty start dying.
    - ☐ **Spirits of the Dead** (1968) Starring Jane Fonda. A trio of Edgar Allan Poe adaptations about a cruel countess haunted by her cousin's stallion, a sadistic soldier haunted by his doppelgänger, and an alcoholic actor haunted by the Devil.
    - ☐ **Two Evil Eyes** (1990) - It is a unique collaboration between two horror masters, George A. Romero and Dario Argento, and is based on stories by Edgar Allan Poe. A duo of Edgar Allan Poe adaptations about a greedy wife's attempt to embezzle her dying husband's fortune, and a sleazy reporter's adoption of a strange black cat.

Poe vs. Corman

Edgar Allan Poe (1809–1849) and Roger Corman (1926-2024) are separated by more than a century, yet together they form one of the most iconic literary-cinematic pairings in horror. Poe, the American master of psychological dread, distilled terror into the intimate spaces of grief, madness, and mortality. Corman, the "Pope of Pop Cinema," transformed that inner darkness into lush, color-saturated visions that captivated mid-20th-century audiences. Where Poe wrote the architecture of the American Gothic imagination, Corman built it on screen, often on recycled sets and tight budgets, but with such operatic intensity that his adaptations defined Gothic cinema for an entire generation.

Poe's Interior Gothic

Poe's works emerged from a life steeped in instability and loss. Orphaned young and plagued by poverty, he watched illness consume nearly every woman he loved. These private agonies became the scaffolding of his fiction. Unlike the European Gothic tradition of ruined castles and external threats, Poe turned horror inward. His haunted chambers were psychological, his narrators unreliable, and his monsters born from obsession, disease, or the collapse of reason itself. In "The Fall of the House of Usher" (1839), a decaying mansion mirrors its owners' doom; in "The Tell-Tale Heart" (1843), madness itself narrates; in "The Masque of the Red Death" (1842), mortality invades even the fortified walls of privilege. Poe's language worked like a spell: rhythmic, incantatory, and claustrophobic drawing readers into an atmosphere where the boundaries between life and death, sanity and delusion, blurred irreversibly. He gave horror its intimate, psychological voice, a legacy that resonated far beyond literature.

Corman's Gothic Factory

Roger Corman emerged from the postwar exploitation boom with a very different background: a producer and director trained in efficiency, marketability, and spectacle. Through American International Pictures, Corman built a reputation for films that were fast, cheap, and eye-catching posters promised lurid thrills, titles sparked curiosity, and the films themselves delivered pulp entertainment with unexpected artistry. Corman's genius lay in his ability to balance exploitation with experimentation. Beneath the surface of shock value and Gothic melodrama, his films often smuggled in visual innovation, psychological tension, or allegorical depth.

It was in his cycle of Edgar Allan Poe adaptations in the early 1960s, starring the inimitable Vincent Price, that Corman found his highest expression. *House of Usher* (1960) inaugurated this series, followed by titles such as *The Pit and the Pendulum* (1961), *The Raven* (1963), and *The Masque of the Red Death* (1964). These films turned AIP's modest budgets into baroque spectacles: cavernous sets drenched in color, surreal dream sequences, and performances that embodied Poe's themes of obsession, grief, and decay. Corman's Gothic cycle was both commercial strategy and artistic statement, showing that even exploitation cinema could rival Hammer Studios in atmosphere and resonance.

The Fusion: Corman Engulfs Poe

The pairing of Poe and Corman was less adaptation than engulfment. Corman did not merely transfer Poe's stories to film; he absorbed their essence and re-expressed them in the visual idioms of his time. Poe's claustrophobic chambers became Corman's vast, color-drenched halls. His unreliable narrators became Vincent Price's haunted aristocrats, whose every gesture suggested grief curdling into madness. Poe's obsession with mortality was heightened by Corman's psychedelic palettes, where plague could be painted in crimson, or terror staged as theatrical allegory.

Importantly, Corman expanded Poe's fragments into full narratives, stretching short stories and poems into feature-length meditations on fear and decay. *The Raven* (1963) even bent Poe's solemn verse into camp comedy, proving the flexibility of his imagery. By engulfing Poe, Corman gave the American Gothic a new cinematic language. One that combined fidelity to the source's atmosphere with the irreverence of exploitation filmmaking.

Legacy of the Gothic Bond

The fusion of Poe and Corman secured Gothic horror's place in mid-century cinema. For audiences of the 1960s, Corman's films reintroduced Poe not as dusty literature but as living nightmare, ripe for allegory in a nuclear age haunted by plague, war, and cultural upheaval. The cycle influenced not only later filmmakers like Guillermo del Toro and Mike Flanagan, but also showed how genre cinema could be both profitable and aesthetically ambitious.

Poe gave horror its psychological interior; Corman gave that interior walls, colors, and motion. Together, they created a Gothic duet. One born in ink, the other in celluloid that continues to echo through the haunted halls of horror.

Parallels and Curiosities

The bond between Edgar Allan Poe and Roger Corman was more than one of writer and adaptor; it was a curious meeting of obsessions. Poe, shaped by loss and illness, wrote from the edge of madness, filling his tales with claustrophobia, grief, and the inexorable pull of death. Corman, by contrast, thrived in the realm of speed and invention, producing films on minimal budgets and breakneck schedules. Each, in his own medium, was consumed by intensity. Poe by private despair, Corman by public demand.

Their partnership also highlights a fascinating transformation of scale. Poe's stories were often no more than a handful of pages, fragments of atmosphere and dread. Corman stretched these fragments into full-length features, inventing characters, romances, and subplots where none existed. Yet the essence remained intact: the dread of confinement, the lure of obsession, and the inevitability of decay. It was less an act of translation than one of expansion. Corman proved that atmosphere alone could sustain an entire cinematic experience.

Vincent Price served as the perfect bridge between the two. Poe's narrators were unreliable, fragile, and fevered, and Price brought them to life with aristocratic poise and velvet menace. In his voice and bearing, the psychological intensity of Poe's words found a physical form, turning literary archetypes into unforgettable cinematic figures.

Even their reputations parallel one another. Poe was often dismissed in his own century as a purveyor of sensationalism, only later to be hailed as the inventor of the American Gothic. Corman's films, too, were once written off as cheap drive-in fare, only to be reassessed as essential milestones in Gothic cinema. Both men left legacies that reached far beyond their immediate audiences. Poe inspiring generations of writers from Lovecraft to Stephen King, Corman launching directors like Coppola, Scorsese, and Cameron. Together, they ensured that Gothic horror would not only endure but evolve, shaping both page and screen in ways still felt today.

- ☐ **Castle of the Living Dead** (1964) – Christopher Lee plays a sinister count hosting a deadly masquerade.
- ☐ **House of Dark Shadows** (1970) – Soap-opera Gothic brought to film, vampiric melodrama at its most atmospheric.
- ☐ **And Now the Screaming Starts!** (1973) - England, 1795: the young Catherine has just married Charles Fengriffen and moves into his castle. She becomes the victim of a curse that was laid on the family long ago. On her wedding night she is raped by a ghost and gets pregnant. Based on the 1970 novella called *Fengriffen,* written by David Case.
- ☐ **Don't Look Now** (1973) – A married couple grieving the recent death of their young daughter are in Venice when they encounter two elderly sisters, one of whom is psychic and brings a warning from beyond.
- ☐ **Lisa and the Devil** (1974) – Bava's dreamlike Gothic about mannequins, death, and an eerie villa.
- ☐ **The Devil's Rain** (1975) – Cults, melting faces, and Gothic occult dread starring Ernest Borgnine.
- ☐ **Don't Be Afraid of the Dark** (1973) - A young couple inherits an old mansion inhabited by small demon-like creatures who are determined to make the wife one of their own.
  - • **ADAPTIONS & SIMILAR FILMS**
    - ☐ **Don't Be Afraid of the Dark** (2010) - This film is a theatrical remake, co-written and produced by Guillermo del Toro, who has stated that the 1973 original was one of the scariest movies he had ever seen. While the core plot is similar, the remake offers a more fleshed-out mythology for the creatures.
    - ☐ **Burnt Offerings** (1976) – A decaying mansion consumes its inhabitants in this American Gothic.
    - ☐ **Lights Out** (2016) - This film explores the fear of what lurks in the dark, with a monster that can only be seen in the shadows. It shares a similar premise of a creature that preys on a protagonist when they are most vulnerable.

Gothic & Revival

- ☐ **House on Haunted Hill** (1959) - A millionaire offers $10,000 to five people who agree to be locked in a large, spooky, rented house overnight with him and his wife.

  - • **ADAPTIONS**
    - ☐ **House on Haunted Hill** (1999) – Remake of the 1959 classic, with Gothic mansions and ghostly carnage.
    - ☐ **Return to House on Haunted Hill** (2007) - Several years after Sara and Eddie escaped the former asylum and its inmates, Ariel, Sara's sister, visits the house looking for answers and the truth behind her sister's insane claims about what happened inside it.
- ☐ **The Changeling** (1980) – After experiencing tragic personal losses, a music professor rents a Seattle mansion, haunted by a slain boy.
  - • **SIMILAR FILMS**
    - ☐ **The Watcher in the Woods** (1980) - When a family moves to a country home, the young girls experience strange happenings that have a link to an occult event years past. The film is a loose adaptation of the young adult mystery novel by Florence Engel Randall. A stage musical version is in development, based on the novel.

☐ **Lady in White** (1988) - An author tells the story of how, as a young boy growing up in a 1960s small town, he was haunted after witnessing the murder of a little girl. The story is told from the perspective of a child, which emphasizes the innocence and vulnerability of the victims and the horror of the world they live in.

☐ **Stir of Echoes** (1999) - After being hypnotized, a man begins to see visions of a missing girl and becomes obsessed with solving her murder.

☐ **The Awakening** (2011, UK) - In 1921, England is overwhelmed by the loss and grief of World War I. Hoax exposer Florence Cathcart visits a boarding school to explain sightings of a child ghost. Everything she believes unravels as the 'missing' begin to show themselves.

☐ **The Woman in Black** (2012) - This gothic horror film features a young lawyer who travels to a remote village and becomes entangled in the vengeful spirit of a woman searching for her child.

☐ **The Shining** (1980) – A family heads to an isolated hotel for the winter where a sinister presence influences the father to become violence, while his psychic son sees horrific forebodings from both past and future. Stanley Kubrick would reportedly call Stephen King at 3:00 a.m. to ask him questions about *The Shining*. According to King, one famous exchange had the director ask the author, "Do you believe in God?" When he replied in the affirmative. Kubrick yelled "I knew it!" and slammed the phone down. **Memorable Quote:** *"Here's Johnny!"*

- **ADAPTIONS & SIMILAR FILMS**

☐ **Doctor Sleep** (2019) - Years following the events of *The Shining* (1980), a now-adult Dan Torrance must protect a young girl with similar powers from a cult known as The True Knot, who prey on children with powers to remain immortal. It is an adaptation of Stephen King's 2013 novel of the same name and a sequel to both the 1980 film and the 1977 novel *The Shining*.

☐ **Next of Kin** (1982) - In a rest home for elderly people, a daughter reads her mother's diary. Soon events that are mentioned in the mother's diary begin to happen to the daughter. Quentin Tarantino famously compared *Next of Kin* to Kubrick's film due to its isolated setting, supernatural undertones, and descent into madness.

☐ **Company of Wolves** (1984) – Angela Carter's fairy-tale Gothic of wolves, sexuality, and surrealism.

☐ **The House of the Spirits** (1993) – While magical realism, its mansion setting and generational curses drip Gothic atmosphere.

☐ **Blood & Donuts** (1995) - A vampire falls for a woman working at a donut shop.

☐ **Beloved** (1998) - The film is a loose adaptation of the 1987 Toni Morrison's Pulitzer Prize-winning novel, drawing on the same source material but translating its powerful, layered narrative to a visual medium. A slave is visited by the spirit of a mysterious young woman.

- **SIMILAR FILMS**

☐ **The Skeleton Key** (2005) – Gothic Southern mystery steeped in Hoodoo and decaying estates.

☐ **Daughters of the Dust** (1991) - This historical drama, like *Beloved*, explores the psychological and generational trauma of slavery within a Gullah Geechee family.

☐ **The Ninth Gate** (1999) – Occult Gothic involving forbidden books and Satanic conspiracies.

☐ **Crimson Rivers** (2000) – A French Gothic-tinged thriller of ritual murders in a remote mountain town.

☐ **Darkness Falls** (2003) – Gothic reimagining of the tooth fairy legend.

☐ **Coraline** (2009) – Animated Gothic fairy tale of shadowy doubles and button-eyed horrors.

☐ **Tell Tale** (2009) - A modern science-fiction horror thriller that uses Poe's story as a launchpad. Produced by Ridley and Tony Scott, it follows a man whose recently transplanted heart drives him to find the donor's killer.

- **ADAPTIONS OF EDGAR'S TELL-TALE HEART**

☐ **The Tell-Tale Heart** (2014) - A more contemporary feature film set in New Orleans that modernizes the story. It stars Rose McGowan and Patrick John Flueger.

☐ **Extraordinary Tales** (2015) - An animated anthology film that adapts five of Poe's stories, including "The Tell-Tale Heart," featuring narration by prominent figures like Sir Christopher Lee and Guillermo del Toro.

Master of Menace

Vincent Price (1911–1993) was horror's velvet voice, its arched eyebrow, its sly smile that hinted at secrets you did not want to know. To call him merely an actor is to undersell his role: he was the face of Gothic cinema in mid-20th-century America, a figure who made menace elegant and dread alluring. Across more than 100 films, Price transformed horror from creaky melodrama into operatic theater, where terror was not just screamed but savored.

Cultivating a Persona

Trained at Yale and the Courtauld Institute of Art in London, Price originally seemed destined for a career in art history, not cinema. That pedigree infused his acting with refinement, an aristocratic bearing that made him instantly distinctive. Unlike the brute force of Boris Karloff or the silent menace of Bela Lugosi, Price specialized in irony, wit, and the psychological curl of language. His voice could drip poison as easily as charm, making him an actor audiences feared and adored in equal measure.

By the late 1940s and 1950s, Price had already earned recognition in dramas and noirs, but it was horror that crowned him. His partnership with director Roger Corman in the 1960s cemented his reputation as the "Master of Menace." In film after film, Price embodied haunted aristocrats, deranged inventors, and mad visionaries, always with a knowing glint that made the grotesque strangely magnetic.

Signature Works

- *House of Wax* (1953) — Price as a vengeful sculptor encasing victims in wax; a 3-D spectacle that became a horror landmark.
- *The Fly* (1958) — A tragic scientist tale that gave Price one of his most sympathetic roles.
- *House on Haunted Hill* (1959) — A camp classic, where Price plays a sinister millionaire staging a deadly party.
- *House of Usher* (1960) — The first of Corman's Poe adaptations, with Price as the doomed Roderick Usher.
- *The Masque of the Red Death* (1964) — Price at his most decadent as Prince Prospero, hosting revels while plague rages outside.
- *The Abominable Dr. Phibes* (1971) — A cult masterpiece where Price plays a masked organist enacting elaborate biblical murders.

These performances ranged from camp to tragedy, yet all carried his unmistakable touch: elegance married to terror, humor shadowing horror.

What He Did for Horror

Price advanced horror by broadening its emotional palette. He made villains cultured and sympathetic, their monstrosity rooted in obsession or grief rather than mere cruelty. He also brought prestige: his theatrical training and refined persona elevated low-budget films into artful spectacles. His ability to oscillate between horror, satire, and melodrama made Gothic cinema feel alive, playful, and modern.

He was also one of horror's first true cross-media icons. Price's voice became a cultural symbol, most famously in Michael Jackson's *Thriller* (1982), where his sinister narration introduced a new generation to Gothic cadence. Beyond film, he appeared in television, radio, and even comedy sketches, proving that horror could adapt to every medium without losing its bite.

Legacy & Amazement

Few actors can claim to have influenced both high culture and pop culture so completely. Price collected art, wrote cookbooks, and appeared on *The Muppet Show*, yet never shed his Gothic aura. He mentored young filmmakers, championed the horror genre when critics dismissed it, and remained self-aware enough to parody his own image. His career stretched over five decades, and through it, horror found sophistication, theatricality, and longevity.

Vincent Price did not just play villains, he defined what a villain could be. He proved that horror did not have to be brutish or crude; it could be decadent, witty, poetic, and timeless. That is why he remains, without question, the Master of Menace.

Modern & Contemporary Gothic

- ☐ **The Blackcoat's Daughter** (2015) – Minimalist Gothic dread in a winterbound girls' school.
- ☐ **A Cure for Wellness** (2016) – Gothic body horror set in an Alpine sanatorium.
- ☐ **The Lodgers** (2017) – Irish Gothic of twins bound by a family curse in a crumbling manor.
- ☐ **Winchester** (2018) – The sprawling, haunted Winchester Mystery House as Gothic labyrinth.
- ☐ **The Little Stranger** (2018) – English estate Gothic of class, trauma, and spectral resentment.
- ☐ **We Have Always Lived in the Castle** (2018) – Adaptation of Shirley Jackson's Gothic family tale.
- ☐ **Gretel & Hansel** (2020) – Fairy tale Gothic with painterly visuals.
  - **SIMILAR FAIRY TALES**
    - ☐ **Pinocchio's Revenge** (1996) - A direct-to-video film about a killer puppet that becomes obsessed with a young boy.
    - ☐ **Rumpelstiltskin** (1996) - A horror film that features the titular character as a grotesque and violent creature.
    - ☐ **Snow White: A Tale of Terror** (1997) - It was adapted from the 1812 German fairy tale collected by the Brothers Grimm and was originally titled "Snow White and the Black Forest."
    - ☐ **The Brother's Grimm** (2005) - This film similarly explores the dark and twisted nature of fairy tales, though with a more adventure-focused and comedic tone.
    - ☐ **Red Riding Hood** (2011) - A romantic fantasy horror film that features a werewolf terrorizing a medieval village and explores themes of love, betrayal, and violence.
    - ☐ **The Lure** (2015, Poland) - A Polish horror musical that follows two mermaid sisters who join a rock band in 1980s Poland and engage in a bloody and sexually charged journey.
    - ☐ **Winnie the Pooh: Blood and Honey** (2023) - A low-budget slasher film that transforms the beloved children's characters into homicidal killers.
    - ☐ **Cinderella's Revenge** (2024) - A direct-to-video slasher film that features a murderous Cinderella character who seeks revenge on her stepfamily.
    - ☐ **The Ugly Stepsister** (2025) - This Norwegian film is a black comedy and body horror story that follows one of Cinderella's stepsisters as she goes to extreme lengths to become beautiful and win the prince's attention.
- ☐ **His House** (2020, UK/SOUTH SUDAN) – A supernatural horror film about a refugee couple from South Sudan who seek asylum in the United Kingdom and are tormented by a malevolent entity from their past.
  - **AFRICAN FOLKLORE & MYSTICISM:** African folklore is a vast, living mythology rooted in oral storytelling, ancestral reverence, and the balance between the spiritual and material worlds. Long before colonial borders, tribal cosmologies across the continent shared common threads: gods who walked among mortals, spirits bound to rivers and forests, and tricksters who tested human virtue. Tales of the *Tokoloshe* in Southern Africa, the *Mamlambo* of the rivers, and West Africa's *Asiman* or *Adze* vampires reflect a world where the unseen is ever-present, and moral law is enforced by the supernatural. These stories emerged as moral compasses and survival codes, shaping communal identity and respect for the land. Modern African cinema still channels these forces transforming folklore into allegory for trauma, faith, and rebirth, proving that mysticism here is not a relic of the past, but a living pulse beneath everyday reality.
    - ☐ **Abro Ne Bayie** (2008) - A Ghanaian film centered around the legend of a wandering demon, a figure that appears throughout African folklore.
    - ☐ **The Lullaby** (2017) - Originally titled *Siembamba*, this South African psychological horror thriller deals with postpartum depression and is named after a traditional Afrikaans folklore song.
    - ☐ **The Tokoloshe** (2018) - This South African horror film centers on a mythological phantom of the same name. A young woman working at a hospital discovers an abandoned girl tormented by the dwarf-like water spirit, a figure from Nguni mythology.
    - ☐ **Atlantics** (2019, Senegal) - This film is a supernatural drama about a group of construction workers who vanish at sea and return as ghosts to haunt the city.
    - ☐ **The Soul Collector** (2019) - Also known as *8: A South African Horror Story*, this film follows a family living on a cursed farmland. They encounter Lazarus, an old man who has been condemned to steal souls forever as penance for sacrificing his own daughter's soul.

- ☐ **Kandisha** (2020, France) - In this French-Moroccan film, a teenage girl accidentally summons a vengeful Moroccan demon after invoking her name.
- ☐ **Pinky Pinky** (2020) - The film revisits this legend, creating a modern take on the campfire story. Different versions of the myth exist, but the story is generally used to explore issues of bullying and fear.
- ☐ **Saloum** (2021, Senegal) - In 2003, a trio of mercenaries escaping a coup in Guinea-Bissau take refuge in a hidden region on the Saloum river of Senegal. But something from beyond the grave awaits them there. It is an original screenplay from Jean Luc Herbulot, though it draws inspiration from African folklore and Western cinema.
- ☐ **Good Madam** (2021) - A South African psychological horror film that delves into the aftermath of apartheid, where a housekeeper's dedication to her dying white employer reveals a deeper, supernatural and generational curse of servitude.
- ☐ **Juju Stories** (2021, Nigeria) - A Nigerian anthology film told in three parts, each exploring different aspects of *juju*, a magical and spiritual practice originating from West Africa. The stories are modern fables set in Lagos.
- ☐ **Nevanji** (2021) - This Zimbabwean film tells the story of a family whose terminally ill son can only be saved by consulting a witch doctor. The film explores the idea of spirits and ancestors from Zimbabwean folklore.
- ☐ **Nanny** (2022) - A psychological horror film written and directed by Nikyatu Jusu, based on Senegalese folklore. A Senegalese immigrant working as a nanny in New York is haunted by a malevolent water spirit, *Mami Wata*, and must confront her own past while caring for her employers' daughter.
- ☐ **The Banishing** (2020, UK) – Gothic haunted house film set in 1930s England. The Banishing tells the story of the most haunted house in England. In the 1930s, a young reverend, his wife and daughter move into a manor with a horrifying secret.
- ☐ **Dawn Breaks Behind the Eyes** (2021, Germany) - A couple spend eternity in a castle until their reality starts to shift, as the unknown moves into their lives.
- ☐ **The Pale Blue Eye** (2022) – Gothic murder mystery entwined with Edgar Allan Poe. A world-weary detective is hired to investigate the murder of a West Point cadet. Stymied by the cadets' code of silence, he enlists one of their own to help unravel the case - a young man the world would come to know as Edgar Allan Poe. Starring Christian Bale.
- ☐ **The Eternal Daughter** (2022, UK) – Joanna Hogg's ghostly Gothic meditation on mothers and memory. Returning to a hotel now haunted by its mysterious past, an artist and her elderly mother confront long-buried secrets in their former family home. Starring Tilda Swinton.
- ☐ **Guillermo del Toro's Cabinet of Curiosities** (2022) – Bizarre nightmares unfold in eight tales of terror in a visually stunning, spine-tingling horror collection curated by Guillermo del Toro.

Gothic Horror Pairing Night: How to Drink It In

Main Course: Silent Expressionist Nightmare + Studio-Era Haunt
The Cabinet of Dr. Caligari (1920) + *The Uninvited (1944)*
How to watch: Start with Caligari's twisted sets and unreliable mindscape, then glide into *The Uninvited*'s refined ghost story where grief seeps through a seaside mansion. Track how painted distortion evolves into elegant restraint while preserving the same dread.

Smartest fact: Caligari's famous twist ending was added at the producers' insistence; The Uninvited is one of the era's most delicate, atmosphere-first hauntings.

Side Dish: Black-and-White Bava + Baroque Color Fever
Black Sunday (1960) + *The Whip and the Body (1963)*
How to watch: Let *Black Sunday* carve fear in stark monochrome, then watch *The Whip and the Body* drench cruelty in jewel-tone color. Notice how Bava shifts from chiseled contrasts to chromatic psychology.

Smartest fact: This pairing maps Italy's move from woodcut-sharp Gothic to saturated, sadomasochistic melodrama — velvet and violence under the same roof.

Dessert: Modern Domestic Gothic + Its Spiritual Ancestor
The Others (2001) + The Innocents (1961)
How to watch: Screen *The Others* first and savor its candlelit minimalism, then trace its DNA back to The Innocents' Turn of the Screw ambiguity. Keep the room dim and let the silences breathe.

Smartest fact: The Others' celebrated twist is a direct conversation with The Innocents. Two generations of repression and revenants speaking across time.

Palate Cleanser: Poe Chamber Piece + Meta Homage
The Pit and the Pendulum (1961) + Young Frankenstein (1974)
How to watch: Trap yourself in Corman-Price's claustrophobic Poe chamber of guilt and stone, then cleanse with Mel Brooks's loving black-and-white send-up of studio Gothic grammar.

Smartest fact: The joke lands because the production design language is sacred text — Brooks riffs directly on the classic Universal look (down to the iconic lab gear lineage).

Nightcap: Science Gothic (Laboratory & Sanatorium)
Corridors of Blood (1958) + A Cure for Wellness (2016)
How to watch: Pair Victorian experimentation's moral slide with a modern Alpine "wellness" clinic where cure becomes curse. Trade cobwebbed keeps for tiled corridors and beakers — the castle reborn as clinic.

Smartest fact: Science Gothic keeps the same sin, trespass against limits, but swaps altars: gaslight surgery theaters give way to spa sterility.

Bonus Pair (Colonial & Southern Gothic Echo)
I Walked with a Zombie (1943) + The Skeleton Key (2005)
How to watch: Move from Lewton's "Jane Eyre with the West Indies" to Louisiana hoodoo and decaying estates; watch folklore, class, and inheritance rot thread the needle.

Smartest fact: Both films reframe Gothic away from castles toward cultural hauntings — plantations and parlor rooms where history itself is the ghost.

Watch the Classic Haunt

Vampire Horror

Vampire horror is the theater of immortality and decay. These stories sit at the crossroads of folklore and modern dread, born from European superstition but evolving into metaphors for sexuality, contagion, addiction, and power. From aristocrats in castles to leather-clad night hunters, the vampire has always been cinema's most adaptable monster. At its heart: the fear of being drained, consumed, or turned into something less (or more) than human.

Why People Are Drawn to Vampire Horror

Because it merges fear with desire. Vampires embody seduction, transgression, and the terror of losing control of your body, your blood, your soul. Unlike werewolves or zombies, they're articulate predators, luring us with beauty before the bite. At its best, vampire horror doubles as allegory: from Victorian fears of foreign invasion (*Dracula*) to the AIDS crisis (*The Hunger*) to addiction (*Let the Right One In*). Audiences return because the vampire is endlessly renewable. Every age gets the monster it deserves.

Essentials

1. **Nosferatu (1922, Germany)** – transformed Bram Stoker's vampire into an expressionist nightmare, with Max Schreck's cadaverous Count Orlok embodying pestilence and decay. Its stark imagery, shadow play, and atmosphere of contagion established the visual language of cinematic horror.
2. **Dracula (1931, USA)** – Crystallized the vampire myth for the sound era, with Bela Lugosi's hypnotic performance defining the Count as both aristocratic and otherworldly. Its theatrical pacing and Gothic imagery set the template for decades of cinematic bloodsuckers.
3. **Horror of Dracula (1958, UK)** – Injected new vitality into the vampire legend, with Hammer Studios' bold use of color, sexuality, and graphic violence. Christopher Lee's feral, magnetic Count and Terence Fisher's dynamic direction reimagined Dracula as both terrifying predator and modern Gothic icon.

4. **Near Dark (1987, USA)** – Reframed the vampire myth through the lens of the American frontier, merging bloodlust with the grit of a modern western. Its sun-scorched landscapes, outlaw family dynamic, and tragic romance gave the genre a raw, unromantic edge that set it apart from traditional Gothic vampire films.
5. **Let the Right One In (2008, Sweden)** – Reimagined the vampire tale as a bleak, tender coming-of-age story set against the frozen isolation of Sweden. Its fusion of innocence and brutality, intimacy and horror, reshaped the genre into something both deeply human and chillingly inhuman.

Deep Cuts

1. **Vampyr (1932, Denmark)** – Is a dreamlike meditation on death and dread, where narrative dissolves into shadow and suggestion. Carl Theodor Dreyer's use of gauzy light, distorted perspective, and ghostly imagery created one of cinema's first true surrealist horrors, more nightmare than story.
2. **Ganja & Hess (1973, USA)** – Reshaped the vampire myth into an allegory of addiction, spirituality, and Black identity. Bill Gunn's surreal, fragmented style turned bloodlust into a metaphor for colonial wounds and existential hunger, making the film a radical, art-house reimagining of horror tradition.
3. **The Hunger (1983, UK/USA)** – Fused vampirism with the sleek decadence of 1980s style, creating a tale where immortality is both erotic and corrosive. Tony Scott's dreamlike visuals and the iconic triangle of Catherine Deneuve, David Bowie, and Susan Sarandon made it a defining work of Gothic sensuality and existential dread.

4. **Thirst (2009, Korea)** – Transposed the vampire myth into a brutal, sensual tragedy, where a priest's infection with vampirism becomes a parable of desire, guilt, and transgression. Park Chan-wook's blend of grotesque violence, dark humor, and aching romance reimagined horror as both sacrilegious and profoundly human.

5. **A Girl Walks Home Alone at Night (2014, Iran/USA)** – Recast the vampire as a feminist avenger, drifting through an Iranian ghost-town on a skateboard beneath a chador. Ana Lily Amirpour's monochrome, genre-blending debut merged Western, noir, and horror into a hypnotic vision of loneliness, justice, and nocturnal power. Dubbed as the "First Iranian Vampire Western."

Critical Essay:

"Vampires Are Mirrors, Not Just Monsters."

Vampire horror has never been about just fangs and coffins. Each generation reinvents the myth to reflect its darkest anxieties: aristocratic exploitation (*Dracula*), Cold War alienation (Hammer and Euro-horror), queer desire and the AIDS crisis (*The Hunger, Interview with the Vampire*), or modern loneliness and trauma (*Let the Right One In, Midnight Mass*). To watch vampire cinema across decades is to trace cultural fears refracted through the same immortal figure. Part monster, part mirror.

Global Spotlight: Japan

Japan's vampire cycle reimagined the Western myth through its own cinematic lenses. Films like *Vampire Doll* (1970), *Lake of Dracula* (1971), and *Evil of Dracula* (1974) formed Toho's so-called "Bloodthirsty Trilogy," blending Hammer-style gothic with J-horror atmosphere. Instead of old castles, these films set vampires against modernity, haunted schools, and cursed families. Their legacy lingers in anime and manga, where vampires became tragic antiheroes as much as villains.

Classic Dracula & Dracula-Inspired Films

☐ **Genuine: The Tragedy of a Vampire** (1920) - Genuine is an ancient and cruel divinity, who seduces men and induce them to kill as a proof of love.

☐ **Dracula's Death** (1921, Hungary) - A girl has frightening visions after visiting an insane asylum where one of the inmates claims to be Drakula and she can not be sure whether they were a nightmare or real.

☐ **Nosferatu** (1922, Germany) – Vampire Count Orlok expresses interest in a new residence and real estate agent Hutter's wife. *Nosferatu: A Symphony of Horror* is itself an unauthorized adaptation of Bram Stoker's novel *Dracula*. The estate of Bram Stoker famously sued the production company, Prana Film, into bankruptcy and most of the original prints were destroyed. However, copies survived, and the film eventually became a revered cult classic. Count Orlok's shadow creeping up the staircase is one of cinema's most iconic images.

- **ADAPTIONS**

  ☐ **Nosferatu the Vampyre** (1979) - A 1979 remake of the film was directed and written by Werner Herzog and starred Klaus Kinski. Although based on the 1922 film, the characters' names are faithful to Bram Stoker novel.

  ☐ **Vampire in Venice** (1988, Italy) - A pseudo-sequel to Werner Herzog's version, again starring Klaus Kinski as the Count. It's a surreal and critically panned film that has little connection to the original beyond Kinski's involvement.

  ☐ **Shadow of the Vampire** (2000, UK) - The filming of Nosferatu: A Symphony of Horror (1922) is hampered by the fact that its star Max Schreck is taking the role of a vampire far more seriously than seems humanly possible. This film is a fictionalized account of the making of the 1922 *Nosferatu*, with Willem Dafoe portraying Max Schreck as an actual vampire. It explores themes of obsession, artistry, and horror.

  ☐ **What We Do in the Shadows** (2014, New Zealand) – Viago, Deacon, and Vladislav are vampires who are struggling with the mundane aspects of modern life, like paying rent, keeping up with the chore wheel, trying to get into nightclubs, and overcoming flatmate conflicts.

☐ **Nosferatu: A Symphony of Horror** (2023) - A more experimental, shot-for-shot remake that overlays new actors onto the original film's footage. Doug Jones played Count Orlok.

☐ **Nosferatu** (2024, Eggers) – Robert Eggers' atmospheric modern remake, hailed as a near-masterpiece of Gothic dread.

F. W. Murnau, German Expressionism, and the Rise of *Nosferatu*

The birth of cinematic horror as we know it can be traced to the fractured landscapes of post–World War I Germany. Out of the rubble of empire, inflation, and collective trauma emerged German Expressionism: a movement that turned inner turmoil into jagged architecture, distorted perspectives, and shadows that seemed to move of their own will. Where realism sought to mirror the world, Expressionism sought to externalize the psyche. Walls tilted, doors warped, and streets narrowed into oppressive labyrinths because that was how the soul felt after war: unstable, claustrophobic, and haunted.

Among the directors who crystallized this movement, none looms larger in horror's lineage than Friedrich Wilhelm Murnau. A former art historian and soldier, Murnau brought to cinema a painter's eye and a poet's sense of mood. His masterpiece *Nosferatu* (1922) remains not only the earliest surviving feature-length vampire film but also one of the most influential works in horror's entire history. Ostensibly an unauthorized adaptation of Bram Stoker's *Dracula*, it transformed Gothic literature into visual language so potent that every vampire narrative since bears its shadow.

German Expressionism and the Architecture of Fear

Expressionist cinema was not born in a vacuum. The horrors of World War I: disfigurement, chemical warfare, authoritarian collapse left German audiences searching for ways to process trauma. Filmmakers responded by bending reality into nightmare. *The Cabinet of Dr. Caligari* (1920) offered a blueprint: angular sets, painted shadows, and a hypnotist's control over a sleepwalker, dramatizing the fragility of free will in a nation reeling from dictatorship. Horror here was political, psychological, and spatial.

Murnau absorbed these aesthetics but moved them into the realm of myth. Instead of allegory alone, he gave the movement its first iconic monster. His Orlok was not Lugosi's suave aristocrat but a grotesque rat-like figure: bald head, clawed fingers, fangs jutting like an animal. This was no decadent invader but a pestilence in human form, a visual embodiment of plague, decay, and death itself. By tying the vampire to disease rather than seduction, Murnau captured the anxieties of a Europe scarred by influenza epidemics and economic collapse.

Nosferatu and the Birth of Cinematic Vampirism

Released in 1922, *Nosferatu* was almost destroyed before its influence could spread. Stoker's widow sued for copyright infringement, and courts ordered every print destroyed. That the film survives at all is a miracle of piracy and preservation, itself echoing the vampire's refusal to stay buried. Its survival allowed Murnau's vision to infect world cinema.

The film's imagery was revolutionary. Shadows became characters: Orlok's elongated hand creeping across a wall toward Ellen's heart remains one of horror's most enduring images. Daylight, previously a neutral setting, became deadly; it was *Nosferatu* that introduced the rule that vampires burn in the sun, a detail absent from Stoker's novel but now a staple of the mythology. The vampire's connection to plague: rats swarming from his ship, coffins piled in the streets reframed him not just as predator but as epidemic. Even geography played into terror: Murnau shot on location in the Carpathians and in German port cities, grounding the supernatural in tangible landscapes. The vampire was no longer confined to Gothic castles; he walked in real streets, carrying disease into ordinary homes.

Influence and Legacy

Nosferatu did more than terrify, it established horror as cinema's most elastic genre. Its blending of myth, allegory, and visual experimentation demonstrated that horror could be both art and popular entertainment. The film's aesthetics directly influenced Universal's *Dracula* (1931), Hammer's Gothic revivals, and Werner Herzog's 1979 reimagining. Beyond the vampire mythos, it codified techniques that filmmakers still deploy: chiaroscuro lighting, the monster as metaphor, and atmosphere as narrative force.

It also proved horror's global reach. Unlike comedy or drama, fear required no translation. Orlok's shadow needed no intertitles. Distributed internationally, *Nosferatu* showed that horror could cross borders faster than any other genre, feeding on universal anxieties about death, disease, and the unknown.

German Expressionism itself soon collapsed under the rise of Nazism, with many of its artists fleeing to Hollywood. Yet its DNA lived on in film noir, Universal monsters, and every horror film that uses shadow as terror. Murnau, who later directed *Sunrise* (1927) in America, would die young in a car accident, but his contribution to horror was immortal. With *Nosferatu*, he gave the genre its first modern icon: a monster not bound by stage or page but by cinema's ability to turn nightmares into moving light.

The Shadow That Never Fades

When audiences watched *Nosferatu* in 1922, they were not just seeing a vampire; they were witnessing horror discovering itself. The film proved that the genre could embody cultural trauma, innovate cinematic form, and haunt popular imagination all at once. Nearly every horror film since, from *Dracula* to *The Exorcist* to *Hereditary*, carries some trace of Murnau's shadow. German Expressionism gave horror its architecture; Murnau gave it its monster. Together, they ensured that horror would never again be a sideshow novelty. It had become cinema's most enduring mirror of fear.

☐ **Dracula** (1931) – Bela Lugosi's iconic portrayal of the vampire aristocrat in Universal's definitive adaptation. **Misquote:** The phrase "I vant to suck your blood" is not actually from the 1931 film Dracula, but is a famous misquotation that appears in the 1994 film Ed Wood, where Martin Landau's character, playing a Lugosi-esque Dracula, says it with a thick accent.

- **SEQUELS & ADAPTIONS**
    - ☐ **Dracula's Daughter** (1936) - When Countess Marya Zaleska appears in London, mysterious events occur that lead Dr. Von Helsing to believe that the Countess must be a vampire.
        - **ADAPTIONS**
            - ☐ **Abigail** (2024) - After a group of criminals kidnap the ballerina daughter of a powerful underworld figure, they retreat to an isolated mansion, unaware that they're locked inside with no normal little girl.
    - ☐ **Son of Dracula** (1943) - When Katherine, a beautiful Southern girl obsessed with thoughts of eternal life, invites Count Alucard to come to her mansion in the U.S., she unleashes a Pandora's box of horror on unsuspecting relatives and neighbors.
    - ☐ **Renfield** (2023) – Director Chris McKay's quasi-sequel starring Nicolas Cage.
    - ☐ **Dracula** (1931, Spain) - Filmed at night on the same sets as the English version, this Spanish-language version is often praised for its superior camera work and more energetic performances.

- **HAMMER ADAPTIONS**
    - ☐ **Horror of Dracula** (1958, UK) – When Jonathan Harker rouses the ire of Count Dracula for accepting a job at the vampire's castle under false pretenses, his friend Dr. Van Helsing pursues the predatory villain. Hammer pushed boundaries of sexuality and gore, scandalizing censors but reviving the genre. **Memorable quote:** *"Listen to them, the children of the night. What music they make."*
        - **SEQUELS**
            - ☐ **The Brides of Dracula** (1960, UK) - This immediate sequel to the 1958 film notably does not feature Count Dracula himself, though he is mentioned. The story focuses on a different vampire.
    - ☐ **Dracula: Prince of Darkness** (1966, UK) - The first of many Hammer sequels to bring back Christopher Lee's count. Ten years after his demise, Count Dracula is resurrected by his servant and preys on four unsuspecting English tourists who have taken shelter in his castle.
    - ☐ **Dracula has Risen from the Grave** (1968, UK) - After a Monsignor accidentally brings Count Dracula back from the dead while exorcising his castle, the vampire preys on the holy man's beautiful niece and her friends.
    - ☐ **Taste the Blood of Dracula** (1970, UK) - After killing his disciple, three English gentlemen unwittingly resurrect Count Dracula, who seeks to avenge his servant by making the trio die at the hands of their own children.
    - ☐ **Scars of Dracula** (1970, UK) - A young man is murdered while spending the night at Count Dracula's castle, prompting his brother to come to the small town where all the traces end to look for him. Christopher Lee has more dialogue in this film than any other in the series except for the first.
    - ☐ **Dracula A.D. 1972** (1972, UK) - This entry brings Dracula and Van Helsing's descendant to modern London. In 1972 London - a century after his final battle with Professor Van Helsing - Count Dracula is resurrected by occultist Johnny Alucard, and goes after his archenemy's descendants.
    - ☐ **The Satanic Rites of Dracula** (1973) – Dracula reimagined as cult leader. this film is the final Hammer Dracula film with Christopher Lee. In it, Dracula poses as a millionaire industrialist in London.
    - ☐ **The Legend of the 7 Golden Vampires** (1974) - A co-production with Shaw Brothers Studio, this film fuses Hammer's gothic horror with kung fu. In it, Van Helsing battles a Chinese cult with a connection to Dracula. Christopher Lee did not reprise his role as Dracula.

72

Dracula in Technicolor: The Hammer Horror Legacy

Hammer Film Productions

Origins & Mission

Founded in 1934 in London, Hammer was a small British studio that exploded into global fame in the 1950s and 60s. Their mission was straightforward: take the familiar monsters of Universal horror: *Dracula, Frankenstein,* the *Mummy* and remake them in bold color, with a distinctly British Gothic sensibility. At a time when Hollywood horror had waned, Hammer reenergized the genre by drenching it in blood, atmosphere, and taboo sexuality.

Signature Style

Hammer is synonymous with Gothic lushness: candlelit castles, velvet capes, foggy graveyards, and a crimson splash of Technicolor blood. They pushed censors with overt sensuality, violence, and the charisma of stars like Christopher Lee and Peter Cushing. Even their non-monster films, psychological thrillers, occult tales carried the same operatic atmosphere.

Essential Titles

- *The Curse of Frankenstein* (1957) – Hammer's breakout hit, introducing Peter Cushing as the obsessed doctor and Christopher Lee as his tragic monster. Revived Gothic horror worldwide.
- *Dracula* (Horror of Dracula) (1958) – Lee's iconic Dracula and Cushing's Van Helsing clash in vivid color, forever redefining the vampire.
- *The Mummy* (1959) – A lavish take on the Egyptian curse, balancing spectacle with grotesque detail.
- *The Devil Rides Out* (1968) – An occult thriller steeped in Satanic ritual, proving Hammer could terrify without fangs or bandages.
- *Quatermass and the Pit* (1967) – Sci-fi horror hybrid exploring alien origins of human evil, showing Hammer's genre range.

Cultural Footprint

Hammer kept horror alive in the post-war years, proving there was an appetite for scarier, bloodier, more adult content. They set the template for international horror co-productions, inspired Italian and Spanish Gothic cinema, and made household names of Cushing and Lee. The lush Gothic they perfected influenced everyone from Tim Burton (*Sleepy Hollow*) to Guillermo del Toro (*Crimson Peak*). Even today, "Hammer Horror" is shorthand for an entire aesthetic: sexy, bloody, and beautiful.

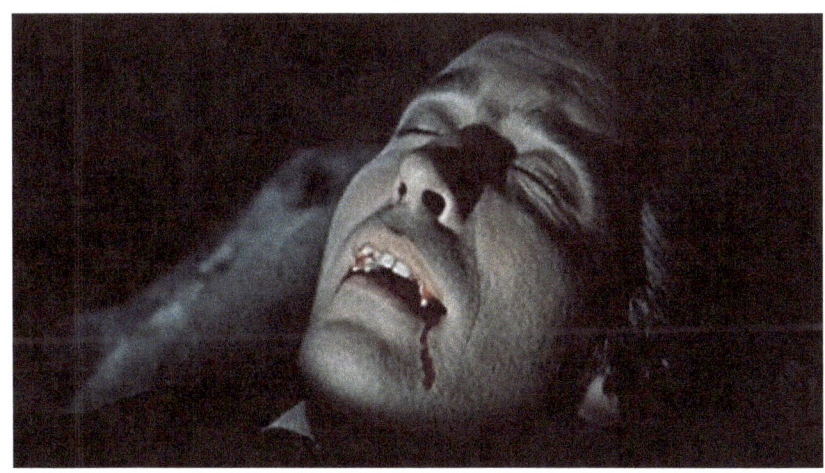

Watchlist – A Hammer Sampler

- *The Curse of Frankenstein* (1957) → Watch how Hammer reinvented the monster myth with shock color and aristocratic menace.
- *Dracula* (1958) → Lee's feral, sensual Dracula is the blueprint for modern vampires.
- *The Devil Rides Out* (1968) → See Hammer stretch into occult territory—rituals, pentagrams, and cosmic evil.

- [ ] **Return of the Vampire** (1943) – When an errant bomb unearths the coffin of a vampire during the London Blitz, a gravedigger unknowingly reanimates the monster by removing the stake from his heart. Tesla was a renegade Romanian scientist from the 18th century who studied the supernatural. The movie starts by showing his initial defeat by Professor Saunders and Lady Jane Ainsley during World War I. It was created to be an unofficial follow-up to Universal's Dracula series. Due to copyright issues with Universal, Bela Lugosi's character was renamed "Armand Tesla" instead of "Count Dracula." It also held back its release for two months so as not to compete with Lon Chaney Jr.'s *Son of Dracula* (1943).

- [ ] **Drackula Instanbul'da** (1953, Turkey) - A rarely-seen Turkish film based on a Turkish adaptation of Stoker's novel, it is possibly the first film to show Dracula with elongated canines. Azmi is a lawyer from Istanbul. Drakula of Romania has assumed a new title. Azmi travels to Romania for legal matters. He is warned of Drakula but Azmi is a strong believer of goodness.

- [ ] **The Return of Dracula** (1958) - After a vampire leaves his native Balkans, he murders a Czech artist, assumes his identity, and moves in with the dead man's American cousins.

- [ ] **Curse of the Blood Ghouls** (1962, Italy) In 19th century Austria, a newlywed couple in an old castle soon are targeted by a savage vampire who is hellbent on destroying both their entire lives when he centers his main focus on the bride. Complications ensue for everyone involved.

  - **SIMILAR THEMES**
    - [ ] **The Vampire and the Ballerina** (1960, Italy) - A troupe of beautiful young dancers find themselves stranded in a sinister, spooky old castle, not knowing that it is home to a group of vampires.
    - [ ] **The Playgirls and the Vampire** (1960) - This film likewise features vampires and seductive women in a castle setting.
    - [ ] **The Ghoul** (1975) - This later British film starring Peter Cushing focuses on a human cannibal, not vampires.

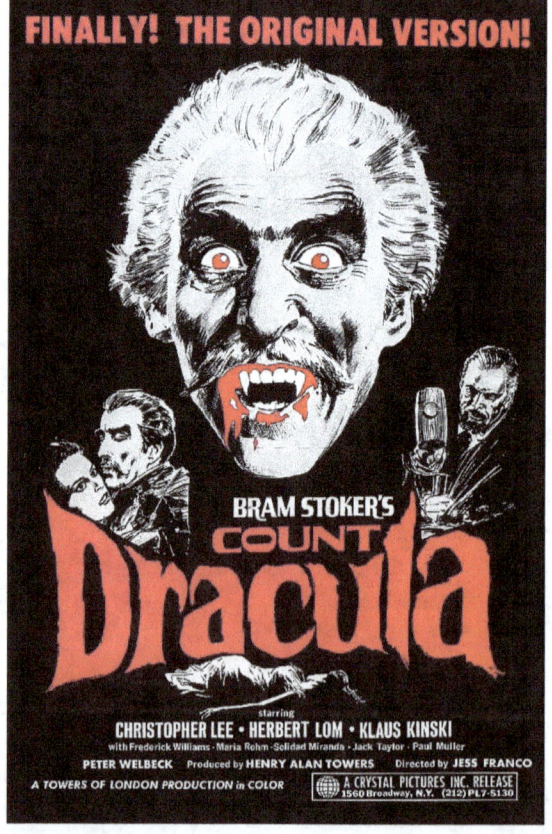

- [ ] **Batman Dracula** (1964) - Andy Warhol's infamous lost campy classic charting the adventures of Batman two years before Adam West donned the Caped Crusader's wings in the classic TV show.

- [ ] **Billy the Kid vs. Dracula** (1966) - Dracula travels to the American Old West, intent on making a young and beautiful female ranch owner his vampire bride. Her fiance, the reformed outlaw Billy the Kid, finds out about it and rushes to save her.[9]

- [ ] **Count Dracula** (1970, Germany) - Count Dracula, a vampire who regains his youth by drinking the blood of maidens, is pursued in London and Transylvania by Professor Van Helsing, Jonathan Harker and Quincey Morris. Christopher Lee plays the count in this version, which is known for its fidelity to Stoker's novel.

---

[9] If you like a blend of western and horror, this is not it according to IMDB with an abysmal ranking of 3.9 out of 10.

- ☐ **Blacula**[10] (1972) - An 18th-century African prince, turned into a vampire by Dracula, finds himself in modern-day Los Angeles.
  - • **SEQUELS**
    - ☐ **Scream Blacula Scream** (1973) - The vampire Mamuwalde (a.k.a. Blacula) is resurrected by voodoo and forced to kill again.
- ☐ **Count Dracula's Great Love** (1973, Spain) - The Transylvanian vampire searches for a virgin sacrifice to resurrect his long-dead daughter.
- ☐ **Blood for Dracula (Andy Warhol's Dracula)** (1974, UK) - An ailing vampire count travels to Italy with his servant to find a bride. It's often associated with the "Eur-Trash" or exploitation subgenre due to its low budget, gratuitous elements, high-camp and satirical take on conventional horror themes. The film mixes horror, humor, and sex, creating a unique blend that appeals to fans of cult cinema. The term "Eur-Trash" also reflects its European production and often unpolished, unconventional style.
  - • **CONNECTION**
    - ☐ **Flesh of Frankenstein** (1973) - Baron Frankenstein creates two "zombies" - one male, one female - planning to mate them in order to create a master race. Although the film is often referred to as "Andy Warhol's Frankenstein," he wasn't directly involved in the production, but allowed the director to use his name. Warhol would make rare visits to the sets and during the editing period.
- ☐ **Dracula** (1979) - In 1913, the charming, seductive and sinister vampire Count Dracula travels to England in search of an immortal bride.
- ☐ **Love at First Bite** (1979) – Disco-era Dracula in modern New York.
- ☐ **Bram Stoker's Dracula** (1992) – Coppola's lush reimagining with operatic Gothic grandeur.
- ☐ **Dracula: Dead and Loving It** (1995) - A Mel Brooks spoof starring Leslie Nielsen as a clumsy, inept Dracula.
- ☐ **Dracula 2000** (2000) - Dracula slakes his blood thirst and renews his search for love in New Orleans.
- ☐ **Guy Maddin's Dracula: Pages from a Virgin's Diary** (2002) – Ballet adaptation as meta-horror.
- ☐ **Dracula Untold** (2014) - As his kingdom is being threatened by the Turks, young prince Vlad Tepes must become a monster feared by his own people in order to obtain the power needed to protect his own family, and the families of his kingdom.
- ☐ **The Last Voyage of Demeter** (2023) - A crew sailing from Varna (Bulgaria) by the Black Sea to England find that they are carrying very dangerous cargo.
- ☐ **Dracula: A Love Tale** (2025, France) - After his wife dies, a 15th century prince renounces God and becomes a vampire. Centuries later in 19th century London, he sees a woman resembling his late wife and pursues her, sealing his own fate.

The Definitive Horror Icon

Bela Lugosi: The Immortal Count

Bela Lugosi (1882–1956) was horror's first aristocrat, its hypnotic gaze, its voice that rolled like thunder from another land. To call him simply an actor is to miss his alchemy: Lugosi transformed horror from silent grotesques into elegant menace. With one role, Dracula, he set the standard for every vampire to follow, turning a folkloric ghoul into cinema's most seductive monster.

Cultivating a Persona

Born Béla Ferenc Dezső Blaskó in Lugos, Hungary, Lugosi trained on the European stage before emigrating to America after World War I. His imposing height, sharp features, and commanding presence made him a natural for dark, magnetic roles. Cast as Count Dracula on Broadway in 1927, Lugosi carried his performance to Tod Browning's *Dracula* (1931), where sound cinema amplified his rolling accent and deliberate cadence. He didn't need makeup to terrify, his stare and voice alone could mesmerize.

Unlike Boris Karloff, who specialized in pathos and prosthetics, Lugosi built horror on elegance and restraint. He was the foreigner made mythic: alluring, dangerous, and unforgettable. His Dracula was not just a character but a template. From Christopher Lee to Gary Oldman, every modern vampire owes a debt to Lugosi's aristocratic predator.

Signature Works

- *Dracula* (1931) — Lugosi's defining role, his cape, accent, and stare shaping the global image of the vampire.
- *White Zombie* (1932) — As the sinister voodoo master Murder Legendre, Lugosi starred in the first feature-length zombie film.
- *The Black Cat* (1934) — A duel of menace with Boris Karloff, blending modernist design with Gothic terror.
- *The Raven* (1935) — Inspired by Poe, Lugosi played a deranged surgeon obsessed with torture devices.
- *Son of Frankenstein* (1939) — As Ygor, he gave one of his most unhinged performances, stealing scenes even from Karloff's Monster.
- *Plan 9 from Outer Space* (1959) — Released after his death, Lugosi's presence (and absence) in Ed Wood's cult film only cemented his mythic aura.

What He Did for Horror

Lugosi gave horror its first true voice. In an era when cinema was still finding its language, he embodied how menace could be spoken—slow, rhythmic, and hypnotic. He shifted horror from makeup and pantomime into psychology and suggestion, teaching audiences that fear could be as much about tone and presence as about blood.

But his gift became his trap. Typecast as Dracula or foreign villains, Lugosi struggled to find varied roles in Hollywood. His later career was marred by poverty, morphine addiction, and exploitation by low-budget productions. Yet even in decline, he remained magnetic. His collaborations with Karloff created some of the 1930s' richest horrors, and his Dracula became the genre's crown jewel.

Legacy & Amazement

Bela Lugosi's life was as tragic as it was legendary. Buried in his Dracula cape, he remains forever entwined with the role that defined him. More than any other actor of his generation, he turned horror into high theater. An elegant dance of accent, posture, and gaze. His influence extends beyond genre films into every Halloween cape, every parody accent, every shadowed silhouette of the vampire.

Lugosi did not just play Dracula. He *became* Dracula. And in doing so, he made horror immortal.

Elizabeth Bathory Films

Countess Elizabeth Báthory (1560–1614), a Hungarian noblewoman often accused of serial murder, has inspired numerous vampire films. Though she was a member of the powerful Báthory family and held vast estates across what is now Hungary, Slovakia, and Romania, the most infamous tales surrounding her emerged only decades after her death. These legends claim she bathed in the blood of young women to preserve her beauty. A story now regarded as folklore rather than fact. Over time, Báthory became a fixture of European mythology, earning enduring nicknames such as "The Blood Countess" and "Countess Dracula." While her notoriety has often been compared to that of Vlad the Impaler, and some have speculated she may have influenced Bram Stoker's *Dracula* (1897), no evidence confirms a direct connection. Her legacy, half history and half legend, continues to blur the line between fact and gothic fiction.

- ☐ **Countess Dracula** (1971, UK) – Hammer's Elizabeth Bathory-inspired tale of blood and aging.
- ☐ **Daughters of Darkness** (1971, Belgium) – While passing through a vacation resort, a newlywed couple encounters a mysterious, strikingly beautiful countess and her aide.
  - • **OTHER LESBIAN VAMPIRE THEMES**
    - ☐ **Vampyros Lesbos** (1971) – Erotic European Gothic vampire tale with surreal flourishes.
    - ☐ **The Velvet Vampire** (1971) - Lee and his wife Susan accept the invitation of mysterious Diane to visit her secluded desert estate. Tensions arise when the couple, unaware that Diane is a vampire, realize that they are both objects of the pale temptress's seductions.
    - ☐ **Vampyres** (1974, UK) – A pair of women lure passers-by to their countryside mansion to feed on them to satisfy their need for blood. The house is Oakley Court, used for exteriors in several Hammer films, and for *The Rocky Horror Picture Show* (1975). It was later turned into a luxury hotel.
      - • **ADAPTIONS**
        - ☐ **Vampyres** (2015) - A Spanish remake, also titled *Vampyres*, was directed by Víctor Matellano. It retains the same setting of two female vampires in an English country house and features a similar plot and tone.
    - ☐ **The Hunger** (1983) – Directed by Tony Scott and starring Catherine Deneuve, David Bowie, and Susan Sarandon, this is a more mainstream, stylish exploration of the lesbian vampire myth. It features modern vampires, high fashion, and a melancholic tone.
- ☐ **Thirst** (1979, Australia) - The descendant of Elizabeth Bathory is abducted by a cult of blood-drinking, self-proclaimed supermen who want her to join them. The Film's unique take on vampire mythology has been praised by fans and critics alike. It is a blend of vampire horror and science fiction, with a plot centered around a modern-day cult that operates a "blood farm" to harvest humans for their blood. The film explores themes of brainwashing and psychological manipulation rather than relying on traditional gothic tropes.
- ☐ **Eternal** (2004, Canada) - Detective Raymond Pope is a detective of questionable morals, searching for his missing wife. His investigation leads him to the wealthy estate of the enigmatic Elizabeth Kane and her young maid Irina.
- ☐ **Stay Alive** (2006) - A group of friends decide to play a killer video game based on the legend of the Countess of Blood, Elizabeth Bathory
- ☐ **The Countess** (2009, France/Germany) - A 17th century Hungarian countess embarks on a murderous undertaking, with the belief that bathing in the blood of virgins will preserve her beauty.
- ☐ **Chasity Bites** (2013) - In the early 1600s, Countess Elizabeth Bathory slaughtered more than 600 young women, believing that if she bathed in the blood of virgins, she would stay young and beautiful forever. Still alive today, she's found a perfect hunting ground for her 'botox' as an abstinence educator in conservative America, and the young ladies of San Griento High are poised to be her next victims. But will her unholy ritual finally be stopped by Leah Ratliff, a feminist blogger and ambitious reporter for the school paper?

Silent & Gothic Foundations

☐ **A Night of Horror** (1916) - The first known full-length motion picture to depict vampires, though the film itself has since been lost.

☐ **London After Midnight** (1927) - The abandoned home of a wealthy man who supposedly committed suicide five years earlier is taken over by ghoulish figures - could they be vampires? The original story is from Tod Browning's short story called "The Hypnotist." It is believed that this film existed until 1965. Inventory records indicated that the only remaining print was being stored in MGM's vault #7 which was destroyed by a fire that year. By that point in time, all other elements had been destroyed or were missing.

- **ADAPTIONS**

☐ **Mark of the Vampire** (1935) - *Mark of the Vampire* is a talkie remake of Tod Browning's silent film, which is now considered a lost film. In the original, Lon Chaney played multiple parts, while in the remake, his roles were split among Lionel Barrymore, Bela Lugosi, and Lionel Atwill. When a nobleman is murdered, a professor of the occult blames vampires, but not all is what it seems. Due to legal action taken by Universal Studios, who claimed that *Mark of the Vampire* infringed on their *Dracula* copyright, there were no sequels or further versions of the story produced at that time. The plot revolves around the mysterious death of Sir Karell Borotyn, who is found with two puncture wounds on his neck and drained of blood. While suspicion falls on Count Mora and his daughter Luna, an expert on the occult, Professor Zelen, is called in to investigate. The film ultimately reveals a twist ending.

☐ **London After Midnight** (2002) - In 2002, Turner Classic Movies (TCM) commissioned restoration producer/expert Rick Schmidlin to produce a 45-minute reconstruction of the famous sought-after lost film, using stills photographs and a surviving original script. A year later, this reconstruction was included "The Lon Chaney Collection" DVD set.

☐ **Vampyr** (1932) - A drifter obsessed with the supernatural stumbles upon an inn where a severely ill adolescent girl is slowly becoming a vampire. An avant-garde horror film. It is a loose and atmospheric adaptation of Joseph Sheridan Le Fanu's 1872 story collection *In a Glass Darkly*. The film takes elements and themes, particularly from the novella *Carmilla*, but alters the plot significantly. The film was poorly received at its premiere, which led director Carl Theodor Dreyer to suffer a nervous breakdown, and his production company went bankrupt. *Vampyr* has a dreamlike, surreal narrative. Its unique, painterly, and hypnotic style differs greatly from the mainstream films of the era.

- **OTHER CARMILLA ADAPTIONS**

☐ **Blood and Roses** (1960, France) - A young heiress - jealous of her cousin's engagement to another woman - becomes obsessed with the legend of a vampire ancestor, who supposedly murdered the young brides of the man she loved.

☐ **Crypt of the Vampire (Terror in the Crypt)** (1963, Italy) - An Italian production starring Christopher Lee as Count Karnstein, this version is a more traditional gothic horror film. Count Karnstein sends for a doctor to help his sick daughter Laura. Her nurse believes she is possessed by the spirit of a dead ancestor, Carmilla.

☐ **The Blood Spattered Bride** (1972, Spain) - Newlywed Susan is haunted by visions of Mircalla Karnstein, a centuries-old bride who murdered her husband on their wedding night.

☐ **Alucarda (Sisters of Satan)** (1977, Mexico) - After the death of her parents, a young girl arrives at a convent and brings a sinister presence with her. Is it her enigmatic imaginary friend, Alucarda, who is to blame? Or is there a satanic force at work?

☐ **The Moth Diaries** (2011) - This film, based on a novel of the same name, features the *Carmilla* book as a plot device and has a very similar storyline involving a new girl at a boarding school.

☐ **The Carmilla Movie** (2017) - A film based on the popular web series of the same name, which is a modern and comedic take on the novella set on a college campus. Five years after they vanquished the apocalypse and Carmilla became human, Laura is a journalist. Then Carmilla begins to show signs of "re-vamping" while Laura has started having bizarre dreams. Sounds like a new supernatural threat.

- ☐ **Carmilla** (2019, UK) - This recent British film is a slow-burn, atmospheric romance focusing on the emotional and repressed desires of the two main characters, while de-emphasizing the supernatural elements.

- **THE KARNSTEIN TRILOGY**
    - ☐ **The Vampire Lovers** (1970) - The first film introduces Countess Mircalla, also known as Carmilla, a vampire who preys on the innocent. Hammer Films' "Karnstein Trilogy," a loosely connected series based on Sheridan Le Fanu's 1872 novella, *Carmilla*.
    - ☐ **Lust for a Vampire** (1971) – Gothic Hammer vampirism in a girls' school setting. In 1830, forty years to the day since the last manifestation of their dreaded vampirism, the Karnstein heirs use the blood of an innocent to bring forth the evil that is the beautiful Mircalla - or as she was in 1710, Carmilla.
    - ☐ **Twins of Evil** (1971) – Hammer Gothic mixing witch-hunting, vampires, and corrupt morality.

☐ **The Vampire Bat** (1933) - When corpses drained of blood begin to show up in a European village, vampirism is suspected to be responsible.

☐ **Isle of the Dead** (1945) - A Greek general takes leave from the 1912 Balkan War to visit a small island in Greece, where his wife is buried. A plague soon breaks out and he is forced to stay when quarantine is declared. It is part of a series of atmospheric horror films made by producer Val Lewton at RKO Pictures. The film was inspired by the famous 19th-century painting *Isle of the Dead* by Arnold Böcklin. The painting is featured prominently behind the title credits. *Isle of the Dead* shares stylistic and thematic elements with other Val Lewton productions, which also often featured Boris Karloff. *Isle of the Dead* is set in 1912 on a small Greek island where a plague breaks out during the Balkan War. The film's core conflict stems from superstition about a vampire-like demon, the vorvolaka, versus the logic of military quarantine.

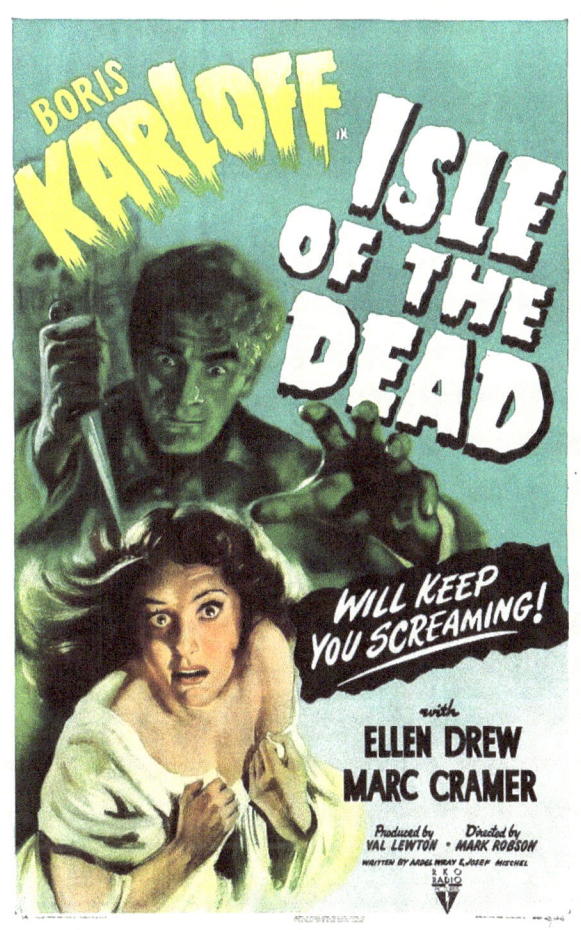

☐ **The Vampire's Ghost** (1945) - In a small African port, a tawdry bar is run by a man named Webb Fallon. Fallon is actually a vampire, but he is becoming weary of his "life" of the past few hundred years. It is notable for its screenplay by legendary sci-fi writer Leigh Brackett, who crafted an original story for the film. *The Vampire's Ghost* stands apart from the Universal monster films of the era by altering some of the standard vampire lore. The vampire in this movie can walk in daylight, though with a sensitivity to light. Instead of a simple wooden stake, a silver-tipped spear is used by the locals to subdue the creature. The vampire, Webb Fallon, is portrayed as a sympathetic and world-weary figure, in contrast to the more overtly sinister vampires of the time. the film's writer, Leigh Brackett, would go on to have a massively successful career in Hollywood, writing classics like *The Big Sleep*, *Rio Bravo*, and an early draft of *Star Wars: Episode V – The Empire Strikes Back*.

☐ **Vampire Moth** (1956, Japan) - The story of a professional nude model stalked by a bizarre, unknown man wearing a hideous mask. Recognized as Japan's first vampire-themed film, though its monster is ultimately revealed to have no supernatural origin.

☐ **The Vampire** (1957) - A kind, small-town doctor mistakenly ingests pills made from vampire bat blood and they turn him into a dangerous fanged creature.

- **The Vampire** (1957, Mexico) - A Mexican girl returns home for an aunt's funeral. She hears town rumors about vampires. She suspects her other aunt and neighbor are involved with vampires.
- **Lust of the Vampire (I vampiri)** (1957, Italy) - Paris. Young girls are found dead, drained of their blood. A journalist investigates these murders while the beautiful Gisele, from a noble family, tries to seduce him.
- **Not of this Earth** (1957) - An alien agent from the distant planet Davana is sent to Earth via a high-tech matter transporter. There, he terrorizes Southern California in an attempt to acquire blood for his dying race, the result of a devastating nuclear war. First film to feature an alien vampire.
  - **SIMILAR FILMS**
    - **Attack of the Crab Monster** (1957) - Released on a double bill with *Not of this World*, this film also produced by Corman. Scientists become trapped on a shrinking island with intelligent, murderous giant crabs.
- **The Vampire's Coffin** (1958) - Graverobbers stumble upon the tomb of a vampire, who turns them into zombies to do his bidding, which is to stalk and capture beautiful women.
- **Curse of the Undead** (1959) - While a malady is claiming the lives of young women in a Western town, a sinister gunslinger-for-hire Drake Robey is really a vampire, and it's up to Preacher Dan to save the town and girlfriend Dolores Carter.
- **The Lady Vampire** (1959, Japan) - A woman who's been missing for twenty years suddenly turns up alive, and looking not a day older than when she vanished. When her daughter sees a painting of a woman identical to her mother, her reporter boyfriend helps her track down the owner.
- **Uncle was a Vampire** (1959, Italy) - A baron down on his luck has to sell his family castle to pay off his mounting debt. After the castle is turned into a hotel, he's hired as a bellboy. But all is not lost, as he discovers he has a rich uncle; unfortunately, he's a vampire.
- **Black Sunday** (1960, Italy) – Mario Bava's Italian Gothic debut, featuring brutal witchcraft and sumptuous shadows. A visual landmark. Decades after being executed for witchcraft, vengeful Princess Asa Vajda and her fiendish servant are resurrected and begin a bloody campaign to possess the body of Asa Vajda's beautiful look-alike descendant Princess Katia. Banned in the UK for eight years due to its graphic violence.
  - **SIMILAR FILMS**
    - **Black Sabbath** (1963, Italy) - Boris Karloff hosts a trio of horror stories about a stalked call girl, a vampire-like monster who preys on his family, and a nurse who is haunted by her ring's rightful owner.
      - **ADAPTIONS:**
        - **The Vourdalak** (2023, France) - Lost in a hostile forest, the Marquis d'Urfé, a noble emissary of the King of France, finds refuge in the home of a strange family.
        - **Night of the Devils** (1972 Italy/Spain) - The patriarch of a wealthy family fears that he will show up one day in vampire form. Should this happen, he warns his family to not let him back into his house, no matter how much he begs them.
    - **Nightmare Castle** (1965, Italy) - Starring Barbara Steele, this is another classic Italian Gothic horror film from the same era. A woman and her lover are tortured and killed by her sadistic husband. The pair return from the grave to seek vengeance. According to its director, Mario Caiano, the film re-uses ideas from Poe's work, such as *The Tell-Tale Heart*.
    - **Castle of Blood** (1964, Italy) – Another Barbara Steele film in which a writer spends a night in a haunted castle and encounters a number of vengeful ghosts. A journalist takes a bet that he can spend the night in a haunted castle on All Hallow's Eve. During his stay, he bears witness to the castle's gruesome past coming to life before him, and falls in love with a beautiful female ghost.
    - **Kill Baby... Kill!** (1966, Italy) – Directed by Mario Bava, this is another classic Italian gothic horror film that focuses on ghosts haunting a small town. A Carpathian village is haunted by the murderous ghost of a little girl, prompting a coroner and a medical student to uncover her secrets

while a witch attempts to protect the villagers. Director Martin Scorsese has cited Bava's use of color in *Kill, Baby, Kill!* as an inspiration for *The Last Temptation of Christ*.

☐ **Kiss of the Vampire** (1963) - When car trouble strands a honeymooning couple in a small Southern European village, an aristocratic family in the area reaches out to help them with sinister consequences.

☐ **The Last Man on Earth** (1964) - When a disease turns all of humanity into the living dead, the last man on earth becomes a reluctant vampire hunter. Richard Matheson, the author of the novel, wrote an early screenplay for the 1964 film but was so unhappy with the final version that he used a pseudonym, "Logan Swanson," in the credits. Despite his dissatisfaction, many viewers and critics consider the Vincent Price version the most faithful adaptation of his novel's tone of melancholy and despair. Established by many reviewers (including director George A. Romero himself) as a graphic blueprint for *Night of the Living Dead* (1968). A post-apocalyptic science fiction horror film based on the 1954 novel *I Am Legend* by Richard Matheson. This novel has been adapted into numerous films such as: *The Omega Man, I am Legend, I am Omega,* and even the comedic television series *The Last Man on Earth.*

☐ **Night of the Vampires** (1964, Germany) - A mad scientist and his bevy of vampires terrorize a German village. A detective and a witch set out to stop them.

☐ **Planet of the Vampires** (1965, Italy) - After landing on a mysterious planet, a team of astronauts begin to turn on each other, swayed by the uncertain influence of the planet and its strange inhabitants. It is based on the 1960 Italian science fiction short story "One Night of 21 Hours" by Renato Pestriniero. the film's visual style and plot elements heavily influenced later, more famous films such as *Alien, Lifeforce, Event Horizon* and *Pitch Black.* It was released in the United States on a double bill with the Boris Karloff film *Die, Monster, Die!* This film marks the first collaboration between Mario Bava and his son/assistant director Lamberto Bava. Lamberto would later become a director himself.

- **INFLUENCE**
  - ☐ **Queen of Blood** (1966) - Some critics have also compared *Queen of Blood* to Mario Bava's Italian horror film, which likewise features astronauts exploring a desolate planet. In 1990, aliens contact Earth announcing their visit. Their ship crashes on Mars. A rescue team from Earth is dispatched to investigate the alien crash site. Resuses special effects footage from the 1963 Soviet film *Mechte Navstrechu.*
  - ☐ **Voyage to the Prehistoric Planet** (1965) - Director Curtis Harrington created this companion film for Corman by splicing new footage with a Russian film, just as he did for *Queen of Blood.*
  - ☐ **Lifeforce** (1985) - A race of space vampires arrives in London and infects the populace, beginning an apocalyptic descent into chaos. Based on the novel, *The Space Vampires,* by Colin Wilson.

☐ **Blood Bath** (1966) - A crazed artist who believes himself to be the reincarnation of a murderous vampire kills young women, then boils their bodies in a vat. The confusing history of *Blood Bath* stems from a failed investment by Roger Corman in a Yugoslavian spy thriller called *Operation: Titian.* Unhappy with the result, he hired directors Jack Hill and Stephanie Rothman to craft three additional versions of the same footage. Given its disjointed and piecemeal creation, *Blood Bath* has no official sequels. Instead, it serves as a unique example of how filmmakers in the low-budget world of American International Pictures would re-edit and reuse existing footage to create new horror films.

- **OTHER REPURPOSED PROJECTS**
  - ☐ **Merlin's Shop of Mystical Wonders** (1996) - This film, starring Ernest Borgnine, pieces together a story using footage from an earlier movie by the same director, *The Devil's Gift* (1984).

- [ ] **A Night to Dismember** (1963) - Director Doris Wishman had to re-edit this film and add a voice-over narrative after much of the original negative was allegedly destroyed by a lab employee.
- [ ] **Face of the Screaming Werewolf** (1964) - Combines footage from two different Mexican horror movies (*La Casa del Terror* and *La Momia Azteca*) to tell a new, nonsensical story.
- [ ] **Creature of the Walking Dead** (1965) - Another example of a Mexican film (*La Marca del Muerto*) heavily re-edited and overdubbed by Warren.
- [ ] **Attack of the Mayan Mummy** (1964) - Warren took the Mexican film *The Aztec Mummy* (1957), cut it down, and inserted new, talking-head scenes to create a new movie.
- [ ] **Blood of Ghastly Horror** (1971) - Adamson took his failed 1965 movie *Psycho a Go-Go!*, re-released it as *Fiend with the Electronic Brain*, and then added more scenes to create this final, re-re-re-released version.
- [ ] **Horror of the Blood Monsters** (1970) - Features new footage combined with clips from various sci-fi and monster movies, tinted to a single color.

- [ ] **The Fearless Vampire Killers** (1967) – Polanski spoofs vampire lore with gothic parody. A noted professor and his dim-witted apprentice fall prey to their inquiring vampires, while on the trail of the ominous damsel in distress.
  - **ADAPTIONS**
    - [ ] **Tanz der Vampire** (1997, Germany) - A German-language musical adaptation of the film was directed by Roman Polanski and premiered in Vienna. It has since been performed in several other countries.

- [ ] **The Torture Chamber of Dr. Sadism** (1967, Germany) - A resurrected count who killed 12 virgins for immortality hunts the daughter of his 13th intended victim and the son of the prosecutor who condemned him, seeking vengeance.
- [ ] **The Blood Beast Terror** (1968, UK) - A scientist genetically engineers a creature that transforms between a Death's-head moth and a woman. The creature poses as the scientist's daughter to lure victims when in human form, then feeds on their blood as a moth.
- [ ] **The Rape of the Vampire** (1968, France) - After a psychoanalyst unsuccessfully tries to convince four sisters that they are not 200-year-old vampires, the Queen of the Vampires promulgates the cause of the Undead.

1970s & European Vampires

- [ ] **The Vampire Doll** (1970, Japan) - Keiko and her friend are trying to find her missing brother after he disappeared visiting his girlfriend, Yuko. For inspiration, director Yamamoto drew upon the horror manga of Kazuo Umezu as well as the Edgar Allan Poe story "The Facts in the Case of M. Valdemar." Yamamoto also cited *Goke, Body Snatcher from Hell* as inspiration.
  - **SEQUELS**
    - [ ] **Lake of Dracula** (1971, Japan) - A doctor investigates the murders of several women at a lakeside resort. His investigation leads him to believe that a vampire is responsible for the murders. He sets out to track the vampire down.
    - [ ] **Evil of Dracula** (1974, Japan) - A teacher assumes a position at a school that's run by a vampire.
- [ ] **Count Yorga, Vampire** (1970) - A couple invites a Count from Hungary, who recently immigrated to America, to conduct a seance for the woman's recently deceased mother, oblivious to the fact that he is actually a vampire.

American International Pictures had planned to revive Count Yorga as an enemy of Dr. Phibes in the film *Dr. Phibes Rises Again* (1972). While this plan was eventually scrapped, Robert Quarry (who played Count Yorga) did appear in the film as Phibes' enemy, only now this enemy was named Darius Biederbeck.

- **SEQUELS AND RELATED PRODUCTIONS**
  - ☐ **The Return of Count Yorga** (1971) - Actor Robert Quarry reprised his role as the titular vampire in this sequel. The story features Count Yorga and his brides, who have been revived by the Santa Ana winds, taking up residence near an orphanage.
  - ☐ **The Deathmaster** (1972) - Quarry is a mysterious, articulate stranger who draws a cult like following of local hippies. Rather than showing them peace and love, he has more sinister plans for them, as he is a vampire.

☐ **The Nude Vampire** (1970, France) - A young man falls in love with a beautiful woman being chased by sinister masked figures at night. He tries to track her down, and learns she's being held captive by his father and colleagues who believe she's a vampire.

- **SIMILAR THEMES**
  - ☐ **Fascination** (1979, France) - A runaway criminal breaks into an eerie chateau, taking its two frightened chambermaids hostage. As night falls, a group of mysterious aristocratic women arrive and the criminal begins to realize the women are hiding a sinister secret. The film is loosely based on a short story titled "The Glass of Blood" by Jean Lorrain, published in 1895.
  - ☐ **The Shiver of the Vampires** (1971, France) - A young honeymooning couple stop for the night at an ancient castle. Unbeknownst to them, the castle is home to a horde of vampires, who have their own plans for the couple. Another Rollin film that features a similarly dreamlike, erotic, and gothic take on vampires.
  - ☐ **The Living Dead Girl** (1982, France) - Rollin's take on the zombie subgenre is infused with his characteristic atmosphere and surrealism. A toxic spill revives a beautiful, dead heiress who, with the help of her childhood friend, must quench her insatiable thirst for blood.

☐ **The She-Butterfly** (1973, Yugoslavia) - A young man wants to marry the beautiful daughter of a landowner who refuses to allow the marriage. To prove his worth, the young man becomes a miller in a vampire-infested local mill.

☐ **Lemora: A Child's Tale of the Supernatural** (1973) - A young girl who returns to her hometown to see her dying father finds herself being drawn into a web of vampirism and witchcraft.

☐ **Captain Kronos: Vampire Hunter** (1974) - A master swordsman and former soldier and his hunchbacked assistant hunt vampires.

☐ **Martin** (1977) - A young man, who believes himself to be a vampire, goes to live with his elderly and hostile cousin in a small Pennsylvanian town, where he tries to suppress his blood-lust. Written and directed by George A. Romero.

- **INTIMATE & UNCONVENTIONAL VAMPIRE FILMS**
  - ☐ **Near Dark** (1987) - A small-town farmer's son reluctantly joins a traveling group of vampires after he is bitten by a beautiful drifter. Despite initially underperforming at the box office, *Near Dark* has earned a strong cult following for its unique blend of the vampire myth with the neo-Western genre. Its raw, gritty style and focus on a nomadic, predatory vampire family have influenced other vampire films that came after it. This film marks Kathryn Bigelow's second feature film and her first as a solo director. This release was early in her career, occurring after her 1981 debut *The Loveless* and before she rose to greater fame with films like *Point Break* (1991).
  - ☐ **The Hamiltons** (2006) - Four young adult siblings, who harbor some dark secrets, try to fend for themselves after the mysterious death of their parents. Directed by the Butcher Brothers.
    - **SEQUELS**
      - ☐ **The Thompsons** (2012) - On the run with the law on their trail, America's most anguished vampire family heads to England to find an ancient vampire clan. What they find instead could tear their family, and their throats, apart forever.
  - ☐ **Let the Right One In** (2008, Sweden) – Swedish Gothic of childhood, vampirism, and isolation. A bullied boy forms a unique friendship with his new neighbor, who is a vampire. Its icy tone and moral ambiguity redefined 21st-century vampire cinema. It is based on the 2004 novel of the same name by Swedish author John Ajvide Lindqvist.

- **ADAPTIONS AND SIMILAR FILMS**
  - ☐ **Let Me In** (2010) - An American film remake, also set in the 1980s, was directed by Matt Reeves. It tells the same story, with the action transplanted to New Mexico.
  - ☐ **All the Moons** (2021, Spain) – Religious cult turns a girl into vampire.
  - ☐ **Let the Wrong One in** (2021, Ireland) - A young supermarket worker discovers that his older brother is a vampire and must choose whether to help him or slay him. It is not a direct adaptation but a creative, Irish-themed twist on classic vampire lore, with the title a comedic nod to the 2008 film *Let the Right One In*.

☐ **Thirst** (2009, Korea) – Through a failed medical experiment, a priest is stricken with vampirism and is forced to abandon his ascetic ways. It is based on the 1867 French novel *Thérèse Raquin* by Émile Zola. The novel is a dark drama about adultery and murder, but it does not contain any vampires. Park Chan-wook reimagined the story by introducing a priest who becomes a vampire, using the supernatural element as a metaphor for unchecked desire and moral decay. The film explores the classic Zola themes of lust, guilt, and vengeance within a modern South Korean setting.

☐ **My Heart Can't Beat Unless You Tell It To** (2020) - Two mysterious siblings find themselves at odds over care for their frail and sickly younger brother.

Punk, Modern & Cult Vampires (1980s–1990s)

☐ **Once Bitten** (1985) – Jim Carrey seduced by a cougar-vampire.

☐ **Transylvania 6-5000** (1985) - Two tabloid reporters are sent to Transylvania to find the Frankenstein monster - or get fired. They are laughed at there, but something suspicious is going on.

☐ **Mr. Vampire** (1985, Hong Kong) – Martial arts + hopping vampires.

- **SEQUELS**
  - ☐ **Mr. Vampire II** (1986) - Also known as *Vampire Family*, this sequel shifts to a modern-day setting, where archaeologists accidentally unearth a family of hopping vampires.
  - ☐ **Mr. Vampire Part 3** (1987) - Returning to a period setting, this film sees Lam's character team up with a fellow priest to fight an evil sorceress and her henchmen.
  - ☐ **Mr. Vampire Saga IV** (1988) - Often referred to as *Uncle Vampire*, this film focuses on two feuding neighbors (a Taoist priest and a Buddhist monk) who must cooperate to face a new vampire threat.
  - ☐ **Mr. Vampire 1992** (1992) - The only true narrative sequel to the original, it reunites the original cast and picks up their story after the events of the first film.
- **SPIN-OFFS, SPIRITUAL SUCCESSORS & TRIBUTES**
  - ☐ **Vampire vs. Vampire** (1989) - This film, directed by Lam Ching-ying himself, introduced a Western vampire into the *jiangshi* universe.
  - ☐ **Magic Cop** (1990) - This features Lam Ching-ying as a cop who uses Taoist magic to solve a modern-day crime.
  - ☐ **The Musical Vampire** (1992) - In this spin-off, a crazy scientist reanimates a corpse, and only music can control it.
  - ☐ **Rigor Mortis** (2013, Hong Kong) – Jiangshi zombie horror tribute. *Rigor Mortis* is an homage to the classic.

☐ **Fright Night** (1985) - *Fright Night* sees a teenager believing that the newcomer in his neighborhood is a vampire. He turns to an actor in a television hosted horror movie show for help to deal with the undead. A legacy sequel to the original 1985 movie is reportedly in development. It is said to be a direct sequel to the 1985 film and *Fright Night Part 2* and will bring back original characters.

- **ADAPTIONS & SEQUELS**
  - ☐ **Fright Night Part 2** (1988) - In this sequel, Charley Brewster (William Ragsdale) has convinced himself that his vampire encounter was a delusion, until Jerry Dandrige's sister, Regine (Julie Carmen), arrives with her own entourage seeking revenge.

- ☐ **Fright Night** (2011) - A remake directed by Craig Gillespie and set in Las Vegas, starring Anton Yelchin, Colin Farrell, and David Tennant. This version has a more aggressive and predatory vampire in Jerry Dandrige and a very different Peter Vincent, who is now a stage magician.
  - ☐ **Fright Night 2: New Blood** (2013) - This film is a low-budget, direct-to-video production. It is a loose remake of the 1988 sequel but is set in Romania and is a sequel to the 2011 remake, ignoring the events of the original *Fright Night Part 2*.
- ☐ **Vampire Hunter D** (1985, Japan, animated) - When Doris Lang is chosen as the next bride for the vampire Count Magnus Lee, she will hire a mysterious vampire hunter known only as D in an attempt to escape her ill-gotten fate.
- ☐ **The Lost Boys** (1987) - After moving to a new town, two brothers discover that the area is a haven for vampires. **My Two Cents:** My mom's favorite horror movie.
  - • **SEQUELS**
    - ☐ **Lost Boys: The Tribe** (2008) – This sequel is set in the same fictional town of Santa Carla, California. It introduces a new group of characters but brings back Corey Feldman as vampire hunter Edgar Frog and features a cameo from Corey Haim as Sam Emerson. Kiefer Sutherland's half-brother, Angus Sutherland, plays the lead vampire.
    - ☐ **Lost Boys: The Thirst** (2010) - The final film in the trilogy focuses on Edgar Frog (Corey Feldman), who joins forces with his estranged brother, Alan Frog (Jamison Newlander), for a "final" battle against the head vampire. Corey Haim was originally slated to return for a fourth film but passed away before production began.
- ☐ **The Lair of the White Worm** (1988) – Ken Russell's bizarre Gothic camp of serpents and sexuality. When an archaeologist uncovers a strange skull in a foreign land, the residents of a nearby town begin to disappear, leading to further inexplicable occurrences.
- ☐ **Vampire's Kiss** (1988) – After an encounter with a neck-biter, a publishing executive thinks that he's turning into a vampire. Some critics have noted similarities between *Vampire's Kiss* and the 2000 film *American Psycho*. Both feature mentally unstable yuppies in a corporate world, and both blur the lines between reality and delusion. The film is widely regarded as a turning point in Nicolas Cage's career, establishing his willingness to embrace chaotic and over-the-top performances that have become a hallmark of his unique style.
- ☐ **Dance of the Damned** (1989) - A vampire selects a suicidal stripper as his prey, but spends the night getting to know her. As they discuss life, she reconsiders her desire to die as the pivotal moment nears.
- ☐ **Sundown: The Vampire in Retreat** (1989) - Vampires residing in a town wear sunscreen. A Van Helsing descendant arrives, leading to humorous situations as their paths intersect. This film is directed by Anthony Hickox who also made a stream of horror comedies in this same era
- ☐ **Rockula** (1990) - A young vampire cannot lose his virginity because of a curse imposed upon him centuries ago.
- ☐ **My Soul is Slashed** (1991, Japan) - A loyal employee of a pharmaceutical company finds himself in intensive care after a critical injury, and is accidentally given a transfusion of Count Dracula's blood.
- ☐ **Subspecies** (1991) - Three students get caught in the struggle between a good vampire and his evil brother in the Transylvanian mountains.
  - • **THE FRANCHISE**
    - ☐ **Bloodstone: Subspecies II** (1993) - This film picks up directly after the first movie and follows Michelle as she flees from Radu and struggles with her newfound vampirism.
    - ☐ **Bloodlust: Subspecies III** (1994) - The story continues immediately, with Michelle being captured by Radu and forced to embrace her vampiric nature.
    - ☐ **Vampire Journals** (1997) - This spin-off centers on a vampire with a conscience who hunts down his own bloodline, which includes a character who later appears in *Subspecies 4*.
    - ☐ **Subspecies IV: Bloodstorm** (1998) - The final film in the original narrative arc concludes the story of Radu's pursuit of Michelle.
    - ☐ **Subspecies V: Blood Rise** (2023) - This is a prequel that explores the origins of the vampire Radu.
- ☐ **Cronos** (1992, Mexico) - A mysterious device designed to provide its owner with eternal life resurfaces after four hundred years, leaving a trail of destruction in its path.
- ☐ **Sleepwalkers** (1992) - A mother-and-son team of strange supernatural creatures move to a small town to seek out a young virgin to feed on. Written by Stephen King.

- ☐ **Innocent Blood** (1992) - Marie is a vampire with a thirst for bad guys. When she fails to properly dispose of one of her victims, a violent mob boss, she bites off more than she can chew and faces a new, immortal danger. Although this entire movie is about vampires, the word "vampire" itself is never actually used.
- ☐ **Interview with the Vampire** (1994) – Gothic vampiric romance and existential dread in a modern adaptation of Anne Rice's novel.
  - **ADAPTIONS & SEQUELS**
    - ☐ **Queen of the Damned** (2002) - In this loose sequel to *Interview with the Vampire* (1994), the vampire Lestat becomes a rock star whose music wakes up the equally beautiful and monstrous queen of all vampires.
- ☐ **Vampire in Brooklyn** (1995) - A Caribbean vampire seduces a Brooklyn police officer who has no idea that she is half-vampire. Directed by Wes Craven and starring Eddie Murphy.
- ☐ **The Addiction** (1995) – Vampirism as psychological allegory for addiction. A New York philosophy grad student turns into a vampire after getting bitten by one, and then tries to come to terms with her new lifestyle and frequent craving for human blood.
  - **SIMILAR THEMES**
    - ☐ **Ganja & Hess** (1973) - After being stabbed with an ancient, germ-infested knife, a doctor's assistant finds himself with an insatiable desire for blood. *Ganja & Hess* is an experimental horror film that had a tumultuous journey after its premiere at the Cannes Film Festival. After its initial box office failure, the film was sold to a grindhouse distributor who re-edited and butchered the original 113-minute runtime into a 78-minute version. This shorter version was released under different titles, including *Blood Couple* and *Double Possession*, and was marketed as a blaxploitation film. Fortunately, a print of the original cut survived and was preserved by the Museum of Modern Art, allowing it to be restored for future audiences.
      - **ADAPTIONS**
        - ☐ **Da Sweet Blood of Jesus** (2014) - Spike Lee's remake. An anthropologist awakes with a thirst for blood after an assistant stabs him with a cursed dagger. Spike Lee used Kickstarter to fund the project. The film is noted for being a mostly faithful, almost shot-for-shot tribute to the original, though it received mixed reviews and failed to capture the original's hypnotic, surreal tone.
    - ☐ **The Funeral** (1996) - This crime drama was released the following year and stars many of the same actors, including Christopher Walken. It is not a vampire film, but it explores related themes of morality and transgression within a different genre context.
    - ☐ **Daybreakers** (2009) - Some film enthusiasts who appreciate the addiction themes in *The Addiction* point to this film as another example of a vampire story that explores the struggles of withdrawal and the decay of a society dependent on blood
- ☐ **From Dusk Till Dawn** (1996) - This film, co-written by Quentin Tarantino and directed by Robert Rodriguez, is also known for a similar tonal shift, moving from a crime drama into an over-the-top vampire movie.
  - **SEQUELS**
    - ☐ **From Dusk Till Dawn 2: The Texas Blood Money** (1999) - A direct-to-video sequel. It follows a new group of criminals who, after a botched robbery, find themselves trapped with vampires in Mexico.
    - ☐ **From Dusk Till Dawn 3: The Hangman's Daughter** (2000) - A direct-to-video prequel that is set in the 19th century and tells the origin story of the Titty Twister bar.
- ☐ **The Night Flier** (1997) – King adaptation about vampire journalist-killer blend.
- ☐ **Blade** (1998) - A half-vampire, half-mortal man becomes a protector of the mortal race, while slaying evil vampires.
  - **SEQUELS AND RELATED FILMS**
    - ☐ **Blade II** (2002) - Directed by Guillermo del Toro, this sequel features Blade teaming up with a group of vampires to fight a new, more dangerous breed of mutant vampires.
    - ☐ **Blade: Trinity** (2004) - The final installment of the original trilogy, written and directed by David S. Goyer, pits Blade against the original vampire, Dracula.
    - ☐ **Deadpool & Wolverine** (2024) - Wesley Snipes returned to the role for a cameo appearance, incorporating his iteration of the character into the Marvel Cinematic Universe.

- **John Carpenter's Vampires** (1998) - Recovering from an ambush that killed his entire team, a vengeful vampire slayer must retrieve an ancient Catholic relic that, should it be acquired by vampires, will allow them to walk in sunlight. Based off the 1992 novel Vampire$ by John Steakley.
  - **TRILOGY**
    - **Vampires: Los Muertos** (2002) - This direct-to-video sequel stars Jon Bon Jovi as a new vampire hunter, Derek Bliss, and was produced by John Carpenter. There are no returning characters from the first film, but there are some loose plot connections.
    - **Vampires: The Turning** (2005) - The third film in the series was also released direct-to-video and stars Colin Egglesfield. It moves the setting to Thailand and does not include any characters or significant plot connections from the previous two films.
- **Habit** (1995) - Set in a gritty, real life New York City, alcoholic Sam meets up with a modern-day succubus who marks him and controls his will. As his world unravels, he slowly figures out what is happening and has to figure out what to do.
  - **FESSENDEN'S MONSTER MASHUP**
    - **Depraved** (2019) - A disillusioned field surgeon suffering from PTSD makes a man out of body parts and brings him to life in a Brooklyn loft.
    - **Blackout** (2023) - A Fine Arts painter is convinced that he is a werewolf wreaking havoc on a small American town under the full moon.

Global & Arthouse Vampires (2000s–Present)

- **Blood: The Last Vampire** (2000, Japan, animation) - Saya is a Japanese vampire slayer whose next mission is in a high school on a US military base in 1960s Japan, where she poses as a student. She uses a katana/samurai sword to kill vampires.
  - **ADAPTION**
    - **Blood: The Last Vampire** (2009, Hong Kong) - A vampire named Saya, who is part of a covert government agency that hunts and destroys demons in a post-WWII Japan, is inserted in a military school to discover which one of her classmates is a demon in disguise.
- **The Forsaken** (2001) - A young man gets embroiled in a war against vampires. Director J.S. Cardone was influenced by Terrence Malick's *Badlands* (1973) and Kathryn Bigelow's vampire film *Near Dark* (1987) when writing *The Forsaken*, and said he wanted to make a "road movie" with vampires.
- **Underworld** (2003) - The first film introduces Selene (Kate Beckinsale), an elite vampire warrior, who falls in love with Michael Corvin (Scott Speedman), a human who becomes a hybrid of both species. There were no special effects used to deepen Kevin Grevioux's (Raze's) voice. His natural speaking voice really is that deep.
  - **SEQUELS**
    - **Underworld: Evolution** (2006) - This sequel picks up where the first film left off, following Selene and Michael as they are hunted by their enemies. The film explores the deeper origins of the vampire-Lycan war.
    - **Underworld: Rise of the Lycans** (2009) - This prequel chronicles the story of the first Lycan, Lucian (Michael Sheen), and his forbidden romance with the vampire Sonja (Rhona Mitra).
    - **Underworld: Awakening** (2012) - The fourth film skips ahead 12 years and finds Selene in a world where humans are aware of and attempting to exterminate both vampires and Lycans.
    - **Underworld: Blood Wars** (2016, Eastern Europe) – Euro-gothic vampire action.
- **BloodRayne** (2005) - In the eighteenth century, a vampire escapes from the freak show, in which she once participated, and teams up with a group of vampire slayers to kill the man who raped her mother. This is based on the video of the same name and maybe trying to capitalize on the success of the female heroine of *Underworld*, but failed miserably. Ben Kinsley also stars in this box office bomb as well as Uwe Boll directing.
  - **SEQUELS**
    - **BloodRayne 2: Deliverance** (2007) – Rayne, the half-human/half-vampire warrior, ventures to America's 1880's Wild West to stop the vampire Billy the Kid and his posse of vampire cowboys.
    - **BloodRayne 3: The Third Reich** (2011) - Rayne joins a resistance group to fight against the Nazis during World War II.
- **Frostbitten** (2006, Sweden) Sweden's first vampire film. Vampires terrorize a city in Norrbotten.

- **Night Watch** (2006, Russia) - A fantasy-horror set in present-day Moscow where the respective forces that control daytime and nighttime do battle. Based on the book series by Sergey Lukyanenko.
  - **SEQUELS**
    - **Day Watch** (2006, Russia) - When Anton, a Warrior of Light, is falsely accused of murdering some vampires, he embarks on a journey to find the real killer and search for an ancient object that has the power to alter destiny.
- **30 Days of Night** (2007) - After an Alaskan town is plunged into darkness for a month, it is attacked by a bloodthirsty gang of vampires.
  - **SEQUELS**
    - **30 Days of Night: Dark Days** (2010) - After surviving the incidents in Barrow, Alaska, Stella Oleson relocates to Los Angeles, where she intentionally attracts the attention of the local vampire population in order to avenge the death of her husband, Eben.
- **Byzantium** (2012) – Gothic vampiric tale of mother-daughter survival. Based on the 2008 stage play *A Vampire Story* by Moira Buffini.
  - **FEMINIST HORROR**
    - **A Girl Walks Home Alone at Night** (2014, Iran) - A stylish indie film that offers a fresh take on the vampire genre with a strong focus on societal decay.
    - **Violation** (2020, Canada) - A deeply unsettling psychological horror film that follows a woman seeking brutal revenge after a traumatic incident.
    - **Jakob's Wife** (2021) - Anne, married to a small-town Minister, feels her life has been shrinking over the past 30 years. Encountering "The Master" brings her a new sense of power and an appetite to live bolder. However, the change comes with a heavy body count.
    - **Medusa** (2021) - In order to resist temptation, Mariana and her girlfriends try their best to control everything and everyone around them. However, the day will come when the urge to scream will be stronger than it ever has been.
- **Kiss of the Damned** (2012) - A beautiful, lonely vampire falls in love with a screenwriter and transforms him into one of the undead, but their budding romance is threatened by her vivacious, troublemaking sister.
- **Vamps** (2012) - Bloodsucking party girls (Alicia Silverstone, Krysten Ritter) find their destinies at stake when one falls for the son of a vampire hunter and the other encounters a long-ago love. *Vamps* is often considered a spiritual or thematic sequel to Heckerling's earlier film *Clueless*. Both films feature Alicia Silverstone and explore themes of friendship and romance in a modern setting, but *Vamps* adds a supernatural, undead twist.
- **Only Lovers Left Alive** (2013) - A depressed musician reunites with his lover. However, their romance, which has already endured several centuries, is disrupted by the arrival of her uncontrollable younger sister.
  - **ROMANCE HORRORS**
    - **Warm Bodies** (2013) - After a highly unusual zombie saves a still-living girl from an attack, the two form a relationship that sets in motion events that might transform the entire lifeless world.
    - **Burying the Ex** (2014) - A guy's regrets over moving in with his girlfriend are compounded when she dies and comes back as a zombie.
    - **Bones and All** (2020) - A young woman embarks on a 1000-mile odyssey through America where she meets a disenfranchised drifter. But all roads lead back to their terrifying pasts and to a final stand that will determine whether love can survive their otherness.
    - **Spontaneous** (2020) - Get ready for the outrageous coming-of-age love story about growing up...and blowing up. When students in their school begin exploding (literally), seniors Mara and Dylan struggle to survive in a world where each moment may be their last.
    - **A Ghost Waits** (2020) - A man's job requires him to clean a house, which turns out to be haunted. In the course of trying to exorcise the ghost, he falls in love with her.
    - **Sorry About the Demon** (2022) - A young man struggling with a broken heart learns that his new place is full of restless spirits.
    - **Humanist Vampire Seeking Consenting Suicidal Person** (2023, Canada) - A young woman vampire is unable to kill to meet her need for blood, but may have found a solution in a young man with suicidal tendencies.

- ☐ **Lisa Frankenstein** (2024) - A coming of RAGE love story about a teenager and her crush, who happens to be a corpse. After a set of horrific circumstances bring him back to life, the two embark on a journey to find love, happiness - and a few missing body parts.
  - ☐ **The Gorge** (2025) - Two operatives are appointed to posts in guard towers on opposite sides of a classified gorge.
- ☐ **Afflicted** (2013) - Two best friends see their trip of a lifetime take a dark turn when one of them is struck by a mysterious affliction. Now, in a foreign land, they race to uncover the source before it consumes him completely.
- ☐ **Vampire Academy** (2014) - Rose Hathaway is a Dhampir, half human-half vampire, a guardian of the Moroi, peaceful, mortal vampires living discreetly within our world. Her calling is to protect the Moroi from bloodthirsty, immortal Vampires, the Strigoi. Based on the novel of the same name by Richelle Mead.
- ☐ **Norway** (2014, Greece) - Photophobic Zano, arrives in the city for the very first time. The year is 1984 and Athens beckons. A vampire and a fine dancer, Zano quickly gets devoured by the dark underbelly of the capital city. All he really wants is a "warm" girl. The movie is presented in a found-footage style.
- ☐ **Bloodsucking Bastards** (2015) - A down on his luck cubicle worker and his slacker best friend discover their new boss is a vampire who is turning their coworkers into the un-dead. *Office Space* meets *Shaun of the Dead*.
- ☐ **He Never Died** (2015) - Jack, a social outcast, is thrust out of his comfort zone when the outside world bangs on his door and he can't contain his violent past.
  - • **SEQUELS**
    - ☐ **She Never Died** (2019) - When a girl goes missing, a woman with a mysterious past tracks down the people responsible.
- ☐ **The Transfiguration** (2016, UK) - When troubled teen Milo, who has a fascination with vampire lore, meets the equally alienated Sophie, the two form a bond that begins to blur Milo's fantasy into reality. Milo references numerous vampire movies in the film including *Martin, Let the Right One In* and *Nosferatu*.
- ☐ **Vampires vs. The Bronx** (2020) - A group of young friends from the Bronx fight to save their neighborhood from gentrification...and vampires.
- ☐ **Morbius** (2022) - Biochemist Michael Morbius tries to cure himself of a rare blood disease, but he inadvertently infects himself with a form of vampirism instead. Starring Jared Leto.
- ☐ **Day Shift** (2022) - A hard-working, blue-collar dad just wants to provide a good life for his quick-witted 10-year-old daughter. His mundane San Fernando Valley pool cleaning job is a front for his real source of income: hunting and killing vampires. Starring Jamie Foxx.
- ☐ **The Invitation** (2022) - Evie's long-lost cousin invites her to a swanky English wedding, where she uncovers a dark and twisted family secret that threatens to upend her life.
- ☐ **El Conde** (2023, Chile) - After living 250 years in this world, Augusto Pinochet, who is not dead but an aged vampire, decides to die once and for all.
- ☐ **Slay** (2024, Canada) - After a booking mistake, four drag queens find themselves performing for a mostly unwelcoming crowd, but when vampires attack, the crowd looks to the queens to save the day.
- ☐ **Sinners** (2025) - Trying to leave their troubled lives behind, twin brothers return to their hometown to start again, only to discover that an even greater evil is waiting to welcome them back. Although horrors are notorious for having sequels, director Ryan Coogler has expressed that he intentionally wanted to move away from franchise filmmaking with this project. He is best known for directing such franchises as *Black Panther* and *Creed*.

Vampire Hybrids & Experiments

- ☐ **Vamp** (1986) - Two fraternity pledges travel to a sleazy bar in search of a stripper for their college friends, unaware it is occupied by vampires. Its story of a strip club populated by vampires has often been noted as a major influence on other films such as *From Dusk Till Dawn* and *A Nightmare on Elm Street 4: The Dream Master*.
- ☐ **My Best Friend is a Vampire** (1987) – High school comedy with vampire puberty allegory.
- ☐ **Def by Temptation** (1990) - An evil succubus is preying on libidinous black men in New York City, and all that stands in her way is a minister-in-training, an aspiring actor, and a cop who specializes in cases involving the supernatural.
- ☐ **Buffy the Vampire Slayer** (1992) - Flighty teenage girl Buffy Summers learns that she is her generation's destined battler of vampires. Although a fun campy movie, it went on to have an even more famous adaption by

the film's screenwriter Joss Wedon and the *Buffy the Vampire* series starring Sarah Michelle Geller, and the even equally successful spin-off, *Angel.*

- ☐ **The Little Vampire** (2000) - A lonely American boy living in Scotland makes a new best friend, a fellow nine-year-old who happens to be a vampire. Based on the German-language book series *Der Kleine Vampir* by Angela-Sommer-Bodenburg.
- ☐ **Twilight** (2008) - When Bella Swan moves to a small town in the Pacific Northwest, she falls in love with Edward Cullen, a mysterious classmate who reveals himself to be a 108-year-old vampire.[11]
  - • **ADAPTIONS & SEQUELS**
    - ☐ **The Twilight Saga: New Moon** (2009) - Edward leaves Bella in an attempt to keep her safe, leading Bella to seek comfort with Jacob Black and his tribe of werewolves.
    - ☐ **The Twilight Saga: Eclipse** (2010) - A vengeful vampire, Victoria, creates an army of "newborn" vampires, forcing an uneasy alliance between the Cullen vampires and the werewolf pack to protect Bella.
    - ☐ **The Twilight Saga: Breaking Dawn Part 1** (2011) - Bella and Edward marry, but their honeymoon is cut short when Bella becomes pregnant with a half-human, half-vampire child, creating conflict with the werewolf pack.
    - ☐ **The Twilight Saga: Breaking Dawn Part 2** (2012) - Bella awakens as a vampire, and the Cullens must gather allies to protect their unique daughter, Renesmee, from the powerful vampire council, the Volturi.
    - ☐ **Vampires Suck** (2010) - In this spoof of vampire-themed movies, teenager Becca finds herself torn between two boys. She and her friends wrestle with endless dramas that crescendo at the prom.
- ☐ **Stake Land** (2010) - In a world of vampires, an expert vampire hunter and his young protégé travel toward sanctuary.
  - • **SEQUELS**
    - ☐ **The Stakelander** (2016) - When his home of New Eden is destroyed by a revitalized Brotherhood and its new Vamp leader, Martin finds himself alone in the badlands of America with only the distant memory of his mentor and legendary vampire hunter, Mister, to guide him.
- ☐ **We are the Night** (2010) - In Berlin, a cop closes in on an all-female vampire trio who just took in a new member, Lena.
- ☐ **Priest** (2011) - A warrior priest disobeys church law to track down a pack of vampires who have kidnapped his niece. This movie is a loose adaptation of a popular Korean manhwa (comic) series of the same name by Hyung Min-Woo.
- ☐ **Abraham Lincoln: Vampire Hunter** (2012) - Abraham Lincoln, the 16th President of the United States, discovers vampires are planning to take over the United States. He makes it his mission to eliminate them. Based on the novel by Seth Grahame-Smith.
- ☐ **Dark Shadows** (2012) - An imprisoned vampire, Barnabas Collins, is set free and returns to his ancestral home, where his dysfunctional descendants are in need of his protection.
  - • **BURTON/DEPP DREAM TEAM PAIRING**
    - ☐ **Edward Scissorhands** (1990) - Edward is taken in by a suburban family and falls in love, but the town's residents turn against him.
    - ☐ **Ed Wood** (1994) - The film follows the eccentric filmmaker's life and his relationship with screen legend Bela Lugosi.
    - ☐ **Sleepy Hollow** (1999) – Tim Burton's fog-drenched Gothic fairy tale of the Headless Horseman. Ichabod Crane is sent to Sleepy Hollow to investigate the decapitations of three people; the culprit is legendary apparition The Headless Horseman.
      - • **INFLUENCE**
        - ☐ **The Headless Horseman** (1922) - An adaptation of Washington Irving's 1820 short story "The Legend of Sleepy Hollow," which tells the tale of the village's legendary ghost, a headless horseman who is said to be searching for the head that he lost in battle.
    - ☐ **Corpse Bride** (2005) - A shy groom is accidentally whisked away to the land of the dead.

---

[11] Yes, I know this is technically not a horror, but it has a cult following and is about vampires.

- ☐ **Charlie and the Chocolate Factory** (2005) - Charlie Bucket wins a golden ticket to tour the mysterious and amazing chocolate factory.
- ☐ **Sweeney Todd: The Demon Barber of Fleet Street** (2007) - The legendary tale of a barber who returns from wrongful imprisonment to 1840s London, bent on revenge for the rape and death of his wife, and resumes his trade while forming a sinister partnership with his fellow tenant, Mrs. Lovett.
- ☐ **Alice in Wonderland** (2010) - A 19-year-old Alice returns to the magical world of her childhood adventure.
- ☐ **Blood Relatives** (2022) - A vampire's loner lifestyle is thrown into disarray when a teenager shows up claiming to be his daughter, and she's got the fangs to prove it. On a road trip across America's blacktops, they decide how to sink their teeth into family life.

Pairing Night Watchlist: Vampire Essentials

1. **Dracula (1931, USA)** – Start with the icon.
   What to watch for: Lugosi's hypnotic delivery and the film's silence between lines — the absence of music makes it eerier.
2. **Horror of Dracula (1958, UK)** – Hammer's Technicolor bloodbath.
   What to watch for: Christopher Lee's animalistic speed — unlike Lugosi, his vampire lunges like a predator.
   Smart note: Hammer's use of color shocked audiences raised on black-and-white horror; censors nearly cut Lee's bloodshot eyes.
3. **Near Dark (1987, USA)** – Vampires hit the open road.
   What to watch for: The bar massacre scene — pure punk nihilism.
   Smart note: Released the same year as *The Lost Boys* (1987), but flopped commercially. Today, it's the critic's favorite.
4. **Let the Right One In (2008, Sweden)** – The coldest romance.
   What to watch for: The swimming pool finale — horror and tenderness collide.
   Smart note: Director Tomas Alfredson avoided CGI where possible; the underwater climax was practically staged with eerie restraint.

Quick Facts to Sound Smart

- **Dracula (1931)** is often called the first "talkie" horror blockbuster, but it contains almost no score. Its quietness makes it strangely dreamlike compared to later Universal hits.
- **Christopher Lee** despised Hammer's scripts for recycling Dracula endlessly. In later films, he delivered his lines *without dialogue written*, improvising menace with just presence.
- **Interview with the Vampire (1994)** reignited gothic decadence in the '90s. Anne Rice originally hated Tom Cruise as Lestat but publicly apologized after seeing his performance.
- **The Lost Boys (1987)** is the first mainstream vampire movie to directly market itself to MTV kids. Its tagline was "Sleep all day. Party all night. Never grow old. Never die. It's fun to be a vampire."
- In **Thirst (2009)**, Park Chan-wook built the vampire's struggle around Catholic guilt, addiction, and lust. It was the first Korean film to win the Jury Prize at Cannes.

Drink the Darkness

Supernatural / Paranormal Horror

Where Gothic horror builds dread from architecture and atmosphere, supernatural horror unleashes what lies beyond natural law: demons, ghosts, cursed objects, and malevolent forces. It thrives on possession, haunting, and spiritual terror. From *The Exorcist* (1973) to *The Conjuring* (2013), the genre explores how the unseen invades the everyday, threatening not just lives but souls.

Why People Are Drawn to It

Supernatural horror terrifies because it strips away control. No weapon, no lock, no rational explanation can protect you. Faith is tested, skepticism punished, and the line between life and afterlife shredded. Audiences return to these stories for the primal shiver: the sense that something invisible may already be in the room with them. It's existential fear in cinematic form.

Essentials

1. **The Exorcist** (1973, USA) – Shattered boundaries by bringing religious terror and bodily corruption into mainstream cinema. Its fusion of theological dread, shocking physical horror, and themes of innocence under siege made it a cultural landmark and one of the most influential films in horror history.
2. **Poltergeist** (1982, USA) – Spielberg/Hooper collaboration where suburban domesticity collapses into ghostly chaos. Blended suburban satire with supernatural spectacle, turning the modern home into a site of spiritual invasion. Its mix of family drama, dazzling effects, and genuine terror captured the fear that even the safest spaces could be haunted by unseen forces.
3. **The Sixth Sense** (1999, USA) – M. Night Shyamalan's slow-burn ghost tale with cinema's most famous twist. Revitalized supernatural horror with quiet restraint, weaving a ghost story through themes of grief, trauma, and communication. Its understated atmosphere and iconic twist turned psychological unease into cultural phenomenon, redefining modern ghost cinema.
4. **The Conjuring** (2013, USA) – Reinvigorated haunted house cinema by grounding its terror in the supposedly true case files of Ed and Lorraine Warren. James Wan's careful pacing, reliance on atmosphere over gore, and use of classic Gothic tropes created a modern franchise template built on dread, faith, and family under siege.
5. **The Omen** (1976, UK) - An occult thriller that taps into apocalyptic anxieties, *The Omen* creates a relentless sense of dread by detailing the chillingly escalating incidents that lead an American diplomat to confront the horrific possibility that his adopted son is the Antichrist.

Deep Cuts

1. **The Amityville Horror** (1979) – Transformed a lurid true-crime backdrop into one of the most famous haunted house films of its era. Its tale of a family besieged by malevolent forces in their new home fused domestic anxiety with supernatural dread, cementing Amityville as a lasting icon of American horror folklore.

2. **The Entity** (1982, USA) – Controversial, based on real-life haunting claims of Doris Bither. Pushed supernatural horror into shocking territory by depicting a woman tormented by an unseen, violent force. Blending parapsychology with raw physical terror, it remains one of the most unsettling explorations of trauma, disbelief, and the body under supernatural assault.

3. **Shutter** (2004, Thailand) – Exemplifies the Thai wave of supernatural horror, merging ghostly vengeance with modern anxieties about photography and guilt. Its chilling use of lingering images and a devastating final reveal cemented it as one of the most influential Asian horror films of the 2000s.

4. **We Are Still Here** (2015, USA) – Fused haunted house tropes with brutal splatter, blending slow-burn atmosphere and sudden violence. Its New England setting, soaked in grief and blood, evokes both Gothic tradition and modern brutality, making the past itself the most vengeful ghost.

5. **The Vigil** (2019, USA) – Brought fresh life to the possession genre by rooting its horror in Jewish mysticism and cultural trauma. Set over one night beside a corpse, it uses claustrophobic atmosphere and folklore to explore grief, faith, and the weight of generational haunting.

Critical Essay

"Supernatural Horror Is Not Just Christianity"

Western audiences often equate supernatural horror with Catholic exorcisms and Christian demons. But the genre is global and plural. Japan's *One Missed Call* (2003) weaponizes cell phones. Thailand's *Shutter* (2004) fuses photography with Buddhist spirit lore. Even within the U.S., films like *The Possession* (2012) draw from Jewish dybbuk folklore. The supernatural is universal but each culture frames its ghosts and demons through its own spiritual lens.

Global Spotlight: Japan & Thailand

Japan's *Ringu* (1998) and *Ju-On: The Grudge* (2002) launched a wave of "J-horror" where technology and tradition intersect: curses traveling through VHS tapes, phone calls, or domestic spaces. These films influenced Hollywood remakes (*The Ring*, *The Grudge*), forever altering global horror aesthetics. Thailand's *Shutter* (2004) introduced international audiences to a uniquely Southeast Asian fear: the ghost caught not in mirrors or shadows but in photographs, binding trauma to physical evidence.

Core Foundations & Modern Hits

☐ **Yotsuya Kaiden** (1912, Japan) - The Japanese ghost story *Yotsuya Kaidan* has been adapted into more films than any other Japanese story, with dozens of versions produced since the early days of cinema. The first film adaptation appeared in 1912, but it is now lost, as are many early adaptations. Numerous versions from 1913 to 1937 were lost. They were likely lost or destroyed during World War II. The visual style and character of Oiwa have had a profound influence on modern Japanese horror (*J-horror*). Filmmakers often point to Oiwa's image: a woman with long hair and a disfigured face seeking revenge as the prototype for modern vengeful ghosts like Sadako in *Ring* and Kayako in *Ju-On*.

- **ADAPTIONS**
    - ☐ **The Ghost of Yotsuya: Part 1 and 2** (1949, Japan) - Directed by Keisuke Kinoshita, this two-part adaptation took a more psychological approach, presenting the ghost of Oiwa as a figment of her husband's guilty imagination rather than a real supernatural entity.
    - ☐ **Yotsuya Kaiden** (1956, Japan) - A version directed by Masaki Mori.
    - ☐ **Ghost Story of Yotsuya** (1959, Japan) - Directed by Kenji Misumi, this version focused on a more balanced and complex portrayal of the characters. It was released just 10 days before another adaptation, creating a direct competition.
    - ☐ **The Ghost of Yotsuya** (1959, Japan) - Directed by Nobuo Nakagawa, this version is widely regarded by critics as one of the best and most faithful adaptations of the kabuki play. It is known for its vivid colors, stylized theatrical direction, and effective use of horror.
    - ☐ **Illusion of Blood** (1965, Japan) - A version produced by Toho, directed by Shirō Toyoda, and starring Tatsuya Nakadai.
    - ☐ **Crest of Betrayal** (1994, Japan) - Directed by Kinji Fukasaku, this film combines the story of *Yotsuya Kaidan* with another famous samurai tale, *Chushingura*.

- ☐ **Over Your Dead Body** (2014) - A film by Takashi Miike, this adaptation tells the story of actors performing a stage production of *Yotsuya Kaidan* whose lives begin to mirror the events of the play.
- ☐ **Fahmann Maria** (1936, Germany) - A beautiful young drifter comes to a small village and battles Death itself to save the man she loves. The film was created with a very limited budget, yet Wisbar managed to create an intensely atmospheric and moody picture.
  - • **ADAPTIONS**
    - ☐ **The Strangler of the Swamp** (1945) - Following the lynching of an innocent man, his vengeful ghost haunts the swamp, preying on the descendants of those responsible until the new ferry operator, a relative of one of the guilty, confronts the spirit.
- ☐ **The Dybbuk** (1937, Poland) - This classic Polish film, with Yiddish dialogue, is a direct adaptation of S. Ansky's influential 1920 play *The Dybbuk*. The mystical love story between Chonen, a poor Talmud student, and Lea, a girl from a wealthy family, depicts the traditional folk culture of Polish Jews before WW2.
  - • **DYBBUK LEGEND FILMS:** The dybbuk is a spirit from Jewish folklore, believed to be the restless soul of someone who died with unfinished business or sin. Rather than haunting places, it clings to and possesses the living, speaking through them and disrupting their lives. Exorcisms by rabbis were said to drive the dybbuk out, making it a legend less about monsters and more about the terror of being overtaken from within.
    - ☐ **The Possession** (2012) – A young girl is overtaken by a dybbuk spirit trapped in an antique box. This American supernatural horror film is perhaps the most well-known modern adaptation.
    - ☐ **Demon** (2015, Poland) - A bridegroom is possessed by an unquiet spirit in the midst of his own wedding celebration, in this clever take on the Jewish legend of the dybbuk.
    - ☐ **Ezra** (2017, India) - A newly married woman brings an antique Jewish box into her home, unaware that the box contains the ghost of Abraham Ezra.
    - ☐ **The Vigil** (2019) – A man providing overnight watch to a deceased member of his former Orthodox Jewish community finds himself opposite a malevolent entity, in writer-director Keith Thomas' electrifying feature debut.
    - ☐ **Dybbuk: The Curse is Real** (2021) - This Indian Hindi-language film is a remake of the 2017 Malayalam film *Ezra*, and it explicitly features an antique Jewish box containing a dybbuk.
    - ☐ **Attachment** (2022) - A Danish actress moves in with her Jewish academic girlfriend in London and meets her controlling mother, uncovering dark secrets rooted in dybbuk lore.
- ☐ **The Picture of Dorian Gray** (1945) - Based on the novel by Oscar Wilde. A critically acclaimed, American supernatural horror-drama film starring Hurd Hatfield as Dorian and George Sanders as Lord Henry Wotton. The film is shot mostly in black and white but famously includes full-color inserts to show the portrait's escalating decay.
  - • **ADAPTIONS & SIMILAR THEMES**
    - ☐ **Dorian Grays Portræt** (1910, Denmark) - A corrupt young man somehow keeps his youthful beauty, but a special painting gradually reveals his inner ugliness to all.
    - ☐ **Dorian Gray** (1970) - An Italian-German-British production that puts a more explicit, sexually charged spin on the story.
    - ☐ **Dorian Gray** (2009) - A British dark fantasy horror film starring Ben Barnes as Dorian and Colin Firth as Lord Henry. This version amps up the supernatural and horror elements with more graphic visuals than earlier adaptations.
    - ☐ **Angel Heart** (1987) – A private investigator is hired by a man who calls himself Louis Cyphre to track down a singer named Johnny Favorite. But the investigation takes an unexpected and somber turn. Writer and director Alan Parker claims that Robert De Niro's performance as Louis

Cyphre was so eerie and realistic that he generally avoided him during his scenes, letting him just direct himself.

- ☐ **Ghostwatch** (1992) - This British "found footage" horror film involves a TV crew investigating a haunted house and a cursed portrait.
- ☐ **Stigmata** (1999) - The film's story is rooted in a stolen artifact—the portrait of a cursed figure from history.
- ☐ **Perfume: The Story of a Murderer** (2006) – Killer seeks the perfect human scent. In 18th-century France, an olfactory genius with no scent of his own becomes obsessed with capturing the ultimate fragrance, leading him to a horrific path of murder.
  - • **ADAPTIONS**
    - ☐ **The Perfumier** (2022) - The story follows a detective with a rare sense of smell who enlists the help of a disturbed perfumier to solve a series of murders.

☐ **The Four Skulls of Jonathan Drake** (1959) - Anthropologist Jonathan Drake believes that the men of his family have been cursed for generations by the native South American tribe he studies. Shortly after his brother, discovers one of the tribe's shrunken heads, he's found murdered.

- • **SIMILAR THEMES**
  - ☐ **Shrunken Heads** (1994) - When three N.Y. kids are murdered, the local Haitian voodoo priest re-animates their shrunken heads to exact revenge. Complications arise between one of the heads and his former girlfriend.

☐ **Asylum** (1972, UK - Amicus) - In order to secure a job at a mental institution, a young psychiatrist must interview four patients inside the asylum.

- • **ANTHOLOGY OF HORROR**
  - ☐ **Dr. Terror's House of Horrors** (1965, UK - Amicus) - Aboard a British train, mysterious fortune teller Dr. Schreck uses tarot cards to read the futures of five fellow passengers.
  - ☐ **Torture Garden** (1967, UK) - Adapted from Robert Bloch stories, with Jack Palance playing a carnival showman who offers his customers a glimpse of their chilling destinies.
  - ☐ **The House that Dripped Blood** (1971, UK) - An anthology of four horror stories revolving around a mysterious rental house in the U.K.
  - ☐ **Tales from the Crypt** (1972, UK - Amicus) - Five strangers get lost in a crypt and, after meeting the mysterious Crypt Keeper, receive visions of how they will die.
    - • **FRANCHISE**
      - ☐ **The Vault of Horror** (1973, UK) - An anthology of five horror stories shared by five men trapped in the basement of an office building.
      - ☐ **Demon Knight** (1995) - This was the first of two films to spin off from the popular HBO television series. It follows a battle between an immortal warrior and a demon for an ancient key.
      - ☐ **Bordello of Blood** (1996) - The second film from the HBO series, this horror-comedy centers on a detective investigating a funeral parlor that is secretly a vampire bordello.
      - ☐ **Ritual** (2002) - The third and final film in the HBO series spin-off, this movie stars Jennifer Grey and Tim Curry. It is based on the film *I Walked With a Zombie*.
      - ☐ **From Beyond the Grave** (1974 - Amicus) - An anthology of four short horror stories revolving around a mysterious antique shop owner and his antique pieces, each of which hides a deadly secret.
      - ☐ **Twilight Zone: The Movie** (1983) - Four horror and science fiction segments, directed by four famous directors, each of them being a new version of a classic story from Rod Serling's landmark television series.

☐ **The Exorcist** (1973) – When a mysterious entity possesses a young girl, her mother seeks the help of two Catholic priests to save her life. The scene where Regan projectile vomits at Father Karras only required one take. The vomit was intended to hit Jason Miller in the chest, but the plastic tubing misfired, hitting him in the face. His reaction of shock and disgust while wiping away the vomit is genuine, and Miller admitted in an interview that he was very angered by this mistake.

- **SEQUELS**
  - ☐ **Exorcist II: The Heretic** (1977) - A teenage girl once possessed by a demon finds that it still lurks within her. Meanwhile, a priest investigates the death of the girl's exorcist.
  - ☐ **The Exorcist III** (1990) - A police lieutenant uncovers more than he bargained for as his investigation of a series of murders, which have all the hallmarks of the deceased Gemini serial killer, leads him to question the patients of a psychiatric ward.
  - ☐ **Exorcist: The Beginning** (2004) - In 1947, having abandoned his faith, Father Merrin joins an archaeological excavation in Kenya, where an ancient church has been unearthed and something much older waits to be awoken.
  - ☐ **Dominion: Prequel to the Exorcist** (2005) - Decades before Father Merrin helped save Regan MacNeil's soul, he first encounters the demon Pazuzu in Kenya. Merrin's initial battle with Pazuzu leads to the rediscovery of his faith.
  - ☐ **The Exorcist: Believer** (2023) - When two girls disappear into the woods and return three days later with no memory of what happened to them, the father of one girl seeks out Chris MacNeil, who's been forever altered by what happened to her daughter fifty years ago.
  - ☐ **The Exorcist: Deceiver** (2025) - Exorcist Father Harris investigates teenage Emily's demonic possession by Asmodeus in Hazelwood. Joined by doctor, mom, he faces visions, deaths, paranoia battling ancient evil threatening to consume the town. (As of now this film may or may not be made).

- **EXORCISM FILMS**
  - ☐ **Requiem** (2006, Germany) – A fictionalized account of the life and death of Anneliese Michel, a German woman who died in 1976 after undergoing multiple exorcisms. The film takes a grounded, docudrama approach, framing the story as a struggle between medical illness (epilepsy) and the protagonist's religious beliefs.
    - **AMERICAN REMAKE**
      - ☐ **The Exorcism of Emily Rose** (2005) – Courtroom drama meets possession horror, inspired by a real case. Unlike the German film, *The Exorcism of Emily Rose* is a horror-legal drama that leaves the cause of the protagonist's condition ambiguous, though it leans more into the supernatural elements.
  - ☐ **The Rite** (2011) - A skeptical seminary student travels to Italy to study exorcism and finds his disbelief challenged.
  - ☐ **The Devil Inside** (2012) - In Italy, a woman becomes involved in a series of unauthorized exorcisms during her mission to discover what happened to her mother, who allegedly murdered three people during her own exorcism.
  - ☐ **Deliver Us from Evil** (2014) – Starring Eric Bana. The film is an adaptation of the 2001 book *Beware the Night* by Ralph Sarchie and Lisa Collier Cool, which recounts Sarchie's own alleged experiences as an NYPD officer who became involved in demonology.
  - ☐ **The Crucifixion** (2017, UK) - When Nicole comes in contact with Father Anton (Corneliu Ulici) more and more inexplicable events occur. The pair begin to believe that the priest lost the battle with a demon. The film is based on the Tanacu exorcism case that took place in Romania in 2005. The incident involved the death of a young nun, Maricica Irina Cornici, during an exorcism, leading to the conviction of the priest and several other nuns.
  - ☐ **The Pope's Exorcist** (2023) – Russell Crowe tackles Vatican-sanctioned possession. In May 2024, producer Jeff Katz confirmed on social media that the sequel had officially been greenlit.

Russell Crowe is expected to reprise his role as Father Gabriele Amorth. The sequel is expected to continue Father Amorth's mission, following up on the conclusion of the first movie.

☐ **Summer of Fear** (1978) - Directed by Wes Craven. A teenage girl's life is turned upside down after her cousin moves into her house, and as time goes by, she begins to suspect that she may be a practitioner of witchcraft. Based on the novel by Lois Duncan.

- **LOIS DUNCAN ADAPTIONS**
  - ☐ **I Know What You Did Last Summer** (1997) – Four young friends bound by a tragic accident are reunited when they find themselves being stalked by a hook-wielding maniac in their small seaside town.
    - **SEQUELS**
      - ☐ **I Still Know What You Did Last Summer** (1998) – The murderous fisherman with a hook is back to once again stalk the two surviving teens, Julie and Ray, who had left him for dead, as well as cause even more murder and mayhem, this time at a posh island resort.
      - ☐ **I'll Always Know What You Did Last Summer** (2006) - This direct-to-video, standalone sequel has a new cast of teenagers who are stalked by the killer after covering up a prank that resulted in a death. It has very little narrative connection to the previous two films.
      - ☐ **I Know What You Did Last Summer** (2025) - This recent legacy sequel brings back Jennifer Love Hewitt and Freddie Prinze Jr. alongside a new, younger cast. The plot is reminiscent of the original, with a group of friends covering up a car accident and then being hunted by a hook-wielding killer.
  - ☐ **Killing Mr. Griffin** (1997) - This TV movie was based on a Duncan novel about students plotting to scare their teacher.
  - ☐ **Down a Dark Hall** (2018) - This supernatural thriller is about a young woman in a mysterious boarding school.

☐ **The Amityville Horror** (1979) – A family's new home becomes a nightmare of demonic possession.

- **SEQUELS**
  - ☐ **Amityville II: The Possession** (1982) - A dysfunctional family moves into a new house, which proves to be satanic, resulting in the demonic possession of their teenage son.
  - ☐ **Amityville 3-D** (1983) - Inquisitive Reveal Magazine journalist John Baxter moves into the Amityville house in defiance of the supernatural events connected to it and finds everyone around him besieged by evil manifestations connected to a demonic presence.
  - ☐ **Amityville Horror: The Evil Escapes** (1989) - The demonic forces in the Amityville house transfer to an ancient lamp, which finds its way to a remote California mansion where the evil manipulates a little girl by manifesting itself in the form of her dead father.
  - ☐ **The Amityville Curse** (1990) - Five people spend the night in an abandoned house, an Amityville haunted house, and soon find themselves terrorized by assorted ghosts, venomous insects and ghostly apparitions.
  - ☐ **Amityville 1992: It's About Time** (1992) - An architect brings home a mysterious old clock, not knowing that it's haunted by the demonic presence of the Amityville house. Soon, the clock begins to alter time and space and starts to possess members of the household.
  - ☐ **Amityville: A New Generation** (1993) - An old mirror from the Amityville house finds its way into a young photographer's home, where the demonic presence soon manifests itself to cause more death and mayhem.

- [ ] **Amityville Dollhouse** (1996) - A children's doll house, which is a miniature of the infamous haunted Long Island house, is given to a young girl where the demonic evil soon comes out to cause more terror.
  - **ADAPTIONS**
    - [ ] **The Amityville Horror** (2005) - Newlyweds are terrorized by demonic forces after moving into a large house that was the site of a grisly mass murder a year before.
    - [ ] **Amityville: The Awakening** (2017) - A desperate single mother moves with her three children into the notorious, supposedly haunted, real-life Amityville house to try and use its dark powers to cure her comatose son. Things go horribly wrong.
  - **NOTES:** There are twenty more sequels, none of which seem worth watching since IMDB.com has them at 2 stars or less out of 10, and that is absolutely terrible. If you want the full list: https://www.imdb.com/list/ls027677338/

- [ ] **Bewitched** (1981, HK) - While possessed by an evil spirit, a man murders his daughter. A police detective investigating the case also becomes possessed. A good monk helps fight the evil spirit.
  - **SIMILAR FILMS**
    - [ ] **The Boxer's Omen** (1983, HK) - While in Thailand to avenge his brother who was crippled in a fight with a corrupt Thai boxer, a man gets caught up in a web of fate, Buddhism and black magic. Considered a thematic follow-up to director Kuei Chih-hung's earlier Shaw Brothers horror film, *Bewitched* (1981).
    - [ ] **Seeding of a Ghost** (1983) - Released in the same year by the Shaw Brothers, this film also features grotesque body horror, supernatural spells, and dark revenge plots.
    - [ ] **The Seventh Curse** (1986) - A Hong Kong horror film that blends action, supernatural curses, and disturbing special effects.
    - [ ] **Black Magic** (1975) - This film features a wizard who uses supernatural spells to cause chaos and murder.
    - [ ] **Mystic in Bali** (1981) - A low-budget Indonesian horror film that similarly features black magic and gruesome, surreal effects.

- [ ] **Poltergeist** (1982) – A family's home becomes the center of paranormal activity that opens a doorway to the "other side." With help, they must cross over to get their daughter back. During the scene where Robbie (Oliver Robins) is being strangled, the clown's arms became extremely tight and Robins started to choke. When he screamed out, "I can't breathe!" Steven Spielberg and Tobe Hooper thought that the boy was ad-libbing and just instructed him to look at the camera. When Spielberg saw Robins' face turning purple, he ran over and removed the clown's arms from Robins' neck. **Memorable Quote:** *"They're here!"*
  - **ADAPTIONS, SEQUELS & SIMILAR FILMS**
    - [ ] **Poltergeist II: The Other Side** (1986) - The Freeling family have a new house, but their troubles with supernatural forces don't seem to be over.
    - [ ] **Poltergeist III** (1988) - Carol Anne is staying with her aunt in a high-rise building, where the supernatural forces haunting her make their return.
    - [ ] **Poltergeist** (2015) - A family whose suburban home is haunted by evil forces must come together to rescue their youngest daughter after the apparitions take her captive.
    - [ ] **Pulse** (1988) - A visiting son tries to warn his father and stepmother that they are being menaced by a living and intelligent pulse of electricity that moves from house to house and terrorizes the residents therein.
    - [ ] **Sweet Home** (1989, Japan) - A TV production crew are making a documentary about the infamous painter Mamiya Ichiro. When they start filming at his old home, they come under attack from the ghost of the painter's wife.

- [ ] **Child's Play** (1988) - A single mother gives her son a much sought-after doll for his birthday, only to discover that it is possessed by the soul of a serial killer.
  - **ADAPTIONS & SEQUELS**
    - [ ] **Child's Play 2** (1990) - Chucky is resurrected at the toy company that made him and continues to target Andy Barclay.
    - [ ] **Child's Play 3** (1991) - Chucky returns to haunt a teenage Andy in military school.
    - [ ] **Bride of Chucky** (1998) – A resurrected Tiffany transfers her soul into a bride doll, becoming Chucky's partner.

- ☐ **Seed of Chucky** (2004) – The story introduces Glen, the child of Chucky and Tiffany.
- ☐ **Curse of Chucky** (2013) - A return to the franchise's straightforward horror roots.
- ☐ **Cult of Chucky** (2017) - Brings together multiple characters from the series' history.
- ☐ **Child's Play** (2019) - A reimagined version of the story where Chucky is a high-tech AI doll from the Kaslan Corporation, not a soul-possessed one.
- • **SIMILAR FILMS**
  - ☐ **Dolls** (1986) - A dysfunctional family of three stop by a mansion during a storm -- father, stepmother, and child. The child discovers that the elderly owners are magical toy makers and have a haunted collection of dolls.
  - ☐ **Puppet Master** (1989) - Produced by Charles Band, this film features a group of psychics stalked by a group of murderous puppets.
  - ☐ **Dolly Dearest** (1991) - A film about a toy factory built on a cursed land, where a demon possesses a doll and then a young girl.
  - ☐ **Demonic Toys** (1992) - A pregnant policewoman, her quarry, and an innocent delivery boy become trapped in a haunted toy warehouse.
  - ☐ **The Boy** (2016) - A modern take on the killer doll trope, featuring a nanny who must care for a porcelain doll.
  - ☐ **M3gan** (2022) - When robotics engineer Gemma becomes the guardian of her orphaned niece, Cady, she thinks her new invention, a robotic AI, will be a good companion. However, M3GAN begins to behave in unexpected and shocking ways.
    - • **ADAPTIONS & SEQUELS**
      - ☐ **M3gan 2.0** (2025) - The story picks up two years after the original, with M3GAN's creator Gemma and her niece Cady facing off against a new threat: a military-grade AI unit called Amelia.
      - ☐ **Soulm8te** (2026) - The story centers on a man who acquires an artificially intelligent android to cope with the death of his wife. When he tries to give the android real sentience, it turns into a deadly killer.
- ☐ **Sometimes They Come Back** (1991) - Teens from hell mark school teacher Jim Norman and his family for destruction. Stephen King's short story, first published in *Cavalier* magazine in 1974 and later collected in *Night Shift* in 1978.
  - • **SEQUELS & SIMILAR FILMS**
    - ☐ **Sometimes They Come Back… Again** (1996) - This follow-up is an original story about a different character, a man who returns to his hometown with his daughter, only to be confronted by the ghosts of three bullies he killed years earlier. It is not directly connected to the plot of the first film, but expands on the theme of supernatural revenge.
    - ☐ **Sometimes They Come Back… For More** (1998) - This second sequel, also a straight-to-video release, is a completely new story involving an isolated army outpost in Antarctica, where a mysterious event awakens a powerful evil. It is not connected to the first two films.
    - ☐ **The Messengers** (2007) - This film similarly explores a haunted family dealing with ghosts and the psychological toll of a tragic past.
- ☐ **The Crow** (1994) - The night before his wedding, musician Eric Draven and his fiancée are brutally murdered by members of a violent gang. On the anniversary of their death, Eric rises from the grave and assumes the mantle of the Crow, a supernatural avenger. Based on the 1989 comic book created by James O'Barr. The on-set death of actor Brandon Lee, who was accidentally shot by a prop gun while filming a scene for *The Crow*, remains one of Hollywood's most tragic moments.
  - • **SEQUELS & ADAPTIONS**
    - ☐ **The Crow: City of Angels** (1996) - The first theatrical sequel, starring Vincent Pérez as Ashe Corven, a new Crow seeking revenge in Los Angeles. The film was largely dismissed by critics for failing to recapture the style or emotional depth of the original.
    - ☐ **The Crow: Salvation** (2000) - This straight-to-video sequel stars Eric Mabius as Alex Corvis, a man framed for his girlfriend's murder who returns for vengeance. It received mixed reviews and was released directly to video after its theatrical release was canceled.

- ☐ **The Crow: Wicked Prayer** (2005) - The final straight-to-video installment stars Edward Furlong as Jimmy Cuervo, an ex-con resurrected to seek revenge on a satanic cult. It was poorly received by critics and fans.
- ☐ **The Crow** (2024) - After years of developmental delays, a new reboot of the film was released in 2024. It stars Bill Skarsgård as Eric Draven and was met with a negative reception from critics and audiences.
- ☐ **The Sixth Sense** (1999) – A boy who communicates with spirits seeks the help of a disheartened child psychologist. Haley Joel Osment auditioned with Shakespeare; Shyamalan said his eyes "already carried the sadness of the story." **Memorable Quote:** *"I see dead people."*
  - • **SPIRITUAL SUCCESSOR ADJACENT**
    - ☐ **Don't Listen** (2020, Spain) - Daniel and Sara have a 9-year-old son, Eric, and they've just moved to a new home not knowing the neighbors call it "the house of the voices". Eric is the first one to notice the odd noises behind each door.
- ☐ **Final Destination** (2000) - A teenager has a premonition of his plane exploding, saving himself and a few others, but Death hunts them down to reclaim their lives.
  - • **ADAPTIONS**
    - ☐ **Final Destination 2** (2003) - One year after the first film, a woman's premonition of a highway pile-up saves another group of strangers, but she must team up with a survivor from Flight 180 to find a way to stop Death.
    - ☐ **Final Destination 3** (2006) - A high school graduate's premonition of a horrific roller coaster crash saves her and her friends, but they must decipher clues from photographs to figure out how Death plans to get them next.
    - ☐ **The Final Destination** (2009) - A young man's premonition of a catastrophic stock car race crash saves his friends and other spectators, who are then hunted by Death with even more elaborate and brutal kills.
    - ☐ **Final Destination 5** (2011) - A premonition of a bridge collapse saves a group of colleagues, but a morbid mortician warns them they can only survive by killing someone else and stealing their remaining lifespan.
    - ☐ **Final Destination: Bloodlines** (2025) - A college student inherits premonitions of a 1960s skyscraper fire from her grandmother and must save her family from a new "bloodline" hit list.
- ☐ **1408** (2007) – A skeptic faces paranormal torment in a haunted hotel room.
- ☐ **Drag Me to Hell** (2009) - An ambitious loan officer must find a way to shatter a curse that threatens her soul with damnation.
- ☐ **Insidious** (2010) – Astral projection, demons, and a terrifying "red-faced" entity lurking in the Further.
  - • **SEQUELS**
    - ☐ **Insidious: Chapter 2** (2013) – Continuation of astral hauntings.
    - ☐ **Insidious: Chapter 3** (2015) – Prequel to the Lambert haunting.
    - ☐ **Insidious: The Last Key** (2018) – Elise's origin story and demons.
    - ☐ **Insidious: The Red Door** (2023) – Family returns to the Further.
  - • **HAUNTED AND POSSESSED HOUSE FILMS**
    - ☐ **The House of the Devil** (2009) – Babysitter tricked into satanic ritual. During the filming of *The House of the Devil*, crew members reported strange experiences at the Yankee Pedlar Inn. This inspired West to write and direct his next film, *The Innkeepers*, a ghost story also starring Sara Paxton.

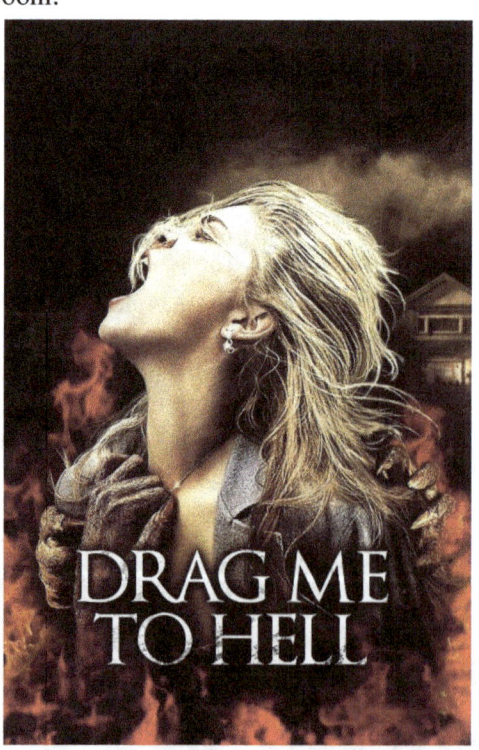

- ☐ **The Pact** (2012) - As a woman struggles to come to grips with her past in the wake of her mother's death and the disappearance of her sister, an unsettling presence emerges in her childhood home.
  - • **SEQUELS**
    - ☐ **The Pact 2** (2014) - This is a direct sequel that brings back protagonist Annie Barlow, who is forced to confront the specter of the "Judas Killer" once again. The sequel received less critical praise than the original.
- ☐ **Sinister** (2012) – A writer finds cursed home movies linked to a pagan entity feeding on children's souls.
  - • **SEQUELS**
    - ☐ **Sinister 2** (2015) - The sequel follows a former deputy (James Ransone) who attempts to stop Bughuul's curse after a new family becomes its next victim.
- ☐ **The Devil's Candy** (2015) - A struggling painter's possessed by dark forces after he and his young family move into their dream home in rural Texas, in this creepy haunted-house tale.
- ☐ **The Closet** (2020, Korea) - After Sang-Won's daughter Yi-Na goes missing in their new home, a mysterious man approaches him and tells him to look for her in the closet.
- ☐ **Son** (2021) - When a young boy contracts a mysterious illness, his mother must decide how far she will go to protect him from terrifying forces in her past.
- ☐ **Mama** (2013) – Orphaned children return to society with a ghostly "mother" in tow.
- ☐ **The Conjuring** (2013) – Paranormal investigators Ed and Lorraine Warren work to help a family terrorized by a dark presence in their farmhouse.
  - • **SEQUELS**
    - ☐ **The Conjuring 2 (**2016) – The Enfield poltergeist case. Ed and Lorraine Warren travel to North London to help a single mother raising four children alone in a house plagued by a supernatural spirit.
    - ☐ **The Conjuring: The Devil Made Me Do It** (2021) - Arne Cheyenne Johnson stabs and murders his landlord, claiming to be under demonic possession while Ed and Lorraine Warren investigate the case and try to prove his innocence.
    - ☐ **The Conjuring: Last Rites** (2025) - Paranormal investigators Ed and Lorraine Warren take on one last terrifying case involving mysterious entities they must confront.
    - ☐ **Annabelle** (2014) – A couple begins to experience terrifying supernatural occurrences involving a vintage doll shortly after their home is invaded by satanic cultists.
    - ☐ **Annabelle: Creation** (2017) – Period-set supernatural doll story.
    - ☐ **Annabelle Comes Home** (2019) – The Warrens' museum of cursed objects awakens.
  - • **SPIN-OFFS**
    - ☐ **The Nun** (2018) – Gothic Catholic imagery in the Conjuring universe.
    - ☐ **The Nun II** (2023) – Continuation of Gothic convent horror.
  - • **THE CONJURING UNIVERSE ADJACENT**
    - ☐ **The Haunting in Connecticut** (2009) - After a family is forced to relocate for their son's health, they begin experiencing supernatural behavior in their new home, and uncover a sinister history.
      - • **SEQUELS**
        - ☐ **The Haunting in Connecticut 2: Ghosts of Georgia** (2013) - This follow-up was produced by the same company, Gold Circle Films, but follows a completely different family and story. It is also based on a supposed true story, this one concerning the Wyrick family in Georgia.
- ☐ **It Follows** (2014) – A sexually transmitted curse pursues its victims with relentless inevitability. Director David Robert Mitchell cited *Island of Terror* as an inspiration for his horror film, noting its sense of "waiting for the creature to pop up."
  - • **SEQUELS**
    - ☐ **They Follow** (2025) – As of the publication, this movie is currently filming.
- ☐ **The Autopsy of Jane Doe** (2016) – A father-son coroner team uncovers paranormal horrors in a mysterious corpse.

Highlights & Global Hauntings

☐ **Village of the Damned** (1960) - A small town's women give birth to unfriendly alien children posing as humans. **Goof:** The action takes place in the 1950s (some characters are wearing medal ribbons for the Korean War), but all of Major General Leighton's campaign ribbons predate 1939; he has no ribbons for World War II. He could have retired before 1939, but he would have been far too old to rejoin after the war.

- **SEQUELS**
  - ☐ **Children of the Damned** (1964) - The story follows a different set of six super-intelligent children from different nations rather than a group from one village as they are brought to London for study.
- **ADAPTIONS**
  - ☐ **Village of the Damned** (1995) - The movie follows the same basic plot of an entire village mysteriously blacking out, leading to several women giving birth to unnervingly identical, pale-haired, glowing-eyed children with powerful psychic abilities.

☐ **The Omen** (1976) – Mysterious deaths surround an American ambassador. Could the child that he is raising actually be the Antichrist? The Devil's own son? **Goof:** The priest's room is "lined with hundreds of crucifixes". In actuality they are just crosses, not crucifixes - crucifixes have an effigy of Jesus affixed to the cross.

- **SEQUELS & ADAPTIONS**
  - ☐ **Damien: Omen II** (1978) - The sequel follows Damien as a young boy, showcasing more explicit deaths with a slasher-like tone.
  - ☐ **Omen III: The Final Conflict** (1981) - Features the adult Damien Thorn as the U.S. Ambassador to the United Kingdom, now played by Sam Neill.
  - ☐ **Omen IV: The Awakening** (1991) - A made-for-TV movie that continues the story, but is often considered a significant downgrade in quality.
  - ☐ **The Omen** (2006) - A remake that is a standalone story and a different version of the original film.
  - ☐ **Damien** (2006) - A television series that serves as a direct sequel to the 1976 film, taking place around thirty years later, but it ignores the sequel films.
  - ☐ **The First Omen** (2024) - A prequel to the original film, exploring the origins of the Antichrist's birth in a new continuity.
- **EVIL CHILDREN**
  - ☐ **The Bad Seed** (1956) - A thriller about a seemingly perfect young girl who is revealed to be a sociopathic killer.
  - ☐ **Bloody Birthday** (1981) - Three children are born at the height of an eclipse of the sun. Ten years later, they begin to murder the people around them - even their family members.
  - ☐ **Mikey** (1992) - The plot focuses on a young boy who appears normal but is actually a psychopathic killer who murders his adoptive families and then seeks out a new one.
  - ☐ **The Good Son** (1993) – Innocent-looking child hides psychopathic darkness. *The Good Son* is often compared to other psychological thrillers and horror films that feature malevolent or sociopathic children.
  - ☐ **Joshua** (2007) - A psychological thriller about a brilliant and malevolent young boy who terrorizes his family.
  - ☐ **The Children** (2008) - A holiday turns into a nightmare for two families when their children suddenly turn against them.

Box Office Opens 6:00 — Show 6:30

TRI-CITY DRIVE-IN — Hwy. 99 Between Colton and Redlands — TU 9-2025 — PY 6-3777

THE STRANGEST STORY SCIENCE-FICTION EVER TOLD!

Behind the blazing eyes of this fair-haired child lurk the demon forces of another planet!

M·G·M Presents

GEORGE SANDERS BARBARA SHELLEY

VILLAGE OF THE DAMNED

- ☐ **Case 39** (2009) – Starring Renee Zellweger and Bradley Cooper. A social worker fights to save a girl from her abusive parents, only to discover that the situation is more dangerous than she expected.
- ☐ **Orphan** (2009) - A husband and wife who recently lost their baby adopt a 9-year-old girl who is not nearly as innocent as she appears. A third *Orphan* film is in development, with Isabelle Fuhrman set to return once again as Esther. Plot details are currently under wraps, but Fuhrman has hinted at even wilder and crazier twists.
  - • **SEQUELS**
    - ☐ **Orphan: First Kill** (2022) - This prequel film explores Esther's backstory, showing how she orchestrated an escape from an Estonian psychiatric facility and successfully impersonated a wealthy family's missing daughter. Isabelle Fuhrman reprises her role as Esther.
- ☐ **The Monitor (Babycall)** (2011, Norway) - After a baby monitor picks up another channel, Anna begins reliving the nightmare she'd recently escaped.
- ☐ **Before I Wake** (2016) - A couple adopt an orphaned child whose dreams - and nightmares - manifest physically as he sleeps.
- ☐ **The Hole in the Ground** (2019) - A single mother living in the Irish countryside with her son begins to suspect he may not be her son at all, and fears his increasingly disturbing behavior is linked to a mysterious sinkhole in the forest behind their house.
- ☐ **Marionette** (2020, Netherlands) - Marionette tells the story of a therapist, who loses her grip on reality when a ten-year-old boy claims he can control her future.
- ☐ **Tin & Tina** (2023, Spain) - A couple who, after a traumatic miscarriage, adopt strange albino siblings with an ultra-Catholic upbringing. The children's bizarre actions make the couple question their reality and morality.
- ☐ **God Told Me To** (1976) - A New York detective investigates a series of murders committed by random New Yorkers who claim that "God told them to."
  - • **THEMATIC FILMS**
    - ☐ **The Mothman Prophecies** (2002) - A supernatural thriller that explores a series of unexplained phenomena in a small town. Much like *God Told Me To*, the protagonist investigates mysterious events and the lines between reality and a powerful, unknown force become blurred.
    - ☐ **Frailty** (2001) - This psychological thriller is about a father who believes he has been tasked by God to kill demons in human form, using his young sons to help him. It shares the theme of religiously-motivated violence and the ambiguous nature of its source.
    - ☐ **Fallen** (1998) This crime thriller, starring Denzel Washington, features a detective investigating a series of murders committed by a supernatural entity that can possess people. It has a similar "what if" paranoia plot structure.
- ☐ **Salem's Lot** (1979) – Stephen King's vampires invade a small town. A novelist and a young horror fan attempt to save a small New England town which has been invaded by vampires.
  - • **ADAPTIONS**
    - ☐ **A Return to Salem's Lot** (1987) - A man and his son vacation to the quiet vampire populated town of Salem's Lot.
    - ☐ **Salem's Lot** (2024) - An author returns to his hometown of Jerusalem's Lot in search of inspiration for his next book, only to discover that the townspeople are being attacked by a bloodthirsty vampire.
- ☐ **Ghost Story** (1981) – Two generations of men find themselves haunted by the presence of a spectral woman. When the son of one of the elderly men returns to his hometown after his brother's mysterious death, they attempt to unravel her story.
- ☐ **The Entity** (1982) – Carla Moran awakens one night to find herself being beaten and raped by an unseen presence. Terrified of what's happening to

103

her, and shunned by friends and family who think she's lost her mind, she seeks help from parapsychologists.

- ☐ **Christine** (1983) – A nerdish boy buys a strange car with an evil mind of its own and his nature starts to change to reflect it.
  - • **MENACING VEHICLES**
    - ☐ **Killdozer** (1974) - A small construction crew on an island is terrorized when a spirit-like being takes over a large bulldozer, and goes on a killing rampage.
    - ☐ **The Cars that Ate Paris** (1974) - The small town of Paris, Australia deliberately causes car accidents, then sells/salvages all valuables from the wrecks as a means of economy.
    - ☐ **The Car** (1977) - A small desert town is terrorized by a powerful, seemingly possessed car, and the local sheriff may be the only one who can stop it.
      - • **SEQUELS**
        - ☐ **The Car: Road to Revenge** (2019) - An unscrupulous District Attorney is savagely murdered and tossed out of a building onto his brand new car. Mysteriously, the District Attorney and his car come back to life as a single being with a thirst for vengeance.
    - ☐ **Maximum Overdrive** (1986) - A group of people try to survive when machines start to come alive and become homicidal. Directed by Stephen King, this film also features technology turning against humanity, though on a much larger scale, involving cars and trucks.
    - ☐ **Black Cadillac** (2003) - Three young men become terrorized in a high-speed car chase with a mysterious pursuant.
- ☐ **Witchboard** (1986) – When his girlfriend becomes dangerously obsessed with a ghost she contacted using a Ouija board, Jim reluctantly joins forces with her ex-his own estranged childhood best friend-to identify and exorcise the evil spirit.
- ☐ **Pet Sematary** (1989) – After tragedy strikes, a grieving father discovers an ancient burial ground behind his home with the power to raise the dead.
  - • **SEQUELS & ADAPTIONS**
    - ☐ **Pet Sematary II** (1992) – A teenage boy and his father move to his recently-deceased mother's hometown, where they encounter the ancient Native American cemetery with the power to raise the dead.
    - ☐ **Pet Sematary** (2019) – Dr. Louis Creed and his wife, Rachel, relocate from Boston to rural Maine with their two young children. The couple soon discover a mysterious burial ground hidden deep in the woods near their new home.
    - ☐ **Pet Sematary: Bloodlines** (2023) - In 1969 a young Jud Crandall and his childhood friends band together to confront an ancient evil that has gripped their hometown of Ludlow.
- ☐ **Shocker** (1989) – A psychotic serial killer is finally caught thanks to a high school football player who has a strange connection to the killer. Right before getting executed, he performs a demonic ritual and uses electricity to come back from the dead.
- ☐ **Wishmaster** (1997) - A demonic djinn attempts to grant its owner three wishes, which will allow him to summon his brethren to Earth.
  - • **SEQUELS**
    - ☐ **Wishmaster 2: Evil Never Dies** (1999) - In this sequel, the Djinn is once again unleashed, this time in a Las Vegas casino, and seeks to collect more souls to complete his prophecy. The original actor, Andrew Divoff, returned to play the Djinn.
    - ☐ **Wishmaster 3: Beyond the Gates of Hell** (2001) - This film features a new actress in the lead role, who must fight the Djinn. Andrew Divoff did not return, and the Djinn was played by John Novak.

- ☐ **Wishmaster: The Prophecy Fulfilled** (2002) - The final installment of the series concludes the Djinn's story, once again starring John Novak as the Djinn.
- • **SIMILAR FILMS & MIDDLE EASTERN FOLKLORE DJINN:** The djinn of Middle Eastern folklore are shape-shifting spirits made of smokeless fire, existing in a world parallel to humans. Neither wholly good nor evil, they can grant favors or wreak havoc, often testing mortals through temptation or trickery. Tales of djinn highlight the unseen forces surrounding daily life, embodying both fear of the unknown and fascination with hidden power.
    - ☐ **The Humans and the Jinns** (1985) – A popular Egyptian horror film where a doctor returns from America and is told by a Jinn that he is in love with her. The Jinn has appeared in many Egyptian films over the decades.
    - ☐ **The Outing** (1987) - A group of teenagers spends the night in a natural history museum and unleashes a deadly, lamp-dwelling force.
    - ☐ **Warlock** (1989) – A male witch seeks apocalypse. This film also features a powerful, supernatural being that manipulates mortals to achieve its goals.
    - ☐ **The Djinn** (2007) - In this movie, a gang of rebels takes an actress hostage in an abandoned ranch, where the caretaker tells them about the Jinn that inhabit the land.
    - ☐ **Red Sands** (2009) - In this film, a group of American soldiers in the Middle East unleashes a monstrous Djinn after destroying a statue.
    - ☐ **Djinn** (2013) - The final film from director Tobe Hooper (*The Texas Chain Saw Massacre*). The plot focuses on a couple in the United Arab Emirates who discover their new home was built on the abode of malevolent Djinn.
    - ☐ **Jinn** (2014) - An action-horror-thriller about a man who discovers an ancient family curse and the powerful Djinn behind it.
    - ☐ **Under the Shadow** (2016, Iran/UK) – A Persian-language psychological horror film set in war-torn Tehran during the 1980s. A mother and daughter are haunted by a malevolent Djinn that thrives on their fear.
    - ☐ **Achoura** (2018) - This Moroccan film explores the myth of the *djinn* or *genie*. Four childhood friends are reunited after one of them reappears after 25 years, and they must confront a monstrous djinn they encountered in their youth.
    - ☐ **Ghibah** (2021) - This Indonesian horror film focuses on college students who get possessed by an Ifrit Djinn after they engage in gossip and malicious talk.
    - ☐ **The Advent Calendar** (2021, Belgium/France) - Eva is a paraplegic. On her birthday, her friend Sophie gives her a strange Advent calendar. It's not the traditional treats you find when you open each drawer, but quirky gifts that are scary and get bloodier.
    - ☐ **The Djinn** (2021) - A modern horror film that similarly explores a protagonist accidentally summoning a demonic entity.
    - ☐ **Qorin** (2022) - An Indonesian horror film that features the concept of "Qorin," the personal jinn that accompany every human. The film explores the terrifying consequences of these entities turning malevolent.
- ☐ **Thirteen Ghosts** (2001) – When Cyrus Kriticos, a very rich collector of unique things, dies, he leaves his house, fortune, and his prized collection of ghosts.
- ☐ **Deathwatch** (2002, UK) - In the middle of World War I, nine British soldiers caught behind enemy lines seek refuge in a complex network of German trenches. What they soon discover is that they aren't alone - and it isn't a German soldier that's hunting them down.
    - • **MILITARY & WAR HORROR**
        - ☐ **The Bunker** (2001, UK) - A British war horror film about German soldiers who believe they are haunted by spirits. Germany, 1944. The forests of the Ardennes. A platoon of battle weary German soldiers, forced into confusion and retreat by advancing Allied forces, take refuge in an isolated Siegfried Line bunker.
        - ☐ **Below** (2002) - A submarine crew is tormented by a supernatural presence during World War II, blurring the line between insanity and a ghost story.
        - ☐ **R-Point** (2004) - During the Vietnam War, a South Korean base receives a radio transmission from a missing squad, presumed dead, and sends a platoon to rescue the lost squad from the R-Point.

- ☐ **The Guard Post** (2008, Korea) - A later Korean military horror film that similarly explores a mysterious massacre at a military guard post in the demilitarized zone (DMZ) between North and South Korea.
- ☐ **The Squad** (2011, Colombia) - After losing contact with a military base, a high mountain unit is sent to investigate. Upon arrival, they find only a woman in chains. Isolation and the impossibility of escape serve to undermine the soldiers' judgment.
- ☐ **Shutter** (2004, Thailand) – When Jane and Tun run over a girl in a car accident, they speed away immediately from the crime scene. However, Tun, a photographer, soon discovers strange shadows in his photos, which unsettles them.
  - • **OTHER FILMS BY SOPHON SAKAPHISIT**
    - ☐ **Alone** (2007, Thailand) - Pim is a Thai woman living in Korea with her husband Wee. At her birthday a friend reads her fortune with a deck of cards and informs that something she has lost will soon return to her. But some lost things are better off staying lost.
      - • **REMAKES**
        - ☐ **Nadiya Kollappetta Rathri** (2007) - An Indian Malayalam film inspired by *Alone*. Railway Anti-Criminal Task Force (RATs) investigates three unrelated murders happened in a train.
        - ☐ **Charrulatha** (2012) - This Indian film in Kannada and Tamil features a similar plot of conjoined twins.
        - ☐ **Guni-Guni** (2012) - A Filipino film that has a similar plot, starring Lovi Poe.
        - ☐ **Geethaanjali** (2013) - A Malayalam remake that was also promoted as a spin-off of the 1993 film *Manichitrathazhu*.
        - ☐ **Alone** (2015, India) - A Hindi-language remake, also dealing with the story of conjoined twins.
        - ☐ **Vaigai Express** (2017) - A Tamil remake of the Malayalam film *Nadiya Kollappetta Rathri*, which was itself loosely based on *Alone*.
        - ☐ **Bhool Bhulaiyaa 2** (2022) - This Hindi film is loosely based on the Malayalam film *Geethaanjali* and features a similar twin dynamic.
    - ☐ **Coming Soon** (2008) - A horror film where two projectionists discover a disturbing, cursed movie. Horror movies can be very scary, with surprise ghosts and unexpected scares. But nothing is scarier than coming home after watching them and feeling the story come to life.
    - ☐ **Laddaland** (2011) - When a family moves to Laddaland, an upscale housing development with large, beautiful homes, they discover life in their new neighborhood isn't so perfect when they encounter a series of terrifying, paranormal events that drives the family to the edge of insanity.
    - ☐ **The Promise** (2017) - A later film directed by Sakdaphisit about a girl who returns to the abandoned, ghost-filled tower where she and her best friend made a suicide pact years earlier.
- ☐ **Silk** (2006, Taiwan) - A team of scientists has managed to capture the energy of a ghost child by using their newly invented device, Menger Sponge. They enlists a lip-reading agent in order to figure out how the child can shed light on life, and life after death.
- ☐ **Exte: Hair Extensions** (2007) - The over-the-top plot, in which a mortician sells cursed hair from an organ-harvesting victim.
  - • **KILLER OBJECTS**
    - ☐ **Rubber** (2010) – A homicidal car tire, discovering it has destructive psionic power, sets its sights on a desert town once a mysterious woman becomes its obsession.
    - ☐ **In Fabric** (2018) - This Peter Strickland film focuses on a haunted red dress that torments its owners, blending horror, satire, and a surreal atmosphere.
    - ☐ **Killer Sofa** (2019, New Zealand) – A killer reclining chair becomes enchanted by a girl and starts committing crimes of passion.
    - ☐ **Deerskin** (2019, France) - A man's obsession with his designer deerskin jacket causes him to blow his life savings and turn to crime.
    - ☐ **Slaxx** (2020) - When a possessed pair of jeans begins to kill the staff of a trendy clothing store, it is up to Libby, an idealistic young salesclerk, to stop its bloody rampage.

King of Horror

Stephen King[12]

Stephen King (b. 1947, Maine, USA) is the most prolific and commercially successful horror writer of all time, often called the "King of Horror." Emerging in the 1970s with *Carrie* (1974), King anchored horror not in distant castles or abstract fears but in small-town America. He has always written with one foot in the everyday: high schools, suburbs, bars, factories and one in the uncanny: telekinesis, vampires, haunted hotels. His horror lens is deeply democratic: if something scares *him*, it will probably scare us.

Signature Works (Curated)

- *Carrie* (1974, novel; 1976, film) — The bullied girl who lashes out with telekinesis; King's debut and a blueprint for modern horror's focus on adolescence.
- *The Shining* (1977, novel; 1980, Kubrick film) — Haunted hotel, psychic child, and Jack Torrance's descent into madness; King's most famous supernatural work.
- *It* (1986, novel; 1990 miniseries; 2017/2019 films) — Small-town kids vs. an ancient evil; Pennywise becomes a pop-culture monster icon.
- *Pet Sematary* (1983, novel; 1989/2019 films) — The line between grief and monstrosity; one of King's darkest stories.
- *Misery* (1987, novel; 1990 film) — Fan obsession turned torture; stripped-down psychological horror.

The Fingerprints

- "The horror next door": small towns as crucibles of evil.
- Children as seers, victims, or heroes (*It*, *Firestarter*).
- Addiction and self-destruction mirrored as supernatural corruption (*The Shining*).
- The ordinary invaded by the extraordinary (*Cujo*, *Christine*).
- Colloquial storytelling voice: characters that feel lived-in, terrified, and resilient.

Legacy & Influence

King made horror mainstream. No one before him had managed both bestseller dominance and cultural omnipresence. He redefined horror for a new generation moving it from gothic castles to everyday America, and inspired countless writers (Joe Hill, Paul Tremblay, Josh Malerman) and filmmakers (Mike Flanagan, Frank Darabont, Andy Muschietti). His work birthed miniseries booms (*It*, *The Stand*), countless feature films, and streaming dominance (*Gerald's Game*, *Doctor Sleep*). "King horror" is practically a genre unto itself.

Pairing Night Watchlist

- *Carrie* (1976) → Watch for the split-screen prom massacre, one of the most iconic sequences in horror film history.
- *The Shining* (1980) → Notice Kubrick's cold, formalist style vs. King's emotional novel — a tension that defines debates around adaptation.
- *It: Chapter One* (2017) → See how Pennywise is updated for CGI spectacle while retaining the core "childhood trauma never dies" theme.

Quick Facts to Sound Smart

- King sold *Carrie* for just $2,500, it changed his life overnight.
- He famously hated Kubrick's *The Shining*, calling it "a fancy car with no engine."
- King has written under the pseudonym Richard Bachman (*The Running Man*, *Thinner*).
- He survived being hit by a van in 1999; he later killed off a similar character in *The Dark Tower*.
- His "constant readers" fandom culture is one of the first true horror communities.

Paranormal Surge

- ☐ **The Eye** (2002, Hong Kong) – A corneal transplant sees ghosts.
    - • **SEQUELS**
        - ☐ **The Eye 2** (2004) - This sequel focuses on a pregnant woman who, after a failed suicide attempt, can also see spirits. While not connected to the first film's plot, it explores a similar theme of clairvoyance.
        - ☐ **The Eye 10** (2005) - Also known as *The Eye Infinity* or sometimes referred to as *The Eye 3*, this film is a supernatural comedy-horror. A group of teenagers in Thailand uses a book of ten ways to see ghosts, which unleashes a series of strange events.
        - ☐ **The Child's Eye** (2010) - This film is another thematic sequel in the series. It follows a group of friends stranded in an old hotel who discover its sinister past.
    - • **ADAPTIONS**
        - ☐ **Adhu** (2004) - A Tamil-language Indian remake of the original *The Eye*.
        - ☐ **Naina** (2005) - A Hindi-language Indian remake starring Urmila Matondkar.
        - ☐ **The Eye** (2008) - The American remake stars Jessica Alba as a classical violinist who gains the ability to see supernatural phenomena after receiving a cornea transplant. The story largely mirrors the original film's plot but with a revised, more crowd-pleasing ending.
    - • **PANG BROTHERS HORROR**
        - ☐ **Ab-Normal Beauty** (2004) - A horror film about a young art student who becomes obsessed with death and photographs the aftermath of gruesome accidents.
        - ☐ **Re-cycle** (2006) - A writer wants to get a glimpse of some genuine supernatural occurrences while doing research for a novel, but her experiences lead her down a dark path as she witnesses vivid hallucinations and begins to lose her grip on reality.
- ☐ **Dead Silence** (2007) – Ventriloquist dolls harbor curses.
- ☐ **Paranormal Entity** (2009) – Found-footage spin on demonic haunting.
- ☐ **Ouija** (2014) – Teens unleash board-game spirits.
    - • **SEQUELS**
        - ☐ **Ouija: Origin of Evil** (2016) – Strong prequel elevates franchise.
- ☐ **1922** (2017) – King's tale of guilt and spectral retribution.
- ☐ **Gerald's Game** (2017) – A couple tries to spice up their marriage in a remote lake house. After the husband dies unexpectedly, the wife is left handcuffed to their bed frame and must fight to survive and break free.
    - • **CONFINED HORROR**
        - ☐ **Till Death** (2021) – Starring Megan Fox. A woman is left handcuffed to her dead husband as part of a sick revenge plot. Unable to unshackle, she has to survive as two killers arrive to finish her off.

Supernatural Evolution

- ☐ **The Tall Man** (2012, France) - When her child goes missing, a mother looks to unravel the legend of the Tall Man, an entity who allegedly abducts children. *The Tall Man* is known for its shocking twist, which reshapes the audience's understanding of the child abductions.
- ☐ **We Are Still Here** (2015) – In the cold, wintery fields of New England, a lonely old house wakes up every thirty years - and demands a sacrifice.
- ☐ **The Windmill Massacre** (2016, Netherlands) - Seven tourists with troubled pasts find themselves trapped at a satanic mill in rural Holland. As they're attacked for their sins one by one, the night becomes a fight for survival.
    - • **DUTCH & EUROPEAN FOLKLORE:** Dutch and European folklore laid the foundation for nearly every horror tradition that followed. Rooted in pre-Christian paganism, oral storytelling, and centuries of superstition, these tales were how people explained the unexplainable: sickness, storms, and sudden death. The result was a continent-wide mythology filled with cursed landscapes, vengeful spirits, shapeshifters, and doomed wanderers, each embodying the fears of their time. In the Netherlands, stories of the Witte Wieven, ghostly women who lured men into the mist, and the Flying Dutchman, the spectral ship condemned to sail forever, mirrored the dangers of seafaring life and moral reckoning. In Central and Eastern Europe, legends of vampires, revenants, and witches gave rise to the Gothic tradition that would later dominate horror literature. These early myths traveled and evolved with migration, war, and

the written word, transforming into the cautionary tales that inspired Bram Stoker's *Dracula*, Mary Shelley's *Frankenstein*, and Murnau's *Nosferatu*. By the 19th century, collectors like the Brothers Grimm and Hans Christian Andersen immortalized these dark folktales, preserving their unease while wrapping them in moral lessons. What began as fireside warnings became the aesthetic backbone of cinematic horror: mist-drenched forests, haunted castles, cursed bloodlines, and the eternal struggle between reason and superstition. European folklore didn't just influence horror, it invented its atmosphere, teaching the genre how to fear the unseen and worship the beautiful decay of the old world.

- ☐ **Thale** (2012, Norway) – Two estranged friends cleaning a crime scene in Norway's woods find a hidden underground chamber with a mute but singing woman. Their discovery draws dangerous attention from those pursuing her.
- ☐ **Moloch** (2022, Netherlands) - Betriek lives on the edge of a bog in the Netherlands. When she and her family are attacked by a stranger one night, Betriek sets out to find an explanation. She discovers that something is chasing her.
- ☐ **Speak No Evil** (2022, Denmark) – Social awkwardness escalates into horror.
  - • **ADAPTIONS**
    - ☐ **Speak No Evil** (2024) - An American family vacationing in Europe meets a British couple and their son. After accepting an invitation to visit the British couple's remote country estate, the American family realizes their hosts have sinister motives.
- ☐ **The Cleansing Hour** (2019) – Another successful "exorcism" streamed online - or so it seems. Can the "exorcist," producer and their team bring the ratings up? Ratings skyrocket, when a real demon gets involved.
- ☐ **Things Heard & Seen** (2021) – A marriage unravels in a haunted farmhouse.
- ☐ **The Unholy** (2021) - A hearing-impaired girl is visited by the Virgin Mary and can suddenly hear, speak, and heal the sick. As people flock to witness her miracles, terrifying events unfold. Are they the work of the Virgin Mary or something much more sinister?
- ☐ **Demonic** (2021) – Possession meets experimental VR exorcism.
- ☐ **The Chalk Line** (2022, Spain) - A couple temporarily adopts a young girl that they found wandering around alone in the high road.
- ☐ **Smile** (2022) – A grinning curse passes victim to victim.
  - • **SEQUELS**
    - ☐ **Smile 2** (2024) - The film follows Skye Riley, a global pop star played by Naomi Scott, who becomes the entity's next victim after witnessing a horrific suicide. Trapped by the pressures of fame and the curse, Skye's mental state rapidly deteriorates. A third *Smile* movie is officially in development.
- ☐ **Cobweb** (2023) – Child suspects monsters in his walls.

Supernatural Horror Pairing Night: How to Channel the Spirits

Main Course (Essentials)
The Exorcist (1973, USA)
How to watch: Alone in the dark if you dare, but it's richer with a group. Watch for the slow build before the shocks.
Smartest fact: Director William Friedkin once fired live gunshots on set to elicit genuine terror from the actors.

Side Dish (Haunted Suburbia)
Poltergeist (1982, USA)
How to watch: Pair with pizza and lights dimmed, then compare Spielberg's sentimental touch to Hooper's grim energy.
Smartest fact: The skeletons in the swimming pool scene were real human skeletons. It was cheaper than making props.

Dessert (Global Flavor)
Shutter (2004, Thailand)
How to watch: Don't scroll your phone, the film weaponizes photography itself. Pay attention to how still images become terrifying.
Smartest fact: After *Shutter*'s release, Thai audiences reported a spike in ghost-photo urban legends.

Palate Cleanser (Modern Hit)

The Conjuring (2013, USA)

How to watch: With skeptics and believers in the room, watch how Wan mixes creaky Gothic with blockbuster jump-scares.

Smartest fact: The real Lorraine Warren visited the set and claimed she sensed spirits still attached to the cursed objects.

After-Dinner Mint (For the Bold)

The Entity (1982, USA)

How to watch: Save this for late-night, when the room is quiet. Its raw subject matter unsettled even seasoned horror fans.

Smartest fact: Based on the real-life case of Doris Bither, who claimed to be assaulted by a spectral force in 1970s California.

Ghost Stories & Midnight Screens

Monster / Creature Horror

Defining the Creature Feature

Monster horror is humanity's mirror through the monstrous. Unlike Gothic ghosts or supernatural spirits, the Creature Feature makes fear tangible: fangs, claws, scales, mutations. From the tragic beasts of the 1930s (*King Kong, Frankenstein's Monster*) to atomic-age kaiju (*Godzilla*), to animal-attack thrillers (*Jaws*), the genre asks: *what if nature or science turned against us?* These creatures embody our anxieties, from industrial progress to nuclear destruction, from genetic experiments to ecological collapse.

Why People Are Drawn to It

People flock to creature horror for spectacle and scale. Monsters are larger than life sometimes literally skyscraper-sized and yet they remain deeply human symbols: greed, ambition, survival instinct. Audiences find catharsis in seeing humanity's arrogance humbled, whether by a towering gorilla on the Empire State Building or a shark circling a beach town. The genre is equal parts wonder and warning: a thrill ride that reminds us we are never the apex predator we believe ourselves to be.

Essentials

1. **King Kong (1933, USA)** – Stop-motion marvel; a tragic love-and-death story of the Eighth Wonder of the World. Blended adventure spectacle with horror, turning the giant ape into both monster and tragic figure. Its groundbreaking special effects and themes of beauty, captivity, and exploitation made it a landmark that reshaped cinematic fantasy and terror alike.
2. **Godzilla (1954, Japan)** – Transformed the monster movie into an allegory of nuclear trauma, with the towering creature embodying Japan's postwar anxieties about atomic destruction. Its blend of spectacle, devastation, and political resonance established kaiju cinema as both thrilling entertainment and cultural reckoning.
3. **Creature from the Black Lagoon (1954, USA)** – Fused science fiction with Gothic romance, presenting its amphibious monster as both terrifying predator and tragic outsider. Its underwater cinematography and themes of evolution, desire, and intrusion into nature made it one of Universal's last great classic monsters.
4. **Jaws (1975, USA)** – Redefined modern horror by turning a seaside town into a stage for primal terror, where an unseen shark became a symbol of nature's unstoppable menace. Its masterful use of suspense, music, and character dynamics created the first true summer blockbuster and a lasting template for creature horror.
5. **Alien (1979, USA/UK)** – Fused science fiction with body horror, transforming deep space into a claustrophobic nightmare. H. R. Giger's xenomorph embodied both technological and biological dread, while Ridley Scott's slow-burn tension and Sigourney Weaver's iconic Ripley reshaped the genre around survival and the terror of the unknown.

Deep Cuts

1. **Freaks (1932, USA)** – Turned the circus sideshow into a site of both exploitation and vengeance, using real disabled performers in a way both radical and controversial. Tod Browning's film shocked audiences with its climactic retribution scene, cementing its legacy as a transgressive classic that blurred the line between sympathy and horror.
2. **The Blob (1958, USA)** – Captured Cold War anxieties through the image of a formless, ever-growing creature that devours everything in its path. Mixing teen rebellion with apocalyptic threat, it became both a drive-in classic and a metaphor for unstoppable, shapeless fear in an age of uncertainty. *See Cosmic Horror for description breakdown.*
3. **The War of the Gargantuas (1966, Japan)** – Cult kaiju with brutal sibling rivalry. Expanded kaiju cinema by shifting from city-smashing spectacle to a tragic clash between two giant humanoid creatures: one gentle, one

violent. Its blend of monster action, eerie atmosphere, and underlying parable of nature corrupted by science gave it a cult reputation far beyond its genre roots.

4. **An American Werewolf in London (1981, UK/USA)** – Black comedy and groundbreaking transformation effects. Revitalized the werewolf myth by combining grisly practical effects with sharp dark humor. John Landis's film balanced shocking transformation sequences with satire and pathos, making it both a technical landmark and a cult classic of modern horror.

5. **The Host (2006, South Korea)** – Fused monster-movie thrills with biting social commentary, using a mutated river creature to critique government negligence and environmental decay. Bong Joon-ho's mix of horror, satire, and family drama made it one of the most acclaimed and politically resonant creature features of the 21st century.

Critical Essay

"Creature Horror Is Not Just Big Monsters"

The Stereotype: Creature Features are all giant beasts stomping cities (*Godzilla*, *King Kong*).

The Reality: Monster horror spans scales and metaphors. A shark (*Jaws*), a parasite (*The Thing*), or even rabbits (*Night of the Lepus*) can embody cultural fears. Some monsters inspire awe (*Mothra*), some sympathy (*Frankenstein's Monster*), and some pure revulsion (*The Blob*). Creature horror thrives because it adapts to every anxiety, scientific hubris, environmental collapse, or the terror of the unknown.

Global Spotlight: Japan

Japan is the heartbeat of kaiju cinema. *Godzilla* (1954) birthed the modern monster movie, blending allegory with spectacle. Toho Studios built an ecosystem of kaiju: Mothra, Rodan, Ghidorah that became global pop icons. Later films like *Shin Godzilla* (2016) reimagined the monster as grotesque evolution and government satire. Meanwhile, *Gamera* (1965–1999) gave audiences a turtle guardian for children, before evolving into a darker trilogy in the 1990s. Japan's monsters are both terrifying and mythic, embodying cultural trauma, resilience, and imagination.

Golden Age & Classic Creature Foundations

☐ **Freaks** (1932) - A circus' beautiful trapeze artist agrees to marry the leader of side-show performers, but his deformed friends discover she is only marrying him for his inheritance. **Memorable Quote:** *"You dirty, slimy, freaks! Freaks, freaks, freaks! You fools! Make me one of you, will you?"*

- **CIRCUS HORROR**
  - ☐ **The Unknown** (1927) - A criminal on the run hides in a circus and seeks to possess the daughter of the ringmaster at any cost.
  - ☐ **Carnival of Souls** (1962) – An independently produced horror film about a woman who survives a car accident but is haunted by a mysterious carnival and its ghost-like figures.
  - ☐ **Vampire Circus** (1972) - As the plague sweeps the countryside, a quarantined village is visited by a mysterious traveling circus. Soon, young children begin to disappear, and the locals suspect the circus troupe might be hiding a horrifying secret.
  - ☐ **Something Wicked This Way Comes** (1983) - In a small American town, a diabolical circus and its demonic proprietor prey on the townsfolk.
  - ☐ **Killer Klowns from Outer Space** (1988) – A cult classic involving aliens who look like

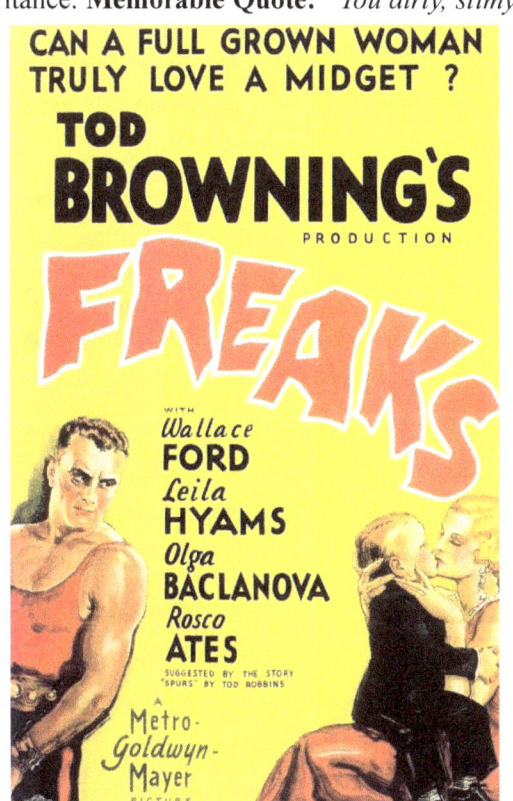

clowns and harvest humans in cotton candy cocoons.

- ☐ **31** (2016) – Directed by Rob Zombie. Five carnival workers are kidnapped and held hostage in an abandoned, hellish compound where they are forced to participate in a violent game, the goal of which is to survive twelve hours against a gang of sadistic clowns.
- ☐ **Hell Fest** (2018) - A masked serial killer turns a horror-themed amusement park into his own personal playground, terrorizing a group of friends while the rest of the patrons believe that it is all part of the show.
- ☐ **Where the Devil Roams** (2023) - Traces a family of murderous sideshow performers as it travels around the world on the dying carnival circuit.

☐ **King Kong** (1933) – A film crew goes to a tropical island for an exotic location shoot and discovers a colossal ape who takes a shine to their female blonde star. He is then captured and brought back to New York City for public exhibition. **Misquote:** "Twas beauty *that* killed the beast." **Actual Quote:** "It was Beauty killed the Beast."

- • **SEQUELS & ADAPTIONS**
- ☐ **Son of Kong** (1933) - RKO released this sequel just nine months after the original. It follows filmmaker Carl Denham's return to Skull Island, where he finds a smaller, more docile, albino ape that he dubs "Little Kong".
- ☐ **King Kong vs. Godzilla** (1962) - Produced by the Japanese studio Toho, this crossover pits King Kong against Godzilla. Toho's version of Kong is larger and gains strength from electricity.
- ☐ **King Kong Escapes** (1967) - Toho's second and final King Kong film is a loose adaptation of the American-Japanese cartoon series *The King Kong Show*. In it, Kong fights his evil robotic doppelgänger, Mechani-Kong.
- ☐ **King Kong** (1976) - Producer Dino De Laurentiis remade the original story for Paramount Pictures. This version is set in the 1970s, with Kong climbing the Twin Towers instead of the Empire State Building.
- ☐ **King Kong Lives** (1986) - A sequel to the 1976 film. It reveals that Kong survived his fall from the World Trade Center and receives an artificial heart. He later meets and mates with a female Kong, Lady Kong.
- ☐ **King Kong** (2005) - Peter Jackson directed this critically acclaimed, big-budget remake that is highly faithful to the original's 1930s setting. It features state-of-the-art CGI and expanded character development.

☐ **The Wolf Man** (1941) - Upon his return to his father's estate, aristocrat Larry Talbot meets a beautiful woman, attends a mystical carnival and uncovers a horrifying curse.

- • **ADAPTIONS**
- ☐ **The Wolfman** (2010) - A more serious and gory remake starring Benicio del Toro as Lawrence Talbot and Anthony Hopkins as his father. The film won an Academy Award for Best Makeup, but its poor box office performance led Universal to cancel a planned sequel.
- ☐ **Wolf Man** (2025) - The newest adaptation in the Universal Monster franchise. It stars Christopher Abbott as the protagonist and is directed by Leigh Whannell.

- • **SIMILAR FILMS**
- ☐ **The Werewolf** (1913) - The earliest werewolf film ever made, featuring a female werewolf, was made in 1913 but is now considered lost.
- ☐ **Wolfblood** (1925) - After wolf blood transfusion, man thinks he's becoming a wolf.
- ☐ **Werewolf of London** (1935) - After botanist Wilfred Glendon travels to Tibet in search of a rare

flower, the Mariphasa, he returns to a London haunted by murders that can only be the work of bloodthirsty werewolves.

- ☐ **The Werewolf** (1956) - Two scientists are involved in a car accident and find an unconscious man in the remains. They take him to their lab and inject him with a serum they have been working with. Sadly, the serum turns the man into a murderous werewolf.
- ☐ **Monster on Campus** (1958) - The blood of a primitive fish exposed to gamma rays causes a benign research professor to regress to an ape-like, bloodthirsty prehistoric hominid.
- ☐ **Wolf** (1994) - Publisher Will Randall becomes a demon wolf and has to fight to keep his job. Starring Jack Nicholson and Michelle Pfeiffer.

☐ **She-Wolf of London** (1946) - A young heiress finds evidence suggesting that at night she acts under the influence of a family curse and has begun committing ghastly murders in a nearby park.

- • **SIMILAR THEMES**
    - ☐ **The Undying Monster** (1942) - This Universal film, released a few years earlier, also focuses on a family curse involving a monster, building suspense and a mystery around a series of attacks.
    - ☐ **The Curse of the Werewolf** (1961) - A Hammer Horror film that follows the tragic life of a man cursed to become a werewolf.

☐ **It Came from Outer Space** (1953) - A spaceship from another world crashes in the Arizona desert and only an amateur stargazer and a schoolteacher suspect alien influence when the local townsfolk begin to act strangely.

- • **ADAPTIONS**
    - ☐ **It Came from Outer Space** (1996) - This made-for-television film, written by Jim and Ken Wheat, is more of a remake than a sequel, despite its title.

☐ **Creature from the Black Lagoon** (1954) – A strange prehistoric beast lurks in the depths of the Amazonian jungle. A group of scientists try to capture the animal and bring it back to civilization for study. Guillermo del Toro modeled *The Shape of Water* on this film, his "love letter" to the Creature.

- • **SEQUELS**
    - ☐ **Revenge of the Creature** (1955) - In this 3D sequel, the Gill-man is captured and transported to a Florida oceanarium. After escaping, he terrorizes the area while pursuing a new love interest. An uncredited Clint Eastwood appears in one of his earliest film roles.
    - ☐ **The Creature Walks Among Us** (1956) - The final film in the original trilogy shows the Gill-man captured again after being badly burned. Scientists perform surgery to make him an air-breather, but the creature struggles with his new existence and eventually escapes.
- • **ADAPTIONS**
    - ☐ **The Monster Squad** (1987) - In this cult classic, the Gill-man appears alongside Dracula, the Wolf Man, and the Mummy as villains who invade a modern-day town.
    - ☐ **The Shape of Water** (2017) - Director Guillermo del Toro, who previously tried to remake the *Creature* film, created this Oscar-winning movie as a love story inspired by the original's themes. The film is about a mute cleaning woman who falls in love with an amphibious creature being held in a secret government laboratory.

☐ **Them!** (1954) – Mutated giant ants wreak havoc in the desert.

- • **GIANT INSECTS**
    - ☐ **Tarantula!** (1955) – A radioactive arachnid terrorizes a small town.
    - ☐ **Rodan** (1956) – Giant pterosaur soars over Japan, part of kaiju canon.
    - ☐ **The Deadly Mantis** (1957) - A giant prehistoric praying mantis, recently freed from the Arctic ice, voraciously preys on American military at the DEW Line and works its way south.
    - ☐ **The Black Scorpion** (1957) - Giant prehistoric scorpions are released by a volcanic eruption.

- ☐ **Attack of the Giant Leeches** (1959) - A backwoods game warden and a local doctor discover that giant leeches are responsible for disappearances and deaths in a local swamp, but the local police don't believe them.
- ☐ **Mothra** (1961) – Benevolent moth goddess battles kaiju threats.
- ☐ **Godzilla** (1954, Japan) – After a dinosaur-like beast - awoken from undersea hibernation by atom bomb testing - ravages Tokyo, a scientist must decide if his similarly dangerous weapon should be used to destroy it. The original's mournful tone is often lost in sequels; it was more dirge than spectacle.
  - • **SHOWA SEQUELS**
    - ☐ **Godzilla Raids Again** (1955) - Introduced the first monster-on-monster battle.
    - ☐ **Mothra vs. Godzilla** (1964) - Another classic monster showdown.
    - ☐ **Ghidorah, The Three-Headed Monster** (1964) – Introduces Godzilla's most iconic nemesis.
    - ☐ **Invasion of Astro-Monster** (1965) - Also known as *Godzilla vs. Monster Zero*, this film involves aliens from Planet X who want to lease Godzilla and Rodan to fight King Ghidorah.
    - ☐ **Ebirah, Horror of the Deep** (1966) - Features Godzilla fighting a giant crab monster.
    - ☐ **Son of Godzilla** (1967) - Portrays Godzilla as a father figure to his adopted son, Minilla, and further solidifies his role as a protagonist.
    - ☐ **Destroy All Monsters** (1968) - Featured an all-out battle with a massive roster of kaiju.
    - ☐ **All Monsters Attack** (1969) - This film largely uses stock footage from previous films but continues the Showa storyline.
    - ☐ **Godzilla vs. Hedorah** (1971) - A toxic, ever-evolving alien life-form from the Dark Gaseous Nebula arrives to consume rampant pollution, and neither humanity nor Godzilla may be able to stop it.
    - ☐ **Godzilla vs. Gigan** (1972) - Godzilla and Anguirus team up to fight alien monsters, Gigan and King Ghidorah.
    - ☐ **Godzilla vs. Magalon** (1973) - Features Godzilla, the robot Jet Jaguar, and Anguirus teaming up against the monster Megalon and Gigan.
    - ☐ **Godzilla vs. Mechagodzilla** (1974) - Godzilla faces his robotic double, Mechagodzilla, who is controlled by aliens.
    - ☐ **Terror of Mechagodzilla** (1975) - This final film of the Showa era is a direct sequel to the 1974 film, featuring Mechagodzilla and the monster Titanosaurus.
  - • **AMERICAN ADAPTIONS**
    - ☐ **Godzilla, King of the Monsters!** (1956) - An American reporter (Raymond Burr) visiting Tokyo becomes a witness to the city's destruction by a dinosaur-like beast awoken from undersea hibernation by atom bomb testing.
    - ☐ **Godzilla 1985** (1985) - Burr reprises his role as Steve Martin, now an international correspondent. His character is not central to the plot but serves as an observer and advisor to the U.S. military.
  - • **HEISEI SERIES**
    - ☐ **The Return of Godzilla** (1985. Japan) - The Japanese government suppresses news of Godzilla's resurrection as political tensions increase between the US and USSR, both of whom willing to bomb Japan to stop the monster.

- ☐ **Godzilla vs. Biollante** (1989) - A mutant plant creature is created from Godzilla's cells.
- ☐ **Godzilla vs. King Ghidorah** (1991) - Features a convoluted plot involving time travel and the creation of King Ghidorah.
- ☐ **Godzilla vs. Mothra** (1992) - Mothra returns to battle Godzilla.
- ☐ **Godzilla vs. Mechagodzilla II** (1993) - Mechagodzilla is created to defend against Godzilla.
- ☐ **Godzilla vs. Space Godzilla** (1994) - Godzilla's cosmic clone arrives on Earth.
- ☐ **Godzilla vs. Destoroyah** (1995) - The series concludes with Godzilla's death.

- • **LEGENDARY PICTURES' MONSTERVERSE**
  - ☐ **Godzilla** (2014) – Legendary reboot of atomic kaiju.
  - ☐ **Kong: Skull Island** (2017) – Vietnam-era soldiers confront a primal Kong. This film re-establishes Kong as a protector of Skull Island in the 1970s. It serves as an origin story for Kong and sets up his inclusion in a shared cinematic universe with Godzilla.
  - ☐ **Godzilla: King of the Monsters** (2019) – Monster mash: Ghidorah, Mothra, Rodan.
  - ☐ **Godzilla vs. Kong** (2021) – Titans clash in neon-soaked mayhem.
  - ☐ **Godzilla x Kong: The New Empire** (2024) - Godzilla and Kong must team up to stop a new threat from the Hollow Earth.
  - ☐ **Godzilla x Kong: Supernova** (2027) - A new installment in the MonsterVerse is currently in production.

- • **TOHO'S REIWA ERA**
  - ☐ **Shin Godzilla** (2016) – Political satire meets grotesque kaiju evolution.
  - ☐ **Godzilla: Planet of the Monsters** (2017) - The first film in a trilogy of anime movies that depict a future Earth overrun by kaiju.
  - ☐ **Godzilla: City on the Edge of Battle** (2018) - The second anime film, in which the humans return to Earth to find it further changed and a new threat has emerged.
  - ☐ **Godzilla: The Planet Eater** (2018) - The third anime film concludes the story with the arrival of King Ghidorah.
  - ☐ **Godzilla Minus One** (2023) - Set in postwar Japan, this award-winning film returns to the original tone of Godzilla as a terrifying, destructive force.

Godzilla Through the Ages: From Showa to MonsterVerse

Few figures in cinema embody the shifting anxieties of modern history quite like Godzilla. Born in 1954 out of nuclear fire and national trauma, the King of the Monsters has lumbered across screens for seventy years, reinventing himself with every cultural tide. Each era of Godzilla is less a sequel chain than a cultural mirror: sometimes camp, sometimes cosmic allegory, sometimes blockbuster spectacle. To watch Godzilla chronologically is to watch the 20th and 21st centuries wrestle with power, disaster, and myth.

The Showa Era (1954–1975): From Terror to Hero
Godzilla's debut in *Gojira* (1954, dir. Ishirō Honda) was no mere monster movie. It was a national exorcism, a metaphor for Hiroshima and Nagasaki. The blackened cityscapes, radiation scars, and solemn tone positioned Godzilla as both dragon and mushroom cloud, unstoppable and indifferent. Yet as sequels multiplied, tone shifted. By the mid-1960s, the King of the Monsters had become a Saturday-matinee hero, battling foes like King Ghidorah and Megalon with pro-wrestling bravado. Showa Godzilla is elastic: at once tragic allegory and camp mascot. To watch these films is to see postwar Japan healing, turning fear into colorful fantasy.

The Heisei Series (1984–1995): Continuity and Consequence
After a nine-year hiatus, *The Return of Godzilla* (1984) rebooted the franchise with sobriety. Gone was the camp; in its place, a darker continuity where each film followed the next. This Godzilla was elemental force — neither savior nor villain, but an ecological disaster made flesh. Films like *Godzilla vs. Biollante* (1989) and *Godzilla vs. Destoroyah* (1995) paired nuclear dread with bioethics and genetic manipulation. The Heisei cycle is sleek, consistent, and operatic, its special effects more advanced, its tone more tragic. Where Showa turned terror into play, Heisei re-anchored Godzilla as a myth of consequence.

The Millennium Era (1999–2004): Experiments in Reinvention
Unlike Heisei's serialized arc, the Millennium films embraced variety. With the exception of a brief duology (*Godzilla Against Mechagodzilla* and *Tokyo S.O.S.*), each entry was a standalone reimagining. *Godzilla 2000* offered a high-tech remix; *Godzilla, Mothra and King Ghidorah: Giant Monsters All-Out Attack* re-cast him as an ancient spirit of vengeance; *Final Wars* (2004) turned into an outrageous kaiju free-for-all. This era is less about continuity than creativity, each director trying on a new mask for an old god. Expect tonal swings, bold experimentation, and a sense that Godzilla can be whatever Japan needs him to be in the moment.

American Adaptations: From Zilla to the MonsterVerse

Hollywood's relationship with Godzilla has been uneven. Roland Emmerich's 1998 *Godzilla* re-imagined the creature as a mutated iguana rampaging through New York. A film panned for misunderstanding the character but still notable as America's first full attempt. Redemption came with Legendary Pictures' *MonsterVerse* (2014–present), beginning with Gareth Edwards' *Godzilla*. Here, kaiju became "Titans," godlike beings locked in ancient combat. Films like *Godzilla: King of the Monsters* (2019) and *Godzilla vs. Kong* (2021) framed them less as allegories and more as superhero-scale myths. These films deliver Hollywood gloss: massive destruction, high-budget spectacle, and an interlinked universe echoing Marvel's template.

The Reiwa Era (2016–present): Reinvention and Reflection

Toho's return with *Shin Godzilla* (2016, dir. Hideaki Anno) jolted the franchise into new relevance. Gone was the cuddly kaiju; this Godzilla was grotesque, mutating mid-film, a living embodiment of bureaucratic paralysis and disaster mismanagement after Fukushima. The Reiwa era embraces auteur vision, bold allegory, and experimentation. Most recently, *Godzilla Minus One* (2023) stripped the monster back to his atomic roots, reframing him against Japan's postwar despair. These films are daring, often political, and unafraid to let Godzilla be terrifying again.

How to Watch, What to Expect

- **Showa Era:** Start for history, charm, and the joy of rubber-suit spectacle.
- **Heisei Series:** For continuity and tragedy, a serialized myth cycle.
- **Millennium Era:** For variety, bold experiments, and genre mash-ups.
- **MonsterVerse:** For Hollywood's epic scope and shared-universe thrills.
- **Reiwa Era:** For modern reinvention, allegory, and cinematic daring.

Across seventy years, Godzilla has been villain, hero, guardian, apocalypse, and mirror. Each incarnation teaches us less about the monster himself than about the people watching him. To trace his universes is to trace history itself: the bomb, the Cold War, the blockbuster, the disaster, and the ever-present fear that nature, once stirred, will not be tamed.

- ☐ **Cult of the Cobra** (1955) - American G.I.s who trespass on a Hindu ceremony are hunted down by a beautiful woman who has the power to transform herself into a cobra.
- ☐ **This Island Earth** (1955) - Aliens come to Earth seeking scientists to help them in their war. Based on the Raymond F Jones' novel of the same name. This film has been referenced in various other productions such as *E.T.* and *Mars Attacks!*
- ☐ **Day the World Ended** (1955) – Directed by Roger Corman. In a post-Apocalyptic world after an atomic war seven disparate people find themselves in a protected valley in the home of a survivalist and his beautiful daughter.
    - • **ROGER CORMAN UNIVERSE**
        - ☐ **It Conquered the World** (1956) - A story about an alien invasion from Venus, also featuring a Paul Blaisdell creature and often cited as another classic Corman production.
        - ☐ **The She-Creature** (1956) - Features a monster conjured through hypnotic regression, also from AIP and featuring another of Blaisdell's creature designs.
        - ☐ **A Bucket of Blood** (1959) - A dark comedy horror film about a beatnik busboy who becomes a serial killer after accidentally killing and covering an animal in clay, also directed by Corman.
- ☐ **The Mole People** (1956) - A party of archaeologists discovers the remnants of a mutant five-millennia-old Sumerian civilization living beneath a glacier atop a mountain in Mesopotamia. In March 2023, Universal acquired a new pitch for a revamp of the 1956 horror film. Robert Kirkman (*The Walking Dead*) and Dave Alpert are producing through their company, Skybound Entertainment.
    - • **SIMILAR FILMS**
        - ☐ **The Kiler Shrews** (1959) - On an isolated island, a small group of people is terrorized by giant voracious shrews during a hurricane.
            - • **ADAPTIONS**
                - ☐ **Return of the Killer Shrews** (2012) - A low-budget sequel was released more than 50 years after the original. It features a returning cast member, James Best, who played Thorne Sherman in the original film. The sequel follows a reality TV crew on the same island, where they are attacked by the offspring of the original killer shrews.
- ☐ **Earth vs. The Flying Saucers** (1956) - Extraterrestrials traveling in high-tech flying saucers contact a scientist as part of a plan to enslave the inhabitants of Earth. Later films, such as *Independence Day* (1996), echoed the visual and narrative cues of *Earth vs. the Flying Saucers*, particularly the destruction of Washington, D.C., by alien spacecraft.

- • **RAY HARRYHOUSEN COLLECTION:** These films are known for their groundbreaking stop-motion effects.
    - ☐ **The Beast from 20,000 Fathoms** (1953) – A ferocious dinosaur awakened by an Arctic atomic test terrorizes the North Atlantic and, ultimately, New York City.
    - ☐ **It Came from Beneath the Sea** (1955) – A giant, radioactive octopus rises from the Philippine Trench to terrorize the North American Pacific Coast.
    - ☐ **20 Million Miles to Earth** (1957) – The first U.S. spaceship to Venus crash-lands off the coast of Sicily on its return trip. A dangerous, lizard-like creature comes with it and quickly grows gigantic.
    - ☐ **Jason and the Argonauts** (1963) - The legendary Greek hero leads a team of intrepid adventurers in a perilous quest for the legendary Golden Fleece.
- ☐ **I Was a Teenage Werewolf** (1957) - A hypnotherapist uses a temperamental teenager as a guinea pig for a serum which transforms him into a vicious werewolf.
    - • **AIP TEEN MONSTER FILMS**
        - ☐ **I Was a Teenage Frankenstein** (1957) - This film features a teenager who is transformed into a monster by a mad scientist. Actor Whit Bissell plays a similar mad-scientist type in both films.

- ☐ **Blood of Dracula** (1957) - Under hypnosis, a young woman turns into a vampire. This retelling of the werewolf story follows a teenage girl who is transformed into a vampire-like creature.
- ☐ **How to Make a Monster** (1958) - A makeup artist is fired from American International Pictures and hypnotizes two actors in their "Teenage Werewolf" and "Teenage Frankenstein" makeup to kill studio executives.
- • **ADAPTIONS**
  - ☐ **Teen Wolf** (1985) - This is a comedic take on the theme of a high school werewolf, starring Michael J. Fox. It is not an official remake or adaptation.
    - • **SEQUELS**
      - ☐ **Teen Wolf Too** (1987) - This is the sequel to the 1985 comedy, starring Jason Bateman as the original hero's cousin.
  - ☐ **Chillerama** (2011) - This comedy horror anthology film features a segment titled "*I Was a Teenage Werebear*," a gay spoof of the original.
- ☐ **The Monster that Challenged the World** (1957) - When a horde of prehistoric mollusk monsters enter the canal system of the California's Imperial Valley and terrorize the populace.
- ☐ **I Married a Monster from Outer Space** (1958) - Aliens arrive on Earth to possess the bodies of humans. One of their first victims is a young man, whose new wife soon realizes something is wrong with him.
- ☐ **It! The Terror from Beyond Space** (1958) - A mission sent to rescue the first manned expedition to Mars is invaded by an unknown life form, which stows away on the rescue ship. Its story and formula are widely cited as a major inspiration for the classic 1979 film *Alien*.
- ☐ **The Birds** (1963) - A wealthy San Francisco socialite pursues a potential boyfriend to a small Northern California town that slowly takes a turn for the bizarre when birds of all kinds suddenly begin to attack people.
  - • **SIMILAR THEMES**
    - ☐ **The Day of the Triffids** (1963) - After an unusual meteor shower leaves most of the human population blind, a merchant navy officer must find a way to conquer tall, aggressive plants which are feeding on people and animals.
    - ☐ **Long Weekend** (1978) - When a suburban couple go camping for the weekend at a remote beach, they discover that nature isn't in an accommodating mood.
      - • **ADAPTIONS**
        - ☐ **Long Weekend** (2008) - This is a direct remake of the original Australian film, also known as *Nature's Grave*. It updates the story and was directed by Jamie Blanks.
    - ☐ **Razorback** (1984) - Another Australian "Ozploitation" horror film, this movie features a giant boar terrorizing the outback and explores the unforgiving nature of the Australian wilderness.

"It could be the most terrifying motion picture I have ever made!"—

"...and remember, the next scream you hear may be your own!"

ALFRED HITCHCOCK'S "The Birds" TECHNICOLOR

ROD TAYLOR · JESSICA TANDY SUZANNE PLESHETTE *and introducing* 'TIPPI' HEDREN *Based on Daphne Du Maurier's Classic Suspense Story!*

A Fascinating New Personality

Screenplay by EVAN HUNTER · Directed by ALFRED HITCHCOCK

- ☐ **Dogora** (1964, Japan) - An amorphous cellular life-form descends from the atmosphere to consume carbon in the form of diamonds. It uniquely blends the monster movie genre with a crime caper, creating a somewhat uneven but memorable narrative. The film was directed by Ishirō Honda and featured special effects by Eiji Tsuburaya, the famous duo behind *Godzilla*.
- ☐ **City in the Sea (War-Gods of the Deep)** (1965) - In 1903 Cornwall, a group of locals discover an underwater city, dating back to 1803, that hides a society of smugglers and aquatic creatures. It shares similar lost world themes such as *20,000 Leagues Under the Sea, Captain Nemo and the Underwater City* and *Latitude Zero*.

☐ **Gamera: The Giant Monster** (1965) – From out of the arctic comes a gigantic flying, fire-breathing turtle that sets its sights on destroying Tokyo.

- • **SEQUELS**
  - ☐ **Gamera vs. Barugon** (1966) - Gamera battles the monstrous lizard Barugon.
  - ☐ **Gamera vs. Gyas** (1967) - Introduced Gamera's most recurring foe, the supersonic flying reptile Gyaos.
  - ☐ **Gamera vs. Viras** (1968) - Gamera fights against a race of squid-like aliens.
  - ☐ **Gamera vs. Guiron** (1969) – Gamera battles the blade-headed monster Guiron on an alien planet.
  - ☐ **Gamera vs. Jiger** (1970) – Gamera faces a demonic beast from Wester Island.
  - ☐ **Gamera vs. Zigra** (1971) – Gamera fights an alien fish monster.
  - ☐ **Gamera: Super Monster** (1980) - A low-budget film made mostly of stock footage from the previous movies, released after the original studio went bankrupt.
- • **ADAPTIONS** This reboot series returned the franchise to a darker, more serious tone, earning critical acclaim and influencing the kaiju genre.
  - ☐ **Gamera: Guardian of the Universe** (1995): A modern reimagining of Gamera's origin, where he is created by the Atlanteans to fight the Gyaos.
  - ☐ **Gamera 2: Attack of Legion** (1996): Gamera must defend Earth from an invasion of insect-like extraterrestrials.
  - ☐ **Gamera 3: Revenge of Iris** (1999): The trilogy concludes with Gamera's darkest and most brutal battle against the creature Iris.

☐ **The War of the Gargantuas** (1966, Japan) – A giant, cannibalistic humanoid's rampage through Tokyo is halted by his more docile twin, but neither their reunion nor their scientist caretakers can prevent their eventual duel. Director Shusuke Kaneko cited *The War of the Gargantuas* as a source of inspiration for his acclaimed trilogy of Gamera films.

- • **ADAPTIONS**
  - ☐ **Frankenstein Conquers the World** (1965) - The film's Japanese title is *Frankenstein's Monsters: Sanda vs. Gaira*. The 1966 film was originally conceived as a direct sequel, but the connection was made "somewhat fuzzy" in the final version to make it a standalone feature. The American cut removed all direct references to the original Frankenstein monster.
- • **INFLUENCED**
  - ☐ **Kill Bill: Volume 2** (2004) - Director Quentin Tarantino, a fan of the film, paid homage to it with a fight scene that he dubbed the "War of the Blonde Gargantuas". The scene also includes a miniature shot of Tokyo, inspired by the special effects of *Gargantuas*.

- ☐ **Attack on Titan Films** (2015) - The Japanese manga and live-action films feature monstrous, giant humanoids. Director Shinji Higuchi confirmed that characters from *Attack on Titan* were based on the Gargantuas.
- ☐ **Island of Terror** (1966) - An isolated remote island community is threatened by an attack by tentacled silicates which liquefy and digest bone and tissue.
  - • **SIMILAR THEMES**
    - ☐ **Night of the Big Heat** (1967) - This film, also directed by Terence Fisher and produced by Planet Films, shares a similar setting and premise. Instead of bone-sucking creatures, an isolated island community is threatened by aliens that thrive in extreme heat.
    - ☐ **The Earth Dies Screaming** (1964) - Another British science fiction film featuring a small group of people trying to survive a mysterious alien invasion.
    - ☐ **Fiend Without a Face** (1958) - This movie, also starring Peter Cushing, involves a scientific experiment gone wrong that creates invisible, brain-eating monsters.
- ☐ **Night of the Lepus** (1972) – Killer giant rabbits terrorize the countryside.
- ☐ **Deliverance** (1972) - Intent on seeing the Cahulawassee River before it's dammed and turned into a lake, outdoor fanatic Lewis Medlock takes his friends on a canoeing trip they'll never forget into the dangerous American back-country.
  - • **SURVIVAL HORROR IN ISOLATED NATURE**
    - ☐ **Wolf Creek** (2005) – Inspired by true events, three backpackers stranded in the Australian outback are plunged inside a hellish nightmare of insufferable torture by a sadistic psychopathic local.
      - • **SEQUELS**
        - ☐ **Wolf Creek 2** (2013) - John Jarratt returned as the sadistic serial killer Mick Taylor. The sequel featured a higher body count and a significant tonal shift towards dark humor and action, following a new set of backpackers who fall victim to the killer.
    - ☐ **The Descent** (2005, UK) – A caving expedition goes wrong when the women exploring the tunnels are trapped and hunted by flesh-eating predators.
      - • **SEQUELS**
        - ☐ **The Descent Part 2** (2009) - This sequel picks up where the original left off, following the sole survivor, Sarah, who is suffering from amnesia. She is forced to return to the caves with a rescue team, only to discover the horrifying truth of what happened and confront the "crawlers" once again.
    - ☐ **Eden Creek** (2008, UK) - When a couple goes to a remote lake for a romantic getaway, their quiet weekend is shattered by an aggressive group of kids. Rowdiness quickly turns to rage as the teens terrorize them, and a weekend outing becomes a battle for survival.
    - ☐ **Frozen** (2010) - Three skiers stranded on a chairlift are forced to make life-or-death choices, which prove more perilous than staying put and freezing to death.
    - ☐ **In Fear** (2013, UK) - Driving to a music festival in Ireland, a new couple become lost and are then set upon by a tormentor with an unknown motive.
    - ☐ **Cub** (2014) - Over-imaginative 12-year-old Sam heads off to the woods to summer scout camp with his pack convinced he will encounter a monster...and he does.
    - ☐ **Harpoon** (2019, Canada) - Rivalries, dark secrets, and sexual tension emerge when three best friends find themselves stranded on a yacht in the middle of the ocean desperate for survival.
    - ☐ **Let It Snow** (2020) - Separated from her fiancé after sneaking onto a restricted slope, Mia, a free-riding snowboarder, must survive not only against nature, but also the masked snowmobile rider in black who is out for her blood.
    - ☐ **The Rental** (2020) - Two couples rent a vacation home for what should be a celebratory weekend get-away.
    - ☐ **Hunter Hunter** (2020) - Joseph and his family live in the remote wilderness as fur trappers, but their tranquility is threatened when they think they are being hunted by the return of a rogue wolf, and Joseph leaves them behind to track it.

- **The Boy Behind the Door** (2020) - After Bobby and his best friend Kevin are kidnapped and taken to a strange house in the middle of nowhere, Bobby manages to escape. But then he hears Kevin's screams for help and realizes he can't leave his friend behind.
    - **REMAKE**
        - **Monster** (2023) - Produced by the Indonesian company Falcon Pictures, this is an official, non-English-language remake of *The Boy Behind the Door*.
- **The Trip** (2021) - A dysfunctional couple head to a remote cabin to reconnect, but each has intentions to kill the other. Before they can carry out their plans, unexpected visitors arrive and they face a greater danger.
- **Don't Say Its Name** (2021) - Shortly after Kharis Redwater, a native anti-mining activist, dies in a hit-and-run, a series of murders occur on the isolated reserve where she lived.
- **A Wounded Fawn** (2022) - A serial killer brings an unsuspecting new victim on a weekend getaway to add another body to his ever-growing count. She's buying into his faux charms, and he's eagerly lusting for blood. What could possibly go wrong?
- **Loop Track** (2023, New Zealand) - an wants to get as far away from humanity as possible and heads into the New Zealand bush, but a four day journey turns into a fight for survival.
- **Jaws** (1975) – When a killer shark unleashes chaos on a beach community, it's up to a local sheriff, a marine biologist, and an old seafarer to hunt the beast down. **Misquote:** "We're going to need a bigger boat." **Actual**

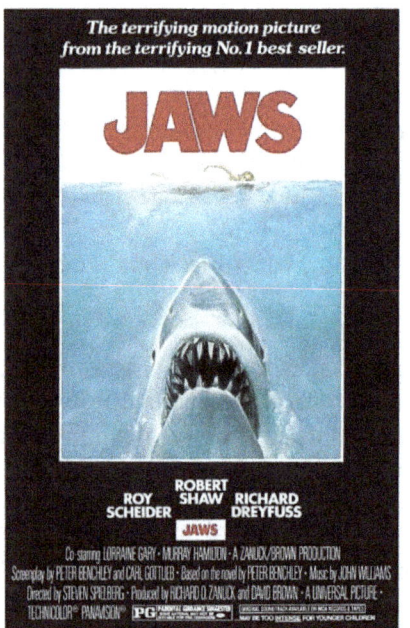

Quote: "*You're* going to need a bigger boat." That quote wasn't actually in the script and was improvised. Author Peter Benchley plays the role of a TV reporter in *Jaws*. Benchley was reportedly thrown off set after continually arguing with Spielberg about the film's ending.

- **SEQUELS**
- **Jaws 2** (1978) – Four years after the first attack, Police Chief Martin Brody (Roy Scheider) must again convince Amity Island officials that another, even larger great white shark is terrorizing the community. The film is known for the memorable tagline, "Just when you thought it was safe to go back in the water...".
- **Jaws 3-D** (1983) – Capitalizing on the 3D craze of the 1980s, this installment follows the now-grown Brody sons, Mike and Sean, at a new Florida sea-themed park called SeaWorld. When a young great white is captured, its 35-foot mother breaks into the park to wreak havoc. The film is remembered for its cheesy 3D effects and poor shark animatronics.
- **Jaws: The Revenge** (1987) - The final installment of the franchise features a now-widowed Ellen Brody (Lorraine Gary) who believes a great white shark is hunting her family out of revenge. The plot, which retroactively ignores the events of *Jaws 3-D*, was widely panned and is often cited as one of the worst sequels of all time.

- **WATER-BASED HORRORS**
    - **Open Water** (2003) – Stranded divers face realistic survival horror. It was inspired by the real-life disappearance of Tom and Eileen Lonergan.
        - **SEQUELS**
            - **Open Water 2: Adrift** (2006) - Released on DVD, this German-made film is not connected to the plot of the first movie. It follows a new group of friends on a yacht who, after jumping into the water, realize they've forgotten to lower the ladder, leaving them stranded.
            - **Open Water 3: Cage Dive** (2017) - This installment is filmed in a "found footage" style and focuses on three friends on a cage-diving excursion in Australia. Like the second film, its story and characters are completely separate from the original.
    - **The Reef** (2010) - Another film inspired by real events, this story focuses on a group of friends whose yacht capsizes, leaving them to swim for their lives while being stalked by a great white shark.

☐ **The Shallows** (2016) – Starring Blake Lively. A mere 200 yards from shore, surfer Nancy is attacked by a great white shark, with her short journey to safety becoming the ultimate contest of wills.

☐ **47 Meters Down** (2017) - Two sisters get trapped in a shark cage at the bottom of the ocean. The film builds intense claustrophobic tension with the looming presence of sharks.

☐ **The Meg** (2018) – Prehistoric Megalodon terrorizes the ocean.
- **SEQUELS**
  - ☐ **Meg 2: The Trench** (2023) - Directed by Ben Wheatley, this sequel brings back Taylor to face not one, but multiple, larger megalodons, in addition to other prehistoric creatures. Despite negative critical reviews, the film was a box office success.

☐ **Dangerous Animals** (2025) - When Zephyr, a savvy and free-spirited surfer, is abducted by a shark-obsessed serial killer and held captive on his boat, she must figure out how to escape before he carries out a ritualistic feeding to the sharks below.

☐ **Kingdom of Spiders** (1977) - In rural Arizona, countless killer tarantulas are migrating through a farm town, killing every living thing in their path. The town's veterinarian will do everything in his power to survive the onslaught.
- **SIMILAR THEMES**
  - ☐ **Arachnophobia** (1990) - A new species of South American killer spider hitches a lift to a California town in a coffin and starts to breed, leaving a trail of deaths that puzzle and terrify young Dr. Ross Jennings, who is newly arrived in town with his family. This film's story of aggressive, venomous spiders attacking a small town has narrative similarities to *Kingdom of the Spiders*. Producer Igo Kantor noted the resemblance but ultimately decided not to sue.
  - ☐ **Eight Legged Freaks** (2002) – Toxic waste mutates spiders into giant killers.
  - ☐ **Infested** (2023, France) - Residents of a rundown French apartment building battle against an army of deadly, rapidly reproducing spiders.

☐ **Piranha** (1978) – Carnivorous fish swarm swimmers in this B-horror gem. When flesh-eating piranhas are accidentally released into a summer resort's rivers, the guests become their next meal.
- **SEQUELS & ADAPTIONS**
  - ☐ **Piranha II: The Spawning** (1982) - A sequel directed by James Cameron in his feature film directorial debut. The plot escalates the threat with genetically engineered flying piranhas terrorizing a Caribbean resort.
  - ☐ **Piranha 3D** (2010) – Directed by Alexandre Aja, this remake is less satirical and more of a gore-filled spectacle. Prehistoric piranhas are unleashed by an underwater tremor during spring break in Lake Victoria, Arizona, resulting in a bloodbath. The film was a critical and commercial success.
  - ☐ **Piranha 3DD** (2012) - This sequel to the 2010 film has the piranhas invading a water park. It received poor reviews and failed commercially.

☐ **Alien** (1979) – A parasitic lifeform evolves into the ultimate predator aboard a spaceship. **Memorable tagline:** "In space, no one can hear you scream."
- **ADAPTIONS & SEQUELS**
  - ☐ **Aliens** (1986) - A more action-oriented sequel directed by James Cameron. Decades after surviving the Nostromo incident, Ellen Ripley is sent out to re-establish contact with a terraforming colony but finds herself battling the Alien Queen and her offspring.
  - ☐ **Alien 3** (1992) - The dark and divisive third installment directed by David Fincher. Returning from LV-426, Ellen Ripley crash-lands on the maximum-security prison Fiorina 161, where she discovers that she has unwittingly brought along an unwelcome visitor.
  - ☐ **Alien Resurrection** (1997) - Directed by Jean-Pierre Jeunet. Two centuries after her death, a powerful human/alien hybrid clone of Ellen Ripley aids a crew of space pirates in stopping the aliens from reaching Earth.
  - ☐ **Alien vs. Predator** (2004) - The first crossover film, exploring the Predator hunting ritual involving Xenomorphs. During an archaeological expedition on Bouvetøya Island in Antarctica, a team of archaeologists and other scientists find themselves caught up in a battle between the two legends. Soon, the team realize that only one species can win.

- ☐ **Alien vs. Predator: Requiem** (2007) - Continues the story from the previous crossover film. Warring Alien and Predator races descend on a rural Colorado town, where unsuspecting residents must band together for any chance of survival.
- ☐ **Prometheus** (2012) - Explores the origins of humanity and the Engineers, a giant humanoid species that created the Xenomorphs. Following clues to the origin of mankind, a team finds a structure on a distant moon, but they soon realize they are not alone.
- ☐ **Alien: Covenant** (2017) - Continues the story from *Prometheus* and further explores the origins of the Xenomorphs. The crew of a colony ship, bound for a remote planet, discover an uncharted paradise with a threat beyond their imagination, and must attempt a harrowing escape.
- ☐ **Alien: Romulus** (2024) - This standalone film is set between the events of the original *Alien* and *Aliens*. It was directed by Fede Álvarez, and a sequel is already in development. While scavenging the deep ends of a derelict space station, a group of young space colonists come face to face with the most terrifying life form in the universe.

☐ **Alligator** (1980) – A pet baby alligator is flushed down a toilet and survives in the city sewers. Twelve years later, it grows to an enormous size thanks to a diet of discarded laboratory dogs injected with growth hormones. Now, humans have entered the menu.
- • **SEQUELS & SIMILAR FILMS**
  - ☐ **Alligator II: The Mutation** (1991) - This direct-to-video sequel was released 11 years after the original. A giant alligator makes a city lake his new feeding ground and must be stopped before he breaks out into the surroundings.
  - ☐ **Lake Placid** (1999) – Massive crocodile terrorizes rural Maine.
  - ☐ **Rogue** (2007, Australia) – Killer crocodile stalks tourists.
  - ☐ **Black Water** (2007) - A boat tour of a mangrove swamp turns into a fight for survival when a group of people are attacked by a ferocious saltwater crocodile.
    - • **SEQUELS**
      - ☐ **Black Water: Abyss** (2020, Australia) – Divers trapped with crocodile in flooded cave.
  - ☐ **Crawl** (2019) – Gigantic alligators swarm around a young woman and her father as hurricane floodwaters engulf their home.

☐ **An American Werewolf in London** (1981) - Two American college students on a walking tour of Britain are attacked by a werewolf that none of the locals will admit exists.
- • **ADAPTIONS & SEQUELS**
  - ☐ **An American Werewolf in Paris** (1997) - This loose sequel follows three American tourists in Paris, one of whom is bitten by a werewolf after a bungee jump from the Eiffel Tower. It was directed by Anthony Waller and features a completely different cast and tone from the original.

☐ **Q: The Winged Serpent** (1982) – Ancient serpent god attacks New York City.
- • **ADAPTIONS & SEQUELS**
  - ☐ **Cry of the Winged Serpent** (2005) - Directed by Jim Wynorski and executive produced by Roger Corman, it was made for television and aired on the Syfy channel. The film features a giant, flying, reptilian creature.

☐ **Cujo** (1983) - Cujo, a friendly St. Bernard, contracts rabies and conducts a reign of terror on a small American town. In March 2025, it was announced that Netflix is developing a new cinematic adaptation of Stephen King's novel.
- • **SIMILAR FILMS**
  - ☐ **White Dog** (1982) - A trainer attempts to retrain a vicious dog that's been raised to attack black people.
  - ☐ **Man's Best Friend** (1993) - A genetically engineered dog escapes from the science facility where it was created. A family takes it in unaware of its deadly instincts which soon emerge. The scientist who created the dog tries to find it before it's too late.

- **Gremlins** (1984) – Cute Mogwai spawns mischievous killer creatures. The original 1984 film was loosely inspired by Roald Dahl's 1943 book, which featured mischievous creatures called gremlins.
  - **SEQUELS**
    - **Gremlins 2: The New Batch** (1990) - The official sequel to the 1984 film Gremlins, released by Warner Bros. The Gremlins are back, and this time, they've taken control of a New York City media mogul's high-tech skyscraper.
    - **Gremlins 3: Dawn of Desmond** (2021) - When 'Gremlins' and 'Gremlins 2' star Gizmo is killed by a gremlin-terrorist hybrid, his half-human, half-gremlin son sets out to take revenge for his fallen superstar father.
- **Silver Bullet** (1985) - In a small town, brutal killings start to plague the close-knit community. Marty Coslaw, a paraplegic boy, is convinced the murders are the doings of a werewolf. The film was adapted from the 1983 novella *Cycle of the Werewolf*, written by Stephen King.
- **Rawhead Rex** (1986) - An ancient creature called Rawhead is awakened from its slumber near an Irish village and goes on a rampage killing anyone in sight. The film is based on a short story of the same name by Clive Barker, which appeared in the third volume of his *Books of Blood* series. Clive Barker hated the film. While he wrote the screenplay and it is mostly faithful to the original story, he was very unhappy with some of the acting and especially with Rawhead Rex's ogre-like design, as he intended the monster to look like a giant phallus. This dissatisfaction inspired him to take a more central role when making *Hellraiser*.
  - **BOOK OF BLOOD ANTHOLOGY MOVIES**
    - **The Yattering and Jack** (1987) - An episode of the television series *Tales from the Darkside* adapts Barker's darkly comedic short story about a demon who tries to torment an oblivious victim.
    - **Candyman** (1992) – Urban Gothic of legend, decay, and haunted spaces. The 1992 film was a loose adaptation of Clive Barker's short story "The Forbidden," which was set in Liverpool, England, and explored themes of class struggle.
      - **SEQUELS**
        - **Candyman: Farewell to the Flesh** (1995) - A direct sequel to the 1992 film, this entry moves the setting to New Orleans to explore more of Candyman's backstory.
        - **Candyman: Day of the Dead** (1999) - The third film in the original trilogy follows the adult daughter of Candyman's lover in Los Angeles as she is targeted by the urban legend.
        - **Candyman** (2021) - A direct sequel to the 1992 original, this film disregards the 1990s sequels. It returns to a gentrified Cabrini-Green and recontextualizes the legend of Candyman as a hive mind connected to multiple victims of racist violence. The 2021 sequel of the same name and other sequels are based on the film's characters rather than directly on Barker's story.
    - **Lord of Illusions** (1995) - Directed by Clive Barker, this film also explores black magic, ritual, and a supernatural presence tied to a hidden cult. Based on the short story "The Last Illusion" from Volume Six.
    - **Quicksilver Highway** (1997) - The Barker segment is a bizarre and comedic tale about a man whose disembodied hands start a revolution. This TV movie anthology features an adaptation of Clive Barker's "The Body Politic" from Volume Four, alongside a story by Stephen King.
    - **The Midnight Meat Train** (2008) - A photographer's obsessive pursuit of dark subject matter leads him into the path of a serial killer who stalks late night commuters, ultimately butchering them in the most gruesome ways. The film is a direct adaptation of Clive Barker's 1984 short story of the same name, which was published in Volume One of his *Books of Blood* collection.
    - **Dread** (2009) - A psychological horror film about a university student's sadistic project to document what people fear most. The film closely follows the dark, character-driven story of the original text. Based on the short story "Dread" from Volume Two.
    - **Book of Blood** (2009, UK) - A paranormal investigator discovers a house at the intersection of "highways" for the dead. It follows a man who becomes a living book written in blood. A low-budget British horror film adapting the framing stories, "The Book of Blood" and "On Jerusalem Street," from Volume One and Volume Six, respectively.

- ☐ **Books of Blood** (2020) - This Hulu original feature is a loose anthology adapting some of the original stories, including elements from "The Book of Blood," while weaving in new material. It is not to be confused with the 2009 film of the same name.
- ☐ **Critters** (1986) – A group of small but vicious alien creatures called Crites escape from an alien prison transport vessel and land near a small farm town on earth, pursued by two shape-shifting bounty hunters.
  - • **SEQUELS**
    - ☐ **Critters 2: The Main Course** (1988) – Eggs of the small but voracious alien creatures called Crites are left behind on earth and, after hatching, set their appetites on the small farm town of Grover's Bend.
    - ☐ **Critters 3** (1991) – Early Leonardo DiCaprio film.
    - ☐ **Critters 4** (1992) – After being cryogenically frozen and waking up on a space station in the near future, the Critters aim to have the unwitting crew for lunch.
- ☐ **Predator** (1987) - A team of commandos on a mission in a Central American jungle find themselves hunted by an extraterrestrial warrior.
  - • **SEQUELS**
    - ☐ **Predator 2** (1990) - This sequel moves the setting from the jungle to the concrete jungle of Los Angeles, where a new Predator hunts amidst a brutal gang war.
    - ☐ **Predators** (2010) - A new group of human killers and mercenaries find themselves hunted for sport on an alien planet that serves as a game preserve for a tribe of Super Predators.
    - ☐ **The Predator** (2018) - In this film, a traumatized group of soldiers and a scientist must stop two different kinds of Predators from invading Earth.
    - ☐ **Prey** (2022) - A prequel set in 1719, this film follows a young Comanche woman who must defend her tribe from a Predator with more primitive weaponry.
    - ☐ **Predator: Badlands** (2025) – Another upcoming film from *Prey* director Dan Trachenberg. A young Predator outcast from his clan finds an unlikely ally on his journey in search of the ultimate adversary.
- ☐ **Pumpkinhead** (1988) – After a tragic accident, a man conjures up a towering, vengeful demon called Pumpkinhead to destroy a group of unsuspecting teenagers.
  - • **SEQUELS**
    - ☐ **Pumpkinhead II: Blood Wings** (1994) - This direct-to-video sequel has no direct character connections to the original film's story. Instead, it revolves around teenagers who resurrect the vengeful demon.
    - ☐ **Pumpkinhead: Ashes to Ashes** (2006) - In this made-for-television film, original star Lance Henriksen reprises his role as Ed Harley, whose mummified body is used by a witch to summon Pumpkinhead.
    - ☐ **Pumpkinhead: Blood Feud** (2007) - A made-for-television movie that pits two feuding families against one another. It features a warning from the ghost of Ed Harley about the demonic curse.
  - • **SIMILAR FILMS**
    - ☐ **DARK NIGHT OF THE SCARECROW** (1981) - In a small Southern town, four vigilantes wrongfully execute a mentally-challenged man, but after the court sets them free mysterious "accidents" begin to kill them off one by one.
      - • **SEQUELS**
        - ☐ **Dark Night of the Scarecrow 2** (2022) - Released more than 40 years after the original, the film follows a single mother and her son who move to the same small town where the events of the first film took place.
    - ☐ **Scarecrows** (1988) - his film features a group of criminals who parachute into a field of killer scarecrows after a heist gone wrong. While more overtly campy and action-oriented, it follows the killer scarecrow trope.
- ☐ **Leviathan** (1989) –Perched on the hull of a wrecked Soviet freighter, a team of deep-sea miners led by head oceanographer Steven Beck comes face to face with a mutant creature that's the product of a failed genetic experiment.
- ☐ **The Relic** (1997) – A homicide detective and an anthropologist try to destroy a South American lizard-like God, who's on a people eating rampage in a Chicago museum.

Universal Classic Monsters

Universal practically invented the "studio horror brand." In the 1930s, at the height of the Great Depression, Carl Laemmle Jr. gambled on Gothic escapism and won. *Dracula* (1931) and *Frankenstein* (1931) didn't just save the studio, they crystallized horror as a profitable Hollywood genre. Drawing from European myths, Gothic novels, and Expressionist visual style, Universal forged monsters that became icons: Dracula's cape, Frankenstein's bolts, the Wolf Man's howl. These weren't just films, they were blueprints. Visual shorthand for fear that still lingers nearly a century later.

Signature Style

- **Architecture of dread:** Crumbling castles, fog-choked graveyards, candlelit laboratories.
- **Star monsters:** Bela Lugosi's aristocratic Dracula, Boris Karloff's sympathetic Frankenstein, Lon Chaney Jr.'s tragic Wolf Man, Claude Rains' invisible menace.
- **Morality plays:** Horror wrapped in melodrama, romance, and cautionary tales about ambition, desire, or fate.
- **Expressionist DNA:** Tilted shadows, jagged sets, chiaroscuro lighting, German émigré filmmakers brought their nightmares to Hollywood soundstages.

Essential Titles

- *Dracula* (1931) — Lugosi's accent, stare, and cape became the template for every vampire to follow.
- *Frankenstein* (1931) — Karloff's lumbering creature embodied both monstrosity and innocence.
- *The Mummy* (1932) — Boris Karloff again, this time as a cursed immortal, wrapping exoticism in resurrection dread.
- *The Invisible Man* (1933) — Claude Rains' mad scientist turned unseen terror into spectacle.
- *The Wolf Man* (1941) — Lon Chaney Jr. gave the werewolf myth a tragic heartbeat.
- *Creature from the Black Lagoon* (1954) — The last great Universal monster, half-man, half-fish, all Cold War allegory.

Cultural Footprint

Universal's monsters transcended their films to become cultural archetypes. They were franchised before franchising was a word. Crossing over in sequels like *House of Frankenstein* and comedy hybrids like *Abbott and Costello Meet Frankenstein*. They haunted Halloween masks, Saturday morning cartoons, Aurora model kits, and cereal boxes. Even in parody, their forms endure. Each generation rediscovers them, whether Stephen Sommers' glossy *Mummy* (1999), Guillermo del Toro citing *Creature* as inspiration, or Blumhouse resurrecting *The Invisible Man* (2020). The monsters proved horror could be serialized, marketed, and global, setting a template every studio brand has chased since.

Watchlist

A perfect Universal marathon: *Dracula* → *Frankenstein* → *Bride of Frankenstein* → *The Wolf Man* → *Creature from the Black Lagoon*. Watch the silhouettes evolve from shadowy Gothic chambers to the sleek rubber-suit spectacle of the 1950s, yet notice how each monster remains a mirror for human fear and desire.

Kaiju Expansions, 80s–90s Creature Features

- ☐ **Tremors** (1990) – Underground Graboids stalk a desert town. Natives of a small isolated town defend themselves against strange underground creatures which are killing them one by one.
  - • **SEQUELS**
    - ☐ **Tremors II: Aftershocks** (1996) – Earl Bassett, now a washed-up ex-celebrity, is hired by a Mexican oil company to eradicate a Graboid epidemic that's killing more people each day. However, the humans aren't the only one with a new battle plan.
    - ☐ **Tremors 3: Back to Perfection** (2001) – Flying "Ass Blasters" emerge.
    - ☐ **Tremors 4: The Legend Begins** (2004) – Prequel: Graboids in the Wild West.
    - ☐ **Tremors 5: Bloodlines** (2015) – Graboids hunt in Africa.
    - ☐ **Tremors: A Cold Day in Hell** (2018) – Arctic mutations of Graboids.
- ☐ **Anaconda** (1997) – Massive snake preys on documentary crew in the Amazon.
  - • **SEQUELS**
    - ☐ **Anacondas: The Hunt for the Blood Orchid** (2004) - This standalone theatrical sequel follows a new group of researchers in Borneo on the hunt for a mystical flower that grants long life.
    - ☐ **Anaconda 3: Offspring** (2008) - In this made-for-television sequel, a genetically engineered snake escapes from a research facility and must be stopped by a team of mercenaries, which includes David Hasselhoff.
    - ☐ **Anacondas: Trail of Blood** (2009) Released directly to television, this sequel continues the story of the genetically enhanced anacondas.
  - • **ADAPTIONS**
    - ☐ **Lake Placid vs. Anaconda** (2015) - This made-for-television movie is a crossover between the *Anaconda* and *Lake Placid* franchises, pitting the giant snake against a giant crocodile.
    - ☐ **Anaconda** (2024) - A Chinese remake of the original film was released in China in 2024 and internationally in early 2025.
    - ☐ **Anaconda** (2025) - A major theatrical reboot is in production starring Jack Black and Paul Rudd and is expected to be a horror-comedy reimagining of the original.
- ☐ **Deep Blue Sea** (1999) – Genetically engineered sharks outsmart scientists.
  - • **SEQUELS**
    - ☐ **Deep Blue Sea 2** (2018) - Released straight to video almost two decades after the original, this sequel follows a new group of scientists experimenting with genetically enhanced bull sharks for a pharmaceutical billionaire. Like the original, the hyper-intelligent sharks turn on their captors. This film was a box office failure and was widely panned by critics.
    - ☐ **Deep Blue Sea 3** (2020) - This third installment continues the story from the second movie. A marine biologist and her crew face a new generation of genetically modified sharks on a remote island as the creatures threaten a flourishing marine nursery. This film was also released on video on demand. In November 2023, actress Tania Raymonde confirmed that a fourth movie in the franchise is actively in development. She stated that she is set to reprise her role from the third film, though the project was delayed by the COVID-19 pandemic and the 2023 writers' and actors' strikes.
- ☐ **Komodo** (1999) – Giant Komodo dragons terrorize stranded survivors.
- ☐ **Bats** (1999) – Mutated bats descend on a small Texas town.
- ☐ **The Mummy** (1999) - At an archaeological dig in the ancient city of Hamunaptra, an American serving in the French Foreign Legion accidentally awakens a mummy who begins to wreak havoc as he searches for the reincarnation of his long-lost love. Brendan Fraser nearly died during a scene where his character is hanged. Rachel Weisz remembered, "He stopped breathing and had to be resuscitated."
  - • **SEQUELS**
    - ☐ **The Mummy Returns** (2001) - Rick and Evelyn, now married with a son, must once again face Imhotep, as well as the newly resurrected Scorpion King (Dwayne "The Rock" Johnson).
    - ☐ **The Mummy: Tomb of the Dragon Emperor** (2008) - In the third installment, the O'Connell family faces a new villain, the mummified Dragon Emperor of China (Jet Li).
    - ☐ **The Scorpion King** (2002) - A spin-off prequel focusing on the origins of the character Mathayus, which was later followed by several direct-to-video sequels.

- **Pitch Black** (2000) – Riddick battles nocturnal alien predators on a distant planet.
  - **SEQUELS**
    - **The Chronicles of Riddick** (2004) - This sequel vastly expands the lore of the *Pitch Black* universe, revealing more about Riddick's homeworld and introducing a new antagonist, the Necromongers.
    - **Riddick** (2013) - The third film brings the franchise back to its roots, focusing on Riddick's survival skills on a desolate, creature-filled planet.
    - **Riddick: Furya** (Upcoming) - A fourth live-action installment is currently in development, with Vin Diesel set to return as the title character.
- **Jeepers Creepers** (2001) – Ancient winged demon feeds every 23 years.
  - **SEQUELS**
    - **Jeepers Creepers 2** (2003) - This sequel follows a bus full of high-school students who become stranded on the Creeper's final day of feeding. It became a commercial success like the first film.
    - **Jeepers Creepers 3** (2017) - This film serves as an interquel, taking place within the events of the original 2001 film. Jonathan Breck reprised his role as the Creeper, and Gina Philips appeared in a cameo role.
    - **Jeepers Creepers: Reborn** (2022) - This film serves as a reboot of the franchise, ignoring the events of the previous sequels. It introduces new characters and a new version of the Creeper. It was widely panned by critics
- **Dog Soldiers** (2002) – Soldiers fight werewolves during training mission. Director Neil Marshall spent years attempting to produce a sequel, with the working title *Dog Soldiers 2: Underdogs*. The project was ultimately abandoned in 2024.
- **Reign of Fire** (2002) – Dragons rise, reducing Earth to scorched ruins. In a 2002 interview, star Christian Bale joked about a possible sequel, and in 2022, he again made a jesting reference to it. In 2022, co-star Matthew McConaughey hinted at a follow-up on social media, reigniting fan discussion.
- **The Host** (2006, Korea) – A monster emerges from Seoul's Han River and begins attacking people. One victim's loving family does what it can to rescue her from its clutches. The cast performed their own stunts, rigging their homes for scares under Savage's remote direction.
- **Cloverfield** (2008) – A group of friends venture deep into the streets of New York on a rescue mission during a rampaging monster attack. A direct sequel to the original 2008 film is in development. While progress has been slow, the project is still moving forward as of 2025.
  - **ADAPTIONS**
    - **10 Cloverfield Lane** (2016) - This psychological thriller follows a young woman trapped in an underground bunker by a man who claims an apocalyptic event has made the surface uninhabitable.
    - **Cloverfield Paradox** (2018) - Released on Netflix immediately after Super Bowl LII, this film reveals that a space station experiment has created tears in the space-time continuum, causing different monster events across multiple dimensions and timelines.
- **Splinter** (2008) – Parasitic spikes infect and consume human hosts.
- **Super 8** (2011) – Kids witness alien escape after train crash.
- **Attack the Block** (2011) – South London teens defend against alien invasion.
  - **BRITISH DARCOMHOR**
    - **Severance** (2006) - Another British horror-comedy involving a group of co-workers who get picked off one by one in a remote location.
    - **The Cottage** (2008, UK) – Kidnap plot turns into slasher-comedy.
    - **Doghouse** (2009) - A group of male friends on a "boys' weekend" travel to a remote village where all the women have been turned into man-eating cannibals.
    - **Cockneys vs. Zombies** (2012) - The title says it all. A gang of bank robbers must fight their way out of a zombie-infested London.
    - **Get Duked!** (2019) - An anarchic, hip-hop inspired comedy that follows four city boys on a wilderness trek as they try to escape a mysterious huntsman.

The Man of a Thousand Faces

Lon Chaney (1883–1930) was horror's first true shapeshifter, its human chameleon, the actor who taught cinema that a face could be as terrifying as any phantom. To call him simply a performer is to undersell his genius: Chaney turned makeup into mythology, transforming himself into grotesques and outsiders with such conviction that his work became the foundation on which Hollywood horror was built. In silence, he gave monsters their first voice.

Cultivating a Persona

Born Leonidas Frank Chaney in Colorado Springs, he grew up the son of deaf parents, which taught him the expressiveness of gesture, mime, and silent communication. This fluency in physical storytelling became his trademark. In an era before sound, Chaney conveyed volumes through posture, glance, and the contortions of his own face. But it was his makeup wizardry that secured his legend. Known as "The Man of a Thousand Faces," he designed and applied his own elaborate prosthetics, enduring physical pain to become hunchbacks, phantoms, legless cripples, and tormented souls.

Where others sought glamour, Chaney sought transformation. His Quasimodo in *The Hunchback of Notre Dame* (1923) turned deformity into tragedy, while his Erik in *The Phantom of the Opera* (1925) gave horror one of its most iconic visages: sunken eyes, skeletal cheeks, and a rictus grin that audiences swore could not be human. Chaney didn't just play monsters; he embodied society's fears of difference, poverty, and exile, giving the "freak" a face both terrifying and heartbreakingly human.

Signature Works

- *The Penalty* (1920) — Chaney strapped his legs into harnesses to play a double-amputee criminal mastermind, enduring excruciating pain to create an unforgettable villain.
- *The Hunchback of Notre Dame* (1923) — As Quasimodo, Chaney fused pathos and spectacle, proving horror could break hearts as well as terrify.
- *The Phantom of the Opera* (1925) — His skull-like visage remains one of cinema's most indelible images, blending romance and dread.
- *London After Midnight* (1927, lost) — Though the film itself is missing, Chaney's image with sharpened teeth, dark cape, and staring eyes has become legendary in horror iconography.
- *West of Zanzibar* (1928) — A revenge tale where Chaney's physical distortion and psychological intensity blurred tragedy and cruelty.

What He Did for Horror

Chaney gave horror its empathy. Before Karloff's Monster or Lugosi's Dracula, Chaney's creatures showed that monsters were more than terrors, they were symbols of isolation, persecution, and yearning. His roles were often outcasts, the deformed and unloved, making audiences recoil in fear only to recognize themselves in pity moments later. He made makeup a storytelling device, elevating prosthetics into psychology.

Yet his art came at a cost. He endured immense physical strain, binding his body, inserting wires, and reshaping his features until he resembled something barely human. He died in 1930, just as sound cinema was arriving, leaving the world to wonder what roles he might have created had his voice joined his faces.

Legacy & Amazement

Lon Chaney remains the primal ancestor of screen horror. His innovations in makeup laid the groundwork for Jack Pierce at Universal, and his portrayals defined how film would forever imagine the monstrous outsider: terrifying, yes, but also tragic. Every sympathetic monster, from Karloff's Frankenstein to Gollum in *The Lord of the Rings*, traces its lineage to Chaney's hunched shoulders and haunted eyes.

He did not need sound. He did not need words. With plaster, paint, and pain, Lon Chaney gave horror its first immortal faces and made cinema itself believe in transformation.

Modern Creature Resurgence

☐ **Grabbers** (2012, Ireland) – Sea monsters attack; alcohol is the only defense.
  - **SIMILAR FILMS**
    - ☐ **Boys from County Hell** (2020, Ireland) - Another Irish horror-comedy that blends local folklore and monsters.
☐ **Pacific Rim** (2013) – Jaegers vs. Kaiju spectacle.
  - **SEQUELS**
    - ☐ **Pacific Rim: Uprising** (2018) – New generation of Jaegers vs. Kaiju.
☐ **The Ritual** (2017) – Friends stalked by a Norse monster in Swedish woods. A direct cinematic sequel is reportedly in development for a 2025 release.
☐ **It** (2017) - In the summer of 1989, a group of bullied kids band together to destroy a shape-shifting monster, which disguises itself as a clown and preys on the children of Derry, their small Maine town. The Duffer Brothers originally wanted to direct the movie, but were overlooked as they were not "established" enough. They went on to create *Stranger Things* (2016), which co-stars Finn Wolfhard (Richie) and pays homage to Stephen King.
  - **ADAPTIONS & SEQUELS**
    - ☐ **It: Chapter Two** (2019) - Twenty-seven years after their first encounter with the terrifying Pennywise, the Losers Club have grown up and moved away, until a devastating phone call brings them back.
    - ☐ **IT** (1990, TV Mini Series) - In 1960, seven pre-teen outcasts fight an evil demon who poses as a child-killing clown. Thirty years later, they reunite to stop the demon once and for all when it returns to their hometown.
☐ **Monster Hunter** (2020) – Soldiers face beasts from another dimension. A second film has been confirmed by those involved, with Paul W. S. Anderson already having written a script by November 2020.
☐ **Love and Monsters** (2020) – Post-apocalypse filled with mutated creatures.
☐ **Shadow in the Cloud** (2020) – WWII gremlin attacks a female pilot mid-flight.
☐ **Blood Red Sky** (2021) – Vampiric mother protects plane from hijackers.

Indie, Global, and Recent Monsters

☐ **Grizzly** (1976) – Killer bear marketed as "Jaws with claws."
☐ **The Boogens** (1981) – Miners awaken subterranean tentacled monsters.
☐ **Shadow Creature** (1995) – Low-budget cult film with night-stalking humanoid terror.
☐ **Ravenous** (1999) – Cannibal soldiers in Sierra Nevada, mixing human monsters and creature hunger. This film uses the Wendigo legend to create a darkly comic and unsettling story about cannibalism and the desire for power during the 19th-century Mexican-American War.
  - **FILMS ABOUT THE WENDIGO LEGEND:** The Wendigo is a figure from Algonquian folklore, a gaunt, cannibalistic spirit of winter and hunger. Said to be born when a person resorts to cannibalism in the cold, the Wendigo becomes an emaciated, towering creature with an endless appetite, its heart iced over by greed and famine. Legends describe it stalking the forests of the Great Lakes and Canada, embodying both the terror of starvation and the warning against unchecked consumption. In horror, the Wendigo endures as a symbol of hunger that can never be satisfied whether literal, moral, or spiritual.
    - ☐ **Frostbiter: Wrath of the Wendigo** (1996) - A more B-movie horror-comedy take on the legend. Two hunters break a sacred circle and unleash the Wendigo, a deer-like skeletal monster that goes on a murderous rampage.
    - ☐ **Wendigo** (2001) - The legend of the Wendigo, a beast from Indian folklore who is half-man, half-deer, and can change itself at will.
    - ☐ **The Last Winter** (2006) - Also directed by Larry Fessenden from *Wendigo*, this film features a team of environmentalists in the Arctic who encounter what may be a Wendigo spirit.
    - ☐ **Dark was the Night** (2014) - A sheriff in a small town investigates a creature preying on livestock and people after a logging company encroaches on nearby woods.
    - ☐ **The Retreat** (2020) - A found-footage horror film where a man's backpacking trip in the Adirondack High Peaks turns into a fight for survival against a mysterious and agile creature of legend.

☐ **Antlers** (2021) – A supernatural horror film about a middle-school teacher who discovers one of her students is harboring a mysterious and dangerous creature.

☐ **Brotherhood of the Wolf** (2001, France) - In 18th-century France, the Chevalier de Fronsac and his Native American friend Mani are sent to the Gevaudan province at the king's behest to investigate the killings of hundreds by a mysterious beast. The film is loosely based on a true story. Between 1764 and 1767, a mysterious wolf-like beast terrorized the French province of Gévaudan, killing more than 100 people. The film uses this historical backdrop but adds elements of action, martial arts, horror, and conspiracy.

- **FILMS BASED ON THE BEAST OF GÉVAUDAN LEGEND:** The Beast of Gévaudan was a mysterious predator that terrorized the French countryside between 1764 and 1767, killing over a hundred people and leaving villages in fear. Described as larger than a wolf, with a reddish hide, massive jaws, and an almost supernatural cunning, the creature defied hunters, soldiers, and royal campaigns sent to destroy it. Some believed it was a monstrous wolf, others a lion, or even a punishment sent by God. The legend endures as one of Europe's most infamous man-eater tales, part history, part myth, where fact and folklore blur into a nightmare of tooth and claw.
    - ☐ **The Beast of Gévaudan** (2003, France) - A French television movie that provides a more straightforward, grounded take on the historical events.
    - ☐ **The Cursed** (2021) - A 19th-century folk horror film that features a beast haunting a remote French village, with clear inspiration from the Beast of Gévaudan legend.

☐ **The Cave** (2005) – Blood-thirsty creatures await a pack of divers who become trapped in an underwater cave network.

☐ **Abominable** (2006) – A man, crippled in a climbing accident, returns to his cabin in the woods as part of his rehabilitation, but he wasn't prepared for the imminent onslaught.

☐ **Monster** (2008, Korea) – After a massive earthquake in Tokyo, two American filmmakers document the true cause of the destruction.

☐ **Pontypool** (2008, Canada) – A radio host interprets the possible outbreak of a deadly virus which infects the small Ontario town he is stationed in.

☐ **Monsters** (2010, UK) - Six years after Earth has suffered an alien invasion, a cynical journalist agrees to escort a shaken American tourist through an infected zone in Mexico to the safety of the U.S. border.

- **SEQUELS**
    - ☐ **Monsters: Dark Continent** (2014) - A direct sequel to the 2010 film, directed by Tom Green and co-written by Green and Jay Basu. Gareth Edwards served as an executive producer but did not return to direct. This film was not as well-received by critics as the original.

☐ **Willow Creek** (2013) – Blair Witch–style found footage, but with Sasquatch.

☐ **Exists** (2014) – group of friends who venture into the remote Texas woods for a party weekend find themselves stalked by Bigfoot.

☐ **Monster** (2014) – Found-footage mother-daughter vs. roadside creature.

☐ **The Pyramid** (2014) – Unearthed Egyptian creature stalks archaeologists.

☐ **Harbinger Down** (2015) – Practical-effects homage to *The Thing*. While studying the effects of global warming on a pod of whales, grad students on a crabbing vessel and its crew uncover frozen Soviet space shuttle and unintentionally release a monstrous organism from it.

☐ **The Hallow** (2015, Ireland) – A family who moved into a remote mill house in Ireland finds themselves in a fight for survival with demonic creatures living in the woods.

☐ **Cold Skin** (2017) – Lighthouse keepers vs. humanoid sea creatures.

☐ **Sea Fever** (2019, Ireland) – Fishing crew trapped with parasitic sea monster.

☐ **Primal Rage** (2018) - A newly reunited young couple's drive through the Pacific Northwest turns into a nightmare as they are forced to face nature, unsavory locals, and a monstrous creature, known to the Native Americans as Oh-Mah. Draws heavily on the Bigfoot legend.

☐ **Werewolf by Night** (2022) - Follows a lycanthrope superhero who fights evil using the abilities given to him by a curse brought on by his bloodline.

☐ **Dust Bunny** (2025) - An eight-year-old girl asks her scheming neighbor for help in killing the monster under her bed that she thinks ate her family.

☐ **Death of a Unicorn** (2025) – Starring Paul Rudd. A father and daughter accidentally hit and kill a unicorn while en route to a weekend retreat, where his billionaire boss seeks to exploit the creature's miraculous curative properties.

Creature Feature Pairing Night: Dinner with Monsters

Main Course (Classic Giant)
King Kong (1933, USA)
How to watch: With the lights low and popcorn ready, marvel at how groundbreaking stop-motion effects still carry pathos.
Smartest fact: It took 18 months to craft the CGI version of the Empire State Building. The real thing was built in 14 months.

Side Dish (Atomic Age Terror)
Godzilla (1954, Japan)
How to watch: In its original Japanese cut (not the Americanized Raymond Burr version). Watch for the mournful tone. zot's less popcorn kaiju, more national trauma.
Smartest fact: The film was banned in some parts of Japan at first for being "too soon" after Hiroshima/Nagasaki.

Dessert (Aquatic Gothic)
Creature from the Black Lagoon (1954, USA)
How to watch: Pair with dim blue lighting and maybe a fishbowl cocktail. Pay attention to underwater cinematography, it was revolutionary.
Smartest fact: The Creature's appearance was based on old seventeenth-century woodcuts of two bizarre creatures called the Sea Monk and the Sea Bishop. The Creature's final head was based on that of the Sea Monk, but the original discarded head was based on that of the Sea Bishop.

Palate Cleanser (Carnival of Grotesques)
Freaks (1932, USA)
How to watch: Not with a crowd of casual horror dabblers, this one's raw and unsettling. Focus on its humanity, not just its shock value.
Smartest fact: Banned in the UK for over 30 years. The cast members were real sideshow performers.

After-Dinner Mint (Creature Surprise)
The Blob (1958, USA)
How to watch: Double-bill with the 1988 remake to compare Cold War paranoia vs. Reagan-era body horror.
Smartest fact: The film's theme song ("Beware of the Blob") was written by Burt Bacharach.

Beasts Unbound: Watch Iconic Monsters

135

Cosmic Horror

Cosmic horror is the vertigo of insignificance. The frame widens, the map keeps going, and whatever stares back does not care if we blink. It is less about monsters than about scale and indifference. Minds crack not because the creature is ugly, but because meaning itself stops holding. In cosmic horror, science, scripture, and sanity are tools that work until they don't. The terror lives in the realization that we were never the protagonists of this story.

Why People Are Drawn to Cosmic Horror

Cosmic horror scratches a different itch than jump scares. It offers awe and dread in the same breath. Viewers chase the feeling of smallness, the eeriness of patterns repeating across time, the way an image or sound can imply an intelligence we cannot parse. It is the genre's purest encounter with limit: language fails, logic frays, yet we keep looking. The reward is a sublime panic that lingers after the credits.

Essentials

1. **The Thing (1982, USA)** – Distilled paranoia into body horror, with John Carpenter's Antarctic outpost becoming a crucible of mistrust and mutation. Its groundbreaking practical effects and relentless atmosphere turned the alien into a symbol of identity collapse and human isolation.
2. **In the Mouth of Madness (1994, USA)** – Publishing as portal. Blurred the line between fiction and reality, channeling Lovecraftian dread through the unraveling psyche of its protagonist. John Carpenter's film turned authorship, insanity, and mass hysteria into cosmic horror, where storytelling itself becomes a contagion.
3. **Quatermass and the Pit (1967, UK)** – Fossil dig, buried spacecraft, ancestral panic. Rational inquiry meets a revelation that rewrites human origins. Hammer, but cosmic. Fused science fiction with ancient terror, unearthing a buried spacecraft that reveals humanity's evolution was shaped by alien influence. Its mix of archaeology, paranoia, and apocalyptic dread made it a cornerstone of British horror, embodying cosmic horror within a modern scientific frame.
4. **Annihilation (2018, USA/UK)** – The Shimmer as ecosystem and mirror. Hypnotic and ruinously beautiful. Explored cosmic horror through the lens of biology, as a team of scientists enter a mysterious zone where nature mutates into surreal, terrifying forms. Its fusion of the uncanny and the beautiful turned self-destruction into both a scientific mystery and an existential mirror.
5. **The Endless (2017, USA)** – Time loops, unseen authors, and the awful politeness of a god that keeps you for the plot. Unfolded cosmic horror on an intimate scale, following two brothers who return to a cult entangled in a time-looping presence beyond comprehension. Its quiet dread, woven with themes of memory, fate, and human insignificance, made the infinite feel both terrifying and achingly personal.

Deep Cuts

1. **Prince of Darkness (1987, USA)** – A church basement, a cylinder, equations that summon. Broadcast dreams from the future and an "anti-God" that is more physics than demon. Pushed John Carpenter's horror into metaphysical territory, blending quantum physics with demonic evil. Its vision of science unlocking ancient darkness turned faith, reason, and reality itself into fragile constructs, making the film a bleak fusion of cosmic and supernatural horror.
2. **Matango (1963, Japan)** – Shipwreck, hunger, and a fungal invitation. Survival slides into spore communion; the island wants you to join the chorus. Transformed shipwreck survival into a nightmarish parable of hunger and decay, as castaways fall victim to hallucinogenic, parasitic fungi. Ishirō Honda's bleak departure from kaiju

spectacle offered a slow, suffocating vision of human corruption, where the line between consumption and transformation dissolves in mold and madness.

3. **The Borderlands [Final Prayer] (2013, UK)** – Vatican investigators, a rural church, and a descent that becomes a birth canal. Found footage with a jaw-drop ending.

4. **The Empty Man (2020, USA)** – Urban legend as misdirection. What begins as slasher folklore opens into cult, conduit, and a message that writes its messenger. Merged found-footage realism with folk horror, as investigators documenting church miracles uncover something far older and more malevolent. Its restrained buildup and shocking descent into subterranean terror make it one of the most unsettling and inventive entries in modern British horror.

5. **Resolution (2012, USA)** – A detox intervention trapped in someone else's edit timeline. The camera is the cage; the cut is the god. Deconstructed horror by trapping two friends in a remote cabin under the gaze of an unseen, storytelling force. Its blend of metafiction, unease, and existential dread laid the groundwork for *The Endless*, turning narrative itself into the source of terror.

Critical Essay

"Cosmic Is Not Just Tentacles"

A common myth reduces cosmic horror to squid gods and sanity meters. In truth, it is an attitude toward knowledge. The engine is epistemic failure: the suspicion that categories like "self," "cause," and "end" are conveniences. Cosmic horror can live in an Arctic station, a suburb, a sanatorium, a national park. What makes it cosmic is not scale alone but the dethroning of human importance. Tentacles help; indifference is essential.

Global Spotlight: Japan

Japanese cinema often approaches cosmic dread through suggestion and contagion rather than exposition. *Matango* reframes consumption as communion. *Cure* (1997) and *Pulse* (2001) suggest an intelligence spreading through language and networks, less villain than vacancy. The fear is not a roaring titan but an idea that will not stop, a melancholy apocalypse where the world keeps running while meaning drains out. Japan proves cosmic horror can whisper and still hollow you out.

- ☐ **The Quatermass Xperiment** (1955) - Professor Bernard Quatermass' manned rocket ship returns to Earth, but two of the astronauts are missing and the survivor seems ill and unable to communicate.
    - • **SEQUELS**
        - ☐ **Quatermass 2** (1957) - Professor Quatermass, trying to gather support for his Lunar colonisation project, is intrigued by mysterious traces that have been showing up.
        - ☐ **Quatermass and the Pit** (1967) - A mysterious artifact is unearthed in London, and famous scientist Bernard Quatermass is called in to divine its origins and explain its strange effects on people. Adapted from Nigel Kneale's BBC serial; its influence threads through British sci-fi and horror for decades.
- ☐ **Invasion of the Body Snatchers** (1956) - Directed by Don Siegel, this classic black-and-white film captures the paranoia of the Cold War and McCarthyism.
    - • **ADAPTIONS & SIMILAR THEMES**
        - ☐ **Invasion of the Body Snatchers** (1978) – Human bodies replaced by alien pods.
        - ☐ **Night of the Creeps** (1986) – Alien parasites create frat-boy zombies.
            - • **ADAPTIONS**
                - ☐ **Zombie Town** (2007) - A film titled *Zombie Town* was marketed in some regions as a sequel to *Night of the Creeps*, using the alternate title *Night of the Creeps 2: Zombie Town*. However, it is an entirely separate, unrelated film.
        - ☐ **The Dark Side of the Moon** (1990) - In 2022, a repair crew is sent to fix an orbital weapon but their spaceship

WALTER WANGER CREATES THE ULTIMATE IN SCIENCE-FICTION!

INVASION OF THE BODY SNATCHERS

KEVIN McCARTHY · DANA WYNTER

SUPERSCOPE

malfunctions and ends up heading towards the dark side of the moon. There, in a mysterious, seemingly abandoned space shuttle, a sinister force lies in wait.

- ☐ **Body Snatchers** (1993) - Directed by Abel Ferrara, this adaptation is set on a military base and focuses on teenage characters. It features an atmospheric, surreal tone and explores themes of conformity.
- ☐ **The Faculty** (1998) - This Robert Rodriguez film is a clear homage, with alien parasites infesting a high school staff and students.
- ☐ **Slither** (2006) – Parasitic alien infestation overtakes small town.
- ☐ **The Invasion** (2007) - A troubled production starring Nicole Kidman and Daniel Craig, this version replaces the pods with a virus that spreads during sleep. A different, more favorable ending was added after extensive reshoots.
- ☐ **Assimilate** (2019) - This low-budget film explicitly draws inspiration from the *Body Snatchers* story, focusing on a group of teens who document their town's unsettling changes.
- ☐ **The Block Island Sound** (2020) - Something lurks off the coast of Block Island, silently influencing the behavior of fisherman, Tom Lynch. After suffering a series of violent outbursts, he unknowingly puts his family in grave danger. The theme of losing control of one's body and mind to an alien presence is a central aspect of both films.

☐ **The Blob** (1958) – A deadly entity from space crash-lands near a small town and begins consuming everyone in its path. Panic ensues as shady government scientists try to contain the horrific creature. Both director Rob Zombie and director Simon West were attached to remake projects that ultimately fell through. But In January 2024, it was announced that David Bruckner would write and direct a new remake of *The Blob*. It is being produced by David S. Goyer and Keith Levine for Warner Bros. and will reportedly change the monster's origin to a man-made phenomenon created with AI and gene-editing.

- • **ADAPTIONS, SEQUELS & SIMILAR THEMES**
  - ☐ **Beware! The Blob** (1972) - Also known as *Son of Blob*, this comedic sequel was directed by Larry Hagman. The Blob is reawakened from its frozen state by a pipeline worker, and a new generation of townsfolk must stop it.
  - ☐ **The Blob** (1988) - Directed by Chuck Russell and co-written by Frank Darabont, this remake is much gorier and has gained a cult following. It reinvents the monster's origin, portraying it as a secret, government-made biological weapon rather than an alien.
  - ☐ **X the Unknown** (1956) - A British film that features a sentient, radioactive mud-like substance that emerges from a fissure and devours living things.
  - ☐ **Caltiki, the Immortal Monster** (1959, Italy) - A team of archaeologists in Mexico encounter an amorphous, blob-like monster that appears to be connected with the collapse of the Mayan civilization.
  - ☐ **The Stuff** (1985) - A delicious, mysterious goo that oozes from the earth is marketed as the newest dessert sensation, but the tasty treat rots more than teeth when zombie-like snackers who only want to consume more of the strange substance at any cost begin infesting the world.
- • **IMPERSONAL UNSTOPPABLE FORCE THEMES**
  - ☐ **The Monolith Monsters** (1957) - Rocks from a meteor which grow when in contact with water threaten a sleepy Southwestern desert community.

- ☐ **The Magnetic Monster** (1953) - In this film, a scientific experiment goes wrong, creating a rapidly growing radioactive isotope that consumes metal and energy and emits deadly radiation. It's a race against the clock for scientists to stop the menace before it grows too large.
- ☐ **Kronos** (1957) - *Kronos* involves a massive, energy-absorbing alien machine that lands on Earth and begins to drain power plants, causing widespread destruction.
- ☐ **The Andromeda Strain** (1971) - A satellite brings back a deadly, fast-mutating extraterrestrial microorganism that threatens to wipe out all life on Earth. A team of scientists works in a high-tech lab to find a cure.
- ☐ **The Ruins** (2008) – Vines invade and consume human flesh.
- ☐ **Life** (2017) – Alien organism evolves rapidly aboard ISS. A deadly, quickly evolving alien organism is discovered on Mars and threatens the crew of a space station. Like *The Monolith Monsters*, the threat is biological and follows its own rules of nature, rather than being intentionally malicious.
- ☐ **Sweetheart** (2019) – Shipwrecked woman vs. island sea beast. The film's story was conceived by director J. D. Dillard, along with writers Alex Hyner and Alex Theurer. Dillard was inspired by a personal experience of looking out at the water and imagining a creature emerging, leading him to develop the concept from there.
- ☐ **Elevation** (2024) - In this sci-fi thriller, a father must take his daughter to safety after a strange, monstrous entity appears, drawing parallels to the unknown, unnatural forces seen in films like *The Monolith Monsters*.

☐ **Matango** (1963, Japan) - Shipwrecked survivors slowly transform into mushrooms. Based on the 1907 short story "The Voice in the Night" by William Hope Hodgson. Several prominent directors such as Steven Soderbergh and John Carpenter have expressed interest in remaking *Matango*, but none have come to fruition due to issues with securing the rights from Toho, the original studio.

☐ **X: The Man with X-Ray Eyes** (1963) - An ambitious scientist invents an eye drop formula that grants him X-ray vision, but his new powers have disastrous consequences.

- • **SIMILAR FILMS**
    - ☐ **The Trip** (1967) - Roger Corman's later film about an LSD trip is stylistically related to *X: The Man with the X-Ray Eyes* due to its psychedelic visuals and themes of altered perception.

☐ **Phase IV** (1974) - Suddenly, desert ants form a group intelligence and wage war on the humans. It's up to a couple of scientists and a girl to stop them. Loosely based on H.G. Wells' 1905 short story "Empire of the Ants."

- • **SIMILAR THEMES**
    - ☐ **Frogs** (1972) - A group of helpless victims celebrate a birthday on an island estate crawling with killer amphibians, birds, insects, and reptiles.
    - ☐ **The Hellstrom Chronicle** (1971) - A pseudo-documentary about insects winning an evolutionary war.
    - ☐ **Phase 7** (2010) - Nicolas Goldbart's science-fiction film includes a scene where *Phase IV* is playing on a television, a direct homage to the original.
    - ☐ **The Swarm** (2020, France) - A single mother's business of a locust farm isn't doing so well. She discovers by accident that blood makes them thrive, and does her best to hide her secrets.

- ☐ **City of the Living Dead** (1980, Italy) – Fulci's surreal gateway-to-hell horror. A reporter and a psychic race to close the Gates of Hell after the suicide of a clergyman caused them to open, allowing the dead to rise from their graves.
  - • **GATES OF HELL TRILOGY**
    - ☐ **The Beyond** (1981, Italy) – Fulci's surreal gore masterpiece. A young woman inherits an old hotel in Louisiana where, following a series of supernatural "accidents," she learns that the building was built over one of the entrances to Hell.
    - ☐ **The House by the Cemetery** (1981, Italy) - This third film concludes the trilogy and again features a new set of characters. The story centers on a family who moves into a new home with a gruesome secret in its basement.
- ☐ **The Fog** (1980) – An unearthly fog rolls into a small coastal town exactly 100 years after a ship mysteriously sank in its waters. Local legend tells of a ship lured on to the rocks of Antonio Bay being enveloped by a supernatural cloud as it sank; the myth says that when this mysterious fog returns, the victims will rise up from the depths seeking vengeance. Starring two scream queen legends Jamie Lee Curtis and Janet Leigh.
  - • **ADAPTIONS & INFLUENCE**
    - ☐ **The Fog** (2005) - This is the most prominent adaptation of the original film, directed by Rupert Wainwright. It retells the story of vengeful ghosts returning to an island town in a thick fog. While it features many of the same plot points, it includes some changes, such as the spirits being awakened by a fire rather than a torn sack and different character development.
    - ☐ **The Crawling Eye** (1958) - A series of decapitations on a Swiss mountainside appear to be connected to a mysterious radioactive cloud. Director John Carpenter has cited *The Crawling Eye* as a direct influence on his horror film, particularly the element of monsters hiding in the clouds. Tom Welling and Selma Blair star in this adaption, but IMDB does not agree with the results as it only got 3.7 stars.
- ☐ **Possession** (1981, Poland/France) – Woman's breakdown spirals into surreal psychosis. Director Ari Aster, known for *Hereditary* and *Midsommar*, has cited *Possession* as a major influence, particularly for its dissection of a family unit and intense emotional horror. Critics and fans frequently draw parallels between *Possession* and David Cronenberg's body horror films, such as *The Brood*. Star Sam Neill once cited Possession as his personal favorite of all the films he'd ever been in.
  - • **ADAPTIONS & SIMILAR THEMES**
    - ☐ **Possession** (2024, Indonesia) - An Indonesian remake of the original film. Faris, who had just returned from his duty as a soldier. Instead of being warm, his return was actually greeted with a request for divorce from his wife, Ratna.
    - ☐ **The Untamed** (2016, Mexico) – Extraterrestrial tentacle creature entwines with human desires. The film's use of a bizarre, otherworldly creature to explore human desire, repressed sexuality, and social issues places it firmly within the cosmic horror genre. The creature is incomprehensible and operates outside of human morality, reflecting the themes of H.P. Lovecraft's work.
    - ☐ **Luz** (2018, Germany) - Luz, a young cabdriver, drags herself into the brightly lit entrance of a run-down police station. A demonic entity follows her, determined to finally be close to the woman it loves.
    - ☐ **Tumbbad** (2018, India) - This Indian mythological horror film follows a family's generations-long obsession with a demonic entity in a hidden chamber. It blends folklore, cosmic elements, and disturbing imagery to create a unique and unsettling atmosphere. Critically acclaimed and one of the highest-rated horror films on IMDB.com with 8.2 stars.
    - ☐ **The Lighthouse** (2019) – Two lighthouse keepers try to maintain their sanity while living on a remote and mysterious New England Island in the 1890s. The claustrophobic atmosphere, isolation, and suggestion of a cosmic entity lurking in the sea echo *Possession's* psychological intensity and sense of inescapable doom. The idea originated with co-writer Max Eggers's attempt to adapt Poe's unfinished story "The Light-House." It was nominated for an Academy Award for Best Achievement in Cinematography in 2020.

- ☐ **Titane** (2021, France) – Following a series of unexplained crimes, a father is reunited with the son who has been missing for ten years. Directed by Julia Ducournau, this French body horror film features a woman with a titanium plate in her head. It is a wild and surreal exploration of body modification, gender, and desire, featuring extreme body horror and a highly unsettling tone.
- ☐ **Frewaka** (2024) - Follow a student of nursing palliative care, who is plagued by a trauma from her past that has a disorienting effect on her present, her relationship, her career and her ability to function.

☐ **Xtro** (1982) - An alien creature impregnates a woman who gives birth to a man who was abducted by aliens three years ago. The man reconnects with his wife and son for a sinister purpose.

- • **SEQUELS**
    - ☐ **Xtro II: The Second Encounter** (1990) - This film has no connection to the first film's plot or characters. Instead, it follows a group of scientists in an underground facility who accidentally unleash a deadly alien entity through a dimensional portal.
    - ☐ **Xtro 3: Watch the Skies** (1995) - The third film is also completely unrelated to its predecessors. In this movie, a platoon of U.S. Marines is sent to a remote island to defuse bombs but is instead terrorized by an alien creature.

☐ **The Thing** (1982) – A research team in Antarctica is hunted by a shape-shifting alien that assumes the appearance of its victims. Bottin was only 22 when he created the film's legendary practical effects working so hard he had to be hospitalized from exhaustion. Released two weeks after *E.T.*, it bombed theatrically before becoming a cornerstone of the genre.

- • **ADAPTIONS**
    - ☐ **The Thing from Another World** (1951) - This is the first film adaptation of the original novella. It portrays the alien as a humanoid creature, distinguishing it significantly from later, more faithful depictions. Based on the 1938 novella "Who Goes There?" by John W. Campbell, Jr.
    - ☐ **The Thing** (2011) - A prequel to the 1982 film, this movie details the events at the Norwegian Antarctic outpost that are only alluded to in Carpenter's version. Despite some clever details, it failed to resonate with audiences and relied heavily on CGI, unlike the 1982 film's famous practical effects.
- • **APOCALYPSE TRILOGY**
    - ☐ **Prince of Darkness** (1987) – A priest, his students, and a group of quantum physics students discover a container of sentient, evil liquid in an old monastery and must try to prevent it from bringing the "anti-God" into the world.

☐ **In the Mouth of Madness** (1994) – An insurance investigator begins discovering that the impact a horror writer's books have on his fans is more than inspirational. The film completes Carpenter's informal "Apocalypse Trilogy" after *The Thing* and *Prince of Darkness*.

- **SIMILAR THEMES**
  - ☐ **Sphere** (1998) - This film, based on the novel by Michael Crichton, also explores the psychological breakdown of scientists confronting an ancient and alien intelligence at a remote, isolated location.
  - ☐ **Apollo 18** (2011) - Decades-old found footage from NASA's abandoned Apollo 18 mission, where three American astronauts were sent on a secret expedition, reveals the reason the U.S. has never returned to the moon.
  - ☐ **Pandorum** (2009) - Two crew members of a spaceship wake up from hypersleep to discover that all their colleagues are missing. Despite this, it appears that they are not alone.
  - ☐ **Black Mountain Side** (2014) - At a cold, desolate, northmost outpost in Canada, an archaeological discovery is made. A specialist arrives Nov. 1. Strange things happen. All contact with the outside world is down. The film is deeply rooted in the themes of cosmic horror developed by H.P. Lovecraft, particularly his novella *At the Mountains of Madness*. The terror arises from confronting an ancient, alien intelligence that operates beyond human comprehension.
  - ☐ **The Alchemist Cookbook** (2016) - Suffering from delusions of fortune, a young hermit hides out in the forest hoping to crack an ancient mystery, but pays a price for his mania. Director Joel Potrykus has stated that his family history of schizophrenia is directly represented in Sean. He used the film as an experiment to see if the audience could care for a character, whom they have just been introduced to, in the middle of a mental breakdown.
  - ☐ **The Void** (2016, Canada) – Cultists trap people in hospital for otherworldly ritual. The film's themes of ancient, incomprehensible beings and the insignificance of humanity are directly drawn from the work of H.P. Lovecraft. It shares a similar claustrophobic setting where characters are isolated and must fight a shape-shifting, monstrous entity as *The Thing*.
  - ☐ **Sputnik** (2020, Russia) – Cosmonaut returns with parasitic alien inside. The film's tense atmosphere and focus on an isolated group dealing with a dangerous alien entity draws comparisons to John Carpenter's film. An English-language remake is in development.
  - ☐ **Slash/Back** (2022, Canada) - In Nunavut, four girls who like horror and alien movies, love their phones and even their poor elders who believe in shapeshifters because "they didn't have the internet" realize local disappearances are linked to a shapeshifting alien. *Slash/Back* openly draws inspiration from this John Carpenter classic. Like *The Thing*, it features an isolated, Arctic-based location and a shapeshifting alien parasite.

☐ **The Keep** (1983) - Nazis are forced to turn to a Jewish historian for help in battling the ancient demon they have inadvertently freed from its prison. Based on the 1981 novel *The Keep* by F. Paul Wilson. Despite its flaws and poor initial reception, the 1983 film has gained a cult following over the years. Many fans appreciate the film's visuals, its moody atmosphere, and the score by Tangerine Dream.

- **SIMILAR THEMES**
  - ☐ **Overlord** (2018) - A small group of American soldiers find horror behind enemy lines on the eve of D-Day. This film blends the D-Day invasion with supernatural horror, creating a similar hybrid of historical and genre storytelling.
  - ☐ **Frankenstein's Army** (2013) - In the dying days of WWII, a battalion of Russian soldiers is lured into the secret lab of a deranged scientist and forced to face off against an army of horrific flesh-and-metal war machines. A found-footage horror film set during World War II that centers on a troop of Russian soldiers discovering a Nazi doctor's experiments.

☐ **Re-Animator** (1985) – After an odd new medical student arrives on campus, a dedicated local and his girlfriend become involved in bizarre experiments centering around the re-animation of dead tissue. Directed by Stuart Gordon, based H.P. Lovecraft's 1922 serial novelette "Herbert West-Reanimator."

- **SEQUELS**
  - ☐ **Bride of Re-Animator** (1990) – Corpses revived anew. Doctors Herbert West and Dan Cain discover the secret to creating human life and proceed to create a perfect woman from dead tissue.

- ☐ **Beyond Re-Animator** (2003) – After 13 years in prison, the mad scientist from *Re-Animator* (1985) gets a new chance to experiment with the arrival of a young prison doctor, who secretly hopes to learn to reanimate dead people. Good intentions turn to horror.
- **GORDON/LOVECRAFT DOMINATION**
  - ☐ **Herbert West-Reanimator** (1985) - This film, based on the Lovecraft novella of the same name, introduced the character of Herbert West, played by Jeffrey Combs. The sequels later place West and his creations into the same narrative world as the events of *From Beyond*.
  - ☐ **From Beyond** (1986) – A group of scientists have developed the Resonator, a machine which allows whoever is within range to see beyond normal perceptible reality. But when the experiment succeeds, they are immediately attacked by terrible life forms. Directed by Stuart Gordon, this film is based on the Lovecraft's short story about a machine that allows scientists to perceive terrifying dimensions of reality.
  - ☐ **Castle Freak** (1995) - A man travels to Italy with his family to live in the castle they have recently inherited. But he soon begins to suspect that they are not the only occupants. Directed by Stuart Gordon and also starring Jeffrey Combs and Barbara Crampton, this film is based on the Lovecraft short story "The Outsider" and is part of the same extended creative family.
    - **ADAPTIONS**
      - ☐ **Castle Freak** (2020) - An Albanian castle with bloodthirsty creatures is inherited by a young blind woman.
  - ☐ **Dagon** (2001) - A boating accident runs a young man and woman ashore in a decrepit Spanish fishing town which they discover is in the grips of an ancient sea god and its monstrous half human offspring. Stuart Gordon's adaptation of Lovecraft's *The Shadow over Innsmouth* is set in a decaying Spanish fishing village.
    - **SHADOW OVER INNSMOUTH**
      - ☐ **The Deep Ones** (2020) - A low-budget film that is a loose and modern take on the source material. A married couple rents a beach side Airbnb only to be surrounded by peculiar neighbors and occurrences. They soon discover that they are in the grip of a mysterious cult and the ancient sea god that they worship.
      - ☐ **The Shadow Over Innsmouth** (1987) - An animated version featured in the Italian anthology film *The Reaping*.
      - ☐ **Suitable Flesh** (2023) - This film, directed by Joe Lynch, is a neo-Lovecraftian thriller that features many members of the Stuart Gordon creative team, including Dennis Paoli and Barbara Crampton, though it is not a direct adaptation of *The Shadow Over Innsmouth*.
  - ☐ **The Resonator: Miskatonic U** (2021) - This web series and later film, produced by Charles Band, acts as a sequel to *From Beyond*. It directly links characters and plot points to the events of the earlier film. Set in the fictional college campus "Miskatonic University" in Arkham, Massachusetts where all sorts of fantastic and unworldly events have been known to unfold in Lovecraft lore. Follows six gifted students as they navigate life after one of them, Crawford Tillinghast, builds a machine known as the "Resonator."
    - **SEQUELS**
      - ☐ **Beyond the Resonator** (2022) - In this sequel to THE RESONATOR: MISKATONIC U, the malevolent inter-dimensional machine is still channeling monsters, but this time things get even more complicated with the arrival of mad med student Herbert West and his dreaded reagent.
      - ☐ **Curse of the Re-Animator** (2022) - The saga of The Resonator winds down into its final acts with this installment, *Curse of the Re-Animator*. Herbert West is totally out of control on campus, sticking his glowing green reagent into every corpse he can find. The living dead are on the loose and looking to kill in this creepy new Lovecraftian shocker.

Cosmical Craft

H.P. Lovecraft

Howard Phillips Lovecraft (1890–1937) was a reclusive writer from Providence, Rhode Island, whose short, troubled life was defined by poverty, illness, and isolation. Out of that bleak existence, he imagined something vast: a universe indifferent to humanity, filled with incomprehensible gods, ancient texts, and creeping madness. His worldview called "cosmic horror" insists that the most terrifying truth isn't death or monsters, but our own insignificance in an uncaring cosmos.

Signature Works (Curated)
- *The Call of Cthulhu* (1928) — Introduced the Great Old One, spawning a mythology of cults and cosmic dread.
- *At the Mountains of Madness* (1931) — Antarctic expedition uncovers alien ruins, blending pulp adventure with existential terror.
- *The Shadow Over Innsmouth* (1931) — A seaside town reveals its pact with monstrous Deep Ones, fusing folklore with racial paranoia.
- *The Colour Out of Space* (1927) — A meteorite unleashes a color that mutates everything it touches; one of the first "environmental horror" tales.

The Fingerprints
- Cosmic indifference: humanity is insignificant against the vast, ancient universe.
- Unknowable entities that warp sanity merely by being perceived.
- Obsession with forbidden knowledge (grimoires, cults, archaeological ruins).
- Decay and degeneration — physical, social, and mental.

Legacy & Influence
Lovecraft's fiction seeded an entire subgenre of "cosmic horror." His mythos was expanded by later writers (August Derleth, Ramsey Campbell) and has influenced filmmakers from John Carpenter (*The Thing, In the Mouth of Madness*) to Richard Stanley (*Color Out of Space*). Even video games (*Bloodborne, Call of Cthulhu*) echo his aesthetics. Directors like Guillermo del Toro and Stuart Gordon have cited him as foundational.

Pairing Night Watchlist
- *The Call of Cthulhu* (2005, silent-film style indie) → watch for how fan filmmakers recreate his 1920s dread.
- *Re-Animator* (1985, dir. Stuart Gordon) → gory, campy, but unmistakably Lovecraft's obsession with science-gone-mad.
- *The Color Out of Space* (2019, dir. Richard Stanley) → perhaps the most faithful modern adaptation of his cosmic vision.

Quick Facts to Sound Smart
- Lovecraft died virtually unknown; his fame exploded only posthumously.
- The term "Cthulhu Mythos" wasn't coined by him but by his literary circle.
- He rarely wrote full novels — his impact comes from short stories and novellas.
- His racial prejudices are controversial today, but critics argue they shaped his horror lens: "the fear of the other" as both metaphor and pathology.

☐ **The Gate** (1987) - Kids left home alone accidentally unleash a horde of malevolent demons from a mysterious hole in their suburban backyard.

- **SEQUELS**
  - ☐ **The Gate II: Trespassers** (1990) - The direct sequel was released in 1990, with Louis Tripp returning to reprise his role as Terry. The plot follows Terry, who, years after the events of the first film, purposefully reopens the gate to use the demonic forces to grant wishes. The sequel was a box office disappointment and was not as well-received as the original.

☐ **The Unnamable** (1988) - College students check out a haunted house where in the 1800's an ugly monster called "the Unnamable" was trapped in a vault. The film is based on H.P. Lovecraft's 1925 short story of the same name, which is a classic piece of cosmic horror literature. However, the film departs significantly from the original story, which is much more subtle and focused on philosophical dread.

- **SEQUELS**
  - ☐ **The Unnamable II: The Statement of Randolph Carter** (1992) - The direct sequel was released in 1992, with many of the original cast members returning. The sequel incorporates elements from another Lovecraft story, "The Statement of Randolph Carter," and focuses more on creature effects and lore expansion than the first film.

☐ **The Lurking Fear** (1994) - The town of Leffert's Corners has been plagued by unearthly beings for decades, and now there is only a few people left... what everyone is not aware of are the humanoid creatures lurking underneath the holy grounds. The film is based on H.P. Lovecraft's 1923 short story "The Lurking Fear." While the source material is a classic piece of cosmic horror literature, the film departs significantly from the original story's focus on philosophical dread and an incomprehensible horror.

- **ADAPTIONS**
  - ☐ **Dark Heritage** (1989) - An independent, low-budget film that also adapts the Lovecraft story.
  - ☐ **Bleeders** (1997) - Also known as *Hemoglobin*, this Canadian film is a loose adaptation of the Lovecraft story and was co-written by Dan O'Bannon, who also wrote *The Resurrected*, another Lovecraft adaptation.
  - ☐ **The Lurking Fear** (2024) - A recent Tubi Original film adaptation.

☐ **Event Horizon** (1997) – A Gothic haunted house, but in space, dripping with infernal imagery.

- **INFLUENCES**
  - ☐ **Solaris** (1972, USSR) - A psychologist is sent to a station orbiting a distant planet in order to discover what has caused the crew to go insane. Director Paul W.S. Anderson drew inspiration from Andrei Tarkovsky's 1972 film *Solaris*, which also deals with a space station crew's psychological torment. It is based on the Stanislaw Lem's novel of the same name.
    - **ADAPTIONS AND INFLUENCED FILMS**
      - ☐ **Solaris** (2002) - Directed by Steven Soderbergh, this American remake starred George Clooney as Chris Kelvin. This version is more streamlined and focuses heavily on the romantic and psychological elements of the story. Author Stanislaw Lem was famously critical of both the 1972 and 2002 films, feeling they misinterpreted his original themes.
      - ☐ **Sunshine** (2007) - A team of international astronauts is sent on a dangerous mission to reignite the dying Sun with a nuclear fission bomb in 2057. Inspired the psychological, isolating atmosphere and the concept of an intelligence near a celestial body that challenges the characters' minds.
      - ☐ **Annihilation** (2018) – Sci-fi cosmic surrealism framed as body/identity horror. Loosely based on a novel, this film involves an extraterrestrial entity that causes bizarre biological and psychological changes to a landscape, creating new, often terrifying, lifeforms. This film's plot, about a mysterious, reality-altering zone and its effect on human consciousness, has clear parallels to the unexplained phenomena of the Solaris ocean. The lighthouse sequence reframes "alien contact" as choreography instead of combat.

☐ **Dark City** (1998, Australia) - A man struggles with memories of his past, which include a wife he cannot remember and a nightmarish world no one else ever seems to wake up from. he film's moody visuals, distorted cityscapes, and unsettling atmosphere draw heavily from films like Fritz Lang's *Metropolis* and Robert Wiene's *The Cabinet of Dr. Caligari*.

☐ **The Call of Cthulhu** (2005) - While sorting the affairs of his late Uncle, a man accidentally stumbles across a series of dark secrets connected to an ancient horror waiting to be freed. A low-budget, black-and-white film created by the H.P. Lovecraft Historical Society that faithfully adapts the original story.

- **ADAPTIONS OF THE CTHULHU MYTHOS:** The Cthulhu Mythos is the shared universe of cosmic horror created by H. P. Lovecraft and later expanded by other writers. Centered on ancient, incomprehensible beings like Cthulhu, Nyarlathotep, and Yog-Sothoth, it depicts a universe where humanity is insignificant and even glimpsing the truth can shatter the mind.

  ☐ **The Mist** (2007) – After a massive thunderstorm, an eerie, unwavering fog descends upon a Maine community. Locals seek refuge in a grocery store from the monstrous creatures now roaming the countryside killing everyone they encounter. While based on a Stephen King novella, its themes of monsters emerging from another dimension into an isolated town have strong Lovecraftian undertones.

  ☐ **Underwater** (2020) – Researchers face Lovecraftian sea monster. A crew of deep-sea researchers encounters ancient, Cthulhu-like creatures after a drilling facility is devastated. Initially, some fans speculated that *Underwater* might be a secret installment of the *Cloverfield* franchise, which often features mysterious monster attacks and viral marketing. However, this theory was debunked, though the film's tone would fit the series.

  ☐ **The Color Out of Space** (2019) – Alien hue mutates land and flesh. It is an adaptation of an H.P. Lovecraft story and the first in a planned trilogy of cosmic horror films from director Richard Stanley.

    - **COLOR OUT OF SPACE ADAPTIONS**

      ☐ **Die, Monster, Die!** (1965) - A young man visits his fiancée's estate to discover that her wheelchair-bound scientist father has discovered a meteorite that emits mutating radiation rays that have turned the plants in his greenhouse to giants. When his own wife falls victim to this mysterious power, the old man takes it upon himself to destroy the glowing object with disastrous results. AIP loved Lovecraft and produced numerous adaptions in the 1960s such as *The Haunted Palace, The Crimson Cult* and *The Dunwich Horror.*

        - **AIP LOVECRAFT ADAPTIONS IN THE 60s**

          ☐ **The Dunwich Horror** (1970) – Lovecraft adaptation with occult overtones and Gothic rituals.

      ☐ **The Curse** (1987) - This film starring Wil Wheaton is a more direct adaptation of Lovecraft's story, also revolving around a farm contaminated by an otherworldly presence from a meteorite.

      ☐ **Die Farbe [The Colour]** (2010) - A boy, looking for his missing father, travels to Germany and uncovers a haunting legacy that a meteorite left behind in the area.

      ☐ **Colour from the Dark** (2008, Italy) - The 2008 film adapts Lovecraft's 1927 cosmic horror story, but sets it in Italy during World War II instead of rural Massachusetts in the 1920s. The core plot, however, remains similar: a strange, otherworldly presence corrupts a family and its environment after a meteorite lands on their farm.

  ☐ **Glorious** (2022) - After a breakup, Wes ends up at a remote rest stop. He finds himself locked inside the bathroom with a mysterious figure speaking from an adjacent stall. Soon Wes realizes he is involved in a situation more terrible than he could imagine. Ghat, voiced by J.K. Simmons, is an eldritch being whose full existence is beyond human understanding. His name is Ghatanothoa, a deity from the Cthulhu Mythos created by H.P. Lovecraft.

- ☐ **Triangle** (2009, UK/Australia) - Five friends set sail and their yacht is overturned by a strange and sudden storm. A mysterious ship arrives to rescue them, and what happens next cannot be explained. In an article for Den of Geek, the film is compared to Stanley Kubrick's *The Shining* for the way its setting functions as a labyrinth, slowly driving the protagonist mad through a supernatural, cyclical reality.
  - • **TIME LOOP HORRORS**
    - ☐ **Lost Things** (2004) - Four teenagers on a surfing weekend find themselves ensnared in a time loop controlled by a demonic entity. The film builds existential dread from its beach setting and a low-budget approach.
    - ☐ **Camp Slaughter** (2005) - A horror-comedy about a group of teens stuck in a never-ending time loop at a summer camp, reliving the same deadly events from an 80s slasher film.
    - ☐ **Timecrimes** (2007, Spain) –A man accidentally gets into a time machine and travels back in time nearly an hour. Finding himself will be the first of a series of disasters of unforeseeable consequences. *Timecrimes* is a low-budget, mind-bending thriller that has earned a cult following. Fans of the film may enjoy other time-travel films with a similar focus on causality and paradoxes.
    - ☐ **Haunter** (2013, Canada) - A teenager is stuck in a time loop that is not quite the same each time. She must uncover the truth, but her actions have consequences for herself and others.
    - ☐ **Blood Punch** (2014) - Three meth-cookers are caught in a time loop at a remote cabin, where they keep killing each other and returning to life in a cycle of drug-fueled horror and black comedy.
    - ☐ **Happy Death Day** (2017) – Slasher meets Groundhog Day comedy. The third film in the series has been in development for several years. After long delays due to budget concerns, it was announced in April 2025 that the film is officially moving forward. The plot will reportedly not take place on the same day as the first two films and will introduce a new genre to the series.
      - • **SEQUELS**
        - ☐ **Happy Death Day 2U** (2019) – Adds sci-fi time loop hijinks.
    - ☐ **Koko-di Koko-da** (2019) - A Swedish/Danish surrealist horror film where a couple relives a camping trip where they are tormented by bizarre nursery rhyme characters.
    - ☐ **In the Tall Grass** (2019) - Based on a novella by Stephen King and Joe Hill, this film follows siblings who enter a large field of grass after hearing a boy's cry for help, only to find themselves trapped in a terrifying time loop.
    - ☐ **Lucky** (2020) - *Lucky*'s core premise involves a woman who is repeatedly attacked by the same masked intruder every night.
    - ☐ **6:45** (2021) - A couple travels to an island town for a romantic getaway, only for their trip to turn into a repeating nightmare when they discover they are trapped in a deadly time loop.
    - ☐ **Totally Killer** (2023) - When the infamous "Sweet Sixteen Killer" returns 35 years after his first murder spree to claim another victim, 17-year-old Jamie accidentally travels back in time to 1987, determined to stop the killer before he can start.
    - ☐ **Time Cut** (2024) - High school student accidentally travels back to 2003 and decides to stop the serial killer who murdered her sister.
    - ☐ **Until Dawn** (2025) - Based on the video game, this survival horror film features a group of friends trapped in a time loop, where mysterious foes chase and kill them in gruesome ways until they can survive until dawn.
- ☐ **Absentia** (2011) - A woman and her sister begin to link a mysterious tunnel to a series of disappearances, including that of her own husband.
- ☐ **The Whisperer in the Darkness** (2011) - This film from the H.P. Lovecraft Historical Society investigates a folklorist's unsettling encounters in rural Vermont. Produced by the HPLHS, this black-and-white feature film is known for its authentic 1930s style and faithfulness to the source material. It adapts the story as if it were released by Universal Pictures in the 1930s, complete with era-appropriate visuals, sound design, and acting. It is worth noting that the HPLHS's adaptation makes a significant change to the original ending to provide a more dramatic,

cinematic climax. While faithful in its stylistic approach, the film alters the fate of the main character, Wilmarth, in a way that is distinctly different from the original story.

- **ADAPTIONS**
  - ☐ **The Whisperer in Darkness** (1975) - The first known fan film adaptation, made on 8mm film. It was restored in 2021 by Arkham Bazaar and Sigh Co. Graphics.
  - ☐ **Necronomicon: Book of the Dead** (1993) - Lovecraft visualizes 3 stories in Necronomicon: The Drowned, The Cold and Whispers, about bringing a dead wife and child back to life, extending life and aliens. The final segment of this anthology horror film, titled "Whispers," was loosely based on Lovecraft's story, though the resemblance is somewhat tenuous due to heavy revisions.

☐ **Dark Skies** (2013) - As the Barrett family's peaceful suburban life is rocked by an escalating series of disturbing events, they come to learn that a terrifying and deadly force is after them, one which may have arrived from beyond the stars. The film, produced by Blumhouse, has a similar domestic horror feel to other properties from the production company, such as *Paranormal Activity* and *Insidious*.

- **SIMILAR THEMES**
  - ☐ **The McPherson Tapes** (1989) - On a typical fall evening in 1983, a young man was videotaping his niece's 5th birthday party. As the night's strange occurrences took place, he kept his video camera running, recording the entire event.
    - **SEQUEL**
      - ☐ **Alien Abduction: Incident in Lake County** (1998) - The official remake of the original, this version was also presented as a true account and is a direct comparison point.
  - ☐ **Fire in the Sky** (1993) - This film, based on a true story, explores a brutal alien abduction experience, a theme shared by *Dark Skies*.
  - ☐ **Signs** (2002) - M. Night Shyamalan's film also centers on a family coping with an unsettling and mysterious alien presence.
  - ☐ **The Fourth Kind** (2009) - The unsolved mystery of a town in Alaska with an extraordinary number of disappearances during the past 40 years, with accusations of a federal cover up. This film similarly explores the terror of an alien entity invading a family home.

☐ **The Borderlands (Final Prayer)** (2013, UK) – Priests face pagan site under church. The film's emphasis on ancient, hidden paganism and cosmic horror has earned comparisons to the works of H.P. Lovecraft.

- **THEMATIC COMPARISONS**
  - ☐ **As Above, So Below** (2014, France) – Parisian catacombs hide cultic secrets. Many horror fans who appreciate the claustrophobic dread of *The Borderlands* often recommend this film, which also involves a found-footage crew uncovering supernatural horrors in a confined, underground space.

☐ **Spring** (2014) – Woman's body cycles through monstrous transformations. Fans of *Spring*'s unique blend of romance and cosmic horror have drawn comparisons to other films, such as *Possession, Bones and All,* and *Color Out of Space.*

- **BENSON & MOORHEAD**
  - ☐ **Resolution** (2012) – Their earlier film has subtle connections to *Spring*, including a character who reappears in their later work.
  - ☐ **The Endless** (2017) – This film most directly ties the universe together, with characters and plot points connecting to both *Resolution* and *Spring*. In *The Endless*, the protagonists watch the *Spring* movie, which exists within their reality as a film based on real events. A companion to the directors' earlier *Resolution*; together they sketch a shared myth of a narrative-hungry entity.
  - ☐ **Synchronic** (2019) - While it is less connected, this film also features a shared universe reference, confirming all four movies occupy the same reality.
  - ☐ **Something in the Dirt** (2022) - Maverick filmmaking duo Justin Benson and Aaron Moorhead offer up a twisted reflection of our paranoid times in this inventive mix of buddy comedy and sci-fi thriller.

☐ **Hidden** (2015) - A family takes refuge in a bomb shelter to avoid a dangerous outbreak. Directed by the Duffer Brothers of *Stranger Things*.

- ☐ **A Quiet Place** (2018) – In a post-apocalyptic world, a family is forced to live in silence while hiding from monsters with ultra-sensitive hearing. Nominated for Best Achievement in Sound Editing at the 2019 Academy Awards.
  - **ADAPTIONS & SEQUELS**
    - ☐ **A Quiet Place Part II** (2021) – Abbott family continues sound-based survival.
    - ☐ **A Quiet Place Part III** (Upcoming, 2027): This third film will continue the Abbott family's story directly after the events of *Part II*. Originally announced for a 2025 release, the project was delayed, but John Krasinski is confirmed to return as director. The new release date is set for July 9, 2027.
    - ☐ **A Quiet Place: Day One** (2024) - A prequel and spinoff film that follows new characters during the initial days of the creature invasion in New York City. It features Lupita Nyong'o and Joseph Quinn and was directed by Michael Sarnoski.
- ☐ **Bird Box** (2018) – Five years after an ominous unseen presence drives most of society to suicide, a mother and her two children make a desperate bid to reach safety.
  - **ADAPTIONS**
    - ☐ **Bird Box Barcelona** (2023) - This is not a direct sequel to the 2018 film but a spin-off that takes place in the same timeline. It explores how the mysterious entities affected other parts of the world, focusing on a new group of characters in Spain.
- ☐ **The Beach House** (2019) - A romantic getaway for two troubled college sweethearts turns into a struggle for survival when unexpected guests - and the surrounding environment - exhibit signs of a mysterious infection. The film draws heavily from the cosmic horror genre, focusing on themes of humanity's insignificance in the face of an incomprehensible and alien force.
- ☐ **Vivarium** (2019, Ireland/Luxembourg) - A young couple looking for the perfect home find themselves trapped in a mysterious labyrinth-like neighborhood of identical houses. Director Lorcan Finnegan has cited several films as influences, including: *2001: A Space Odyssey, Lost Highway, The Twilight Zone,* and Art from painters like René Magritte and M.C. Escher, which provided the inspiration for the housing development's uniform and otherworldly aesthetic.
  - **SIMILAR THEMES**
    - ☐ **Under the Skin** (2013, UK) – Alien seduces men and liquefies bodies. An alien takes human form to prey on men in Scotland, creating a film with a detached, unsettling tone and themes of isolation.
- ☐ **Psycho Goreman** (2020) - After unearthing a gem that controls an evil monster looking to destroy the Universe, a young girl and her brother use it to make him do their bidding. If you like Steven Kostanski he co-directed *The Void, Frankie Freako,* and *Deathstalker.* Kostanski has been compared to the director of this film by a critic.
  - **KOSTANKSI PROJECTS**
    - ☐ **Frankie Freako** (2024) - Workaholic yuppie Conor is in an existential rut until one night he catches a bizarre ad for a party hotline hosted by a strange dancing goblin: Frankie Freako. Could this be just the recipe to spice up his boring life?
- ☐ **The Empty Man** (2020) - On the trail of a missing girl, an ex-cop comes across a secretive group attempting to summon a terrifying supernatural entity. Based on the Boom! Studios graphic novel series. The film draws inspiration from the cosmic horror genre and writers like H.P. Lovecraft. It explores themes of contagious thoughts, psychic transmission, and the creation of reality through belief, particularly the concept of a *tulpa* (a being created by collective thought).
- ☐ **She Dies Tomorrow** (2020) - A woman becomes strangely convinced she will die the next day. Her friend initially disbelieves her before becoming paranoid herself that she too will die the next day. Released during the early days of the COVID-19 pandemic, the film was praised for its timely exploration of viral anxiety and paranoia, a theme that felt very relevant to the moment.
  - **COVID-ERA PARANOIA**
    - ☐ **Sick** (2022) - Due to the pandemic, Parker and her best friend decide to quarantine at the family lake house alone - or so they think.
- ☐ **Mad God** (2021) - The Assassin travels through a nightmare underworld of tortured souls, ruined cities and wretched monstrosities forged from the primordial horrors of the unconscious mind of Phil Tippett, the world's preeminent stop-motion animator.

- **Skinamarink** (2022) – Two children wake up in the middle of the night to find their father is missing, and all the windows and doors in their home have vanished. Ball crowdsourced childhood nightmare descriptions on YouTube to inspire the film's imagery.
  - **SURREAL HORROR**
    - **Come True** (2020) - A teenage runaway takes part in a sleep study that becomes a nightmarish descent into the depths of her mind and a frightening examination of the power of dreams.
    - **Stopmotion** (2023) - A stop-motion animator struggles to control her demons after the loss of her overbearing mother.
- **The Outwaters** (2023) – Four travelers encounter menacing phenomena while camping in a remote stretch of the Mojave Desert. Much of the sound design was created from distorted field recordings of desert wildlife.
- **No One Will Save You** (2023) - An exiled anxiety-ridden homebody must battle an alien who's found its way into her home.

Cosmic Horror Pairing Night: How To Stare Into It

Main Course: Identity Erosion
The Thing (1982) + The Endless (2017)
How to watch: Paranoia first, patterns second. Track how assimilation terror evolves into authorship terror.
Smartest fact: Both films weaponize uncertainty about who is "you," one at the cellular level, one at the editorial level.

Side Dish: Science As Summoning
Quatermass and the Pit (1967) + Prince of Darkness (1987)
How to watch: Pair British rationalism with American metaphysics. Fossils rewrite origins, equations rewrite theology.
Smartest fact: Kneale distrusted pulp demons; Carpenter makes the demon an equation you can accidentally solve.

Dessert: Ecology Will Have You Now
Annihilation (2018) + Matango (1963)
How to watch: Consume a modern shimmer of refracted DNA, then an older fable of mushrooms and appetite.
Smartest fact: Both treat "infection" as an invitation to join a larger system, which is the kindest and cruelest idea in the genre.

Nightcap: The Story That Eats You
Resolution (2012) + The Empty Man (2020)
How to watch: Two tales of characters trapped by narratives that want outcomes. One small and intimate, one sprawling and cultic.
Smartest fact: Each suggests the antagonist is a curator, not a killer. The horror is being arranged.

Beyond the Stars

Mad Scientist Horror

Mad Scientist Horror makes the laboratory the haunted castle. Where Gothic tales warned of curses, the mad scientist warns of discovery itself: lightning-charged labs, test tubes bubbling with hubris, surgical tables where ethics dissolve. Here, terror comes not from the supernatural but from human ambition unbound. The arrogance to tamper with life, mind, and body until monstrosity is inevitable. From Frankenstein's stitched creature to atomic mutations and cybernetic nightmares, the mad scientist charts our anxieties about progress, technology, and the thin line between genius and madness.

Why People Are Drawn to It

Because mad scientist horror is both warning and seduction. It asks: *What if knowledge goes too far?* The thrill lies in watching intellect mutate into obsession, science become sorcery. Audiences are lured by invention's spectacle: flashing coils, grotesque hybrids, invisibility serums, but also by the moral drama: hubris punished, humanity betrayed. It speaks to the unease of every age, whether fears of electricity, eugenics, nuclear fallout, or artificial intelligence. We crave the spectacle of genius undone, the reminder that progress always carries a cost.

Essentials

1. **Frankenstein (1931, USA)** –Gave cinematic form to Mary Shelley's Gothic novel, turning the stitched-together Creature into a tragic icon of horror. James Whale's stylized direction and Boris Karloff's poignant performance made it a landmark of both monster cinema and modern myth.
2. **The Invisible Man (1933, USA)** – H.G. Wells adapted with sadistic wit: science turns body to vapor and mind to mania. Revolved scientific ambition into horror, with Claude Rains's chilling performance embodying the madness of unchecked power. James Whale's inventive special effects and dark humor made invisibility both a spectacle and a parable of isolation and moral collapse.
3. **Island of Lost Souls (1932, USA)** – Brought H. G. Wells's *The Island of Dr. Moreau* to the screen with startling perversity, steeping its tale of human-animal hybrids in atmosphere both exotic and grotesque. Charles Laughton's sinister Dr. Moreau and the infamous "House of Pain" turned scientific hubris into nightmare, making it one of the most transgressive pre-Code horrors.
4. **The Fly (1958, USA)** – Cold War mutation: a brilliant experiment in teleportation fuses man and insect, tragedy and reveal. Turned scientific hubris into body horror, as a botched teleportation experiment fuses a man with an insect. Its tragic mix of domestic melodrama and grotesque transformation made it a cornerstone of 1950s sci-fi horror, blending pathos with shock.
5. **Re-Animator (1985, USA)** – Turned H.P. Lovecraft's tale of scientific obsession into outrageous splatter comedy, pushing horror into gleefully transgressive extremes. Stuart Gordon's mix of gore, dark humor, and Jeffrey Combs's manic performance created a cult classic that redefined the mad scientist for the VHS generation.

Deep Cuts

1. **Dr. Jekyll and Mr. Hyde (1931, USA)** – Transformation as science and allegory; repression bottled, then unleashed. Visualized the duality of human nature with startling intensity, using innovative makeup and camera tricks to show the doctor's transformation into his monstrous double. Rouben Mamoulian's adaptation fused moral cautionary tale with early cinematic shock, making it a cornerstone of psychological and body horror.
2. **Eyes Without a Face (1960, France)** – Fused poetic lyricism with surgical horror, telling the story of a guilt-ridden doctor who mutilates young women in hopes of restoring his daughter's disfigured face. Georges Franju's

haunting mix of beauty and brutality created a surreal meditation on obsession, identity, and the violence hidden beneath devotion.

3. **The Brain That Wouldn't Die (1962, USA)** – Epitomized drive-in schlock, combining mad science with lurid exploitation. Its tale of a severed head kept alive while the scientist hunts for a new body pushes pulp horror into camp, remembered as much for its grotesque premise as for its cult reputation.

4. **Altered States (1980, USA)** – Fused psychedelic imagery with body horror, following a scientist whose sensory-deprivation experiments unleash primal states of human evolution. Ken Russell's surreal visuals and William Hurt's intense performance turned scientific inquiry into a nightmarish descent through consciousness, identity, and transformation.

5. **Tetsuo: The Iron Man (1989, Japan)** – Exploded cyberpunk and body horror into a frantic industrial nightmare, where flesh mutates violently into scrap metal. Shinya Tsukamoto's raw, experimental style turned technology, desire, and dehumanization into a relentless assault, making it a cornerstone of extreme and avant-garde horror.

Critical Essay
"The Lab is the New Castle: Hubris, Obsession, and Scientific Horror."
Myth: The mad scientist is only a cackling caricature in a white coat.
Reality: The archetype is cultural critique. From Shelley's Frankenstein to Cronenberg's *The Fly*, these stories embody the shadow of progress: eugenics, radiation, AI, bioengineering. The laboratory replaces the crypt, but the theme is unchanged: forbidden knowledge punishes its seeker. The mad scientist is both visionary and villain, a mirror of society's own ambivalence about discovery.

Global Spotlight: Britain & Japan
- **Britain**: Hammer Films recharged Frankenstein through Peter Cushing's ruthless Baron — no tragic idealist, but a cold manipulator. Films like *The Curse of Frankenstein* (1957) and sequels made science itself monstrous.
- **Japan**: From *Matango* (1963, fungus-mutated castaways) to *Akira* (1988, psychic science gone nuclear), Japanese cinema linked experiments to postwar trauma and mutation. Here the mad scientist often symbolizes authority unchecked, progress collapsing into apocalypse.

Gothic & Classic Foundations
☐ **Homounculus** (1914, Germany) - A group of scientists, led by a Professor Ortmann, produce a living human child using scientific processes - a "homunculus." This creature is human in every way, except that he cannot experience love.

- **ADAPTIONS & INFLUENCES**
    - ☐ **Metropolis** (1927, Germany) - Director Fritz Lang, who worked as an assistant on *Homunculus*, later explored similar themes of a malevolent automaton stirring up a workers' revolt in his 1927 masterpiece.
    - ☐ **The Golem** (2018, Israel) – Jewish folk myth of clay protector. During an outbreak of a deadly plague in Lithuania, a mystical woman must save her tight-knit Jewish community from a gang of ruffians led by a local landowner, but the entity she conjures to protect them is a far greater evil.
        - **OTHER GOLEM MOVIES:** The golem is a figure from Jewish folklore, a being sculpted from clay or mud and brought to life through sacred ritual or divine words. Created to protect Jewish communities from danger, the golem embodies both miraculous power and the danger of unchecked creation, often growing uncontrollable once it gains strength.

- **Der Golem** (1915, Germany) - The first of Wegener's films, this mostly lost silent movie was set in modern times and portrayed the Golem falling in love and going on a jealous rampage.
- **The Golem: How He Came into the World** (1920, Germany) - A classic German silent horror film that is perhaps the most famous adaptation of the golem story. Wegener's most famous and best-preserved film was a prequel set in 16th-century Prague. It cemented the core story of Rabbi Löw creating a clay giant to protect the Jewish community from persecution.
- **The Golem** (1936, Czech) - Early adaptation of Jewish folklore.
- **It!** (1967, UK) - A British horror film in which a museum owner uses a revived Golem to take revenge on his enemies.

- **The Cabinet of Dr. Caligari** (1920, Germany) – Expressionist nightmare where a hypnotist uses a somnambulist to commit murders. Drenched in eerie visuals and twisted architecture. **Censorship:** Minimal, though criticized

for "perverting" German morality. Its twist ending was an afterthought, demanded by producers.

- **A Blind Bargain** (1920) – Based on the novel *The Octave of Claudius*. In return for money and medical aid for his invalid mother, struggling author Robert Sandell agrees to subject himself to experiments by Dr. Lamb, who claims he is trying to extend the human lifespan. Because the 1922 version is lost, director Paul Bunnell released a modern reimagining of the film starring Crispin Glover. It updates the story to 1970 but keeps the core premise of a desperate man making a deal with a mad doctor.
- **The Monster** (1925) - The horror revolves around a brilliant but deranged surgeon, Dr. Ziska (Lon Chaney), who runs a secluded sanitarium and conducts bizarre experiments on his patients.

Director Roland West's later works continue the "old dark house" style, and the film's star, Lon Chaney, was prolific in silent horror during this period. Roland west went on to direct *The Bat* and *The Bat Whispers* while Lou Chaney had a banner year with the releases of *Phantom of the Opera* and *The Unholy Three* as well.

- **The Magician** (1926) - A magician/alchemist, seeking to create life, finds that he needs the "blood of a virgin" to continue his experiments. He sends out his dwarf assistant to pick out the right girl. Based on the novel by W. Somerset Maugham. The character of Oliver Haddo was reportedly based on the real-life occultist Aleister Crowley. Several historians have noted the film's influence on Whale's classic monster films, including *Frankenstein* (1931), *Bride of Frankenstein* (1935) and *The Black Cat* (1934).

  - **THEMES OF ALEISTER CROWLEY:** Known as the wickedest man in the world. Aleister Crowley (1875–1947) was a British occultist, writer, and ceremonial magician who founded the religion of Thelema. Known for his motto "Do what thou wilt," Crowley's influence stretched beyond esoteric circles, shaping modern occultism, countercultural spirituality, and even the imagery of rock and pop culture.

    - **Curse of the Demon** (1957) - The central occultist figure in this British horror film, Julian Karswell, is also believed to be based on Crowley.
    - **Abbey of Thelema** (2007) - This film explores Crowley's occult commune in Cefalù, Sicily, during the 1920s.
    - **In Search of the Great Beast 666** (2007) - A documentary that explores Crowley's life, ideas, and his influence on the spiritual world.

153

- ☐ **Chemical Wedding** (2008, UK) - Written by Iron Maiden frontman Bruce Dickinson, this British horror film features a virtual reality experiment that accidentally resurrects Aleister Crowley's soul inside a university professor.
- ☐ **Aleister Crowley: Legend of the Beast** (2013) - A low-budget biographical drama depicting Crowley's life story from his deathbed. A haunting look into the world most famous occultist's journey - from his devout Christian upbringing through his many aspirations, Aleister Crowley looks back on the many triumphs and pains of how he lived and loved.
- ☐ **A Dark Song** (2016, Ireland) – Occult ritual spirals into obsession. A psychological horror film centered on a complex occult ritual that draws heavily from real magical practices, including some known to have been used by Crowley.
  - • **SIMILAR THEMES**
    - ☐ **The Haunting of Bly Manor** (2020) - Director Liam Gavin directed two episodes of this Netflix horror series, which also features supernatural themes and a claustrophobic atmosphere.
    - ☐ **The Dark and the Wicked** (2020) – On a secluded farm in a nondescript rural town, a man is slowly dying. His family gathers to mourn, and soon a darkness grows, marked by waking nightmares and a growing sense that something evil is taking over the family.
    - ☐ **From Black** (2023) - Another horror film that involves a woman dealing with grief and resorting to a dark ritual, a premise similar to *A Dark Song*. A guilt-ridden mother gets an offer to uncover her missing son's fate, but at a disturbing cost. Her decision on how far she'll go for redemption drives the story.
- ☐ **The Confessions of Aleister Crowley** (2020) - A low-budget horror film featuring three mysterious figures embark on a road trip up to Loch Ness in Scotland, with the mission of completing Aleister Crowleys infamous Abramelin spell.
- ☐ **Nightmare Alley** (2021) - Guillermo del Toro's psychological thriller deals with themes of mysticism and manipulation, with some viewers noting similarities to Crowley's influence in spiritualism.
- ☐ **A Daughter of Destiny** (1928, Germany) - A scientist with an interest in genetics impregnates a sex worker with the seed of a hanged murderer. The sex worker gives birth to a child who has no concept of love, whom the scientist adopts. Based on the 1911 novel, *Alraune* by Hanns Heinz Ewers.
  - • **ADAPTIONS**
    - ☐ **Alraune** (1918, Hungary) - This earlier version, also based on the same novel, is now considered a lost film. A mad scientist "creates" a beautiful but demonic woman, the result of a forced sexual union between a woman and a mandrake root, a plant said to have magical powers due to its uncanny resemblance to the human body.
    - ☐ **Alraune** (1930, Germany) - Brigitte Helm, who starred in the 1928 version, reprised her role in this sound film remake. A scientist, Professor Jakob ten Brinken, interested in the laws of heredity, impregnates a prostitute in a laboratory with the semen of a hanged murderer. The prostitute conceives a female child who has no concept of love, whom the professor adopts. The girl, Alraune, suffers from obsessive sexuality and perverse relationships throughout her life. She learns of her unnatural origins and she avenges herself against the professor.
    - ☐ **Alraune** (1952, West Germany) - This later remake starred Hildegard Knef as Alraune and Erich von Stroheim as her misguided mentor. A scientist creates

a beautiful "perfect woman", but since she is artificial, she seems soul-less and with no sense of morality, she brings ruin to all around her.

☐ **Frankenstein** (1931) – Shelley's tragic monster comes to life; Gothic themes of creation, isolation, and unintended horror. Condemned in multiple states for its "Playing God" theme. **Memorable Quote:** *"It's Alive!"*

- **SEQUELS**
    - ☐ **Bride of Frankenstein** (1935) – A baroque and emotionally resonant sequel, often regarded as superior to its predecessor. Whale laced the sequel with camp and satire, making it one of the first knowingly queer horror films. **Memorable Quote:** *"To a new world of gods and monsters!"*
    - ☐ **Son of Frankenstein** (1939) - Returning to the ancestral castle long after the death of the monster, the son of Dr. Frankenstein meets a mad shepherd who is hiding the comatose creature.
    - ☐ **The Ghost of Frankenstein** (1942) - Dr. Frankenstein's plans to replace the brain of his monster are hijacked by his scheming and malevolent assistant Ygor.
    - ☐ **Frankenstein Meets the Wolf Man** (1943) - The resurrected Wolf Man, seeking a cure for his malady, enlists the aid of a mad scientist, who claims he will not only rid the Wolf Man of his nocturnal metamorphosis, but also revive the frozen body of Frankenstein's inhuman creation.
    - ☐ **House of Frankenstein** (1944) - A deranged scientist escapes from prison and recruits Dracula, Frankenstein's Monster and the Wolf Man to get revenge on his behalf.
    - ☐ **House of Dracula** (1945) - The Wolf Man and Count Dracula beg Dr. Edelman to cure them of their killing instincts but Dracula schemes to seduce the doctor's nurse.
- **HAMMER ADAPTIONS**
    - ☐ **The Curse of Frankenstein** (1957) – Hammer's first color horror film; vivid gore and Gothic dread define this reimagining of Shelley's tale. BBFC demanded cuts to the gore. Its box office success saved Hammer and launched two decades of Gothic revival.
    - ☐ **The Revenge of Frankenstein** (1958) - Having escaped execution and assumed an alias, Baron Frankenstein transplants his deformed underling's brain into a perfect body, but the result proves to be mortally perilous.
    - ☐ **The Evil of Frankenstein** (1964) - In a soft reboot, a penniless Victor Frankenstein returns to his village, finds his old monster frozen, and uses a hypnotist to control it.
    - ☐ **Frankenstein Created Woman** (1967) - Baron Frankenstein transfers the soul of his executed assistant into the body of the assistant's lover, who then seeks revenge on those who wronged them.

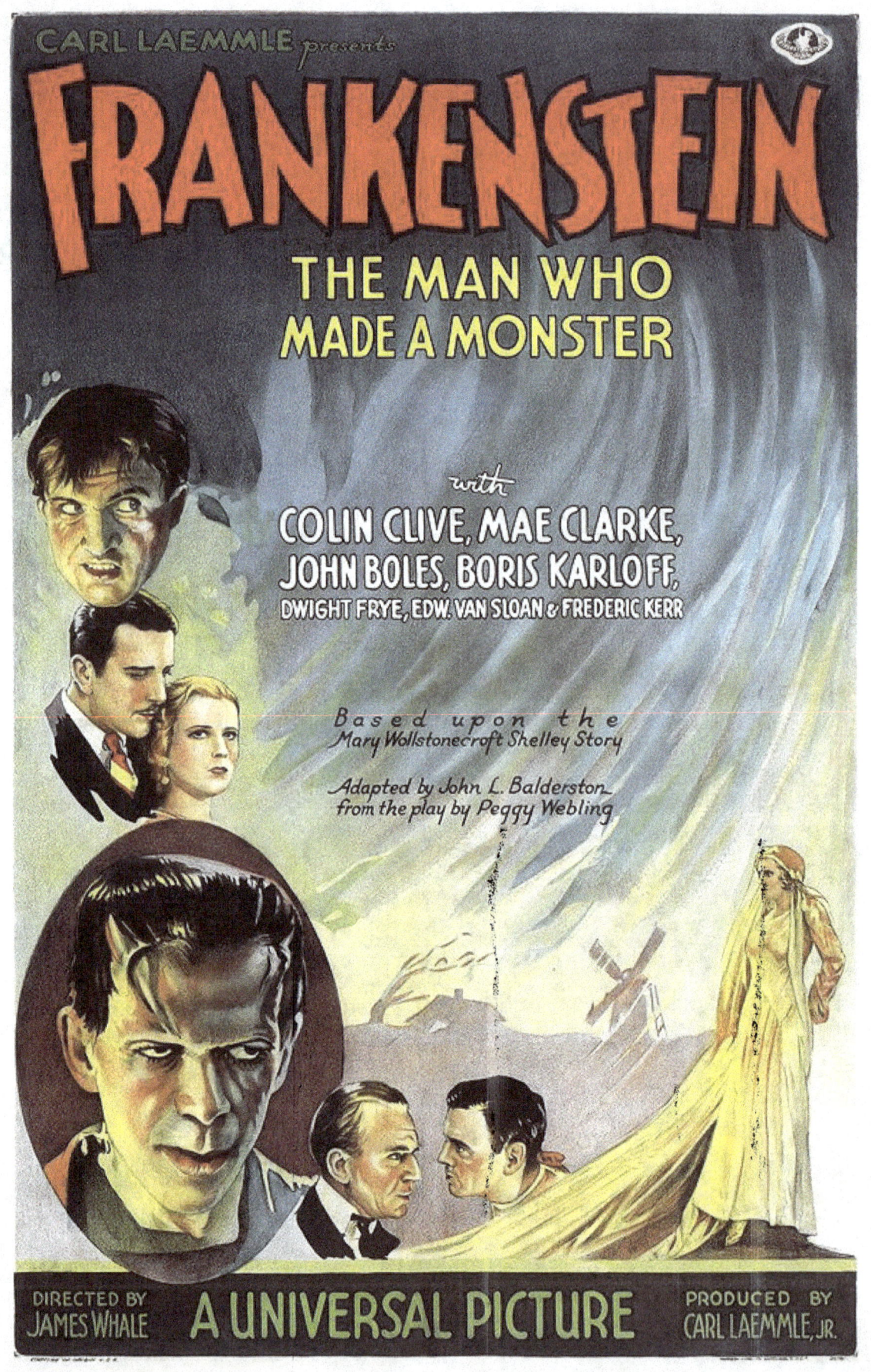

□ **Frankenstein Must Be Destroyed** (1970) - Baron Frankenstein, with the aid of a young doctor and his fiancée, kidnaps the mentally sick Dr. Brandt in order to perform the first brain transplant operation.

□ **Frankenstein and the Monster from Hell** (1974) - In the final film of the series, a Baron Frankenstein hiding in an asylum uses a young doctor to help him reanimate the dead.

- **OTHER ADAPTIONS**
  □ **Frankenstein** (1910) - The first filmed adaptation of the classic Mary Shelley novel, this silent short details the creation of the monster.
  □ **The Horror of Frankenstein** (1970) - A comedic remake of the original story, featuring Ralph Bates as a younger, more ruthless Baron Frankenstein.
  □ **Lady Frankenstein** (1971, Italy) - Baron Frankenstein's daughter and his assistant/her lover continue his experiments in an attempt to rebuild his legacy after he is killed by his psychotic, murderous first monster.

  □ **Frankenstein: The True Story** (1973) - When the brilliant but unorthodox scientist Dr. Victor Frankenstein rejects the artificial man that he has created, the Creature escapes and later swears revenge.
  □ **Young Frankenstein** (1974) – Mel Brooks' affectionate send-up of Universal horror.
  □ **Terror of Frankenstein** (1977) - Victor Frankenstein's search for the secret of life leads to the creation of a monster that consumes his life and family.
  □ **Gothic** (1986) – Ken Russell's surreal imagining of the night Mary Shelley conceived *Frankenstein*. Dreamlike and disturbing.
  □ **Frankenstein Unbound** (1990) - The ultimate weapon, which was meant to be safe for mankind, produces global side effects including time slides and disappearances. The scientist behind the project, and his car, are zapped from the year 2031 to 1817's Switzerland.
  □ **Mary Shelley's Frankenstein** (1994) – Branagh directs an extravagant, faithful Gothic adaptation.
  □ **Frankenhooker** (1990) - This film's story of a man who builds a new girlfriend from the body parts of prostitutes shares a similar low-budget, comedic, and gruesome tone to *Brain Damage*.
  □ **Frankenstein** (1994) - When the brilliant but unorthodox scientist Dr. Victor Frankenstein rejects the artificial man that he has created, the Creature (Robert De Niro) escapes and later swears revenge.
  □ **Van Helsing** (2004) - The famed monster hunter is sent to Transylvania to stop Count Dracula, who is using Dr. Frankenstein's research and a werewolf for nefarious purposes.
    - **VAN HELSING THEMES**
      □ **Nadja** (1994) - A vampire family deals with their father's death in NYC while being pursued by Van Helsing and his nephew. Love and destruction clash in this modern vampire story. The film begins after Van Helsing has already killed Dracula, effectively exploring what happens to the vampire family when their iconic patriarch is gone.
  □ **I, Frankenstein** (2014) - Frankenstein's creature finds himself caught in an all-out, centuries-old war between two immortal clans.
  □ **Victor Frankenstein** (2015) – Starring Daniel Radcliff, told from Igor's perspective, we see the troubled young assistant's dark origins, his redemptive friendship with the young medical student Viktor Von Frankenstein.

- **The Angry Black Girl and Her Monster** (2023) - Vicaria's a brilliant teenager. After the brutal murder of her brother, she embarks on a dangerous journey to resurrect him. It is a direct and modern adaptation of Mary Shelley's classic novel *Frankenstein*. The film also joins a wave of horror films that incorporate social commentary and explore themes of systemic pressure, grief, and generational trauma.
- **Frankenstein** (2025) - A brilliant but egotistical scientist brings a creature to life in a monstrous experiment that ultimately leads to the undoing of both the creator and his tragic creation.
- **The Bride** (2026) - In 1930s Chicago, Frankenstein asks Dr. Euphronius to help create a companion. They give life to a murdered woman as the Bride, sparking romance, police interest, and radical social change.

- **The Devil-Doll** (1931) - An escaped convict uses miniaturized humans to wreak vengeance on those who framed him. The film was adapted from the novel *Burn, Witch, Burn!* by Abraham Merritt, though the movie significantly changed the plot. The book centered on witchcraft and supernatural themes, whereas the film explained its shrinking phenomenon through science.
  - **SIMILAR THEMES**
    - **The Unholy Three** (1925/1930) - Directed by Tod Browning, this film shares striking similarities with *The Devil-Doll*. Both feature the main character, an elderly woman in disguise, operating a shop to aid in their criminal activities. In *The Unholy Three*, the disguise was for a pet shop; in *The Devil-Doll*, it's a doll shop.
    - **Dr. Cyclops** (1940) - A mad scientist working in the South American jungle miniaturizes his colleagues when he feels his megalomania is threatened. The first science fiction film to be shot in three-strip Technicolor.

      - **The Incredible Shrinking Man** (1957) - This sci-fi horror film expanded on the central concept of miniaturization and survival in a giant world. After Scott Carey begins to shrink because of exposure to a combination of radiation and insecticide, medical science is powerless to help him.
  - **ADAPTIONS**
    - **The Incredible Shrinking Woman** (1981) - A comedic remake of *The Incredible Shrinking Man* starring Lily Tomlin and directed by Joel Schumacher. While a parody, it is based on the same source material. The original film's screenwriter, Richard Matheson, reportedly disliked this comedic take on the story.
    - **Innerspace** (1987) - Director Joe Dante, a fan of the original film, included William Schallert (who played a doctor in the original) in a small role in this film about a miniaturized person injected into a human body.
    - **Honey, I Shrunk the Kids** (1989) - This family comedy adapted the basic premise into a family-friendly adventure. The scientist father of a teenage girl and boy accidentally shrinks his and two other neighborhood teens to the size of insects. Now the teens must fight diminutive dangers as the father searches for them.
- **Dr. Jekyll and Mr. Hyde** (1931) – Early mad-science Gothic featuring terrifying transformations and moral decay. Dr. Jekyll faces horrible consequences when he lets his dark side run wild with a potion that transforms him into the animalistic Mr. Hyde.
  - **ADAPTIONS**
    - **The Duality of Man** (1910, UK) - Embodies early cinema's fascination with psychology and morality, using rudimentary effects to externalize the inner battle between good and evil. Its silent imagery reflects how film first grappled with the fractured self, anticipating decades of horror rooted in identity and repression.

- **The Head of Janus** (1920, Germany) - A lost film and an unauthorized adaptation of Robert Louis Stevenson's 1886 novella *Strange Case of Dr. Jekyll and Mr. Hyde*. It is a prime example of German Expressionist horror. Two opposing characters are hidden in the person of the inconspicuous London gentleman Dr. Warren and Janus.
- **Dr. Jekyll and Mr. Hyde** (1912) - An early adaptation of the Robert Louis Stevenson novella, it explores the dark and monstrous side of human nature through scientific experimentation. Dr. Henry Jekyll experiments with scientific means of revealing the hidden, dark side of man and releases a murderer from within himself.
- **Dr. Jekyll and Mr. Hyde** (1941) A remake of the 1931 movie, it stars Spencer Tracy, Ingrid Bergman, and Lana Turner. Dr. Jekyll allows his dark side to run wild after he drinks a potion that turns him into the evil Mr. Hyde.
- **The Son of Dr. Jekyll** (1951) - The son of the notorious Dr. Henry Jekyll is determined to prove that his father's reputation has been unjustly deserved. He sets out to develop his father's formula in order to prove that he was a brilliant scientist rather than a murderous monster.
- **My Friend, Dr. Jekyll** (1960) - Italy, Il mio amico Jekyll - comedy
- **The Two Faces of Dr. Jekyll** (1960) - U.K. film released in the U.S. as House of Fright and Jekyll's Inferno. A lurid love triangle and explicit scenes of snakes, opium dens, rape, murder and bodies crashing through glass roofs.
- **The Mistress of Dr. Jekyll** (1964) - A mad scientist creates a hideous monster to carry out his murderous plans.
- **Dr. Jekyll and Ms. Hyde** (1995) - A scientist creating perfumes inherits his great grandfather Dr. Jekyll's formula and decides to use modern technology to improve it. He ends up as an ambitious, ruthless woman.
- **Jekyll** (2007) - starring Matt Keeslar, Jonathan Silverman, Alanna Ubach, and directed by Scott Zakarin. Brilliant scientist Tom Jackman shares his body with a wicked alter ego while an ancient organization monitors their conflict. Tom uses technology to watch over his sinister half and keep his family safe, as a centuries-old plan unfolds.
- **Doctor Jekyll** (2023) - A modern re-imagining of the infamous Dr. Jekyll from Robert Louis Stevenson's 1886 novella The Strange Case of Dr. Jekyll and Mr. Hyde.
- **Doctor X** (1932) - A wisecracking New York reporter intrudes on a research scientist's quest to unmask The Moon Killer. Based on the 1931 play *The Terror* by Howard W. Comstock and Allen C. Miller.
  - **ADAPTIONS & SEQUELS**
    - **The Return of Doctor X** (1939) - The later film, starring Humphrey Bogart in his only science-fiction or horror role, involves a scientist who is revived with artificial blood and requires more to survive.
    - **Night Monster** (1942) - Kurt Ingston, a rich recluse, invites the doctors who left him a hopeless cripple to his desolate mansion in the swamps as one by one they meet horrible deaths. This Universal Pictures film starring Lionel Atwill is considered by many critics to be a loose, uncredited remake of *Doctor X*. The film also reunites Atwill with Bela Lugosi, who appeared in the original.

- **The Island of Lost Souls** (1932) - A mad doctor conducts ghastly genetic experiments on a remote island in the South Seas, much to the fear and disgust of the shipwrecked sailor who finds himself trapped there. It is the first major film adaptation of H.G. Wells's 1896 novel *The Island of Doctor Moreau*.
  - **ADAPTIONS**
    - **Terror is a Man** (1959) - A Filipino exploitation horror film that follows the same basic story of a shipwrecked man discovering a mad doctor's animal-man experiments.
    - **The Twilight People** (1972) - Another Filipino film from the director of *Terror is a Man*, this one stars Pam Grier in an action-oriented version of the story.
    - **The Island of Dr. Moreau** (1977) - A higher-budget production starring Burt Lancaster as Moreau and Michael York as the shipwrecked man.
    - **The Island of Dr. Moreau** (1996) - A famously troubled production starring Marlon Brando and Val Kilmer. It was heavily criticized, and its original screenwriter Richard Stanley was removed during filming.
- **The Invisible Man** (1933) - A scientist finds a way of becoming invisible, but in doing so, he becomes murderously insane.
  - **ADAPTIONS & SEQUELS**
    - **The Invisible Man Returns** (1940) - A man wrongly condemned for murder uses the invisibility formula to clear his name. This film notably stars a young Vincent Price.
    - **The Invisible Woman** (1940) - This film was a departure from the horror genre, using the invisibility formula as a plot device for a screwball comedy.
    - **Invisible Agent** (1942) - The invisibility serum is used for a patriotic spy adventure during World War II.
    - **The Invisible Man's Revenge** (1944) - A new character, also named Griffin, uses the formula to take revenge on his business partners.
    - **The Invisible Man** (2020) - When Cecilia's abusive ex takes his own life and leaves her his fortune, she suspects his death was a hoax. As a series of coincidences turn lethal, Cecilia works to prove that she is being hunted by someone nobody can see.
- **The Walking Dead** (1936) - After hapless pianist and ex-con John Elman (Boris Karloff) is framed for murder and wrongly executed, he is resurrected by a scientist. He then seeks revenge on the gangsters who framed him. Blends gangster crime with supernatural horror.
- **The Man They Could Not Hang** (1939) - When Dr. Savaard's experiment in cryonics is interrupted by the short-sighted authorities, his volunteer dies, and he is condemned to death. He vows vengeance if he can survive his own hanging. The film was inspired by the real-life biochemist Robert Cornish, who experimented with reviving animals after clinical death in the 1930s. He hoped to eventually apply his techniques to humans but was refused permission. The film's plot also draws heavily from the 1936 Warner Bros. film *The Walking Dead*, which also stars Boris Karloff as a wrongly executed man who is revived and seeks revenge on those who framed him.
  - **THEMATIC SEQUELS**
    - **The Man with Nine Lives** (1940) - A medical researcher visits the deserted home of a pioneer in cryogenic science who disappeared 10 years earlier and finds him frozen in ice but still alive.
    - **Before I Hang** (1940) - Another "mad doctor" tale featuring Karloff as a physician who, before his own hanging, tests a serum from a murderer on himself, with dangerous side effects.
    - **The Devil Commands** (1940) - In this film, Karloff's character tries to communicate with the dead after a personal tragedy, leading to horrific results.
    - **The Boogie Man Will Get You** (1942) - This finale to the series is a horror-comedy in which Karloff spoofs the menacing mad scientist roles he had made famous.

☐ **Black Friday** (1940) - Dr. Sovac transplants the brain of a gangster into his professor friend's body to save his life, but there is a side effect that causes a dangerous split personality.

- **ADAPTIONS**
    - ☐ **The Lady and the Monster** (1944) - A millionaire's brain is preserved after his death, and telepathically begins to take control of those around him.
    - ☐ **Donovan's Brain** (1953) - Three scientists unlawfully remove the still living brain of a dead tycoon and experiment with it but the evil brain begins to telepathically control the lead scientist.
- **OTHER BRAIN TRANSPLANT HORROR**
    - ☐ **The Man Who Lived Again** (1936) – Also starring Boris Karloff, who is known for playing mad scientists. Dr. Laurience, a brilliant but unstable scientist experimenting with transferring minds, becomes vengeful when his magnate patron withdraws his support.
    - ☐ **The Brain** (1962) - After the mysterious crash of a millionaire's private airplane, three scientists secretly harvest the dying man's brain and keep it alive in a laboratory in order to communicate with it through telepathy.
    - ☐ **The Brain that Wouldn't Die** (1962) – A doctor experimenting with transplant techniques keeps his girlfriend's head alive when she is decapitated in a car crash, then goes hunting for a new body. Reportedly, Virginia Leith hated the film so much she refused to return for post-production. At least a few of her lines were dubbed by Doris Brent, who played a nurse.
    - ☐ **Monstrosity** (1963) - A rich but unscrupulous old woman plots with a scientist to have her brain implanted in the skull of a sexy young woman.

Atomic Age & Mutations

☐ **Creature with an Atom Brain** (1953) - An ex-Nazi mad scientist uses radio-controlled atomic-powered zombies in his quest to help an exiled American gangster return to power. Writer Curt Siodmak, who penned the screenplay, was also the author of the novel *Donovan's Brain*. The film features a former Nazi scientist named Wilhelm Steigg. The use of a Nazi scientist, a common trope in Cold War-era fiction, was used to demonize the misuse of science. *Creature with the Atom Brain* and other films from its era helped to establish the zombie film as a genre. Though the zombies in this film are controlled by radio waves rather than driven by hunger, the sight of reanimated corpses as antagonists was a significant step forward for the genre.

- **SIMILAR FILMS**
    - ☐ **Invisible Invaders** (1959) - Directed by the same person, Edward L. Cahn, this movie featured a similar concept. Instead of a mad scientist, alien invaders take over the reanimated corpses of humans to use as their army.
    - ☐ **Universal Soldier** (1992) - The original film, directed by Roland Emmerich, introduces Luc Deveraux (Van Damme) and Andrew Scott (Lundgren), two soldiers killed in Vietnam and later resurrected as UniSols. After their memories begin to return, they clash again.
        - **SEQUELS**
            - ☐ **Universal Soldier: Regeneration** (2009) - This sequel brings back Van Damme and Lundgren, acting as a direct continuation of the first movie and ignoring the events of later films. Deveraux is reactivated to stop a new generation of UniSols led by a revived Scott.
            - ☐ **Universal Soldier: Day of Reckoning** (2012) - This film, with a surreal, nightmarish tone, features a new protagonist (Scott Adkins) and places Deveraux and Scott in more villainous, leadership roles of a rogue UniSol army.

☐ **Bride of the Monster** (1955) - A mad doctor attempts to create atomic supermen. The film was a low-budget B-movie directed by Edward D. Wood Jr., and starred Bela Lugosi in his last speaking role.

- **SEQUELS AND ADAPTIONS**
    - ☐ **Night of the Ghouls** (1959) - A phony spiritualist raises the dead.

- ☐ **The Amazing Colossal Man** (1957) - A military officer survives a nuclear blast, only to begin to uncontrollably grow into an increasingly unstable giant.
  - • **SEQUELS, ADAPTIONS & SIMILAR THEMES**
    - ☐ **War of the Colossal Beast** (1958) - A direct sequel produced and directed by Bert I. Gordon, the same filmmaker behind the original.
    - ☐ **The Nth Man** (1928) - *The Amazing Colossal Man* is an uncredited adaptation of this short science fiction novel by Homer Eon Flint.
    - ☐ **The Cyclops** (1957) - Released the same year, this film also stars Dean Parkin as a giant mutant monster.
    - ☐ **Attack of the 50 Foot Woman** (1958) - When an abused socialite grows to giant size because of an alien encounter and an aborted murder attempt, she goes after her cheating husband with revenge on her mind. The film's director, Nathan Juran, drew inspiration from the kaiju genre when creating the sequence where the giant woman attacks the power lines. The film has been referenced in numerous animated series episodes where a female character becomes giant, including *The Simpsons*, *Phineas and Ferb*, and *Harley Quinn*. Artists such as Belinda Carlisle, Go West, and Lana Del Rey have created music videos inspired by the film's imagery. A movie poster for *Attack of the 50 Foot Woman* appears as a set dressing in films like *Pulp Fiction* and *Raising Dion*.
      - • **SIMILAR FILMS AND THEMATIC INFLUENCES**
        - ☐ **Attack of the 60 Foot Centerfold** (1995) - This is a direct parody of the 1958 film, produced by Fred Olen Ray. It features two female models who grow to giant size due to a beauty-enhancing formula.
        - ☐ **Attack of the 50 Foot Cheerleader** (2012) – Camp parody of giant-woman films.
        - ☐ **Attack of the 50 Foot CamGirl** (2022) - This modern adult parody directed by Jim Wynorski features Ivy Smith and Christine Nguyen.
        - ☐ **The 30-Foot Bride of Candy Rock** (1959) - A comedy starring Lou Costello, this film centers on a woman who accidentally grows to giant size after exposure to radiation.
        - ☐ **Monsters vs. Aliens** (2009) - The DreamWorks animated film explicitly homages *Attack of the 50 Foot Woman* with the character Susan Murphy/Ginormica, who grows to a monstrous size after being hit by a meteorite.
        - ☐ **Colossal** (2016) – This film starring Anne Hathaway provides a more serious and introspective take on the giant monster subgenre, with a woman discovering she is psychically connected to a kaiju attacking Seoul.
    - ☐ **Village of the Giants** (1965) - Gordon directed this movie about a group of teenagers who grow to giant size after eating a substance called "goop."
    - ☐ **The Food of the Gods** (1976) - A loose adaptation of an H.G. Wells novel, this film features giant rats and other animals mutated by a strange substance.
- ☐ **The Fly** (1958) – A scientist has a horrific accident when he tries to use his newly invented teleportation device.
  - • **SEQUELS & ADAPTIONS**
    - ☐ **Return of the Fly** (1959) - The scientist's son attempts to complete his father's work with the teleportation device, leading to another tragic accident. Vincent Price returns in a supporting role.
    - ☐ **Curse of the Fly** (1965) - The third film in the original series is more of a sci-fi mystery. It follows another member of the same family who is

162

working on teleportation experiments with disastrous consequences.

- ☐ **The Fly** (1986) – Scientist's DNA fuses with insect, body decays. A new film set within the universe of Cronenberg's 1986 remake has been announced. Announced in November 2024, this project will be set within Cronenberg's universe but is not a direct remake. Nikyatu Jusu, known for the film *Nanny*, is attached to write and direct.
- ☐ **The Fly II** (1989) –The almost-human son of "Brundlefly" searches for a cure to his mutated genes while being monitored by a nefarious corporation that wishes to continue his father's experiments.

☐ **The Alligator People** (1959) - A woman in a hypnotic state recounts to two doctors the details of a horrific experience from her past life that began with the mysterious and sudden disappearance of her husband. Stan Lee noted the similarity between *The Alligator People* and the origin story for the Spider-Man villain The Lizard, but said it was possibly a subconscious influence.

☐ **The Black Pit of Dr. M** (1959, Mexico) - Two doctors make a pact in which they swear that the first to die will return - if possible - to tell the other how to get a glimpse of the afterlife while still alive.

- • **MEXICAN MACABRE COLLECTION:** The Mexican Macabre is not a singular monster or myth but rather a cycle of mid-20th century horror films from Mexico that fused Gothic atmosphere with local folklore. Emerging in the 1950s and 1960s, these films blended vampires, mummies, witches, and luchador heroes into stories that were as theatrical as they were uniquely regional, cementing Mexico's place in the global horror canon. Other films included in this repertoire are: *The Vampire* (1958), *The Vampire's Coffin* (1958), and *The Curse of the Crying Woman* (1963), featured in the appropriate sections.
  - ☐ **The Robot vs. the Aztec Mummy** (1958) - A mad doctor builds a robot in order to steal a valuable Aztec treasure from a tomb guarded by a centuries-old living mummy.
  - ☐ **The Living Coffin** (1959) - A cowboy and his sidekick meet a ranching family that is haunted by spirits and vampires.
  - ☐ **The Witch's Mirror** (1962) - This film starts as a story of witchcraft and revenge but evolves into a gothic horror story that includes themes reminiscent of *Frankenstein* and *Eyes Without a Face*.
  - ☐ **The Brainiac** (1962) - In this monster movie, a 17th-century baron convicted of witchcraft returns 300 years later as a monstrous creature to exact revenge on the descendants of his accusers. The monster uses its elongated tongue to suck out its victims' brains.

☐ **The Man Who Could Cheat Death** (1959) - A centenarian artist and scientist in 1890 Paris maintains his youth and health by periodically replacing a gland with that of a living person. Based on the 1937 stage play *The Man in Half Moon Street* by Barré Lyndon.

- • **ADAPTIONS & SIMILAR THEMES**
  - ☐ **The Man in Half Moon Street** (1945) - A film adaptation of the play was made by Paramount Pictures, starring Nils Asther as the immortal doctor. A scientist who has found a way to prolong life (he is 120 years old) finds himself in a dilemma: he has fallen in love, and he has also discovered that if he doesn't get new glands, he will die.
  - ☐ **The Asphyx** (1972) - English country squire Sir Hugo Cunningham searches for immortality by literally 'bottling up' the Spirit of the Dead, or Asphyx.
  - ☐ **The Lazarus Effect** (2015) - A group of medical researchers discover a way to bring dead patients back to life.

The King of Horror

Boris Karloff

Boris Karloff (1887–1969) was horror's quiet revolutionary. Born William Henry Pratt in London, he transformed himself into one of cinema's most enduring icons. Not through elegance, like Lugosi, but through an alchemy of makeup, physicality, and unexpected tenderness. When James Whale cast him as the Monster in *Frankenstein* (1931), Karloff carried thirty pounds of prosthetics on his shoulders and still gave a performance of aching vulnerability. The Monster's outstretched hands, childlike stumbles, and haunted eyes turned what could have been a lumbering brute into a tragic figure audiences pitied as much as they feared. Horror had never known empathy like this.

Cultivating a Persona

Unlike his contemporary Lugosi, Karloff was not defined by a single accent or aristocratic bearing. His gift was adaptability. He specialized in prosthetics and pathos, vanishing into roles that demanded both menace and humanity. In *The Mummy* (1932), he embodied the ancient sorcerer Imhotep with hypnotic restraint; in *The Black Cat* (1934), he went toe-to-toe with Lugosi in a battle of psychological sadism. Even in lighter fare, like *Abbott and Costello Meet the Killer, Boris Karloff* (1949), he wielded his screen presence with knowing authority.

Signature Works

- **Frankenstein (1931)** — Karloff's defining role, a monster stitched from corpses yet played with heartbreaking fragility.
- **The Mummy (1932)** — As Imhotep, he brought menace through stillness, proving that silence and restraint could terrify more than shrieks.
- **The Black Cat (1934)** — A modernist nightmare pairing Karloff and Lugosi in one of horror's most stylish duels of sadism.
- **Bride of Frankenstein (1935)** — Returned as the Monster, deepening the character into a figure of pathos, comedy, and tragedy.
- **The Body Snatcher (1945)** — In Val Lewton's psychological chiller, Karloff gave one of his most chillingly human performances as a grave robber.
- **Black Sabbath (1963)** — Hosted and starred in Mario Bava's anthology, bridging classic Gothic with modern Italian horror.
- **How the Grinch Stole Christmas! (1966)** — Narrated and voiced the Grinch, showing that even outside horror, his voice could define cultural icons.

What He Did for Horror

Karloff gave horror its depth. Where silent grotesques once relied on shock, he proved that monsters could also embody tragedy, compassion, and social allegory. His performances expanded horror in several key ways:

- **Humanized the Monster** — By playing Frankenstein's creature with vulnerability, he showed that audiences could fear and pity simultaneously, a template for every sympathetic monster to follow.
- **Elevated Prosthetics into Art** — His willingness to endure grueling makeup work turned latex and greasepaint into tools for character rather than gimmick, influencing generations of effects-driven performances.
- **Bridged Horror Movements** — From Universal's Gothic cycle to Val Lewton's psychological horrors and Mario Bava's Italian Gothic, Karloff's presence gave continuity and credibility across eras and styles.
- **Created the Horror "Brand Actor"** — His name on a marquee became a seal of fear, proving that horror stars could carry franchises, not just individual films.
- **Balanced Fear with Prestige** — Unlike many horror actors sidelined by typecasting, Karloff moved between prestige projects, thrillers, and children's entertainment, showing horror could be versatile and enduring.

Bridging Eras

Beyond his famous monsters, Karloff was horror's great connector. He carried the genre from the silent grotesques of the 1920s into the Gothic spectacles of the 1930s, then reinvented himself again in Val Lewton's restrained psychological horrors of the 1940s, and later in Mario Bava's stylish European experiments of the 1960s. No other actor of his generation navigated so many horror traditions so seamlessly. This ability to move between styles and decades meant that Karloff was not just the King of Horror in his prime—he was its guardian, ensuring the genre adapted, survived, and remained vital across the shifting landscape of cinema.

The Untold Legacy

What most people don't realize is how much Karloff humanized horror offscreen as well. He served as president of the Screen Actors Guild during its early years, fighting for fair conditions even while spending hours under makeup that left scars on his body. Offscreen, he was known for his gentleness and generosity, so much so that colleagues joked that "the kindest man in Hollywood" made his living terrifying audiences. This duality: monster onscreen, mentor offscreen deepened the resonance of his performances.

Legacy & Amazement

Karloff gave horror its conscience. He proved that monsters could be metaphors, that fear could coexist with sympathy, and that prosthetics could be a gateway to performance rather than a mask. His work paved the way for everything from Lon Chaney Jr. to Doug Jones and Andy Serkis. More than "the King of Horror," Karloff was its soul—an artist who

taught us that the scariest creatures are often the most human of all.

European & Arthouse Experiments

☐ **Blood of the Vampire** (1958, UK) - In 1870s Transylvania, scientist Dr. Callistratus is put to death by villagers who wrongly believe he's a vampire. However, his horribly disfigured henchman, Carl is on hand to orchestrate a life-saving heart transplant.
- **SIMILAR THEMES**
  - ☐ **Red Blooded American Girl** (1990) - Another film exploring the idea of a medical condition that requires a blood substitute to survive.
  - ☐ **Aaron's Blood** (2016) - A film where a single father must find a way to stop his son from becoming a vampire after a blood transfusion.

☐ **Eyes Without a Face** (1960) – A surgeon causes a car accident which leaves his daughter disfigured and goes to extreme lengths to give her a new face. The film significantly influenced later horror, inspiring specific imagery and broader themes like: *Halloween, The Skin I Live In,* and *Face/Off.* It inspired a subgenre of "mad doctor" exploitation films in the 1960s, such as *The Awful Dr. Orlof* (1962) and *The Brain That Wouldn't Die* (1962). As well as the 1984 Billy Idol hit "Eyes Without a Face."
- **INSPIRATIONS**
  - ☐ **Atom Age Vampire** (1960, Italy) - This sci-fi horror film centered on Dr. Alberto Levin, a scientist who creates a special serum to restore the disfigured face of a beautiful nightclub dancer named Jeanette.
  - ☐ **The Awful Dr. Orlof (Gritos en la noche)** (1962, Spain) - Dr. Orlof, a former prison doctor, abducts beautiful women from nightclubs and tries to use their skin to repair his daughter's fire-scarred face.
  - ☐ **Mansion of the Doomed** (1976) - A mad scientist fills his basement dungeon with victims in an insane attempt to restore his daughter's eyesight. Listed on the Video Nasties section 3 list of non- persecuted films.
  - ☐ **Face/Off** (1997) - To foil a terrorist plot, an FBI agent assumes the identity of the criminal who murdered his son via facial transplant surgery, but the crook wakes up prematurely and vows revenge.
  - ☐ **The Skin I Live In** (2011, Spain) – Surgeon crafts captive's new body.

☐ **Circus of Horrors** (1960, UK) - Dr. Rossiter, a plastic surgeon wanted by the police, flees to France and under an assumed name acquires, by murder, a run-down circus. His first recruit is a woman criminal. He transforms her face by surgery and trains her. The film, penned by writer George Baxt, is considered part of a "Sadian trilogy" that focused on cruelty and sadism rather than supernatural horror.
- **SADIAN TRILOGY:** Other horrors in this Trilogy include *Peeping Tom* and *Freaks.*
  - ☐ **Horrors of the Black Museum** (1959) - Directed by Arthur Crabtree, this film is considered the first entry in the so-called trilogy and, like *Circus of Horrors*, focuses on a series of grisly murders rather than the supernatural.
- **INSPIRATIONS**
  - ☐ **The Mutations** (1974, UK) - This British film, starring Donald Pleasence and Tom Baker, features a botanist who uses kidnapped people as hybrid human-plant experiments that he exhibits in a traveling freak show.

☐ **The Horrible Dr. Hichcock** (1962, Italy) - In 1897 London, a woman weds a necrophiliac doctor whose first wife died under mysterious circumstances - and who might be returning from the grave to torment her successor. The title is a cheeky nod to director Alfred Hitchcock, and Riccardo Freda's direction incorporates many suspenseful techniques popularized by the "Master of Suspense." he film draws heavily from classic gothic romance and horror literature, such as the works of Edgar Allan Poe.
- **SIMILAR FILMS**
  - ☐ **The Ghost** (1963) - Directed by Freda and starring Steele, this movie is a gothic thriller that features Steele's character dealing with a haunting in a remote estate, echoing the atmosphere and plot of *The Horrible Dr. Hichcock*. The films are otherwise unrelated in plot, although the character of John Hitchcock is played by Robert Flemyng, who played the lead in the 1962 film.

- **ADAPTIONS**
    - ☐ **Do Gaz Zameen Ke Neeche** (1972, India) - Eerie things start happening after a disloyal wife kills her handicapped husband with the help of her lover.
- ☐ **The Whip and the Body** (1963, Italy) – Mario Bava's lush Gothic of sadomasochism and spectral revenge. This Gothic horror film by Mario Bava, another master of Italian horror, shares the same atmosphere and themes of obsession and a haunted estate.

☐ **Horror Hospital** (1973, UK) - Jason Jones and Judy Peters, young British people, meet on a train heading to the country. They stay with odd characters in a secluded mansion, where deranged Dr. Christian Storm is using his guests for surgical mind-control experiments.

☐ **The Creeping Flesh** (1973, UK) - A Victorian-age scientist returns to London with his paleontological bag-of-bones discovery from Papua New Guinea. Unfortunately, when exposed to water, flesh returns to the bones unleashing a malevolent being on the scientist's family and friends.

- **SIMILAR FILMS**
    - ☐ **Horror Express** (1972) - This film, released just a year before *The Creeping Flesh*, also stars Christopher Lee and Peter Cushing and features an ancient alien being that is resurrected and causes terror.

1970s American Drive-In & Grindhouse

☐ **The Thing with Two Heads** (1972) - Doctors are forced to transplant the head of terminally ill, arthritic racist surgeon Maxwell Kirshner onto the body of African American Death Row inmate Jack Moss because there is no other donor.

- **THEMATIC INFLUENCES**
    - ☐ **The Manster** (1959, Japan) - An earlier film featuring a two-headed creature, though in this case, the second head is a mutated growth rather than a transplant.
    - ☐ **The Incredible 2-Headed Transplant** (1971) - Dr. Roger Girard, a mad scientist who dares to combine two heads onto one body, despite serious consequences. This earlier exploitation film from the same studio, American International Pictures, is often paired with *The Thing with Two Heads* on DVD releases.
    - ☐ **The Man with Two Heads** (1972) - This film, originally titled *Dr. Jekyll and Mr. Blood*, was retitled by its producer to capitalize on the success of *The Thing with Two Heads*. It is not actually about a two-headed person. Serum obtained from a brain after a mass murder transforms the good Dr. Jekyll of London into the evil Mr. Blood.

☐ **Sssssss** (1973) - A college student becomes lab assistant to a scientist who is working on a serum that can transform humans into snakes.

- **SIMILAR FILMS**
    - ☐ **Tusk** (2014) – Kevin Smith's independent horror film, in which a man is surgically transformed into a walrus, is often cited as a more modern, spiritual successor to *Sssssss*. The director himself acknowledged the comparison.
    - ☐ **Prophecy** (1979) – Mutated bear rampages through wilderness. The film's environmentalist message—that humanity's pollution is corrupting nature—was also a popular theme in other horror films of the decade, such as *Prophecy*, which features a mutant bear created by industrial waste.

☐ **Horror Rises from the Dead** (1973, Spain) - A warlock's severed head is unearthed centuries after his execution. Reanimated, it seeks to reunite with its body, wreaking havoc as a group encounters its sinister quest.

- **SEQUELS, INFLUENCES & RELATED FILMS**
    - ☐ **Panic Beats** (1982) - A sequel to *Horror Rises from the Tomb* was released nearly a decade later. Paul Naschy returned to his role as the warlock Alaric de Marnac, who is once again resurrected to continue his deadly rampage.
    - ☐ **The Thing that Wouldn't Die** (1958) - The film was inspired by this Universal Pictures monster movie, where an ancient head is discovered and brought back to life.
    - ☐ **The Exterminating Angel** (1962) - Paul Naschy himself cited Luis Buñuel's surrealist film as an influence on the plot device of characters being trapped in a house.
    - ☐ **The Hanging Woman** (1973, Spain) - Another Spanish horror film starring Paul Naschy, released the same year.

- ☐ **Blue Eyes of the Broken Doll** (1974, Spain) - This Spanish horror film, also starring Naschy, was inspired by the historical serial killer Gilles de Rais, who was also an influence on *Horror Rises from the Tomb.*

☐ **Embryo** (1976) - A scientist (Rock Hudson) doing experiments on a human fetus discovers a method to accelerate the fetus into a mature adult in just a few days. All is not well though as the child begins to exhibit some horrific tendencies. *Embryo* is considered a modern retelling of Mary Shelley's classic story. In both works, a scientist creates an artificial being, but the "creation" ultimately proves to be a monster with murderous tendencies. *Embryo* was re-released in the 1980s under the more lurid title "*Created to Kill.*" This was a common practice for low-budget horror films at the time to make them seem more sensational

- • **SIMILAR PREMISES**
    - ☐ **Demon Seed** (1977) - The following year, a similar film was released involving a fetus grown in an artificial uterus, though with a different story involving artificial intelligence.
    - ☐ **Splice** (2009) – Scientists create disturbing human-animal hybrid.
    - ☐ **Replicas** (2018) - This movie deals with a neuroscientist who clones his dead family, but with deadly consequences.

☐ **Scanners** (1981) – Exploding heads become iconic gore imagery. A scientist trains a man with an advanced telepathic ability called "scanning" to stop a dangerous Scanner with extraordinary psychic powers from waging war against non-Scanners. A remake was in development in 2007, with Darren Lynn Bousman attached to direct and David S. Goyer to write the script. The project was ultimately abandoned after Bousman stated he would not make the film without David Cronenberg's approval, which was not granted.

- • **SEQUELS & ADAPTIONS**
    - ☐ **Scanners II: The New Order** (1991) - In this film, a veterinary student discovers his "scanner" abilities after unknowingly stopping a robbery. He is recruited by a corrupt police commander to exploit his powers, only to find himself embroiled in a larger conspiracy.
    - ☐ **Scanners III: The Takeover** (1992) - This entry follows a young female scanner who uses an experimental drug to boost her telepathic powers. The drug turns her into a killing machine, and she begins a campaign to take over the world through television signals.
    - ☐ **Scanners Cop** (1994) - This spin-off follows Sam Staziak, a rookie police officer and scanner who suppresses his telepathic abilities with medication. After a series of cop killings, he is forced to use his powers to hunt down the murderer.
    - ☐ **Scanners: The Showdown** (1995) - Also known as *Scanner Cop II*, this film is a sequel to *Scanner Cop*. Sam Staziak returns to face a new scanner antagonist who is murdering fellow scanners and harvesting their brain fluid to boost his own powers.

Japanese Cyberpunk & Mutation

☐ **Horrors of Malformed Men** (1969, Japan) - After escaping from an insane asylum, a medical student assumes the identity of a mysterious dead man, who appeared to be his doppelganger, and gets lured to a sinister island ruled by a mad scientist and his malformed men.

- • **SIMILAR FILMS**
    - ☐ **Tetsuo: The Iron Man** (1989, Japan) – A businessman accidentally kills The Metal Fetishist, who gets his revenge by slowly turning the man into a grotesque hybrid of flesh and rusty metal. This experimental Japanese horror film shares a similarly surreal, industrial, and nightmarish quality.
        - • **SEQUELS**
            - ☐ **Tetsuo II: Body Hammer** (1992, Japan) – Cyberpunk mutations return.
            - ☐ **Tetsuo: The Bullet Man** (2009, Japan) - The third film shifts gears, becoming a more action-oriented story and using English dialogue.
        - • **RELATED PROJECTS**
            - ☐ **Tokyo Fist** (1995, Japan) – Explores urban angst and violence through a story of two friends who are driven to obsessive and destructive boxing matches.
            - ☐ **Bullet Ballet** (1998, Japan) - Another fast-paced, black-and-white film that deals with obsession and urban decay, though without the metal fetishism.

- ☐ **Audition** (1999, Japan) – Torture and surgical obsession revealed. Takashi Miike's shocking psychological horror film has been compared to *Horrors of Malformed Men* for its disturbing and unsettling nature.
  - • **OTHER FILMS BY TAKASHI MIIKE**
    - ☐ **Ichi the Killer** (2001, Japan) – Miike's ultraviolent yakuza splatter.
    - ☐ **Visitor Q** (2001, Japan) – Miike's grotesque family gore experiment.
    - ☐ **Gozu** (2003, Japan) – Miike's surreal gangster-horror hybrid.
- ☐ **Black Lizard** (1969, Japan) - In this flamboyant and surreal Japanese crime film, a mysterious master jewel thief named Black Lizard enters a high-stakes game of wits with a brilliant detective, a contest of mind games and romance that escalates into kidnapping and violence. The story originated as a 1934 pulp novel by Japanese author Rampo Edogawa, a master of mystery and suspense.
  - • **SPIRITUAL SUCCESSOR**
    - ☐ **Black Rose Mansion** (1969, Japan) - A year after the release of *Black Lizard*, director Kinji Fukasaku released *Black Rose Mansion*, also starring Akihiro Miwa (who played Black Lizard). It is not a direct sequel but carries over many of the original's decadent and gothic themes in a more melancholic story.
- ☐ **Blind Beast** (1969, Japan) - A blind sculptor and his mother kidnap a young model. This film is a loose adaption of the 1931 novel, *Moju* by Edogawa Ranpo.
- ☐ **Rubber's Lover** (1996, Japan) - Scientists use a brain-altering drug to conduct experiments, after one such project goes astray, they need to find another test subject.
  - • **PREQUEL**
    - ☐ **964 Pinocchio** (1991, Japan) - While released five years earlier, *Rubber's Lover* is often interpreted as a prequel. It depicts a group of renegade scientists experimenting on human test subjects to unlock their latent psychic abilities. The ending of *Rubber's Lover* has even been noted to segue directly into the events of *964 Pinocchio*, which follows the fate of one of the scientists' brainwashed and modified human guinea pigs.
- ☐ **Parasite Eve** (1997, Japan) - A scientist realizes his dead wife is an organization of mitochondria bent on making a new species that will wipe out humanity. Based off the novel by Hideaki Sena.
- ☐ **Meatball Machine** (1999, Japan) - This 70-minute, low-budget, independent film was directed by Jun'ichi Yamamoto. An alien parasite invades Earth, transforming humans into biomechanical, grotesque fighters known as "NecroBorgs" who are forced to battle each other to the death, a fate that befalls a young couple who must then engage in a deadly, splatter-filled showdown.
  - • **ADAPTIONS**
    - ☐ **Meatball Machine** (2005, Japan) – Bio-mechanical parasite splatter.
    - ☐ **Meatball Machine: Kodoku** (2017, Japan) - This direct sequel to the 2005 film was directed by Yoshihiro Nishimura and follows a different plot and set of characters.

Monsters of Psychology & Paranoia

- ☐ **Hollow Man** (2000) – Scientist turns invisible, loses humanity. Both *Hollow Man* and its sequels are loosely based on this classic H.G. Wells novel, which explores themes of science-gone-wrong and the corruption of power. Nominated for an Academy Award for Best Effects, Visual Effects.
  - • **SEQUELS**
    Hollow Man 2 (2006) - This standalone sequel was released directly to video. It features a new story about a soldier who is also made invisible, played by Christian Slater.
- ☐ **Upgrade** (2018) – Set in the near-future, technology controls nearly all aspects of life. But when the world of Grey, a self-labeled technophobe, is turned upside down, his only hope for revenge is an experimental computer chip implant.
  - • **MEMORY MANIPULATION**
    - ☐ **Black Box** (2020) - After losing his wife and his memory in a car accident, a single father undergoes an agonizing experimental treatment that causes him to question who he really is.
- ☐ **Masking Threshold** (2021, Austria) - Conducting a series of experiments in his makeshift home-lab, a skeptic IT worker tries to cure his harrowing hearing impairment.

☐ **The A-Frame** (2024) - A quantum physicist develops a machine that creates a tunnel to a subatomic universe. In his quest to prove the machine's efficacy, he inadvertently discovers a radical treatment for cancer.

Offbeat, Cult, and Forgotten Gems

☐ **The Invisible Ray** (1936) - A scientist becomes murderous after discovering, and being exposed to the radiation of, a powerful new element called Radium X.

- **RELATED PRODUCTIONS**
  - ☐ **The Phantom Creeps** (1939) - Universal reused footage from *The Invisible Ray* in its 1939 science fiction serial, *The Phantom Creeps*, starring Bela Lugosi. The scenes where Boris Karloff's character, Dr. Janos Rukh, descends into a fiery pit were incorporated into the serial.
  - ☐ **The 4D Man** (1959) - Considered a semi-remake of *The Invisible Ray*. Both films feature a scientist who gains dangerous powers after an experiment involving a special type of ray or energy goes wrong, and then uses his abilities to seek revenge.

☐ **Chamber of Horrors** (1940) - A murder is found to be connected to a false heir and a secret underground torture chamber. Based on the novel *The Door with Seven Locks* by Edgar Wallace.

- **INFLUENCES & SIMILAR THEMES**
  - ☐ **The Most Dangerous Game** (1932) - Leslie Banks, who plays the sadistic Dr. Manetta in *Chamber of Horrors*, also played the equally sadistic Count Zaroff in this earlier film. His performance as the flamboyant, torture-device-collecting villain is a clear throwback to that role.

☐ **The Mad Ghoul** (1943) - A university chemistry professor experiments with an ancient Mayan gas on a medical student, turning the would-be surgeon into a murdering ghoul.

- **SIMILAR THEMES**
  - ☐ **Man-Made Monster** (1941) - This Universal film, starring Lon Chaney Jr., follows a mad scientist who experiments with electricity, turning his subject into a superhuman but obedient killer. It shares the theme of a mad scientist creating a mindless servant.
  - ☐ **The Mad Doctor of Market Street** (1942) - Starring George Zucco (who plays the mad scientist in *The Mad Ghoul*), this film features a doctor who flees to a tropical island to continue his bizarre experiments, where he uses native subjects for his work.
  - ☐ **The Strange Case of Doctor Rx** (1942) - This film, released the year before *The Mad Ghoul*, features a mystery where a series of murderers are discovered to be the result of a doctor's sinister plan involving brain transplants.

☐ **Captive Wild Woman** (1943) - An insane scientist doing experimentation in glandular research becomes obsessed with transforming a female gorilla into a human...even though it costs human life.

- **SEQUELS**
  - ☐ **Jungle Woman** (1944) - A direct sequel that uses flashbacks to explain the story. It centers on a coroner's inquest that seeks to determine if Paula Dupree, who has apparently been killed, was a human or an animal.
  - ☐ **The Jungle Captive** (1945) - A third and final film in the series. A different scientist revives the dormant Ape Woman and attempts to cure her monstrous side.
- **SIMILAR THEMES**
  - ☐ **The Monster and the Girl** (1941) - After a young woman is coerced into prostitution and her brother framed for murder by an organized crime syndicate, retribution in the form of an ape visits the mobsters.

- ☐ **Murders in the Rue Morgue** (1932) - In this film, a mad scientist performs experiments in Paris with an ape. Based on the Edgar Allan Poe's short story.
  - • **ADAPTIONS**
    - ☐ **Phantom of the Rue Morgue** (1954) - When several women are found mutilated and murdered, the Paris police are baffled as to who the killer may be. All evidence points to Dupin, but soon it becomes apparent that it is someone (or something) stronger and deadlier than a human.
- ☐ **The Black Sleep** (1956) - Sir Joel Cadman, a mad scientist, kidnaps his victims and cuts open their brains in an effort to discover a means to cure his wife's brain tumor. The movie is also notable for bringing together several legendary horror actors from the "golden age" of Universal monster movies, such as Basil Rathbone, Bela Lugosi, Lon Chaney Jr., and John Carradine, though some have only minor roles.
- ☐ **The Abominable Dr. Phibes** (1971) – Vincent Price as a Gothic antihero exacting revenge with baroque cruelty.
  - • **SEQUELS**
    - ☐ **Dr. Phibes Rises Again** (1972) – Phibes continues his ornate quest with Egyptian Gothic flourishes.
  - • **VINCENT PRICE FILMS WITH SIMILAR THEMES**
    - ☐ **Madhouse** (1974) - A horror movie star (Vincent Price) returns to his famous role after years in a mental institution. But the character seems to be committing murders independent of his will. Based on the 1969 novel *Devilday* by Angus Hall.
    - ☐ **Theatre of Blood** (1973) - In this film, Price plays an actor who kills the critics who panned his work, staging the murders to reflect scenes from Shakespeare's plays. *Madhouse* followed a year later and is considered by some critics to be a "disappointing follow-up" that takes itself too seriously compared to the campy *Theatre of Blood*.
- ☐ **Brainstorm** (1983) - Researchers develop a system where they can jump into people's minds. But when people involved bring their personal problems into the equation, it becomes dangerous - perhaps deadly.
  - • **SPIRITUAL SEQUELS & INFLUENCED FILMS**
    - ☐ **Dreamscape** (1984) – Entering dreams becomes a psychological war. The film's concept of entering and influencing dreams has appeared in other films, many of which were released in the same era or came out years later.
    - ☐ **Flatliners** (1990) - This film follows a group of medical students who experiment with near-death experiences, inspired by the afterlife themes in *Brainstorm*.
    - ☐ **Strange Days** (1995) - Written by James Cameron and directed by Kathryn Bigelow, this film features a sleeker, more modern version of *Brainstorm*'s headgear technology, used to record and replay human experiences.
    - ☐ **Paprika** (2006, Japan) - In this anime, a device that allows therapists to enter their patients' dreams is stolen and weaponized.
    - ☐ **Rememory** (2017) - This film focuses on a new technology that allows users to record and re-experience their memories.
    - ☐ **Double Blind** (2023, Ireland) - After an experimental drug trial goes awry, the test subjects face a terrifying side effect: if you fall asleep you die. Trapped in an isolated facility, panic ensues as they try to escape and somehow stay awake.

Mad Scientist Pairing Night: How to Play God and Lose

Main Course: The Birth of Hubris
Frankenstein (1931) + Dr. Jekyll and Mr. Hyde (1931)

How to watch: Begin with creation, then turn inward. Frankenstein externalizes hubris as stitched monstrosity; Jekyll embodies it as self-inflicted duality.

Smartest fact: These two films established the archetype: hubris punished either by the creature you made or the one already inside you.

Side Dish: Invisibility and Isolation
The Invisible Man (1933) + Hollow Man (2000)

How to watch: Whale's witty invisibility unravels into mania; Verhoeven's glossy update strips away humanity until nothing remains but predator instinct.

Smartest fact: Both films weaponize transparency—scientific progress that erases empathy as well as flesh.

Dessert: Surgical Obsession
Eyes Without a Face (1960) + The Brain That Wouldn't Die (1962)

How to watch: Pair French lyricism with American schlock. One treats surgery as poetry, the other as drive-in grotesque.

Smartest fact: Both confront the same terror: the body as raw material, love and devotion twisted into mutilation.

Nightcap: Mutation as Tragedy
The Fly (1958) + Altered States (1980)

How to watch: Watch Cold War fusion horror give way to psychedelic regression. One is tragedy of domestic horror, the other a descent through evolution itself.

Smartest fact: Both hinge on transformation as spectacle—the horror isn't just the monster revealed, but the dissolution of the self.

Bonus Shot: Excess and Extremes
Re-Animator (1985) + Tetsuo: The Iron Man (1989)

How to watch: End your night by leaping into extremes. One campy and gore-splattered, the other experimental and industrial.

Smartest fact: Both redefine the mad scientist for their moment: the VHS generation's gleeful splatter, and Japan's cyberpunk nightmare of technology fused with flesh.

Unleash the Lab

Splatter / Gore / Extreme Horror

Splatter (or "gore") horror makes the body the battlefield. Where other subgenres imply, splatter shows: torn flesh, erupting viscera, liquefied limbs, and transgressive set-pieces engineered to shock, satirize, or confront taboo. From Herschell Gordon Lewis's grindhouse origins to 1980s latex wizardry and 2000s "torture" cycles, splatter tracks our anxieties about medicine, war, surveillance, and the limits of empathy filtered through the craft of special effects.

Why People Are Drawn to It

Because splatter is visceral truth or dare. It tests boundaries (How much can I handle?), spotlights FX artistry (How did they do that?), and often smuggles in satire under the gush (consumerism in *Dawn of the Dead*, class disgust in *Society*). In a crowd, gore becomes communal catharsis; alone, it's a confrontation with mortality our soft, perishable selves.

Essentials

1. **Blood Feast** (1963, USA) –Bright-red grindhouse gore and a mad caterer serving Egyptian ritual murder. Often hailed as the first splatter film, pushing horror into new extremes of graphic violence and gore. Herschell Gordon Lewis's low-budget shocker was crude yet groundbreaking, setting the stage for exploitation cinema and the gore-driven horror boom that followed.
2. **The Last House on the Left** (1972) – Brutal revenge classic; "to avoid fainting, keep repeating…" Dragged horror into the raw brutality of the Vietnam era, blurring the line between exploitation and social commentary. Wes Craven's debut shocked audiences with its mix of sadism, realism, and revenge, establishing a template for transgressive modern horror.
3. **The Evil Dead** (1981, USA) –Unleashed a storm of low-budget ingenuity, turning a cabin in the woods into a playground of gore, demonic possession, and camera trickery. Sam Raimi's frenetic style and relentless intensity made it a cult classic that redefined independent horror through sheer energy and audacity.
4. **Hellraiser** (1987, UK) –Fused supernatural horror with sadomasochistic imagery, introducing the Cenobites as emissaries of pleasure and pain beyond human limits. Clive Barker's vision of desire, flesh, and damnation created a new mythology that pushed horror into realms of both the erotic and the grotesque.
5. **Saw** (2004, USA) – Puzzle-box cruelty reinvents 2000s gore; moral traps, industrial grime, and franchise endurance. Reshaped horror for the 21st century, introducing the grim puzzle of morality under duress. Its mix of psychological terror, inventive traps, and a shocking twist birthed the "torture-porn" cycle while reestablishing low-budget ingenuity as a force in mainstream horror.

Deep Cuts

1. **The Wizard of Gore** (1970, USA) – Epitomized Herschell Gordon Lewis's splatter aesthetic, staging elaborate illusions of mutilation that blur performance and reality. Its Grand Guignol excess and metafictional edge turned stage magic into a grotesque spectacle, cementing its cult status in grindhouse horror.
2. **Maniac** (1980, USA) – NYC grindhouse realism; scalpels, sweat, and Savini's explosive head gag. Pushed slasher horror into grimy urban realism, following a disturbed killer through New York's decaying streets. Its unflinching violence, psychological focus, and Tom Savini's notorious effects made it both reviled and revered as one of the most disturbing portraits of madness in 1980s horror.
3. **Pieces** (1982, Spain/USA) – Cheerfully tasteless campus chainsaw carnage; the tagline says it all. A Spanish-American slasher infamous for its mix of absurdity and brutality, following a killer assembling a human jigsaw puzzle from his victims. Its outrageous gore, sleazy tone, and campy dialogue gave it enduring cult status as one of exploitation horror's most unhinged spectacles.
4. **Society** (1989, USA) – Class satire culminates in a body-melding finale you can't unsee. Satirized class privilege through grotesque body horror, revealing the wealthy elite as a literally shape-shifting, flesh-consuming cult. Brian Yuzna's climactic "shunting" sequence turned social critique into surreal, transgressive spectacle, cementing the film as a cult classic of 1980s excess.
5. **Tokyo Gore Police** (2008, Japan) – Splatterpunk fever dream: bio-weapons, arterial fountains, cyberpunk absurdity. Pushed splatter into surreal excess, depicting a dystopian world where grotesque mutations and bio-

mechanical body horror erupt in fountains of blood. Its outrageous violence, satirical edge, and inventive practical effects made it a defining entry in Japan's extreme gore cinema.

Critical Essay

"Splatter Isn't Mindless: It's Craft, Satire, and Limits-Testing."

Myth: Gore = mindless shock.

Reality: The best splatter is formal showmanship and cultural critique. Lewis's candy-colored blood was a distribution hack; Romero's entrails indict consumption; 80s latex maestros (Bottin, Savini, Nicotero) advanced cinematic illusion; French extremity (*Inside, Martyrs*) interrogates pain, faith, and spectatorship. Even when it plays as midnight-movie mayhem, splatter asks a serious question: *What makes us look away and why?*

Global Spotlight: Japan & France

- **Japan (Splatterpunk & Cyber-gore):** From *Meatball Machine* (2005) to *Tokyo Gore Police* (2008) and *Helldriver* (2010), Japanese splatterpunk embraces cartoonish excess, bio-engineered body mods, arterial geysers, and comic-book world-building. It's punk anarchy with VFX bravado.
- **France (New French Extremity):** *High Tension* (2003), *Inside* (2007), *Martyrs* (2008), and *Frontier(s)* (2007) trade camp for philosophical cruelty: clean framing, punishing realism, and bodies as sites of ideology. Not just gore, but arguments carved in flesh.

Grindhouse Origins & Aftershocks (Mini-Timeline)

Grindhouse gore emerged from the low-budget exploitation circuit of the 1960s and 70s, when drive-ins and urban theaters specialized in films too transgressive for the mainstream. Rooted in the Grand Guignol's stage blood and fueled by the collapse of the Production Code, these films emphasized explicit violence, dismemberment, and shock as both marketing hook and audience dare. Directors like Herschell Gordon Lewis (*Blood Feast*, 1963) pioneered the splatter aesthetic, while later grindhouse fare pushed boundaries with sadism, taboo sexuality, and outrageous body mutilation. Developed outside Hollywood's polished studio system, grindhouse gore thrived on its disreputability. Films were cheaply made, luridly advertised, and unapologetically visceral, shaping the blueprint for modern splatter and torture horror.

Grindhouse gore's aftershocks rippled into later decades, resurfacing in the "video nasty" era of the 1980s and inspiring the torture-horror revival of the 2000s. Films like *Saw* (2004) and *Hostel* (2005) carried forward its ethos of spectacle and shock, now with higher budgets and global reach. What once played in sticky-floored theaters became multiplex events, proving that the raw, visceral thrills of grindhouse never truly disappeared, they just evolved with new audiences and technologies.

- **1963 – Blood Feast (USA).** Herschell Gordon Lewis sprays Technicolor gore across drive-ins, inventing the "splatter film." Cheap, crude, but revolutionary.
- **1972 – Last House on the Left (USA).** Wes Craven fuses exploitation sadism with Vietnam-era malaise. Brutality framed as both grindhouse shock and cultural mirror.
- **Late 1970s–Early 80s – Italian Gut-Punches.** Lucio Fulci (*House by the Cemetery*), Dario Argento (*Tenebrae*), and Juan Piquer Simón (*Pieces*) push gore into operatic excess: eyeballs punctured, intestines feasted, fountains of crimson.
- **1980s – Latex Boom.** Practical FX masters unleash geysers and transformations: Raimi's *Evil Dead II* (slapstick blood), Barker's *Hellraiser* (sadomasochistic splatter), Brian Yuzna's *Society* (body-melt orgy).
- **2000s – Torture Cycles.** *Saw* and *Hostel* turn splatter into mainstream multiplex fare—moral traps, tourist terrors, and endless sequels.
- **2000s–2010s – Global Extremity.** France (*High Tension, Inside, Martyrs*) and Japan (*Tokyo Gore Police, Meatball Machine*) redefine gore as either grim realism or comic-book excess.

Effects Hall of Fame

Tom Savini – Practical Gore Realism. Vietnam veteran turned FX pioneer. Savini brought combat-level authenticity to entrails, decapitations, and bullet hits (*Dawn of the Dead, Maniac, The Burning*). His mantra: "If you can imagine it, you can make it." He proved gore could be artistry, not just shock.

Rob Bottin – Transformations. Prodigy under Rick Baker. At 22, Bottin masterminded *The Thing* (1982): pulsating dogs, spider-head, flesh as metamorphosis. His work turned gore into surreal sculpture. Body horror as living gallery.

KNB EFX Group (Kurtzman, Nicotero, Berger) – Hybrid FX Dynasty. From *Evil Dead II* to *Kill Bill* to *The Walking Dead*, KNB became Hollywood's gore factory. Known for blending latex, animatronics, and later CGI, they carried splatter into the 90s–00s mainstream while honoring practical traditions.

Viewer's Toolkit: Reading Gore

Consumption: Zombies eat us (*Dawn of the Dead*) = critique of consumer culture devouring itself.
Class: *Society* (1989) literalizes wealth as parasitic flesh orgy. Gore exposes who gets consumed and who feeds.
Faith: *Martyrs* (2008) weaponizes torment as spiritual transcendence. Gore becomes theology.
State Violence: *Hostel* channels post-9/11 anxieties and outsourced torture, global capitalism as slaughterhouse.
Ratings & Censorship:
- 1960s: Gore flourishes outside the MPAA (drive-ins, grindhouses).
- 1970s–80s: Cuts demanded for mainstream release (*My Bloody Valentine, Friday the 13th*).
- 1980s UK "Video Nasties" list bans (*Cannibal Holocaust, The Evil Dead*).
- 2000s: "Unrated" DVD boom markets gore as forbidden fruit. Censorship didn't kill gore—it taught fans to hunt down "uncut" versions, fueling cult status.

Foundations & Grindhouse Gore

- ☐ **Blood Feast** (1963) – An Egyptian caterer kills various women in suburban Miami to use their body parts to revive a dormant Egyptian goddess while an inept police detective tries to track him down. Shot for peanuts in Miami; its shock marketing ("Nothing so appalling in the annals of horror!") built the blueprint for exploitation hype.
  - **SEQUELS**
    - ☐ **Blood Feast 2: All You Can Eat** (2002) - Directed by Herschell Gordon Lewis, this sequel was released 39 years after the original. It features the grandson of the original killer, Fuad Ramses, continuing his grandfather's cannibalistic ways under the influence of the same Egyptian goddess, Ishtar.
- ☐ **Two Thousand Maniacs!** (1964) – Lewis again, with a Southern town exacting Civil War revenge.
  - **ADAPTIONS**
    - ☐ **2001 Maniacs** (2005) - This is a comedy horror remake of the original film, with a significantly larger budget. Directed by Tim Sullivan, it stars Robert Englund as Mayor George W. Buckman. It largely follows the original plot of Northerners being lured into a Southern town for a centennial celebration, which turns into a deadly trap.
    - ☐ **2001 Maniacs: Field of Screams** (2010) - A direct-to-video sequel to the 2005 remake. In this installment, the maniacs of Pleasant Valley leave their town and embark on a road trip to find more "Yankees" to torment.
- ☐ **The Wizard of Gore** (1970) – A TV talk-show hostess and her boyfriend investigate a shady magician who has the ability to hypnotize and control the thoughts of people in order to stage gory on-stage illusions using his powers of mind bending.
  - **ADAPTIONS**
    - ☐ **The Wizard of Gore** (2007) - This remake, directed by Jeremy Kasten, is more of a reimagining than a straightforward reboot.
- ☐ **The Gore Gore Girls** (1972) – Strip club massacres, Lewis's farewell to gore.

IT'S THE FIRST... **HILLBILLY HORROR SHOW!**
YOU SAW THE BLOOD FEAST...
NOW SEE THE BARBECUED BLONDE!
MEANT FER THE YOUNG-UNS! (SOUTHERN STYLE)
TWO THOUSAND MANIACS!
GRUESOMELY STAINED IN BLOOD COLOR!
ADULTS ONLY!
★ NOW SHOWING ★
OPEN 11 AM PARIS All Seats 75¢
CE 2-4201

- ☐ **The Last House on the Left** (1972) – Two teenage girls heading to a rock concert for one's birthday try to score marijuana in the city, where they are kidnapped and brutalized by a gang of psychopathic convicts. A mixture of red and blue food coloring mixed with caramel syrup was used for the fake blood, which contrary to most film "blood," actually looks real.
  - • **ADAPTIONS**
    - ☐ **The Last House on the Left** (2009) - In the remake, one of the teenage victims, Mari, survives her brutal assault and is nursed by her doctor parents. The ending, while still brutal, was designed to provide some sense of hope, a change from the unrelentingly grim conclusion of the original.
  - • **RAPE-REVENGE HORRORS**
    - ☐ **The Virgin Spring** (1960, Sweden) - The art-house predecessor to many rape-revenge films, this Swedish film is based on a medieval ballad about a family's revenge for their daughter.
    - ☐ **I Spit on Your Grave** (1978) - An aspiring writer is repeatedly assaulted, humiliated, and left for dead by four men she systematically hunts down to seek revenge.
    - ☐ **Baise-moi** (2000, France) - A French film following two marginalized women on a nihilistic, destructive tour of sex and violence across the country.
    - ☐ **Irreversible** (2002, France) – A brutal story of a rape and the subsequent revenge in reverse chronological order. The director cited several films as influences, including *Betrayal* (1983) for its reverse chronology. Other films known for their controversial content, such as *In the Realm of the Senses* (1976), *A Clockwork Orange* (1971), and *Straw Dogs* (1971), also influenced the film.
    - ☐ **A Serbian Film** (2010, Serbia) – An infamous and highly controversial film that depicts extreme violence within the context of a snuff film production. Infamous for taboo-breaking gore, which led to it being banned or heavily censored in numerous countries.
    - ☐ **American Mary** (2012) – This film follows a surgical student who, after a traumatic experience, enters the world of underground body modification and uses her skills for revenge against those who wronged her.
    - ☐ **Bound to Vengeance** (2015) - A horror-thriller where a young girl escapes her confinement in a basement and discovers other victims, leading her to turn the tables on her captor and seek revenge.
    - ☐ **Elle** (2016 France/Germany/Belgium) - A French-German thriller directed by Paul Verhoeven. A successful businesswoman tracks down the man who assaulted her, engaging in a complex and disturbing game of cat and mouse.
    - ☐ **Revenge** (2017) - Never take your mistress on an annual guys' getaway, especially one devoted to hunting - a violent lesson for three wealthy married men.
    - ☐ **The Nightingale** (2018) - Directed by Jennifer Kent (*The Babadook*), this Australian film is a brutal period piece set in 1825. It follows a young convict who seeks revenge on the British officer who harmed her family.
- ☐ **Deep Red** (1975, Italy) – A jazz pianist and a wisecracking journalist are pulled into a complex web of mystery after the former witnesses the brutal murder of a psychic. Directed by Dario Argento.
- ☐ **Maniac** (1980) – Two strangers are drawn to a mysterious pharmaceutical trial for a drug that they're assured will, with no complications or side-effects whatsoever, permanently solve all of their problems. Things do not go as planned. **Memorable Quote:** *"It's not that I'm sick. It's that I don't matter."*

  - • **ADAPTIONS & CHARACTER STUDIES**
    - ☐ **Maniac** (2012) – Elijah Wood remake told from killer's POV.
    - ☐ **The Stylist** (2020) - A lonely hair stylist becomes obsessed with the lives of her clients and descends into murderous madness.

- ☐ **My Bloody Valentine** (1981) – Pickaxe-wielding slasher with juicy kills. In May 2024, reports indicated that Blumhouse Productions is developing a new reboot of the franchise as part of a multi-picture pact with Lionsgate.
  - • **ADAPTIONS**
    - ☐ **My Bloody Valentine 3D** (2009) - The remake introduces new characters and changes a sizable portion of the plot, though it centers on the same premise of a killer wearing mining gear.
- ☐ **Pieces** (1982, Spain) – The co-eds of a Boston college campus are targeted by a mysterious killer who is creating a human jigsaw puzzle from their body parts. *"You don't have to go to Texas for a chainsaw massacre!"* The film draws heavily from the Italian giallo horror subgenre, with its black-gloved killer and mystery elements, as well as American slasher films like *Psycho* and *The Texas Chain Saw Massacre.*
- ☐ **Basket Case** (1982) – Mutant twin wreaks gore-soaked revenge. This film is part of a larger universe of low-budget, often campy, horror films created by Charles Band. A young man carrying a big basket that contains his extremely deformed, formerly conjoined twin brother seeks vengeance on the doctors who separated them against their will.
  - • **SEQUELS**
    - ☐ **Basket Case 2** (1990) - The first sequel picks up immediately after the events of the original film. Duane and his deformed brother, Belial, are taken in by Granny Ruth, who runs a home for "unique individuals" like Belial.
    - ☐ **Basket Case 3: The Progeny** (1991) - The second sequel, which concludes the trilogy, focuses on Belial as he is about to become a father. The film notably amps up the bizarre comedy and practical effects.
  - • **FULL MOON FEATURES**
    - ☐ **Head of the Family** (1996) - The "head" of the family is literally that - a giant head on a tiny body, who psychically controls the rest of his even more unusual family.
      - • **SEQUELS:**
        - ☐ **Bride of the Head of the Family** (2020) - A direct sequel was finally produced and released in 2020 as part of the Full Moon Features series, *Deadly Ten.* While plans for a sequel had been discussed for over two decades, it took until 2020 to be made.
    - ☐ **The Gingerdead Man** (2005) - Starring Gary Busey as a murderer whose soul is transferred into a gingerbread cookie.[13]
      - • **THE KILLER COOKIE CHRONICLES**
        - ☐ **Gingerdead Man 2: Passion of the Crust** (2008) - This sequel focuses on the killer cookie attacking a low-budget movie set. The deranged cookie murderer known as the The Gingerdead Man is about to crash a studio lot and leave behind a trail of bloody murder and hilarious mayhem.
        - ☐ **Gingerdead Man 3: Saturday Night Cleaver** (2011) - The Gingerdead Man travels back in time to 1976 to continue his murder spree at a roller disco.
        - ☐ **Gingerdead Man vs. Evil Bong** (2013) - A crossover with another Full Moon franchise, *Evil Bong*, where the killer cookie faces off against a demonic bong.
        - ☐ **The Gingerweed Man** (2021) - This spin-off is the fifth installment and a sequel to the *Evil Bong* series.
      - • **EVIL BONG SERIES:** Just because I am a glutton for punishment and this book is already insanely long, but hey, it is an anthology.
        - ☐ **Evil Bong** (2006) - A group of stoner college roommates acquires an old, giant bong with evil, magical powers. When they smoke it, they are sent to a bizarre and trippy alternate realm. Starring Tommy Chong.

---

[13] These are absolutely horrendous movies barely getting above three stars on IMDB. I honestly think they made these films just because they thought of clever titles. That is the best thing about these films.

- ☐ **Evil Bong 2: King Bong** (2009) - The surviving characters travel to South America to find an antidote to Eebee's curse. They discover an even more powerful, malevolent entity named King Bong.
- ☐ **Evil Bong 3D: The Wrath of Bong** (2011) - An alien bong crashes on Earth, and it is up to the returning characters to stop its plan for global domination.
- ☐ **Evil Bong 420** (2015) - The character Rabbit, having escaped the Bong World, opens a topless bowling alley, only to be pursued by Eebee.
- ☐ **Evil Bong: High 5** (2016) - With the heroes trapped in the Bong World, Eebee again sets her sights on world domination.
- ☐ **Evil Bong 666** (2017) - Eebee is resurrected through a blood sacrifice and teams up with the proprietor of a head shop who has some sinister plans of her own.
- ☐ **Evil Bong 777** (2018) - Eebee travels to Las Vegas with her human companions, but trouble follows them.
- ☐ **Evil Bong 888: Infinity High** (2022) - The series continues, with the characters trying to make a name for themselves in the restaurant business, with weed on the menu.

☐ **Demons** (1985, Italy) – Written by Dario Argento. A group of random people are invited to a screening of a mysterious movie, only to find themselves trapped in the theater with ravenous demons. The building used for the exteriors of the Metropol theater still stands in Berlin. It's a club called Goya that's been host to several horror conventions thanks to its appearance in this film.

- • **SEQUELS**
  - ☐ **Demons 2** (1986) - This is the only official sequel, directed by Lamberto Bava and produced by Dario Argento. The story follows demons invading the real world through a television broadcast, turning the residents of an apartment building into monsters.
  - ☐ **The Ogre** (1988) - Released outside Italy as *Demons III: The Ogre*. Although directed by Lamberto Bava, and the title suggestion, it is not related to the Demons film series. It tells the story of horror novelist Cheryl, whose childhood nightmares of an ogre in an Italian villa come to life when she moves into a similar villa with her family.
  - ☐ **The Church (La Chiesa)** (1989, Italy) – Medieval church becomes site of demonic cult awakening. Originally conceived as *Demons 3* before being rewritten as a standalone film by director Michele Soavi and written by Dario Argento. An old Gothic cathedral built over a mass grave develops strange powers that trap a number of people inside with ghosts from a 12th Century massacre seeking to resurrect an ancient demon from the bowels of the Earth.
  - ☐ **The Sect (La Setta)** (1991, Italy) – A lonely kindergarten teacher discovers a secret well in the basement of her house, and soon finds herself being followed by a murderous Satanic cult. Also known as *Demons 4*.
  - ☐ **The Mask of Satan** (1989) – Marketed as *Demons 5*. Also known as Black Sunday, which goes more in depth in the Vampire Horror section.
  - ☐ **The Black Cat** (1989) – Marketed as *Demons 6*. An actress starts seeing visions of a witch character called Levana, which she's supposed to play in an upcoming horror movie, and slowly begins to discover a supernatural plot against her life.

☐ **Street Trash** (1987) – Melting hobos in technicolor gore comedy. A liquor store owner sells alcoholic beverages to homeless people, unaware of what the bottles actually contain: toxic brew.

- • **REMAKE**
  - ☐ **Street Trash** (2024) - Ryan Kruger's take on the original film continues his style, blending dark humor with visceral effects and focusing on society's underbelly. A group of homeless misfits must fight for survival when they discover a plot to exterminate every homeless person in the city.

☐ **Bad Taste** (1987) – The population of a small town disappears and is replaced by aliens that chase human flesh for their intergalactic fast-food chain. Peter Jackson's splatter debut, alien invaders + guts. After directing *Braindead* in 1993, Peter Jackson approached the New Zealand Film Commission with plans to make *Bad Taste 2* and *Bad Taste 3* back-to-back. Jackson put the sequels aside to focus on other projects, including *Meet the Feebles* and *Braindead*. Jackson made all the alien latex masks in his mother's kitchen. As he frequently used her oven to harden the latex, his family was forced to have sausages for dinner.

Prince of Horror

Clive Barker[14]

Clive Barker (b. 1952, Liverpool, UK) is a writer, painter, and filmmaker whose work fuses eroticism, grotesquerie, and the fantastical. Emerging in the 1980s with *Books of Blood*, Barker broke from gothic tradition and pulp horror alike, insisting that horror could be both literate and transgressive. His worldview: the body and imagination are limitless playgrounds, but also prisons. Barker's horror lens is unapologetically sensual, queer, and surreal, often blurring the line between pain and pleasure, flesh and spirit.

Signature Works (Curated)

- *Books of Blood* (1984–85, short stories) — The launching pad: splatterpunk vignettes of lust, violence, and cosmic grotesquery.
- *Hellraiser* (1987, film, based on novella *The Hellbound Heart*) — The birth of the Cenobites, where desire and damnation meet; one of the most iconic horror mythologies.
- *Nightbreed* (1990, film & novel *Cabal*) — Outcasts, monsters, and queer allegory wrapped in fantasy-horror.
- *Candyman* (1992, film, based on "The Forbidden") — Urban legend and racial/urban tension collide; Tony Todd becomes a horror icon.

The Fingerprints

- Flesh as canvas: hooks, scars, transformations.
- Desire and pain intertwined: horror as erotic.
- Monsters as sympathetic outsiders often more humane than humans.
- Myth-making: Barker builds entire universes (the Cenobites, Midian, the Art Trilogy) rather than one-off scares.

Legacy & Influence

Barker reshaped horror in the late 20th century, coining the term "splatterpunk" alongside peers but pushing it further into art and sexuality. *Hellraiser* gave horror its most enduring 80s/90s icon outside Freddy/Jason/Michael. His queer lens paved the way for later horror that treated sexuality and identity as integral to fear (*Jennifer's Body*, *Raw*, *Thelma*). Filmmakers like Guillermo del Toro cite Barker's fearless fusion of grotesque and beautiful as an influence. His imprint also extends into video games (*Clive Barker's Undying*, *Jericho*).

Pairing Night Watchlist

- *Hellraiser* (1987) → Watch for the fusion of domestic melodrama and sadomasochistic nightmare. Notice how Pinhead isn't a villain but an indifferent functionary of desire.
- *Candyman* (1992) → Look for the intersection of folklore and systemic injustice; the mirror motif is layered with symbolism about representation and history.
- *Nightbreed* (1990) → Watch how Barker humanizes his monsters; Midian is a sanctuary, not a threat.

Quick Facts to Sound Smart

- *Hellraiser*'s most famous line, "We'll tear your soul apart," was improvised on set.
- The Cenobites were never intended to be "villains." Barker described them as "explorers in the further regions of experience."
- Barker's paintings and illustrations inform much of his fiction; monsters often appear first on his canvas before his page.
- *Candyman*'s bees were real. Tony Todd negotiated a $1,000 bonus for every sting.
- Barker was one of the first openly gay horror creators at a mainstream level, embedding queer identity in his monsters long before the genre embraced it.

---

[14] "Author Clive Barker talks about what makes him tick Nov. 5, 2007 at the EMP/ Sci Fi Museum in Seattle." Steven Friederich (https://www.flickr.com/people/60581440@N00, Creative Commons Attribution 3.0)

1980s Splatter Renaissance

☐ **The Evil Dead** (1981) – Blood geysers begin. Five friends travel to a cabin in the woods, where they unknowingly release flesh-possessing demons. The original script called for all the characters to be smoking marijuana when they are first listening to the tape. The actors decided to try this for real, and the entire scene had to be later re-shot due to their uncontrollable behavior. Karo syrup and coffee grounds powered its infamous "blood." The MPAA forced a self-release unrated strategy.

- **SEQUELS & ADAPTIONS**
  - ☐ **Evil Dead II** (1987) – Ash Williams, the lone survivor of an earlier onslaught of flesh-possessing spirits, holes up in a cabin with a group of strangers while the demons continue their attack. Raimi choreographed the fights like Three Stooges routines complete with cartoon sound cues.
  - ☐ **Army of Darkness** (1992) – When Ash Williams is accidentally transported to 1300 A.D., he must retrieve the Necronomicon and battle an army of the dead in order to return home. This film is a major cult classic. An issue of the magazine "Fangoria" can be seen in the car's trunk. This was director Sam Raimi showing his gratitude for the publication's including the original *The Evil Dead* when it initially premiered.
  - ☐ **Evil Dead** (2023) - Five friends head to a remote cabin, where the discovery of a Book of the Dead leads them to unwittingly summon up demons living in the nearby woods.

- **INFLUENCE ON OTHER FILMS**
  - ☐ **Evil Dead Trap** (1988, Japan) - A late night TV presenter receives a snuff tape, in which a woman is brutally killed. She decides to take a crew out to a location indicated in the tape, but only death and despair await them. The title is a deliberate attempt to capitalize on the success of Sam Raimi's *The Evil Dead* (1981). However, the film is stylistically and tonally different from Raimi's series.
    - **SEQUELS**
      - ☐ **Evil Dead Trap 2** (1992, Japan) - The first official sequel was directed by Izo Hashimoto and is a standalone story. It follows a young theater projectionist who becomes obsessed with a ghostly boy and spirals into madness.
  - ☐ **Evil Toons** (1992) - Burt has a cleaning company and hires four women to clean an isolated house. They find an old book, a dagger and a soul shred and when one of them, Megan, reads an incantation, she unleashes an evil beast in our world. The film pokes fun at genre conventions, particularly the cabin-in-the-woods trope found in films like *The Evil Dead*.
  - ☐ **Cube** (1997) – Traps shred flesh in abstract geometrical terror. The low-budget, high-concept nature of *Cube* has influenced numerous other films and shows that involve characters trapped in a deadly, mysterious setting including the billion-dollar franchise *Saw*.
    - **SEQUELS & ADAPTIONS**
      - ☐ **Cube 2: Hypercube** (2002) - This sequel was released directly to video. It follows a new group of strangers who awaken in a hypercube, where the laws of physics and time are manipulated.
      - ☐ **Cube Zero** (2004) - A prequel to the original, *Cube Zero* was also a direct-to-video release. It delves into the mysterious origins of the cube, revealing the operators who oversee the deadly maze and their own fate.
      - ☐ **Cube** (2021) - A Japanese remake, also titled *Cube*, was released in 2021. It reimagines the story with a new cast and a more sanitized approach compared to the raw, visceral tone of the original.
  - ☐ **Kolobos** (1999) - Five young individuals live in an isolated lodge, filming their daily activities, but the house is locked down, and they encounter a murderous serial killer.
  - ☐ **My Little Eye** (2002) - A found-footage film that similarly follows a group of people in a remote house for a reality TV show, only to become victims of a more sinister plot.
  - ☐ **Malefique** (2002, France) - Four prisoners find an ancient diary in the wall of their cell which might be the key to getting out.
  - ☐ **Devil** (2010) - A group of people are trapped in an elevator and the Devil is mysteriously amongst them. The film's premise of a group of people with guilty pasts being trapped and killed

off one by one is acknowledged by M. Night Shyamalan as a nod to Agatha Christie's 1939 novel *And Then There Were None*.

- [ ] **Cabin in the Woods** (2012) – A group of kids go to a remote cabin in the woods where their fate is unknowingly controlled by technicians as part of a world-wide conspiracy where all horror movie clichés are revealed to be part of an elaborate sacrifice ritual. The thermal coffee mug/bong was a fully functional mug and bong as portrayed in the film, the prototype of which cost $5000 to make.
- [ ] **The Maze Runner** (2014) – A sci-fi series about teenagers trapped in a giant maze. Thomas is deposited in a community of boys after his memory is erased, soon learning they're all trapped in a maze that will require him to join forces with fellow "runners" for a shot at escape.
- [ ] **The Platform** (2019) – A Spanish film about prisoners in a vertical prison. In a prison where inmates are fed on a descending platform, those on the upper levels take more than their fair share while those below are left to starve on scraps and one man decides to change the system.
- [ ] **Escape Room** (2019) - A horror film centered on a series of deadly escape rooms. Six strangers find themselves in a maze of deadly mystery rooms and must use their wits to survive.

- [ ] **Guinea Pig: Devil's Experiment** (1985, Japan) - The first film, which features a group of masked men torturing a young woman as a scientific experiment. The original films are notorious for their graphic content and controversial history, including a famous incident involving actor Charlie Sheen mistaking one for a genuine snuff film. Due to the "snuff film" controversy, behind-the-scenes documentaries were produced to show the special effects used to create the gore in the Japanese films. The series' reputation for extreme violence, and the Charlie Sheen incident, made it too controversial for traditional sequels or mainstream adaptations. The series and its legacy are kept alive by a loyal cult following of horror fans. These fans appreciate the independent, effects-driven nature of the films and support the homage series and rereleases.

- • **SEQUELS & AMERICAN ADAPTIONS**
  - [ ] **Guinea Pig 2: Flower of Flesh and Blood** (1985, Japan) – Infamous dismemberment short. Late at night, a woman is kidnapped by an unknown assailant and taken back to his blood-spattered dungeon, where he turns her into a "flower of blood and flesh" through a series of dismemberment and evisceration.
  - [ ] **Guinea Pig 3: He Never Dies** (1986, Japan) - A more darkly comedic entry about a salaryman who discovers he cannot die and proceeds to mutilate himself to shock a coworker. After being dumped by his girlfriend for a friend, he attempts suicide - which turns up pain-free - and decides to scare the guy by literally throwing his own guts at him.
  - [ ] **Guinea Pig: Devil Woman Doctor** (1986, Japan) - A black comedy featuring a female drag queen doctor performing bizarre and painful experiments on her patients.
  - [ ] **Guinea Pig: Mermaid in a Manhole** (1988, Japan) – Body melt grotesque. An artist rescues a mermaid in a sewer, who develops bleeding sores all over her body. He paints a portrait with what oozes from her body, and eventually dismembers her.
  - [ ] **Guinea Pig: Android of Notre Dame** (1988, Japan) - The story of a dwarf scientist who conducts gruesome experiments on a human body in an attempt to cure his sister's grave illness.
  - [ ] **American Guinea Pig: Bouquet of Guts and Gore** (2014) – Tribute to notorious Japanese Guinea Pig series. Two women are abducted by a group of snuff filmmakers and brought into a Hellish nightmare of unmistakable brutality, viciousness and destruction that will leave every viewer shocked, amazed and awestruck.
  - [ ] **American Guinea Pig: Bloodshock** (2015) - Another entry in the homage series, featuring a man who is subjected to torture by a deranged doctor. A man is imprisoned by a psychotic doctor who tortures him in increasingly gruesome ways in order to extract chemicals from his bloodstream. Along the way, he develops a relationship with a female prisoner.
  - [ ] **American Guinea Pig: The Song of Solomon** (2017) - A supernatural-themed installment involving an exorcism. The Catholic Church is trying to save an innocent soul from the ravages of satanic possession. Wave after wave of holy men are sent to confront the possessed.
  - [ ] **American Guinea Pig: Sacrifice** (2017) - This film features a man who engages in self-mutilation to summon a goddess.

- [ ] **Hellraiser** (1987) – A woman discovers the newly resurrected, partially formed, body of her brother-in-law and lover. She starts killing for him to revitalize his body and escape the demonic beings that are pursuing him after he escaped their underworld. The original title was *The Hellbound Heart* (Barker's novella). A producer jokingly suggested *Sadomasochists From Beyond the Grave*.

- **HELL SAGA**
  - ☐ **Hellbound: Hellraiser II** (1988) – More Cenobite gore in labyrinthine hell. Kirsty is brought to an institution after the horrible events of *Hellraiser* (1987), where the occult-obsessive head doctor resurrects Julia and unleashes the Cenobites and their demonic underworld.
  - ☐ **Hellraiser III: Hell on Earth** (1992) - In this film, Pinhead is freed from the puzzle box and begins tormenting a television reporter.
  - ☐ **Hellraiser: Bloodline** (1996) - This film spans multiple centuries, exploring the origin of the puzzle box and concluding with its destruction in the future.
  - ☐ **Hellraiser: Inferno** (2000) – A shady police detective becomes embroiled in a strange world of murder, sadism and madness after being assigned a murder investigation against a madman known only as "The Engineer".
  - ☐ **Hellraiser: Hellseeker** (2002) - A partial continuation of the Kirsty Cotton storyline. After a car crash, a shady stockbroker suffers from amnesia. This leaves him in a hazy limbo of sex and murder. But, as in a predestined journey, he takes the bait and follows the marked-out clues all the way to Pinhead.
  - ☐ **Hellraiser: Deader** (2005) – A journalist uncovers an underground group who can bring back the dead and slowly becomes drawn into their world.
  - ☐ **Hellraiser: Hellworld** (2005) – Gamers playing a MMORPG based on the *Hellraiser* films find their lives endangered after being invited to a rave, the host of which intends to show them the truth behind the Cenobite mythos.
  - ☐ **Hellraiser: Revelations** (2011) – Two college friends unwittingly release Pinhead and his minions.
  - ☐ **Hellraiser: Judgment** (2018) – Detectives Sean and David Carter are on the case to find a gruesome serial killer terrorizing the city. Joining forces with Detective Christine Egerton, they dig deeper into a spiraling maze of horror that may not be of this world.
- **ADAPTIONS & SIMILAR THEMES**
  - ☐ **Hellraiser** (2022) - This film, executive produced by Clive Barker, reinvents the story with a new cast and new lore for the Cenobites. It was directed by David Bruckner and features a female Pinhead.
  - ☐ **Baskin** (2015, Turkey) – Cops descend into hellish dimension. Evrenol has cited influences from 1970s and 1980s Italian horror, including the works of Dario Argento and Lucio Fulci, in its dreamlike imagery and gore. The film's depiction of a hellish dimension, presided over by a deformed sadist known as "Baba" (the Father), is heavily inspired by Clive Barker's creation.

☐ **Opera** (1987, Italy) – Argento's needles-to-eyes gore opera. A young opera singer on the cusp of stardom is hounded by a psychopath with a connection to her past, who forces her to watch as he brutally murders her friends and colleagues. The idea of the pins-under-the-eyes torture device came from a joke of Argento's. Argento said it would annoy him when people would look away during the scary scenes in his films. He would jokingly suggest taping pins under people's eyes so they couldn't look away from the film. It would late materialize on the screen for this film.

☐ **Society** (1989) – An ordinary teenage boy discovers his family is part of a gruesome orgy cult for the social elite. The scene where Billy sees Jenny's body distort in the shower was added during the production because director Brian Yuzna felt another shocking scene was needed earlier in the film.

☐ **Intruder** (1989) – Supermarket slasher with over-the-top practical gore. The overnight stock crew of a local supermarket find themselves being stalked and slashed by a mysterious maniac.

☐ **Meet the Feebles** (1989, New Zealand) – Jackson's puppet splatter musical. Multiple animals and insects experience the sleazier side of show business while working on a variety show.

☐ **Dead Alive (Braindead)** (1992, New Zealand) – Peter Jackson's goriest; lawnmower massacre legend. A young man's mother is bitten by a Sumatran rat-monkey. She gets sick and dies, at which time she comes back to life, killing and eating dogs, nurses, friends, and neighbors.

☐ **Body Melt** (1993, Australia) – Australian splatter of grotesque mutations. Residents of peaceful Pebbles Court, Homesville, are being used unknowingly as test experiments for a new 'Body Drug' that causes rapid body decomposition (melting skin etc.) and painful death.

The Wizard of Blood & Latex

Tom Savini[15]

Tom Savini (b. 1946) stands as one of horror cinema's most influential figures, a master craftsman who transformed gore from crude shock into an art form. Raised in Pittsburgh, Pennsylvania, Savini was drawn to cinema early, inspired by Lon Chaney's transformative makeup work and the gritty local productions of George A. Romero. His life took a detour when he served as a combat photographer in Vietnam, an experience that would shape his approach to horror. Witnessing the visceral reality of war left him with an unflinching eye for detail, and later, an insistence on authenticity in the illusions he created for film.

Savini's breakthrough came with Romero's *Dawn of the Dead* (1978), where he orchestrated balletic carnage on a scale never before seen. From exploding heads to hordes of zombies torn apart, his work didn't just shock audiences, it convinced them. The realism, grounded in his war experience and sharpened by his theatrical imagination, made violence in horror tangible rather than abstract. He went on to refine and escalate this style in *Friday the 13th* (1980), *Creepshow* (1982), and *Day of the Dead* (1985), where his groundbreaking animatronics and prosthetics earned him industry legend status.

Savini revolutionized horror by making gore both spectacle and narrative device. His effects didn't just decorate a scene; they told a story. A machete kill, a bite wound, a corpse reanimated, all carried weight because Savini made the unreal feel real. He elevated special makeup effects into a discipline of innovation, training generations of artists through his school and spreading his philosophy that horror's power comes from the interplay of illusion, timing, and audience psychology.

Beyond his technical genius, Savini has also acted (*From Dusk Till Dawn*, 1996; *Maniac*, 1980) and directed (*Night of the Living Dead*, 1990 remake), but his enduring legacy is the way he redefined how horror looked and felt. In an industry often divided between artistry and exploitation, Savini proved that gore could be both shocking and beautiful, grotesque and essential. His fingerprints are on every modern horror effect that strives for realism, his influence bleeding into cinema history as indelibly as the creatures he brought to life.

Signature Works

- *Dawn of the Dead* (1978) – Savini's breakthrough, establishing new standards for zombie gore and makeup realism.
- *Friday the 13th* (1980) – Introduced the slasher's iconic practical effects, from inventive kills to shocking reveals.
- *Creepshow* (1982) – A playful yet gruesome anthology showcasing Savini's range in stylized horror imagery.
- *Day of the Dead* (1985) – His magnum opus of practical gore, featuring jaw-dropping dismemberments and animatronic wizardry.
- *From Dusk Till Dawn* (1996) – Demonstrated his dual talents as both effects maestro and cult-favorite actor.

Legacy

Beyond his filmography, Tom Savini cemented his impact by training future generations of effects artists through the Tom Savini Special Makeup Effects Program in Pittsburgh. Many of today's leading practical effects creators trace their lineage back to his school, carrying forward his philosophy of innovation, detail, and realism. His work ensured that practical gore remained vital even in the age of CGI, making him not just the Godfather of Gore but also its most enduring teacher.

---

[15] Tom Savini at Spooky Empire's Ultimate Horror Weekend 2014 held in Orlando, Florida. Sam Howzit (https://www.flickr.com/people/12508217@N08, Creative Commons Attribution 2.0)

1990s–2000s Gore Wave

☐ **Nekromantik** (1987, Germany) – Corpse-love splatter. A necrophiliac has a hard time finding fulfillment in life. Jörg Buttgereit said in an interview that he never intended to be a director and Nekromantik was just a film to rebel against the German film rating system, trying to shock as many people as possible.

- • **SEQUELS**
  - ☐ **Nekromantik 2** (1991, Germany) – Continuation of corpse-romance gore. A female nurse desperately tries to hide her feelings of necrophilia from her new boyfriend, but still has pieces of the corpse of the first movie's hero in her possession.

☐ **Schramm** (1993, Germany) – From the Nekromantik director, gore-soaked killer portrait. As serial killer Lothar Schramm lies dying in his own blood, horrific memories of his miserable life of paranoia, self-harm and rejection flash before his eyes. A tragic look into the mind of a serial killer.

☐ **Saw** (2004) – Two strangers awaken in a room with no recollection of how they got there, and soon discover they're pawns in a deadly game perpetrated by a notorious serial killer. Shot largely in one room in 18 days; the short-film proof-of-concept landed the feature. In order to make the actors feel what the characters were going through, all of the bathroom scenes were shot in chronological order. Worldwide ticket sales for the *Saw* franchise put it at just shy of a billion dollars, making it the highest earning horror franchise globally. **Memorable quote:** *"I want to play a game."*

- • **THE JIGSAW FILES**
  - ☐ **Saw II** (2005) – Traps grow bloodier. A detective and his team must rescue eight people trapped in a factory by a man known as Jigsaw.
  - ☐ **Saw III** (2006) – Peak of gore traps. Jigsaw abducts a doctor in order to keep himself alive while he watches his new apprentice put an unlucky citizen named Jeff through a brutal test.
  - ☐ **Saw IV** (2007) – Torture legacy continues. Despite Jigsaw's death, and in order to save the lives of two of his colleagues, Lieutenant Rigg is forced to take part in a new game, which promises to test him to the limit.
  - ☐ **Saw V** (2008) – Elaborate blood-soaked puzzles. Following Jigsaw's grisly demise, Mark Hoffman is commended as a hero, but Agent Strahm is suspicious, and delves into Hoffman's past. Meanwhile, another group of people are put through a series of gruesome tests.
  - ☐ **Saw VI** (2009) – Health insurance twist on gore. Agent Strahm is dead, and FBI agent Erickson draws nearer to Hoffman. Meanwhile, a pair of insurance executives find themselves in another game set by Jigsaw.
  - ☐ **Saw 3D** (2010) – 3D blood spectacle. As a deadly battle rages over Jigsaw's brutal legacy, a group of Jigsaw survivors gathers to seek the support of self-help guru and fellow survivor Bobby Dagen, a man whose own dark secrets unleash a new wave of terror.
  - ☐ **Jigsaw** (2017) – This spin-off takes place a decade after Kramer's death, as police hunt a new killer with a familiar modus operandi. Police search for a supposed to be dead killer who forces his victims to play sadistic games of life and death.
  - ☐ **Spiral: From the Book of Saw** (2021) – Chris Rock's spin on gore traps. In this new chapter from the Book of Saw, a detective and his partner investigate grisly murders that are eerily reminiscent of the past.
  - ☐ **Saw X** (2023) – This prequel, set between the events of *Saw* and *Saw II*, sees a terminally ill John Kramer seeking revenge on con artists who scammed him. A sick and desperate John travels to Mexico for a risky and experimental medical procedure in hopes of a miracle cure for his cancer only to discover the entire operation is a scam to defraud the most vulnerable.

☐ **Calvaire** (2006, Belgium) - Marc, a traveling entertainer, is on his way home for Christmas when his van breaks down in the middle of a jerkwater town with some strange inhabitants.

- • **OTHER NEW FRENCH EXTREMITY FILMS**
  - ☐ **In My Skin** (2002, France) – Woman compulsively mutilates herself. A woman grows increasingly fascinated with her body after suffering a disfiguring accident.
  - ☐ **High Tension (Haute Tension)** (2003, France) – Visceral slasher with extreme gore. Best friends Marie and Alexia decide to spend a quiet weekend at Alexia's parents' secluded farmhouse. But on the night of their arrival, the girls' idyllic getaway turns into an endless night of horror.

- **Sheitan (Satan)** (2006, France) - A group of youngsters go out to a disco on Christmas Eve and accidentally run into a shepherd who has prepared himself for a night of pure insanity.
- **Frontier(s)** (2007, France) – Neo-Nazis + extreme gore. A gang of young thieves flee Paris during the violent aftermath of a political election, only to hole up at an Inn run by neo-Nazis.
- **Inside (À l'intérieur)** (2007, France) – Pregnant woman vs. intruder, notorious gore. Four months after the death of her husband, a woman on the brink of motherhood is tormented in her home by a strange woman who wants her unborn baby.
  - **ADAPTION & FOLLOW-UPS**
    - **Inside** (2017) - The American remake follows the same premise as the original: a pregnant woman is stalked by a mysterious stranger on Christmas Eve.
    - **Livid** (2011, France) - The suggestion of a big treasure hidden somewhere inside Mrs Jessel's once renowned classical dance academy will become an irresistible lure to a fiendish trap for Lucie and her friends. *Livid* was the follow-up to the directors' controversial 2007 debut, *Inside*.
- **Martyrs** (2008, France) – A young woman's quest for revenge against the people who kidnapped and tormented her as a child leads her and a friend, who is also a victim of child abuse, on a terrifying journey into a living hell of depravity. **Censorship:** Refused classification in several countries. Its American remake (2015) softened the ending, stripping it of existential bite.
  - **ADAPTIONS**
    - **Martyrs** (2015) - A woman and her childhood friend seek out revenge on those who victimized and abused them.
- **Hostel** (2005) – Three backpackers head to a Slovak city that promises to meet their hedonistic expectations, with no idea of the hell that awaits them. Banned in several countries for "excessive cruelty." Quentin Tarantino produced the film, branding it under his name for shock appeal. A "modern adaptation" and "reinvention" of the franchise is in development at Peacock.
  - **SEQUELS**
    - **Hostel: Part II** (2007) – Women victims fight back against gore tourism.
    - **Hostel: Part III** (2011) - This direct-to-video sequel was directed by Scott Spiegel and is not considered canon by Eli Roth. It is set in Las Vegas, where a bachelor party becomes the newest target for Elite Hunting.
- **Turistas** (2006) – Organ-harvest gore thriller.
- **Tokyo Gore Police** (2008) – In future Tokyo, a young woman in the privatized police force tracks down her father's killer while battling against mutant rebels known as engineers.
  - **ADAPTIONS**
    - **63 Minutes Later** (2009) - This spin-off is an anthology film focusing on three characters from the main film. It provides short stories that explain how each character became an "Engineer".
- **The Machine Girl** (2008, Japan) – Schoolgirl avenger with a machine-gun arm. *The Machine Girl* is part of a Japanese splatterpunk movement that also produced films like *Tokyo Gore Police* (2008) and *Meatball Machine* (2005).
  - **ADAPTIONS**
    - **Shyness Machine Girl (The Hajirai Machine Girl)** (2009) - It is a brief side-story or *gaiden*, not a direct sequel, that follows a different schoolgirl named Yoshie who also gets a machine-gun prosthetic.
    - **Rise of the Machine Girls** (2019) - This is a reboot of the original film, not a direct sequel. Outfitted with special weapons, two sisters take on the boss of an organ-harvesting ring and her army of henchmen.
- **Mutant Girl Squad** (2010) – Girls mutate with grotesque powers. After a high-school girl discovers that she descends from a long line of mutants, she joins other mutants to battle anti-mutants. Ordinary humans that can't run fast get caught in the slaughter.
- **Helldriver** (2010, Japan) – Splatterpunk apocalyptic zombie mayhem. *Helldriver* was produced by Nishimura's company, Nishimura Eizo, and features the director's signature style of over-the-top gore and absurd humor. It is part of a Japanese splatterpunk movement that also produced films like *Tokyo Gore Police* and *Meatball Machine: Kodoku*.

Torture-Horror Pioneers

Eli Roth[16] & Alexandre Aja[17]

The early 2000s saw horror shift toward extremes of brutality, realism, and endurance, fueled by global unrest and anxieties about voyeurism, violence, and survival. Two directors stood at the forefront: Eli Roth, the American provocateur whose *Hostel* (2005) put "murder tourism" into the cultural imagination, and Alexandre Aja, the French stylist whose *High Tension* (2003) helped define the "New French Extremity." Together, they pushed horror beyond supernatural threats and into the realm of raw human cruelty.

Eli Roth emerged from the American indie scene with *Cabin Fever* (2002), but it was *Hostel* that made him a household name and a lightning rod. Dubbed the "godfather of torture porn," Roth specialized in weaponizing sadism, voyeurism, and cultural fears of globalization. His films suggest that the worst monsters are not otherworldly, but humans empowered by wealth and privilege to indulge in cruelty. Roth's unflinching depictions of pain mirrored post-9/11 anxieties about torture, surveillance, and the commodification of suffering, making his work both controversial and timely.

Alexandre Aja, meanwhile, came from France's art-horror tradition, where extremity was not just spectacle but philosophy. *High Tension* (2003) marked him as a leading voice in the "French Extremity," a movement that confronted audiences with unrelenting violence and moral collapse. Aja's horror is immersive and claustrophobic, often trapping characters in impossible survival scenarios (*The Hills Have Eyes*, 2006). He relies on practical effects and visceral soundscapes to anchor brutality in realism, crafting films that feel like waking nightmares rather than stylized exercises.

Together, Roth and Aja redefined horror's boundaries in the 2000s, popularizing what critics derisively called "torture porn" but what fans recognized as a return to horror's ability to disturb, provoke, and mirror the darkest parts of society. Their legacy lies not just in gore, but in forcing audiences to confront why they watch, what they fear, and how violence functions as both spectacle and reflection.

Signature Works
- *Cabin Fever* (2002, Roth) – Flesh-eating virus as gory black comedy.
- *Hostel* (2005, Roth) – Murder tourism and the commercialization of cruelty.
- *High Tension* (2003, Aja) – A brutal home invasion that epitomized the New French Extremity.
- *The Hills Have Eyes* (2006, Aja) – Remake that intensified survival horror with savage realism.

Aftershocks
The extremes of Roth and Aja sparked waves across global horror. In America, their success fueled studios to bankroll ever bloodier spectacles, from the *Saw* sequels to imitators like *Turistas* (2006). In Europe, their influence dovetailed with films such as *Inside* (2007) and *Martyrs* (2008), which pushed the New French Extremity toward even more transgressive ends. Together, they legitimized brutality as a mainstream draw. What once lived in grindhouses now dominated multiplexes, video shelves, and streaming queues.

Legacy
Though often dismissed under the pejorative "torture porn," the work of Roth and Aja reflected a world steeped in images of war, terror, and Abu Ghraib. For some, their films were exploitation; for others, they were the most honest mirror of a violent age. Roth cemented himself as a provocateur who mined human cruelty for shock and satire, while Aja emerged as a stylist who gave brutality a philosophical edge. Their legacy is twofold: they proved horror could disturb on a global scale, and they ensured that violence, whether as spectacle or inquiry, remains central to how the genre tests its audiences.

Modern Extreme, Indie, and Cult Gore

☐ **Trouble Every Day** (2001, France) – Erotic gore and vampirism. Two American newlyweds in Paris experience a love so strong, it almost devours them.

☐ **August Underground** (2001) – The first film, known for its extreme found-footage style, directed by Fred Vogel, follows a serial killer named Peter and his accomplice, who document their murders and tortures on video. The films' graphic violence and subject matter, intentionally designed to disturb viewers, made them unsuitable for mainstream cinematic release or adaptation. The series' reputation for extreme content has made it a focal point of controversy and debate within the horror community.

- **SEQUELS**
  - ☐ **August Underground's Mordum** (2003) – Even nastier sequel. Two friends bring along a newcomer to go on a killing spree. [18]
  - ☐ **August Underground's Penance** (2007) – Trilogy closes in depravity. The third film in the series. This time a couple go on a killing spree in their local area.

☐ **Murder-Set-Pieces** (2004) – Serial killer gore excess. A fashion photographer exposes his demented childhood and zooms his evil lens on the oldest profession under the moon, in quite possibly the most notorious serial killer film ever made.

☐ **Slaughtered Vomit Dolls** (2006, Canada) – The films focus on the character Angela Aberdeen, a bulimic stripper whose life descends into a series of grotesque and surreal hallucinations. The *Vomit Gore* series is part of a subgenre of extreme and controversial horror films that push the boundaries of decency and content. It is often compared to other "shock cinema" films, such as *August Underground*, which was released around the same time.[19]

- **VOMIT GORE TRILOGY**
  - ☐ **ReGOREgitated Sacrifice** (2008) - In the first sequel, Angela is shown in hell, where she is subjected to violent and sexual torture.
  - ☐ **Slow Torture Puke Chamber** (2010) - This film concludes the trilogy by showing Angela escaping hell and attempting to find another victim, mirroring her fate from the original.
  - ☐ **Vomit Gore 4: Black Mass of the Nazi Sex Wizard** (2015) - The series was continued with a fourth film, which follows a new character who becomes the focus of Angela's torment.
  - ☐ **The Angela Chapters** (2020) - An anthology film featuring previously unseen and unused footage of the character Angela Aberdeen.

☐ **Deadgirl** (2008) – Necrophilia and gore in coming-of-age nightmare. Two high school boys discover an imprisoned woman in an abandoned mental asylum who cannot die.

☐ **Thanatomorphose** (2012, Canada) – Woman decomposes alive in her apartment. A Hellenic word referring to the visible signs of an organism's decomposition caused by death. One day, a young and beautiful girl wakes up and finds her flesh rotting.

☐ **Found** (2012) – Disturbing child's-eye view of gore obsession. A horror-obsessed boy discovers his older brother is a serial killer. The bulk of this movie was shot with a hand-held camera.

- **ADAPTIONS:**
  - ☐ **Headless** (2015) – Faux grindhouse splatter spawned from *Found*. After unearthing the lost slasher film from 1978 in Found (2012), the now-grown-up skull-masked boy abducts and tortures helpless women. Now, he needs one more victim. Will her blonde-haired head end up as the Killer's latest trophy?

☐ **Green Room** (2015) - A punk rock band is forced to fight for survival after witnessing a murder at a neo-Nazi skinhead bar.

☐ **Project Wolf Hunting** (2022, Korea) – Prison ship becomes bloodbath. Follows dangerous criminals on a cargo ship who are transported from the Philippines to South Korea, as they unleash a sinister force after an escape attempt leads to a riot.

---

[18] All though these films have gotten horrible reviews on IMDB, they are vastly known in the horror world. This film, however, is the worst in the series.

[19] This may be a porn with horror undertones. I am sorry in advance if you watch this as it is a staggering 2.3 on IMDB, making it not a good horror and an even worse porn. This film does have a blending of genres and is a staple for the vomit horror category.

The New Master of Horror

James Wan[20]

Born in Malaysia in 1977 and raised in Australia, James Wan emerged from indie horror into one of the most commercially successful directors in the genre. His background in art and film school sharpened his eye for precision scares and visual rhythm. Wan's horror is about *control*: the architecture of a scare, the orchestration of sound and silence, and the creation of franchises that become cultural juggernauts.

Signature Works (Curated)

- *Saw* (2004) — Low-budget puzzle-box horror that spawned a multi-billion-dollar franchise; introduced the concept of moral trap-based gore.
- *Insidious* (2010) — Family haunted by astral projection and demonic forces; cemented Wan's reputation for elegant jump scares.
- *The Conjuring* (2013) — Based on the Warrens' case files; blended haunted house traditions with period realism, launching the "Conjuring Universe."
- *The Conjuring 2* (2016) — Set in London's Enfield haunting; expanded Wan's craft with operatic Gothic set pieces.
- *Malignant* (2021) — A wild, giallo-inspired return to experimental horror; campy and inventive with its infamous "Gabriel" twist.

The Fingerprints

- The "Wan Cam": fluid camera movements that creep, flip, and circle to embody the presence of the supernatural.
- Silence-to-slam jump scares: perfectly timed audio dropouts and sudden blasts.
- Focus on family vulnerability: parents and children as horror's core unit.
- Franchise world-building: creating interconnected horror universes (*Saw, Insidious, Conjuring*).

Legacy & Influence

Wan reinvented the jump scare as an art form, making it about choreography rather than cheap shock. His *Conjuring Universe* became the Marvel of horror spin-offs (*Annabelle, The Nun*) proved horror could sustain sprawling cinematic universes. Beyond horror, Wan bridged into blockbusters (*Aquaman, Fast & Furious 7*), showing that horror filmmakers could dominate Hollywood tentpoles. His influence is everywhere: from Blumhouse's business model to A24 directors borrowing his camera craft.

Pairing Night Watchlist

- *Saw* (2004) → Notice how most of the film takes place in one room. Tension is built from editing and moral stakes, not spectacle.
- *Insidious* (2010) → Pay attention to how Wan uses sound design and off-screen space for some of his most effective scares.
- *The Conjuring* (2013) → Look for his use of 1970s period detail and long takes that transform ordinary domestic space into Gothic terror.

Quick Facts to Sound Smart

- *Saw* was shot in just 18 days on a $1.2M budget, grossing over $100M and birthing one of horror's biggest franchises.
- Wan storyboarded *Insidious* himself, including exact sound cues for every scare.
- The real Perron family (from *The Conjuring*) visited the set. Crew reported strange phenomena during filming.
- Wan is a master of *scale*: starting with micro-budget horror, then scaling into billion-dollar blockbusters without losing his signature style.
- He and Leigh Whannell (his longtime collaborator) originally wanted *Saw* to be a short film, and now its expansion changed horror history.

[20] "James Wan in 2019" by Daniel Benavides (https://www.flickr.com/people/52309209@N02, Creative Commons Attribution 2.0)

Splatter & Gore Horror Pairing Night

How to Watch
Think of this as a rollercoaster: start with goofy crimson excess, dive into serious gut-punches, then end with neon-drenched madness. Best enjoyed with practical snacks (red Jell-O, spaghetti "intestines," tomato soup shooters).

1. *Blood Feast* **(1963, USA)**
Why start here: It's crude, campy, and the "first" splatter film. Sets the tone: you're watching horror history evolve.
Smart Fact to Drop: Herschell Gordon Lewis made it for $24,000, and critics called it "an insult to the intelligence." He laughed all the way to the drive-in bank.

2. *Maniac* **(1980, USA)**
Why here: Tom Savini's exploding head FX made people faint in theaters. Raw, sleazy New York grindhouse energy.
Smart Fact to Drop: Savini himself plays the doomed driver who gets his head blown apart. Talk about making your own mark.

3. *Evil Dead II* **(1987, USA)**
Why here: This is when gore turns funny. Buckets of blood, chainsaws, and slapstick splatter. The perfect "palate cleanser" after Maniac's grit.
Smart Fact to Drop: Raimi invented a camera rig called the "shaky cam" by duct-taping the camera to a 2x4 and running through the woods.

4. *Hellraiser* **(1987, UK/USA)**
Why here: Body-ripping sadomasochism with hooks, chains, and Pinhead. Shifts the night into operatic splatter.
Smart Fact to Drop: The Cenobites were inspired by 1980s underground fetish clubs Clive Barker visited in New York.

5. *Martyrs* **(2008, France)**
Why here: The room goes quiet. This is New French Extremity—gore not for laughs, but for philosophy. It's torture as transcendence.
Smart Fact to Drop: Critics called it "the last horror film that matters." Barker himself praised its audacity.

6. *Tokyo Gore Police* **(2008, Japan)**
Why here (finale): You end with cyberpunk splatter absurdity—mutant weapons, arterial fountains, and tongue-in-cheek insanity. The only way to stumble out smiling after Martyrs.
Smart Fact to Drop: Director Yoshihiro Nishimura was once a makeup FX artist, which explains why every blood geyser feels like an art installation.

Pro Tips to Sound Like the Smartest Person in the Room
- "Splatter cinema always comes in waves. Lewis in the 60s, Italy in the 80s, France & Japan in the 00s."
- "Censorship made gore *more* iconic. If it's banned, people *want* it."
- "Notice how gore changes: from spectacle (*Blood Feast*) → sleaze (*Maniac*) → comedy (*Evil Dead II*) → erotic pain (*Hellraiser*) → existential philosophy (*Martyrs*) → cartoon excess (*Tokyo Gore Police*). That arc is the genre's DNA."

Bleed Screen

Slasher Horror

Where supernatural horror traffics in the unseen and Gothic horror builds from atmosphere, slasher horror is blunt-force carnage distilled into formula: a masked (or otherwise unstoppable) killer, a group of vulnerable victims, and a trail of creative deaths. At its core, slashers are morality plays disguised as bloodbaths, punishing youthful excess, rewarding resilience, and birthing the "Final Girl" archetype.

The genre's DNA traces back to *Psycho* (1960) and *Peeping Tom* (1960), both notorious for daring to put audiences inside the killer's gaze. From there, Italy's *A Bay of Blood* (1971) carved up inventive kills, *Black Christmas* (1974) introduced the holiday-themed maniac, and *Halloween* (1978) lit the fuse for the 1980s explosion. By the time Jason donned his hockey mask and Freddy invaded dreams, the slasher was as iconic as Dracula or Frankenstein.

Why People Are Drawn to It

Slashers terrify because they're stripped-down, intimate, and relatable. No cosmic gods, no demons, just a blade in the dark, a face at the window, or footsteps too close behind. Audiences return for the catharsis: the adrenaline of the chase, the jump-scare scream, the relief when the killer is stopped… or the shock when they aren't.

There's also ritual in the formula. Viewers *know* the rules: sex, drugs, and arrogance often spell doom but part of the thrill is watching filmmakers subvert those rules, from Sidney Prescott's survival in *Scream* to Erin Harson's fight-back in *You're Next*. Slashers are rollercoasters of blood, suspense, and rebellion.

Essentials

1. **Psycho (1960, USA)** – Hitchcock's shower scene didn't just stab Marion; it carved horror into the modern age. Shattered classical Hollywood conventions, blending psychological horror with shocking violence and narrative misdirection. Hitchcock's stark imagery and Norman Bates's fractured psyche redefined what horror and cinema itself could dare to show.
2. **The Texas Chain Saw Massacre (1974, USA)** – Raw, sweaty terror that redefined rural horror. Dragged horror into raw, documentary-like terror, with its grainy realism and relentless brutality. Tobe Hooper's vision of cannibalism, decay, and industrial collapse redefined the slasher and cemented itself as one of the most disturbing and influential horror films ever made.
3. **Halloween (1978, USA)** – Created the blueprint: masked killer, babysitters, suburbia. Distilled slasher horror into its purest form, with John Carpenter's minimalist direction and haunting score turning suburbia into a landscape of dread. Michael Myers's blank mask and unstoppable presence created an archetype of modern terror, launching a wave of imitators and cementing the film as a genre cornerstone.
4. **Friday the 13th (1980, USA)** – Crystal Lake's bloody legacy cemented the summer-camp massacre as slasher staple. Capitalized on the slasher boom with a summer-camp setting where youthful freedom met brutal punishment. Its inventive kills and shocking ending made it a box-office hit, establishing the Jason Voorhees legend and cementing the formula for 1980s slasher franchises.
5. **A Nightmare on Elm Street (1984, USA)** – Wes Craven fuses slasher tropes with supernatural dream logic. Freddy Krueger became a pop icon. Solidified the slasher formula with surreal dream logic, introducing Freddy Krueger as a killer who strikes in the subconscious. Wes Craven's blend of inventive effects, psychological terror, and supernatural menace redefined 1980s horror and created one of the genre's most iconic villains.

Deep Cuts

1. **Peeping Tom (1960, UK)** – The voyeuristic proto-slasher that destroyed Michael Powell's career, now revered as essential. Turned the camera itself into an instrument of terror, following a killer who films his victims' final moments. Michael Powell's controversial film anticipated the slasher by exposing horror's voyeuristic gaze, blurring the line between spectator and perpetrator.
2. **A Bay of Blood (1971, Italy)** – Mario Bava's proto-*Friday the 13th*; its kills were directly copied by later slashers. Also known as *Twitch of the Death Nerve*, is Mario Bava's most vicious and influential work, laying the groundwork for the slasher boom that followed. Its shocking set-piece murders, inheritance-driven plot, and

cynical tone made it a blueprint for films like *Friday the 13th*, proving that horror could be both stylish and ruthlessly exploitative.

3. **Black Christmas (1974, Canada)** – The first holiday horror; its anonymous phone calls remain chilling. Fused urban legend with holiday dread, turning a sorority house into a trap stalked by an unseen killer. Bob Clark's film pioneered the slasher's DNA: phone calls, first-person POV, and "the killer inside the house" years before *Halloween* refined the formula.

4. **The Prowler (1981, USA)** – Tom Savini's gore effects turn this WWII-themed slasher into a cult classic. Stands out among early slashers for its unflinching brutality and Tom Savini's grisly practical effects. Set against a postwar trauma backdrop, its masked killer delivers some of the era's most infamous murders, cementing the film as a cult classic of slasher extremity.

5. **Sleepaway Camp (1983, USA)** – Disguised itself as a routine summer-camp slasher before shocking audiences with one of horror's most infamous twist endings. Its mix of campy tone, brutal kills, and transgressive finale secured its cult status and lasting place in slasher history.

Critical Essay

"Slashers Didn't Start with Halloween"

Many credit John Carpenter's *Halloween* (1978) as the first true slasher, but the groundwork was already in place. Hitchcock's *Psycho* (1960) established the killer-next-door, *Peeping Tom* (1960) weaponized the camera as murder weapon, and Bava's *A Bay of Blood* (1971) perfected the body-count template. Even *Black Christmas* (1974) hit the beats of holiday setting, anonymous killer, and Final Girl survival. Carpenter synthesized these elements into a clean, terrifying package but he didn't invent them. The slasher was a genre waiting to be named.

Global Spotlight: Italy & Canada

- **Italy:** The giallo films of Dario Argento (*Deep Red*, *Tenebrae*) and Bava (*A Bay of Blood*) bridged mystery and murder, emphasizing elaborate kills and killer POV shots. Their fingerprints are all over American slashers.
- **Canada:** Before Hollywood seized the mask, Canada delivered *Black Christmas* (1974) and *Prom Night* (1980), both starring Jamie Lee Curtis. These films married slasher tropes with cultural specificity: long winter nights, sorority houses, and small-town claustrophobia.

Viewer's Toolkit

- **Final Girl Archetype:** Look for how she's framed: resourceful, cautious, morally "clean," she becomes the survivor by design.
- **The Mask:** It's anonymity made flesh. From Michael's Shatner mask to Ghostface's Scream visage, masks are shorthand for the unknowable.
- **The Kill Count:** Slashers invite viewers to track creativity: machetes, drills, claws, chainsaws—each death becomes a set piece.
- **Meta Evolution:** From *New Nightmare* (1994) to *Scream* (1996), slashers eventually became self-aware, mocking their own formulas while still delivering scares.

Slasher Horror: Grindhouse Origins & Aftershocks (Mini-Timeline)

1960 – Foundations
- *Psycho* (1960, Hitchcock) – The shower scene shocks censors and audiences. Introduces psychological killers, voyeurism, and the seeds of the slasher formula.
- *Peeping Tom* (1960, Powell) – Killer POV camera work, so disturbing it destroyed Powell's career. Later canonized as proto-slasher DNA.

1970s – Proto-Slasher Surge
- *A Bay of Blood* (1971, Bava) – Inventive kills and multi-victim structure.
- *Black Christmas* (1974, Clark) – Killer-in-the-house template, obscene phone calls, sorority setting.
- *The Texas Chain Saw Massacre* (1974, Hooper) – Grindhouse rawness; rural terror and cannibal family dynamics.

1978 – The Template
- *Halloween* (1978, Carpenter) – Michael Myers creates the suburban slasher mold: masked killer, Final Girl, holiday setting, unstoppable evil.

1980s – Golden Age of Body Counts
- *Friday the 13th* (1980, Cunningham) – Gore-forward camp massacre; Jason Voorhees emerges as franchise icon.
- *A Nightmare on Elm Street* (1984, Craven) – Surrealism and supernatural slashers invade dreams.
- *Sleepaway Camp* (1983), *Silent Night, Deadly Night* (1984) – Slashers invade holidays and camps, each with shocking twists.
- Proliferation: *Prom Night, The Prowler, Slumber Party Massacre* — low-budget slashers flood video stores.

Late 80s/Early 90s – Decline & Self-Parody
- Sequels multiply (*Friday the 13th Part VII, Halloween V*), gore escalates, plots thin out.
- Cult entries like *Maniac Cop* and *Stagefright* stretch the formula.
- Audiences burn out; slashers mocked as cliché.

1996 – Meta Revival
- *Scream* (1996, Craven) – Revives the genre by dissecting its own rules. Ghostface reboots the teen slasher for the irony-saturated 90s.
- *I Know What You Did Last Summer* (1997), *Urban Legend* (1998) – Copycat hits ride the wave.

2000s – Globalized & Extreme
- *American Psycho* (2000) – Satirical "yuppie slasher."
- *Cold Prey* (2006, Norway) – Euro-slashers prove the template is universal.
- *Hatchet* (2006, USA) – Back-to-basics splatter, self-aware but traditional.

2010s–Present – Legacy & Viral Slashers
- *Halloween (2018)* – Direct sequel to the 1978 original; Laurie vs. Michael redux.
- *Terrifier* (2016–2024) – Indie gore clown Art goes viral, proving slashers thrive in streaming and social media eras.
- *The Strangers* (2008), *Hush* (2016), *You're Next* (2011) – Hybrid home-invasion and survival slashers push the genre into realism and grit.

Slasher Horror: Effects Hall of Fame

Tom Savini – The Godfather of Gore (but also Slashers)
- Vietnam combat photographer turned SFX maestro.
- Defined the practical gore of *Friday the 13th* (1980), arrow through the throat, axe in the face with shocking realism.
- His "art of the kill" turned slashers into playgrounds for creative carnage.

Dean Cundey – Carpenter's Eye
- Cinematographer of *Halloween* (1978).
- Invented the slow "Shape POV" tracking shots, making the camera itself a stalker.
- His mastery of shadow and frame defined the suburban slasher's atmosphere.

Rick Baker & Kevin Yagher – The Dream Team
- Baker's creature work and Yagher's makeup effects brought Freddy Krueger's melted visage to life in *A Nightmare on Elm Street* sequels.
- They transformed Freddy into both a nightmare clown and a grotesque horror icon.

KNB EFX Group (Nicotero, Berger, Kurtzman)
- Took over in the late 80s/90s, keeping slashers gory during the decline.
- Provided blood, guts, and inventive deaths for films like *Halloween: The Curse of Michael Myers* and *Scream*.
- Blended classic prosthetic gore with emerging digital tools.

Slasher Horror: Viewer's Toolkit

How to Read Slashers
- *Sex & Survival*: Slashers often punish hedonism, rewarding the "Final Girl" but critics argue this reflects cultural anxieties, not morality.
- *Masks as Metaphor*: Michael's blank face = pure evil. Jason's hockey mask = everyman turned monster. Masks hide individuality, turning killers into symbols.
- *Suburban Fear*: Slashers thrive in "safe" spaces (suburbs, summer camps, sorority houses) corruption of the familiar is the point.
- *Kill Creativity*: Watch for escalation. Early stabbings give way to over-the-top gimmick deaths (sleeping bag slam in *Friday the 13th Part VII*, drill in *Slumber Party Massacre*).

Censorship & Ratings Battles

- 1980s MPAA cracked down, forcing filmmakers to trim gore, often making slashers oddly bloodless (*Friday the 13th Part VII*).
- The UK "Video Nasties" list banned *The Driller Killer* and *Silent Night, Deadly Night*, cementing slashers as cultural outlaws.
- Today, unrated streaming cuts (*Terrifier 2*) prove gore sells when free of ratings shackles.

Why We're Drawn to Slashers

- They're cathartic morality plays: chaos punished, innocence rewarded (or shattered).
- They make fear fun: a crowd can cheer a creative kill, then scream when the lights flicker.
- They're endlessly adaptable: slashers survive every era by reflecting its anxieties — from 70s counterculture (*Texas Chain Saw*) to 90s irony (*Scream*) to Gen Z viral horror (*Terrifier*).

Foundations & Early Slashers

- ☐ **The Leopard Man** (1943) - A seemingly-tame leopard used for a publicity stunt escapes and kills a young girl, spreading panic throughout a sleepy New Mexico town. Based on the 1942 novel *Black Alibi* by Cornell Woolrich. The film's influential narrative style has inspired other filmmakers and genres. For example, the use of a hidden human killer and shocking plot twists makes it a precursor to later slasher films and giallo horror. Filmmakers like William Friedkin (who directed *The Exorcist*) have cited its influence on their work.

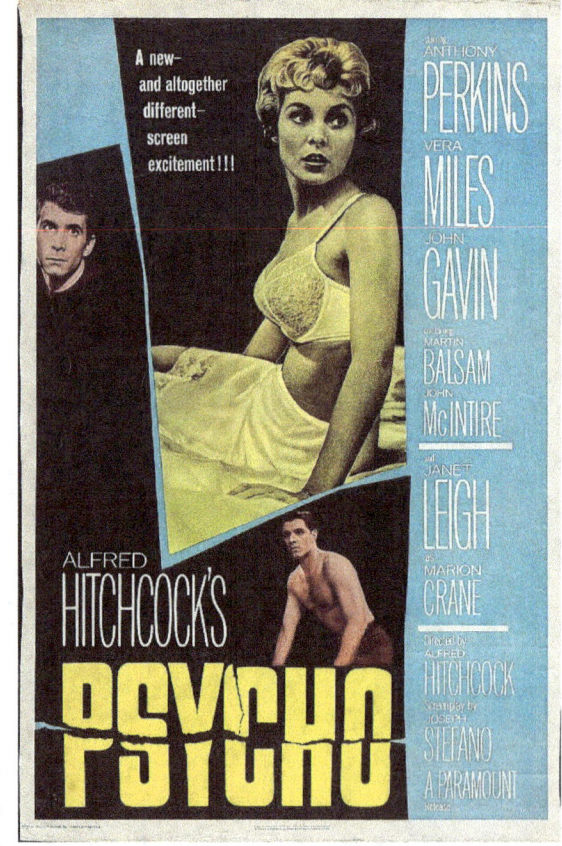

- ☐ **Psycho** (1960) – A Phoenix secretary embezzles forty thousand dollars from her employer's client, goes on the run, and checks into a remote motel run by a young man under the domination of his mother. This is the most famous adaption of the 1959 novel of the same name by Robert Bloch. Resisted Production Code oversight by self-financing and independent distribution. First U.S. film to show a toilet flushing. Hitchcock considered it scandalous enough to add suspense. Hitchcock bought up copies of Robert Bloch's novel to preserve the film's twist ending. Hitchcock's famous shower scene endures as a work of art unto itself, albeit one with a minor mistake. As Janet Leigh's character lies dead on the floor, her pupils are contracted when they're supposed to be dilated. After learning of the error, Hitchcock reportedly consulted with a handful of ophthalmologists, who recommended that he use belladonna eye drops when depicting murder victims. **Memorable Quote:** *"A boy's best friend is his mother."*
  - • **SEQUELS & ADAPTIONS**
    - ☐ **Psycho II** (1983) - Released 23 years after the original, this film brings Anthony Perkins back as Norman Bates, who is released from a mental institution. Norman returns to his home and motel, seemingly rehabilitated, but soon finds himself tormented by his past and a new series of murders. The sequel was a surprise success and is generally well-regarded among fans.
    - ☐ **Psycho III** (1986) - Anthony Perkins returned to direct and star in this sequel, which continues Norman's story shortly after the events of *Psycho II*. Leaning more into the slasher genre, the film finds Norman falling for a suicidal ex-nun, which causes his "Mother" persona to become jealous and violent.
    - ☐ **Psycho IV: The Beginning** (1990) - This film serves as both a sequel and prequel. It follows an adult Norman, now married and seemingly sane, as he reflects on his traumatic childhood during a radio talk show. The film uses flashbacks to show the psychological abuse and manipulation

by his mother, Norma Bates. The screenplay was written by Joseph Stefano, the screenwriter of the original *Psycho*.

- ☐ **Psycho** (1998) - Director Gus Van Sant helmed this shot-for-shot, color remake of the original film. Starring Vince Vaughn as Norman and Anne Heche as Marion Crane, it was largely panned by critics and failed at the box office.

- **OTHER ROBERT BLOCK WORK**
  - ☐ **The Night Walker** (1964) - A lawyer advises a blind man's rich widow tormented by nightmares.
  - ☐ **The Skull** (1965) - A collector comes into possession of the skull of the Marquis de Sade and learns it is possessed by an evil spirit.

- **MOTEL HORROR**
  - ☐ **Motel Hell** (1980) - A seemingly friendly farmer and his sister kidnap unsuspecting travelers and bury them alive, using them to create the "special meat" they are famous for.
  - ☐ **The Hitcher** (1986) – A sadistic drifter stalks a young man.
    - **ADAPTIONS & SEQUELS**
      - ☐ **The Hitcher II: I've Been Waiting** (2003) – Direct-to-video continuation.
      - ☐ **The Hitcher** (2007) - Produced by Michael Bay and directed by Dave Meyers, this remake is a bloodier, more action-oriented version of the original.
  - ☐ **Vacancy** (2007) – Starring Luke Wilson and Kate Beckinsale. Stranded in an isolated motel, a couple become the unsuspecting subjects of a snuff film.
    - **The VACANCY COLLECTION**
      - ☐ **Vacancy 2: The First Cut** (2008) - This is a direct-to-video prequel to the 2007 film. It depicts how the snuff film enterprise at the motel began, with a new group of unsuspecting victims.
      - ☐ **Terror Trap** (2010) - While driving, an estranged couple's car is hit twice. A sheriff takes them to a motel where they hear disturbing noises from a room, realizing they're part of a deadly game. While not an official trilogy, some releases include a third film, *Terror Trap* (2010), as part of the *Vacancy* collection, due to its similar plot of a couple being terrorized at a roadside motel.
  - ☐ **The Night** (2020) - An Iranian couple living in the US become trapped inside a hotel when insidious events force them to face the secrets that have come between them, in a night that never ends.

- ☐ **Peeping Tom** (1960, UK) – A young man murders women, using a movie camera to film their dying expressions of terror. Critics like Derek Malcolm later hailed it as "Britain's *Citizen Kane* of horror."
  - **INFLUENCE ON OTHER FILMS**
    - ☐ **The Last Horror Film** (1982) – This film directly spoofs the voyeuristic camera shots from the killer's perspective.
    - ☐ **Last Night in Soho** (2021) - Edgar Wright's film was heavily inspired by *Peeping Tom* in its themes and cinematic style.

- ☐ **Dementia 13** (1963) - A scheming widow hatches a bold plan to acquire her late husband's inheritance, unaware that she is being targeted by an ax murderer who lurks in the family's estate. This Gothic horror and mystery thriller is widely known as the feature film debut of director Francis Ford Coppola. The movie draws heavily from the psychological thrillers of Alfred Hitchcock, specifically *Psycho*, and combines elements of a "haunted castle" picture with a whodunit plot involving a series of brutal axe murders. The film is considered a proto-slasher for its depiction of bloody axe murders, which predated the slasher boom of the 1970s and '80s. In 2021, Coppola released a restored "director's cut" of his original 1963 film. This version removes scenes that were added by producer Roger Corman, who took over after production and insisted on adding more violence to make the film more commercially viable. he director's cut presents the version that Coppola originally intended and provides a clearer insight into his early filmmaking vision. George Lucas, a friend of Coppola's, included a nod to *Dementia 13* in his 1973 film *American Graffiti* by putting the title on a movie marquee in a background shot.

- **ADAPTIONS**
  - ☐ **Dementia 13** (2017) - At a wealthy family's estate, extortionists go after their matriarch and her inheritance while a ghost and an ax-wielding figure lurk in the shadows.

☐ **Blood and Black Lace** (1964, Italy) - A masked, shadowy killer brutally murders the models of a scandalous fashion house in Rome. The film's setting in a fashion boutique and its use of mannequins have been noted as an homage to Mario Bava's influential giallo. **Memorable Quote:** *"Perhaps the sight of beauty makes him lose control of himself, so he kills."*

- **RELATED FILMS & INFLUENCE**
  - ☐ **The Girl Who Knew Too Much (The Evil Eye)** (1963, Italy) - A mystery novel-loving American tourist witnesses a murder in Rome, and soon finds herself and her suitor caught up in a series of killings. Director Martin Scorsese intentionally reconstructed one of Bava's camera shots from *The Girl Who Knew Too Much* as a homage.
  - ☐ **The Bird with the Crystal Plumage** (1970, Italy) - An American writer vacationing in Rome attempts to unmask a serial killer he witnessed in the act of an attempted murder, and who is now hunting him and his girlfriend.
    - **ADAPTIONS AND SEQUELS**
      - ☐ **The Cat o' Nine Tails** (1971) - This second film in the trilogy focuses on a newspaper reporter and a blind puzzle-maker investigating a series of genetic-related murders.
      - ☐ **Four Flies on Grey Velvet** (1971) - The third film centers on a drummer who is blackmailed after he believes he has committed a murder.
      - ☐ **Screaming Mimi** (1958) - Virginia Wilson saw a man get shot right after he tried to kill her, so she goes to psychiatrist Dr. Greenwood. He falls in love with her and takes over her life, but she insists on continuing her career as a stripper.
  - ☐ **Black Belly of the Tarantula** (1971, Italy) - An inspector investigates a string of murders, which are committed by paralyzing the victims before eviscerating them - the same way a wasp kills a tarantula - and are connected to a spa.
  - ☐ **Amer** (2009, Belgium) - a highly experimental homage to the Italian *giallo* genre. As a young girl Ana was a rebellious child. She was also tormented by images of death and a shadowy, ominous figure in black. Now an adult, she is once again tormented by shadowy, other-worldly forms.

☐ **I Saw What You Did** (1965) – Starring Joan Crawford. Based on the Ursula Curtis' novel *Out of the Dark*. Teenagers Libby and Kit innocently spend an evening making random prank calls that lead to murderous consequences.

- **OTHER WILLIAM CASTLE HORRORS**
  - ☐ **13 Ghosts** (1960) - A family inherits a house with 12 ghosts who want a 13th.
  - ☐ **Homicidal** (1961) - This film is about a murderous woman with a shocking secret. For the climax, Castle offered a "Fright Break" and a refund to patrons too scared to see the ending. Those who left were given a yellow card to sign and escorted out along a yellow line painted on the theater floor.
  - ☐ **Mr. Sardonicus** (1961) - In this gothic thriller, a man's face is frozen into a terrifying grin. The "Punishment Poll" gimmick gave the audience a chance to vote for the villain's fate using glow-in-the-dark cards. An alternate ending showing mercy was filmed, but audiences always chose the gruesome punishment.

- ☐ **The Old Dark House** (1963) - This comedic horror film is a remake of the 1932 classic. It features an American car salesman in London who gets caught up in a series of family murders at a secluded mansion.
- ☐ **Let's Kill Uncle** (1966) - After inheriting a fortune, a young boy is targeted by his villainous, ex-military uncle. The film's dark, playful tone is typical of Castle's work.

☐ **The Slasher is a Sex Maniac!** (1972, Italy) - A serial killer is on the loose. His victims are unfaithful wives and he always leaves compromising photographs at the crime scene. A re-edited version released in the U.S. was called "Penetration", and featured hardcore porno footage with adult-film stars Harry Reems and Tina Russell. It was advertised as a porno featuring actor Farley Granger, who was in the original film but had nothing to do with the re-edited version. Granger threatened the distributors with a major lawsuit for the unauthorized use of his name in the new version, and they subsequently withdrew the film from US distribution, but not from Europe.

☐ **Don't Torture a Duckling** (1972, Italy) - When a southern Italian town is rocked by a string of child murders, the police and two urban outcasts search for the culprit amid scapegoating within the superstitious community. The film offers a powerful critique of religious hypocrisy, sexism, and mob violence. The Catholic church and the village's backwards, superstitious nature are presented as central to the tragic events. This film is one of Fulci's earlier works to showcase the gruesome violence he would become known for. It is an original giallo film.

- • **SIMILAR FILMS**
  - ☐ **What Have You Done to Solange** (1972, Italy) - A giallo film released in the same year, also featuring a mystery surrounding a series of murders and the dark secrets of a Catholic school.
  - ☐ **Alice, Sweet Alice** (1976) - This American giallo explores a series of brutal murders within a Catholic community, with an eerie child at the center of the mystery. It shares the themes of religious hypocrisy and violence.

☐ **Torso** (1973) – Giallo/slasher hybrid with stylish gore.

☐ **Black Christmas (Silent Night, Evil Night)** (1974, Canada) – Sorority sisters stalked by a mysterious phone caller. Directed by Bob Clark.

- • **ADAPTIONS**
  - ☐ **Black Christmas** (2006) - This remake, stylized as *Black X-Mas*, was directed by Glen Morgan and is far more graphic and direct than the original.
  - ☐ **Black Christmas** (2019) - This Blumhouse production was directed by Sophia Takal and is a more politically charged and supernatural take on the premise.
- • **HOLIDAY HORRORS**
  - ☐ **Christmas Evil** (1980) - A toy factory worker, mentally scarred as a child upon learning Santa Claus is not real, suffers a nervous breakdown after being belittled at work, and embarks on a Yuletide killing spree.
    - • **LATER WORKS & HOMAGES**
      - ☐ **Better Watch Out** (2016) - On a quiet suburban street, a babysitter must defend a twelve-year-old boy from intruders, only to discover it's far from a normal home invasion.
      - ☐ **Joker** (2019) - Some fans have drawn thematic comparisons between the protagonist's descent into madness in *Christmas Evil* and the origin story of the Joker.
  - ☐ **New Year's Evil** (1980) - During New Year's celebrations, a killer calls a disc jockey as he murders one reveler at midnight in each time zone.
  - ☐ **Silent Night, Deadly Night** (1984) – Killer Santa causes controversy.
    - • **SEQUELS & ADAPTIONS**
      - ☐ **Silent Night, Deadly Night Part 2** (1987) – "Garbage Day!" cult sequel.

CINEMA North 455-6624 STARTS LAKESHORE 457-1520
NORTHERN LIGHTS TODAY! DRIVE-IN LIVERPOOL
AT 7:30 AND 9:30 SHOW STARTS 8:50

If this picture doesn't make your skin crawl...it's on TOO TIGHT.

Christmas is coming early this year. And it's murder.

SILENT NIGHT EVIL NIGHT

R RESTRICTED OLIVIA HUSSEY · KEIR DULLEA

2nd HIT! LAKESHORE! *TALES FROM THE CRYPT* A REAL TREAT FOR HORROR FANS

- ☐ **Silent Night, Deadly Night 3: Better Watch Out!** (1989) - Also released direct-to-video, this film brings back Ricky Caldwell, who, after awakening from a coma, stalks a blind clairvoyant on Christmas Eve.
- ☐ **Silent Night, Deadly Night 4: Initiation** (1990) - This sequel abandons the killer Santa plot for a new storyline involving a cult of witches. It was directed by Brian Yuzna and features effects by Screaming Mad George.
- ☐ **Silent Night, Deadly Night 5: The Toy Maker** (1991) - The final entry in the original series focuses on a new villain, a murderous toy maker.
- ☐ **Silent Night** (2012) - A loose theatrical remake that features a new killer Santa and new characters.
- ☐ **Silent Night, Deadly Night** (2025) - A new film "reimagining" of the original was announced by Cineverse in 2024 and is set for a December 2025 release. Rohan Campbell was cast in the lead role of Billy Chapman in April 2025

- ☐ **Rare Exports: A Christmas Tale** (2010) - In the depths of the Korvatunturi mountains, 486 meters deep, lies the closest ever guarded secret of Christmas. The time has come to dig it up. This Christmas everyone will believe in Santa Claus.
- ☐ **It's a Wonderful Knife** (2023) - A recent horror-comedy that blends Christmas themes with meta-commentary on the slasher genre.

- **KRAMPUS FOLKLORE:** Krampus is a horned, goat-like figure from Central European folklore, originating in Alpine pagan traditions and later integrated into Christian customs. He serves as the counterpart to St. Nicholas, punishing misbehaving children on Krampusnacht (December 5) with whips, chains, or by carrying them off in baskets. His role reflects the seasonal balance of reward and punishment, with St. Nicholas rewarding the good and Krampus disciplining the wicked.
    - ☐ **Krampus und Angelika** (1965) - A German TV film that featured the characters of Krampus and St. Nicholas, likely in a less horrifying context than later interpretations.
    - ☐ **Krampus: The Christmas Devil** (2013) - A low-budget horror film about a policeman who believes Krampus is responsible for a string of child abductions.
        - **SEQUELS**
            - ☐ **Krampus: The Devil Returns** (2016) - A sequel to 2013's *Krampus: The Christmas Devil*, this film features a cop on the trail of Krampus.
    - ☐ **A Christmas Horror Story** (2015) - This Canadian anthology horror features interwoven holiday-themed stories, including a violent encounter between Santa Claus and Krampus.
    - ☐ **Krampus** (2015) - A boy who has a bad Christmas accidentally summons a festive demon to his family home. Despite earlier films, the 2015 movie Krampus is the most widely known and influential of the modern era. It was the first high-budget, theatrical release in the United States to bring the creature to a mainstream audience.
    - ☐ **Krampus: The Reckoning** (2015) - A low-budget film about a child psychologist investigating a link between a young girl and Krampus.
    - ☐ **Krampus Unleashed** (2016) - Fortune hunters in the desert accidentally unearth a summoning stone that unleashes a bloodthirsty Krampus upon them.
    - ☐ **Krampus: Origins** (2018) - This film gives the Krampus an origin story, taking place during WWI.

- ☐ **Mother Krampus** (2017) - Based on the German legend of Frau Perchta, a witch who punishes naughty children, this film was inspired by the Krampus trend.
  - • **SEQUELS**
    - ☐ **Mother Krampus 2: Slay Ride** (2018) – A campy sequel with a Kim Kardashian lookalike. With an abysmal 3.1 on IMDB. It's safe to avoid.
- ☐ **The Texas Chain Saw Massacre** (1974) – Leatherface's chainsaw defines rural slasher horror. Yes, that is spelled correctly and the other ones are two. They must have changed how to spell chainsaw somewhere in the mix. banned or cut in several countries for its relentless tone. Though famous for gore, it shows remarkably little blood onscreen. Horror lives in suggestion and sound design.
  - • **SEQUELS**
    - ☐ **The Texas Chainsaw Massacre 2** (1986) - Also directed by Hooper, this sequel is a black comedy with an increased budget and gory effects by Tom Savini. It follows a radio host targeted by Leatherface and his family.
    - ☐ **Leatherface: The Texas Chainsaw Massacre** (1990) - This film from New Line Cinema is an alternate sequel that mostly ignores the comedic tone of the second movie. A couple driving through Texas is stalked by Leatherface and his new family, which includes a young Viggo Mortensen.
    - ☐ **Texas Chainsaw Massacre: The Next Generation** (1995) - Originally titled *The Return of the Texas Chainsaw Massacre*, this fourth installment features a younger Renée Zellweger and Matthew McConaughey. It reimagines the killer family as members of an Illuminati-like cult and has loose ties to the original.
  - • **ADAPTIONS**
    - ☐ **The Texas Chainsaw Massacre** (2003) - This remake re-envisions the events of the 1974 film, with a group of friends encountering the Hewitt family and a different version of Leatherface.
    - ☐ **The Texas Chainsaw Massacre: The Beginning** (2006) - A prequel to the 2003 remake, this film explores Leatherface's origins and the formation of his cannibalistic family.
    - ☐ **Texas Chainsaw 3D** (2013) - A direct sequel to the 1974 original, this film follows a young woman who inherits a Texas mansion and discovers she is related to Leatherface.
    - ☐ **Leatherface** (2017) - A prequel to the original film and *Texas Chainsaw 3D*, this story focuses on a teenage Leatherface's origins as an escaped mental patient.
    - ☐ **Texas Chainsaw Massacre** (2022) - This Netflix release is a direct sequel to the 1974 film, ignoring all prior installments. It follows a group of young entrepreneurs who inadvertently encounter an elderly Leatherface in a remote Texas town.
- ☐ **Criminally Insane** (1975) - An obese woman recently released from an insane asylum kills anyone who attempts to get her to stop eating.
  - • **ADAPTIONS & SEQUELS**
    - ☐ **Criminally Insane 2** (1987) - Fatty, fatty 4X4, can't get in the kitchen door!
    - ☐ **Crazy Fat Ethel** (2016) - A modern remake was released, also featuring the title character. Director Brian Dorton used the opportunity to address some of the issues with the original film, providing better gore effects and more character development for Ethel.
- ☐ **The Hills Have Eyes** (1977) – Cannibal family terrorizes stranded travelers.
  - • **ADAPTIONS & SEQUELS**
    - ☐ **The Hills Have Eyes Part II** (1984) – Sequel continues mutant cannibal kills.
    - ☐ **Mind Ripper** (1995) - This film, produced by Wes Craven, was originally conceived as *The Hills Have Eyes III* but was rewritten to remove direct connections to the franchise.
    - ☐ **The Hills Have Eyes** (2006) – Brutalized remake amplifies gore.

- ☐ **The Hills Have Eyes 2** (2007) – Soldiers vs. cannibal mutants.
- ☐ **Halloween** (1978) – Carpenter's Michael Myers becomes the slasher template. Fifteen years after murdering his sister on Halloween night 1963, Michael Myers escapes from a mental hospital and returns to the small town of Haddonfield, Illinois to kill again. The Michael Myers face mask in Halloween is just a Captain Kirk/William Shatner face mask. They spray-painted the face white, teased out the hair, and reshaped the eye holes. **Memorable Quote:** "You can't kill the boogeyman."
  - • **SEQUELS**
    - ☐ **Halloween II** (1981) - While Dr. Loomis hunts for Michael Myers, a traumatized Laurie is rushed to Haddonfield Memorial Hospital, and The Shape is not far behind her.
    - ☐ **Halloween III: Season of the Witch** (1982) – Kids all over America want Silver Shamrock masks for Halloween. Doctor Daniel Challis seeks to uncover a plot by Silver Shamrock owner Conal Cochran.
    - ☐ **Halloween IV: The Return of Michael Myers** (1988) – Ten years after his original massacre, the invalid Michael Myers awakens on Halloween Eve and returns to Haddonfield to kill his seven-year-old niece. Can Dr. Loomis stop him?
    - ☐ **Halloween V: The Revenge of Michael Myers** (1989) – One year after the events of Halloween 4: The Return of Michael Myers (1988), the Shape returns to Haddonfield once again in an attempt to kill his now-mute niece.
    - ☐ **Halloween: The Curse of Michael Myers** (1995) - Six years after Michael Myers last terrorized Haddonfield, he returns there in pursuit of his niece, Jamie Lloyd, who has escaped with her newborn child, for which Michael and a mysterious cult have sinister plans.
    - ☐ **Halloween H20: 20 Years Later** (1998) – Laurie Strode returns to face Michael.
    - ☐ **Halloween: Resurrection** (2002) – Michael stalks reality show in his house.
  - • **ADAPTIONS**
    - ☐ **Halloween** (2007) – Rob Zombie's remake. After being committed for 15 years, Michael Myers, now a grown man and still very dangerous, escapes from the mental institution and immediately returns to Haddonfield to find his baby sister, Laurie.
    - ☐ **Halloween II** (2009) – Rob Zombie's killer sequel. Laurie Strode struggles to come to terms with her brother Michael's deadly return to Haddonfield, Illinois; meanwhile, Michael prepares for another reunion with his sister.
    - ☐ **Halloween** (2018) – Laurie Strode confronts her long-time foe, Michael Myers, the masked figure who has haunted her since she narrowly escaped his killing spree on Halloween night four decades ago.
    - ☐ **Halloween Kills** (2021) – Surviving victims of Michael Myers form a vigilante mob and vow to end his reign of terror.
    - ☐ **Halloween Ends** (2022) - The plot follows the outcast Corey Cunningham who falls in love with Laurie Strode's granddaughter while a series of events, including crossing paths with Michael Myers, drives him to become a serial killer.
- ☐ **Tourist Trap** (1979) - A group of young friends stranded at a secluded roadside museum are stalked by a masked assailant who uses his telekinetic powers to control the attraction's mannequins.
- ☐ **Friday the 13th** (1980) – Camp Crystal Lake bloodbath begins. A group of camp counselors are stalked and murdered by an unknown assailant while trying to reopen a summer camp which was the site of a child's drowning and a grisly double murder years before. Composer Harry Manfredini's "ki-ki-ki, ma-ma-ma" was created by whispering and echoing "kill" and "mommy." Jason may or may not be the killer in this one. A future prequel movie titled Crystal Lake set to be released in 2026, according to IMDb.
  - • **SEQUELS & ADAPTIONS**
    - ☐ **Friday the 13th Part 2** (1981) – Jason takes over, sack-mask debut. Five years after the events of the first film, a summer camp next to the infamous Camp Crystal Lake is preparing to open, but the legend of Jason is weighing heavy on the proceedings.
    - ☐ **Friday the 13th Part III** (1982) – Jason dons iconic hockey mask. Jason Voorhees stalks a group of friends who have just arrived to spend the weekend at a cabin near Crystal Lake.
    - ☐ **Friday the 13th: The Final Chapter** (1984) – Gore-heavy "ending" of Jason. After being announced dead and taken to a morgue, Jason Voorhees spontaneously revives, escapes from the hospital, and stalks a group of friends renting a house in the countryside near Crystal Lake.

- ☐ **Friday the 13th: A New Beginning** (1985) – Jason copycat slays again. Still haunted by his past, Tommy Jarvis, who, as a child, killed Jason Voorhees, is sent to a secluded halfway house in the countryside, where the killing of a young man triggers a brutal series of murders in the area.
- ☐ **Friday the 13th Part VI: Jason Lives** (1986) – Meta-humor and zombie Jason. Tommy Jarvis exhumes Jason Voorhees to cremate his corpse, but inadvertently brings him back to life instead. The newly revived killer seeks revenge, and Tommy may be the only one who can stop him.
- ☐ **Friday the 13th Part VII: The New Blood** (1988) – Jason vs. telekinetic girl. Jason Voorhees is accidentally freed from his watery prison by a telekinetic teenager. Now, only she can stop him.
- ☐ **Friday the 13th Part VIII: Jason Takes Manhattan** (1989) – Jason on a cruise to NYC. Jason Voorhees is accidentally awakened from his watery grave and ends up stalking a ship full of graduating high-school students headed to Manhattan, New York.[21]
- ☐ **Jason Goes to Hell: The Final Friday** (1993) – Demon-Jason body hopping and his supernatural origins are revealed.
- ☐ **Jason X** (2001) – Jason in space; futuristic kills. Jason Voorhees is cryogenically frozen at the beginning of the 21st century, and is discovered in the 25th century and taken to space. He gets thawed, and begins stalking and killing the crew of the spaceship that's transporting him.
- ☐ **Freddy vs. Jason** (2003) – Horror icons clash in gore-soaked showdown. Freddy Krueger and Jason Voorhees return to terrorize the teenagers of Elm Street. Only this time, they're out to get each other, too.
- ☐ **Friday the 13th** (2009) - A group of young adults visit a boarded-up campsite named Crystal Lake where they soon encounter the mysterious Jason Voorhees and his deadly intentions.

- ☐ **A Nightmare on Elm Street** (1984) – The monstrous spirit of a slain child murderer seeks revenge by invading the dreams of teenagers whose parents were responsible for his untimely death. Trimmed gore in initial releases. Johnny Depp's film debut. Heather Langenkamp beat over 200 actresses for the role of Nancy Thompson, among them Jennifer Grey, Demi Moore, and Courteney Cox. In the original script, Freddy was a child molester. However, the decision was made to change him into being a child murderer to avoid accusations of exploiting a series of child molestations in California around the time of production. He was re-written as a child molester in the 2010 remake starring Jackie Earle Haley. **Memorable quote:** *"Whatever you do, don't fall asleep."*
  - • **SEQUELS & ADAPTIONS**
    - ☐ **A Nightmare on Elm Street 2: Freddy's Revenge** (1985) – Subtext-heavy sequel. A teenage boy is haunted in his dreams by deceased child murderer Freddy Krueger, who is out to possess him in order to continue his reign of terror in the real world.
    - ☐ **A Nightmare on Elm Street 3: Dream Warriors** (1987) – Fan-favorite; kids fight back. A psychiatrist, familiar with the knife-wielding dream demon Freddy Krueger, helps teens at a mental hospital battle the killer who is invading their dreams.
    - ☐ **A Nightmare on Elm Street 4: The Dream Master** (1988) – Freddy's quippy peak. Freddy Krueger returns once again to terrorize the dreams of the remaining Dream Warriors, as well as those of a young woman who may be able to defeat him for good.
    - ☐ **A Nightmare on Elm Street 5: The Dream Child** (1989) – Surreal dream imagery. The pregnant Alice finds Freddy Krueger striking through the sleeping mind of her unborn child, hoping to be reborn into the real world.
    - ☐ **Freddy's Dead: The Final Nightmare** (1991) – 3D finale of original saga. Dream-haunting Freddy Krueger returns once again to prowl the nightmares of Springwood's last surviving teenager, and of a woman whose personal connection to Krueger may mean his doom.
    - ☐ **Wes Craven's New Nightmare** (1994) – Meta Freddy returns to haunt actors. A demonic force has chosen Freddy Krueger as its portal to the real world. Can Heather Langenkamp play the part of Nancy one last time and trap the evil trying to enter our world?
    - ☐ **A Nightmare on Elm Street** (2010) – Gritty remake of Freddy's debut, starring Rooney Mara. The spectre of a disfigured man haunts the children of the parents who murdered him, stalking and killing them in their dreams.

---

[21] If you want to write a good horror, always *"Accidentally Awaken the killer…again."*

The Slasher Pioneer

Tobe Hooper

Born in Austin, Texas in 1943, Tobe Hooper was a documentary filmmaker before he shocked the world with one of the most infamous horror films of all time. His style grew out of cinéma vérité grit, Southern Gothic folklore, and countercultural paranoia. Hooper's films often blur the line between realism and nightmare, grounding supernatural or grotesque horror in ordinary American landscapes: dusty highways, suburban homes, TV broadcasts. Where others leaned into gothic fantasy, Hooper dragged horror into the harsh daylight of small-town America.

Signature Works (Curated)

- *The Texas Chain Saw Massacre* (1974) — A low-budget indie that redefined horror: sunlit terror, chainsaw hysteria, and Leatherface. A landmark in brutality and atmosphere.
- *Salem's Lot* (1979) — TV miniseries adaptation of Stephen King; creepy small-town vampire tale, cemented Hooper's skill in longer forms.
- *Poltergeist* (1982) — Spielberg-produced suburban haunting; famous for its mix of family melodrama, cutting-edge effects, and uncanny terror.
- *The Funhouse* (1981) — Carnival horror with voyeurism, mutants, and grindhouse energy.
- *Lifeforce* (1985) — Space vampires invade Earth in this gonzo sci-fi/horror mashup, infamous for its ambition and excess.

The Fingerprints

- Sunlit horror: terror often set in daylight (*Texas Chain Saw*).
- Americana twisted: suburban homes, roadside diners, small towns turned sinister.
- Grotesque families: dysfunction and cannibalism as cultural metaphors.
- A documentary-like realism that heightens the surreal when horror arrives.
- Spectacle meets grit: practical effects and visceral chaos woven with social commentary.

Legacy & Influence

Hooper's *Texas Chain Saw Massacre* remains one of the most imitated and studied horror films ever made inspiring slashers, grindhouse cinema, and even art-house reappraisals. His mix of vérité grit and surreal violence shaped everything from Rob Zombie's *House of 1000 Corpses* to the *Wrong Turn* franchise. *Poltergeist* set the standard for suburban supernatural horror, echoed decades later in films like *Insidious* and *The Conjuring*. His career proves horror can be both unflinching and wildly imaginative.

Pairing Night Watchlist

- *The Texas Chain Saw Massacre* (1974) → Notice how little gore there actually is; the terror comes from sound, editing, and atmosphere.
- *Poltergeist* (1982) → Watch for the blend of domestic comedy, escalating horror, and the influence of Spielberg's fingerprints.
- *Lifeforce* (1985) → Look for Hooper's wild ambition; this is pulp spectacle colliding with cosmic horror.

Quick Facts to Sound Smart

- *Texas Chain Saw Massacre* was banned in several countries but contains very little on-screen gore; its reputation came from suggestion and atmosphere.
- The film's sound design — buzzing chainsaws, squealing pigs — is as unsettling as the visuals.
- There's long-standing debate about how much of *Poltergeist* was directed by Hooper versus Spielberg, though cast members later defended Hooper's control on set.
- Hooper also directed a music video: Billy Idol's "Dancing with Myself."
- Leatherface was loosely inspired by real-life murderer Ed Gein, who also inspired *Psycho* and *Silence of the Lambs*.

Complete List of Video Nasties

The *video nasty* scare wasn't really about gore alone, it was about power. In early 1980s Britain, the explosion of home video created a legal grey zone: unlike theatrical releases, VHS tapes didn't go through the BBFC's certification process. Suddenly, lurid horror titles were being rented next to family films at local shops. Campaigners like Mary Whitehouse framed these tapes as a moral threat to children, stoking tabloid headlines of "horror in the living room." The resulting prosecutions had less to do with what people were actually watching, and more to do with who controlled the new medium. In hindsight, the panic looks less like censorship of content and more like the state reasserting its grip over technology. Ironically, the ban only cemented these films as forbidden fruit, giving them cultural afterlives far beyond what their original directors could have imagined.

Of the 72 films targeted during the *video nasty* panic, 39 were ultimately prosecuted under the Obscene Publications Act. The other 33 faced less severe outcomes. Many had their cases dropped or were handled under Section 3, which allowed authorities to seize and confiscate tapes without pursuing full criminal charges. This created a patchwork of rulings where some films were branded criminally obscene while others were quietly pulled from circulation.

In the decades that followed, cultural attitudes and censorship standards shifted. With the introduction of the Video Recordings Act of 1984 and the later reassessments by the British Board of Film Classification, many of these once-banned titles were revisited. Edited versions were released, restrictions were lifted, and some films were eventually reclassified entirely. What had once been demonized as corrupting material found its way back into mainstream circulation, often carrying with it the notoriety of having been suppressed in the first place.

- ☐ **Absurd (Rosso Sangue)** (1981, Italy) – Italian "Video Nasty" adjacent to zombie tradition. A priest-doctor chasing a man with supernatural regenerative abilities, who has recently escaped from a medical lab, reaches a small town where the mutant goes on a killing spree.
- ☐ **Anthropophagus** (1980, Italy) - A group of friends and a hitchhiker become stranded on a tourist island where they are stalked by a disfigured cannibalistic killer who is prowling the island after killing its residents.
- ☐ **Axe (Lisa, Lisa)** (1977) - Three criminals on a murder spree arrives at a farmhouse, where a girl is living with her paralyzed grandfather.
- ☐ **A Bay of Blood (Twitch of the Death Nerve)** (1971, Italy) – The murder of a wealthy countess triggers a chain reaction of brutal killings in the surrounding bay area as several unscrupulous characters try to seize her large estate. *Friday the 13th* (1980) and *Friday the 13th Part 2* (1981) pay homage to this movie by lifting two murders from it (one in each movie), almost shot-for-shot. The locations in all three movies look similar.
- ☐ **The Beast in Heat** (1977, Italy) - A beautiful, nefarious senior female SS officer/doctor creates a genetic, mutant human hybrid; the beast is a, squat, mongoloid hyper-sexually-driven fiend which she uses to torture and molest female prisoners while getting fellow Nazis to watch.
- ☐ **The Beyond** (1981, Italy) – *See Gates of Hell Trilogy for complete entry.
- ☐ **Blood Feast** (1963) – *See Foundations & Grindhouse Gore for complete entry.
- ☐ **Blood Rites (The Ghastly Ones)** (1968) - Three married couples must spend three nights in a secluded Victorian mansion to claim an inheritance, but a hooded killer begins to murder them one by one. Horror author Stephen King claims in his book "Danse Macabre" that this film is "the work of morons with cameras."
- ☐ **Bloody Moon** (1981, Germany) - Girls are killed at a language-school in Spain. Banned in Germany up until March 2023. With the removal of the ban, the FSK gave the uncut version a "not under 18" rating.
- ☐ **The Boogeyman** (1982) - A man tries to explain to his psychiatrist that the Boogeyman is real and has been killing his children. Lester Billings is a man tormented by an unseen entity destroying his family one by one, until he is forced to confront the evil taking over his soul. With the help of Dr.Harper, Lester relives his horrific past in a desperate attempt to save his own life.

- **Boogeyman II (Revenge of the Boogeyman)** (1983) - Lacey travels to Hollywood, to the home of a film director, where she brings along the last surviving haunted mirror shard from the end of the first movie as proof to her horrifying experiences.
- **The Burning** (1981) – Slasher with extreme Tom Savini gore effects. Abusive former summer camp caretaker Cropsy, horribly burned from a prank gone wrong five years earlier, lurks around upstate NY summer Camp Stonewater with garden shears and bent on killing the teenagers responsible for his disfigurement.
  - **ADAPTIONS**
    - **Madman** (1981) - A legendary psychopathic murderer stalks a summer camp.
    - **Cropsey** (2009) - Realizing that the urban legend of their youth has actually come true, two filmmakers delve into the mystery surrounding five missing children and the real-life boogeyman linked to their disappearances. The 1981 film *The Burning* is a classic slasher, while the 2009 film *Cropsey* is a documentary that explores the real-life crimes that inspired the legend.
    - **The Cropsey Incident** (2018) - A found-footage horror film inspired by the legend, but otherwise unrelated.
- **Butcher, Baker, Nightmare Maker** (1981) - An orphaned teenager finds himself being dominated by his aunt who's hell-bent on keeping him with her at all costs.
- **Cannibal Apocalypse (Cannibal in the Streets)** (1980, Italy) - A Vietnam War veteran, bitten by a cannibalistic soldier, discovers he has an infectious craving for human flesh, which he uncontrollably spreads throughout Atlanta.
- **Cannibal Ferox** (1981, Italy) - Three friends embark on a trip through the Amazon jungle to disprove cannibalism, where they meet a pair of fugitive drug smugglers forcing a vicious cannibal tribe to harvest cocaine. A notoriously gory cannibal film that features a mix of jungle adventure and cannibalistic horror. *See also *Zombie Holocaust*.
- **Cannibal Holocaust** (1980, Italy) – *See Found Footage Horror for complete entry.
- **The Cannibal Man (La semana del asesino)** (1972, Spain) - A meat factory worker accidentally kills a taxi driver, and begins gradually killing people close to him in order to cover up his original crime. He starts getting rid of the mounting corpses stored in his bedroom through his day job.
- **Cannibal Terror (Terreur cannibal)** (1980, France) - After botching a kidnapping, two criminals hide with their victim in a friends house in the jungle. After one of them rapes the friend's wife, they're left to be eaten by a nearby cannibal tribe.
- **Contamination** (1980, Italy) - A former astronaut helps a government agent and a police detective track the source of mysterious alien pod spores, filled with lethal flesh-dissolving acid, to a South American coffee plantation controlled by alien pod clones.
- **Dead & Buried** (1981) – Town conceals murderous cult practices. Sheriff Dan Gillis investigates eerie deaths in a sleepy coastal town.
- **Eaten Alive (UK title: Death Trap)** (1977, Italy) – Motel owner feeds victims to his pet crocodile. Psychotic redneck Judd owns a dilapidated hotel in rural East Texas, where he murders people who upset him or his business, and then feeds their remains to his large pet crocodile in the swamp beside his hotel.
- **Deep River Savages (Il paese del sesso Selvaggio)** (1972, Italy) - After killing a man in a bar fight, a British photographer flees into the rainforest, where he is captured by a native tribe and is forced to adapt to their brutal customs before he is accepted.
- **Delirium** (1979) - An ex-soldier is hired by local right-wingers as a vigilante to clean up criminals and street people. However, he freaks out and starts killing off everybody.
- **Devil Hunter (El caníbal)** (1980, Spain) - A Vietnam veteran is hired to rescue a kidnapped model from a gang in a remote jungle, only to discover the area is also inhabited by a cannibalistic tribe and their flesh-eating "Devil God."
- **Don't Go in the House** (1979) – A disturbed young man who was burned as a child by his sadistic mother stalks women with a flamethrower. Due to its graphic content, particularly a scene where a nude woman is burned alive, the film became infamous and was banned in several countries, including the United Kingdom, where it was considered a "video nasty."
- **Don't Go in the Woods** (1981) - Four friends camping in the woods inadvertently stumble upon the domain of a maniacal killer.

- **Don't Go Near the Park** (1979) - Two siblings cursed in prehistoric times survive for millennia by feasting on the entrails of young people, prowling in what eventually becomes a park in contemporary Los Angeles.
- **Don't Look in the Basement** (1973) - A young psychiatric nurse goes to work at a remote asylum following a murder. There, she experiences varying degrees of torment from the patients.
- **The Dorm that Dripped Blood** (1982) - Four college students are stalked by an unknown assailant while staying on campus over the Christmas holidays to help clear out a dormitory which is to be demolished.
- **The Driller Killer** (1979) - An artist slowly goes insane while struggling to pay his bills, work on his paintings, and care for his two female roommates, which leads him taking to the streets of New York after dark and randomly killing derelicts with a power drill.
- **The Evil Dead** (1981) - *See 1980s Splatter Renaissance for complete entry.
- **Evilspeak** (1981) - An outcast military cadet taps into a way to summon demons and cast spells on his tormentors through his computer.
- **Exposé (House on Straw Hill, Trauma)** (1976, UK) A paranoid novelist, suffering from writer's block, hires a new secretary, who unleashes a wave of violence and revenge after settling into his secluded cottage.
- **Faces of Death** (1978) - A collection of death scenes, ranging from TV material to homemade super 8 movies.
- **Fight for Your Life** (1977) - After escaping from jail, three convicts terrorize a black minister and his family in their secluded home, subjecting them to racist abuse and violence until the family fights back.
- **Flesh for Frankenstein** (1973, Italy/France) - Baron Frankenstein creates two "zombies" - one male, one female - planning to mate them in order to create a master race. Although the film is often referred to as "Andy Warhol's Frankenstein," he wasn't directly involved in the production, but allowed the director to use his name. Warhol would make rare visits to the sets and during the editing period. The gory special effects are an early example of the work of Carlo Rambaldi who would later go on to do the special effects for E.T. the Extra-Terrestrial (1982).

- **Frozen Scream** (1975) - Mad scientists turn people into frozen zombies and the zombies wreak havoc and kill people.
- **The Funhouse** (1981) - Teenage Amy Harper, her boyfriend Buzz Dawson, and their friends Richie Atterbury and Liz Duncan visit a local carnival for a night of innocent amusement, but soon witness a fortune teller's murder and find that the exits are locked.
- **The Gestapo's Last Orgy (L'ultima orgia de Ill Reich)** (1977, Italy) - A Jewish woman who survived the horrors of a concentration camp revisits the ruins of the camp, along with a former SS officer, and recollects the humiliation, the torture, and the constant abuse she went through.
- **Hell of the Living Dead (Virus)** (1980, Italy/Spain) - After an experiment gone wrong, a virus that turns people into zombies spreads throughout New Guinea. A female reporter and her cameraman, and a team of four commandos sent to investigate try to survive the onslaught.
- **The House by the Cemetery** (1981, Italy) - *See Gates of Hell Trilogy for complete entry.
- **The House on the Edge of the Park (La casa sperduta nel parco)** (1980, Italy) - Two low-life punks are invited to a party at a posh villa and take everyone hostage after being humiliated by their snobbish guests, subjecting them to rape, torture and mayhem.

- **Human Experiments** (1979) - A demented prison doctor performs gruesome shock therapy experiments on inmates.
- **I Miss You, Hugs and Kisses** (1978, Canada) - A woman is murdered and her millionaire husband is accused. But is he guilty?
- **Inferno** (1980, Italy) - An American student investigates the disappearance of his sister and the death of a friend, both connected from New York to Rome by an old alchemy book. All of the murderer's hands in the movie were Dario Argento's.
- **Island of Death (Ta paidiá tou Diavólou)** (1976, Greece) - A couple of perverted and maniac killers get loose on a Greek island. Nico Mastorakis was inspired to make this film after seeing *The Texas Chain Saw Massacre* (1974). He noticed how much money that film made, and decided to make a more violent and perverse film in order to make even more money. He even admitted in an interview on the DVD that money was his only motivation for making this film. To finish the money motivation, he wrote the script in a week.
- **The Killer Nun (Suor Omicidi)** (1979, Italy) - Legendary Swedish sex bomb Anita Ekberg stars as Sister Gertrude, a cruel nun who discovers depraved pleasure in a frenzy of drug addiction, sexual degradation and sadistic murder.
- **The Last House on the Left** (1972) - *See Foundations & Grindhouse Gore for complete entry.
- **Late Night Trains (Night Train Murders)** (1975, Italy) - Two teenage girls traveling on a train from Germany to Italy are terrorized and brutalized by three criminals, who later unknowingly seek shelter at the home of one of the girls' parents, leading to a savage revenge.
- **The Living Dead at Manchester Morgue (Let Sleeping Corpses Lie)** (1974, Spain/Italy) – Environmental zombies in rural England. A cop chases two hippies suspected of a series of Manson family-like murders. Unbeknownst to him, the real culprits are the living dead, brought to life with a hunger for human flesh by ultrasonic radiation being used for pest control.
- **Love Camp 7** (1969) - Two female Army agents go undercover at a Nazi prison camp to get information from a scientist being held there. One of the first in the "Nazisploitation" subgenre and pioneered a cycle of similar exploitation films that followed in the 1970s.
- **Madhouse (There was a Little Girl)** (1981) - A woman is pursued by her murderous, psychopathic twin sister in the days leading up to their birthday. Producer Ovidio G. Assonitis had to fire and subsequently fill in for the original director who was hired to do this film ten days into the production. However, it was later revealed that the same had happened on *Beyond the Door* (1974), and he would famously do it again with James Cameron on *Piranha II: The Spawning* (1982). Cameron claimed that Assonitis only hired an American director to get studios to finance his productions; he would then declare that director 'incompetent' just so he could fire them and direct the movie himself.
- **Mardi Gras Massacre** (1978) - Police try to capture someone who is committing ritual murders of women during Mardi Gras in New Orleans.
- **Night of the Bloody Apes (La horripilante bestia humana)** (1969, Mexico) - A doctor tries to save his son's life through a complicated heart transplant operation, the involuntary donor being a gorilla. Eventually, the young man turns into a violent hybrid beast.
- **Night of the Demon** (1980) - An anthropologist and his students attempt to track down a Bigfoot responsible for a rash of violent murders, only to uncover something even more sinister.

- **Night of the Howling Beast (The Werewolf and the Yeti)** (1975, Spain) - Daninsky joins a Yeti expedition in the Himalayas but gets captured by cannibalistic nymphs guarding a Buddhist temple. They turn him into a werewolf where he encounters a sadistic bandit while roaming the mountains.
- **Night School (Terror Eyes)** (1981) - Who's been decapitating the innocent girls at a local night school? The police are baffled.
- **Nightmare (Nightmare in a Damaged Brain)** (1981) - A mental patient embarks on a murder spree upon escaping from an institution. *Make sure to see the uncut version as per reviews. That is probably a given for this whole list.
- **Possession** (1981, Poland/France) - *See Cosmic Horror for complete entry.
- **Slave of the Cannibal God (La montagna del dio cannibal)** (1978, Italy) - A woman is aided by her brother, a professor and an explorer as they search the jungles of New Guinea for her anthropologist husband, who vanished near a mountain that is said to be cursed.
- **The Slayer** (1982) - Two couples become stranded on a rugged isle, and are haunted by a supernatural beast, drawn to the wife of one of the couples, who dreams of its killings. J.S. Cardone claims that the story was inspired by H.P. Lovecraft due to elements of dreams vs. reality, though few, if any, actual Lovecraft tropes anywhere in the film.
- **Snuff** (1975, Argentina) - A so-called "snuff" film involving the exploits of a cult leader leading a gang of bikers in a series of supposedly real killings on film. The simulated murder scene of a female cast member at the end of the film was shot in the New York production studio of pornography film director Carter Stevens.
- **SS Experiment Love Camp (Lager SSadis Kastrat Kommandantur)** (1976, Italy) - Near the end of WW2, prisoners of war are used in experiments to perfect the "Aryan" race.
- **Tenebrae** (1982, Italy) – Argento's stylish giallo with fountains of blood. An American novelist visiting Rome to promote his latest book is stalked and harassed by an obsessed fan who is committing a string of murders that appear to be tributes to his work.
- **The Toolbox Murders** (1978) - A ski-masked maniac kills apartment complex tenants with the contents of a toolbox. The film was marketed as being a dramatization of a true story. According to journalist Linda Gross, the screenplay was loosely based on a string of serial killings in Michigan committed by a man who attacked women using various tools.
- **Toxic Zombies** (1980) - Marijuana growers deep in the woods are hit with a new toxic herbicide, and they turn into mindless cannibals killing everyone they come into contact with.
- **Unhinged** (1982) - Three young women who crash their car during a rainstorm are taken in by a bizarre family at their large, rural estate. The film had already received notoriety in the UK after being featured on the BBC News as part of a report concerning the availability of uncertified video films. Even though the film had received a cinema certificate by the BBFC this led to it being banned and included on the DPP list of 72 video nasties. The film was eventually passed uncut in the UK in 2005.
- **Visiting Hours** (1982, Canada) - A deranged, misogynistic killer assaults a journalist. When he discovers that she survived the attack, he follows her to the hospital to finish her off.
- **The Witch Who Came from the Sea** (1976) - A disturbed woman is haunted by memories of childhood abuse, which culminates in a murder spree. This film originally received an X rating from the MPAA. Several cuts had to be made in order to secure an R rating. One of the 72 films banned in Britain as a "Video Nasty" during the early 1980s. The film was finally released completely uncut in the UK in 2006.
- **Women Behind Bars (Des diamants pour l'enfer)** (1975, France) - A criminal attempts insurance fraud and diamond heist. His girlfriend kills him, gets imprisoned, and undergoes involuntary electric shock treatments.

A Tale of Two Directors

Craven[22] and Carpenter[23]

If Alfred Hitchcock detonated the genre with *Psycho*, it was Wes Craven and John Carpenter who built the slasher into a cathedral of modern horror. Their films stand as companion pillars: Carpenter's *Halloween* (1978) codifying the rules of suburban terror, and Craven's *A Nightmare on Elm Street* (1984) exploding them with dream-logic surrealism. Both directors transformed horror with unmistakable fingerprints. So distinct that any seasoned viewer could identify the hand behind the camera within minutes.

Carpenter worked like a minimalist architect. His frames were stripped to essentials: widescreen shots of empty streets, silence punctuated by his own pulsing synthesizer scores, faceless evil embodied in Michael Myers' blank mask. Horror, for Carpenter, came through subtraction. What was left unsaid, unseen, unstressed. Craven, by contrast, thrived on rupture. A former humanities professor, he mined philosophy and psychology, smuggling trauma, repression, and satire into his films. Where Carpenter gave horror its purest slasher grammar, Craven deconstructed that grammar from the inside, turning killers like Freddy Krueger and Ghostface into symbols of cultural anxiety as much as characters.

Eerily, the two were united by their fascination with boundaries: Carpenter's evil was faceless, impossible to comprehend, while Craven's horror leaked from the unconscious, forcing repressed fears into daylight. Both directors also shared an instinct for reinvention. Carpenter blended horror with westerns (*Assault on Precinct 13*), sci-fi (*The Thing*), and satire (*They Live*), while Craven revived the genre repeatedly shifting from grindhouse brutality (*Last House on the Left*) to self-aware meta-horror (*Scream*). Yet their legacies diverge in tone: Carpenter, the punk craftsman with a rock 'n' roll ethos, and Craven, the philosopher-professor turned cultural trickster.

What many miss is how both men redefined horror's relationship to its audience. Carpenter weaponized silence and empty space, making viewers scan the frame for movement that may never come. Craven, conversely, made the audience complicit, from *Peeping Tom*–inspired voyeurism in *Last House* to *Scream's* knowing wink that horror fans themselves were part of the cycle. Together, they didn't just terrify audiences, they taught them how to watch horror differently.

Their legacy is not only in the killers they birthed: Michael Myers, Freddy Krueger, Ghostface, but in the grammar of fear itself. Carpenter proved that atmosphere could be weapon enough; Craven proved that horror could think about itself without losing its edge. Between them lies the blueprint of the slasher: structure and subversion, silence and satire, the knife in the dark and the nightmare in the mind.

Box Office vs. Cult Status

Carpenter and Craven both lived through the strange economics of horror. Carpenter's *The Thing* was dismissed on release as too bleak and too gory in the shadow of *E.T.*, only to later be canonized as one of the greatest horror films ever made. Craven's *Last House on the Left* was banned or censored in several countries but built its reputation as forbidden cinema, fueling the very notoriety that kept it alive. Their careers show how horror's commercial failures can often be its cultural victories.

---

[22] "Filmregisseur, Drehbuchautor, Produzent und Schauspieler Wes Craven, 2010" Bob Bekian (https://www.flickr.com/people/53771684@N04) Creative Commons Attribution-Share Alike 2.0

[23] "John Carpenter" Kyle Cassidy Creative Commons Attribution-Share Alike 4.0

Self-Portraits of the Director

Carpenter frequently described himself as a "blue-collar filmmaker," more interested in craft than prestige, yet his stripped-down aesthetic became the prestige style of modern horror. Craven, meanwhile, often inserted himself into his films' intellectual games: his appearance in *New Nightmare* as a director who literally dreams Freddy into being is one of horror's most striking meta-cameos. Both used cinema to comment on themselves as much as the genre.

The Politics of Fear

Each director reflected the anxieties of his era. Carpenter's *They Live* distilled Reagan-era consumerism and media manipulation into one of horror's most quoted satires. Craven's *The Hills Have Eyes* reflected 1970s dread of nuclear collapse and family breakdown. Their films weren't just stories of killers; they were essays in disguise, embedding cultural critique inside spectacle.

Unlikely Common Ground

Though their sensibilities diverged, both men loved westerns. Carpenter remade Howard Hawks' *Rio Bravo* as *Assault on Precinct 13*; Craven infused *The Hills Have Eyes* with frontier-style survivalism. This shared DNA explains why their slashers feel mythic: Myers as the faceless outlaw, Freddy as the trickster spirit haunting the frontier of dreams.

Globalization of the Slasher

Craven and Carpenter didn't just redefine American horror, they gave the template that spread worldwide. Carpenter's *Halloween* was the model for Italian giallo directors transitioning into slashers in the late 70s and 80s, while Craven's *Elm Street* influenced Japan's *Dream Cruise* and Korea's surreal horror boom. Even when remade (*Halloween* in 2007, *Elm Street* in 2010), their DNA remained visible, showing how their visions became transnational grammar for horror.

From Marginal to Mainstream

Both directors helped shift horror from cultural pariah to mainstream conversation. Carpenter's Michael Myers became a Halloween costume staple within a year of release, while Craven's *Scream* made horror self-aware enough to be quoted on sitcoms and late-night shows. What was once grindhouse taboo now became multiplex event and cultural shorthand. Their combined legacy is that horror didn't stay in the shadows, it became a shared language across generations, part of the fabric of popular culture.

Influence

Craven and Carpenter's fingerprints are everywhere. Carpenter's stripped-down style inspired James Wan (*The Conjuring*, *Insidious*), David Gordon Green's Halloween trilogy, and indie directors who use silence and negative space as terror itself. His synth scores influenced musicians from Trent Reznor to Stranger Things' Kyle Dixon and Michael Stein. Craven's meta-horror cracked open new genres, paving the way for Drew Goddard (*Cabin in the Woods*), Jordan Peele (*Get Out*), and even prestige television like *Buffy the Vampire Slayer*. Together, they trained filmmakers to see horror as both playground and mirror. Pure entertainment and sharp cultural commentary in the same breath.

Pairing Night Watchlist

- *Halloween* (1978, Carpenter) → Watch how long takes and silence turn suburbia into a killing ground.
- *The Hills Have Eyes* (1977, Craven) → Notice how America's cultural fears bleed into cannibal clans and desert landscapes.
- *The Thing* (1982, Carpenter) → Study paranoia as atmosphere; evil is trust itself dissolving.
- *A Nightmare on Elm Street* (1984, Craven) → Focus on dream logic breaking the rules of slashers; Freddy as repressed trauma incarnate.
- *They Live* (1988, Carpenter) + *Scream* (1996, Craven) → A double bill in satire: one skewering consumerism, the other skewering horror itself.

Quick Facts to Sound Smart

- Craven had a master's degree in philosophy and literature; his academic lens made horror feel both primal and intellectual.
- Carpenter wrote the *Halloween* theme in 5/4 time to mimic a heartbeat. Minimal, but unforgettable.
- Freddy Krueger was inspired by both a childhood bully and real medical cases of teenagers dying in their sleep.
- *The Thing* (1982) was a critical flop on release but is now considered one of the greatest horror films of all time.
- Craven almost left horror altogether before *Elm Street* pulled him back permanently.
- Carpenter has often said he's less a horror director than a "jobbing filmmaker" but horror became his canvas because it allowed the most freedom.

Golden Age of 80s Slashers

☐ **Prom Night** (1980) – High school dance massacre starring Jamie Lee Curtis. At a high-school senior prom, a masked killer stalks four teenagers who were responsible for the accidental death of a classmate six years previously.

- • **SEQUELS & ADAPTIONS**
    - ☐ **Hello Mary Lou: Prom Night II** (1987) - This first sequel, originally intended as a standalone film, was repackaged to capitalize on the original's success. It introduces the supernatural element of Mary Lou Maloney, a vengeful prom queen who possesses a student 30 years later.
    - ☐ **Prom Night III: The Last Kiss** (1990) - The third film continues the story of Mary Lou Maloney as she returns from hell to seek a new prom king.
    - ☐ **Prom Night IV: Deliver Us from Evil** (1992) - The fourth film features a new plotline, with a group of teenagers being tormented by a possessed priest at an abandoned seminary.
    - ☐ **Prom Night** (2008) - This loose remake follows a teenager and her friends who are stalked by an obsessed serial killer on her prom night. The story and characters are mostly different from the original, with the only connection being the prom setting.

☐ **He Knows You're Alone** (1980) - A young bride-to-be is being stalked upon by a serial killer in Staten Island. She gets help from a former lover, but will they manage to escape? The movie's most well-known trivia is that it features Tom Hanks in his first film role, playing a character who famously discusses the psychology of fear. His character was originally scripted to be killed, but the filmmakers liked him so much they let him live.

☐ **The Boogey Man** (1980) - Through the reflection in the mirror, a girl witnesses her mother's boyfriend's murder.

☐ **Terror Train** (1980) – College kids stalked on a moving train.

- • **ADAPTIONS & SEQUELS**
    - ☐ **Terror Train: The Revenge of Alex** (2007) - This sequel, produced by Lionsgate and released directly to video, has no direct narrative connection to the original film.
    - ☐ **Terror Train** (2022) - Tubi and Incendo produced a made-for-TV movie remake in 2022, which follows a new group of college students on a New Year's Eve party train, where a killer from their past returns to hunt them.

☐ **Happy Birthday to Me** (1981) – Birthday party killings with inventive deaths.

☐ **The Prowler** (1981) –An unknown killer, clad in World War II U.S. Army fatigues, stalks a small California town, bent on reliving a 35-year-old double murder by focusing on a group of college kids holding an annual graduation dance.

☐ **Graduation Day** (1981) – Track team targeted by a masked killer.

☐ **Hell Night** (1981) – College hazing in haunted mansion turns deadly.

☐ **Final Exam** (1981) - An unknown, nameless, psycho killer shows up on a college campus to slash up pretty co-eds and dumb jocks on the final day of exams.

☐ **Just Before Dawn** (1981) – Mountain wilderness hides killers. Five young people venture into the backwoods of Oregon to claim a property, and find themselves being stalked by a hulking, machete-wielding psychopath.

☐ **Alone in the Dark** (1982) – Escaped asylum patients target a doctor

☐ **Girls Nite Out** (1982) - At a remote Ohio college, a killer dressed in the school's bear mascot suit stalks several young women participating in an all-night scavenger hunt.

☐ **Deadly Games** (1982) - A woman falls to her death after getting attacked by a black-clad assailant. Her sister arrives in town and starts dating a police detective, who's friends with a strange movie theater curator, as other women fall prey to the killer.

☐ **Incubus** (1982) – Based on the Ray Russell novel of the same name. A small town's doctor takes matters into his own hands after a series of gruesome and bizarre rape crimes perplex the clueless authorities.

- **EXPLORING THE MYTH OF THE INCUBUS:** The incubus is a male demon from European folklore believed to attack women in their sleep, often with sexual intent. Rooted in ancient Mesopotamian spirits like the *lilu* and adapted into Christian demonology, the myth was used to explain sleep paralysis, nightmares, and nocturnal emissions, reflecting cultural fears of sexuality and loss of control.
  - ☐ **The Summoned** (1992) - In this film, a woman who tries to conjure a dream lover during a séance ends up bringing forth a murderous incubus.
  - ☐ **Paranormal Attraction** (2020) - A woman moves into a house with a tragic past and discovers she is being haunted by a demonic entity.
- ☐ **Mortuary** (1982) - A young woman investigates the seemingly accidental death of her father, revealing many unsettling secrets and putting her in mortal danger.
  - **SIMILAR THEMES**
    - ☐ **Phantasm** (1979) - This cult classic features a mortuary and an undertaker at its center, with plenty of supernatural and bizarre occurrences.
    - ☐ **One Dark Night** (1983) - In this film, a group of teenagers spends a night in a mausoleum, where a necromancer's reanimated corpse is kept
- ☐ **The Slumber Party Massacre** (1982) – Feminist satire disguised as power-drill slasher.
  - **SEQUELS**:
    - ☐ **Slumber Party Massacre II** (1987) – Rock 'n' roll slasher comedy.
    - ☐ **Slumber Party Massacre III** (1990) – Return to grim slasher basics.
  - **ADAPTIONS:**
    - ☐ **Slumber Party Massacre** (2021) - This Syfy original movie is a "modern reimagining" and standalone sequel that pays homage to the original films. It is a self-aware horror-comedy that subverts many of the genre's tropes while still delivering scares and gore.
    - ☐ **Sorority House Massacre** (1986) – College girls stalked by killer.
      - **SEQUELS**
        - ☐ **Sorority House Massacre II** (1990) – Campy sequel; more slasher chaos.
        - ☐ **Sorority House Massacre III: Hard to Die** (1990) - The final direct-to-video sequel, also directed by Jim Wynorski, features many of the same actors as the second film. It is essentially a remake of the second film with a slightly altered plot and a different setting.
    - ☐ **Cheerleader Massacre** (2003) - This film, directed by Jim Wynorski, was originally intended to be *Slumber Party Massacre 4*. When it was retitled, the script was altered, but it still features a cameo from Brinke Stevens, reprising her role from the original *Slumber Party Massacre*. It was released direct-to-video.
      - **SEQUELS**
        - ☐ **Cheerleader Massacre 2** (2011) - A separate direct-to-video sequel directed by Brad Rushing. It has no narrative connection to the first *Cheerleader Massacre*.
    - ☐ **Sharkansas Women's Prison Massacre** (2015) - A standalone film connected to the wider Massacre franchise. When a fracking environmental accident rips apart the earth's crust, the resulting hole lets out prehistoric sharks from underground that target a group of women and trap them in a cabin.
- ☐ **The House on Sorority Row** (1983) – Sorority prank gone wrong sparks slaughter.
  - **ADAPTIONS**
    - ☐ **Sorority Row** (2009) - The story follows a group of sorority sisters who cover up the accidental death of a fellow sister and are later hunted by a masked killer seeking revenge during their graduation party.
- ☐ **Sleepaway Camp** (1983) – Bunks and showers are a mad stabber's beat at a summer camp strictly for teens. This is Mike Kellin's final film. He was sick during filming, but did his best to conceal it. He died of lung cancer in August 1983, three months before the film's release.
  - **SEQUELS**
    - ☐ **Sleepaway Camp II: Unhappy Campers** (1988) – Angela returns with wisecracks and gore.
    - ☐ **Sleepaway Camp III: Teenage Wasteland** (1989) – More Angela-led camp carnage.

- ☐ **Sleepaway Camp IV: The Survivor** (2012) - This film was shot in 1992 but never completed. Decades later, the available footage was combined with archive footage from the first three films and released online as a completed movie.
  - • **ADAPTIONS & SIMILAR FILMS**
    - ☐ **Return to Sleepaway Camp** (2008) - This direct sequel to the original film was made by the original director, Robert Hiltzik, and ignores the events of the Michael A. Simpson sequels. It has a different tone and received generally poor reviews.
    - ☐ **Summer Camp Nightmare** (1986) - A group of campers revolt against their strict camp director and take over the camp for themselves.
- ☐ **The Initiation** (1984) - An amnesiac sorority member who has been plagued by a recurring nightmare is stalked alongside other coeds by a killer in a deserted department store where they are completing a hazing ritual.
  - • **SIMILAR FILMS**
    - ☐ **Initiation** (2020) - The film follows a group of students targeted by a killer during a high-profile homecoming party.
- ☐ **The Mutilator** (1984) - A college student, who accidentally killed his mother as a child, decides to take his friends to his father's fishing cabin during fall break, not knowing that his crazed father is stalking the place.
  - • **SEQUELS**
    - ☐ **Mutilator 2** (2023) - The storyline involves a remake of the first film, where the cast and crew, including some returning actors from the original, gather for a wrap party and are attacked by a new killer.
- ☐ **Killer Party** (1986) - In order to join a sorority, three friends go to a hazing party in an old house where a sadistic bloodthirsty demonic spirit is lying in wait. Many of the bloodier death scenes were censored by MGM before release, as evidenced by photos published in *Fangoria* magazine, but these scenes have never been restored.
- ☐ **April Fool's Day** (1986) - Nine college students staying at a friend's remote island mansion begin to fall victim to an unseen murderer over the April Fool's Day weekend, but nothing is as it seems.
  - • **ADAPTIONS**
    - ☐ **April Fool's Day** (2008) - This remake has a completely different plot and set of characters, though it retains the core idea of a deadly prank. The story follows a group of wealthy, partying teens who find themselves targeted by a killer exactly one year after a harmless April Fool's prank resulted in the accidental death of one of their friends.
- ☐ **Stagefright** (1987) – Owl-masked killer slays theater troupe.
- ☐ **American Gothic** (1987) - After their seaplane malfunctions, a group of travelers make an emergency landing on an island in the Pacific Northwest and stumble across an isolated and psychopathic family.
- ☐ **Berserker** (1987) - Six people renting a cabin in the woods of Utah run afoul of a legendary viking warrior who dons the claws and mouth of a bear, with no help in sight.
- ☐ **Maniac Cop** (1988) – Undead police officer slashes corrupt city.
  - • **SEQUELS**
    - ☐ **Maniac Cop 2** (1990) – Lustig and Cohen returned for this sequel, which continues Cordell's rampage across New York City. The film is often considered an improvement on the original, with a bigger budget and more elaborate action sequences. It was released direct-to-video.
    - ☐ **Maniac Cop III: Badge of Silence** (1993) - The final entry in the original trilogy was also directed by William Lustig, although he was credited under the pseudonym "Alan Smithee" due to creative disagreements. The plot involves a voodoo priest resurrecting Cordell to protect an innocent female cop who has been wrongly accused.
- ☐ **Amsterdamned** (1988) - A hard-boiled police detective sets out to capture a gruesome serial killer terrorizing the canals of Amsterdam. A long-awaited sequel was announced in 2024, with director Dick Maas and star Huub Stapel (who plays Detective Eric Visser) both returning. It is scheduled to be released in December 2025.
- ☐ **Hide and Go Shriek** (1988) - A group of teenagers spend the night in a furniture store for a graduation party. A psycho killer starts hunting them down one by one.
- ☐ **The Last Slumber Party** (1988) - Linda, Tracy, and Chris are a trio of teenage girls who decide to celebrate the last day of high school by having a slumber party at Linda's house. A few guys also show up to further enhance the merry festivities. However, things take a turn for the worse when a homicidal maniac who has just escaped from a mental hospital crashes the bash.

The House that Freddy Built

New Line Cinema

NEW LINE CINEMA

Origins & Mission

Founded in 1967 as a distributor of art films and exploitation flicks, earning the nickname "The House That Freddy Built" in the 1980s. New Line Cinema stands as one of the few studios whose very survival was built on horror. While many major companies treated the genre as a side market, New Line embraced it as its backbone. *A Nightmare on Elm Street* (1984) not only spawned a billion-dollar franchise but transformed a struggling distributor into a Hollywood contender and a horror powerhouse. Freddy Krueger was more than a character, he was a brand, merchandised into toys, lunchboxes, and TV appearances, proving that horror icons could break into mainstream pop culture.

The studio's influence didn't stop there. New Line carved out a niche for horror that mixed surrealism with accessibility: slashers that doubled as teen melodramas, franchises that could balance terror with camp. Their willingness to gamble on high-concept ideas with modest budgets paved the way for *Final Destination* (2000), which turned death into a Rube Goldberg spectacle, and later, *The Conjuring* (2013) and its spinoffs, which redefined supernatural horror for modern audiences. Along the way, New Line kept older classics alive, re-releasing *The Texas Chain Saw Massacre* (1974) to solidify its reputation as a genre guardian.

New Line's legacy lies in proving that horror could be the financial foundation of a studio. Where others saw risk, New Line saw franchise potential, turning nightmares into steady revenue and cementing horror's place as both a cultural phenomenon and an industrial engine.

Signature Style
- Embrace of the outrageous, surreal, and youth-driven.
- Willingness to gamble on high-concept ideas with modest budgets.
- Horror blended with camp, comedy, and teen angst.

Essential Titles
- *A Nightmare on Elm Street* (1984) — Wes Craven's dream demon Freddy Krueger launched a billion-dollar franchise.
- *Freddy vs. Jason* (2003) — Franchise mashup spectacle.
- *The Texas Chain Saw Massacre* (1974) — Though produced independently, New Line later helped distribute and re-release it, amplifying its legend.
- *Final Destination* (2000) — Teen-death-as-Rube-Goldberg meta-horror.
- *The Conjuring Universe* (later distribution via Warner Bros. and New Line) cemented New Line's pivot into modern horror franchises.

Cultural Footprint
New Line proved horror could fund an entire studio. Freddy Krueger became a pop-culture antihero, appearing on talk shows and lunchboxes. Their 2000s output (*Final Destination*, *The Conjuring* spinoffs) carried the same DNA: accessible, teen-friendly, franchise-able.

Watchlist
A Nightmare on Elm Street → *Final Destination* → *The Conjuring* (2013) sampler: see how the studio shifted from surreal slashers to polished supernatural blockbusters.

90s Slasher Revival & Meta Era

☐ **Popcorn** (1991) - A master of disguise deranged killer begins killing off the college students who are organizing a horror-movie marathon in an abandoned theater. The film is a loving homage to B-movie schlock producer William Castle, who famously used interactive gimmicks in theaters to promote his films. *Popcorn* features its own set of films-within-the-film, complete with their own gimmicks.
- **INFLUENCE**
  - ☐ **13 Fan Boy** (2021) - This slasher film centers on a killer stalking real-life "scream queens" from the *Friday the 13th* franchise. It shares the meta, fan-obsessed killer trope with *Popcorn*.

☐ **Trauma** (1993, Italy) - A young man tries to help a teenage girl find the serial killer who murdered her parents before the killer comes after them.

☐ **Scream** (1996) – Wes Craven reinvents the slasher with meta satire. A masked killer targets a past victim's daughter. At the beginning of the movie when Casey's (Drew Barrymore's) parents come home to find something is wrong, her father tells her mother to "go to the McKenzies'," which is the same thing Laurie (Jamie Lee Curtis) told Lindsey (Kyle Richards) and Tommy (Brian Andrews) to do in *Halloween* (1978), of which this movie contains many references. The party scene near the end of the film runs forty-two minutes long. It was shot over the course of twenty-one days from the time the sun set to the time it rose. After it wrapped, the crew had t-shirts made that read "I SURVIVED SCENE 118" (which was the name of the scene during shooting). The cast and crew jokingly called it "The longest night in horror history." **Memorable Quote:** *"What's your favorite scary movie?"*
- **SEQUELS**
  - ☐ **Scream 2** (1997) – Bigger body count, college setting.
  - ☐ **Scream 3** (2000) – Hollywood-set whodunnit.
  - ☐ **Scream 4** (2011) – Reboot satire for social media age.
  - ☐ **Scream** (2022) – Legacy sequel; Ghostface returns.
  - ☐ **Scream VI** (2023) – Ghostface stalks New York.
  - ☐ **Scream 7** (2026) - The upcoming installment is set to bring back original cast members Neve Campbell, Courteney Cox, and David Arquette, with Kevin Williamson directing.

☐ **Cure** (1997, Japan) - A frustrated detective deals with the case of several gruesome murders committed by people who have no recollection of what they've done.

☐ **Jack Frost** (1997) - After an accident that left murderer Jack Frost dead in genetic material the vengeful killer returns as a murderous snowman to exact his revenge on the man who sent him to be executed.
- **SEQUELS**
  - ☐ **Jack Frost 2: Revenge of the Mutant Killer Snowman** (2000) - The villainous snowman, Jack Frost, is accidentally resurrected during an experiment and follows his nemesis, Sheriff Sam Tiler, to a tropical island.

☐ **Campfire Tales** (1997) - Teens entertain one another by telling an anthology of famous urban legends with a modern twist; including makeout-point, monsters, psychopaths, and ghosts.
- **ADAPTIONS**
  - ☐ **Darna Mana Hai** (2003) - After their car breaks down in the middle of the night, seven friends find shelter and tell one another stories to kill time till dawn. Loosely based on the 1997 film.

☐ **Urban Legend** (1998) – A college student suspects a series of bizarre deaths are connected to certain urban legends. Staring Jared Leto and Rebecca Gayhart. The SUV driven in the beginning was originally supposed to be a Land Rover. It was changed to the Ford Expedition, the largest 4x4 available at the time, because the filmmakers discovered they couldn't swing an axe inside of a Land Rover. Sarah Michelle Gellar accepted the role of Sasha, but had to back out due to schedule conflicts with *Buffy the Vampire Slayer* (1997).
- **SEQUELS**
  - ☐ **Urban Legends: Final Cut** (2000) – Film school killings.
  - ☐ **Urban Legends: Bloody Mary** (2005) - The final entry in the original trilogy was released straight to video. Unlike the previous films, this entry shifts from a "whodunit" slasher format to supernatural horror, focusing on the legend of Bloody Mary.
    - **BLOODY MARY LEGEND:** A piece of European and American folklore rooted in mirror superstitions and ritual invocation. Originating as early as the 19th century, the ritual involved young women gazing into a mirror by candlelight. Often during marriage

divination rites believing they might glimpse their future husband or, if cursed, a spectral figure instead. Over time this practice evolved into the modern children's dare: chanting "Bloody Mary" before a mirror to summon a vengeful spirit, sometimes said to be the ghost of a murdered woman, a witch, or even Queen Mary I of England, remembered for her executions of Protestants. The tale endures as one of the most famous urban legends, merging folk ritual with adolescent fear of the supernatural.

- ☐ **The Legend of Bloody Mary** (2008) - In this film, a young man and a cleric must battle a malevolent spirit they find trapped in a mirror.
- ☐ **Curse of Bloody Mary** (2021) - A low-budget horror film where a group of friends reunites and accidentally unleashes the titular curse after performing the ritual.

☐ **Valentine** (2001) – Masked killer seeks revenge on old crushes. Five women are stalked by an unknown assailant while preparing for Valentine's Day. Starring Denise Richards and David Boreanaz. Director Jamie Blanks was inspired by Jack Sholder's film *Alone in the Dark* (1982) for the killer's bloody nose gag.

☐ **Wrong Turn** (2003) – Chris and a group of five friends are left stranded deep in the middle of the woods after their cars collide. As they venture deeper into the woods, they face an uncertain and bloodcurdling fate. The female lead character, Jessie Burlingame, was named after the heroine in Stephen King's novel, *Gerald's Game*. Director Rob Schmidt said on the commentary that he considers this film to be his own personal tribute to the classics like *The Texas Chain Saw Massacre* (1974) and *The Hills Have Eyes* (1977). The only film in the series that does not contain any sex or nudity.

- **SEQUELS, ADAPTIONS & ROAD TRIP HORRORS**
  - ☐ **Wrong Turn 2: Dead End** (2007) –A group of reality show contestants find themselves fighting for their survival against a family of hideously deformed inbred cannibals who plan to ruthlessly butcher them all.
  - ☐ **Wrong Turn 3: Left for Dead** (2009) –When their transfer bus crashes in a West Virginia forest, a group of convicts and a corrections officer meet a rafter who is on the run from cannibalistic hillbillies who have murdered her friends.
  - ☐ **Wrong Turn 4: Bloody Beginnings** (2011) – Origins of cannibal family. A group of college students gets lost in a storm during their snowmobiling trip and takes shelter in an abandoned sanitarium which, unbeknown to them, is home to deformed cannibals.
  - ☐ **Wrong Turn 5: Bloodlines** (2012) – Another prequel, this film focuses on the cannibals' family patriarch. A group of college students, on a trip to the Mountain Man Festival on Halloween in West Virginia, encounter a clan of cannibals.
  - ☐ **Wrong Turn 6: Last Resort** (2014) - This loose sequel and soft reboot has a new group of characters. An inheritance leads a young man and his friends to an abandoned resort inhabited by two sketchy caretakers and a clan of mutant cannibals.
  - ☐ **Wrong Turn** (2021) – Folk-horror reboot of franchise. Friends hiking the Appalachian Trail are confronted by 'The Foundation', a community of people who have lived in the mountains for hundreds of years.
  - ☐ **Joy Ride** (2001) - Three friends on a cross-country road trip taunt a trucker over a CB radio, with terrifying consequences when the trucker, who turns out to be a serial killer, starts hunting them.
  - ☐ **Dead End** (2003) - Christmas Eve. On his way to his in-laws with his family, Frank Harrington decides to try a shortcut, for the first time in 20 years. It turns out to be the biggest mistake of his life.
  - ☐ **Wind Chill** (2007) - A supernatural horror film about two college students who are stranded on a remote, snow-covered highway on Christmas Eve and are haunted by spirits.
  - ☐ **No One Lives** (2012) - A gang of ruthless highway killers kidnap a wealthy couple traveling cross country only to shockingly discover that things are not what they seem.
  - ☐ **The Monster** (2016) - A mother and daughter must confront a terrifying monster when they break down on a deserted road.
  - ☐ **Coming Home in the Dark** (2021) - A schoolteacher is forced to confront a brutal act from his past when a pair of ruthless drifters take his family and him on a nightmare road trip.

The Scream Queens

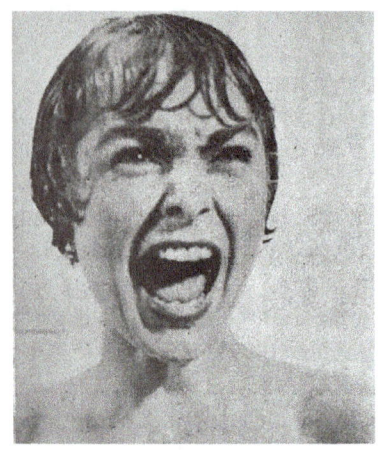

The "Scream Queen" became horror's most enduring archetype: the woman who survives, resists, or suffers at the center of terror, her voice and body carrying the audience's fear. The term originally described actresses typecast in horror films, but it quickly evolved into a badge of honor. Scream Queens embodied vulnerability and resilience in equal measure: running from killers, fighting back, or enduring ordeals that branded them as icons of the genre.

Types of Scream Queens
- **The Innocent Survivor** – Naïve but resourceful, defined by the *Final Girl* trope (e.g., Laurie Strode in *Halloween*).
- **The Endurance Queen** – Women subjected to relentless torment across multiple films (*Texas Chain Saw Massacre's* Marilyn Burns).
- **The Gothic Heroine** – Rooted in earlier horror, often imperiled by supernatural or psychological threats (*Psycho's* Janet Leigh).
- **The Meta Queen** – Characters who know the rules of horror, bridging satire and survival (*Scream's* Neve Campbell).

The Icons
- **Jamie Lee Curtis** – Crowned the ultimate Scream Queen after *Halloween* (1978), she reprised Laurie Strode across decades, cementing her as horror's reigning survivor. Curtis appeared in multiple slashers (*Prom Night*, *Terror Train*, *The Fog*) during the late 70s–80s boom, making her career inseparable from the genre. Her longevity and repeated returns to Laurie's trauma made her reign "Scream Queen Supreme."
- **Janet Leigh** – *Psycho* (1960) positioned her as an early archetype; her shocking shower murder remains one of cinema's most iconic horror images.
- **Marilyn Burns** – As Sally Hardesty in *The Texas Chain Saw Massacre* (1974), she defined the endurance archetype, surviving the unrelenting terror of Leatherface's family.
- **Neve Campbell** – Revitalized the role in the 1990s as Sidney Prescott in the *Scream* series, embodying meta-awareness while still grounded in genuine peril.
- **Other Notables** – Fay Wray (*King Kong*, 1933), Linnea Quigley (*Return of the Living Dead*, 1985), and Heather Langenkamp (*A Nightmare on Elm Street*, 1984) expanded the lineage, each adding new shades of vulnerability, humor, or grit.

Legacy
Scream Queens were more than victims, they were cultural touchstones. They reflected shifting views of women in horror, from passive damsels to active survivors. Their cries, their endurance, and their survival instincts became the heartbeat of slasher cinema, and their roles continue to evolve in modern horror.

Quick Facts to Sound Smart
- Jamie Lee Curtis's *Halloween* debut in 1978 was also her first credited film role, instantly launching her into horror royalty.
- Janet Leigh received an Oscar nomination for Best Supporting Actress for *Psycho* (1960), a rare recognition for a horror performance at the time.
- Curtis is the daughter of Janet Leigh, star of *Psycho* (1960). Their mother-daughter connection created a lineage of scream queens, highlighted when they appeared together in *The Fog* (1980)
- Neve Campbell turned down *Scream 6* (2023) over pay disputes, a decision that sparked industry-wide discussions on gender equity in horror franchises.
- The term "Scream Queen" first gained traction in the 1970s exploitation boom, but its roots stretch back to silent-era actresses like Fay Wray (*King Kong*, 1933), who was called the "Queen of Screams."

Modern & Global Slashers

☐ **Camp Blood** (2000) - Out and about on a camping trip in the woods without a care in the world, four campers found themselves in an unknown world. With the death of their guide and at the mercy of a cold-blooded killer, the trip of fun in the sun soon took a wrong turn. With friends slowly disappearing, so does the chance of getting out alive. These films, especially the sequels, have the worst ratings on IMDB. I would suggest passing on them unless you want make a drinking game out of it. There also may or may not be more sequels or adaptions, but we will leave this list at that.

- **SEQUELS**
  - ☐ **Camp Blood 2** (2000) - Released the same year as the original, it follows the traumatized survivor returning to the infamous camp.
  - ☐ **Within the Woods** (2005) - An unofficial sequel sometimes referred to as *Camp Blood 3*. Is the legendary Clown back, or is one of the group willing to kill for the prize?
  - ☐ **Camp Blood: First Slaughter** (2014) - A later installment directed by Mark Polonia, sometimes referred to as *Camp Blood 3* or *4* depending on the list.
  - ☐ **Camp Blood 4** (2016) - A bunch of college friends stop at the notorious Camp Blood on their way to a rock concert. But there is someone lurking in the woods nearby, ready to arrange one hell of a night for unfortunate campers.
  - ☐ **Camp Blood 5** (2016) - Raven, the only survivor of a previous massacre, returns to the forest to avenge her fallen friends and stop Camp Blood Killer once and for all.
  - ☐ **Camp Blood 666** (2016) - The Camp Blood Killer Clown returns from hell to search for fresh victims. Betsy goes looking for her missing brother who joined a Satanic Clown Cult, only to find horrors beyond her imagination. Will she end up on the end of a machete wielded by an insane, creepy clown. Will anyone survive Camp Blood 666?!?
  - ☐ **It Kills: Camp Blood 7** (2017) - A group of college kids on Fall break find themselves in a bad situation when they become stranded at the infamous Camp Blood.
  - ☐ **Ghost of Camp Blood** (2018): A spin-off film. Infamous Blackwood Forest is still haunted by the numerous deaths at the hands of a masked clown killer, but now, it's haunted by something else. The vengeful spirit of the recently deceased Camp Blood Killer is out for revenge from beyond the grave.
  - ☐ **Camp Blood 8: Revelations** (2019) - When a team of volleyball players get lost in the woods, they encounter a killer clown and his psychotic exhibitionist mother. Will he kill them all or will they find a way to defeat him?
  - ☐ **Children of Camp Blood** (2020) - A group of emotionally disturbed teenagers attend a remote retreat to work through their fears of the infamous "Camp Blood Killer". But could this local legend be all too real? And if so who will survive?

☐ **The Pool** (2001, Germany) - International students at an elite Prague school are stalked and murdered while holding a party in an abandoned water park.

- **ADAPTIONS**
  - ☐ **The Pool 2** (2005) - The movie released as *The Pool 2* was not a true sequel, but rather the 2001 film *Do You Wanna Know a Secret?* which was retitled for an Italian release.

☐ **Wilderness** (2006) - Juvenile delinquents are sent to a small British island after a fellow prisoner's death, where they have to fight for survival.

☐ **Hatchet** (2006) – When a group of tourists in a New Orleans haunted swamp tour find themselves stranded in the wilderness, their evening of fun and spooks turns into a horrific nightmare.

- **SEQUELS**
  - ☐ **Hatchet II** (2010) – More splatter and Crowley kills.
  - ☐ **Hatchet III** (2013) – Crowley's rampage escalates.
  - ☐ **Victor Crowley** (2017) – Fourth entry, Crowley unleashed again.

☐ **Cold Prey** (2006, Norway) – Five young Norwegians head up to the mountains to snowboard. One breaks his leg and it's getting dark soon, so they spend the night in a big, abandoned hotel, closed 30 years ago. They are not alone. An American Remake is in the works. In 2017, WWE Studios acquired the rights for an English-language remake, with Casey La Scala attached to write the screenplay. As of 2024, the remake has not been produced.

- SEQUELS
  - ☐ **Cold Prey 2** (2008) – Survivors hunted in hospital.
  - ☐ **Cold Prey 3** (2010) – Prequel to Norwegian cult slasher.
- ☐ **Laid to Rest** (2009) – ChromeSkull hunts in brutal fashion.
  - SEQUELS
    - ☐ **ChromeSkull: Laid to Rest 2** (2011) – Masked killer's cult grows.
- ☐ **High Lane** (2009) - A group of friends decide to venture onto a trail high up in the mountains that has been closed for repairs. The already dangerous adventure turns into horror when they realize they are not alone.
- ☐ **Julia's Eyes** (2010) - Julia, a woman suffering from a degenerative sight disease, finds her blind sister Sara hung in a basement. Despite all signs pointing to suicide, Julia decides to investigate what she intuitively feels is a murder case.
  - ADAPTIONS
    - ☐ **Blurr** (2022) - This Indian film is a Hindi-language remake, co-produced by and starring Taapsee Pannu. The story follows the same plot of a woman investigating her twin sister's death while losing her own eyesight.
    - ☐ **Adrushya** (2021, India) - A Marathi-language remake featuring actors Riteish Deshmukh and Manjari Fadnnis.
- ☐ **Bloody Homecoming** (2013) - Three years after a tragic accident leaves a student dead at the annual Homecoming dance, a group of senior friends anxious about the return of Homecoming Night to their sleepy Southern town find themselves visited by a deadly presence from their past in the dark and desolate halls of their very own high school.
- ☐ **Pieces of Talent** (2014) – Underground slasher praised for brutality.
- ☐ **The Redwood Massacre** (2014) - What begins as a exciting camping trip to the legendary Redwood murder site, takes a terrifying turn when the innocent campers discover the legend is about to become a nasty and bloody reality.
  - SEQUELS
    - ☐ **The Redwood Massacre: Annihilation** (2020) - The storyline centers on a group of bereaved family members who venture into the wilderness in search of the notorious killer who murdered their loved ones in the first film.
- ☐ **The Funhouse Massacre** (2015) - Six of the world's scariest psychopaths escape from a local Asylum and proceed to unleash terror on the unsuspecting crowd of a Halloween Funhouse, whose themed mazes are inspired by their various reigns of terror. The movie is a homage to the slasher films of the 1980s and has been compared to *The Funhouse, The Texas Chain Saw Massacre* and *Scream*. The movie was released direct-to-video, and its cult status was not enough to warrant a franchise.
- ☐ **Terrifier** (2016) – A maniac named Art the Clown terrorizes two friends on Halloween and everyone who gets in his way.
  - SEQUELS
    - ☐ **Terrifier 2** (2022) – Even gorier sequel, viral phenomenon.
    - ☐ **Terrifier 3** (2024) - This third film shifts the setting to the Christmas season and continues the story of Sienna Shaw and Art the Clown.
    - ☐ **Terrifier 4** (TBD) - A fourth installment is in active development, with Damien Leone planning to conclude the overall narrative and dive deeper into Art's origins.
- ☐ **Hush** (2016) – Deaf writer stalked by masked killer.
- ☐ **Fear Street: Part One – 1994** (2021) - A circle of teenage friends accidentally encounter the ancient evil responsible for a series of brutal murders that have plagued their town for over 300 years. Welcome to Shadyside.
  - SEQUELS
    - ☐ **Fear Street: Part Two – 1978** (2021) - Shadyside, 1978. School's out for summer and the activities at Camp Nightwing are about to begin. But when another Shadysider is possessed with the urge to kill, the fun in the sun becomes a gruesome fight for survival.
    - ☐ **Fear Street: Part Three – 1666** (2021) - In 1666, a colonial town is gripped by a witch hunt that has deadly consequences for centuries to come, while teenagers in 1994 try to put an end to their town's curse before it is too late.
    - ☐ **Fear Street: Prom Queen** (2025) - When the "it" girls competing for prom queen at Shadyside High start to disappear, a gutsy outsider discovers she's in for one hell of a prom night.

- ☐ **They/Them** (2022) - A group of teenagers at an LGBTQ+ conversion camp endures unsettling psychological techniques while being stalked by a mysterious masked killer.
- ☐ **Candy Land** (2022) - A seemingly naive and devout young woman navigates her way into the underground world of truck stop sex workers a.k.a. "lot lizards."

Slasher Horror: Pairing Night

The Lineup (6 Films, 1 Night → or split into 2 mini-marathons)

1. **Psycho (1960, USA)** – The proto-slasher; Hitchcock's shower scene that changed horror forever. *Watch for:* How Hitchcock cuts before the knife pierces flesh. Your mind supplies the violence.
2. **Black Christmas (1974, Canada)** – Holiday horror before *Halloween*. *Watch for:* The killer's obscene phone calls, an early use of "the call is coming from inside the house" trope.
3. **Halloween (1978, USA)** – Carpenter's precision-made suburban terror. *Watch for:* The use of Steadicam and silence; Michael Myers is most terrifying in the negative space.
4. **Friday the 13th Part 2 (1981, USA)** – Jason's sack-mask debut. *Watch for:* How it leans harder on gore than *Halloween*, foreshadowing the 80s body-count craze.
5. **A Nightmare on Elm Street (1984, USA)** – The supernatural slasher twist. *Watch for:* Freddy as both monster and comedian. A villain who talks, unlike his mute peers.
6. **Scream (1996, USA)** – The postmodern revival that mocks (and honors) everything before it. *Watch for:* How Kevin Williamson's script replays slasher rules in real-time: "Never say I'll be right back."

Quick "Sound Smart" Facts

- Black Christmas (1974) inspired *Halloween* — Carpenter admitted he wanted to take the "killer in a house" idea and expand it.
- Michael Myers' mask in *Halloween* was a $1.98 William Shatner mask, spray-painted white.
- Jason Voorhees doesn't get the hockey mask until *Friday the 13th Part III*. In Part 2, it's a burlap sack.
- Freddy Krueger's name came from a childhood bully of Wes Craven's.
- Drew Barrymore was supposed to star in *Scream* but asked to play the opening victim so audiences knew nobody was safe.

Viewing Tips: How to Read Slashers Like a Scholar

- **Final Girl:** Spot her early. Cautious, observant, morally coded to survive. She evolves from Laurie Strode (*Halloween*) to Sidney Prescott (*Scream*).
- **Cultural Anxiety:** Each decade's slashers mirror real fears: Vietnam-era rural America (*Texas Chain Saw Massacre*), 80s teen rebellion (*Friday the 13th*), 90s ironic detachment (*Scream*).
- **Point-of-View Shots:** Slashers pioneered killer-POV camera work, forcing audiences into complicity.
- **Censorship Battles:** Slashers were prime targets of the MPAA and "video nasty" crackdowns. What you *don't* see is as important as what you do.

Slash & Stare

Intermission: Masks of Horror

Ancient and Cultural Origins

Masks have haunted human imagination long before the invention of cinema. In Greek tragedy, the actor's mask was both a tool and a symbol: a way to project voice in vast amphitheaters, but also a vessel for gods, archetypes, and moral allegories. In Japanese *Noh* theater, the mask's subtle tilt could suggest multiple emotions, a lesson horror would later borrow when blank faces carried infinite menace. Across African and Indigenous traditions, ritual masks embodied spirits, ancestors, or demons, giving ceremonies the uncanny force of the supernatural. European carnival and Halloween rites transformed masking into a yearly inversion of order, where the living could mimic the dead and the powerful could be mocked by the powerless. Horror cinema inherits all of this: the mask as transformation, as anonymity, as license to become something other.

Silent-Era Horrors

The power of masks entered horror cinema almost immediately. In *The Phantom of the Opera* (1925), Lon Chaney's partial mask was at once shield and prison, hiding deformity but hinting at the tragedy beneath. The moment Christine unmasks the Phantom remains one of silent cinema's great shocks, proving how much fear a simple face covering could withhold. Elsewhere, films like *Häxan* (1922) used witch masks to visualize medieval superstition, bringing folkloric dread into cinematic form. In these early works, masks carried the dual weight of concealment and revelation, shaping horror's visual grammar before the sound era even began.

Mid-20th Century Preludes

By the 1960s, the horror mask had moved beyond Gothic deformity into a symbol of unsettling beauty. Georges Franju's *Eyes Without a Face* (1960) presented one of the most haunting images in European horror: a young woman's flawless, doll-like

mask, blank but fragile, covering a face destroyed by surgery. Here, the mask was no longer monstrous but poetic, embodying the horror of perfection without humanity. At the same time, regional cinemas from Mexico to Japan were experimenting with masked demons and monsters. In *The Brainiac* (1962), a grotesque mask-like visage became a folkloric horror made flesh. In Japan's *Onibaba* (1964), a stolen samurai mask becomes cursed, fusing folk superstition with body horror. Before the slasher boom, masks had already established themselves as vessels of tragedy, allegory, and cultural specificity. Not just disguises, but symbols of horror's oldest fears.

The Red Death – Masquerade of Doom

In Roger Corman's *The Masque of the Red Death* (1964), adapted from Edgar Allan Poe, the mask serves as both metaphor and omen. The mysterious Red Death arrives at a decadent masquerade, wearing a crimson skull mask that conceals pestilence itself. When the mask is lifted, death is revealed—unstoppable, egalitarian, divine. This film reconnected horror's visual language to its Gothic and allegorical roots, where the mask signifies both sin and inevitability.

Michael Myers – The Blank Shape

When *Halloween* (1978) arrived, the mask changed horror forever. John Carpenter and production designer Tommy Lee Wallace purchased a cheap Captain Kirk mask, stripped it of its eyebrows, widened the eye holes, and spray-painted it ghostly white. What emerged was not William Shatner's likeness but a void: a faceless, unreadable entity. Carpenter himself dubbed Myers "The Shape," because the mask reduced him to an outline of human form without soul or identity. Unlike Dracula's aristocracy or Frankenstein's tragedy, Myers' mask erased character entirely. It terrified because it said nothing, a reflection of our own dread. Audiences didn't see Michael's face; they saw the possibility of evil in any darkened hallway. Beyond the screen, the mask redefined Halloween night itself, turning a simple plastic disguise into the archetype of modern horror.

220

Jason Voorhees[24] – The Hockey Juggernaut

Jason Voorhees didn't begin with a mask. In *Friday the 13th Part 2* (1981), he wore a crude burlap sack. But when Part III (1982) introduced the hockey mask, horror history shifted. A piece of sporting equipment became the face of inevitability. The mask's cold plastic, punched with ventilation holes, stripped Jason of humanity and gave him the look of a laborer turned executioner. It also distinguished him visually from Myers, carving his own mythology. By the mid-1980s, Jason's hockey mask rivaled Dracula's cape and Frankenstein's bolts as shorthand for "horror" in popular imagination. It spawned Halloween costumes, toys, and endless imitators, transforming a once-generic slasher into a franchise juggernaut. Jason's mask showed horror how iconography itself could sell fear.

Leatherface[25] – Masks of Flesh

No mask in horror is more grotesque or more layered than Leatherface's. In *The Texas Chain Saw Massacre* (1974), he crafts masks from human skin, each one embodying a different "persona": butcher, maternal caretaker, even clown. Tobe Hooper conceived Leatherface as mentally unstable, hiding his own face to "become" whoever his family needed. The horror here is not only in the grotesque image of stitched flesh but in the psychology: identity as costume, humanity erased and rewritten with each skin-mask. Unlike Myers or Jason, whose masks render them symbols, Leatherface's masks implicate the audience in the violence of the body. To look at Leatherface is to see horror's obsession with flesh made literal. His mask is not a void but a reminder: the killer wears us.

Hannibal Lecter – The Muzzle of the Mind

In *The Silence of the Lambs* (1991), Hannibal Lecter's mask is not one of concealment, but containment. The metal muzzle, designed to protect others from his bite, became a visual shorthand for intellect restrained by madness. Unlike other killers, Lecter doesn't hide behind the mask; it hides the world from him. The image of him wheeled upright, strapped and masked, reframed horror: evil not as faceless brute force, but as articulate genius behind a cage.

Ghostface[26] – Commodity Turned Killer

Ghostface's mask has a different story. It wasn't designed for *Scream* (1996), it was already hanging on drugstore racks as a novelty Halloween item, inspired loosely by Edvard Munch's *The Scream*. Wes Craven and screenwriter Kevin Williamson turned it into a genius device: a mask anyone could wear. Unlike Myers' one-man shape or Jason's hockey emblem, Ghostface is interchangeable. Every film reveals a different killer (or killers) behind the mask, turning the disguise into a meta-commentary on horror itself. The mask's cartoonish droop allows it to be both terrifying and ridiculous, perfect for *Scream's* tone. In doing so, it blurred the line between real Halloween costumes and cinematic icons: Ghostface is both the joke kids wear and the nightmare that kills.

Masks Beyond the Icons

Burlap and the Everyman Terror

Before Jason's hockey mask, the burlap sack made anonymity horrifying. *The Town That Dreaded Sundown* (1976) introduced the "Phantom Killer," whose pillowcase-like hood with crude eye holes looked disturbingly homemade. The mask of someone who could live next door. *Friday the 13th Part 2* (1981) recycled the look for Jason, emphasizing the slasher's roots in rural paranoia.

Decades later, *The Strangers* (2008) would echo this by giving its killers simple sack and doll masks, leaning into the terror of the banal: killers who could make horror out of hardware-store supplies. These masks work because they are not icons polished by merchandising; they are terrifying precisely because they are crude, ordinary, and possible.

Animal Faces and the Predator Within

Animal masks carry primal associations, stripping humanity and suggesting predation. Michele Soavi's *Stagefright* (1987) used a massive owl mask, absurd yet grotesque, turning a costume-party prop into a looming symbol of inescapable death. In *You're Next* (2011), killers wear sleek fox, lamb, and tiger masks, blending home invasion with feral instinct. The animal visage works as shorthand: predators among us, cloaked in false innocence. These films remind audiences that behind the mask may not be supernatural evil but ordinary humans choosing brutality and that choice is far more unsettling.

The Clown as Mask

Though clowns technically wear paint rather than masks, horror treats the painted face as a mask of its own. *Killer Klowns from Outer Space* (1988) turned circus grotesques into latex-faced nightmares, while Art the Clown (*Terrifier*, 2016–present) modernized the archetype into a sadistic mime whose painted leer never changes. The clown mask works by corrupting the familiar: what once entertained children becomes a fixed, grinning death's head. By divorcing emotion from expression, clown masks evoke the same uncanny fear as Myers' blank face, laughter drained into menace.

Dr. Decker – The Psychologist as Monster

David Cronenberg's portrayal of Dr. Philip Decker in *Nightbreed* (1990) gave horror one of its most chillingly clinical masks: a stitched-mouth burlap sack with button eyes and a zipper grin. The mask looks handmade, improvised, yet disturbingly precise, like a surgical experiment gone rogue. Decker's disguise externalizes his psyche: the rational man suppressing monstrous impulses until they break free. In Clive Barker's mythology, the mask doesn't just conceal, it *creates* the killer, suggesting the self as something literally sewn shut to contain its own chaos.

Folkloric and Festival Masks

Some horror masks root themselves in folklore rather than slasher tradition. Sam in *Trick 'r Treat* (2007) dons a burlap-sack head with button eyes, embodying the spirit of Halloween itself. His mask, once removed, reveals a pumpkin-skull demon, a folkloric guardian ensuring traditions are obeyed. The *Purge* franchise (2013–2018) extended this into satire: its killers wear grotesque carnival masks, a Mardi Gras of violence where anonymity licenses atrocity. These films show how masks are not just disguises but ritual objects. Celebrations of inversion, when rules collapse and chaos reigns.

Frank the Rabbit[27] – The Time-Loop Harbinger

Frank's cracked, metallic rabbit mask turned psychological horror into metaphysical prophecy in *Donnie Darko*. Its grotesque distortion of a children's costume mirrors Donnie's unraveling mind and the film's apocalyptic undertones. The mask became a cult symbol for early-2000s existential dread. A haunting of suburbia by surreal inevitability. Horror had entered the dream-logic era, where the mask is no longer a disguise but a riddle: a signal that reality itself is fractured.

Jigsaw's Billy Puppet – The Mechanical Messenger

While John Kramer never wears a mask himself, *Saw* (2004–) reintroduced the mask-as-avatar through Billy the Puppet, whose chalk-white face, spiraled cheeks, and red eyes became one of modern horror's most recognizable images. Billy isn't alive, but his mask channels Kramer's philosophy: justice through cruelty, morality through pain. In a genre obsessed with identity, Billy's mechanical smile is both performance and prophecy: the mask that delivers judgment.

ChromeSkull – The Digital Age Killer (*Laid to Rest*, 2009)

ChromeSkull's mirror-finished mask is both armor and reflection, a literal screen that turns the audience's gaze back on itself. In the found-footage era of horror, he represents the killer as content creator, filming his murders with cinematic precision. The chrome mask refracts light like a camera lens, making violence both performative and self-documenting. Where Leatherface wore humanity and Ghostface wore irony, ChromeSkull wears *surveillance*. He is the 21st-century monster: polished, industrial, and aware that the kill only counts if it's captured.

The Babadook – The Paper Mask of Grief
From *The Babadook* (2014), Jennifer Kent's creation redefined what a mask could mean. The Babadook's black top hat, chalk-white face, and grotesque paper grin aren't a literal mask but a storybook manifestation, grief personified. What makes it iconic is that it merges the psychological mask (repression, denial) with the visual mask (the monster's paper-cutout features). It's not worn, but projected. The inner demon externalized. In modern horror, this marks the genre's turn inward: the mask no longer hides the killer's identity but exposes the protagonist's soul.

Leslie Vernon – The Meta Mask of Becoming
Leslie's Kabuki-inspired mask is a clever homage to every killer before him: smooth like Myers, pale like Jason, stylized like theatre. But unlike them, Leslie removes the mask mid-film, letting us see the performer beneath the archetype. His story flips the genre inside-out: the mask isn't a curse, it's *a goal.* He wants to *earn* his place among legends. The result is a film that turns horror mythology into apprenticeship, and the mask into graduation. The moment a man becomes myth.

The Man in the Red Mask – The Family's Shame (*Eyes Wide Shut*, 1999)
Though Kubrick's film is more erotic nightmare than traditional horror, the Venetian-style masks worn during the orgy sequence tap into the genre's primal terror of exposure and anonymity. The Man in the Red Mask, presiding over ritual humiliation, becomes a figure of moral decay wrapped in elegance. These masks draw directly from European carnival tradition, turning opulence into menace. In horror's visual lineage, they bridge Poe's plague masquerade and modern psychological dread, civilization wearing its own corruption as costume.

The Red Hood – Ritual and Rebellion (*Midsommar*, 2019)
Ari Aster's *Midsommar* reimagined masking as collective ritual. The villagers' floral and animal disguises, and particularly the Red Hood worn during sacrifice, function as ceremonial absolution. Anonymity in the name of belief. Unlike slasher masks that isolate a killer, these unify a community in horror. The mask here is not the mark of insanity but of devotion, blurring where faith ends and violence begins. It's folk horror's ultimate inversion: horror not from the mask's wearer, but from the crowd wearing it together.

The Psychology of the Mask in Horror
Masks terrify because they deny the most basic human instinct: the search for a face. We read expression for intent, safety, empathy. Remove it, and every encounter becomes unknowable. Horror exploits this rupture. Michael Myers' mask is terrifying because it is blank, an empty page for our fear. Leatherface horrifies because his stitched flesh mask is grotesquely expressive, a parody of identity itself. Ghostface unnerves because it is too exaggerated, a scream frozen forever. Whether blank, crude, cartoonish, or grotesque, the mask strips away personality and replaces it with archetype. The killer ceases to be a man and becomes myth, facelessness standing in for the void.

Legacy: From Screen to Halloween
Masks did more than shape horror cinema, they reshaped Halloween and global popular culture. By the early 1980s, Michael's white mask and Jason's hockey mask were as common in suburban streets as plastic pumpkins, turning cinematic killers into holiday mascots. They gave horror not just films but rituals: to wear the mask was to join the myth. Ghostface completed the cycle by becoming both a real-world party mask and a cinematic killer, collapsing the distance between culture and commodity. Today, masks remain horror's purest iconography, whether in multiplex blockbusters or homemade indie nightmares. They travel from folklore to film to festival, proving that the faceless killer still holds the oldest, most primal power in storytelling: to frighten not with what is seen, but with what is hidden.

Body Horror

Where splatter explodes bodies from the outside, body horror lets them rot, warp, and betray from within. It's the genre of parasites, mutations, surgical obsession, and techno-flesh fusion. The moment when your skin, your organs, your whole sense of self becomes unstable. David Cronenberg codified it, but Japan, France, and global filmmakers pushed it further: merging human and machine, infection and desire, identity and abjection. If horror is about losing control, body horror is the nightmare of losing control *of your own body*.

Why People Are Drawn to It
Because body horror makes the intimate alien. It takes what we think of as "me" skin, blood, mind, appetite and renders it porous. These films confront disease, sexuality, technology, and trauma by literalizing them in flesh. Audiences squirm because it's personal: we recognize our own bodies in every bulging vein and suppurating wound. The thrill is double-edged: disgust at what we could become, fascination at the creativity of transformation. To watch is to admit we are meat, mutable and mortal.

Essentials
- **Shivers (1975, Canada)** – Cronenberg's parasite-as-STD classic. Fuses body horror with social satire, turning a Montreal apartment complex into a petri dish where a parasite spreads both sexual liberation and violent contagion. Its mix of eroticism and infection makes it a chilling study of how desire and disease intertwine, launching Cronenberg's career-long obsession with the body as battleground.
- **The Brood (1979, Canada)** – Divorce therapy spawns mutant children. David Cronenberg externalizes psychological trauma into monstrous form, with repressed rage literally birthing deformed children. Blending domestic melodrama with body horror, the film turns family dissolution into a grotesque allegory of how inner wounds manifest in flesh.
- **Videodrome (1983, Canada)** – Television signal infects flesh; long live the new flesh. *Fun fact*: James Woods improvised against Cronenberg's bizarre props, including the infamous "flesh gun." A hallucinatory fusion of body horror and media critique, where television itself becomes a mutating infection that reshapes flesh and mind. With its mantra "long live the new flesh," the film turns technology into parasite, warning that mass media doesn't just influence us, it consumes us.
- **The Thing (1982)** – Directed by John Carpenter. Stands as one of the most visceral achievements in body horror, where alien assimilation transforms the human form into grotesque spectacle. Rob Bottin's groundbreaking effects turn bodies inside out. Limbs sprouting claws, faces splitting open, viscera becoming teeth, making paranoia inseparable from the terror of watching flesh betray itself. Here, the horror is not only that anyone could be the monster, but that the body itself is mutable, unstable, and horrifyingly untrustworthy.
- **Eraserhead (1979)** - David Lynch's *Eraserhead* is a surreal, dreamlike expression of anxiety centered on a new father's fears of responsibility, sex, and parenthood, which manifest as grotesque biological horror in a desolate, industrial urban landscape.

Deep Cuts
- **Possession (1981, Poland/France)** – Isabelle Adjani's breakdown as performance art, complete with writhing monster. Andrzej Żuławski pushes body horror into the realm of psychological and marital collapse, where emotional disintegration manifests in convulsive performances and abject, inhuman transformations. Most infamous for its subway miscarriage scene and the creature born of adultery, the film equates love, betrayal, and obsession with bodily mutation, making intimacy itself a site of horror.
- **Brain Damage (1988)** – A parasite offers euphoric highs in exchange for brains. Frank Henenlotter marries splatter comedy with body horror, following a young man addicted to a phallic, parasite-like creature that injects euphoric chemicals while demanding human victims in return. The film's gooey practical effects and grotesque metaphors turn drug dependency into literal body invasion, satirizing pleasure, control, and decay in equal measure.

- **Akira (1988, Japan)** – Animated mutation apocalypse, teen power as grotesque flesh. Katsuhiro Ōtomo translates psychic power into grotesque body horror, climaxing in Tetsuo's mutation into a seething mass of uncontrollable flesh and machinery. Its imagery of bodies fusing with technology and expanding beyond recognition makes the film a nightmarish allegory of unchecked power, scientific hubris, and the collapse of human identity in the face of mutation.
- **American Mary (2012, Canada)** – Underground surgeries turn trauma into art. Jen and Sylvia Soska reframe body horror through the lens of underground surgery, following a medical student who turns to extreme body modification to survive. With its clinical detachment and feminist edge, the film explores agency, exploitation, and transformation, making the altered body both a site of power and grotesque spectacle.
- **Titane (2021, France)** – A woman fuses with machinery, pregnancy, and identity fluidity. Julia Ducournau pushes body horror into surreal territory, merging car crash fetishism with themes of gender, identity, and transformation. Winner of the Palme d'Or, the film blurs human and machine, pregnancy and mutation, using grotesque metamorphosis to question what it means to inhabit and redefine a body.

Critical Essay

"Body Horror Isn't Just Gore, It's Philosophy."

Myth: Body horror is about gross-out effects.

Reality: It's allegory in skin. *Videodrome* interrogates media and technology. *The Thing* is Cold War paranoia in latex. *Possession* dissects divorce and madness. *Akira* channels nuclear trauma through teenage mutation. Even the outrageous *Human Centipede* and *Tusk* are modern fables about control and dehumanization. Behind every ooze, puncture, and parasite is a question: what defines the self when the body stops cooperating?

Global Spotlight: Japan & France

- **Japan (Cyberpunk Flesh & Fetish).** From *Tetsuo: The Iron Man* (1989) to *Tokyo Gore Police* (2008), Japanese cinema embraced mutation as punk rebellion. Industrial metal welded to skin, arterial geysers reimagined as performance art. Miike's *Audition* (1999) took body horror into domestic spaces, where intimacy becomes surgical terror.
- **France (New Extremity).** *Inside* (2007), *Martyrs* (2008), and *Raw* (2016) reframed the body as a site of ideology: motherhood, martyrdom, appetite. With cool aesthetics and philosophical bite, these films pushed past gore into existential violation. In France, flesh is not just spectacle, it's debate carved into the skin.

Foundations & Cronenberg Core

- ☐ **The Penalty** (1920) - A deformed criminal mastermind plans to loot the city of San Francisco as well as revenge himself on the doctor who mistakenly amputated his legs.
- ☐ **Invaders from Mars** (1953) - A young boy learns that space aliens are taking over the minds of earthlings. The film's exploration of cold war paranoia and the idea of loved ones being replaced by emotionless impostors influenced Don Siegel's 1956 film *Invasion of the Body Snatchers*. The visual style and plot device of experiencing an alien invasion from a child's vulnerable perspective have influenced filmmakers such as Steven Spielberg (*E.T.*) and Brad Bird (*The Iron Giant*). Director Don Coscarelli has cited *Invaders from Mars* as an influence on his cult horror film *Phantasm* (1979).
  - • **ADAPTIONS**
    - ☐ **Invaders from Mars** (1988) - The basic premise is the same: a young boy (Hunter Carson) witnesses a flying saucer land and observes his parents acting strangely, prompting him to seek military assistance to defeat the aliens. The most direct remake was directed by horror icon Tobe Hooper (of *The Texas Chain Saw Massacre* and *Poltergeist* fame).

☐ **The Tingler** (1959) - An obsessed pathologist discovers and captures a parasitic creature that grows when fear grips its host.

- **SIMILAR THEMES**
  - ☐ **Shivers** (1975) – Parasites spread through sexual contact in a high-rise. *Shivers* and its focus on an infectious agent turning people into sexually-crazed fiends is considered a landmark for the body horror genre. Its influence has been cited in later horror films that feature similar themes of infection and social decay. Canadian funding bodies nearly buried the film after its controversy, but its success made Cronenberg a cult name.
    - **CRONENBERG THEMES**
      - ☐ **Rabid** (1977) – A young woman develops a taste for human blood after experimental plastic surgery, and her victims turn into blood-thirsty zombies, leading into a city-wide epidemic.
      - ☐ **The Brood** (1979) – A man tries to uncover an unconventional psychologist's therapy techniques on his institutionalized wife, amidst a series of brutal murders. Cronenberg wrote it during his own divorce, channeling domestic rage into bodily metaphor.
      - ☐ **Videodrome** (1983) – A programmer at a Toronto TV station that specializes in adult entertainment searches for the producers of a dangerous and bizarre broadcast. Numerous academic analysis and historical context essays have been made dissecting the film. The Criterion Collection releases feature in-depth essays, such as "Videodrome: The Slithery Sense of Unreality," which explore the film's themes and enduring relevance. A feature on the Roger Ebert website, "A Vision of the Future: On David Cronenberg's Videodrome," provides additional analysis of the film's prophetic nature.
        - **ADAPTIONS**
          - ☐ **eXistenZ** (1999) – Bio-organic game consoles fuse with spines.
      - ☐ **Dead Ringers** (1988) – Twin surgeons spiral into surgical psychosis.
      - ☐ **Crash** (1996) – Car crash survivors eroticize wounds and scars.
      - ☐ **Crimes of the Future** (2022) - Humans adapt to a synthetic environment, with new transformations and mutations. With his partner Caprice, Saul Tenser, celebrity performance artist, publicly showcases the metamorphosis of his organs in avant-garde performances.
  - ☐ **The Hidden** (1987) – Parasitic alien leaps from host to host.
    - **SEQUELS**
      - ☐ **The Hidden II** (1993) - Released six years after the original, this sequel was distributed directly to video. It was not well-regarded by critics or fans and featured a new cast, aside from using a few minutes of footage from the first movie.
  - ☐ **Brain Damage** (1988) – Parasitic creature trades euphoria for brains.

☐ **The Wasp Woman** (1959) - The head of a major cosmetics company experiments on herself with a youth formula made from royal jelly extracted from wasps, but the formula's side effects have deadly consequences.

- **ADAPTIONS & SIMILAR THEMES**
  - ☐ **Rejuvenatrix** (1988) - Also known as *The Rejuvenator*, this film was inspired by Corman's original. Some critics have even called it the "1988 version of *The Wasp Woman*," though it replaced the wasp enzymes with alien ones.
  - ☐ **The Wasp Woman** (1995) - This television remake was produced by Corman for Showtime as part of his *Roger Corman Presents* series. It

starred Jennifer Rubin and was directed by Jim Wynorski, who was heavily influenced by the original.

- ☐ **Catwoman** (2004) - Some viewers have noted similarities between *The Wasp Woman* and the 2004 film *Catwoman*, particularly in the aspect of a cosmetics executive developing superpowers after a lab experiment.
- ☐ **The Substance** (2024) - This body horror film starring Demi Moore is a "remake of *Wasp-Woman* from 1958," according to its director. The film adapts the premise of a woman taking an experimental substance to regain her youth, only to have it transform her into a monster.

☐ **The Incredible Melting Man** (1977) – Astronaut melts into radioactive slime. While the film was critically panned upon release, the impressive special effects by a young Rick Baker have influenced other works such as *RoboCop*, *Street Trash* and featured on *Myster Science Theater 3000*. Due to its cult status and enduring popularity with bad movie fans, a remake is often considered.

☐ **Eraserhead** (1977) – Lynch's surreal body horror; grotesque infant imagery. Henry Spencer tries to survive his industrial environment, his angry girlfriend, and the unbearable screams of his newly born mutant child.

- **SURREALIST & PSYCHEDELIC HORROR**
  - ☐ **John Dies at the End** (2012) - An alien takes control of a drug-addicted man's body, leading to debauchery and chaos as the visitor explores humanity through Cape Town's underworld of drugs, sex, and violence.
  - ☐ **Climax** (2018, France) – Dance troupe descends into drug-fueled body collapse.
  - ☐ **Mandy** (2018) – Starring Nicolas Cage. The enchanted lives of a couple in a secluded forest are brutally shattered by a nightmarish hippie cult and their demon-biker henchmen, propelling a man into a spiraling, surreal rampage of vengeance.
  - ☐ **Fried Barry** (2020) - An alien takes control of a drug-addicted man's body, leading to debauchery and chaos as the visitor explores humanity through Cape Town's underworld of drugs, sex, and violence.

☐ **Blue Sunshine** (1977) - A bizarre series of murders begins in Los Angeles, where people start going bald and then become homicidal maniacs. But could the blame rest on a particularly dangerous form of LSD called Blue Sunshine the murderers took ten years before?

☐ **Swamp Thing** (1982) – Directed by Wes Craven. After a violent incident with a special chemical, a research scientist is turned into a swamp plant monster. Based on the DC Comics character.

- **SEQUELS**
  - ☐ **The Return of the Swamp Thing** (1989) - This is the direct sequel to the 1982 film. Directed by Jim Wynorski, it features a much lighter, more campy tone than its predecessor. Dick Durock and Louis Jourdan reprised their roles as Swamp Thing and the villainous Anton Arcane, respectively.
  - ☐ **Swamp Thing** (2019) - A new, darker live-action series premiered on the DC Universe streaming service. The show received a positive reception from horror fans for its emphasis on horror and gore but was canceled after one season.

☐ **Slugs** (1988) - Killer slugs on the rampage in a rural community. Based on the novel of the same name by Shaun Hutson.

- **SIMILAR THEMES**
  - ☐ **Squirm** (1976) - This earlier film also features a small town besieged by mutated, flesh-eating worms after a downed power line energizes the soil.
  - ☐ **The Nest** (1987) - A movie in which cockroaches become carnivorous and start to prey on humans.

☐ **Akira** (1988, Japan) – A secret military project endangers Neo-Tokyo when it turns a teenage biker gang member into a rampaging psychic psychopath who can only be stopped by his best friend.

The Father of Body Horror

David Cronenberg[28]

Born in Toronto in 1943, David Cronenberg is the godfather of *body horror*. The subgenre where flesh, technology, and psychology mutate into grotesque new forms. Starting with Canadian indie features in the 1970s, he developed a reputation for clinical precision and disturbing originality. Cronenberg's work obsesses over how the body betrays the mind, how technology rewires biology, and how desire and disease intermingle. A self-professed rationalist, his horror isn't about ghosts or demons, it's about science, sex, and evolution gone wrong.

Signature Works (Curated)

- *Shivers* (1975) — A parasite spreads through an apartment complex, turning residents into sex-crazed predators. Controversial on release, now seen as the beginning of body horror cinema.
- *Videodrome* (1983) — A TV executive discovers a broadcast signal that causes hallucinations, tumors, and violent new realities. "Long live the new flesh."
- *The Fly* (1986) — Scientist fuses with a fly in a teleportation experiment; tragic love story and grotesque metamorphosis.
- *Dead Ringers* (1988) — Identical twin gynecologists spiral into addiction, obsession, and surgical nightmare.
- *Crash* (1996) — Adaptation of J.G. Ballard's novel about car-crash fetishists. Banned, censored, and revered as fearless transgression.

The Fingerprints

- The body as battlefield: cancer, parasites, deformity, transformation.
- Fusion of flesh and machine (*Videodrome*, *Crash*, *eXistenZ*).
- Detached, clinical tone: horror dissected like a medical case study.
- Sexuality + pathology: desire inseparable from decay.
- Evolutionary anxiety: humanity transforming into something unrecognizable.

Legacy & Influence

Cronenberg defined the *body horror* lexicon inspiring everyone from Clive Barker (*Hellraiser*) to contemporary filmmakers like Julia Ducournau (*Raw*, *Titane*) and Brandon Cronenberg (*Possessor*, *Infinity Pool*). His influence stretches beyond horror: filmmakers like David Lynch, Darren Aronofsky, and even medical thrillers owe him a debt. "Cronenbergian" is now a shorthand for any mix of biology, sex, and technology in disturbing collapse.

Pairing Night Watchlist

- *Videodrome* (1983) → Watch for its prophetic themes: media addiction, body-tech fusion, reality collapse.
- *The Fly* (1986) → Pay attention to the balance of tragedy and grotesque transformation; it's a love story as much as a monster film.
- *Dead Ringers* (1988) → Study the doubling of identity and the surgical imagery; it's horror as psychological pathology.

Quick Facts to Sound Smart

- *The Fly* won an Academy Award for Best Makeup. A rare Oscar win for a horror film.
- Cronenberg turned down directing *Return of the Jedi* to make *Videodrome*.
- The phrase "long live the new flesh" from *Videodrome* has become a pop-culture mantra about media evolution.
- He frequently casts actors who embody vulnerability and obsession from Jeff Goldblum to Viggo Mortensen.
- Cronenberg himself often cameos in films. He plays a doctor in *The Fly* and a gynecologist in *The Fly II*.

80s/90s Extremes & Global Experiments

☐ **The Howling** (1981) - After a bizarre and near deadly encounter with a serial killer, a television newswoman is sent to a remote mountain resort whose residents may not be what they seem. Based *The Howling* novel series by Gary Brandner.

- **ADAPTIONS, SEQUELS & SIMILAR FILMS**
  - ☐ **Howling II: Your Sister is a Werewolf (**1985) - The only direct sequel to the 1981 film. It follows the brother of the original film's heroine, Karen, as he teams up with a paranormal investigator (played by Christopher Lee) to travel to Transylvania and battle the werewolf queen.
  - ☐ **Howling III: The Marsupials** (1987) - An unrelated story set in Australia, exploring a colony of marsupial werewolves. The tone is more of a strange, B-movie horror comedy.
  - ☐ **Howling IV: The Original Nightmare** (1988) - A more faithful adaptation of the original Gary Brandner novel, though it makes some alterations. It follows a successful horror author who travels to a remote town and is plagued by visions and werewolves.
  - ☐ **Howling V: The Rebirth** (1989) - A whodunit mystery set in an old Hungarian castle, where a group of strangers is trapped by a werewolf.
  - ☐ **Howling VI: The Freaks** (1991) - A werewolf becomes part of a traveling carnival freak show. The plot includes elements of the third novel and a vampire vs. werewolf fight.
  - ☐ **Howling: New Moon Rising** (1995) - This film attempts to tie the previous three movies together but is notoriously low-budget, with some scenes reportedly shot on video.
  - ☐ **The Howling: Reborn** (2011) - A reboot of the series aimed at a younger audience. The story focuses on a teenager who discovers his werewolf heritage.
  - ☐ **Wolfen** (1981) - A New York cop investigates a series of brutal deaths that resemble animal attacks. *The Howling* and *American Werewolf in London* were released in the same year and contributed to a revival of the werewolf subgenre. *Wolfen* stands out for its unique take on the monster mythology, focusing on the supernatural aspect rather than the lycanthropy trope.
  - ☐ **The Wolf of Snow Hollow** (2020) - Terror grips a small mountain town as bodies are discovered after each full moon. Losing sleep, raising a teenage daughter, and caring for his ailing father, officer Marshall struggles to remind himself there's no such thing as werewolves.

☐ **They Live** (1988) - They influence our decisions without us knowing it. They numb our senses without us feeling it. They control our lives without us realizing it. They live.

☐ **Primal Rage** (1988, Italy) - A scientist at a Florida University accidentally creates a "rage virus" while conducting experiments to restore dead brain tissue in baboons. The virus soon spreads.

☐ **Begotten** (1989) - Presented in a surreal, gory and entirely visual manner, Begotten tells of the death of religion, the abuse of nature by Man and a nihilistic outlook on what life ultimately is.

☐ **Hardware** (1990) – Reassembled robot fuses with human prey.

☐ **Nightbreed** (1990) - A troubled young man is drawn to a mythical place called Midian where a variety of friendly monsters are hiding from humanity. Meanwhile, a sadistic serial killer is looking for a patsy.

☐ **Poison** (1991) - Inspired by the writings of French author Jean Genet and has since become an influential art-house film. A boy shoots his father and flies out the window. A man falls in love with a fellow inmate in prison. A doctor accidentally ingests his experimental sex serum, wreaking havoc on the community.

☐ **Ticks** (1993) - A group of troubled teenagers are led by social workers on a California wilderness retreat, not knowing that the woods they are camping in have become infested by mutated, blood-sucking ticks. *Ticks* was part of a throwback to the "angry nature" creature features of the 1970s and 1980s.

☐ **Species** (1995) - A group of scientists try to track down and trap a killer alien seductress before she successfully mates with a human.

- **SEQUELS**
  - ☐ **Species II** (1998) - This is the direct theatrical sequel to the original film. The plot follows a returning astronaut infected with alien DNA from Mars, causing him to go on a killing spree. Scientists team up with a more docile clone of the original alien to track him down.
  - ☐ **Species III** (2004) - This made-for-television film continues the story after the events of *Species II*. An alien-human hybrid searches for other hybrids to mate with as the species begins to suffer from genetic decay.

- **Species: The Awakening** (2007) - This made-for-television film is considered a standalone entry rather than a direct follow-up to the first three films. It follows a scientist's desperate attempt to save his niece, a human-alien hybrid, from a genetic breakdown in Mexico.
- **Thinner** (1996) - An obese attorney is cursed by a gypsy to rapidly and uncontrollably lose weight. Based on the 1984 horror novel by Stephen King.
- **Mimic** (1997) –Genetically modified roaches evolve to mimic humans. Starring Mira Sorvino. Three years ago, entomologist Dr. Susan Tyler genetically created an insect to kill cockroaches carrying a virulent disease. Now, the insects are out to destroy their only predator, mankind.
  - **SEQUELS**
    - **Mimic 2** (2001) – Directed by Jean de Segonzac, this sequel follows school teacher Remi (played by Alix Koromzay, who had a supporting role in the first film) as she is targeted by the evolved "Judas" insects.
    - **Mimic 3: Sentinel** (2003) - This third film, directed by J.T. Petty, is only loosely connected to the events of the previous two films. It focuses on a reclusive young man who observes the killer insects from his apartment window.
- **Deep Rising** (1998) - A group of heavily armed hijackers board a luxury ocean liner in the South Pacific Ocean to loot it, only to do battle with a series of large-sized, tentacled, man-eating sea creatures who had already invaded the ship. It has been widely rumored that the roar was meant to lead into a potential King Kong reboot, which never came to fruition.
- **Virus** (1999) - After outrunning a typhoon at sea, a strong-willed tugboat navigator and her crew discover a high-tech alien life form that's taken control of a Russian research vessel and aims to destroy on a massive scale.
- **Uzumaki** (2000, Japan) – Town cursed by spirals that warp bodies. The population of Kurouzu is slowly driven mad by their growing obsessions with spiral shapes, finding them everywhere with shocking and horrifying results.
- **Suicide Club** (2001, Japan) – Mass deaths in body-drenched imagery. A detective is trying to find the cause of a string of suicides.
  - **ADAPTIONS & OTHER FILMS BY SION SONO**
    - **Noriko's Dinner Table** (2005) - It attempts to provide more answers to the ambiguities of *Suicide Club* by exploring the life of Noriko, a rural teenager who runs away to Tokyo and joins a cult-like "family rental" service.
    - **Strange Circus** (2005) - The erotic novelist Taeko is writing a morbid story of a family destroyed by incest, murder and abuse. Her assistant, Yuji, sets on a mission to uncover the reality of this story, but the reality might be too much to bear.
    - **Cold Fish** (2010) - The lives of a bored suburban couple are changed forever when a seemingly nice old man gives their daughter a job at his fish store, and soon his gruesome hobbies are brought to light.
    - **Why Don't You Play in Hell?** (2013) - A renegade film crew becomes embroiled with a yakuza clan feud. Another film by Sion Sono.
- **Altered** (2006) – Alien abduction survivors scarred by experiments.
- **Teeth** (2007) – Teenage girl develops vagina dentata.
- **The Human Centipede (First Sequence)** (2009) – Three people surgically conjoined. The films' controversial premise and graphic content, particularly in the second film, made them unsuitable for a wide theatrical release. *The Human Centipede 2* was initially refused classification by the British Board of Film Classification, making a mainstream franchise impossible.
  - **SEQUELS**
    - **The Human Centipede II (Full Sequence)** (2011) – Meta sequel escalates grotesquery.
    - **The Human Centipede III (Final Sequence)** (2015) – Prison-wide centipede experiment.
- **Grotesque** (2009, Japan) – Extreme surgical mutilation endurance test.
- **Contracted** (2013) – STD mutates a woman's body grotesquely. After being drugged and raped at a party, a young woman contracts what she thinks is an STD; but, it's actually something much worse.
  - **SEQUELS**
    - **Contracted: Phase II** (2015) – Infection spreads in horrifying detail.
    - **Contracted Redux** (2017) – Alternate cut of infection saga.

2000s–2010s Body Breakdown

- ☐ **Ginger Snaps** (2000) - Two death-obsessed sisters, outcasts in their suburban neighborhood, must deal with the tragic consequences when one of them is bitten by a deadly werewolf.
- ☐ **May** (2002) – A psychological horror film about a socially awkward young woman who, after repeated rejections, tries to construct a "perfect friend" from the body parts of others.
  - **HIGH SCHOOL HORRORS**
    - ☐ **The Loved Ones** (2009) - When Brent turns down his classmate Lola's invitation to the prom, she concocts a wildly violent plan for revenge.
- ☐ **Cabin Fever** (2002) - Five college graduates rent a cabin in the woods and begin to fall victim to a horrifying flesh-eating virus, which attracts the unwanted attention of the homicidal locals.
  - **ADAPTIONS & SEQUELS**
    - ☐ **Cabin Fever 2: Spring Fever** (2009) - Directed by Ti West, this sequel follows a high school prom where the flesh-eating virus, spread through a contaminated water supply, wreaks bloody havoc.
    - ☐ **Cabin Fever: Patient Zero** (2014) - Serving as a prequel to the series, this film shows the origin of the flesh-eating virus on a remote Caribbean island, where a bachelor party stumbles upon a research facility.
    - ☐ **Cabin Fever** (2016) - This film is a remake that uses the same script as the original 2002 movie. It was widely criticized for adding little new to the story, although some reviewers considered its more serious tone a different take.
- ☐ **Bug** (2006) – Lovers descend into shared parasite delusion. Starring Ashley Judd. An unhinged war veteran holes up with a lonely woman in a spooky Oklahoma motel room. The line between reality and delusion is blurred as they discover a bug infestation.
- ☐ **Antiviral** (2012) – In a blackly satirical near future, a thriving industry sells celebrity illnesses to their obsessed fans. Employee Syd March's attempts to exploit the system backfire when they involve him in a potentially deadly mystery. As the son of David Cronenberg, Brandon's work often draws comparisons to his father's body horror films, such as *Videodrome* and *eXistenZ*.
  - **OTHER BRANDON CRONENBERG'S WORKS**
    - ☐ **Possessor** (2020) – An agent works for a secretive organization that uses brain-implant technology to inhabit other people's bodies - ultimately driving them to commit assassinations for high-paying clients.
    - ☐ **Infinity Pool** (2023) – James and Em Foster are enjoying an all-inclusive beach vacation in the fictional island of La Tolqa, when a fatal accident exposes the resort's perverse subculture of hedonistic tourism, reckless violence and surreal horrors.
- ☐ **Honeymoon** (2014) - A newlywed couple finds their lake-country honeymoon descend into chaos after Paul finds Bea wandering and disoriented in the middle of the night.
  - **RELATIONSHIP HORROR**
    - ☐ **The One I Love** (2014) - A couple on the brink of divorce stays at a secluded retreat to save their marriage, only to discover a bizarre and unsettling phenomenon involving doppelgängers.
    - ☐ **What Keeps You Alive** (2018) - A horror film with a similar plot about a couple on a lakeside getaway that descends into violence and manipulation.
    - ☐ **After Midnight** (2019) - When his girlfriend suddenly disappears, leaving a cryptic note as her only explanation, Hank's comfortable life and his sanity begin to crack. Then, from the woods surrounding his house, something terrible starts trying to break in.
- ☐ **Swallow** (2019) – A psychological thriller about a seemingly perfect newlywed who begins compulsively swallowing dangerous objects. It explores themes of female autonomy and control within a toxic relationship.
  - **RELATIONSHIP DECAY HORROR**
    - ☐ **Significant Other** (2022) - A sci-fi horror film where a couple on a remote hike is terrorized by an alien presence. It explores themes of codependency and the fear that you never really know the person you love.
    - ☐ **Together** (2025) - Years into their relationship, Tim and Millie find themselves at a crossroads as they move to the country. With tensions already flaring, an encounter with an unnatural force threatens to corrupt their lives, their love and their flesh.

Modern Body Horror & Global Visions

- ☐ **Three** (2002, South Korea) - An anthology consisting of three horror shorts from different Asian directors: Memories by Kim Jee-woon, The Wheel by Nonzee Nimibutr, and Going Home by Peter Chan.
  - • **SPIRITUAL SEQUELS**
    - ☐ **Three... Extremes** (2004, South Korea) - An Asian cross-cultural trilogy of horror films from accomplished indie directors.
    - ☐ **Dumplings** (2004) - Aunt Mei's famous homemade dumplings provide amazing age-defying qualities popular with middle-aged women. But her latest customer - a fading actress - is determined to find out what the secret ingredient is.
- ☐ **Taxidermia** (2006, Hungary) – Generational grotesqueries: gluttony, speed-eating, body art.
- ☐ **Dogtooth** (2009, Greece) – Body mutilation in oppressive family isolation.
- ☐ **Beneath the Skin** (2013) – Short, experimental body-disintegration tale.
- ☐ **Evolution** (2015, France) – Boys on island undergo strange bodily experiments.
- ☐ **Sequence Break** (2017) – Arcade machine fuses with human flesh.
- ☐ **Kuso** (2017) – Surreal body grotesqueries from Flying Lotus.
- ☐ **The House That Jack Built** (2018) – Serial killer's philosophy dissected in brutal body imagery. This film's structure, involving a serial killer recounting his murders to the character "Verge," echoes the framing narrative of Thomas Kyd's play *The Spanish Tragedy*, where the ghost of Andrea and the figure of Revenge watch the events unfold.
  - • **THE SPANISH TRAGEDY DNA**
    - ☐ **The Revenant** (2015) - A modern take on the ultimate revenge story, which many critics have compared to *The Spanish Tragedy*.
    - ☐ **The Revenger's Tragedy** (2002) - A film based on Thomas Middleton's play of the same name, which was itself influenced by Kyd's work. It is a dark, stylized, and violent tale of revenge.
- ☐ **Huesera: The Bone Woman** (2022, Mexico) - Valeria has long dreamed about becoming a mother. After learning that she's pregnant, she expects to feel happy, yet something's off. The film is often compared to other "reproductive horror" films like *Rosemary's Baby* and *The Babadook* that explore anxiety and motherhood.
- ☐ **Hatching** (2022, Finland) - A young gymnast, who tries desperately to please her demanding mother, discovers a strange egg. She hides it and keeps it warm, but when it hatches, what emerges shocks them all.
- ☐ **Swallowed** (2022) - Follows two best friends on their final night together, with a nightmare of drugs, bugs, and horrific intimacy.
- ☐ **When Evil Lurks** (2023, Argentina) - In a remote village, two brothers find a demon-infected man just about to "give birth" to evil itself. They decide to get rid of the body, only to end up unintentionally spreading chaos.
- ☐ **Him** (2025) - A young athlete descends into a world of terror when he's invited to train with a legendary champion whose charisma curdles into something darker.

Body Horror Pairing Night: *Into the Flesh Spiral*

How to Watch
Don't marathon these like slashers. Body horror works best in waves: watch one, sit with it, feel it under your skin, then dive back in. Keep snacks ironic (gelatin, spaghetti, anything that wiggles). Dim lights, lean into discomfort, and let the unease linger between films.

What to Look For
- **Texture**: Latex, slime, prosthetics. Body horror is tactile cinema.
- **Metaphor**: Infection as addiction (*Shivers*), mutation as trauma (*The Brood*), flesh as media (*Videodrome*).
- **Performance**: From Adjani's infamous subway scene in *Possession* to Jeff Goldblum's insect decay in *The Fly* (a bonus!), the body is the script.
- **Sound**: Squishes, snaps, and the industrial clank of machinery fusing with flesh. Listen as much as you look.

Starter Platter (Warm the Palate)
- **Shivers (1975)** – Parasites + sex = Cronenberg's first viral infection. Notice how the sterile modern apartment block becomes a pressure cooker for desire.
- **The Brood (1979)** – Mutant children born of therapy. Watch how domestic arguments turn into literal monsters.

Main Course (The New Flesh)
- **Videodrome (1983)** – TV eats its audience. Look for how screens, tapes, and wounds blur together. Cronenberg warning us about media decades early.
- **The Thing (1982)** – Bottin's Antarctic nightmare. Watch the transformations frame by frame: every effect is handmade, every goo deliberate.

Late-Night Dessert (Global Extremes)
- **Possession (1981)** – Isabelle Adjani gives the most feral performance in horror history. The subway freakout isn't just hysteria, it's the body as battlefield of marriage, politics, and faith.
- **Tetsuo: The Iron Man (1989)** – Pure cyberpunk nightmare. Industrial sound, stop-motion, and surreal edits turn flesh into steel.

Quick Facts to Sound Like the Smartest in the Room
- *Videodrome*'s "long live the new flesh" wasn't in the original script. Cronenberg wrote it on set to give the film its manifesto.
- *The Thing* used gallons of KY jelly, bubblegum, and offal from butcher shops for its effects.
- Isabelle Adjani reportedly needed therapy after filming *Possession*; her subway scene took multiple takes and nearly broke her.
- *Tetsuo* was shot on weekends for almost two years, guerrilla-style, with cast members literally sleeping in abandoned buildings between takes.

Flesh Becomes Art

Comedy Horror

When Horror Learned to Laugh (and Still Scare)

Where gothic chills and splatter shocks aim straight at fear, horror-comedy thrives in the uneasy middle: the grotesque and the ridiculous. It doesn't mock horror so much as bend it, exaggerating tropes until they become absurd, then pulling the rug out with genuine scares. From parody classics to cult camp and modern meta, the subgenre thrives on tonal whiplash: you're laughing one second, then shrieking the next.

Why People Are Drawn to It

Because fear and laughter live in the same nervous system. Both rely on tension and release, the sudden jolt of the unexpected. Horror-comedy gives permission to scream *and* cackle, often within the same breath. It's also the genre most likely to go viral or become cult, because quoting lines, singing songs (*Rocky Horror*), or bonding over absurd kills (*Scary Movie*, *Shaun of the Dead*) makes horror a party.

Essentials

- **The Rocky Horror Picture Show (1975, UK/USA)** – Campy rock musical of mad science and gender-bending parody. Transforms horror tropes into camp spectacle, blending Frankenstein pastiche with glam rock, drag, and sexual liberation. Its cult status lies in turning the monster movie inside out, celebrating excess and queerness while mocking the rigidity of genre itself.
- **Ghostbusters (1984, USA)** – A satirical take on entrepreneurship and the American Dream, *Ghostbusters* explores how three down-on-their-luck, discredited scientists successfully turn their esoteric research into a thriving ghost-catching business by responding to a supernatural crisis that the government is incapable of handling.
- **Beetlejuice (1988, USA)** – Ghost couple + obnoxious bio-exorcist = gothic comedy classic. Tim Burton turns the afterlife into a grotesque comedy, where death is bureaucratic, ghoulish, and absurd. Mixing gothic visuals with slapstick surrealism, it reimagines horror imagery as playful spectacle, making the macabre mischievous rather than terrifying.
- **Shaun of the Dead (2004, UK)** – The ultimate "rom-zom-com": pub mates vs. zombie apocalypse. Edgar Wright reinvents the zombie film as a romantic comedy, using sharp satire and kinetic editing to balance genuine gore with affectionate parody. Its success proved horror could be self-referential and hilarious without losing emotional weight, cementing it as the blueprint for modern horror-comedy.
- **Tucker & Dale vs. Evil (2010, USA/Canada)** – Hillbillies mistaken for slashers by panicked college kids. Flips slasher conventions on their head, casting two well-meaning hillbillies as the mistaken "killers" while college kids meet grisly accidental deaths. By parodying horror stereotypes with heart and humor, it exposes how much of the genre relies on perspective, turning villains into victims and clichés into comedy.

Deep Cuts

- **Saturday the 14th (1981, USA)** – A haunted-house spoof marketed as "the day after the scariest night of the year." Spoofs the slasher and monster craze of its era, cramming vampires, werewolves, and haunted houses into a deliberately absurd send-up. While never truly scary, its campy humor and parody of genre clichés reflect how deeply horror had permeated pop culture by the early 80s.
- **Vampire's Kiss (1988, USA)** – Nicolas Cage's unhinged descent into vampiric delusion; a comedy by accident and design. Uses the trappings of vampire horror as psychological satire, following Nicolas Cage's unhinged performance as a man who may be turning into a vampire or simply losing his mind. Blurring delusion with gothic excess, the film critiques toxic masculinity and urban alienation while descending into grotesque, darkly comic madness.
- **Idle Hands (1999, USA)** – Blends stoner comedy with supernatural horror, as a teenager's possessed hand embarks on a murderous rampage. Equal parts gory and goofy, the film satirizes slacker culture while reveling in campy practical effects, making possession both absurd and splatter-filled.

- **What We Do in the Shadows (2014, New Zealand)** – Mockumentary of vampire roommates bickering over chores. Transforms the vampire mythos into deadpan mockumentary, following centuries-old bloodsuckers struggling with roommates, chores, and modern life. By grounding the supernatural in mundane absurdities, it lovingly satirizes horror traditions while creating one of the most enduring horror-comedies of the 21st century.
- **WolfCop (2014, Canada)** – A drunk cop becomes a werewolf and still has to file paperwork. Embraces grindhouse camp, following a small-town cop who transforms into a werewolf yet keeps fighting crime, often messily. With its mix of gore, humor, and retro B-movie flair, the film turns lycanthropy into both a grotesque spectacle and a tongue-in-cheek badge of justice.

Critical Essay

"If You're Laughing, Is It Still Horror?"

Myth: Comedy dilutes horror.

Reality: It often heightens it. By disarming the audience with humor, horror-comedy primes them for sharper scares (think *An American Werewolf in London*). Humor also makes taboo subjects palatable: cannibalism in *Eating Raoul*, necromancy in *Re-Animator*, even the end of the world in *Shaun of the Dead*. And in cult contexts (*Rocky Horror*), the laughter isn't a release from fear, it's the creation of a community around it.

Global Spotlight

- **UK – The Cornetto Trilogy (Wright & Pegg).** *Shaun of the Dead (2004), Hot Fuzz (2007), The World's End (2013).* British wit collides with horror tropes, making genre satire its own global export.
- **New Zealand – Deadpan Absurdity.** *What We Do in the Shadows (2014), Housebound (2014).* Kiwi horror-comedy finds laughs in understatement, awkwardness, and domestic chaos alongside bloodshed.
- **USA – Slapstick Splatter.** From Raimi's *Evil Dead II* to *Scary Movie* parodies and *Happy Death Day*, American horror-comedy embraces excess whether it's gore-as-cartoon or satire-as-sledgehammer.

Foundations & Parody Classics

- ☐ **Haunted Spooks** (1920) - After numerous failed attempts to commit suicide, our hero (Lloyd) runs into a lawyer who is looking for a stooge to stand in as a groom in order to secure an inheritance for his client (Davis). The inheritance is a house, which her scheming uncle "haunts" so that he can scare them off and claim the property.
- ☐ **The Gorilla** (1927) - An ape is suspected of committing a series of murders. The film is primarily a spoof of the conventions of "old dark house" films. The original 1927 version was long considered a lost film until a print was rediscovered at the Cineteca Milano in Italy. A restored version was shown at the 2024 San Francisco Silent Film Festival.
  - **ADAPTIONS**
    - ☐ **The Gorilla** (1930) - The first sound remake was produced by First National Pictures. The plot was reportedly closer to the original stage play and featured Walter Pidgeon in a different role.
    - ☐ **The Gorilla** (1939) - The most well-known remake was directed by Allan Dwan and starred the Ritz Brothers and horror legend Bela Lugosi. This version was a classic horror-comedy and spoofed many of the conventions of the genre.

- ☐ **The Cat and the Canary** (1927) - Relatives of an eccentric millionaire gather in his spooky mansion on the 20th anniversary of his death for the reading of his will.

- ☐ **The Ghost Breakers** (1940) – Starring Bob Hope. A radio broadcaster, his quaking manservant and an heiress investigate the mystery of a haunted castle in Cuba. Based on the stage play of the same name by Paul Dickey and Charles W. Goddard. The film has been influential on later horror-comedies. Dan Aykroyd has stated that the classic Hollywood horror-comedy films, including *The Ghost Breakers*, were an inspiration for his idea to combine comedy with the paranormal in his film *Ghostbusters*.
  - • **ADAPTIONS**
    - ☐ **The Ghost Breaker** (1914) - A silent film adaptation directed by Cecil B. DeMille.
    - ☐ **The Ghost Breaker** (1922) - Another silent version directed by Alfred E. Green.
    - ☐ **Scared Stiff** (1953) - Director George Marshall remade his own 1940 film with Dean Martin and Jerry Lewis in the lead roles. Bob Hope and Bing Crosby made cameo appearances.
- ☐ **Hold that Ghost** (1941) – Starring Abbott and Costello. After inheriting a fortune from a gangster, two dim-witted service station attendants find themselves stranded in a haunted house.
  - • **ABBOTT AND COSTELLO SPOOFS**
    - ☐ **The Time of their Lives** (1946) - A psychiatrist stays in a mansion haunted by prankish ghosts from the Revolutionary War.
    - ☐ **Abbott and Costello Meet Frankenstein** (1948) – Legendary comedians face Dracula, Wolf Man, and Frankenstein.
    - ☐ **Abbott and Costello Meet the Killer, Boris Karloff** (1949) - The duo becomes entangled in a murder mystery at a resort run by a sinister hypnotist played by Boris Karloff.
    - ☐ **Abbott and Costello Meet the Invisible Man** (1951) - This was a semi-remake of *The Invisible Man Returns*, using the invisible formula as a backdrop for a murder mystery comedy.
    - ☐ **Abbott and Costello Meet Dr. Jekyll and Mr. Hyde** (1953) - The duo travels to London and runs into the notorious Dr. Jekyll and his murderous alter ego.
    - ☐ **Abbott and Costello Meet the Mummy** (1955) - In their final film for Universal, they travel to Egypt to recover a cursed medallion and encounter a revived mummy.
- ☐ **Francis in the Haunted House** (1956) – Starring Mickey Rooney. Francis the Talking Mule witnesses a murder. He takes a bumbling reporter named David Prescott under his wing and the two of them set out to solve the crime.
- ☐ **The Comedy of Terrors** (1963) - Dishonest undertaker Waldo Trumbull and his sidekick Felix Gillie are creating their own customers when they cannot find willing ones. Starring Vince Price and Boris Karloff.
- ☐ **The Ghost and Mr. Chicken** (1966) - A timid typesetter hasn't a ghost of a chance of becoming a reporter--until he decides to solve a murder mystery and ends up spending a fright-filled night in a haunted house.
  - • **SIMILAR FAMILY FRIENDLY HORRORS**
    - ☐ **The Spirit is Willing** (1967) - A family-friendly haunted house comedy also produced by Universal, this film stars Sid Caesar and was directed by William Castle. It has a similarly light-hearted, ghostly tone.
    - ☐ **Casper** (1995) – Friendly ghost with comic villains.
      - • **SEQUELS**
        - ☐ **Casper: A Spirited Beginning** (1997) - This film is a prequel to the 1995 movie, detailing how Casper became a friendly ghost and met the Ghostly Trio. It is widely regarded as a stand-alone story, as it contradicts some of the plot from the original film.
        - ☐ **Casper Meets Wendy** (1998) - This sequel to *A Spirited Beginning* brings in another comic book character, Wendy the Good Little Witch, played by Hilary Duff in her first major role. Cathy Moriarty, who played the villainess in the 1995 film, also returned in a different role.
        - ☐ **Casper's Haunted Christmas** (2000) - This film is a direct-to-video, computer-animated movie in which Casper must learn to scare someone before Christmas or be banished to the "Dark."
    - ☐ **Nightbooks** (2021) - Alex, a boy obsessed with scary stories, is imprisoned by an evil young witch in her contemporary New York City apartment.

- **Schlock (Banana Monster)** (1973) - A small town is terrorized by "The Banana Killer," which turns out to be the missing link between man and ape.
  - **SIMILAR MOVIES**
    - **The Kentucky Fried Movie** (1977) - An anthology film that features several comedic sketches, including some that parody monster and horror films. It was produced by David Zucker, Jim Abrahams, and Jerry Zucker, who were known for their comedy.
- **The Rocky Horror Picture Show** (1975) – A newly-engaged couple have a breakdown in an isolated area and must seek shelter at the bizarre residence of Dr. Frank-n-Furter. Tim Curry's Frank-N-Furter was his stage role before the film and he wore the original corset from the play.
  - **ADAPTIONS**
    - **Shock Treatment** (1981) - This film, directed by Jim Sharman and co-written by Richard O'Brien, was billed as "not a sequel... not a prequel... but an equal". It is a standalone story that features Brad and Janet, though played by different actors, navigating a surreal TV network in their hometown of Denton. It is not considered a true sequel by most fans, and O'Brien has been critical of it.
    - **The Rocky Horror Picture Show: Let's Do the Time Warp Again** (2016) - It used the original script and songs but was framed by a modern audience watching the movie in a theater.
  - **SIMILAR HORROR MUSICALS**
    - **Little Shop of Horrors** (1986) – Musical comedy of man-eating plant Audrey II.
      - **ADAPTIONS**
        - **The Little Shop of Horrors** (1960) - The story was first told in the low-budget Roger Corman film *The Little Shop of Horrors*.
    - **The Happiness of the Katakuris** (2001, Japan) - A farcical horror-comedy musical. A family moves to the country to run a rustic mountain inn when, to their horror, the customers begin befalling sudden and unlikely fates.
    - **Repo! The Genetic Opera** (2008) - A worldwide epidemic encourages a biotech company to launch an organ-financing program similar in nature to a standard car loan. The repossession clause is a killer, however.
    - **The Devil's Carnival** (2012) - This musical follows three dead souls who are sent to a carnival-themed hell and are forced to face their mortal sins.
    - **Stage Fright** (2014) - A slasher-musical about a theater camp terrorized by a masked killer who has a vendetta against musical theater.
    - **Anna and the Apocalypse** (2017) – Christmas zombie musical.
    - **The Guy Who Didn't Like Musicals** (2018) - From the internet theater company Team StarKid, this musical is about a man in a small town who must survive a sudden outbreak of singing and dancing, with a sinister alien threat behind it.
- **Attack of the Killer Tomatoes** (1978) – Sentient tomatoes attack humanity.
  - **SEQUELS**
    - **Return of the Killer Tomatoes** (1988) – Sequel amps up the absurdity. Crazy old Professor Gangreen has developed a way to make tomatoes look human for a second invasion.
    - **Return of the Killer Tomatoes III: Killer Tomatoes Strike Back!** (1990) – Third entry goes full parody.
    - **Return of the Killer Tomatoes IV: Killer Tomatoes Eat France!** (1991) – Franchise finale.
    - **Attack of the Killer Tomatoes: Organic Intelligence** (2025) - he fifth film in the franchise is scheduled for release in 2025. Original creator Costa Dillon serves as an executive producer.
- **Student Bodies** (1981) – Meta-slasher spoof decades before Scream.

- **Saturday the 14th** (1981) – A family inherits an old mansion which houses the dangerous 'Book of Evil' that has all the monsters of the world trapped inside it.
  - **SEQUELS**
    - **Saturday the 14th Strikes Back** (1988) - The sequel features a different family moving into a haunted house, where they unleash a new set of monsters. Like the first film, it is a parody of the horror genre, specifically classic monster movies and 1950s sci-fi films.
- **Creepshow** (1982) - Five grisly tales from a kid's comic book about a murdered father rising from his grave, a bizarre meteor, a vengeful husband, a mysterious crate's occupant, and a plague of cockroaches. Adapted from several short stories by Stephen King and heavily inspired by the EC horror comics of the 1950s. A comic book adaptation of the film was also released in 1982.
  - **SEQUELS**
    - **Creepshow 2** (1987) - The first official sequel, directed by Michael Gornick and with a screenplay by George A. Romero based on stories by Stephen King. It includes three stories: "Old Chief Wood'nhead," "The Raft," and "The Hitchhiker."
    - **Creepshow 3** (2006) - An unofficial sequel made without the involvement of Romero or King. This second sequel to Creepshow (1982) features five new tales of horror: "Alice," "The Radio," "Call Girl," "The Professor's Wife," and "Haunted Dog." This critically panned anthology featured new stories and characters.
    - **Tales from the Dark Side – The Movie** (1990) - To stall a witch plotting to eat him, a boy reads her horror tales dealing with a collegian's resurrection of a mummy, a murderous cat, and an artist's pact with a gargoyle. The film is a spin-off of the anthology television series of the same name, which was created by George A. Romero. Since *Creepshow 3* (2006) did not include any of the original creative team, many fans and effects artist Tom Savini consider *Tales from the Darkside: The Movie* the unofficial *Creepshow 3*. Directed by Romero and based on stories by Stephen King, among others, it continues the same EC Comics anthology style.
  - **SIMILAR FILMS**
    - **The Uncanny** (1977) - Wilbur Gray, a horror writer, has stumbled upon a terrible secret, that cats are supernatural creatures who really call the shots. In a desperate attempt to get others to believe him, Wilbur spews three tales of feline horror.
    - **The Monster Club** (1981) - A horror writer is summoned to a "monster club" by an enigmatic elder. There, three macabre tales unfold before him, interspersed with musical interludes. The convergence of storytelling and performance creates an eerie atmosphere. A later anthology film that has a more comedic, campy tone similar to the final story in *Cat's Eye*.
    - **Cat's Eye** (1985) - A stray cat guides us through each tale in this Stephen King-based anthology horror film. These stories are adapted from King's 1978 collection *Night Shift*.
    - **Body Bags** (1993) – An anthology hosted horror movie with John Carpenter as "The Coroner," who spent three hours in the make-up chair for his role as The Coroner.
    - **Tales from the Hood** (1995) - A funeral director tells four strange tales of horror with an African American focus to three drug dealers he traps in his place of business.
      - **SEQUELS**
        - **Tales from the Hood 2** (2018) - Released straight to video, this sequel brings back the wraparound story's undertaker, Mr. Simms (Keith David). The anthology follows new characters and tackles new social issues with supernatural twists.
        - **Tales from the Hood 3** (2020) - Also a straight-to-video release, this film continues the tradition of linking horror stories with a grim wraparound narrative. The themes explored are similar, with tales focusing on topics like greedy real estate, racism, and domestic violence.
    - **Trick 'r Treat** (2007) - A horror anthology that intertwines four stories on Halloween night, with a shared theme and supernatural atmosphere.
    - **Tales of Halloween** (2015) - A more recent horror anthology, this film features segments by multiple directors, all centered around Halloween.

- **Strangler vs. Strangler** (1984, Yugoslavia) - A mentally-disturbed flower seller starts killing young girls on the streets of Belgrade. While the frustrated police inspector is trying to stop him, an aspiring musician finds his life and work deeply intertwined with that of a killer.
  - **SIMILAR DARK COMEDIES**
    - **Man Bites Dog** (1992) - This dark, mockumentary-style film similarly explores the media's obsession with a serial killer, blurring the line between comedy and horrifying violence.
- **Ghostbusters** (1984) - Three parapsychologists forced out of their university funding set up shop as a unique ghost removal service in New York City, attracting frightened yet skeptical customers. When Louis Tully mingles with his party guests (commenting on the price of the salmon, and so on), the scene is one continuous shot, and almost entirely improvised. Opening titles give the name of the movie as "Ghost Busters" (two words). But in nearly all media/ads and even packaging/casing for home video releases, it is spelled as "Ghostbusters" (one word).
  - **ADAPTIONS & SEQUELS**
    - **Ghostbusters II** (1989) - The original cast returns five years later to find their ghost-catching business shuttered. They must team up again to stop a river of supernatural slime that is threatening to destroy New York City.
    - **Ghostbusters** (2016) - A timeline reboot featuring a new all-female team of paranormal investigators. The original cast members make cameo appearances as new characters.
    - **Ghostbusters: Afterlife** (2021) - A direct sequel to the 1984 and 1989 films, this movie moves the action to Oklahoma, where the estranged family of the late Egon Spengler discovers their supernatural heritage.
    - **Ghostbusters: Frozen Empire** (2024) - The Spengler family returns to the iconic New York City firehouse to join the original Ghostbusters in battling an ancient evil that threatens a new ice age
- **Trick or Treat** (1986) - A bullied teenage boy is devastated after the death of his heavy metal idol, Sammi Curr. But as Halloween night approaches, he discovers that he may be the only one who can stop Sammi from making a Satanic comeback from beyond the grave.
  - **SIMILAR THEMES**
    - **Rock'n'Roll Nightmare** (1987) - A low-budget Canadian horror film about a heavy metal band recording an album in a secluded farmhouse where they are terrorized by demons.
    - **Black Roses** (1988) - This film similarly features a heavy metal band with a sinister, otherworldly agenda that turns a town's teenagers against their parents.
- **Class of Nuke 'Em High** (1986) - The pupils at a high school next to a nuclear power plant start acting and looking strange after buying contaminated drugs from a plant worker.
  - **SEQUELS**
    - **Class of Nuke 'Em High 2: Subhumanoid Meltdown** (1991) - The sequel is largely unrelated to the original film, with a new cast and storyline centered on a college's shady nuclear facility.
    - **Class of Nuke 'Em High 3: The Good, the Bad and the Subhumanoid** (1994) – This third installment continues the storyline from the second film. Taking place after the events of part two, where Roger Smith's twin sons Adlai and Dick are born; one of them is suddenly kidnapped and taught to be evil while Adlai is determined to foil the fiendish plot and save Tromaville.
    - **Return to Nuke 'Em High Volume I** (2013) - Co-directed by Lloyd Kaufman, this film is a more direct sequel/remake of the original. It features a new group of students at Tromaville High who must face off against the mutant "Cretins."
    - **Return to Return to Nuke 'Em High AKA Volume 2** (2017) - This completes the story from the 2013 film.
  - **THE TROMAVERSE:** The shared cinematic universe of Troma Entertainment, the cult indie studio founded in 1974 by Lloyd Kaufman and Michael Herz. Defined by ultra-low budgets, gleefully offensive humor, and punk DIY energy, Troma built a following through splatter gore, absurd comedy, and satire targeting consumerism, pollution, and authority. Its interconnected world of mutants, toxic avengers, and misfit heroes is tied together by recurring characters and crossovers, with *The Toxic Avenger* as its central icon.
    - **Mother's Day** (1980) - A more serious horror film (directed by Lloyd Kaufman's brother, Charles Kaufman) about a demented mother who forces her sons to abduct and brutalize women.

☐ **The Toxic Avenger** (1984) – Troma's mutant janitor splatters punks.

- **SEQUELS & ADAPTIONS**
  - ☐ **The Toxic Avenger Part II** (1989) – In this sequel, Toxie travels to Tokyo to find his father, leaving Tromaville vulnerable to attack from an evil corporation.
  - ☐ **The Toxic Avenger Part III: The Last Temptation of Toxie** (1989) - Filmed concurrently with *Part II* due to an abundance of footage, this film sees Toxie fighting evil after being corrupted by a deal with a villainous corporation. A reconstructed edit of *Part II* and *Part III* was released in 2025 under the title *Mr. Melvin*.
  - ☐ **Citizen Toxie: The Toxic Avenger IV** (2000) - A third, more independent sequel features Toxie facing an evil, alternate-universe version of himself, the Noxious Offender.
  - ☐ **The Toxic Avenger** (2024) - A modern reimagining of the original film, this remake was directed by Macon Blair and stars Peter Dinklage as Winston Gooze, the new Toxic Avenger. It was produced by Legendary Pictures with the original's directors, Lloyd Kaufman and Michael Herz, as producers. The film premiered in 2023 and received a theatrical release in the US on August 29, 2025.

☐ **Redneck Zombies** (1989) – Troma's shot-on-video trash zombie cult gem. When a barrel of toxic waste poisons a moonshine still, it turns local rednecks into flesh-eating zombies.

☐ **Troma's War** (1988) - A satire of 1980s action films in which a group of everyday people must fight against terrorists plotting to overthrow the U.S. government.

☐ **Sgt. Kabukiman N.Y.P.D** (1990) - Another Troma superhero film following a bumbling New York detective who gains mystical powers.

☐ **Cannibal! The Musical** (1993) - An early film from *South Park* creators Trey Parker and Matt Stone, which Troma helped to distribute.

☐ **Tromeo and Juliet** (1996) - A twisted, irreverent, and gore-filled adaptation of Shakespeare's classic play.

☐ **Terror Firmer** (1999) - A meta-slasher film set on the set of a Troma movie, where the cast and crew are targeted by a serial killer.

☐ **Poultrygeist: Night of the Chicken Dead** (2006) - A musical horror comedy about a fast-food chicken restaurant built on an ancient Native American burial ground.

☐ **Elvira: Mistress of the Dark** (1988) – Camp icon inherits a haunted house.

- **SEQUELS**
  - ☐ **Elvira's Haunted Hills** (2001) - The story is set in 1851 Carpathia, with Elvira and her maid passing through a mysterious castle on their way to Paris.

☐ **Leprechaun** (1993) - A malevolent and murderous leprechaun goes on a rampage in North Dakota to reclaim his stolen pot of gold, killing anyone who stands in his way. As of 2024, a new reboot is in development with a new creative team and direction.

- **SEQUELS**
  - ☐ **Leprechaun 2** (1994) - The leprechaun (Warwick Davis) travels to modern-day Los Angeles in search of a new bride after his last attempt was thwarted 1,000 years prior.
  - ☐ **Leprechaun 3** (1995) - The leprechaun is accidentally freed from a statue in a Las Vegas pawn shop, causing mayhem in his quest to find a wish-granting gold coin.
  - ☐ **Leprechaun 4: In Space** (1997) - Set in the future, the leprechaun stalks and kills a group of space marines while trying to claim a space princess as his bride.
  - ☐ **Leprechaun in the Hood** (2000) - After being freed from a stone statue, the leprechaun wreaks havoc on a group of aspiring rappers in Compton, California.
  - ☐ **Leprechaun: Back 2 tha Hood** (2003) - The leprechaun returns to the hood, and a young woman and her friends who stole his gold must fight for their lives.
  - ☐ **Leprechaun: Origins** (2014) - A reboot of the franchise, starring Dylan Postl as the leprechaun, with a more serious and conventional monster horror approach.
  - ☐ **Leprechaun Returns** (2018) - A direct sequel to the original film, which ignores the other films in the series and features the leprechaun returning to terrorize a sorority.

- **Scary Movie** (2000) – Spoof of *Scream* and 90s slashers. The new *Scary Movie*, which will be the sixth film in the series, is scheduled for a June 12, 2026 theatrical release.
  - **SEQUELS**
    - **Scary Movie 2** (2001) – Haunted house parody.
    - **Scary Movie 3** (2003) – *Aliens*, *The Ring*, and *Signs* spoofed.
    - **Scary Movie 4** (2006) – *War of the Worlds* and *Saw* spoofed.
    - **Scary Movie 5** (2013) – *Paranormal Activity* spoof.
  - **ADAPTIONS**
    - **Date Movie** (2006): Spoofs romantic comedies.
    - **Epic Movie** (2007): Parodies fantasy adventure films.
    - **Meet the Spartans** (2008): Pokes fun at the historical fantasy film *300*.
- **Shriek If You Know What I Did Last Friday the 13th** (2000) – Another slasher parody. A reporter investigates a series of murders, dubbed the Spring Break Massacre, which leads to further mayhem.

80s Camp & Cult Horror-Comedy

- **Ghoulies** (1985) – Toilet-dwelling creatures terrorize partygoers. The *Ghoulies* series is often mistakenly seen as a rip-off of *Gremlins*. The original *Ghoulies* was in production at the same time and was intended for an earlier release, but funding issues allowed *Gremlins* to hit theaters first. In March 2024, the original creators announced a new trilogy of *Ghoulies* films.
  - **SEQUELS**
    - **Ghoulies II** (1988) – Ghoulies invade a carnival funhouse.
    - **Ghoulies III: Ghoulies Go to College** (1991) - The creatures are summoned to a college campus, where their mayhem is initially dismissed as pranks.
    - **Ghoulies 4** (1994) - The final installment of the original run brings back the protagonist from the first film, now a police officer, to battle the demons once again.
- **Spookies** (1986) – Haunted mansion filled with bizarre comedic monsters. A wicked sorcerer tries to sacrifice a group of people inside his house with the intention of using their vitality to keep his wife alive.
- **House** (1986) – Vietnam vet's haunted house is surreal comedy-horror. A reboot of the *House* franchise is reportedly in development.
  - **SEQUELS**
    - **House II: The Second Story** (1987) – Bizarre comedic fantasy-horror sequel.
    - **House III: The Horror Show** (1989) – Serial killer returns from the dead.
    - **House IV: The Repossession** (1992) – Final haunted house comedy entry.
- **The Witches of Eastwick** (1987) - Three bored single women in a small New England town discover they have supernatural powers after they all unwittingly summon a charismatic and mysterious stranger who unleashes their hidden potential and dark desires. The film was adapted from John Updike's 1984 novel of the same name. Two different television series have been adapted including one starring Rebecca Romijn, as well as another reboot in development.
- **Beetlejuice** (1988) – The spirits of a deceased couple are harassed by an unbearable family that has moved into their home, and hire a malicious spirit to drive them out. Michael Keaton improvised much of Beetlejuice's manic dialogue; he's only in the film for 17 minutes but dominates pop culture memory. Won Best Makeup at the 1989 Academy Awards. Following the commercial success of the 2024 film, Warner Bros. officially confirmed a third movie is in the works. The tentative release window is around 2027.
  - **SEQUELS**
    - **Beetlejuice Beetlejuice** (2024) - After decades of development, this sequel was released, with Michael Keaton, Winona Ryder, and Catherine O'Hara all reprising their original roles. The plot features Lydia Deetz returning to Winter River with her teenage daughter, Astrid.
- **Spontaneous Combustion** (1990) – Tobe Hooper's oddball fiery horror-comedy. A young man finds out that his parents had been used in an atomic-weapons experiment shortly before he was born, and that the results have had some unexpected effects on him.
- **The People Under the Stairs** (1991) - When Fool breaks into the home of his family's landlords, he discovers that they have mutilated several boys and kept them imprisoned under stairs. As Fool attempts to flee, he meets their daughter, Alice. Can Fool and Alice escape?

- [ ] **The Addams Family** (1991) –Con artists plan to fleece an eccentric family using an accomplice who claims to be their long-lost uncle. Nominated for Best Costume Design at the Academy Awards.
  - **SEQUELS**
    - [ ] **Addams Family Values** (1993) – Even funnier, darker sequel. The Addams Family try to rescue their beloved Uncle Fester from his gold-digging new love, a black widow named Debbie.
    - [ ] **Addams Family Reunion** (1998) - This direct-to-video film was a standalone reboot, starring Tim Curry and Daryl Hannah, and served as a pilot for *The New Addams Family* series.
- [ ] **Death Becomes Her** (1992) – Immortality potion brings slapstick dismemberment. When a fading actress learns of an immortality treatment, she sees it as a way to outdo her long-time rival. The film won an Academy Award for Best Visual Effects for its groundbreaking use of computer-generated imagery.
- [ ] **Hocus Pocus** (1993) – Disney witch comedy with cult following. After the success of the 2022 sequel, Disney confirmed a third film is in development. The original cast members have expressed interest, but talks have been slow. The story is still in the planning stages.
  - **SEQUELS**
    - [ ] **Hocus Pocus 2** (2022) - Released 29 years after the original, this sequel brings back the Sanderson sisters after they are summoned by three high school students. The movie became a huge streaming success on Disney+.
- [ ] **Tucker & Dale vs. Evil** (2010) – Affable hillbillies Tucker and Dale are on vacation at their dilapidated mountain cabin when they are mistaken for murderers by a group of preppy college students. Every "kill" is really an accident. A satire of slasher logic flipped inside out.
  - **SIMILAR FILMS**
    - [ ] **Vicious Fun** (2020, Canada) - Joel, a caustic 1980s film critic for a national horror magazine, finds himself unwittingly trapped in a self-help group for serial killers. With no other choice, Joel attempts to blend in or risk becoming the next victim.
- [ ] **Frankenweenie** (2012) – Feature-length animated version.
- [ ] **A Haunted House** (2013) – Spoofs *Paranormal Activity.*
  - **SEQUELS**
    - [ ] **A Haunted House 2** (2014) – Found-footage parody sequel.

2000s–2010s Horror-Comedy Resurgence

- [ ] **Bubba Ho-Tep** (2002) - When residents of their nursing home start dying of dubious causes, an aged Elvis and an African-American senior who claims to be President John F. Kennedy discover that the perpetrator is an Egyptian mummy with murderous intentions.
- [ ] **Monster Man** (2003) - Two guys and a female hitchhiker are terrorized by a monstrous looking man driving a giant monster truck. The film draws heavily from other horror and action movies, including *Jeepers Creepers*, *Duel*, and *The Texas Chain Saw Massacre*.
- [ ] **Shaun of the Dead** (2004) – The uneventful, aimless lives of a London electronics salesman and his layabout roommate are disrupted by the zombie apocalypse. George A. Romero loved it so much he gave Edgar Wright a cameo in *Land of the Dead*.
  - **THE CORNETTO TRILOGY**
    - [ ] **Hot Fuzz** (2007) – Action-horror hybrid with cult conspiracies.
    - [ ] **The World's End** (2013) – Alien invasion meets pub crawl comedy.
  - **ADAPTIONS**
    - [ ] **Juan of the Dead** (2011, Cuba) – Satirical zombie apocalypse in Havana.
- [ ] **Black Sheep** (2006) - An experiment in genetic engineering turns harmless sheep into bloodthirsty killers that terrorize a sprawling New Zealand farm.
  - **KILLER CUTE ANIMALS**
    - [ ] **Zombeavers** (2014) - A spoof film about zombie beavers attacking a group of college students in a secluded cabin.
    - [ ] **Cocaine Bear** (2023) - A black comedy-horror about a real-life American black bear who goes on a murderous rampage after ingesting a large amount of cocaine.

- ☐ **Dead Snow** (2009, Norway) – A ski vacation turns horrific for a group of medical students, as they find themselves confronted by an unimaginable menace: Nazi zombies.
  - • **SEQUELS**
    - ☐ **Dead Snow 2: Red vs. Dead** (2014) – Zombie Nazis vs. zombie Russians.
- ☐ **My Super Psycho Sweet 16** (2009) - A spoiled teen's birthday bash turns killer after she convinces her parents to re-open a roller-skating rink where murders took place.
- ☐ **Cooties** (2014) – Teachers vs. zombie-infected schoolkids. Starring Elijah Wood and Rainn Willson. A mysterious virus hits an isolated elementary school, transforming the kids into a feral swarm of mass savages. An unlikely hero must lead a motley band of teachers in the fight of their lives.
- ☐ **Summer of Blood** (2014) - In this critically acclaimed comedy, an emotionally stunted New Yorker's miserable love life turns around when he meets a deadbeat vampire and becomes a blood-sucker himself.
- ☐ **Housebound** (2014, New Zealand) – House arrest + haunted house comedy.
- ☐ **The Voices** (2014) – Starring Ryan Reynolds. A likable guy pursues his office crush with help from his evil talking pets, but things turn sinister when she stands him up for a date.
- ☐ **Scouts Guide to the Zombie Apocalypse** (2015) – Boy Scouts battle zombies.
- ☐ **The Love Witch** (2016) - A modern-day witch uses spells and magic to get men to fall in love with her, with deadly consequences. The film is a loving homage to 1960s Technicolor horror, melodramas, and exploitation films. The aesthetic, cinematography, and dialogue were all meticulously designed to capture the feel of classic Hollywood.
- ☐ **The Babysitter** (2017) – Teen discovers his babysitter leads a cult.
  - • **SEQUELS**
    - ☐ **The Babysitter: Killer Queen** (2020) – Sequel amps up camp.
- ☐ **Little Evil** (2017) – Stepfather suspects his stepson is the Antichrist.
- ☐ **Mom and Dad** (2017) – Starring Nicolas Cage and Selma Blair. A teenage girl and her younger brother must survive a wild 24 hours during which a mass hysteria of unknown origin causes parents to turn violently on their own kids.
- ☐ **Scary Stories to Tell in the Dark** (2019) – Youthful dark humor mixed with horror.
- ☐ **Ready or Not** (2019) – Bride hunted by in-laws in deadly hide-and-seek.
  - • **SEQUELS**
    - ☐ **Ready or Not 2: Here I Come** (2026) - The sequel will expand upon the first film's mythology.
- ☐ **Extra Ordinary** (2019, Ireland) – Driving instructor with paranormal talents faces cult.

Recent Horror-Comedy & Global Cult Favorites

- ☐ **Night of the Comet** (1984) – Valley girls survive apocalyptic comet.
- ☐ **Chopping Mall** (1986) – Security robots kill mall teens with lasers.
- ☐ **Stitches** (2012, Ireland) – Zombie clown kills kids at birthday party.
- ☐ **30 Nights of Paranormal Activity with the Devil Inside the Girl with the Dragon Tattoo** (2013) - After a stint in a psychiatric hospital, a young woman returns to the house where her father killed the entire cast of The Artist during his exorcism.
- ☐ **Suburban Gothic** (2014) – Camp ghost story with snarky protagonist.
  - • **SIMILAR THEMES**
    - ☐ **Excision** (2012) - Bates's directorial debut shares a similarly dark and satirical tone.
    - ☐ **Trash Fire** (2016) - This black comedy follows a couple dealing with their twisted past.
    - ☐ **Tone-Deaf** (2019) - Also starring Matthew Gray Gubler, this horror-comedy explores themes of social and political commentary.
    - ☐ **Life After Beth** (2014) - A rom-zom-com released the same year, exploring similar themes of dead-end suburban life and the undead.
- ☐ **WolfCop** (2014) – Werewolf cop fights crime with campy gore. As a series of strange and violent events begin to occur, an alcoholic policeman realizes that he has been turned into a werewolf as part of a larger plan.
  - • **SEQUELS**
    - ☐ **Another WolfCop** (2017) – Sequel amps up absurdity. Alcoholic werewolf cop Lou Garou springs into action when an eccentric businessman with evil intentions seduces Woodhaven's residents with a new brewery and hockey team in this outrageous horror-comedy sequel.

- ☐ **Freaks of Nature** (2015) - In the town of Dillford, humans, vampires and zombies were all living in peace - until the alien apocalypse arrived. Now three teenagers - one human, one vampire, and one zombie - have to team up to figure out how to get rid of the visitors.
- ☐ **The Belko Experiment** (2016) - In a twisted social experiment, eighty Americans are locked in their high-rise corporate office in Bogotá, Colombia, and ordered by an unknown voice coming from the company's intercom system to participate in a deadly game of kill or be killed.
  - • **OTHER SURVIVAL GAMES**
    - ☐ **Battle Royale** (2000, Japan) - In the future, the Japanese government captures a class of ninth-grade students and forces them to kill one another under the revolutionary "Battle Royale" act.
    - ☐ **13: Game of Death** (2006, Thailand) – Based on the 1999 comic book *The 13th Quiz Show* by Eakasit Thairatana. After losing his job, his car and his money, Phuchit, Krissada Sukosol, races against time to complete 13 tasks ordered by an anonymous caller who promised 100,000,000 Thai Baht upon completion.
      - • **REMAKE**
        - ☐ **13 Sins** (2014) - A cryptic phone call sets off a dangerous game of risks for Elliot, a down-on-his-luck salesman. The game promises increasing rewards for completing 13 tasks, each more sinister than the last.
    - ☐ **The Tournament** (2009) - In this film, a group of the world's most dangerous assassins compete in a free-for-all death match held in a single city.
    - ☐ **Would You Rather** (2012) - A group of people at a dinner party must play a deadly game of "would you rather."
    - ☐ **As the Gods Will** (2014, Japan) - Directed by Takashi Miike, this Japanese film features a high school setting where students are forced to play bizarre, deadly children's games.
    - ☐ **Circle** (2015) - A psychological take on the genre, in which 50 strangers wake up in a room and must vote for who among them should be killed every two minutes.
    - ☐ **Most Beautiful Island** (2017) - Most Beautiful Island is a chilling portrait of an undocumented young woman's struggle for survival as she finds redemption from a tortured past in a dangerous game.
    - ☐ **Bodies Bodies Bodies** (2022) - A party game at a remote family mansion during a hurricane turns deadly for a group of wealthy 20-somethings.
- ☐ **Mayhem** (2017) – Office tower infected with rage virus.
- ☐ **Office Uprising** (2018) – Corporate energy drink turns employees psychotic.
- ☐ **DeadTectives** (2018) – Fake ghost-hunters encounter real hauntings.
- ☐ **The VelociPastor** (2018) – Pastor turns into dinosaur to fight ninjas.
  - • **SEQUELS**
    - ☐ **The VelociPastor 2** (2025) - The sequel follows Father Doug Jones and his sidekick Carol as they travel to Milan to solve a string of murders committed by a masked slasher. The plot will also involve Soviet spies and Interpol.
- ☐ **Scare Package** (2019) – Anthology of horror-comedy shorts.
  - • **SEQUELS**
    - ☐ **Scare Package II: Rad Chad's Revenge** (2022) - The sequel follows the survivors of the first film as they attend the funeral of their friend and horror aficionado, "Rad Chad" Buckley. A mysterious figure traps the mourners in a series of deadly games, forcing them to use the "rules of horror" to survive.
- ☐ **Villains** (2019) – Burglars trapped in home of eccentric killers.
- ☐ **Bloody Hell** (2020, Australia) – Man trapped with cannibal family uses wit to survive.
- ☐ **Scare Me** (2020) - During a power outage, two strangers tell scary stories. The more Fred and Fanny commit to their tales, the more the stories come to life in their Catskills cabin. The horrors of reality manifest when Fred confronts his ultimate fear.
- ☐ **Sweetie, You Won't Believe It** (2020, Kazakhstan) - Dastan can no longer stand the constant nagging of his highly pregnant wife and decides to run away for at least one day with his friends. The men go fishing, which would have gone smoothly, if not for a series of unforeseen events.

- ☐ **Werewolves Within** (2021) - A new awkward park ranger arrives in a small town, and murder and havoc soon follows. The paranoid townsfolk soon suspect each other, but a devious, shapeshifting werewolf becomes their prime suspect. But who is it?
- ☐ **The Blackening** (2022) - Seven friends go away for the weekend and end up trapped in a cabin with a killer who has a vendetta. Will their street smarts and knowledge of horror movies help them stay alive? Probably not.
- ☐ **Fresh** (2022) - After quitting dating apps, a woman meets the supposedly perfect man and accepts his invitation to a romantic weekend getaway, only to find that her new paramour has been hiding some unusual appetites.
- ☐ **Flux Gourmet** (2022, UK) - Set at an institute devoted to culinary and alimentary performance, a collective finds themselves embroiled in power struggles, artistic vendettas, and gastrointestinal disorders.
- ☐ **The Coffee Table** (2022, Spain) - Jesus and Maria are a couple going through a difficult time in their relationship. Nevertheless, they have just become parents. To shape their new life, they decide to buy a new coffee table. A decision that will change their existence.
- ☐ **Good Boy** (2025) - A loyal dog moves to a rural family home with his owner, only to discover supernatural forces lurking in the shadows. As dark entities threaten his human companion, the brave pup must fight to protect the one he loves most.

Horror-Comedy Pairing Night

Horror-comedy works best with friends, drinks, and the kind of audience that *wants* to shout at the screen. Here's a ready-made marathon to turn your living room into a midnight movie theater.

The Smart Starter

Shaun of the Dead (2004). *What to look for:* Watch how Edgar Wright edits jokes and scares with the same rhythm: quick cuts, sound cues, and visual gags timed like jump scares. *Quick flex fact:* Romero himself gave Wright and Pegg cameos in *Land of the Dead*.

The Camp Classic

The Rocky Horror Picture Show (1975). *What to look for:* Audience participation: this is a cult film because fans *perform* it. Listen for double entendres, and note how parody flips into sincerity during the ballads. *Quick flex fact:* The "Time Warp" wasn't in the original stage play, it was added to pad the runtime.

The Gore Gag

Evil Dead II (1987). *What to look for:* How Raimi uses slapstick camera tricks (Dutch tilts, POV zooms, wild pans) to make gore funny instead of just grotesque. *Quick flex fact:* Raimi's "splatstick" style directly influenced *Peter Jackson's* early gore comedies (*Dead Alive*).

The Meta Wink

Tucker & Dale vs. Evil (2010) *What to look for:* Every "kill" is a misunderstanding. Pay attention to how the film parodies *slasher tropes* while still delivering gore. *Quick flex fact:* College kids impaling themselves is a deliberate inversion of Friday the 13th logic: dumb teens aren't victims of killers, but their own panic.

The Midnight Oddball

Idle Hands (1999). *What to look for:* The late-90s stoner/slacker vibe mashed with supernatural possession. It's very much a time capsule. *Quick flex fact:* This is where Jessica Alba got one of her earliest breakout roles. Yes, in a stoner-hand-horror.

Bonus Party Picks (Swap in Depending on Vibe)

- **What We Do in the Shadows (2014):** Mockumentary vampires + deadpan Kiwi humor.
- **Attack of the Killer Tomatoes (1978):** The gold standard of absurd food horror.
- **Beetlejuice (1988):** Only 17 minutes of Keaton, yet pure cult energy.

How to Wet Your Palate:

Start with Shaun to look clever, drop "splatstick" when Evil Dead II rolls, and then seal your cult status by singing along to *Rocky Horror*. By the time Tucker & Dale plays, you'll be the one explaining *meta-horror* before anyone else gets it.

Quick Facts to Sound Like the Smartest Person in the Room

- **The Rocky Horror Picture Show (1975)**. It wasn't just a film, it invented the concept of the "midnight movie." Audience participation, costumes, and call-backs kept it in theaters for *decades*.
- **Waxwork (1988)** Inspired partly by the German silent film *Waxworks* (1924), it plays like an anthology inside a single setting. The museum's exhibits are basically pocket dimensions.
- **Beetlejuice (1988)**. Michael Keaton is only on screen for about 17 minutes, yet he defines the whole film. That's efficiency in chaos.
- **Shaun of the Dead (2004)**. Simon Pegg and Edgar Wright pitched it as a "rom-zom-com" (romantic zombie comedy), coining a term that critics now use for an entire sub-subgenre.
- **Scary Movie (2000)**. Its success was so huge it briefly revived parody cinema in Hollywood. A sixth entry is already slated for 2026. Twenty-six years after the first.
- **Happy Death Day (2017)**. Marketed as "*Groundhog Day* meets *Scream*." Its sequel leaned harder into sci-fi than slasher, proving horror-comedy can stretch into time loop mechanics.
- **Dead Snow (2009, Norway)**. Nazi zombies aren't just a gag: the film riffs on Norway's real WWII occupation history, giving absurd splatter a national trauma undertone.
- **Tucker & Dale vs. Evil (2010)**. A perfect inversion: the "killers" are just hapless hillbillies, while the college kids accidentally kill themselves. Critics call it "the kindest horror movie ever made."
- **Killer Tomatoes (1978)**. The absurdity was deliberate. It was written to be "the worst possible monster movie." Yet it spawned four sequels and a *Saturday morning cartoon*.

Laugh Before You Scream

Serial Killer / Realistic Horror

While slashers turn murder into formula and supernatural tales lean on the unseen, serial killer horror thrives on proximity to real events. These films unsettle not because they show monsters, but because they reveal humans as the true predators. From Ed Gein's grave-robbing to Ted Bundy's manipulations, serial killer cinema translates headlines into nightmares, collapsing the divide between documentary and drama.

Why People Are Drawn to It
Because realism cuts deepest. We watch with morbid fascination: Could this neighbor, this drifter, this lover, be capable of atrocity? Serial killer horror feeds voyeurism and fear, but also functions as cultural processing: explaining crimes, interrogating evil, and testing how far empathy can bend before snapping. It is horror without safety nets: no supernatural force to blame, only ourselves.

Essentials
- **M (1931, Germany)** – Fritz Lang's *M* is a suspenseful thriller that uses the hunt for a child murderer to explore themes of mob justice, vigilantism, mass hysteria, the nature of evil, and the moral ambiguities of punishment. The film's use of sound and German Expressionist visuals create a haunting atmosphere that reflects the anxieties and societal decay of Germany during the Weimar Republic.
- **The Boston Strangler (1968, USA)** –A stark police procedural that dramatizes the Albert DeSalvo case with Tony Curtis delivering a transformative performance far removed from his "pretty boy" image. The film's use of split-screen techniques mirrors the paranoia and disorientation of a city under siege, while critics later compared Curtis's method-style intensity to Robert De Niro's work a decade afterward
- **Henry: Portrait of a Serial Killer (1986, USA)** – Shot with flat lighting and stripped of cinematic cues to deny audiences catharsis. Its unflinching realism, so bleak the MPAA refused it a rating not for gore but for its "tone of moral bleakness" turns the film into a disturbing character study that blurs the line between documentary and nightmare
- **Se7en (1995, USA)** – Fincher's rain-soaked neo-noir where sins become staged tableaux. Each murder staged around the seven deadly sins becomes a grotesque morality play, pushing the detective genre into existential horror. Fincher's meticulous direction and suffocating atmosphere make the film less about catching a killer than confronting the rot of a world where justice itself feels impossible
- **Zodiac (2007, USA)** – Fincher again, reconstructing the case that baffled San Francisco. This chilling docudrama transforms the real-life case into a meditation on obsession, following a cartoonist turned amateur detective consumed by the hunt for the Zodiac Killer. Fincher meticulously recreated 1970s San Francisco, street by street, grounding the film's procedural dread in an almost forensic realism, and turning the act of investigation itself into the true horror

Deep Cuts
- **The Honeymoon Killers (1970, USA)** – A stark, unglamorous depiction of the "Lonely Hearts" murders, following an embittered nurse and her conman lover as they lure and kill women through personal ads. Shot with documentary-like grit and emotional brutality, the film strips away romance and sensationalism, making their toxic codependency as unsettling as the crimes themselves
- **10 Rillington Place (1971, UK)** – A chilling dramatization of British serial killer John Christie, with Richard Attenborough's understated performance capturing the banality of evil. Beyond its true-crime horror, the film carries historic weight: the wrongful execution of Timothy Evans, depicted here, fueled public outrage and helped end capital punishment in the UK.
- **Angst (1983, Austria)** – An Austrian descent into pure psychosis, following a recently released convict on a frenzied killing spree rendered with jittery camerawork and invasive close-ups. Based on the real murderer Werner Kniesek, the film's relentless subjectivity traps viewers inside the killer's manic perspective, making it one of the most disturbing and technically audacious portraits of violence ever filmed.

- **Citizen X (1995, USA/HBO)** – A grim procedural about the years-long hunt for Andrei Chikatilo, the "Butcher of Rostov," who murdered over fifty children and women in Soviet Russia. Stripped of sensationalism, the HBO film focuses on the dogged investigators battling bureaucracy and denial, showing how systemic failures allowed one of history's most prolific killers to thrive
- **Memories of Murder (2003, Korea)** – Bong Joon-ho's poetic retelling of Korea's first serial killer case, blending crime drama, dark comedy, and tragedy into a story of obsession and futility. Its unsettling power lies in how it denies resolution, leaving viewers with the same gnawing uncertainty that haunted investigators until the real killer was identified decades later.

Critical Essay

"Serial Killer Horror Isn't Just Exploitation"

Myth: These films are cheap thrills feeding off tragedy.

Reality: At their best, they interrogate systems and societies. *In Cold Blood* (1967) is about media and empathy. *Se7en* is about moral decay. *Zodiac* becomes a meditation on obsession. Even exploitation fare reflects its time: *The Town That Dreaded Sundown* mirrors 1970s fears of law enforcement's limits, while *River's Edge* channels Gen-X alienation.

Global Spotlight: Korea & Germany

- **Korea**: *Memories of Murder* (2003) and *I Saw the Devil* (2010) turn real cases and revenge cycles into philosophical explorations of justice, fate, and obsession.
- **Germany**: *M* (1931) and *The Golden Glove* (2019) bookend nearly a century. Fritz Lang using expressionism to interrogate mob justice, Fatih Akin exposing the grotesque reality of Fritz Honka's crimes in 1970s Hamburg.

Foundations & True-Crime Inspired Classics

☐ **M** (1931, Germany) – When the police in a German city are unable to catch a child-murderer, other criminals join in the manhunt. This is Fritz Lang's first sound film and before making this, Peter Lorre had mainly been a comedic actor. Contrary to popular belief, Fritz Lang did not change the title from *The Murderers are Among Us* to *M* due to fear of persecution by the Nazis. He changed the title during filming, influenced by the scene where one of the criminals writes the letter on his hand. Lang thought *M* was a more interesting title.

- **ADAPTIONS**
    - ☐ **M** (1951) - An American remake was directed by Joseph Losey. The plot was largely unchanged, but it was reset in Los Angeles. No credit is given to the classic 1931 German production (whic was directed by Fritz Lang and starred Peter Lorre) of which this film is a remake. Lang was very angry about this remake, and was savagely critical of its director, Joseph Losey, although Losey did consult him about the film before agreeing to do it.
    - ☐ **The Black Vampire** (1953, Argentina) - A Latin American version, directed by Román Viñoly Barreto, retells the story in Argentina, making the killer a vampire. This "feminist" reworking focuses on the mothers of children stalked by a deranged pedophile.
- **SIMILAR FILMS & INFLUENCES**
    - ☐ **Tenderness of the Wolves** (1973) - Using his status as a police informant to procure his victims, baby-faced, shaven-headed Fritz Haarmann dismembers their bodies after death and sells the flesh to restaurants, dumping the remainder out of sight. The film is based on the real-life German serial killer Fritz Haarmann, also known as the "Butcher of Hanover" or "the Vampire of Hanover." Director Ulli Lommel and producer Rainer Werner Fassbinder were inspired by Fritz Lang's classic German thriller *M* (1931), which was also influenced by Haarmann's case.
    - ☐ **The Golden Glove** (2019, Germany) – Portrait of Fritz Honka, grotesque barfly killer. A serial killer strikes fear in the hearts of residents of Hamburg during the early 1970s. The film explores Honka's motivations through his pathetic existence, his heavy drinking, and his sexual dysfunction, rather than providing a psychological justification for his crimes. The film is an adaptation of the 2016 novel of the same name by Heinz Strunk. Actor Jonas Dassler portrayed Honka, using heavy makeup to match the serial killer's disfigured appearance.

☐ **In Cold Blood** (1967) – Stark retelling of Clutter family murders. Two ex-cons murder a family in a robbery attempt, before going on the run from the authorities. The police try to piece together the details of the murder in an attempt to track down the killers.

- **ADAPTIONS**
  - ☐ **Capote** (2005) - This film focuses on author Truman Capote's (Philip Seymour Hoffman) experience researching and writing his book, including his complex relationship with killer Perry Smith.
  - ☐ **Infamous** (2006) - Another film exploring Truman Capote's writing process, with Toby Jones as Capote and Daniel Craig as Perry Smith. It also covers the crimes and their investigation.

☐ **The Boston Strangler** (1968) – Tony Curtis as real-life strangler Albert DeSalvo. A series of strangulation murders of Boston women sparks a protracted complex manhunt. Law professor John Bottomley leads a multi-jurisdictional task force in the investigation, with help from surviving victim Diane Cluny. The film uses split-screen techniques to reflect paranoia and disorientation.

- **ADAPTIONS**
  - ☐ **Boston Strangler** (2023) - This Hulu film, starring Keira Knightley and Carrie Coon, centers on the two journalists who first connected the murders. Unlike the 1968 film, it focuses on the media investigation rather than the police procedural.
  - ☐ **The Boston Strangler** (2006) and **Boston Strangler: The Untold Story** (2008) - These are low-budget films that explore the case with a less polished approach. The 2006 film, for instance, raises doubts about DeSalvo's guilt, while the 2008 film also deviates from the straightforward narrative.
  - ☐ **The Strangler** (1964) - This fictional horror film was inspired by the unsolved murders but was not a direct adaptation of the case itself.
  - ☐ **No Way to Treat a Lady** (1968) - Both the 1964 novel and the 1968 film of the same name were inspired by the multiple-killer theories that circulated during the Strangler investigation.
  - ☐ **The Front** (2010) - This TV film suggests that DeSalvo was not the only perpetrator and explores a detective reopening the unsolved case of a woman who may have been the first victim.

☐ **The Honeymoon Killers** (1970) – True story of "Lonely Hearts Killers." An obese, embittered nurse doesn't mind if her toupee-wearing boyfriend romances and fleeces other women, as long as he takes her along on his con jobs.

- **ADAPTIONS OF THE LONELY HEARTS KILLERS:** The "Lonely Hearts Killers" were Raymond Fernández and Martha Beck, a couple who lured victims through personal ads in the 1940s before robbing and, in some cases, murdering them. Fernández used his charm to seduce women seeking companionship, while Beck, fiercely jealous, often accompanied him and ensured control over their victims. Between 1947 and 1949, they are believed to have killed around 20 women across several states, though they were convicted of three murders. Their bizarre, toxic partnership and the sensational trial that followed captivated the public.
  - ☐ **Lonely Hearts** (1991) - A TV movie starring Eric Roberts and Beverly D'Angelo as the killer couple.
  - ☐ **Deep Crimson** (1996, Mexico) - This Mexican-language adaptation, directed by Arturo Ripstein, updates the setting and characters.
  - ☐ **Lonely Hearts** (2006) - Starring Jared Leto and Salma Hayek, with John Travolta and James Gandolfini as the detectives on their trail.
  - ☐ **Alleluia** (2014, Belgium/France) - A French-language film directed by Fabrice Du Welz that modernizes the story.

- ☐ **10 Rillington Place** (1971, UK) – Based on serial killer John Christie. What happened to the women at 10 Rillington Place? The story of British serial killer John Christie, who committed most or all of his crimes in the titular terraced house, and the miscarriage of justice involving Timothy Evans. The crimes of John Christie were so significant that they had a major impact on British law. The wrongful execution of Timothy Evans, who was hanged for a crime committed by Christie, led to a public outcry that contributed to the eventual abolition of capital punishment in the UK.

  - • **ADAPTIONS BASED JOHN CHRISTIE:** John Christie was a British serial killer whose crimes in the 1940s and early 1950s shocked the nation and left a lasting mark on legal history. Living at 10 Rillington Place in London, Christie murdered at least eight women, including his wife, luring many of his victims with false promises of medical help before strangling them. He became infamous not only for the brutality of his acts but also for the miscarriage of justice linked to his case, as Timothy Evans, who lived in the same building, was wrongly convicted and executed for one of the murders Christie committed, and the revelation of Christie's guilt and Evans's innocence played a pivotal role in turning public opinion against the death penalty in the United Kingdom.
    - ☐ **Rillington Place** (2016, UK) - This three-part BBC biographical crime drama mini-series tells the story of the murders from the perspectives of Christie (Tim Roth), his wife Ethel (Samantha Morton), and Timothy Evans (Nico Mirallegro).
    - ☐ **See How They Run** (2022, UK) - A nod to the Christie murders, mentioning the case as the real-life incident police were busy with while a fictional murder mystery took place.
- ☐ **Zodiac Killer** (1971) – Low-budget contemporary exploitation of real case. The Riddler in *The Batman* was explicitly modeled on the Zodiac killer, complete with cryptic messages and symbols. *Dirty Harry,* the critically acclaim Clint Eastwood film, was influenced by the Zodiac Case. Also, in *The Batman* (2022), the Riddler, is an homage to the Zodiac Killer. He uses cryptograms and leaves behind cards to taunt the authorities.
  - • **ADAPTIONS OF THE ZODIAC KILLER:** The Zodiac Killer was an unidentified serial killer who terrorized Northern California in the late 1960s and early 1970s, claiming responsibility for at least five murders but hinting at many more. He became infamous not only for the brutality of his attacks but for the taunting letters, ciphers, and phone calls he sent to newspapers and police, demanding public attention and mocking investigators. His cryptic messages, some of which remain unsolved, cemented his place in true-crime history and inspired decades of speculation, making the Zodiac one of the most notorious uncaught killers of the 20th century.
    - ☐ **Zodiac** (2005) - A different film, also named *The Zodiac*, focused on the impact of the case on a Vallejo detective.
    - ☐ **Zodiac** (2007) – Fincher's meticulous, chilling docudrama. Between 1968 and 1983, a San Francisco cartoonist becomes an amateur detective obsessed with tracking down the Zodiac Killer, an unidentified individual who terrorizes Northern California with a killing spree. Every letter in the film was recreated from actual Zodiac case files, down to the handwriting.
    - ☐ **Curse of the Zodiac** (2007) - Another film directed by Ulli Lommel, this is a very loose and sensationalized retelling of the murders.
    - ☐ **Awakening the Zodiac** (2017) - This film follows a couple who find old film reels of the Zodiac killer's murders and try to track him down for a reward.
  - • **DOCUMENTARIES**
    - ☐ **This is the Zodiac Speaking** (2007) – A documentary that includes interviews with the real-life people involved with the investigation and victims.
    - ☐ **The Hunt for the Zodiac Killer** (2017) - A docuseries that re-examines the evidence in the cold case.

- ☐ **Myth of the Zodiac Killer** (2023) - A Peacock docuseries that explores a controversial theory that there was no single Zodiac Killer.
- ☐ **This is the Zodiac Speaking** (2024) - A Netflix docuseries that also points to Arthur Leigh Allen as the probable killer.

☐ **The Night Stalker** (1972) – An abrasive Las Vegas newspaper reporter investigates a series of murders committed by a vampire. This film predates the Richard Ramirez murders, but arises because Ramirez adopted the nickname given to him by the media. While we are on the subject and in the serial killer chapter…

- • **SERIAL KILLER RICHARD RAMIREZ, WHO WAS KNOWN AS THE NIGHT STALKER:** Richard Ramirez, known as the "Night Stalker," was an American serial killer, rapist, and burglar who terrorized California between 1984 and 1985. His crimes were marked by extreme violence and satanic imagery, breaking into homes at night to assault and murder his victims, who ranged widely in age. Ramirez's lack of pattern in victim selection, along with his chilling courtroom displays and devoted cult-like following after his arrest, made him one of the most infamous serial killers of the 20th century.

  - ☐ **Night Stalker: The Hunt for a Serial Killer** (2021) - This four-part Netflix docuseries is a comprehensive look at the hunt for Ramirez. It is told from the perspective of the two Los Angeles County detectives who pursued him and features archival footage and interviews with survivors.
  - ☐ **Richard Ramirez: The Night Stalker Tapes** (2024) - A Peacock docuseries that includes exclusive audio interviews with Ramirez on death row, as well as with his family and wife.
  - ☐ **Manhunt: Search for the Night Stalker** (1989) - A made-for-TV movie that recreated the events of Ramirez's crime spree just a few years after his conviction.
  - ☐ **The Night Stalker: Richard Ramirez** (2024) - A recent Amazon Prime Video documentary exploring the case
  - ☐ **The Night Stalker** (2016) - This psychological thriller is based on the events but contains fictional elements. It stars Lou Diamond Phillips as Ramirez and Bellamy Young as an attorney who tries to get him to confess to a past murder.
  - ☐ **Nightstalker** (2002) - A low-budget horror film based on the case, directed by Chris Fisher.
  - ☐ **Nightstalker** (2009) - A fictionalized horror film about Ramirez, directed by Ulli Lommel.[29]

☐ **The Night Strangler** (1973) - A reporter hunts down a 144-year-old alchemist who is killing women for their blood.

☐ **Badlands** (1973) – Terrence Malick retells Starkweather's killing spree. An impressionable teenage girl from a dead-end town, and her older greaser boyfriend, embark on a killing spree in the South Dakota Badlands. *Badlands* is widely considered one of the most influential films in the "New Hollywood" movement, with its style and themes directly inspiring other films such as *Bonnie and Clyde, Natural Born Killers, True Romance, The Frighteners,* and *The Boys Next Door.*

- • **ADAPTIONS OF STARKWEATHER & FUGATE:** Charles Starkweather was a 19-year-old spree killer who, along with his 14-year-old girlfriend Caril Ann Fugate, embarked on a killing rampage across Nebraska and Wyoming in 1957–58 that left 11 people dead. Starkweather's brooding, rebellious persona and the shocking involvement of a teenage girl made the case a media sensation. While Starkweather was executed in 1959, Fugate's role has remained controversial. She claimed she was a hostage rather than a willing accomplice, a debate that continues to shape her legacy in true-crime history.

  - ☐ **The Sadist** (1963) - This low-budget, stark thriller is perhaps the most direct exploitation-style film based on the spree. It focuses on a sadist and his girlfriend who terrorize a group of people.
  - ☐ **Murder in the Heartland** (1983) - Also known as *Stark Raving Mad*, this is a fictionalized account of the murder spree.

---

[29] I was in a Ulli Lommel horror. I would recommend not watching any of his movies. They are $100 horror films, that anyone with a camera can produce. And I never got paid.

- [ ] **The Boys Next Door** (1985) – Starring Charlie Sheen. Roy and Bo leave their small California town the weekend after graduation for a short road trip to Los Angeles. Soon, they find themselves lashing out and leaving a trail of bodies behind them. The violence escalates throughout.
- [ ] **Kalifornia** (1993) – Journalists road-trip with a psychopath. This thriller explicitly parallels the true story. Two couples, a writer researching serial killers and his girlfriend, and a recently paroled psychopath and his unstable girlfriend, travel together across the country.
- [ ] **Natural Born Killers** (1994) – Media satire through spree-killer couple. This highly controversial Oliver Stone film is the most famous to draw inspiration from the Starkweather and Fugate case.
- [ ] **The Frighteners** (1996) – Ghost con artist faces real supernatural threat. Directed by Peter Jackson, this film stars Michael J. Fox as a "ghost hunter" who discovers he can see real ghosts. The killer and his ghostly accomplice are heavily inspired by Starkweather and Fugate.
- [ ] **Starkweather** (2004) - This direct-to-video horror film is another dramatization of the killing spree.

- [ ] **Deranged** (1974) – Based on Ed Gein's murders and body desecrations. Alfred Hitchcock's horror classic *Psycho* was famously inspired by Gein's story, though the plot was significantly altered. Also, *The Texas Chain Saw Massacre* and *The Silence of the Lambs* were inspired by the Ed Gein's crimes. It also inspired Rob Zomie's films *House of 1000 Corpses* and *The Devil's Rejects*. Specifically, the character Otis Driftwood wears the flayed skin of his victims, similar to Gein's skin suits.
  - **ADAPTIONS OF THE ED GEIN MURDERS:** Ed Gein was a reclusive murderer and body snatcher from Plainfield, Wisconsin, whose crimes in the 1950s horrified the public and left a lasting cultural legacy. He exhumed corpses to fashion trophies and clothing from human remains, and his murders revealed a grotesque obsession with death and his deceased mother. Gein became infamous not only for the macabre details of his crimes but for how they inspired some of horror's most iconic characters.
    - [ ] **Ed Gein and His Dead Mother** (1993) - A dark comedy starring Steve Buscemi, this film takes a more satirical approach to the theme of an Oedipal son and his dead mother. The protagonist resurrects his dead mother, but she soon develops a monstrous appetite for destruction.
    - [ ] **Ed Gein** (2000) - A more fact-based film starring Steve Railsback as Gein.
    - [ ] **Ed Gein: The Butcher of Plainfield** (2007) - A straight-to-video horror film also based on Gein's crimes.

- [ ] **The Town That Dreaded Sundown** (1976) – Hooded killer terrorizes Texarkana. Sixty-five years after a masked serial killer terrorized the small town of Texarkana, the so-called "moonlight murders" begin again. Is it a copycat or something even more sinister? A lonely high-school girl may be the key to catching him.
  - **ADAPTIONS OF THE PHANTOM KILLER:** The Phantom Killer was an unidentified assailant who terrorized Texarkana in 1946, attacking eight people and killing five in what became known as the "Moonlight Murders." Striking lovers' lanes at night while wearing a white hood with slits for eyes, he created a climate of fear that gripped the twin cities on the Texas-Arkansas border. The case was never solved, and its eerie blend of small-town paranoia and masked brutality.
    - [ ] **The Town That Dreaded Sundown** (2014) - The 2014 version is set in the present day in Texarkana, where a new killer begins to reenact the original "Phantom Killer" murders after a yearly screening of the 1976 movie.

- [ ] **Angst** (1983, Austria) – Disturbing psychodrama based on real killer Werner Kniesek. A troubled man gets released from prison and starts taking out his sadistic fantasies on an unsuspecting family living in a secluded house.
  - **INFLUENCES OF WERNER KNIESEK:** Werner Kniesek was an Austrian murderer whose shocking crimes in 1980 cemented his reputation as one of Europe's most disturbing killers. After being released from prison, he invaded the home of a family in St. Pölten, torturing and murdering a mother and her two children in a frenzied attack. His sadistic violence and lack of remorse made him infamous, and his case later inspired the harrowing Austrian film *Angst* (1983), which is still regarded as one of the most unsettling cinematic explorations of a killer's psyche.
    - [ ] **In a Violent Nature** (2024, Canada) - When a locket is removed from a collapsed fire tower in the woods that entombs the rotting corpse of Johnny, a vengeful spirit spurred on by a horrific 70-year-old crime, his body is resurrected and becomes hellbent on retrieving it. Nash cited

Angst as a key inspiration for portraying the killer's actions in a brutal, matter-of-fact way. A sequel, *In a Violent Nature 2*, has been officially announced and is in the early stages of development.

- **Manson Family Movies** (1984) - In response to the legend that the "Manson Family" may have filmed themselves in some of their exploits, this film is a re-creation of a film of what may have been filmed. When they Occupied Spahn Movie Ranch in 1969. The film, shot in an unsystematic fashion, is an intentionally amateurish "home movie" of the events leading up to, and including, the infamous Tate-LaBianca murders on August 9th into the 10th, 1969.

  - **ADAPTIONS OF THE CHARLIE MANSON MURDERS:** Charles Manson was the manipulative cult leader of the "Manson Family," a quasi-commune of disaffected young followers in 1960s California who treated him as a messianic figure. Preaching a warped blend of apocalyptic prophecy, racism, and Beatles-inspired delusions he called "Helter Skelter," Manson orchestrated a series of murders carried out by his followers in 1969, most infamously the brutal killings of actress Sharon Tate and others in Los Angeles. Though he never physically committed the crimes, his ability to command others to kill made him a symbol of the dark underbelly of the counterculture era and one of the most notorious figures in American criminal history. Charles Manson and his followers were convicted of nine murders including the Tate-LaBianca killings and the earlier deaths of Gary Hinman and Donald "Shorty" Shea.
    - **Once Upon a Time in Hollywood** (2019) - Quentin Tarantino's film offers a fictional alternate ending to the Manson murders. Charles Manson and his family appear as characters, with the story centered on Hollywood in 1969.
    - **Charlie Says** (2018) - Directed by Mary Harron, this film tells the story from the perspective of the female followers, focusing on Leslie Van Houten and a graduate student who tries to deprogram them in prison.
    - **The Haunting of Sharon Tate** (2019) - A supernatural horror film that fictionalizes the Tate murders. It was widely criticized for its exploitative premise.
    - **Manson's Lost Girls** (2016) - A made-for-TV movie focusing on the experiences of Linda Kasabian and other Manson Family members in the summer of 1969.
    - **The Other Side of Madness** (1971) - One of the first movies to cash in on the Manson murders, it mixes documentary-style footage with dramatizations.
    - **Manson** (1973) - A documentary that includes original footage of Manson and his family filmed at Spahn Ranch and other locations.
    - **Charles Manson Superstar** (1989) - A documentary featuring interviews with Manson from San Quentin Prison, focusing on his philosophies and worldview.
    - **The Six Degrees of Helter Skelter** (2009) - Hosted by Hollywood historian Scott Michaels, this documentary visits numerous locations connected to the case.
    - **Inside the Manson Cult: The Lost Tapes** (2018) - This TV documentary uses original, 16mm archival footage to retell the Manson story.
    - **Helter Skelter: An American Myth** (2020) - A comprehensive, six-part documentary series about Manson, his family, and the trial.
    - **Making Manson** (2024) - This docuseries uses previously unheard conversations with Manson to offer unfiltered insights into his personality and crimes.

- **Citizen X** (1995) – Hunt for Russian serial killer Andrei Chikatilo. During the 1980s, Soviet authorities hunt for a serial killer who picks his victims in railway stations and commuter trains and lures them into the woods.
  - **ADAPTIONS OF SERIAL KILLER ANDREI CHIKATILO:** Andrei Chikatilo, known as the "Butcher of Rostov," was a Soviet serial killer who brutally murdered and mutilated at least 52 women

and children between 1978 and 1990. A seemingly ordinary teacher and family man, he lured victims with promises of food or work, then attacked them in forests or secluded areas, often displaying extreme sexual sadism. His long, unchecked killing spree was enabled by bureaucratic denial and investigative missteps within the Soviet system, and his eventual capture and trial revealed one of the most horrifying criminal cases of the 20th century.

- ☐ **Evilenko** (2004, Italy) - The story portrays Chikatilo (renamed Andrei Evilenko and played by Malcolm McDowell) as a disgraced communist schoolteacher who becomes a brutal serial killer.
- ☐ **Child 44** (2015) - It features a fictionalized version of the killer, whose character was inspired by Chikatilo, but changes the setting to the Soviet Union of the 1950s.
- ☐ **The Hunt for the Red Ripper** (1993) - An early documentary about the case.
- ☐ **The Butcher of Rostov** (2004) - A documentary that focuses on Chikatilo's crimes and features interviews with those involved in his capture.
- ☐ **Murderous Minds** (2018) - An episode of this series is dedicated to the case, titled "The Rostov Ripper"

☐ **Henry: Portrait of a Serial Killer** (1986) – Cold, matter-of-fact depiction of murderers. Arriving in Chicago, Henry moves in with ex-con acquaintance Otis and starts schooling him in the ways of the serial killer. Michael Rooker got the part after an audition so intense the director thought he was dangerous. Loosely inspired by Henry Lee Lucas.

- • **SEQUELS & ADAPTIONS OF HENRY LEE LUCAS:** Henry Lee Lucas was an American drifter and convicted murderer who became notorious in the 1980s after claiming responsibility for hundreds of killings across the United States. While many of his confessions were later proven false or exaggerated, he was ultimately convicted of 11 murders, including the killing of his mother. Lucas gained infamy not only for the brutality of his crimes but for the media spectacle surrounding his shifting confessions, which exposed flaws in law enforcement's reliance on coerced or fabricated statements. His disturbing legacy lives on through the film.

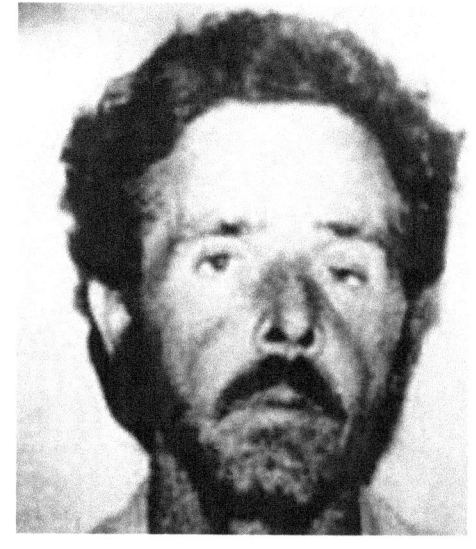

  - ☐ **Henry: Portrait of a Serial Killer, Part 2** (1996) - The sequel picks up after the events of the first film, with Henry (now played by Neil Giuntoli instead of Michael Rooker) finding a new victim in a small town.
  - ☐ **Confessions of a Serial Killer** (1985) - This low-budget horror film also details a serial killer based on Henry Lee Lucas. The story focuses on a man who, after being arrested, confesses to the murders of over 200 women.
  - ☐ **Drifter: Henry Lee Lucas** (2009) - This movie, starring Antonio Sabato Jr., is a more traditional biopic that attempts to cover Lucas's entire life. It explores his troubled childhood and the events that led to his infamous killing spree, and it does so in a more restrained way compared to the disturbing nature of *Henry*.
  - ☐ **The Confession Killer** (2019) - This five-part Netflix docuseries focuses on the consequences of the Henry Lee Lucas investigation. Instead of dramatizing his murders, it examines how law enforcement, eager to close cold cases, believed his numerous, often fabricated, confessions and the devastating impact this had on justice.

☐ **River's Edge** (1986) – Based on real California teen murder. Starring Keanu Reeves. A high school slacker commits a shocking act and proceeds to let his friends in on the secret. However, the friends' reaction is almost as ambiguous and perplexing as the crime itself. The Marcy Conrad murder case in Milpitas, California has been the subject of numerous podcasts and true-crime articles.

☐ **Anguish** (1987, Spain) – Meta-serial killer film about cinema's hypnotic power. The first part of the film is a horror movie called *The Mommy*, which the audience in the theater is watching. It's a story about a mentally disturbed man who is hypnotized by his overbearing mother into killing people and gouging out their eyeballs.

The second half of the movie reveals that a real-life killer is in the same movie theater as the onscreen audience, paralleling the action of *The Mommy* and creating a terrifying meta-horror experience.

- ☐ **Killer: A Journal of Murder** (1995) – True story of prison killer Carl Panzram, starring James Woods. A prison guard at Leavenworth with lofty ideals and hopes of reform struggles to understand a violent, hateful and conscienceless convict. The result is a written testimonial to a crime that no one could have predicted.
    - • **ADAPTIONS OF THE CARL PANZRAM CASE:** Carl Panzram was an American serial killer, rapist, arsonist, and thief active in the early 20th century, whose life of relentless violence and nihilism made  him one of the most notorious criminals in U.S. history. Born in 1891, he spent most of his life in reform schools and prisons, where he endured severe abuse that he later claimed shaped his hatred of humanity. Panzram confessed to killing 21 people and committing thousands of burglaries, assaults, and acts of arson, though exact numbers remain uncertain due to the scale of his claims. His autobiography, written while in prison before his execution in 1930, revealed chilling details of his crimes and philosophy, making him infamous long after his death and the subject of several film adaptations.
        - ☐ **The Most Brutal Serial Killer** (2023) - This documentary explores the life of Carl Panzram, detailing his horrifying crimes and delving into how he became one of the most violent serial killers in American history.
        - ☐ **Serial Killer Doc** (2020) - A documentary that includes information and analysis of the Carl Panzram case, using historical records and psychological context.
        - ☐ **Carl Panzram: The Spirit of Hatred and Vengeance** (2011) - This is a documentary film directed by John Borowski that tells the true story of Panzram's life and crimes. It includes voiceover narration of Panzram's own writing from his autobiography.
- ☐ **Paradise Lost: The Child Murders at Robin Hood Hills** (1996) – True-crime doc that feels like horror. A horrific triple child murder leads to an indictment and trial of three nonconformist boys based on questionable evidence.
    - • **SEQUELS**
        - ☐ **Paradise Lost 2: Revelations** (2000) - A follow-up that explores new evidence and raises further doubts about the convictions. It also documents the rise of a grassroots movement to free the teenagers.
        - ☐ **Paradise Lost 3: Purgatory** (2011) - The final installment covers the release of the West Memphis Three from prison in 2011, after they accepted an Alford plea. It was nominated for an Academy Award for Best Documentary Feature.
    - • **ADAPTIONS OF THE WEST MEMPHIS 3:** The West Memphis Three refers to Damien Echols, Jason Baldwin, and Jessie Misskelley Jr., three teenagers from West Memphis, Arkansas, who were convicted in 1994 for the brutal murders of three young boys. The case became infamous because the prosecution leaned heavily on claims of Satanic ritual, despite scant physical evidence, and the teens' outsider status: black clothing, heavy metal music, and interest in the occult was used against them. Over time, growing doubts, new DNA evidence, and a wave of public support led to their release in 2011 after 18 years in prison, under an Alford plea that allowed them to maintain innocence while accepting a guilty verdict. Their story, captured in documentaries and dramatizations, stands as one of the most controversial miscarriages of justice in modern American history.
        - ☐ **West of Memphis** (2012) - This documentary was produced by Peter Jackson and Amy Berg. It features interviews with new witnesses, explores alternative theories, and details new DNA evidence uncovered by a private investigation. The film was produced with the cooperation of Damien Echols.

- ☐ **The Forgotten West Memphis Three** (2020) - A television mini-series produced by ID that explores the crime, the trial, and the eventual release of the West Memphis Three.
- ☐ **The West Memphis Three: An ID Murder Mystery** (2020) - A television series that delves into the details of the case.
- ☐ **Devil's Knot** (2013) - This biographical crime drama, directed by Atom Egoyan, stars Colin Firth and Reese Witherspoon. It is based on the 2002 book *Devil's Knot: The True Story of the West Memphis Three* by Mara Leveritt.

☐ **Summer of Sam** (1999) –Spike Lee's take on the "Son of Sam" murders in New York City during the summer of 1977 centering on the residents of an Italian-American Northeast Bronx neighborhood who live in fear and distrust of one another. Starring John Leguizamo, Adrien Brody and Mira Sorvino.

- • **ADAPTIONS OF THE SON OF SAM MURDERS:** David Berkowitz, infamously known as the "Son of Sam," was a serial killer who terrorized New York City in 1976–77 by shooting couples in parked cars with a .44 caliber revolver, ultimately killing six people and wounding seven others. What made him notorious was not only the randomness of his attacks but also the taunting letters he sent to police and newspapers, mocking investigators and signing them "Son of Sam." His capture ended a reign of fear that had gripped the city, and his case became a media spectacle, cementing him as one of America's most infamous killers. His crimes and the hysteria around them have since been dramatized in films and series.
  - ☐ **Out of the Darkness** (1985) - A made-for-television movie starring Martin Sheen as a detective on the Son of Sam task force. The film focuses on the police investigation to find Berkowitz, who is played by Robert Trebor.
  - ☐ **The Bronx Is Burning** (2007) - This ESPN miniseries focuses on the New York Yankees baseball team during the summer of 1977 but also covers the Son of Sam manhunt and the tense atmosphere in the city.
  - ☐ **Son of Sam** (2008) - A low-budget horror film by director Ulli Lommel, who also made several films inspired by the Zodiac Killer. The story recounts Berkowitz's crimes and his later claim that he was influenced by a satanic cult.
  - ☐ **The Lost Tapes: Son of Sam** (2016) - This Smithsonian Channel episode uses archival footage, news reports, and recordings to tell the story of the murders in near real-time.
  - ☐ **Son of Sam: The Killer Speaks** (2017) - This TV special features an interview with Berkowitz conducted by CBS journalist Maurice DuBois. Berkowitz discusses his troubled past and religious conversion in prison.
  - ☐ **Mindhunter** (2017–2019) - In the second season of this Netflix series, FBI agents conduct criminal profiling interviews with David Berkowitz in prison.
  - ☐ **The Sons of Sam: A Descent into Darkness** (2021) - A Netflix docuseries that re-examines the murders through the investigation of journalist Maury Terry. Terry spent decades trying to prove Berkowitz did not act alone.
  - ☐ **Conversations with a Killer: The Son of Sam Tapes** (2025) - The latest Netflix docuseries in this anthology features previously unheard interviews with Berkowitz from the 1970s.
☐ **Der Samurai** (2014, Germany) – Surreal small-town slasher about repression and violence. The surreal and unsettling atmosphere of *Der Samurai* has been compared to Lynch's work, such as *Eraserhead* (1977) and *Lost Highway* (1997).

Home Invasion Horror

☐ **Wait Until Dark** (1967) - A home invasion thriller starring Audrey Hepburn as a blind woman trapped in her apartment. Like *Dead of Winter*, it creates suspense by putting a vulnerable character in a confined space with a dangerous threat.

☐ **Straw Dogs** (1971, UK) Starring Dustin Hoffman. A classic film about a man and his wife who are terrorized by a local gang after moving to a rural town, causing the husband to violently defend his home.

- **Funny Games** (1997, Austria) – Two violent young men take a mother, father, and son hostage in their vacation cabin and force them to play sadistic "games" with one another for their own amusement.
  - **ADAPTIONS**
    - **Funny Games** (2007, US) – Haneke's shot-for-shot remake.
- **Them (Ils)** (2006, France) – A French horror film about a couple in a secluded house who are tormented by a gang of hooded figures.
- **The Strangers** (2008) - This American home-invasion film is often considered an unofficial remake or a film heavily influenced by *Them*. It stars Liv Tyler and Scott Speedman and follows a similar plot of masked intruders terrorizing a couple in their secluded vacation home.
  - **SEQUELS AND REMAKES**
    - **The Strangers: Prey at Night** (2018) – Neon-soaked sequel. A family of four staying at a secluded mobile home park for the night are stalked and then hunted by three masked psychopaths.
    - **The Strangers: Chapter 1** (2024) – This first installment follows a new couple on a road trip who are forced to stay in an isolated Airbnb and are terrorized by the masked strangers.
    - **The Strangers: Chapter 2** (2025) – Scheduled for release on September 26, 2025, this film will continue the story immediately after the events of *Chapter 1*, with the survivor delving deeper into the mystery of the killers.
    - **The Strangers: Chapter 3** (2026) - The third and final installment of the trilogy is planned for release in 2026 and will conclude the narrative arc begun in the first two chapters.
- **Kidnapped** (2010, Spain) - Three hooded Eastern-European criminals burst into a home in a Madrid gated community, holding the family hostage in their home, and forcing the father to empty his credit cards.
- **Sleep Tight** (2011, Spain) – This unique and disturbing home invasion film is from the perspective of the invader. A bitter apartment concierge takes pleasure in making the life of one of his tenants a living hell without her ever knowing he's in her home.
  - **ADAPTIONS**
    - **Door Lock** (2018, South Korea) - The original film is told from the perspective of the concierge, César, as he torments his tenant, Clara. The remake tells the story from the perspective of the female victim, providing a new take on the terrifying events.
- **You're Next** (2011) – When the Davison family comes under attack during their wedding anniversary getaway, the gang of mysterious killers soon learns that one of the victims harbors a secret talent for fighting back. When the Davison family comes under attack during their wedding anniversary getaway, the gang of mysterious killers soon learns that one of the victims harbors a secret talent for fighting back.
- **In Their Skin** (2012) - The Hughes' cottage vacation is violently interrupted by a family on a murderous and identity-stealing journey, in search of the "perfect" life.
- **The Purge** (2013) - A film in which a family is hunted inside their home by a masked group during a lawless night.
  - **SEQUELS**
    - **The Purge: Anarchy** (2014) - This sequel moves the setting from a confined home to the city streets, following a group of strangers trying to survive the night together.
    - **The Purge: Election Year** (2016) - Set in 2040, a former police sergeant becomes the head of security for a presidential candidate who vows to end the Purge.
    - **The First Purge** (2018) - A prequel exploring how the annual event originated as a sociological experiment on Staten Island.
    - **The Forever Purge** (2021) - The fifth film sees the end of the annual Purge, but an anti-immigration group continues to commit crimes, launching a never-ending Purge.
- **Intruders** (2015) - Anna suffers from agoraphobia so crippling that when a trio of criminals break into her house, she cannot bring herself to flee. But what the intruders don't realize is that agoraphobia is not her only problem.
- **Don't Breathe** (2016) - A home invasion thriller where thieves are hunted by a vengeful homeowner.
- **For the Sake of Vicious** (2020, Canada) - An overworked nurse returns home to find a maniac hiding out with a bruised and beaten hostage. When an unexpected wave of violent intruders descend upon her home, it becomes a fight for survival.

- **Motherly** (2021, Canada) - Kate (Lora Burke) and her daughter Beth live alone in an isolated farmhouse in the woods, but when Kate slowly begins to suspect that something sinister is happening, her motherly instincts are put to the test.
- **Knock at the Cabin** (2021) – While vacationing, a girl and her parents are taken hostage by armed strangers who demand that the family make a choice to avert the apocalypse. An adaptation of Paul G. Tremblay's 2018 novel, *The Cabin at the End of the World*. Director M. Night Shyamalan made significant changes to the book's famously ambiguous and grim ending, giving the movie a more definitive and hopeful, yet still tragic, conclusion.
- **Little Bone Lodge** (2023) - Set during a vicious storm, two criminal brothers on the run seek refuge in a desolate farmhouse. Taking the resident family captive, they find the house holds dark secrets of its own.

Psychological Serial Killer Horror

- **Manhunter** (1986) – Former FBI profiler Will Graham returns to service to pursue a deranged serial killer dubbed "the Tooth Fairy" by the media.
  - **SEQUELS**
    - **The Silence of the Lambs** (1991) – Hannibal Lecter helps track Buffalo Bill. A young F.B.I. cadet must receive the help of an incarcerated and manipulative cannibal killer to help catch another serial killer, a madman who skins his victims. Won five Academy Awards in 1992 including Best Picture, Best Actor in a Leading Role, Best Actress in a Leading Role, Best Director, and Best Writing, Screenplay Based on Material Previously Produced or Published.
    - **Hannibal** (2001) – Lecter returns, balancing horror and art. Living in exile, Dr. Hannibal Lecter tries to reconnect with now disgraced F.B.I. Agent Clarice Starling, and finds himself a target of revenge from a powerful victim.
    - **Red Dragon** (2002) – Lecter prequel with "Tooth Fairy" killer.
    - **Hannibal Rising** (2007) - This film, based on the novel of the same name, is a prequel that details Lecter's origins.
- **Se7en** (1995) – Two detectives, a rookie and a veteran, hunt a serial killer who uses the seven deadly sins as his motives. The shocking "head in the box" ending was almost cut by the studio; Brad Pitt refused to do the movie without it.
  - **SEQUELS**
    - **Solace** (2015) - The movie follows a psychic FBI agent (Anthony Hopkins) who is brought in to help track a serial killer with similar abilities (Colin Farrell).
  - **NEO- NOIR & PSYCHOLOGICAL HORROR SIMILAR THEMES**
    - **Jacob's Ladder** (1990) - Mourning his dead son, a haunted Vietnam War veteran attempts to uncover his past while suffering from a severe case of dissociation. To do so, he must decipher reality and life from his own dreams, delusions, and perceptions of death.
    - **Cape Fear** (1991) - A convicted rapist, released from prison after serving a fourteen-year sentence, stalks the family of the lawyer who originally defended him.
- **Copycat** (1995) – Sigourney Weaver & Holly Hunter vs. copycat killer.
  - **SIMILAR FILMS**
    - **Nightwatch** (1997) - A law student is suspected of serial killings.
      - **ADAPTIONS**
        - **Nattevagten** (1994) - The original Danish film, also directed by Ole Bornedal. The 1997 American version is a shot-for-shot remake of this original, with Bornedal directing both.
        - **Nightwatch: Demons are Forever** (2023) - A direct sequel to the 1994 Danish original, released 30 years after the first film. Bornedal returned to write and direct the sequel, which features the returning cast and focuses on the legacy of the original killer.
    - **The Bone Collector** (1999) - Involves a bedridden detective who must work with a rookie officer to track down a serial killer.
    - **In Dreams** (1999) - This film similarly explores the psychological effects of a serial killer on a protagonist who has a psychic connection to the killer's crimes.

258

- ☐ **Kiss the Girls** (1997) – Detective tracks serial kidnapper in North Carolina.
  - • **ADAPTIONS AND SEQUELS**
    - ☐ **Along Came a Spider** (2001) – Alex Cross vs. a sadistic kidnapper.
    - ☐ **Alex Cross** (2012) - This film was a reboot of the Alex Cross movie franchise. It starred Tyler Perry in the title role and was based on Patterson's 2006 novel *Cross*.
    - ☐ **Cross** (2024) - Aldis Hodge took over the role of Alex Cross for this TV series on Prime Video.
- ☐ **Dahmer** (2002) – Jeremy Renner as the infamous Milwaukee killer. Biopic about notorious American serial killer Jeffrey Dahmer, taking place in both the past and the present. Jeremy Renner was cast because of his resemblance to Jeffrey Dahmer and because not many actors wanted to portray the serial killer.
  - • **ADAPTIONS OF THE DAHMER MURDERS:** Jeffrey Dahmer, known as the "Milwaukee Cannibal," was an American serial killer and sex offender who murdered 17 young men between 1978 and 1991. His crimes were especially shocking for their gruesome details: rape, dismemberment, necrophilia, and cannibalism, often carried out in his apartment where police later discovered human remains, photographs, and preserved body parts. Dahmer's calm demeanor during his trial, combined with the horrific nature of his acts, made him one of the most infamous killers of the 20th century, and his story has since been retold in numerous documentaries and dramatizations.
    - ☐ **The Secret Life: Jeffrey Dahmer** (1993) - A low-budget biographical crime drama, one of the earliest films to cover Dahmer's story.
    - ☐ **Raising Jeffrey Dahmer** (2006) - A drama focusing on the killer's troubled family life in the lead-up to his crimes.
    - ☐ **The Jeffrey Dahmer Files** (2012) - An indie documentary that tells the story through archival footage, interviews, and re-enactments.
    - ☐ **My Friend Dahmer** (2017) – Coming-of-age portrait of Jeffrey Dahmer.
    - ☐ **Dahmer – Monster: The Jeffrey Dahmer Story** (2022) - A Netflix biographical crime drama series starring Evan Peters, which explores Dahmer's life and the perspective of his victims.
    - ☐ **Conversations with a Killer: The Jeffrey Dahmer Tapes** (2022) - lso on Netflix, this docuseries features previously unheard audio recordings of Dahmer's interviews with his legal team.
- ☐ **Memories of Murder** (2003, Korea) – Bong Joon-ho's masterpiece about Korea's first serial killer. In a small Korean province in 1986, two detectives struggle with the case of multiple young women being found raped and murdered by an unknown culprit.
  - • **ADAPTIONS OF THE HWASEONG CASE:** The Hwaseong serial murders were a string of killings that took place between 1986 and 1991 in Hwaseong, South Korea, where ten women were brutally murdered, ranging in age from teenagers to grandmothers. The case baffled police for decades, becoming Korea's most infamous unsolved serial killings until 2019, when advances in DNA analysis linked convicted rapist Lee Chun-jae to the crimes, which he later confessed to.
    - ☐ **Gap-dong** (2014, Korea) - This television series was loosely inspired by the Hwaseong case, featuring a serial killer returning after a long period of dormancy.
    - ☐ **Signal** (2016, Korea) - This police procedural series also drew inspiration from the Hwaseong murders as one of its cold case storylines.
    - ☐ **Tunnel** (2017, Korea) - This television series features a detective from 1986 who travels through time to solve the Hwaseong murders in 2016.
    - ☐ **Footfairy** (2020, India) - This Bollywood film was loosely based on the 2003 film.
- ☐ **Monster** (2003) – Based on the life of Aileen Wuornos, a Daytona Beach prostitute who became a serial killer. Starring Charlize Theron, who won Best Actress at the 2004 Academy Awards.
  - • **ADAPTIONS OF THE AILEEN WUORNOS CASE:** Aileen Wuornos was a Florida prostitute-turned-serial killer who murdered seven men between 1989 and 1990, claiming they attempted to assault her while she was working. Her case drew international attention not only for the brutality of the crimes, shooting her victims at point-blank range, but also because she was framed as both a victim of lifelong

abuse and a remorseless killer. Wuornos became one of the most infamous female serial killers in history, her trial and eventual execution in 2002 fueling debates over trauma, justice, and exploitation.

- ☐ **Aileen Wuornos: The Selling of a Serial Killer** (1993) - An early documentary by Nick Broomfield featuring interviews with Wuornos and her adoptive mother.
- ☐ **Aileen: Life and Death of a Serial Killer** (2003) - A follow-up documentary by Nick Broomfield that covers Wuornos' final days on death row, released the same year as the film *Monster*.
- ☐ **Aileen Wuornos: American Boogeywoman** (2021) - A prequel film exploring the serial killer's earlier life, with a different cast and production.

☐ **Mindhunters** (2004) – FBI trainees hunted by one of their own.

☐ **The Girl Next Door** (2007) – Based on Sylvia Likens' torture case. In a quiet suburban town in the summer of 1958, two recently orphaned sisters are placed in the care of their mentally unstable Aunt Ruth. But Ruth's depraved sense of discipline will soon lead to unspeakable acts of abuse and torture. Stephen King called it "the first authentically shocking American film I've seen since *Henry: Portrait of a Serial Killer*."

- • **ADAPTIONS OF THE SYLVIA LIKENS' TORTURE CASE:** The Sylvia Likens case is one of the most harrowing crimes in American history, involving the prolonged torture and eventual murder of a 16-year-old girl in Indianapolis in 1965. Left in the care of Gertrude Baniszewski while her parents traveled for work, Sylvia endured months of abuse, humiliation, and violence at the hands of Baniszewski, her children, and neighborhood youths. Her death exposed shocking failures of community intervention and became a symbol of unchecked cruelty.
  - ☐ **An American Crime** (2007) - A separate biographical crime drama starring Catherine Keener and Ellen Page that is also based on the Sylvia Likens case.

☐ **I Saw the Devil** (2010, Korea) – A secret agent exacts revenge on a serial killer through a series of captures and releases.

- • **REVENGE THRILLERS**
  - ☐ **Sympathy for Mr. Vengeance** (2002, Korea) - The first film in Park Chan-wook's Vengeance Trilogy, this movie explores a man's misguided attempts at revenge and the violent fallout.
  - ☐ **Oldboy** (2003, Korea) - This highly acclaimed Park Chan-wook film follows a man released after 15 years of captivity and forced to seek out his mysterious tormentor. The second film in the Vengeance Trilogy.
  - ☐ **Lady Vengeance** (2005, Korea) - After being wrongfully imprisoned for thirteen years and having her child taken away from her, a woman seeks revenge through increasingly brutal means. The last film in the Vengeance Trilogy.
  - ☐ **The Chaser** (2008, Korea) - This thriller, also starring Choi Min-sik, is a cat-and-mouse chase between a serial killer and a disgraced ex-policeman.
  - ☐ **Bedevilled** (2010, Korea) - A woman subject to mental, physical and sexual abuse on a remote island seeks a way out.
  - ☐ **The Man from Nowhere** (2010, Korea) - A pawnshop owner with a dark past is pushed to violence when he must rescue a young girl who is his only friend.
  - ☐ **Confessions** (2010, Japan) - Yuko, a teacher of middle-school, is shattered to see her four-year-old daughter dead. She returns back to the school and finds out that her students are responsible for her daughter's murder.
  - ☐ **Lesson of the Evil** (2012, Japan) - Another Japanese film set in a high school, this one follows a charismatic teacher who is secretly a psychopath and serial killer.

☐ **Snowtown** (2011, Australia) – Based on true events, 16-year-old Jamie, a vulnerable and abused teenager, who is groomed and manipulated by his mother's new boyfriend, a charismatic but deeply disturbed serial killer. A relationship that leads to a spree of torture and murder.

- • **ADAPTIONS OF SNOWTOWN:** The Snowtown case, also known as the "Bodies in Barrels" murders, was a series of killings in South Australia between 1992 and 1999 that left 12 victims dead. Masterminded primarily by John Bunting, along with accomplices Robert Wagner, James Vlassakis, and Mark Haydon, the crimes targeted individuals they labeled as pedophiles, homosexuals, or social outcasts, though motives often masked personal grudges and sadism. The victims' bodies were discovered in barrels filled with acid inside a disused bank vault in the town of Snowtown, a revelation that shocked the nation for both its brutality and scale.

☐ **Snowtown: Bodies in the Barrels** (2007) - An episode from a television series detailing the discovery of the bodies and the investigation that followed.

☐ **Extremely Wicked, Shockingly Evil and Vile** (2019) – A chronicle of the crimes of Ted Bundy from the perspective of Liz, his longtime girlfriend, who refused to believe the truth about him for years. Starring Zac Efron and Lily Collins.

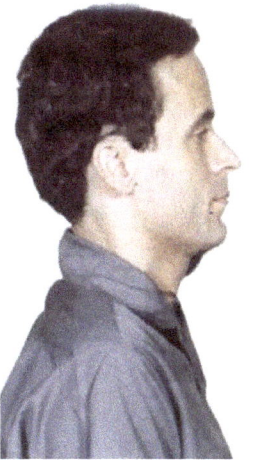 

- **ADAPTIONS OF THE TED BUNDY STORY:** Ted Bundy was an American serial killer who confessed to murdering more than 30 young women across multiple states in the 1970s, though the true number of his victims is believed to be higher. Charismatic and outwardly charming, Bundy lured women into traps by feigning injury or impersonating authority figures, then abducted, assaulted, and killed them, often returning to the bodies for further acts. His ability to escape custody, his televised Florida trial, and his execution in 1989 turned him into one of the most infamous criminals of the 20th century. Bundy's case has since been examined in countless books, documentaries, and films, cementing his place as the archetype of the "charming monster" in true-crime lore.

  ☐ **Ted Bundy** (2002) - An independent film starring Michael Reilly Burke.

  ☐ **The Strangler Beside Me** (2003) - A made-for-TV film based on the book by Ann Rule, a former colleague of Bundy's.

  ☐ **Conversations with a Killer: The Ted Bundy Tapes** (2019) - A docuseries from the same director as *Extremely Wicked*, Joe Berlinger, which features archival footage and interviews with Bundy.

  ☐ **Ted Bundy: Falling for a Killer** (2020) - A miniseries that examines the case from the perspective of the women who survived and knew Bundy.

  ☐ **No Man of God** (2021) - This film stars Elijah Wood as an FBI agent who interviews Bundy on death row.

  ☐ **Ted Bundy: American Boogeyman** (2021) - Another film exploring Bundy's life and crimes.

☐ **BTK: A Killer Among Us** (2019) – Small-town hunt for Dennis Rader. For 31 years Dennis Rader aka BTK killer was able to live a double life. This documentary chronicle's comprehensive interviews with law enforcement, victim's family members, reporters and his daughter Kerri Rawson.

- **ADAPTIONS OF THE BTK KILLER:** Dennis Rader, known as the BTK Killer (Bind, Torture, Kill), was an American serial killer who murdered 10 people in Kansas between 1974 and 1991. He gained notoriety not only for the cruelty of his crimes but for the taunting letters and poems he sent to police and the media, describing his killings and mocking investigators. Living a seemingly normal life as a family man, church leader, and compliance officer, Rader evaded capture for decades until 2005, when renewed communication with authorities led to his arrest. His double life and long evasion of justice made him one of the most infamous and unsettling serial killers in American history.

  ☐ **The Hunt for the BTK Killer** (2005) - A made-for-TV film that recreates the events leading to Rader's capture.

  ☐ **B.T.K.** (2008) - A low-budget horror film inspired by the murders, but not a straight documentary.

  ☐ **A Good Marriage** (2014) - A film based on a Stephen King novella. The story is a fictional account of a woman discovering that her husband is a serial killer, which was directly inspired by the BTK case.

  ☐ **Feast of the Assumption: BTK and the Otero Family Murders** (2022): A documentary-drama focusing on the first known murders committed by Dennis Rader in 1974.

  ☐ **The Clovehitch Killer** (2018) – Teen suspects his father is a serial murderer. The film was heavily inspired by the true story of Dennis Rader, the "BTK Killer."

80s/90s Serial Killer Exploitation & Hybrids

- ☐ **Rampage** (1987) – Fictionalized court drama about a mass murderer. Alex is an outwardly normal man who goes on killing and mutilating sprees. When he is finally captured and brought to trial, the district attorney is torn between his own liberal ideals on guilt and the crimes the accused is being tried.
  - • **SEQUELS**
    - ☐ **Rampage** (2009) – Uwe Boll's spree killer with armor suit.
    - ☐ **Rampage: Capital Punishment** (2014) – Sequel continues spree.
  - • **ADAPTIONS ABOUT THE RICHARD CHASE CASE:** Richard Chase, known as the "Vampire of Sacramento," was an American serial killer who murdered six people in California in the late 1970s. He earned his nickname because of his gruesome compulsion to drink his victims' blood and his necrophilic acts, stemming from severe mental illness and delusions that his blood was turning to powder. Chase's crimes shocked the nation for their brutality and randomness, as he often selected victims at random and killed in their homes.
    - ☐ **Lore: Deadly Obsession** (2011) - This low-budget TV movie dramatizes the story of Richard Chase. Critics note that while it may have abysmal acting and cinematography, it attempts to capture the horror of the case.
    - ☐ **World's Most Evil Killers** (2020) - An episode of this series, titled "Richard Chase - The Vampire of Sacramento," provides a detailed profile of the serial killer.
    - ☐ **Conversations With a Serial Killer** (2018) - An episode of this series is dedicated to Richard Chase, exploring his crimes through psychic and journalistic investigations.
    - ☐ **Vampire: The Richard Chase Murders** (2012) - This documentary and book by Kevin M. Sullivan offers a detailed look into the case, including interviews with those involved.
- ☐ **The Stepfather** (1987) – Family annihilator slasher-thriller. After murdering his entire family, a man marries a widow with a teenage daughter in another town and prepares to do it all over again.
  - • **ADAPTIONS & SEQUELS**
    - ☐ **The Stepfather II: Make Room for Daddy** (1989) – Killer seeks new family. After escaping the insane asylum in which he was incarcerated, Jerry Blake (Terry O'Quinn) impersonates a marriage counselor and manages to win over a patient (Meg Foster) and her young son (Jonathan Brandis).
    - ☐ **Stepfather III** (1992) - In this TV movie, the role of the stepfather is played by Robert Wightman, with the character's new appearance explained by plastic surgery. The movie follows his continued efforts to find the ideal family.
    - ☐ **The Stepfather (2009)** – Remake of identity-shifting killer. Starring Penn Badgley and Dylan Walsh. Michael Harding returns home from military school to find his mother Susan happily living with her new boyfriend David. As Michael and David get to know each other, Michael becomes more and more suspicious of this new guy.
- ☐ **Jennifer 8** (1992) – Blind woman stalked by serial killer.
- ☐ **8MM** (1999) – Private investigator uncovers snuff film network.
  - • **SEQUELS**
    - ☐ **8MM 2** (2005) - The story follows a couple who become embroiled in a blackmail plot involving a sex tape, a storyline with no relation to the snuff film investigation of the first film.
  - • **SIMILAR FILMS**
    - ☐ **Hardcore** (1979) - A father searches for his runaway daughter, who is believed to be involved in the making of snuff films.
    - ☐ **The Counselor** (2013) - A lawyer becomes involved in a drug trafficking scheme, which is shown to involve snuff films.
    - ☐ **Tesis** (1996, Spain) - A film student discovers a snuff film and begins to investigate its origins, putting her own life in danger.
- ☐ **Switchblade Romance** (2003, France) – Brutal serial killer twist film. *Switchblade Romance* is known for its polarizing plot twist, which has led to intense audience debate. The ending fundamentally recontextualizes the film's events. The film has also faced plagiarism accusations due to its similarities to the 1996 novel *Intensity* by Dean Koontz.

☐ **Gacy** (2003) – Model citizen, devoted father, loving husband and serial killer John Wayne Gacy - a man with over 30 dead men and boys entombed in the crawl space underneath his family house. Based on a true story.

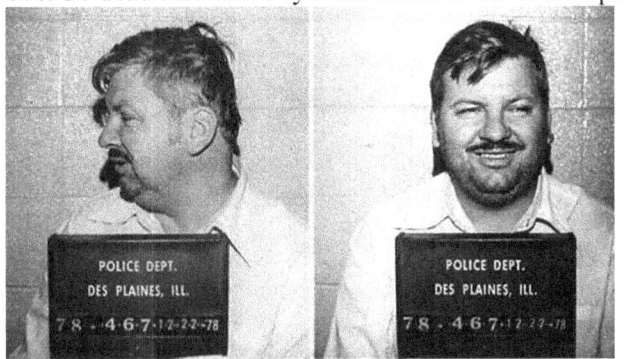

● **ADAPTIONS ABOUT THE JOHN WAYNE GACY'S CRIMES:** John Wayne Gacy was an American serial killer and sex offender who murdered at least 33 young men and boys in the 1970s, many of whom he lured to his Chicago home before assaulting, killing, and burying them in the crawl space beneath his house. By day, Gacy was a seemingly respectable businessman and community member, even performing at children's parties as "Pogo the Clown," but his double life hid one of the most prolific killing sprees in U.S. history. His case shocked the nation both for the scale of his crimes and for the grotesque discovery of bodies in his home, cementing him as one of America's most infamous killers.

☐ **To Catch a Killer** (1992) - This television film focuses on the detectives who hunted Gacy and features Brian Dennehy in an Emmy-nominated performance as the killer.

☐ **Dear Mr. Gacy** (2010) - A Canadian film based on the memoir *The Last Victim* by Jason Moss, a college student who corresponded with Gacy on death row.

☐ **Devil in Disguise: John Wayne Gacy** (2025) - A forthcoming Peacock scripted series that aims to focus on the stories of Gacy's victims and expose the systemic failures that allowed his crime spree.

☐ **John Wayne Gacy: Devil in Disguise** (2021) - A six-part Peacock documentary series that includes interviews with Gacy himself, survivors, and investigators.

☐ **Conversations with a Killer: The John Wayne Gacy Tapes** (2022) - A three-part Netflix docuseries that features previously unreleased audio tapes of Gacy's conversations with his lawyers, as well as interviews with those who knew him.

☐ **The John Wayne Gacy Murders: Life and Death in Chicago** (2024–) - A documentary series exploring Gacy's life and crimes, featuring footage from his interviews with filmmakers.

Modern Global & Indie Realistic Horrors

☐ **Elephant** (2003) – School shooting as clinical horror. Several ordinary high school students go through their daily routine as two others prepare for something more malevolent.

● **DEATH TRILOGY BY GUS VAN SANT**

☐ **Gerry** (2002) - Explores death at the hands of a friend. Starring Casey Affleck and Matt Damon. The friendship between two young men is tested when they go for a hike in the desert but forget to bring any food or water.

☐ **Last Days** (2005) - Explores death at one's own hands, and is inspired by the death of Kurt Cobain.

● **OTHER FILMS ABOUT COLUMBINE**

☐ **Duck! The Carbine High Massacre** (1999) - An independent film made shortly after the real-life events.

☐ **Bowling for Columbine** (2002) - A documentary by Michael Moore about gun violence in America, with a major focus on the Columbine massacre.

☐ **Zero Day** (2003) - Another film inspired by the massacre, also released in 2003.

☐ **The Only Way** (2004) - An independent film inspired by the massacre.

☐ **Mass** (2021) - Explores the aftermath of a school shooting, focusing on the parents of a victim and one of the perpetrators.

● **SIMILAR FILMS**

☐ **Massacre at Central High** (1976) - A high-school transfer student pushed to the edge by a trio of brutal bullies resorts to murder to reclaim the school from oppression, and later turns against the students wanting to fill the vacuum of their oppressors.

- ☐ **Tormented** (2009) - A bullied teenager comes back from the dead to take revenge on his classmates.
- ☐ **We Need to Talk About Kevin** (2011) – Mother faces aftermath of her son's massacre.
- ☐ **The Dirties** (2013, Ireland) - A found-footage film that explores the toxic power dynamics and violence of high school through a fictionalized story of two film students.
- ☐ **M.O.M. Mothers of Monsters** (2020) - A distraught mother suspects her teenage son of plotting a school shooting, but when the system ignores her, she's forced to take matters into her own hands.

☐ **Suspect Zero** (2004) – FBI agent hunts mythic "super-killer."

☐ **Behind the Mask: The Rise of Leslie Vernon** (2006) – Meta mock-doc about serial killer legend. This meta-slasher film explores the mechanics of a "gimmick killer" as a documentary crew follows a fictional slasher-in-training.

- • **SIMILAR FILMS**
  - ☐ **Dr. Giggles** (1992) - A madman who believes he's a doctor comes to the town where his crazy father was killed, and soon begins murdering people and becoming infatuated with a teenage girl who has a heart condition.
  - ☐ **The Dentist** (1996) - This film similarly features a seemingly respectable medical professional who loses his sanity and uses his professional tools for sadistic murder. It also employs a comedic and gory tone.
    - • **SEQUELS**
      - ☐ **The Dentist 2: Brace Yourself** (1998) - This straight-to-video sequel continues the story of the murderous Dr. Feinstone (Corbin Bernsen), who has escaped from the mental institution and fled to a new town. When he discovers his new love interest being unfaithful, he begins another gruesome rampage.
  - ☐ **Ice Cream Man** (1995) - This film features a deranged ice cream man who murders people, and like *Dr. Giggles*, is a fun, lighthearted slasher film.

☐ **Dear Zachary: A Letter to a Son About His Father** (2008) – True-crime doc turned real-life nightmare. A filmmaker decides to memorialize a murdered friend when his friend's ex-girlfriend announces she is expecting his son.

☐ **Chained** (2012) – Vincent D'Onofrio raises a boy to be a killer. A young man held prisoner by a cab-driving serial killer must make a life-or-death choice between following in his captor's footsteps or breaking free.

- • **SIMILAR FILMS**
  - ☐ **Bereavement** (2010) - This film has been compared to *Chained* because it also features a kidnapped child being trained by a serial killer.
  - ☐ **In a Glass Cage** (1986) - A Spanish film where a former Nazi doctor, a sexual predator, is paralyzed and cared for by a young man who becomes his accomplice.
  - ☐ **The Collector** (2009) - A former thief becomes trapped in a house he was robbing when a psychopath begins torturing the family.

☐ **The Frozen Ground** (2013) – Nic Cage hunts Alaskan serial killer Robert Hansen. An Alaska State Trooper partners with a young woman who escaped the clutches of serial killer Robert Hansen to bring the murderer to justice. Based on actual events. Also starring Vanessa Hudgens and John Cusack.

- • **ADAPTIONS OF THE ROBERT HANSEN CASE:** Robert Hansen, known as the "Butcher Baker," was an Alaskan serial killer who abducted, raped, and murdered at least 17 women during the 1970s and early 1980s. A well-liked local baker and avid hunter, Hansen targeted women, often sex workers, whom he would fly into the Alaskan wilderness, release, and then hunt down with a rifle like game. His chilling double life shocked the nation, and his crimes were later dramatized in films and documentaries, most notably *The Frozen Ground* (2013), which brought wider attention to the horrifying story of his predatory "human hunts."

- ☐ **Butcher Baker: Mind of a Monster** (2020) - A documentary that aired on Investigation Discovery.
- ☐ **Very Scary People: The Butcher Baker** (2022) - This two-part special on the Crime and Investigation network details Hansen's murders and the girls who got away.
- ☐ **Naked Fear** (2007) - This film, about a serial killer who hunts and abducts women, is loosely based on Hansen's crimes.
- ☐ **Dexter: New Blood** (2021): The character of Kurt Caldwell in this limited series, who hunts and kills women, was loosely based on Hansen's crimes.
- ☐ **Nightcrawler** (2014) – Paparazzi descent into predatory voyeurism.
- ☐ **Creep** (2014) – Videographer stalked by a deeply unsettling man.
  - • **SEQUELS AND INFLUENCES**
    - ☐ **Creep 2** (2017) – Sequel with even darker manipulation.
    - ☐ **Death Line** (1972) - When a government official disappears in the London tunnels, after several reports of missing people in the same location, Scotland Yard start to take the matter seriously, along with a couple who stumble into a victim by accident. The film's plot, about a stalker terrorizing a woman in the London Underground, is so similar that many consider it an unofficial remake of *Death Line*.
- ☐ **Hounds of Love** (2016, Australia) – Teen abducted by sadistic couple. Vicki Maloney is randomly abducted from a suburban street by a disturbed couple. As she observes the dynamic between her captors she quickly realizes she must drive a wedge between them if she wants to survive.
  - • **ADAPTIONS OF THE DAVID & CATHERINE BIRNIE CASE:** David and Catherine Birnie were an Australian couple who became infamous as the perpetrators of the "Moorhouse Murders" in 1986. Operating out of their home in Perth, the pair abducted, raped, and murdered four women, with a fifth victim narrowly escaping and alerting police, leading to their capture. Their case horrified the public not only for the sadistic nature of the crimes but also for the chilling partnership between husband and wife, whose shared fantasies and compulsions drove their killing spree. The murders remain one of Australia's most shocking examples of a killer couple acting in tandem.
    - ☐ **Crime Investigation Australia** (2006, Australia) - An episode of this documentary series, titled "The Moorhouse Horrors," focuses on the Birnie case. It details the abduction, torture, and murder of four women in the Birnies' home on Moorhouse Street in Perth.
    - ☐ **Australian Families of Crime** (2010, Australia) - An episode of this series is dedicated to the Birnie case, featuring interviews and insights into the killer couple's history.
    - ☐ **Beyond the Darklands** (2009, Australia) - This documentary features analysis of the Birnie case, providing insight into their personalities and crimes through interviews with people who knew them.
- ☐ **The Snowman** (2017) – Adaptation of Jo Nesbø's serial killer thriller. Detective Harry Hole investigates the disappearance of a woman whose scarf is found wrapped around an ominous-looking snowman.
- ☐ **You Were Never Really Here** (2017) – PTSD-hit enforcer blurs justice and brutality.
- ☐ **Super Dark Times** (2017) – Teen accident spirals into paranoia and violence.
  - • **SIMILAR FILMS**
    - ☐ **Donnie Darko** (2001) - A cult classic featuring a troubled suburban teenager dealing with disturbing visions and the breakdown of reality.
    - ☐ **The Virgin Suicides** (1999) - Explores the mysterious lives and tragic fate of five teenage sisters in a detached, suburban community.
    - ☐ **Mean Creek** (2004) - Features a group of teenagers who plan to humiliate a bully, which spirals into a horrific confrontation.
    - ☐ **Hypochondriac** (2022) - A young potter's life devolves into chaos as he loses function of his body while being haunted by the physical manifestation of his childhood trauma.
- ☐ **Extremity** (2018) – Woman enters extreme haunt, blurring killer and victim roles.
  - • **OTHER EXTREME HAUNT MOVIES**
    - ☐ **The Houses October Built** (2014) and its sequel (2017) - Found footage films that follow a group of friends who seek out the most extreme Halloween haunted houses.
    - ☐ **Haunters: The Art of the Scare** (2017) - A documentary that explores the subculture of extreme haunts.

☐ **Haunt** (2019) - A group of friends is hunted by masked figures in a terrifying haunted house.

☐ **The Good Nurse** (2022) – Based on Charles Cullen, killer nurse. Starring Eddie Redmayne. An infamous caregiver is implicated in the deaths of hundreds of hospital patients.

- **ADAPTIONS ON CHARLES CULLEN:** Charles Cullen, often called "The Angel of Death," was a nurse who became one of the most prolific serial killers in American history, believed to have murdered up to 400 patients over a 16-year career in New Jersey and Pennsylvania. Using his position of trust, he administered lethal doses of drugs such as insulin and digoxin to vulnerable patients, often under the guise of providing care. While Cullen claimed at times he was ending suffering, his killings were indiscriminate, and systemic failures within hospitals allowed him to move between facilities despite red flags. His crimes came to light in the early 2000s, and his chilling story was later depicted in the book *The Good Nurse* (2013) and its 2022 film adaptation.

  ☐ **Capturing the Killer Nurse** (2022) - This documentary provides a detailed account of the investigation and includes interviews with Loughren and the detectives involved in the case.

☐ **Strange Darling** (2023) - Nothing is what it seems when a twisted one-night stand spirals into a serial killer's vicious murder spree.

Pairing Night Watchlist: Realism Bites Back

Theme of the Night: *"Are you sure you want to know?"*

Serial killer and realistic horror films work best when they make you lean in, only to remind you this isn't a monster with fangs, it's someone with car keys, a job, maybe even a smile. This pairing night is about stripping away the supernatural to face the dread of human predators.

The Lineup

1. **Psycho (1960)** – Start the night with Hitchcock's pivot point: horror as psychological breakdown. Look for how Hitchcock weaponizes editing (the shower scene) and how Norman Bates' "normalcy" is the true terror.
   o *Smart fact to drop:* Paramount Pictures refused to fund the film's controversial story. In response, Hitchcock financed it himself for under $1 million and shot it in black and white.
2. **Henry: Portrait of a Serial Killer (1986)** – Follow with something unflinching. This film feels like a police file: flat lighting, no music cues, no glamor. Watch how it denies you catharsis.
   o *Smart fact to drop:* The MPAA refused to rate it not for gore, but for its "tone of moral bleakness."
3. **Se7en (1995)** – Shift into stylized procedural dread. The deadly sins structure lets you see how serial killer films became modern morality plays.
   o *Smart fact to drop:* The role of David Mills was originally offered to Denzel Washington, who found the script "too dark and evil" and turned it down. He later admitted he regretted the decision.
4. **Zodiac (2007)** – By this point, you've left "slasher fun" behind and entered obsession. Watch how Fincher turns the act of investigation into the horror itself.
   o *Smart fact to drop:* Fincher digitally recreated 1970s San Francisco street by street to make the film's "reality" seamless.
5. **Memories of Murder (2003)** – End on Bong Joon-ho's masterpiece. Notice how he blends genre. Sometimes comedy, sometimes tragedy, but leaves you unsettled by unsolved dread.
   o *Smart fact to drop:* The real killer was identified only in 2019, over 30 years later.

How to Watch: Dim the lights, no phones. Keep snacks minimal. Popcorn feels too frivolous here. Think bourbon neat or black coffee. After each film, ask not "Who did it?" but "Why do we keep watching?"

Quick Facts: Serial Killer & Realistic Horror

- **The Boston Strangler (1968)** – Tony Curtis took the role to shake off his "pretty boy" image; critics at the time compared his performance to De Niro's method work a decade later.
- **Ed Gein's legacy** – Three icons were directly inspired by him: Norman Bates (*Psycho*), Leatherface (*Texas Chain Saw Massacre*), and Buffalo Bill (*Silence of the Lambs*). One small-town killer, three cultural juggernauts.
- **In Cold Blood (1967)** – The film was shot in the *real Clutter family house* where the murders occurred. Many found it disturbingly voyeuristic at the time.

- **Henry: Portrait of a Serial Killer (1986)** – Roger Ebert called it "a great film" but admitted he never wanted to see it again. That's the measure of its impact.
- **Se7en (1995)** – The color palette intentionally never shows sunlight until the final scene, then it's harsh desert light, not comforting warmth.
- **Zodiac (2007)** – Fincher had actors do dozens of takes per scene not for performance, but so he could digitally composite the "perfect" micro-expressions.
- **Memories of Murder (2003)** – The final shot, with the detective staring into the camera, was improvised. Bong Joon-ho told the actor to just "look into the audience and ask them if they know."
- **Natural Born Killers (1994)** – Oliver Stone used 18 different film stocks (including Super 8 and black-and-white) to mimic the overstimulation of American media.
- **Monster (2003)** – Charlize Theron gained 30 pounds and wore prosthetic teeth and contacts; the transformation was so extreme some crew members didn't recognize her on set.
- **Bundy & Gacy Trivia** – Both Ted Bundy and John Wayne Gacy once worked for political campaigns. Bundy as a Republican campaign aide, Gacy as a Democratic precinct captain. Serial killers and politics aren't that far apart.

Real Monsters. Real Crimes

Psychological Horror

Where splatter spills blood and supernatural horror calls on demons, psychological horror attacks the mind itself. It thrives on paranoia, repression, hallucination, trauma, and the fragile line between perception and reality. Whether it's the crumbling sanity of *Repulsion* (1965), the obsessive cruelty of *Misery* (1990), or the dream logic of *Mulholland Drive* (2001), psychological horror unsettles by turning inward: what if the real monster is our own mind?

Why People Are Drawn to It

Because it destabilizes certainty. Psychological horror strips away the safety of knowing what's real. The monster may be imaginary or worse, it may not. Audiences are seduced by the tension of unreliable narrators, claustrophobic settings, and characters who mirror their own fears of madness, grief, or obsession. It forces us to ask: If we can't trust our senses, our family, or ourselves… who can we trust?

Essentials

- **Diabolique (1955, France)** – A psychological thriller of relentless suspense, *Diabolique* masterfully explores themes of greed, deceit, and manipulation through the intricate plot by a wife and mistress to murder their cruel husband/lover, only to have their crime spiral into paranoid terror when his body mysteriously disappears.
- **Repulsion (1965, UK)** – Roman Polanski's claustrophobic psychological horror film follows a sexually repressed young woman's nightmarish descent into madness, where her fears of men and sexual trauma manifest as terrifying hallucinations that transform her apartment into a menacing, predatory environment.
- **Carrie (1976, USA)** – Stephen King's bullied teen channels trauma into telekinetic destruction. Brian De Palma fuses teen melodrama with supernatural horror, using split screens and operatic style to turn adolescent humiliation into apocalyptic vengeance. Its infamous prom climax makes repressed rage and religious guilt explode in blood, fire, and psychic devastation.
- **Misery (1990, USA)** – A masterful psychological thriller that explores the dark side of fandom and the struggle between an artist's creative freedom and a consumer's obsessive demands, as a best-selling author is held captive and tortured by his "number one fan."
- **Black Swan (2010, USA)** – Darren Aronofsky transforms artistic ambition into psychological and bodily horror, following a ballerina's descent into obsession, self-destruction, and metamorphosis. Blurring reality with hallucination, the film uses body distortion and doppelgänger imagery to show how perfection can consume identity.

Deep Cuts

- **Eyes Without a Face (1960, France)** – A haunting blend of lyricism and surgical horror, where a surgeon's quest to restore his daughter's disfigured face leads to chilling experiments on abducted women. Its eerie masks and poetic brutality make it a landmark in body horror, balancing clinical detachment with gothic melancholy.
- **The Haunting of Julia (1977, UK)** – Also known as *Full Circle*. Richard Loncraine channels grief into supernatural dread, following a mother who becomes haunted after the accidental death of her child. With its subdued pacing and atmosphere of melancholy, the film blurs mourning with ghostly presence, making loss itself the source of horror.
- **Session 9 (2001, USA)** – Brad Anderson transforms an abandoned asylum into a labyrinth of psychological and supernatural terror, where a hazmat crew unravels under mounting paranoia. Its slow-burn tension, eerie sound design, and suggestion of possession make it a modern classic of atmospheric horror rooted in madness and decay.
- **The Reflecting Skin (1990, UK/Canada)** – A surreal gothic set against the wide skies of rural America, where childhood innocence warps into nightmare. Mixing vampiric delusion, grotesque imagery, and apocalyptic dread, it frames coming-of-age as a hallucinatory descent into death-haunted fantasy.
- **Goodnight Mommy (2014, Austria)** – Severin Fiala and Veronika Franz weaponize domestic space, trapping twin boys in paranoia as they suspect their bandaged mother is an impostor. With its sterile aesthetic and escalating cruelty, the film blurs maternal intimacy with menace, turning family bonds into a crucible of dread.

Critical Essay

"Psychological Horror Isn't Just Slow Burns."

Myth: It's all atmosphere, nothing happens.

Reality: The best psychological horror is kinetic. It weaponizes pacing, identity shifts, and subjective perspective to disorient the viewer. From Hitchcock's editing experiments to Lynch's dream logic, psychological horror plays with cinematic form itself. The horror is not the absence of action but the collapse of meaning.

Global Spotlight: Europe & Asia

- **Europe**: Ingmar Bergman's *Hour of the Wolf* (1968) and Robert Altman's *Images* (1972) mined marital collapse and artistic madness, influencing later auteurs like David Lynch. Austrian exports like *Angst* (1983) and *Goodnight Mommy* (2014) pushed the genre into stark realism and surreal cruelty.
- **Asia**: Japan's *Kairo* (2001) reframed loneliness as viral dread through the internet, while South Korea's *Memories of Murder* (2003) blurred procedural with existential despair. Both prove psychological horror is not bound to Western neuroses but is a global lens on isolation, obsession, and truth unraveling.

Classics & Foundations

- ☐ **Pikovaya Dama** (1910, Russia) – Based on the 1834 novella by Alexander Pushkin. Driven by a desire to know a secret that guarantees fortune at cards, a young officer's obsession leads him to terrorize and accidentally kill an old countess before he is driven mad by his greed.
  - **ADAPTIONS**
    - ☐ **The Queen of Spades** (1916, Russia) - This Russian silent film is known for its high production values and artistic direction.
    - ☐ **The Queen of Spades** (1949, UK) - A British version starring Anton Walbrook and Edith Evans. An army officer becomes obsessed with learning the secret to a card game for which an elderly countess sold her soul years earlier.
    - ☐ **The Queen of Spades** (1960, Soviet Union) - A Soviet-era adaptation.
    - ☐ **Queen of Spades: The Dark Rite** (2015, Russia) - A modern Russian horror film that reinterprets the story with a new mythology. Legend has it that any mirror may become a portal into the world of the dead. The oldest ritual known to humankind is the summoning of The Queen of Spades. Four teenagers decide to call the Queen of Spades as a joke. But they cannot even begin to imagine the horrors they condemned themselves and their loved ones to. The evil entity won't stop until she gets their souls...
      - **SEQUELS**
        - ☐ **Queen of Spades: Through the Looking Glass** (2018, Russia) - A direct sequel to *The Dark Rite*.
- ☐ **The Student of Prague** (1913, Germany) - Widely considered the first German "art film" and the first feature-length horror movie. It is considered one of the first examples of psychological horror, featuring themes of duality and existential dread. A poor student, Balduin (played by Paul Wegener, who also co-directed), sells his reflection to a sorcerer in exchange for wealth. His newly freed double, or doppelgänger, proceeds to torment and ruin his life. It was one of the first films to use optical effects to show an actor interacting with himself on screen.

  - **ADAPTIONS**
    - ☐ **The Student of Prague** (1926, Germany) - This version is a cornerstone of the German Expressionist movement.
    - ☐ **The Student of Prague** (1935, Germany) - This German film was directed by Arthur Robison and stars Anton Walbrook as the student. This is the first sound version.

- ☐ **Warning Shadows** (1923, Germany) - A wealthy man invites the local wealthy bachelors over for a puppet show about men who covet another man's wife. The puppeteer is actually a witch and gives the men nightmares about what could happen if they date the lady of the house.
- ☐ **The Phantom of the Opera** (1925) - A mad, disfigured composer seeks love with a lovely young opera singer.
  - **ADAPTION**
    - ☐ **Phantom of the Opera** (1943) - This adaptation, starring Claude Rains, is less of a horror film and more of a grand opera spectacle. In this version, the Phantom's disfigurement is caused by a music publisher throwing acid in his face.
    - ☐ **The Phantom of the Opera** (1989) - This gory, horror-tinged version stars Robert Englund, best known as Freddy Krueger.
    - ☐ **The Phantom Lover** (1995) - A Hong Kong-produced remake of the 1937 Chinese film, featuring Leslie Cheung.
    - ☐ **The Phantom of the Opera** (2004) - A film adaptation of the Andrew Lloyd Webber musical, starring Gerard Butler as the Phantom and Emmy Rossum as Christine.
- ☐ **The Lodger: A Story of the London Fog** (1927) - A landlady suspects that her new lodger is the madman killing women in London. Based on the 1913 novel *The Lodger: A Story of the London Fog* by Marie Belloc Lowndes.
  - **ADAPTIONS**
    - ☐ **The Lodger** (1932) - A sound version directed by Maurice Elvey.
    - ☐ **The Lodger** (1944) - A landlady suspects that her new lodger is Jack the Ripper.
    - ☐ **Man in the Attic** (1953) - A remake starring Jack Palance and directed by Hugo Fregonese.
    - ☐ **The Lodger** (2009) - A modern version starring Alfred Molina and Simon Baker, directed by David Ondaatje.
  - **OTHER FILMS ON JACK THE RIPPER:** The legend of Jack the Ripper originates in London's Whitechapel district in 1888, when a series of brutal murders of women, primarily prostitutes, captured the public imagination. The killer's identity was never discovered, but the combination of gruesome mutilations, taunting letters sent to police, and sensational press coverage transformed the crimes into enduring folklore. Jack the Ripper became the archetypal modern boogeyman: faceless, elusive, and symbolic of both urban fear and society's fascination with violent mystery.
    - ☐ **Jack the Ripper** (1958) - One of the first films to heavily feature gore, this movie focuses on Scotland Yard's hunt for the killer.
    - ☐ **A Study in Terror** (1965) - Pits Sherlock Holmes against the Ripper in a fictionalized case.
    - ☐ **Hands of the Ripper** (1971) - A Hammer film in which the Ripper's daughter, now grown up, goes on murderous rampages when she sees her father's face.
    - ☐ **Murder by Decree** (1979) - Also featuring Sherlock Holmes, this film suggests a conspiracy involving the royal family to cover up the murders.
    - ☐ **New York Ripper** (1982) – A giallo film directed by Lucio Fulci in which a serial killer stalks New York, using a voice like Donald Duck and inspired by the original Ripper.
    - ☐ **Jack's Back** (1988) - A man becomes the prime suspect in a series of murders that replicate the original Ripper killings 100 years later. He must find the real killer to clear his name.
    - ☐ **Edge of Sanity** (1989) - An exploitation film starring Anthony Perkins as a Jekyll-and-Hyde character who also becomes a Ripper-like killer.
    - ☐ **From Hell** (2001) – Jack the Ripper tale steeped in Gothic Victorian grime. Based on the graphic novel by Alan Moore and Eddie Campbell, this film stars Johnny Depp as a detective with psychic visions and links the Ripper's murders to a conspiracy involving the British royal family.
    - ☐ **Ripper** (2001) - College students are hunted by a serial killer who emulates the Ripper's methods.
    - ☐ **Razors: The Return of Jack the Ripper** (2016) - A writer who acquires the knives used by the original Ripper discovers they are cursed and possess people.

- **Svengali** (1931) - Through hypnotism and telepathic mind control, a sinister music maestro controls the singing voice, but not the heart, of the woman he loves. Based on the novel *Trilby* by George du Maurier.
  - **ADAPTIONS OF TRILBY**
    - **Trilby** (1912, Austria) - An early Austrian silent film, now considered lost.
    - **Trilby** (1915) - An American production starring Wilton Lackaye, who had previously originated the role of Svengali on stage.
    - **Trilby** (1923) - An American film directed by James Young.
    - **Svengali** (1927, Germany) - A German silent film starring Paul Wegener.
    - **The Mad Genius** (1931) - Starring John Barrymore, the same actor who played Svengali in the 1931 film, this movie features a similar theme of a manipulator controlling a young protégé.
    - **Svengali** (1954, UK) - A British film adaptation with Donald Wolfit in the title role and Hildegard Knef as Trilby.
    - **Svengali** (1983) - A made-for-television movie starring Peter O'Toole and Jodie Foster.
    - **Svengali** (2013, UK) - A modern British comedy film that loosely adapts the premise of a "Svengali-like" figure controlling a band.
- **Murders in the Zoo** (1933) - A monomaniacal zoologist is pathologically jealous of his beautiful but unfaithful wife Evelyn and will not stop short of murder to keep her. Because the film was produced before the full enforcement of the Motion Picture Production Code in 1934, it contains shocking and gruesome violence that was rare in later decades. The opening scene, where a man's mouth is sewn shut with a needle and thread, is a famous example.
  - **RELATED FILMS**
    - **The Black Zoo** (1963) - Directed by Herman Cohen, this film shares thematic similarities with *Murders in the Zoo*, including a vengeful animal handler at a zoo, but it is not a remake.
    - **Willard** (1971) - A social misfit uses his only friends, his pet rats, to exact revenge on his tormentors. Based on characters from the 1968 novel *Ratman's Notebooks* by Stephen Gilbert.
      - **SEQUELS, ADAPTIONS & SIMILAR FILMS**
        - **Ben** (1972) - A lonely boy befriends Ben, the leader of a violent swarm of killer rats.
        - **Willard** (2003) - Starring Crispin Glover. Loosely based on the original 1971 film and incorporated elements from *Ben*. A version of the theme song "Ben" was recorded by Crispin Glover for the soundtrack.
        - **Of Unknown Origin** (1983) - In this film, a man's home is invaded by a large, aggressive rat, leading to a suspenseful and claustrophobic battle.
    - **The Black Zoo** (1989) - This direct-to-video film is sometimes cited as a low-budget remake, but it is not officially connected.
- **Cat People** (1942) - The original film, directed by Jacques Tourneur and produced by Val Lewton, introduces the Serbian fashion designer Irena, who fears a family curse that turns her into a panther when sexually aroused. It is praised for its suspenseful atmosphere and use of suggestion rather than on-screen horror. Production Code office forced cuts to overt sexual references. The swimming pool sequence, with rippling shadows and growls, invented the modern jump scare.
  - **SEQUELS**
    - **The Curse of the Cat People** (1944) - This is a direct sequel but has a very different tone and plot. It follows the widower Oliver Reed and his new family. The story focuses on his daughter Amy, who befriends the ghost of Irena, her father's deceased first wife.

- ☐ **The Seventh Victim** (1943) - This film is often described as an unofficial spin-off. It features the same *Dr. Judd* character from *Cat People*, even though the character died in the first film, suggesting a convoluted effort to capitalize on the original's success.
  - • **ADAPTIONS & SIMILAR FILMS**
    - ☐ **Cat People** (1982) – Sexual repression reimagined as transformation dread. A woman who was orphaned from a young age finally reunites with her older brother. Matters start to go awry when she slowly discovers the true nature of her family.
    - ☐ **Tormented** (1960) - This film follows a man haunted by the ghost of his ex-lover whom he murdered. It shares the same noir-like atmosphere, seaside setting, and exploration of psychological guilt and paranoia.
    - ☐ **Night Tide** (1961) - A young sailor is attracted to a mysterious mermaid performing at a carnival, but soon suspects that the girl is actually a siren who draws men to their watery deaths during the full moon.
- ☐ **Calling Dr. Death** (1943) - A neurologist suffering from amnesia wonders if he is the culprit behind his wife's brutal murder. Using hypnosis, he and his nurse attempt to piece together the truth.
  - • **INNER SANCTUM MYSTERIES:** The series is known for its recurring framing device in which a disembodied head (David Hoffman) addresses the audience from within a crystal ball and introduces the unsettling tale to come.
    - ☐ **Weird Woman** (1944) - A university professor's scientific beliefs are challenged by his new wife, who was raised in the South Seas and practices voodoo. Strange and deadly incidents occur after she is ostracized by his colleagues, prompting the question of whether it's magic or human malice at play.
    - ☐ **Dead Man's Eyes** (1944) - An artist is blinded in an accident, and when his benefactor—who promised to donate his eyes—dies under suspicious circumstances, the artist becomes the prime suspect. The mystery deepens when his own eyes are stolen before the transplant.
    - ☐ **The Frozen Ghost** (1945) - A stage mentalist involved in a mysterious death and a discredited plastic surgeon are among the assorted characters involved in mysterious goings-on in an eerie wax museum.
    - ☐ **Strange Confession** (1945) - A scientist, driven to madness by his unscrupulous boss, goes to his attorney to deliver a confession. In a flashback, he recounts a tale of corporate greed, betrayal, and revenge.
    - ☐ **Pillow of Death** (1945) - The series finale involves a lawyer and his secretary who are having an affair. When the lawyer's wife is found suffocated, he is drawn into a web of suspicion and séances as more people close to him are murdered.
- ☐ **The Spiral Staircase** (1944) - In 1906, a shadowy serial killer is targeting women with "afflictions"; one night during a thunderstorm, the mute Helen feels menaced. Based on the British novel *Some Must Watch* by Ethel Lina White.
- ☐ **Hangover Square** (1945) – Loosely adapted of the 1941 novel by Patrick Hamilton. A promising classical musician finds his life poisoned by a music hall dancer and by the strange gaps in his memory.
- ☐ **Bedlam** (1946) - Nell Bowen, the protégé of Lord Mortimer, wants to help change the conditions of notorious St. Mary's of Bethlehem Asylum (Bedlam). Though she tries to reform Bedlam, the cruel Master Sims who runs it has her committed there, but ultimately, it's the lunatics who've taken over the asylum. The movie's plot and setting were inspired by the 1732–1734 painting series *A Rake's Progress* by William Hogarth. The final painting in the series, which depicts the famous asylum known as Bedlam, was a direct source of inspiration. *Bedlam* is the last film in a series of B-movie horror films produced by Val Lewton for RKO Radio Pictures, following other low-budget hits like *Cat People* and *Isle of the Dead*. The film focuses on the abuse and manipulation of the institutionalized and the helplessness of those without agency. The terrifying aspects come from the constant threat of violence, the sadistic cruelty of the asylum master (played by Boris Karloff), and the fear of losing one's sanity in a degrading environment.

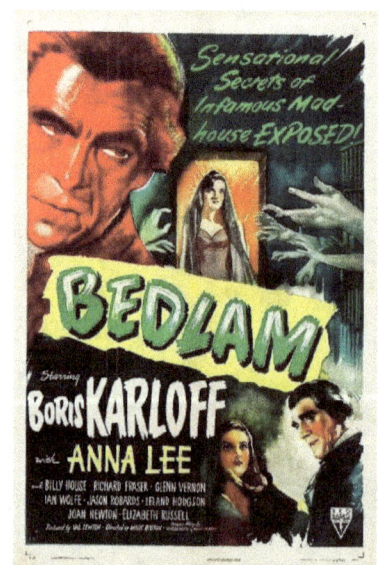

- **Dementia** (1955) - This film, with no dialogue at all, follows a psychotic young woman's nightmarish experiences through one skid-row night. This film received scant distribution. It became well known when footage from it was used in the theatre sequence of the highly popular release *The Blob* (1958).
  - **ADAPTIONS**
    - **Daughters of Horror** (1957) - The original film was released with no dialogue, only music. After its initial limited theatrical release, the film was re-edited and re-released with narration voiced by Ed McMahon and a different score. This version was retitled *Daughter of Horror*. The film is famously featured in the 1958 film *The Blob*. In one scene, it is the movie playing in the theater when the titular monster attacks.
    - **Dementia 3D** (2025) - A 3D conversion of the film, titled *Dementia 3D*, was released in 2025.
- **The Night of the Hunter** (1955) - A self-proclaimed preacher marries a gullible widow whose young children are reluctant to tell him where their real dad hid the $10,000 he'd stolen in a robbery. The film is a faithful but highly stylized adaptation of Davis Grubb's acclaimed novel, which in turn was inspired by the true story of serial killer Harry Powers.
  - **SIMILAR FILMS**
    - **The Innocents** (1961) – A young governess for two children becomes convinced that the house and grounds are haunted. Truman Capote co-wrote the screenplay.
      - **ADAPTIONS**
        - **The Turn of the Screw** (2020) – Modern Gothic adaptation of James's novella.
    - **The Little Girl Who Lives Down the Lane** (1976) – Starring Jodie Foster. A thirteen-year-old girl, who lives with her absentee father, befriends a disabled teenage amateur magician and invites him, gradually, into her tenuous struggle against a predatory local neighbor.
    - **The Killer Inside Me** (1976, 2010) - Adaptations of Jim Thompson's novel about a charming, small-town deputy who is secretly a sadistic serial killer. Like *Night of the Hunter*, the films feature a human monster hiding in plain sight.
- **Diabolique** (1955, France) - A mistress and the frail wife of a brutal headmaster plot his murder, but their conspiracy unravels when his corpse mysteriously disappears. *Diabolique* (original title: *Les Diaboliques*) is a blend of several genres, most accurately categorized as a psychological thriller with strong elements of suspense and horror. It was a highly influential film of its time, paving the way for later psychological thrillers, including Alfred Hitchcock's *Psycho*.
  - **ADAPTIONS**
    - **Reflections of Murder** (1974) - This made-for-television film adaptation starred Joan Hackett, Sam Waterston, and Tuesday Weld. It was a well-received, but little-seen, version of the story.
    - **House of Secrets** (1993) - Another TV movie adaptation of the story.
    - **Diabolique** (1996) - This American film stars Sharon Stone, Isabelle Adjani, and Chazz Palminteri. Directed by Jeremiah Chechik, it was a high-profile remake that received largely negative reviews and is generally considered inferior to the original.
    - **The Boarding School** (1978) - This Spanish thriller directed by Narciso Ibáñez Serrador borrows heavily from the original film, featuring a cruel headmaster and a similar school setting.
- **The Abominable Snowman** (1957) - A kindly English botanist and a gruff American scientist lead an expedition to the Himalayas in search of the legendary Yeti. The film raises questions about who the real "monsters" are: the yetis, who only seek peace, or the humans, who invade their territory out of greed.
- **I Bury the Living** (1958) - Cemetery director Robert Kraft discovers that by arbitrarily changing the status of plots from empty to occupied on the planogram causes the death of the plots' owners. As the film progresses and Kraft gradually comes to believe that the map controls him, the map on the wall becomes slightly larger in each progressive scene, symbolizing it slowly controlling him. Stephen King says he was thinking about this film when he wrote his short story "Obits," about a young writer who discovers he can kill people by writing an obituary about them. The short story is in King's Bazaar of Bad Dreams collection. He references the film in the foreword to the short story.

- ☐ **The Housemaid** (1960, South Korea) - A composer and his wife are thrown into turmoil when a housemaid becomes more than they bargained for.
  - **HOUSEMAID TRILOGY**
    - ☐ **Woman of Fire** (1971, South Korea) - A color remake that retells the original story, though with some changes to the narrative. The lives of a composer and his wife, who live on a chicken farm, are thrown into turmoil when a femme fatale joins their household.
    - ☐ **Woman of Fire '82** (1982, South Korea) - Another color remake that completes the trilogy.
  - **ADAPTIONS & SIMILAR FILMS**
    - ☐ **The Housemaid** (2010) - Remade by director Im Sang-soo and starred Jeon Do-yeon. This adaptation was more explicit and emphasized the extreme class divisions within Korean society.
    - ☐ **Empire of Passion** (1978, Japan) - A married woman and her lover murder her husband and dump his body into a well, but his ghost returns to haunt them as the local gossip intensifies.
      - **THEMATIC COMPANION**
        - ☐ **In the Realm of the Senses** (1976, Japan) – Loosely based on the novel *The ghost of Love* by Itoko Nakamura. A fictionalized retelling of the story of Sada Abe, whose affair with her master quickly turned obsessive and sadomasochistic.
    - ☐ **Fatal Attraction** (1987) - A married man's one-night stand comes back to haunt him. More than 20 directors passed on directing the movie, before Adrian Lyne agreed. According to Glenn Close, people still come up to her to tell her "Thanks, you saved my marriage!" Nominated for six Oscars including: Best Picture, Best Actress, Best Supporting Actress, Best Director, Best Adapted Screenplay and Best Film Editing.
    - ☐ **The Servant** (1963, UK) - A British film that explores the unsettling power shift between a wealthy man and his new manservant, resulting in a psychological breakdown of the household.
- ☐ **What Ever Happened to Baby Jane** (1962) - A former child star torments her paraplegic sister in their decaying Hollywood mansion. The film was nominated for five Oscars including Best Actress in a Leading Role (Bette Davis), Best Actor in a Supporting Role (Victor Buono), Best Cinematography, Best Sound, and won for Best Costume Design. According to Bette Davis in her book "This N' That," the film was originally going to be shot in color. Davis opposed this, saying that it would just make a sad story look pretty.

  - **ADAPTIONS & SIMILAR THEMES**
    - ☐ **Hush… Hush, Sweet Charlotte** (1964) - Though not a sequel to *Baby Jane*, this film reunites director Robert Aldrich with Bette Davis in a similar Southern Gothic

thriller. It was originally intended to reunite Davis and Joan Crawford, but Crawford was replaced by Olivia de Havilland due to illness. The project was initially titled *What Ever Happened to Cousin Charlotte?* but was changed by Davis to avoid being seen as a direct sequel.

    - ☐ **What Ever Happened to Aunt Alice** (1969) - Produced by Aldrich, this film is part of the same "psycho-biddy" cycle, though it is not a direct sequel to *Baby Jane*. An aging widow hides a deadly secret which she will do anything to keep buried.
    - ☐ **Scream, Pretty Peggy** (1973) – Starring Bette Davis. A sculptor hires young college girls to take care of his elderly mother and his supposedly insane sister, both of whom live in the old family mansion with him.
    - ☐ **The Screaming Woman** (1972) - A wealthy former mental patient goes home to her estate to rest and recuperate. While walking the grounds one day she hears the screams of a woman coming from underneath the ground who has been buried alive. Her family, however, refuses to believe her story, and sees the incident as an opportunity to prove the woman's mind has snapped so they can take control of her money.

- **PSYCHO-BIDDY FILMS:** Also called "hagsploitation," are a subgenre of horror-thrillers from the 1960s and 70s that feature aging actresses in grotesque, often deranged roles. Sparked by *What Ever Happened to Baby Jane?* (1962), these films exploit themes of faded stardom, madness, and confinement, turning once-glamorous women into objects of both pity and terror.
  - ☐ **Scream of Fear** (1961) - A wheelchair-bound young woman returns to her father's estate after 10 years, and although she's told he's away, she keeps seeing his dead body on the estate.
    - **SIMILAR THEMES**
      - ☐ **What Lies Beneath** (2000) - The wife of a university research scientist believes that her lakeside Vermont home is haunted by a ghost - or that she is losing her mind. Influenced by the work of Alfred Hitchcock.
      - ☐ **Paranoiac** (1963) - Another thriller from Hammer Films that, like *Scream of Fear*, deals with manipulation and madness within a family.
      - ☐ **Gaslight** (1944) - The classic film about a woman manipulated by her husband into thinking she is going insane is a major precursor to *Scream of Fear*.
  - ☐ **Berserk** (1967) - A scheming circus owner finds her authority challenged when a vicious killer targets the show. Joan Crawford's role as a menacing, unstable older woman fits a trend she helped popularize with her earlier film *What Ever Happened to Baby Jane?* This was her second-to-last feature film appearance before she retired from acting. Her final film was the 1970 monster movie *Trog*.
    - **JOAN CRAWFORD**
      - ☐ **Trog** (1970) - A sympathetic anthropologist uses drugs and surgery to try to communicate with a primitive troglodyte who is found living in a local cave.
  - ☐ **Straight-Jacket** (1964) - A thriller about a woman released from an asylum who returns home to find a new string of murders, starring Joan Crawford. (This is also noted from a Robert Bloch novel.
  - ☐ **The Nanny** (1965) - Bette Davis stars as a seemingly prim and proper caregiver who may be a dangerous threat to the child in her care.
  - ☐ **Greta** (2018) - A young woman's friendship with a lonely widow takes a dark turn toward a terrifying obsession.
- ☐ **At Midnight I'll Take Your Soul** (1964, Brazil) - A gravedigger prowls the city in search of a female to bear him a son.
  - **COFFIN JOE TRILOGY**
    - ☐ **The Night I'll Possess Your Corpse** (1967, Brazil) - This is the second film in the trilogy, continuing the story of the sociopathic undertaker Coffin Joe (Zé do Caixão), who survived his encounter at the end of the first movie. The film expands on his blasphemous quest and features an infamous sequence where he is dragged to a nightmarish, frozen vision of Hell.
    - ☐ **Embodiment of Evil** (2008, Brazil) - The third and final installment concludes the trilogy after a 40-year hiatus. Coffin Joe is released from prison and resumes his depraved mission to sire a son.
    - ☐ **The Strange World of Coffin Joe** (1968, Brazil) - This is a horror anthology featuring three stories, one of which sees Coffin Joe kidnapping a couple and putting them through a series of sadistic trials.
- ☐ **Repulsion** (1965) – A withdrawn manicurist who disapproves of her sister's boyfriend sinks into depression and experiences horrific visions of violence. *Repulsion* is considered the first installment of Polanski's unofficial "Apartment Trilogy." Catherine Deneuve's performance became a touchstone for later portraits of female psychological unraveling.
  - **SEQUELS**
    - ☐ **Rosemary's Baby** (1968) – Paranoia and satanic conspiracy blur reality. A young couple trying for a baby moves into an aging, ornate apartment building on Central Park West, where they find themselves surrounded by peculiar neighbors.
    - ☐ **The Tenant** (1976) – Polanski plays a man consumed by identity paranoia.
- ☐ **Spider Baby or, the Maddest Story Ever Told** (1967) - A caretaker devotes himself to three demented siblings after their father's death.

- ☐ **Hour of the Wolf** (1968) – Bergman's painter descends into nightmarish visions. *Hour of the Wolf* is considered the first of a thematic trilogy of films by Bergman, sometimes called the "Fårö trilogy" after the island where they were filmed. The films explore violence intruding on ordinary lives and the psychology of troubled relationships, though they are not narratively connected. The film has been cited as an influence on other works in the horror and psychological thriller genres with such movies as *The Fly, Lost Highway* and *The Witches*.
  - • **FÅRÖ TRILOGY**
    - ☐ **Shame** (1968) - Also starring Max von Sydow and Liv Ullmann, this film explores a couple's marital strife in the context of a civil war.
    - ☐ **The Passion of Anna** (1969) - The third film in the trilogy, featuring the same two lead actors, deals with psychological violence and relationships.
- ☐ **Duel** (1971) - A business commuter is pursued and terrorized by the malevolent driver of a massive tractor-trailer. Directed by Steven Spielberg and won a Primetime Emmy. According to Richard Matheson, he was inspired to write the original short story "Duel" after an encounter with a tailgating truck driver on November 22, 1963, the day that John F. Kennedy was assassinated.
- ☐ **The Other** (1972) – Twin boys blur innocence and evil. A series of gruesome accidents plague a small American farming community in the summer of 1935, encircling two identical twin brothers and their family.
- ☐ **Images** (1972) – Woman hallucinates doppelgängers and breakdowns. *Images* is considered part of an unofficial trilogy of films by Robert Altman that deal with identity and psychological distress, though they are not narratively connected.
  - • **SIMILAR FILMS**
    - ☐ **3 Women** (1977) - This film, also directed by Altman, explores a similar theme of identity blurring and psychological instability.
    - ☐ **A Cold Day in the Park** (1969) - A less-known Altman film that is sometimes included in the trilogy due to its focus on a woman under extreme psychological stress.
- ☐ **The Baby** (1973) – Disturbing psychodrama of infantilized adult man. The film's themes of dysfunctional family dynamics, abuse, and psychological horror have led to comparisons with other films, such as *What Ever Happened to Baby Jane?* (1962), *Spider Baby* (1967), and *Orphan* (2009).
- ☐ **It's Alive** (1974) - The Davises are expecting a baby, which turns out to be a monster with a nasty habit of killing people whenever it is scared. And it is easily scared.
  - • **SEQUELS, EVIL BABY & MATERNAL ANXIETY FILMS**
    - ☐ **It Lives Again** (1978) - An epidemic of monster babies sweeps across America.
    - ☐ **The Unborn** (1991) - Features a mother who discovers that the new baby she's been carrying is part of a dark genetic experiment.
    - ☐ **Grace** (2009) - After losing her unborn child, Madeline Matheson insists on carrying the baby to term. Following the delivery, the child miraculously returns to life with an appetite for human blood. Madeline is faced with a mother's ultimate decision.
    - ☐ **Prevenge** (2016, UK) - Widow Ruth is seven months pregnant when, believing herself to be guided by her unborn baby, she embarks on a homicidal rampage, dispatching anyone who stands in her way.
    - ☐ **Still/Born** (2017) - A mother gives birth to one healthy twin but is tormented by a supernatural entity she believes wants to take her living child.
    - ☐ **Birth/Rebirth** (2023) - Explores themes of stillbirth and motherhood through a story about a morgue technician who successfully reanimates a child.
- ☐ **The Night Porter** (1974) – Trauma and obsession blur love and horror. A concentration camp survivor rekindles her sadomasochistic relationship with an ex-SS officer working as a night porter at a Vienna hotel, but his former associates begin stalking them.
- ☐ **Dead of Night (Deathdream)** (1974) - A young soldier killed in the Vietnam War inexplicably shows up at his family home on the night of his death. Loosely inspired by the classic 1902 W. W. Jacobs short story "The Monkey Paw." Directed by Bob Clark.
  - • **SIMILAR FILMS**
    - ☐ **Sole Survivor** (1984) - A lone survivor of a plane crash is haunted by a feeling unworthy of survival. Dead people start coming after her to collect her.
    - ☐ **The Survivor** (1981, Australia) - An Australian horror film that also focuses on a plane crash's lone survivor, a pilot, who is haunted by the ghosts of dead children.

☐ **House of Whipcord** (1974) – Woman trapped in sadistic pseudo-reform institution. *House of Whipcord* is considered the first in a trilogy of horror films directed by Pete Walker and written by David McGillivray, although the films are not narratively connected. The film shares similarities with other exploitation films of the era, particularly the "women in prison" subgenre.

- **SEQUELS**
  - ☐ **Frightmare** (1974) - The second film, featuring a cannibalistic elderly couple, explores similar themes of moral decay and social deviance.
  - ☐ **House of Mortal Sin** (1976) - The third film focuses on a corrupt priest and the misuse of institutional power.

☐ **The Stepford Wives** (1975) – Paranoid housewife suspects suburban perfection hides horror. Joanna Eberhart has come to the quaint little town of Stepford, Connecticut with her family, but soon discovers there lies a sinister truth in the all too perfect behavior of the female residents.

- **SEQUELS & ADAPTIONS**
  - ☐ **Revenge of the Stepford Wives** (1980) - A television reporter (played by Sharon Gless) investigates the suspiciously happy women of Stepford.
  - ☐ **The Stepford Children** (1987) - The story revisits Stepford, with the men now also transforming their rebellious children into obedient drones.
  - ☐ **The Stepford Husbands** (1996) - This film reverses the original story's premise, with the women of the town brainwashing their husbands.
  - ☐ **The Stepford Wives** (2009) - The secret to a Stepford wife lies behind the doors of the Men's Association.

☐ **The Amusement Park** (1975) - Directed by George A. Romero. The film was originally commissioned as a public service announcement about ageism and was considered lost for decades. An elderly gentleman goes for what he assumes will be an ordinary day at the amusement park, only to find himself in the middle of a hellish nightmare.

☐ **Obsession** (1976) – De Palma's Hitchcockian tale of fixation and doubles. A wealthy New Orleans businessman becomes obsessed with a young woman who resembles his late wife.

- **DE PALMA FILMS**
  - ☐ **Sisters** (1973) – Conjoined-twin psychology fuels a murder mystery.
  - ☐ **Dressed to Kill** (1980) - Another De Palma thriller, this film similarly uses psychological suspense and shocking twists. A mysterious blonde woman kills one of the patients of a psychiatrist and then goes after the high-class hooker who witnessed the murder.
  - ☐ **Body Double** (1984) - The last film in De Palma's Hitchcockian trilogy, this movie explores themes of voyeurism and obsession. A young actor's obsession with spying on a beautiful woman who lives nearby leads to a baffling series of events with drastic consequences.
  - ☐ **Raising Cain** (1992) - The oncologist wife of a prominent child psychologist suspects her husband has an unhealthy scientific obsession with their child, unaware of what - or who - is really going on inside his head. It is a high-concept, twist-filled film in the vein of De Palma's other psychological thrillers. The horror is rooted in mental illness and extreme psychological manipulation, with a uniquely perverse tone.
    - **SIMILAR FILMS**
      - ☐ **Primal Fear** (1996) - This film features a seemingly timid altar boy accused of murder who reveals a violent alter ego during his trial. It capitalizes on the same anxieties around multiple personality disorder.
      - ☐ **Identity** (2003) – Strangers trapped at motel, minds unravel. This film features a complex and twist-filled plot involving a series of murders committed by the multiple personalities of a single individual.
      - ☐ **Open Grave** (2013) - A man wakes up with no memory in a pit full of dead bodies in the wilderness and must determine if the murderer is one of the strangers who rescued him, or if he himself is the killer.
      - ☐ **Split** (2016) - M. Night Shyamalan's psychological horror similarly features a protagonist with multiple personalities, including a terrifying and violent one, though with a supernatural twist.

- ☐ **Carrie** (1976) – Carrie White, a shy, friendless teenage girl who is sheltered by her domineering, religious mother, unleashes her telekinetic powers after being humiliated by her classmates at her senior prom. Brian De Palma split screens during the prom massacre to show both the horror and Carrie's perspective simultaneously. In 2024, Amazon announced a new television series based on the novel, with Mike Flanagan attached to develop it. It is described as a "bold and timely reimagining" of the story.
  - • **ADAPTIONS**
    - ☐ **The Rage: Carrie 2** (1999) - This sequel focuses on Rachel Lang, a new telekinetic teenager who is revealed to be Carrie's half-sister. The film follows a similar plot as Rachel, like Carrie, faces humiliation that leads to a violent, telekinetic rampage.
    - ☐ **Carrie** (2002) - This made-for-TV movie starred Angela Bettis in the title role. It attempted to be more faithful to King's novel but altered the ending significantly, leaving Carrie alive in a potential setup for a TV series that never materialized.
    - ☐ **Carrie** (2013) - Directed by Kimberly Peirce, this theatrical remake starred Chloë Grace Moretz as Carrie and Julianne Moore as her mother, Margaret White.
  - • **SIMILAR FILMS**
    - ☐ **The Fury** (1978) - A former CIA agent uses the talents of a young psychic to help retrieve his telekinetic son from a shadowy secret government agency.
    - ☐ **The Medusa Touch** (1978) - A telekinetic novelist causes disasters simply by thinking about them.
    - ☐ **Patrick** (1978, Australia) - A young nurse who's just started working at a public clinic begins to suspect that a comatose young man may possess the powers of psychokinesis.
    - ☐ **The Visitor** (1979) - The soul of a young girl with telekinetic powers and her mother become the prize in a battle between good ETs and evil ETs.
    - ☐ **Firestarter** (1984) – Starring Drew Barrymore. A young girl with pyrokinesis, the ability to create and control fire with her mind, must go on the run with her father from a relentless and secretive government agency that wants to weaponize her power. Based on the 1980 Stephen King novel of the same name.
      - • **ADAPTIONS & SEQUELS**
        - ☐ **Firestarter 2: Rekindled** (2002) - This two-part TV miniseries, released on the Sci Fi Channel, serves as a direct sequel to the 1984 film. It follows a grown-up Charlie McGee (played by Marguerite Moreau) as she continues to hide from "The Shop" but is eventually drawn into a confrontation with her old nemesis, John Rainbird.
        - ☐ **Firestarter** (2022) - This film is a remake of the original 1984 movie, with Zac Efron and Ryan Kiera Armstrong in the lead roles. It updates the story for a modern audience but generally follows the same core plot of Charlie and her father on the run. Despite talk of expanding the film into a franchise, its poor box office performance makes a direct sequel unlikely.
- ☐ **The Haunting of Julia** (1977) – Starring Mia Farrow. After her daughter's death, wealthy American homemaker Julia Lofting moves to London to restart her life. All seems well until she is haunted by the ghosts of other children while mourning for her own.
- ☐ **When a Stranger Calls** (1979) - A psychopathic killer terrorizes a babysitter, then returns seven years later to menace her again. Throughout the opening segment, director Fred Walton gradually increases the feeling of suspense by making each subsequent phone call ring a bit louder than the previous one. They escalate from eerie to jarring and finally infuriating.
  - • **ADAPTIONS & SEQUELS**
    - ☐ **When a Stranger Calls Back** (1993) - This made-for-television sequel reunites the original film's director Fred Walton with actors Carol Kane and Charles Durning. The story revisits the trauma of the first film while following a new woman being stalked by a killer.
    - ☐ **When a Stranger Calls** (2006) - This theatrical remake expands the suspenseful opening of the original film to a full feature length. It modernizes the setting with cell phones but keeps the core plot of a babysitter terrorized by a mysterious caller.

The Master of Suspense

Alfred Hitchcock

Alfred Hitchcock (1899–1980) was the "Master of Suspense," an English director whose career spanned silent films to Hollywood dominance. While not a horror specialist, his thrillers redefined cinematic fear, influencing every horror filmmaker who followed. Hitchcock's Catholic upbringing, fascination with guilt and voyeurism, and meticulous technical control shaped films that turned everyday spaces — showers, staircases, birds on a wire — into primal nightmares.

Signature Works (Curated)
- *Psycho* (1960) — Motel, mother, shower. Broke taboos on violence, sexuality, and narrative structure; essentially launched modern horror.
- *The Birds* (1963) — Nature's revolt without explanation; pure dread.
- *Rear Window* (1954) — Voyeurism as suspense, with horror undertones of powerlessness.
- *Vertigo* (1958) — Obsession and identity collapse; psychological horror dressed as romance.
- *Frenzy* (1972) — His return to London, exploring graphic murder through dark comedy.

The Fingerprints
- Voyeurism: audiences made complicit in looking (*Rear Window*, *Psycho*).
- "The wrong man" trope: innocents trapped by fate (*North by Northwest*).
- Everyday spaces turned uncanny: showers, birds, staircases.
- Precision editing: montage as terror (the shower scene cut into 78 shots).
- Cold blonde heroines as both victims and enigmas.

Legacy & Influence
Hitchcock created the grammar of modern horror and thrillers. *Psycho* birthed the slasher. *The Birds* anticipated apocalyptic horror. His manipulation of audience empathy — killing off the supposed protagonist halfway through *Psycho* — shattered narrative conventions. Directors from Brian De Palma to David Lynch, John Carpenter to Dario Argento, all borrow Hitchcock's DNA in camera movement, suspense-building, and psychological dread. Even Jordan Peele has cited Hitchcock as an influence in making horror socially resonant.

Pairing Night Watchlist
- *Psycho* (1960) → Look for how the film weaponizes editing and sound; the shower scene is as much about suggestion as gore.
- *The Birds* (1963) → Notice the lack of musical score — Hitchcock forces you to sit with silence and shrieks.
- *Rear Window* (1954) → Pay attention to how your perspective is trapped with James Stewart's; every cut implicates you as the voyeur.

Quick Facts to Sound Smart
- Hitchcock financed *Psycho* himself and used his TV crew to keep costs down; it became one of the most profitable films ever made.
- He made cameo appearances in nearly all his films, a running in-joke for audiences.
- Hitchcock never won a competitive Oscar for directing, despite his massive influence.
- He pioneered "the MacGuffin" a plot device that drives the story but ultimately doesn't matter.

1980s-1990s Psychological Mastery

☐ **The Dead Zone** (1983) – Psychic powers destroy a man's mental state.
☐ **C.H.U.D.** (1984) – Psychological decay of the city underbelly.
- **SEQUELS**
  - ☐ **C.H.U.D. II: Bud the C.H.U.D.** (1989) - The plot centers on two friends who accidentally unleash a C.H.U.D. in a new suburban town. The creature, named Bud, creates a zombie-like epidemic by biting residents.
☐ **Blue Velvet** (1986) – Lynch's suburbia hides darkness and obsession.
- **RELATED DAVID LYNCH PROJECTS:**
  - ☐ **Wild at Heart** (1990) - This film, released four years after *Blue Velvet*, also stars Laura Dern and was directed by Lynch. Like *Blue Velvet*, it examines the psychological violence and depravity hidden within seemingly innocent scenarios.
  - ☐ **Twin Peaks: Fire Walk with Me** (1992) - Some theorize the world of *Blue Velvet* could be a prequel to Lynch's *Twin Peaks* franchise, but there is no official narrative link. Both projects share a thematic focus on the sinister underbelly of small-town American life.
  - ☐ **Lost Highway** (1997) – Lynch's fractured identity nightmare.
  - ☐ **Mulholland Drive** (2001) – Surrealism, dream logic, and Hollywood nightmare.
  - ☐ **Twin Peaks: The Missing Pieces** (2014) - Twin Peaks before *Twin Peaks* (1990) and at the same time not always and entirely in the same place as *Twin Peaks: Fire Walk with Me* (1992).
☐ **The Reflecting Skin** (1990) – In the 1950s, a young boy living with his troublesome family in rural USA fantasizes that a neighboring widow is actually a vampire, responsible for a number of disappearances in the area. The film is considered the first of an unofficial trilogy of horror films by Philip Ridley that explore distorted, subjective realities, though they are not narratively connected.
- **SEQUELS**
  - ☐ **The Passion of Darkly Noon** (1995) - Ridley's follow-up film explores similar themes of violence and psychological turmoil in a rural American setting.
  - ☐ **Heartless** (2009) - This later film also presents a subjective, sometimes delusional, interpretation of reality, though its narrative concludes differently.
☐ **Misery** (1990) – After a famous author is rescued from a car crash by a fan of his novels, he comes to realize that the care he is receiving is only the beginning of a nightmare of captivity and abuse. Kathy Bates won Best Actress in a Leading Role at the 1991 Academy Awards, the first (and still rare) Academy recognition for the horror genre. Many prominent actresses were considered for the role of Annie Wilkes, including Bette Midler, who turned it down because she found it too violent. Kathy Bates was suggested by screenwriter William Goldman. Many well-known actors, such as Harrison Ford, Kevin Kline, and Jack Nicholson, turned down the role of Paul Sheldon. Nicholson reportedly declined because of a bad experience with Stanley Kubrick while filming another King adaptation, *The Shining*. A new film, described as a "loose remake" of *Misery*, was announced in 2024. Starring Jenna Ortega, Barry Keoghan, and The Weeknd, the project has reportedly faced challenges finding a distributor.
- **SIMILAR FILMS**
  - ☐ **My Name is Julia Ross** (1945) - Through a nosy employment agency, Julia Ross secures employment with a wealthy widow, Mrs. Hughes, and goes to live at her house. Two days later, she awakens in a different house, in different clothes, and with a new identity. She's told she is the daughter-in-law of Mrs. Hughes and has suffered a nervous breakdown. Is Julia really "Julia," or is it true that she's lost all memory of who she is?
  - ☐ **The Fan** (1982, West Germany) – A West German horror thriller about a teenage girl whose obsessive love for a pop singer turns to murderous rage.
  - ☐ **Dead of Winter** (1987) - A fledgling actress is lured to a remote mansion for a screen-test, soon discovering she is actually a prisoner in the middle of a blackmail plot. Loosely based on the 1941 novel *The Women in Red* by Anthony Gilbert.
  - ☐ **Shirley** (2020) – Starring Elizabeth Moss. A famous horror writer finds inspiration for her next book after she and her husband take in a young couple. Based on the 2014 novel *Shirley* by Susan Scarf Merrell. The film focuses on a fictional young couple who moves in with Shirley Jackson and her husband, creating a psychological story in the style of Jackson's own work.

- ☐ **Pacific Heights** (1990) – Tenant from hell manipulates landlords psychologically.
  - • **SIMILAR THEMES**
    - ☐ **Fear** (1996) - Focuses on a family terrorized by their teenage daughter's seemingly charming new boyfriend.
    - ☐ **Lakeview Terrace** (2008) - A police officer terrorizes a new interracial couple who moves in next door.
- ☐ **Single White Female** (1992) – Obsessive roommate morphs into identity horror. In 2025, reports confirmed that a new remake of *Single White Female* is in development at Sony's 3000 Pictures. Jenna Ortega and Taylor Russell are reportedly in talks to star and produce the new version.
  - • **SEQUELS**
    - ☐ **Single White Female 2: The Psycho** (2005) - The story follows a young woman whose life spirals out of control after her new roommate becomes dangerously obsessed with her and begins plotting against her friends.
- ☐ **The Hand That Rocks the Cradle** (1992) – Nanny manipulates a family with precision cruelty.
  - • **ADAPTIONS & SIMILAR FILMS**
    - ☐ **Khal-Naaikaa** (1993, India) - An Indian film remake was released in 1993, just one year after the original.
    - ☐ **The Hand that Rocks the Cradle** (2025) - The upcoming American remake is directed by Michelle Garza Cervera and stars Maika Monroe as the nanny and Mary Elizabeth Winstead as the mother. It is scheduled to be released on Hulu in October 2025.
    - ☐ **The Guardian** (1990) - A young couple with a newborn son don't realize that their new nanny is a magical Druid sacrificing infants to an evil tree. The film is based on the novel of the same name by Dan Greenburg. William Friedkin, known for directing *The Exorcist* (1973), was brought in to direct and significantly rewrote the script, adding the supernatural "Druid" mythology to the story.
- ☐ **The Dark Half** (1993) – Directed by George A. Romero. The film is based on Stephen King's 1989 novel of the same name. The story is semi-autobiographical, reflecting King's own time writing under the pseudonym Richard Bachman. A writer's fictional alter ego wants to take over his life...at any price.
  - • **SIMILAR FILMS**
    - ☐ **The King of Comedy** (1982) - A satirical film that also explores the darker side of obsession and ambition, with a similar focus on a protagonist who wants to be noticed by the world.
    - ☐ **Fight Club** (1999) - This film similarly explores the theme of a protagonist with a suppressed, violent alter ego that takes over his life.
    - ☐ **American Psycho** (2000) – A wealthy New York City investment banking executive, Patrick Bateman, hides his alternate psychopathic ego from his co-workers and friends as he delves deeper into his violent, hedonistic fantasies. Looking for a way to create the character of Patrick Bateman, Christian Bale stumbled onto a Tom Cruise appearance on the Late Show with David Letterman (1993). According to co-writer and director Mary Harron, Bale saw in Cruise "this very intense friendliness with nothing behind the eyes," and Bale subsequently based the character of Bateman on that. Interestingly, Tom Cruise is actually featured in the novel. He lives in the same apartment complex as Bateman, who meets him in an elevator and gets the name of Cocktail (1988) wrong, calling it "Bartender." Based on the novel, *American Psycho* by Bret Easton Ellis.
      - • **SEQUELS**
        - ☐ **American Psycho 2** (2002) - Starring Mila Kunis, this film has almost no connection to the original. The story follows a criminology student who kills her classmates to secure a position as a teaching assistant.
    - ☐ **Secret Window** (2004) – Writer haunted by his own doppelgänger. Also based on a Stephen King story, this film features a writer who is accused of plagiarism and haunted by a man who claims he stole his idea. It shares the theme of authorship and psychological unraveling.
    - ☐ **Mr. Brooks** (2007) – Kevin Costner as a respected businessman/serial killer. A film that follows a seemingly normal man who secretly has a murderous alter ego.
    - ☐ **Malignant** (2021) - Madison is paralyzed by shocking visions of grisly murders, and her torment worsens as she discovers that these waking dreams are in fact terrifying realities. The

film's twist involving a malignant, homicidal alter ego has been explicitly compared to *The Dark Half* by fans.

- ☐ **The Beta Test** (2021) - A married Hollywood agent receives a mysterious letter for an anonymous sexual encounter and becomes ensnared in a sinister world of lying, murder and infidelity.

☐ **Mute Witness** (1995) – Mute woman trapped in psychological snuff-film paranoia.
- • **SIMILAR FILMS**
  - ☐ **Ms. 45** (1981) - A classic exploitation film about a mute woman who, after being assaulted, becomes a spree killer targeting men in New York City.
  - ☐ **Beyond the Black Rainbow** (2010) – In 1983, a young mute woman with psychic abilities is held captive within the Arboria Institute, a secluded futuristic facility run by a sinister doctor with an unraveling mind and a growing obsession with her.
  - ☐ **The Seasoning House** (2012) - Sold at a brothel deep in the woods to work as a caretaker, a hapless deaf girl must summon the courage to fight for her life.

☐ **The Prophecy** (1995) – Angel war framed in psychological terms. Directed by Gregory Widen, stars Christopher Walken as the archangel Gabriel, who comes to Earth to find a powerful soul to end the heavenly war.
- • **SEQUELS**
  - ☐ **The Prophecy II** (1998) - This sequel sees Gabriel (Walken) return to Earth from Hell to stop the birth of a Nephilim, a child of a human and an angel.
  - ☐ **The Prophecy 3: The Ascent** (2000) - In the third installment, Gabriel (Walken) has become human. The story follows the adult Nephilim from the previous film, who must face a genocidal angel.
  - ☐ **The Prophecy: Uprising** (2005) - This film moves away from the previous plotline and does not feature Christopher Walken. A new protagonist must protect a mystical book of prophecies, the Lexicon, from an aggressive demon.
  - ☐ **The Prophecy: Forsaken** (2005) - Continuing directly from *Uprising*, the final film follows the same protagonist as she tries to protect the Lexicon, which reveals the name of the Antichrist
- • **SIMILAR RELIGIOUS HORROR FILMS**
  - ☐ **Constantine** (2005) - This film also features a protagonist navigating a hidden supernatural war on Earth between angelic and demonic forces.
  - ☐ **Legion** (2010) - In this movie, the archangel Michael arrives on Earth to protect a pregnant woman whose child is humanity's last hope against an angelic apocalypse.

☐ **The Stendhal Syndrome** (1996, Italy) - A detective falls under hallucinatory spells while trying to capture the sadistic man who raped her.
- • **SEQUELS**
  - ☐ **The Card Player** (2004) - A direct sequel was planned, following Detective Anna Manni on another case. However, when actress Asia Argento was unavailable, the character's name was changed, and the resulting film was *The Card Player*.

☐ **Open Your Eyes** (1997, Spain) – Dreams and reality blur in identity crisis.
- • **ADAPTIONS**
  - ☐ **Vanilla Sky** (2001) – US remake of *Open Your Eyes*.

☐ **Pi** (1998) – Obsession with numbers drives mathematician into breakdown. Aronofsky's subsequent films explore similar themes of obsession and the self-destructive nature of pursuing a single-minded goal such as *Requiem for a Dream.*
- • **SIMILAR ARONOFSKY FILMS**
  - ☐ **Mother!** (2017) – Allegorical fever dream of psychological abuse.
  - ☐ **The Fountain** (2006) - A sprawling romantic fantasy about a man desperately trying to save his dying wife by finding the Tree of Life. It explores themes of love, death, and reincarnation in a spiritual, mystical way.
  - ☐ **Black Swan** (2010) - A psychological horror film about a ballerina's intense dedication to her role, which causes her to lose her grip on reality. Natalie Portman trained for over a year and performed many of her own dance sequences.

The Architect of Grief

Ari Aster[30]

Born in New York in 1986, Ari Aster studied at the AFI Conservatory before shocking the world with his debut feature. He mines horror not from monsters, but from family, grief, and ritual turning the domestic into the demonic. His films are emotional exorcisms: grief curdled into terror, relationships collapsed into nightmare. Aster has become synonymous with "elevated horror," but his work is as savage and gutting as anything in the genre's history.

Signature Works (Curated)
- *Hereditary* (2018) — A family cursed by grief and a demonic pact; a modern classic that combines possession, trauma, and psychological despair.
- *Midsommar* (2019) — A breakup horror wrapped in sunlit ritual; cult violence blossoms in broad daylight.
- *Beau Is Afraid* (2023) — A surreal odyssey through anxiety, guilt, and maternal control; less horror than absurdist dread, but still a nightmare.

The Fingerprints
- Horror as grief: death, trauma, and dysfunctional families always at the center.
- Ritual and inevitability: characters can't escape fate, only spiral into it.
- Daylight dread: where most horror hides in the shadows, Aster makes sunlight blinding and terrifying.
- Operatic emotion: screaming matches, breakdowns, and raw human anguish.
- Meticulous set design: every symbol, tapestry, and background detail contributes to the story's dread.

Legacy & Influence
Aster helped cement A24's dominance in modern horror alongside Robert Eggers. *Hereditary* is often called the scariest film of the 2010s, reviving slow-burn supernatural terror with raw emotional grounding. *Midsommar* became a cultural event, spawning memes, Halloween costumes, and breakup metaphors. His blending of melodrama and horror has influenced new indie filmmakers and provoked debate about the direction of horror itself—arthouse spectacle or gut-punch genre.

Pairing Night Watchlist
- *Hereditary* (2018) → Watch Toni Collette's performance; it's not just possession, it's a howl of grief. Look for how the camera frames the house as a dollhouse trap.
- *Midsommar* (2019) → Track how the cult's rituals double as metaphors for Dani's breakup—terror and liberation entwined.
- *Beau Is Afraid* (2023) → Consider how absurdist comedy turns into existential horror; paranoia stretched to mythic proportions.

Quick Facts to Sound Smart
- Aster first gained attention with disturbing short films like *The Strange Thing About the Johnsons* (2011), about taboo abuse in a family.
- The treehouse in *Hereditary* was built entirely on a soundstage; its unnatural glow was deliberate.
- Florence Pugh shot *Midsommar* back-to-back with *Little Women*. Two wildly different takes on womanhood and community.
- Aster calls *Beau Is Afraid* his "Jewish *Lord of the Rings*," though many fans saw it as a 3-hour panic attack.
- He has cited Ingmar Bergman and Michael Haneke as major influences, especially in fusing family drama with existential dread.

2000s Psychological Thrillers

- ☐ **The Cell** (2000) - An F.B.I. Agent persuades a social worker, who is adept with a new experimental technology, to enter the mind of a comatose serial killer in order to learn where he has hidden his latest kidnap victim.
  - • **SEQUELS**
    - ☐ **The Cell 2** (2009) - This low-budget, direct-to-video sequel has a similar premise to the original, with a psychic investigator using technology to enter the mind of a serial killer.
- ☐ **Session 9** (2001) – Tensions rise within an asbestos cleaning crew as they work in an abandoned mental hospital with a horrific past that seems to be coming back.
  - • **HOSPITAL & INSTITUTION HORROR**
    - ☐ **Gothika** (2003) - A psychiatrist awakens as a patient in a mental institution, with no memory of the murder she's accused of committing. As she tries to regain her memory, a vengeful spirit manipulates her.
    - ☐ **Fragile** (2005, Spain) - At her new job in a rundown children's hospital, a nurse desperately tries to keep her patients safe from a plague of random, mysterious attacks.
    - ☐ **The Jacket** (2005) – Amnesia and time-slips in asylum. A Gulf war veteran is wrongly sent to a mental institution for insane criminals, where he becomes the object of a doctor's experiments, and his life is completely affected by them.
    - ☐ **The Ward** (2010) - A woman confined to a psychiatric ward begins to experience a terrifying haunting.
    - ☐ **6 Souls** (2010) - A forensic psychiatrist discovers that all but one of her patient's multiple personalities are murder victims. She will have to find out what's happening before her time is finished.
    - ☐ **Unsane** (2018) - A young woman is involuntarily committed to a mental institution, where she is confronted by her greatest fear - but is it real or a product of her delusion?
    - ☐ **Yummy** (2019, Belgium) - An orgy of blood, violence and fun in which a young couple travel to a shabby Eastern European hospital for plastic surgery. Once there things unravel.
    - ☐ **12 Hour Shift** (2020) - Bodies start to pile up when a drug-user nurse and her cousin try to find a replacement kidney for an organ trafficker.
    - ☐ **The Power** (2021) - In 1970s London, a trainee nurse spends her first night at a hospital during power outages, where she is haunted by a supernatural presence.
    - ☐ **Knocking** (2021) - A woman leaves a psychiatric ward after a nervous breakdown, only to start hearing mysterious knocking sounds in her apartment.
    - ☐ **The Rule of Jenny Pen** (2024) - Confined to a secluded rest home and trapped within his stroke-ridden body, a former Judge must stop an elderly psychopath who employs a child's puppet to abuse the home's residents with deadly consequences.
- ☐ **Dark Water** (2002, Japan) – A mother going through a divorce moves into a run down apartment with her daughter. A persistent leak from above, visions of a missing girl, and other eerie phenomena become increasingly menacing as clues to a past tragedy come to light.
  - • **ADAPTION**
    - ☐ **Dark Water** (2005) – Starring Jennifer Connelly. A mother and daughter, still wounded from a bitter custody dispute, hole up in a run-down apartment building, where they are targeted by the ghost of a former resident.
- ☐ **The Machinist** (2004) – Insomniac's paranoia warps his perception of reality. The producers of the film claim that Christian Bale dropped from about 173 pounds in weight down to about 110 pounds in weight to make this film. They also claim that Bale actually wanted to drop down to 100 pounds, but that they would not let him go below 120 out of fear that his health could be in too much danger if he did. His diet consisted of one can of tuna and an apple per day. His 63-pound weight loss is said to be a record for any actor for a movie role. He regained the weight in time for his role in *Batman Begins* (2005).
- ☐ **The Forgotten** (2004) – Gaslighting conspiracy of abducted children, starring Julianne Moore. After being told that their children never existed, a man and woman soon discover there is a much bigger enemy at work.
- ☐ **Hide and Seek** (2005) – As a widower tries to piece together his life in the wake of his wife's suicide, his daughter finds solace, at first, in her imaginary friend. Starring Robert De Niro and Dakota Fanning.

☐ **Hard Candy** (2005) – Hayley's a smart, charming teenage girl. Jeff's a handsome, smooth fashion photographer. An Internet chat, a coffee shop meet-up, an impromptu fashion shoot back at Jeff's place. Jeff thinks it's his lucky night. He's in for a surprise.

☐ **Stay** (2005) – Mind-bending psycho-thriller of reality collapse. A psychiatrist attempts to prevent one of his patients from committing suicide while trying to maintain his own grip on reality.

☐ **Silent Hill** (2006) - Rose Da Silva takes her adopted daughter, Sharon, to the town of Silent Hill in an attempt to cure her of her ailment. After a violent car crash, Sharon disappears and Rose begins a horrific journey to get her back. Based on the popular video game series.

- **SEQUELS**
    - ☐ **Silent Hill: Revelation** (2012) - When her adoptive father disappears, Sharon Da Silva is drawn into a strange and terrifying alternate reality that holds answers to the horrific nightmares that have plagued her since childhood.
    - ☐ **Return to Silent Hill** (2026) - When a mysterious letter calls him back to Silent Hill in search of his lost love, James finds a once-recognizable town and encounters terrifying figures both familiar and new, and begins to question his own sanity.

☐ **The Skeptic** (2009) – Lawyer inherits house, doubts his own sanity.

☐ **The Eclipse** (2009, Ireland) – Melancholic ghost story steeped in psychology.

☐ **Goodnight Mommy** (2014, Austria) – Twin boys move to a new house with their mother after she has face-changing cosmetic surgery, but under the bandages is someone the boys don't recognize.

☐ **The Invitation** (2015) – A psychological thriller where a man attends a dinner party at his ex-wife's house and begins to suspect that her new partner and their friends are part of a sinister cult.

- **DINNER PARTY HORROR**
    - ☐ **The Cook, The Thief, His Wife & Her Lover** (1989) - This film's macabre final dinner scene is a brutal and visceral culmination of its violent story.
    - ☐ **The Last Supper** (1995) – Starring Cameron Diaz. A group of idealistic but frustrated liberals succumb to the temptation of murdering right-wing pundits for their political beliefs.
    - ☐ **Monster Party** (2018) - Three young thieves crash a Malibu dinner party, only to find themselves trapped in a night far more dangerous than they planned.
    - ☐ **The Dinner Party** (2020) - A couple attends a dinner party with a group of eccentric elites. Their unsettling evening is driven by the hope of securing funding for a play, but they soon discover their hosts' dark intentions.
    - ☐ **Hosts** (2020, UK) - A family invite their neighbors over for Christmas dinner with disastrous consequences.
    - ☐ **Barbarians** (2021, UK) - A dinner party in a country house that sees four friends come together for a birthday celebration. But as the night progresses secrets emerge and unsettling events begin to unfold around them.
    - ☐ **The Feast** (2021, UK) - Follows a young woman serving privileged guests at a dinner party in a remote house in rural Wales. The assembled guests do not realize they are about to eat their last supper.
    - ☐ **Silent Night** (2021, UK) – Starring Keira Knightley. Nell, Simon, and their 3 sons are ready to welcome friends and family for what promises to be a perfect Christmas gathering. Perfect except for one thing: everyone is going to die.
    - ☐ **The Menu** (2022) - A young couple travels to a remote island to eat at an exclusive restaurant where the chef has prepared a lavish menu, with some shocking surprises.
    - ☐ **Who Invited Them** (2022) - A wealthy couple hosts a housewarming party, only to find an uninvited couple lingering after the other guests have left. They claim to be friendly neighbors, but their bizarre behavior suggests something more sinister.
    - ☐ **Soft & Quiet** (2022) - Playing out in real time, an elementary school teacher organizes a mixer of like-minded women, when she encounters a woman from her past, leading to a volatile chain of events.
    - ☐ **Brooklyn 45** (2023) - Five military veterans, best friends since childhood, gather together to support their troubled host, and the metaphoric ghosts of their past become all-too-literal.

☐ **The Gift** (2015) – A couple's past resurfaces in psychological torment.

The Poet of Shadows

Val Lewton

Val Lewton (1904–1951) was horror's whisperer, its master of the unseen. Where Universal gave monsters faces and fangs, Lewton gave them implication. Working as a producer at RKO during the 1940s, he redefined the genre by proving that fear could live in silence, suggestion, and shadow. With budgets too small for spectacle, he transformed limitation into liberation, turning repression itself into a style.

Cultivating a Persona

Born Vladimir Ivan Leventon in Yalta, Russia, Lewton emigrated to America as a child and found his way into Hollywood as a novelist and story editor. In 1942, RKO handed him a mandate to make low-budget horror films to compete with Universal's monsters. What emerged was a cycle of films unlike anything before them. Working with directors Jacques Tourneur, Robert Wise, and Mark Robson, Lewton stripped horror of its Gothic excess. Instead of castles, he used city streets; instead of monsters, he used psychology. He made audiences fear not what they saw, but what they imagined.

Lewton's films blurred into film noir, trading vampires and werewolves for paranoia, repression, and alienation. In his hands, horror became modern. The monster was no longer a medieval relic, it might be your neighbor, your lover, or the secret inside your own mind.

Signature Works

- *Cat People* (1942) — A woman fears her passion will turn her into a panther; the "Lewton Bus" sequence, where a hiss of brakes punctures silence, invented the modern jump scare.
- *I Walked with a Zombie* (1943) — A reimagining of *Jane Eyre* set in the Caribbean, weaving Gothic romance with voodoo ritual and colonial unease.
- *The Seventh Victim* (1943) — A bleak story of Satanic cults in New York, filled with existential dread.
- *The Body Snatcher* (1945) — Starring Boris Karloff, a chilling meditation on grave robbing, medicine, and ethics.
- *Bedlam* (1946) — A harrowing look at cruelty inside an asylum, merging history and horror with psychological terror

What He Did for Horror

Lewton gave horror its grammar of suggestion. Forbidden by censors from showing gore or sexuality, he mastered implication. A shadow across a wall, a footstep in silence, or a sudden hiss of brakes became as terrifying as any monster. His films taught audiences that fear lives in the imagination—that the unseen is scarier than the seen.

By tying horror to psychology, repression, and modern settings, Lewton moved the genre out of the Gothic past and into the anxieties of the present. He showed that horror could whisper, and be even more terrifying than when it screamed.

Legacy & Amazement

Though he died young, Lewton's influence endures in every horror film that relies on atmosphere, subtlety, and psychological dread. The jump scare owes him. The marriage of noir shadows and horror unease owes him. Directors from Hitchcock to Aster work in his lineage.

Val Lewton proved that horror didn't need fangs, masks, or monsters to endure. It only needed a shadow, a silence, and the imagination of the audience to make the ordinary terrifying.

Modern & Global Psychological Horror

- ☐ **The Babadook** (2014, Australia) – Manifestation of grief and depression. A single mother and her child fall into a deep well of paranoia when an eerie children's book titled "Mister Babadook" manifests in their home. Festival campaigns highlighted its "arthouse monster" status. Netflix once mistakenly listed it under "LGBT films," fueling the meme.
  - • **GENERATIONAL TRAUMA & FAMILY SECRETS**
    - ☐ **What Josiah Saw** (2021) - A family with buried secrets reunite at a farmhouse after two decades to pay for their past sins.
    - ☐ **You are Not My Mother** (2021) - In a North Dublin housing estate Char's mother goes missing. When she returns Char is determined to uncover the truth of her disappearance and unearth the dark secrets of her family.
    - ☐ **Relic** (2020, Australia) – A daughter, mother and grandmother are haunted by a manifestation of dementia that consumes their family's home.
    - ☐ **Anything for Jackson** (2020) – Satanic grandparents summon wrong spirit.
    - ☐ **The Lodge** (2019) – Stepchildren and isolation spiral into paranoia.
    - ☐ **Hereditary** (2018) – A grieving family is haunted by tragic and disturbing occurrences. The decapitation scene was so shocking it trended worldwide on Twitter opening weekend.
    - ☐ **The Wind** (2018, USA) – Pioneer woman tormented by prairie spirits. Critics also likened *The Wind* to this film, noting the similar focus on how grief and isolation can manifest into psychological and supernatural horror.
    - ☐ **Pyewacket** (2017) – Teen's occult ritual awakens sinister cultic power.
    - ☐ **Slapface** (2021) - A boy deals with the loss of his mother by creating a dangerous relationship with a monster rumored to live in the woods.
    - ☐ **Nocturna: Side A – The Great Old Man's Night** (2021, Argentina) - Ulysses is a hundred-year-old man, battling for redemption on his last night on earth. Faced with imminent death, he is forced to rethink his past, his present and his take on reality.
      - • **SEQUEL**
        - ☐ **Nocturna: Side B – Where the Elephants Go to Die** (2021) - A woman narrates the final night on earth of a 100-year-old man, whom fights for redemption from his life's misdeeds.
    - ☐ **Starve Acres** (2023) - An idyllic rural family life of a couple is thrown into turmoil when their son starts acting out of character.
    - ☐ **Sleep** (2023, Korea) - A young, expectant wife must figure out how to stop her husband's nightmarish sleepwalking habits before he harms himself or his family.
    - ☐ **Went Up the Hill** (2024, Australia/New Zealand) - Jack ventures to remote New Zealand for the funeral of his estranged mother and meets her widow, Jill. But his mother's spirit returns to inhabit each of their bodies, instigating a life-threatening three-way nocturnal dance.
- ☐ **The Neon Demon** (2016) - An aspiring model, Jesse, is new to Los Angeles. However, her beauty and youth, which generate intense fascination and jealousy within the fashion industry, may prove themselves sinister.
- ☐ **It Comes at Night** (2017) – Paranoia tears apart families in post-apocalypse.
  - • **POST-APOCALYPTIC HORRORS**
    - ☐ **The Rover** (2014) - A film that depicts a desolate, post-apocalyptic world in which a man pursues a group of thieves across the Australian Outback.
    - ☐ **Coherence** (2013) – Dinner party fractures under quantum paranoia.
    - ☐ **The Battery** (2012) - The personalities of two former baseball players clash as they traverse the rural back roads of a post-plague New England teeming with the undead.
    - ☐ **The Divide** (2011) - Survivors of a nuclear attack are grouped together for days in the basement of their apartment building, where fear and dwindling supplies wear away at their dynamic.
    - ☐ **The Road** (2009) - This post-apocalyptic film about a father and son traveling across a desolate landscape, based on the Cormac McCarthy novel, shares the same overwhelming sense of hopelessness and dread.
    - ☐ **Testament** (1983) - The aftermath of a nuclear war is examined through the eyes of a single family in a small, isolated California town.

- ☐ **On the Beach** (1959) - After a global nuclear war, the residents of Australia must come to terms with the fact that all life will be destroyed in a matter of months.
- ☐ **The World, the Flesh and the Devil** (1959) - A miner trapped in a cave-in resurfaces, and upon discovering mankind has been wiped out in a nuclear holocaust, sets out to find other survivors.
- ☐ **Five** (1951) - The world is destroyed in a nuclear holocaust. Only five Americans survive, including a pregnant woman, a neo-Nazi, a black man and a bank clerk.

☐ **The Killing of a Sacred Deer** (2017) – Surreal punishment destabilizes family psychology. Steven, a charismatic surgeon, is forced to make an unthinkable sacrifice after his life starts to fall apart, when the behavior of a teenage boy he has taken under his wing turns sinister. Starring Nicole Kidman and Colin Farrell)

☐ **The Perfection** (2018) – Musical obsession turns into psychological warfare.

☐ **Run** (2020) – Munchausen by proxy becomes gaslighting terror.

☐ **Resurrection** (2022) – Woman's past abuser returns, gaslighting her sanity.

- • **SIMILAR THEMES**
  - ☐ **Heretic** (2024) – Starring Hugh Grant. Two young religious women are drawn into a game of cat-and-mouse in the house of a strange man.
  - ☐ **Men** (2022, UK) – A young woman goes on a solo vacation to the English countryside following the death of her ex-husband.
  - ☐ **Saint Maud** (2019) – A psychological Gothic about religiosity, isolation, and mental collapse. Eerie and deeply unsettling.

☐ **Watcher** (2022) – Woman abroad suspects a stalker, reality questioned.

☐ **The Cleaning Lady** (2018) - As a means to distract herself from an affair, a love-addicted woman befriends a cleaning lady, badly scarred by burns. She soon learns, these scars run much deeper than the surface.

☐ **The Black Phone** (2021) - After being abducted and locked in a basement, a boy starts receiving calls on a disconnected phone from the killer's previous victims.

- • **SEQUELS**
  - ☐ **Black Phone 2** (2025) - As Finn, now 17, struggles with life after his captivity, his sister begins receiving calls in her dreams from the black phone and seeing disturbing visions of three boys being stalked at a winter camp known as Alpine Lake.
- • **PHONE HORRORS**
  - ☐ **The Caller** (2011) - A young divorcee is getting her life back together by moving into an apartment. But what will she do when a strange person repeatedly calls her, and threatens to change her new life around?
    - • **REMAKE**
      - ☐ **The Call** (2020, Korea) – The critically-acclaimed remake. Two people live in different times. Seo-Yeon lives in the present and Young-Sook lives in the past. One phone call connects the two, and their lives are changed irrevocably.

☐ **X** (2022, New Zealand) - In 1979, a group of young filmmakers set out to make an adult film in a rural Texas farm, but when their reclusive, elderly hosts catch them in the act, the crew find themselves fighting for their lives.

- • **ADAPTIONS & SEQUELS**
  - ☐ **Pearl** (2022, New Zealand) - In 1918, a young woman on the brink of madness pursues stardom in a desperate attempt to escape the drudgery, isolation, and lovelessness of life on her parents' farm.
  - ☐ **MaXXXine** (2024) - In 1980s Hollywood, adult film star and aspiring actress Maxine Minx finally gets her big break. But as a mysterious killer stalks the starlets of Hollywood, a trail of blood threatens to reveal her sinister past.

☐ **Barbarian** (2022) - A woman staying at an Airbnb discovers that the house she has rented is not what it seems. Zach Cregger's next horror film, *Weapons*, is set in the same universe as *Barbarian*, although it is not a direct sequel. An in-universe viral website launched for the film references the events of *Barbarian*.

- • **RELATED FILMS**
  - ☐ **Weapons** (2025) – Starring Julia Garner and Josh Brolin. When all but one child from the same class mysteriously vanishes on the same night at exactly the same time, a community is left questioning who or what is behind their disappearance.

☐ **Longlegs** (2024) - In pursuit of a serial killer, an FBI agent uncovers a series of occult clues that she must solve to end his terrifying killing spree.

- **RELATED FILMS**
  - ☐ **The Monkey** (2025) - Osgood Perkins' next directorial project is an adaptation of a Stephen King short story, which is also distributed by Neon, the company behind *Longlegs*. When twin brothers Bill and Hal find their father's old monkey toy in the attic, a series of gruesome deaths start. The siblings decide to throw the toy away and move on with their lives, growing apart over the years.

☐ **Dead Mail** (2024) - An ominous help note finds its way to a 1980s post office, connecting a dead letter investigator to a kidnapped keyboard technician.

Pairing Night Watchlist

Want to taste-test psychological horror like a connoisseur? Try these curated double-features with prompts on what to watch for:

- **Classic Breakdown**: *Psycho* (1960) + *Repulsion* (1965). Look for Hitchcock's use of cuts and sound vs. Polanski's silence and claustrophobic frames. Both ask how much madness is perception and how much is reality.
- **Grief as Monster**: *Carrie* (1976) + *The Babadook* (2014). Both weaponize grief—Carrie's humiliation, Amelia's depression—and transform them into externalized horrors. Watch how domestic spaces twist into prisons.
- **Obsession & Isolation**: *Misery* (1990) + *Black Swan* (2010). From Annie Wilkes' fan obsession to Nina's perfectionism, both are tales of devotion mutating into destruction. Track how bodies bear the scars of psychological collapse.
- **Dream Logic & Surreal Terror**: *Mulholland Drive* (2001) + *Goodnight Mommy* (2014). David Lynch and Austrian auteurs both toy with doubling, fractured identity, and cinematic gaslighting. Watch for how editing itself becomes a psychological weapon.

Quick Facts to Sound Like the Smartest Person in the Room

- *Repulsion* was shot almost entirely in a single apartment, turning walls and space into psychological antagonists.
- In *Misery,* Kathy Bates, who has a background in theater, was used to rehearsing frequently, while James Caan preferred less rehearsal. Director Rob Reiner told Bates to use her frustration with Caan to fuel her performance.
- *Black Swan* was partly inspired by *Perfect Blue* (1997), a Japanese anime about fractured identity and performance pressure.
- *Eyes Without a Face* directly inspired the mask design of Michael Myers in *Halloween*.
- *Session 9* was filmed in the abandoned Danvers State Hospital, infamous for its real-life psychiatric history.
- In *Carrie*, the blood dump scene was filmed in one take. Sissy Spacek refused to wash off the pig's blood for continuity, staying covered for three days of shooting.

Scan for Sanity

Cult / Underground Horror

Cult horror thrives on secrecy, ritual, and group psychology. Unlike the lone killer or supernatural entity, these films terrify by showing the power of collective belief, how devotion curdles into violence. From cornfield children to seaside towns, cults strip individuals of autonomy and place them at the mercy of dogma, ritual, and mob hysteria.

Why People Are Drawn to It

Cults scare because they mirror real-world fears of manipulation, brainwashing, and community gone wrong. Viewers are unsettled by the idea that ordinary neighbors could harbor esoteric rituals or that family itself could be weaponized for sacrifice. At its core, cult horror asks: *How much of ourselves would we give up for belonging and what happens when belief demands blood?*

Essentials

- **Race with the Devil (1975, USA)** – A blend of road action and occult horror, *Race with the Devil* builds paranoid tension by pitting two normal couples on an RV vacation against an entire countryside full of Satanists after they accidentally witness a human sacrifice
- **Messiah of Evil (1973, USA)** – Blending eerie American Gothic atmosphere with surreal, psychedelic visuals, *Messiah of Evil* follows a young woman to a mysterious seaside town where she finds the residents possessed by a mysterious evil, blurring the lines between waking nightmares, undead folklore, and unsettling reality
- **Children of the Corn (1984, USA)** – Stephen King's story of kids worshipping "He Who Walks Behind the Rows." A horror story that explores themes of cults and isolation in rural America, adapted into a film series that has received mixed critical reception.
- **The Believers (1987, USA)** – A detective in Manhattan uncovers Santería-inspired murders. Blending psychological thriller with occult horror, *The Believers* follows a recently widowed police psychologist in New York City who becomes embroiled in a terrifying conspiracy involving a sinister Santeria cult that sacrifices children for success and wealth.
- **Midsommar (2019, Sweden/USA)** – Ari Aster's folk-horror of grief, ritual, and sunlit terror. As a breakup film disguised as folk horror, *Midsommar* follows a grieving and emotionally fragile young woman who finds catharsis and a perverse sense of belonging by embracing the violent rituals of a rural Swedish pagan cult.

Deep Cuts

- **The Brotherhood of Satan (1971, USA)** – Blends small-town paranoia with occult horror, trapping a family in a desert community secretly controlled by a satanic cult. Its eerie atmosphere and themes of generational sacrifice reflect early 70s anxieties about power, faith, and the corruption lurking beneath Americana.
- **Mark of the Devil (1970, West Germany)** – Witch-hunting framed as cultic corruption; infamous for its barf bags in theaters. A brutal West German exploitation film that exposes the cruelty of witch hunts, depicting torture and corruption with unprecedented graphic detail. Marketed with vomit bags in theaters, it shocked audiences by turning historical horror into visceral spectacle, cementing its reputation as one of the most infamous "video nasties."
- **The Sect (1991, Italy)** – Produced by Dario Argento, fuses occult horror with surreal imagery, following a schoolteacher ensnared by a Satanic cult that believes she is destined to give birth to their messiah. Mixing dreamlike visuals, insect symbolism, and Lovecraftian unease, the film reflects Italy's late–giallo shift into supernatural paranoia.
- **Sound of My Voice (2011, USA)** – A quiet, unsettling cult thriller where journalists infiltrate a sect led by a woman claiming to be from the future. Its minimalist style and ambiguous revelations blur belief and deception, turning the audience into participants in the question of faith versus manipulation.
- **The Other Lamb (2019, Poland/Ireland)** – Uses folk-horror aesthetics to depict an all-female cult ruled by a single patriarch known as the Shepherd. Through its stark imagery and ritualistic atmosphere, the film critiques

gendered power, isolation, and indoctrination, turning coming-of-age into a revolt against spiritual and bodily control.

Critical Essay

"Cult Horror Isn't Just Satanic."

Myth: Cult horror = devil worship.

Reality: Cults take many forms: religious, political, social, even secular. *Children of the Corn* uses agrarian faith. *The Believers* reflects Santería panic. *Midsommar* weaponizes communal grief in a folk setting. *Sound of My Voice* reframes it as millennial time-travel spirituality. What unites them isn't Satan, it's the surrender of self to collective power.

Global Spotlight: Indonesia & Japan

- **Indonesia – Satan's Slaves (2017) / Satan's Slaves 2 (2022).** Rooted in Islamic and folk traditions, Joko Anwar's reimagining of the 1982 cult classic ties resurrection horror to cultural fears of family, ritual, and spiritual inheritance.
- **Japan – Tag (2015) & The Forest of Love (2019).** Japanese cult horror leans surreal: from fate-warped schoolgirls to manipulative cult leaders, blending psychological collapse with cosmic absurdity. Miike's *The Forest of Love* draws directly from real cult scandals.

Classics & Foundations

- ☐ **The Apostle (El Apóstol)** (1939, Spain) – Early Spanish surrealist cult parable.
- ☐ **To the Devil a Daughter** (1953) - The film is an adaptation of the novel of the same name by Dennis Wheatley. However, the film's screenplay made so many changes to the original story that Wheatley openly disapproved of the film.
    - **ADAPTIONS & RELATED FILMS**
        - ☐ **To the Devil a Daughter** (1976) – Cult grooms a girl for sacrifice. A novelist fights a priest who plots with Satan.
        - ☐ **The Devil Rides Out** (1968) – Occult rituals summon dark forces. Devil worshipers plan to convert two new victims.
        - ☐ **The Resident** (2011) - This was Christopher Lee's final film with Hammer Films, marking his return to the production company decades after his work on *To the Devil a Daughter*.
- ☐ **Mark of the Devil** (1970, West Germany) – In 1700s Austria, a witch-hunter's apprentice has doubts about the righteousness of witch-hunting when he witnesses the brutality, the injustice, the falsehood, the torture and the arbitrary killing that go with the job. The only official sequel is *Mark of the Devil Part II*. Several unrelated films were retitled to capitalize on the notoriety of *Mark of the Devil* such as Mexico's *Alucarda (Sisters of Satan)*, Spain's Blind Dead Series rounding out Part IV and V as *The Ghost Galleon* (1974) and *Night of the Seagulls* (1975), respectively.
    - **SEQUELS**
        - ☐ **Mark of the Devil Part II** (1973) - This is the only official, producer-sanctioned sequel to the 1970 film. A tribunal interrogates, tortures and murders "witches" and "heretics" during the Inquisition.
        - ☐ **Mark of the Devil 666: The Moralist** (1995) - An American-made, low-budget VHS release. A serial killer slaughters those he feels are responsible for society's ills, while a cop and reporter are hot on his grisly trail.
        - ☐ **Mark of the Devil 777: The Moralist, Part 2** (2022) - A horror-spoof style film with some character connections to the 1995 American sequel. Twenty-five years after she first encountered evil, reporter Meredith O'Brien again finds herself in danger, only now her daughter and other victims who survived near death assaults years ago are on the hit list of a bumbling Satanic Cult.
- ☐ **The Brotherhood of Satan** (1971) – A family is trapped in a desert town by a cult of senior-citizens who recruit the town's children to worship Satan.
- ☐ **The Mephisto Waltz** (1971) – Satanic cult targets pianist for possession.

- **Messiah of Evil** (1973) – A young woman goes searching for her missing artist father. Her journey takes her to a strange Californian seaside town governed by a mysterious undead cult. The film draws heavily from literary and cinematic influences such as H.P Lovecraft and George A. Romero. Long overlooked, it's now considered one of the great American nightmares of the 70s, cited by Guillermo del Toro as an influence.
  - **SIMILAR FILMS**
    - **Let's Scare Jessica to Death** (1971) – Woman suspects reality slipping into madness.
    - **Offseason** (2022) - A modern horror film that has been compared to *Messiah of Evil* for its similar themes of a secluded town, mysterious secrets, and rising dread.
- **Race with the Devil** (1975) – Two couples vacationing together in an R.V. from Texas to Colorado are terrorized after they witness a murder during a Satanic ritual. Peter Fonda reportedly did many of his own stunts in the RV chase scenes, adding grit to the paranoia.
  - **ADAPTIONS**
    - **Kazhugu** (1981, India) - This Tamil-language action film is a remake of *Race with the Devil*. The plot follows a group of treasure hunters who are pursued by villains after a secret is revealed.
    - **Red State** (2011) - Director Kevin Smith has stated that his film was strongly influenced by *Race with the Devil*. *Red State* similarly explores the paranoia of a small-town cult by focusing on a group of teenagers who become the targets of a fundamentalist church.
    - **Drive Angry** (2011) - Starring Nicolas Cage, this action film was also based on *Race with the Devil*. It is an over-the-top, supernatural action movie featuring a man who escapes from Hell to take revenge on the cult that murdered his daughter.
    - **Party Bus to Hell** (2017) - This film serves as a homage to *Race with the Devil*. It features characters named after the actors and roles from the original, and its story involves people on a party bus being attacked by a satanic cult in the desert.
- **Children of the Corn** (1984) – A young couple is trapped in a remote town where a dangerous religious cult of children believes that everyone over age 18 must be killed. Based on the Stephen King short story "Children of the Corn" published in the March 1977 issue of Penthouse. **Memorable quote:** *"Outlander! We have your woman!"*
  - **SEQUELS**
    - **Children of the Corn II: The Final Sacrifice** (1992) – Cult influence spreads.
    - **Children of the Corn III: Urban Harvest** (1995) – Corn cult comes to the city.
    - **Children of the Corn IV: The Gathering** (1996) – New town overtaken by child cult.
    - **Children of the Corn V: Fields of Terror** (1998) – Teens stumble into rural cult.
    - **Children of the Corn 666: Isaac's Return** (1999) – Isaac revives to continue the cult.
    - **Children of the Corn: Revelation** (2001) – Elderly complex hides a corn cult.
    - **Children of the Corn: Genesis** (2011) - A couple on a road trip encounters a sinister preacher who is in control of a mysterious child.
    - **Children of the Corn: Runaway** (2018) – Survivor hunted by cult again.
  - **ADAPTIONS**
    - **Children of the Corn** (2009) – Syfy remake of King's tale.
    - **Children of the Corn** (2020) - A theatrical reboot and prequel directed by Kurt Wimmer, exploring the massacre of the adults in the town.
- **The Believers** (1987) – Cal Jamison, a police psychologist, is forced to deal with a series of ritualistic murders and a malevolent cult. Based on the 1982 novel *The Religion* by Nicholas Conde. Also, loosely based on real ritual-crime headlines from the 1980s, adding a tabloid edge to the narrative.
  - **SIMILAR MOVIES**
    - **The Serpent and the Rainbow** (1988) - An anthropologist goes to Haiti to research a drug that makes someone appear dead by suspending all vital signs. The film is a loose adaptation of ethnobotanist Wade Davis's non-fiction book of the same name. The book details Davis's investigation into Haitian Vodou and the case of Clairvius Narcisse, a man allegedly poisoned, buried alive, and later revived as a zombie. While rooted in true events, the film adds more sensational and supernatural horror elements.
    - **Perdita Durango** (1997) - This film, also inspired by the same true events, follows a bank robber and a Santería priestess who kidnap a couple for a ritual sacrifice.
    - **Borderland** (2007) – Backpackers kidnapped by narco-satanic cult.

Cult Expansion

- ☐ **Satan's Slave** (1982, Indonesia) – Cult-driven resurrection horror. After the death of his wife, a businessman and his two kids are plagued by visions of ghosts and demons, and soon, people around them start to die, which all started after the arrival of their new and mysterious housekeeper.
  - • **ADAPTIONS AND SEQUELS:**
    - ☐ **Satan's Slaves** (2017, Indonesia) – Acclaimed remake rooted in cult horror. After dying from a strange illness that she suffered for 3 years, a mother returns home to pick up her children.
    - ☐ **Satan's Slaves 2** (2022, Indonesia) - This is a direct sequel to the 2017 remake, continuing the story of the family as they move into a new, densely populated apartment building, only to find themselves haunted by an even bigger threat. Following the release of *Satan's Slaves 2: Communion*, director Joko Anwar indicated that plans for a third installment of the trilogy. in the series were in development.
  - • **DIRECTOR'S OTHER WORK**
    - ☐ **Impetigore** (2019, Indonesia) – Woman uncovers cursed village legacy.
    - ☐ **The Queen of Black Magic** (2019, Indonesia) - Written by Joko Anwar, this is a remake of the 1981 film of the same name and is also a standalone horror movie.
    - ☐ **Grave Torture** (2024, Indonesia) - An expansion of his 2012 short film.
- ☐ **Murder-Rock: Dancing Death** (1984, Italy) – Giallo with cultic ritual undertones. The owner of a prestigious New York ballet school teams up with a male model to solve a series of bizarre murders of a few of the students. Directed by Lucio Fulci.
- ☐ **The Unholy** (1988) – Demon cult threatens Catholic priest. A priest battles a demon that kills sinners in the act of sinning.
- ☐ **Servants of Twilight** (1991) - Based on the novel by Dean R. Koontz, this action-packed thriller features Bruce Greenwood as a private detective hired to protect a little boy from a fanatical religious cult that believe he is the antichrist foretold in the book of Revelations.
  - • **RELATED FILMS**
    - ☐ **Bless the Child** (2000) – A nurse discovers that her sister's son has supernatural powers and is the target of a Satanic cult.
- ☐ **Eyes Wide Shut** (1999) – Secret elite orgy cult hides sinister truths. A Manhattan doctor embarks on a bizarre, night-long odyssey after his wife's admission of unfulfilled longing. Stanley Kubrick died just four days after presenting Warner Bros. with what was reported to be a final cut of the film, after a legendarily long shoot. His friends and family, as well as the cast and crew of the film, all claimed that Kubrick's death was completely unexpected and that he never seemed to be in poor health while making the film.
- ☐ **The Innkeepers** (2011) – During the final days at the Yankee Pedlar Inn, two employees determined to reveal the hotel's haunted past begin to experience disturbing events as old guests check in for a stay.
- ☐ **Sound of My Voice** (2011) – Two documentary filmmakers attempt to penetrate a cult who worships a woman who claims to be from the future. While a direct sequel never materialized, Batmanglij and Marling created the Netflix series *The OA*, which many fans consider to be a spiritual successor to *Sound of My Voice*.
- ☐ **Jug Face** (2013) – Rural cult sacrifices victims to a pit. When she learns the supernatural pit worshiped by her remote community in the woods has demanded her as a blood sacrifice, Ada struggles to find a way to survive, while the pit lashes out in anger.
  - • **SIMILAR FILMS**
    - ☐ **Dementer** (2019) - Explores similar folk horror themes involving a woman who escapes a backwoods cult.
- ☐ **Starry Eyes** (2014) – Aspiring actress seduced by Hollywood satanic cult. A hopeful young starlet uncovers the ominous origins of the Hollywood elite and enters into a deadly agreement in exchange for fame and fortune. The film started as a Kickstarter project and was aided by the support of author Chuck Palahniuk's (*Fight Club*) fans. 100 donors to the project had their names thanked in Chuck's 2014 novel 'Beautiful You.' Co-writer/co-director Dennis Widmyer runs Chuck's official website and manages his social media.
  - • **SIMILAR FILMS**
    - ☐ **She Will** (2021, UK) - An aging film star retreats to the Scottish countryside with her nurse to recover from surgery. While there, mysterious forces of revenge emerge from the land where witches were burned.

- **Midsommar** (2019, Sweden) – A couple travels to Northern Europe to visit a rural hometown's fabled Swedish mid-summer festival. What begins as an idyllic retreat quickly devolves into an increasingly violent and bizarre competition at the hands of a pagan cult. Shot in Hungary during near-constant daylight. Many scenes used practical sunlight rather than studio lighting.
  - **SIMILAR FILMS**
    - **Apostle** (2018) – Man infiltrates remote island cult in 1905.
    - **Holy Ghost People** (2013) – Backwoods church conceals manipulative cult.
      - **DOCUMENTARY**
        - **Holy Ghost People** (1967) - Directed by Peter Adair. The documentary is a factual account of a Pentecostal community in rural West Virginia whose church service includes faith healing, snake handling, and speaking in tongues.
    - **Sacrifice** (2020, Norway) – Pagan sea cult demands blood.
    - **The Shrine** (2010, Canada) – Journalists uncover statue-worshipping cult.

Modern Global Cult Horrors

- **House of 1000 Corpses** (2003) – Firefly family's murder-cult carnival. Two young couples traveling across the backwoods of Texas searching for urban legends of murder end up as prisoners of a bizarre and sadistic backwater family of serial killers.
  - **THE FIREFLY TRILOGY**
    - **The Devil's Rejects** (2005) - This sequel follows three surviving members of the Firefly family as they go on the run from the police. The tone shifts from the first film's stylized, chaotic horror to a grittier, more grounded road movie.
    - **3 from Hell** (2019) - In the final installment of the trilogy, the incarcerated Firefly family members escape from prison and resume their killing spree. This was the last film released by actor Sid Haig before his death.
- **Regression** (2015) – Satanic panic explored through cult accusations. A detective and a psychoanalyst uncover evidence of a satanic cult while investigating a young woman's terrifying past. Starring Ethan Hawke and Emma Watson.
- **Tag** (2015, Japan) – A girl's life cascades into chaos as everyone around her suffers a gruesome fate while she becomes less certain of who she is and her once-once normal life.
  - **OTHER ADAPTIONS OF THE YUSUKE YAMADA'S NOVEL**
    - **The Chasing World** (2008, Japan) - The first film adaptation of the novel. Teenager is transported to a parallel world where everyone who shares his family name is being hunted down by the dictatorial government.
    - **The Chasing World 2** (2010, Japan) - A direct sequel to the 2008 film. Teenager Tsubasa Sato returns to the parallel universe where demons are out to kill every person with the last name of Sato.
    - **The Chasing World 3** (2012, Japan) - Set in the year 3000 in New Tokyo where this time round, human beings with blood type B are being targeted.
    - **The Chasing World 4** (2012, Japan) - One day it's decided that all people with blood type B have to be killed.
    - **The Chasing World 5** (2012, Japan) - When good-for-nothing employee Daichi, who has a crush on his senior associate Nozomi, is attending to a backlog of work with colleagues, a frightening game of tag targeting people with blood type B begins.
    - **The Chasing World: The Origin** (2013, Japan) - A television series adaptation of the novel.
- **The Ghoul** (2016, UK) – Investigator falls into psychological cult web. A homicide detective goes undercover as a patient to investigate a psychotherapist he believes is linked to a strange double murder. As his therapy sessions continue the line between fantasy and reality begins to blur.
- **The Heretics** (2017) – Woman kidnapped by cult preparing her transformation.
  - **OTHER CHAD ARCHIBALD'S FILMS**
    - **Bite** (2015) - A body horror film about a young woman who, after being bitten by a bug, undergoes a grotesque transformation.

- ☐ **I'll Take Your Dead** (2018) - A supernatural thriller about a man who disposes of bodies for criminals, only to discover that the spirits of the victims are haunting his home.
- ☐ **Belzebuth** (2017, Mexico) – Cult sacrifices children to summon evil. After a personal tragedy, a police detective investigates a school massacre committed by a student - and another massacre. Are the 3 tragedies linked to demon possession?
- ☐ **The Other Lamb** (2019, Poland/Ireland) – A girl born into an all-female cult led by a man in their compound begins to question his teachings and her own reality.
- ☐ **The Wretched** (2019) – Boy discovers neighbor part of witch cult.
- ☐ **The Forest of Love** (2019, Japan) – A small group of student filmmakers and a shy young girl with strict parents are simultaneously manipulated, seduced and abused by an older man. They follow his bidding, even when murder is involved.
  - • **SIMILAR FILMS**
    - ☐ **Cult** (2013, Japan) – Documentary-style horror of possession rituals.
    - ☐ **Occult** (2009, Japan) – Mass murder leads to cosmic cult revelations
    - ☐ **We Are Little Zombies** (2019, Japan) – Postmodern grief satire with horror aesthetics.

Obscure, Exploitation, & Recent

- ☐ **The Demon Lover** (1977) – Cult horror low-budget exploitation.
- ☐ **The Burning Moon** (1992, Germany) – Underground splatter cult parables.
- ☐ **Offspring** (2009) - Against the backdrop of grisly murders and child abductions, a clan of cannibalistic savages which plague the North-east Coast since 1858, is after an unsuspecting family and their innocent baby girl. Do they have what it takes to survive? his film, based on Ketchum's 1991 novel of the same name.
  - • **SEQUELS**
    - ☐ **The Woman** (2011) - When a successful country lawyer captures and attempts to "civilize" the last remaining member of a violent clan that has roamed the Northeast coast for decades, he puts the lives of his family in jeopardy.
    - ☐ **Darlin'** (2019) - This standalone sequel was written and directed by actress Pollyanna McIntosh, who also reprised her role as The Woman. It continues the story of the feral child from the first film, Darlin', who is taken into a Catholic boarding school.
- ☐ **We Are What We Are** (2010, Mexico) – When the patriarch of the family passes away, the teenage children must take responsibility for the family chores: the preparation of the rituals, the hunting and putting the all-important meat on the table. These newfound responsibilities are even more daunting, however, when you live in the city and happen to be a family of cannibals.
  - • **ADAPTIONS & SIMLIAR FILMS**
    - ☐ **We Are What We Are** (2013, US) – American remake with same themes.
    - ☐ **Raw** (2016, France) – Cannibal awakening, bloody coming-of-age.
- ☐ **The Master** (2012) – Paul Thomas Anderson's drama of charismatic cult leader. The film was partially inspired by the life of L. Ron Hubbard, the founder of Scientology. The "Cause" movement in the film mirrors some of Scientology's early practices and philosophy.
- ☐ **Children of Sorrow** (2012) – Woman infiltrates destructive cult.
- ☐ **V/H/S** (2012) - When a group of misfits are hired by an unknown third party to burglarize a desolate house and acquire a rare VHS tape, they discover more found footage than they bargained for. Unlike the *Camp Blood* Franchise, this franchise holds steady with a 5.3-star and above rating on almost all films except *V/H/S: Viral*, which only has a measly 4.2.
  - • **SEQUELS**
    - ☐ **V/H/S/2** (2013) – Found-footage of Indonesian death cult.
    - ☐ **V/H/S: Viral** (2014) - A Los Angeles police chase sends a fame-obsessed man on a wild ride to save his girlfriend from a cybernetic terror.
    - ☐ **V/H/S/94** (2021) - A police S.W.A.T. team investigate a mysterious VHS tape and discover a sinister cult that has pre-recorded material which uncovers a nightmarish conspiracy. A "soft reboot" set in 1994, with different segments.

- ☐ **V/H/S/99** (2022) - Witness a hellish vision of 1999, as social isolation, analog technology and disturbing home videos fuse into a nightmare of found footage savagery. The fifth installment, set in 1999.
- ☐ **V/H/S/85** (2023) - Unveiled through a made-for-TV documentary, five tales of found footage horror emerge to take viewers on a terrifying journey into the grim underbelly of the 1980s. The sixth installment, featuring segments set in 1985.
- ☐ **V/H/S/Beyond** (2024) - Six bloodcurdling tapes unleash horror in a sci-fi inspired hellscape, pushing the boundaries of fear and suspense.
- ☐ **V/H/S/Halloween** (2025) - A collection of Halloween-themed videotapes unleashes a series of twisted, blood-soaked tales, turning trick-or-treat into a struggle for survival.
  - • **SPIN-OFFS & SPIRITUAL SUCCESSORS**
    - ☐ **Southbound** (2015) - Five interlocking tales of terror follow the fates of a group of weary travelers who confront their worst nightmares - and darkest secrets - over one long night on a desolate stretch of desert highway.
    - ☐ **Siren** (2016) - A bachelor party becomes a savage fight for survival when the groomsmen unwittingly unleash a fabled predator upon the festivities.
    - ☐ **Kid vs. Aliens** (2022) - An all-time rager of a teen house party turns to terror when aliens attack, forcing two warring siblings to band together to survive the night.
- ☐ **Faults** (2014) – Cult deprogrammer battles a manipulative sect.
- ☐ **Kill Command** (2016) – Tech cult worships rogue AI.
- ☐ **Holy Hell** (2016) – Doc on real cult's manipulation.
  - • **OTHER DOCUMENTARIES ABOUT CULTS**
    - ☐ **Wild Wild Country** (2018) – Netflix doc on Rajneesh cult in Oregon.
    - ☐ **The Source Family** (2012) - A documentary about a hippie spiritual commune in the Hollywood Hills, featuring a charismatic leader and archival footage.
    - ☐ **The Vow** (2020) - An HBO docuseries about the NXIVM cult and its leader Keith Raniere.
    - ☐ **Heaven's Gate: The Cult of Cults** (2020) - A docuseries detailing the Heaven's Gate cult and its mass suicide.
- ☐ **The Devil's Doorway** (2018, Ireland) – Found-footage in Magdalene asylum with cult-like nuns.
- ☐ **1BR** (2019) – Woman discovers her new apartment complex is a cult.

Pairing Night: Cult Horror

- **Starter Drink:** Spiced wine or herbal tea — communal, ritualistic, and a little unsettling.
- **Double Feature:**
  1. *Race with the Devil* (1975) — Look for how paranoia builds on open highways, flipping Americana into terror.
  2. *Midsommar* (2019) — Pay attention to how horror is staged in daylight, not shadow.
- **Discussion Points (Smart Room Tricks):**
  - o Cult horror often plays on *real-world moral panics* from Santería in the 80s to Satanic Panic in the 90s.
  - o Note how group chants or rituals often drown out individual identity, it's sound design as brainwashing.
  - o Ask: Does belonging itself become the monster?

Quick Facts to Sound Smart

- **Cult Horror isn't just satanic.** While U.S. films leaned heavily on Satanic panic (*Children of the Corn, House of the Devil*), global cult horror reflects regional fears: Santería in *The Believers*, narco-satanism in *Borderland*, pagan traditions in *Midsommar*, and ancestor rituals in Indonesia's *Satan's Slaves*.
- **Race with the Devil (1975)** influenced more than horror. It's considered a proto–action-horror hybrid, blending car-chase spectacle with occult dread, paving the way for grindhouse crossovers like Tarantino's Death Proof.
- **Messiah of Evil (1973)** is sometimes dubbed "the American Giallo." Its dreamlike editing, seaside setting, and painterly visuals owe as much to Argento and Bava as to Romero.
- **Children of the Corn** has more sequels and reboots (11 and counting) than almost any Stephen King adaptation despite King's original short story being barely 20 pages long.

- **Mark of the Devil (1970)** was marketed with vomit bags in theaters. The gimmick worked: it became one of the most infamous exploitation titles of the era, sparking a wave of rebranded "sequels" that weren't really sequels at all.
- **Midsommar (2019)** was shot almost entirely in broad daylight. A deliberate inversion of horror convention, where terror usually thrives in the dark.
- **Cults as Metaphor:** Academic critics often argue that cult horror mirrors real social fears of the time from Cold War conformity (*The Stepford Wives*) to Reagan-era paranoia about satanic daycare (*The Believers*) to millennial anxieties about community vs. individuality (*Midsommar, 1BR*).

Obsession and Obedience

Postmodern / Meta Horror

Where classic horror seeks immersion, postmodern horror constantly reminds you that you're watching a movie. These films blur reality and performance, bend genre conventions, and weaponize self-awareness. From psychedelic surrealism (*Hausu, Santa Sangre*) to meta-deconstruction (*Scream, The Final Girls*), the effect is unsettling: the horror is not just on-screen, it's in the act of watching, remembering, and questioning the story itself.

Why People Are Drawn to It

Because meta horror makes the viewer complicit. The scares aren't just jump cuts or monsters, they're the realization that our own expectations, cultural references, and consumption of horror are part of the trap. Surreal postmodern films bend logic, forcing us to confront disorientation. Meta-slashers parody what we've already laughed at, then remind us the joke can still kill. It's playful, but also destabilizing: we never know where the floor is.

Essentials

- **Persona (1966, Sweden)** –Ingmar Bergman's *Persona* is an avant-garde psychological drama that explores the shattering of identity and the transference of personality between a silent actress and her talkative nurse, creating an ambiguous and deeply unsettling study of selfhood, duality, and the permeable boundaries of the human psyche.
- **House (Hausu) (1977, Japan)** – The surreal and psychedelic Japanese film *House* is a chaotic, dreamlike horror comedy that follows a group of schoolgirls who visit a sinister, man-eating country home, only to be devoured one by one in a series of bizarre and inventive ways.
- **Santa Sangre (1989, Mexico/Italy)** – Directed by Alejandro Jodorowsky, *Santa Sangre* is a surreal, grotesque, and visually stunning exploration of childhood trauma and Oedipal complexes, as a former circus artist escapes a mental institution and becomes the murderous "arms" of his armless, religiously fanatical mother.
- **The Final Girls (2015, USA)** –A horror-comedy meta-parody, *The Final Girls* uses a loving homage to 1980s slasher films to tell a surprisingly heartfelt story about a grieving daughter who, after being sucked into one of her late mother's movies, gets a second chance to spend time with her.
- **Skinamarink (2022, Canada)** – A minimalist, liminal horror. Shot like a found-footage nightmare, *Skinamarink* is an experimental horror film that traps two young siblings in their home as reality melts around them, effectively tapping into deep-seated childhood fears of abandonment, darkness, and the unknown.

Deep Cuts

- **Performance (1970, UK)** –Blurs crime drama with psychedelic horror, as a London gangster hides out in a rock star's mansion and descends into hallucinatory identity collapse. Its fragmented style, occult undertones, and fluid merging of violence, sex, and transformation make it a haunting exploration of self-erasure and the masks we wear.
- **Detention (2011, USA)** – A hyper-stylized horror-comedy mashup where slasher tropes collide with teen satire, time travel, and pop culture overload. Its frenetic pace and self-aware absurdity turn the high school setting into a meta-commentary on genre recycling and millennial anxieties.
- **One Cut of the Dead (2017, Japan)** – A zombie movie that transforms into a joyful, meta ode to low-budget filmmaking. Shin'ichirō Ueda begins as a low-budget zombie movie shot in a single take, only to reveal itself as a clever, layered comedy about filmmaking itself. By blending splatter, farce, and heartfelt ingenuity, it transforms what seems like exploitation into a joyous celebration of creativity and collaboration.
- **Censor (2021, UK)** – Prano Bailey-Bond situates its horror in Britain's "video nasties" era, following a film censor who becomes obsessed with a mysterious movie that seems tied to her past. Blurring repression, memory, and exploitation aesthetics, it turns the act of editing images into a descent into madness where the line between fiction and reality disintegrates.
- **In the Mouth of Madness (1994, USA)** – John Carpenter's Lovecraftian experiment where fiction devours reality. A descent into metafictional horror, where a missing author's work infects readers with madness and

reshapes reality itself. Combining cosmic dread with satirical digs at publishing and fandom, it suggests that stories don't just reflect the world, they can rewrite it.

Critical Essay

"Meta Horror Isn't Just Parody"

Myth: Meta horror exists only to make fun of horror.

Reality: The best meta horror uses self-awareness as a scalpel. *Scream* (1996) redefined the slasher not by mocking it, but by showing how cultural rules shape life-and-death choices. Jodorowsky and von Trier bend narrative itself into a weapon, turning surrealism into psychological assault. *Skinamarink* strips horror down to ambient experience, questioning what a "movie" even is. Postmodern horror isn't a gag, it's a mirror that asks us why we're laughing, why we're scared, and why we can't look away.

Global Spotlight: Surreal Europe & Japan

- **Czechoslovakia**: *Valerie and Her Week of Wonders* (1970) and *The Cremator* (1969) fuse fairy tale and fascism, showing how political oppression can be refracted through surreal allegory.
- **Japan**: From *Hausu* (1977) to *Tag* (2015), Japanese filmmakers embrace absurdity, turning surreal horror into a uniquely national expression of both play and apocalypse.
- **Spain**: *Timecrimes* (2007) and *The Nameless* (1999) inject surreal paranoia into tight genre frameworks, making the uncanny feel grounded.

Foundations of Meta & Surreal Horror

- ☐ **The Saragossa Manuscript** (1965, Poland) – Labyrinthine narratives folding into horror dreamscapes. Upon finding a book that relates his grandfather's story, an officer ventures through Spain meeting a wide array of characters, most of whom have a story of their own to tell.
- ☐ **Persona** (1966) – A nurse is put in charge of a mute actress and finds that their personae are melding together. Bergman's exploration of identity, psychological breakdown, and the blurring of boundaries between two women has influenced a wide range of filmmakers such as Robert Altman's *3 Women*, David Crohenberg's *Dead Ringers*, David Lynch's *Mulholland Drive*, Darren Aronofsky's *Black Swan*, Peter Strickland's *The Duke of Burgundy*, and Alex Ross Perry's *Queen of Earth*.
  - **INFLUENCE**
    - ☐ **Queen of Earth** (2015) - Two women who grew up together discover they have drifted apart when they retreat to a lake house together.
- ☐ **Targets** (1968) - An aging horror star contemplates retirement amid the modern culture of random violence, while a disturbed young gun collector embarks on an unprovoked killing spree.
- ☐ **Performance** (1970) – A violent East London gangster undergoes a transformation of identity while hiding from his former colleagues in the home of a jaded Bohemian rock star and his two girlfriends. It explores themes of identity, masculinity, sexual ambiguity, and the dissolution of reality. The film uses a non-linear narrative structure and stylistic elements that were groundbreaking at the time. It features a psychedelic visual style, influenced by pop art and the counterculture of the late 1960s. Director Ingmar Bergman wrote the screenplay while recovering from a serious illness in a hospital and later called the film a "life-saver". He felt he had gone as far as he could artistically and was "all washed up" until he found the strength to make this film. The film's conception was inspired by a photograph of his two leading actresses, Liv Ullmann and Bibi Andersson, sunbathing together. He saw an "uncanny resemblance" between them and visualized them placing their hands next to each other, which became a key image in the film. Bergman fell in love with Liv Ullmann during the filming. The pair would go on to have a long romantic and professional relationship that produced a child and many more films together. Bergman allowed the script to develop as the production proceeded. The famous and sexually frank monologue delivered by Bibi Andersson's character, Alma, was partially rewritten by Andersson herself, who felt the original dialogue was too obviously written by a man.
  - **FILMS INFLUENCED BY**
    - ☐ **Altered States** (1980) – Sensory-deprivation regresses scientist to primal form. Nominated for two Academy Awards including Best Sound and Best Music, Original Score.

- ☐ **Bad Timing** (1980) - A psychological thriller by Nicolas Roeg, again exploring themes of questionable sexuality and the investigation of a character's questionable sex and sexuality.
- ☐ **The Limey** (1999) - Steven Soderbergh's film, also featuring a gangster coming to terms with his past, is reminiscent of *Performance* in its non-linear narrative.

☐ **The Man Who Fell to Earth** (1976) – Sci-fi blending alienation and surreal horror tone. Based on the science fiction novel of the same name by Walter Tevis. An alien must pose as a human to save his dying planet, but a woman and greed of other men create complications. Starring David Bowe and Rip Torn.

- • **ADAPTIONS**
  - ☐ **The Man Who Fell to Earth** (1987) - A made-for-television film version was produced but did not achieve the same cult status as the 1976 movie.
  - ☐ **The Man Who Fell to Earth** (2022) - This Showtime series is a direct, standalone sequel to the 1976 film.

☐ **House (Hausu)** (1977, Japan) – A schoolgirl and six of her classmates travel to her aunt's country home, which turns out to be haunted. The film was pitched using ideas from Obayashi's 10-year-old daughter.

☐ **Santa Sangre** (1989, Mexico) – A former circus artist escapes from a mental hospital to rejoin his armless mother - the leader of a strange religious cult - and is forced to enact brutal murders in her name as he becomes "her arms."

- • **OTHER FILMS BY ALEJANDRO JODOROWSKY**
  - ☐ **The Holy Mountain** (1973, Mexico) – Cult, surrealism, and body-transcendent imagery. In a corrupt, greed-fueled world, a powerful alchemist leads a messianic character and seven materialistic figures to the Holy Mountain, where they hope to achieve enlightenment.
  - ☐ **El Topo** (1970, Mexico) – Surrealist western with grotesque horror touches.

☐ **Dead Man** (1995) – Jarmusch's surreal western with horrific visions of death.

Meta-Horror, Self-Awareness, & Deconstruction

☐ **Detention** (2011) – As a copycat killer named after movie villain Cinderhella stalks the student body at Grizzly Lake High School, a group of co-eds band together to survive while serving detention.

- • **HIGH SCHOOL HORRORS & SATIRES**
  - ☐ **Cutting Class** (1989) – Pre-meta slasher parody with Brad Pitt.
  - ☐ **Heathers** (1989) - This film also satirizes high school life, though with a different tone and focus on black comedy.
  - ☐ **Cherry Falls** (2000) – Virginity becomes target in high school killings.
  - ☐ **Jennifer's Body** (2009) - A newly-possessed high-school cheerleader turns into a succubus who specializes in killing her male classmates. Can her best friend put an end to the horror? While not an official sequel, there is a series of four found-footage films, known as "The Jennifer Quadrilogy," that were inspired by the original film.
  - ☐ **The Final Girls** (2015) – A young woman grieving the loss of her mother, a famous scream queen from the 1980s, finds herself pulled into the world of her mom's most famous movie. Reunited, the women must fight off the film's maniacal killer.
  - ☐ **Tragedy Girls** (2017) - A twist on the slasher genre, following two death-obsessed teenage girls who use their online show about real-life tragedies to send their small mid-western town into a frenzy, and cement their legacy as modern horror legends.
  - ☐ **Thoroughbreds** (2017) - This film, while not supernatural, features two high-school girls who bond over their shared darkness and a plot to kill someone.
  - ☐ **Freaky** (2020) – Body-swap comedy meets slasher gore.
  - ☐ **Sissy** (2022) - Teen best friends Cecilia and Emma run into each other after a decade. Cecilia is invited to Emma's bachelorette weekend, where she gets stuck in a remote cabin with her high school bully and gets a taste for revenge.
  - ☐ **Piggy** (2022, Spain) - An overweight teen is bullied by a clique of cool girls poolside while holidaying in her village. The long walk home will change the rest of her life. Following the success of *Piggy*, Carlota Pereda is set to direct her first English-language film, *The Edge of Normal*, a psychological thriller starring Chloë Grace Moretz.

☐ **Re-Cut (a.k.a. Found Footage 3D)** (2016) – A found-footage film that knows it's a found-footage film.

The Prophet of Paranoia

Jordan Peele[31]

Born in New York City in 1979, Jordan Peele first rose to fame through comedy (*Key & Peele*), but his pivot to horror revealed him as one of the genre's most vital modern voices. Rooted in satire, sketch, and cultural observation, his films fuse social critique with dread, showing how systemic fears and personal identity crises are scarier than any monster. Peele's horror lens comes from being both an observer and insider: someone who dissects the everyday anxieties of race, class, and spectacle, then mutates them into uncanny nightmares.

Signature Works (Curated)

- *Get Out* (2017) — A young Black man meets his white girlfriend's family, uncovering a chilling form of body-snatching racism. Won the Oscar for Best Original Screenplay.
- *Us* (2019) — A family is hunted by their doppelgängers; a sharp allegory about inequality and America's hidden underclass.
- *Nope* (2022) — Siblings run a California horse ranch while facing an otherworldly predator; a critique of spectacle, exploitation, and the gaze.
- *Candyman* (2021, producer/writer) — A direct sequel to the 1992 film, tying urban legend horror to gentrification and racial trauma.

The Fingerprints

- Social horror: systemic racism, class divides, cultural trauma reframed as supernatural.
- Doppelgängers & mirrors: identity fractured and reflected.
- Satire in horror form: humor softens the edges but deepens the unease.
- The uncanny in the everyday: teacups, scissors, cloud formations turned into terrors.
- Strong sound design & silence as narrative tools (the deer hit, the Tethered's guttural speech, the UFO's "scream").

Legacy & Influence

With *Get Out*, Peele redefined "social horror" for the mainstream, proving that horror could carry urgent political discourse without losing mass appeal. He became the first Black screenwriter to win the Oscar for Best Original Screenplay. Peele's production company, Monkeypaw, has nurtured bold new voices (*Candyman* reboot, *Lovecraft Country*, *Wendell & Wild*). His work reshaped expectations: studios now actively seek elevated horror with sociopolitical teeth, and his DNA is visible in filmmakers like Nia DaCosta and even Robert Eggers/Ti West in how they balance art-house and genre.

Pairing Night Watchlist

- *Get Out* (2017) → Notice how microaggressions, seemingly polite, turn into life-or-death threats. The "Sunken Place" is now cultural shorthand for silenced oppression.
- *Us* (2019) → Watch the symbolism: scissors, rabbits, and the Hands Across America motif. Allegory meets pure slasher tension.
- *Nope* (2022) → Track how Peele builds dread not from gore but from absence. What you *don't* see in the sky is as terrifying as what you do.

Quick Facts to Sound Smart

- Peele originally considered making *Get Out* with a dark ending where Chris is arrested; he changed it post–Obama era to strike a balance between realism and catharsis.
- *Get Out* made over $250M worldwide on a $4.5M budget.
- Peele cites *The Stepford Wives*, *The Shining*, and Hitchcock as key influences.
- "The Sunken Place" became a viral cultural metaphor beyond film used in politics, social media, and music.
- Peele was once considered for *Akira* but chose to focus on original projects, stating he wants to tell new stories, not recycle old ones.

---

31 "Key and Peele with their Peabody Award." Peabody Awards (https://www.flickr.com/people/79383703@N08, Creative Commons Attribution 2.0)

Surreal Experiments & Reality-Bending Horror

- ☐ **The Cremator** (1969, Czechoslovakia) – Set in Central Europe during World War II, a demented cremator believes cremation relieves earthly suffering and sets out to save the world.
  - **INFLUENCED FILMS**
    - ☐ **Morgiana** (1972, Czechoslovakia) - Director Herz was forced to shelve other projects due to political circumstances but later revisited some of the stylistic excesses of *The Cremator* in this film.
    - ☐ **The Zone of Interest** (2023) - This film, about the family of Auschwitz commandant Rudolf Höss, has been compared to *The Cremator* for its unsettling portrayal of complicity in totalitarian atrocities.
- ☐ **Valerie and Her Week of Wonders** (1970, Czechoslovakia) – Surreal dream-like tale that combines several themes into one fantastical world.
- ☐ **The Man Who Sleeps** (1974, France) – Ennui as existential surreal horror.
- ☐ **Southland Tales** (2006) – Genre-collapsing apocalyptic satire.
  - **SIMILAR THEMES**
    - ☐ **A Scanner Darkly** (2006) - This film, also starring Keanu Reeves, uses a similar retrofuturistic, surreal aesthetic to explore drug use, paranoia, and identity.
    - ☐ **Synecdoche, New York** (2008) - This Charlie Kaufman film shares a similar narrative style that delves into existential angst and the nature of reality.
    - ☐ **Sorry to Bother You** (2018) - This satirical film explores capitalism, systemic racism, and corporate greed in a surreal, allegorical way.
- ☐ **Antichrist** (2009) – Von Trier's surrealist descent into grief and violence. It is thematically the first film in von Trier's unofficial "Depression Trilogy."
  - **DEPRESSION TRILOGY**
    - ☐ **Melancholia** (2011) – Apocalyptic dread framed as psychological breakdown.
    - ☐ **Nymphomaniac** (2013) - The final film in the trilogy is a two-part erotically charged drama that explores female sexuality and liberation.
- ☐ **The Duke of Burgundy** (2014) – A woman who studies butterflies and moths test the limits of her relationship with her lesbian lover.
  - **SIMILAR FILMS**
    - ☐ **The Handmaiden** (2016) - This South Korean erotic psychological thriller, directed by Park Chan-Wook, features a complex plot involving deception, power dynamics, and a lesbian relationship in a secluded estate.
- ☐ **Get Out** (2017) – Satirical deconstruction of social horror. A young African-American visits his white girlfriend's parents for the weekend, where his simmering uneasiness about their reception of him eventually reaches a boiling point. Peele originally wrote a bleak ending where Chris is arrested instead of rescued. Won an Oscar for Best Original Screenplay. It was nominated for three other Academy Awards including: Best Picture, Best Actor, and Best Directing. **Memorable Quote:** *"Now you're in the sunken place."*
  - **THE MIND OF JORDAN PEELE**
    - ☐ **Us** (2019) – Doppelgängers as allegory of American horror identity. In order to get away from their busy lives, the Wilson family takes a vacation to Santa Cruz, California. At night, four strangers break into Adelaide's childhood home. The family is shocked to find out that the intruders look like them.
    - ☐ **Hunters** (2020) - An Amazon series about a group of Nazi hunters. Peele served as an executive producer.
    - ☐ **Lovecraft County** (2020) - An HBO series about a young Black man traveling through the segregated American South in the 1950s, encountering both supernatural and racial horrors.
    - ☐ **Monkey Man** (2024) - This action-horror film, starring and directed by Dev Patel, was produced by Monkeypaw Productions.
    - ☐ **Nope** (2022) – Peele's genre-deconstruction of spectacle and horror. The residents of a lonely gulch in inland California bear witness to an uncanny and chilling phenomenon.
    - ☐ **Wendell & Wild** (2022) - A stop-motion animated horror comedy, co-written and co-produced by Peele.

- ☐ **Under the Silver Lake** (2018) – Surreal paranoia and Hollywood conspiracies.
  - • **SIMILAR FILMS**
    - ☐ **Inherent Vice** (2014) - Another stoner noir film, also adapted from a Thomas Pynchon novel and directed by Paul Thomas Anderson.
    - ☐ **The Long Goodbye** (1973) - Robert Altman's film is a key reference point for *Under the Silver Lake* and is considered one of its closest antecedents.
    - ☐ **Kiss Kiss Bang Bang** (2005) - A satirical neo-noir film featuring a convoluted plot and sardonic tone.
    - ☐ **The Big Lebowski** (1998) - This Coen Brothers film is another example of a slacker protagonist getting drawn into a convoluted plot, though it is more comedic.
    - ☐ **Enemy** (2013) - A surreal psychological thriller starring Jake Gyllenhaal, which explores similar themes of identity and paranoia.
- ☐ **Censor** (2021, UK) –After viewing a strangely familiar video nasty, Enid, a film censor, sets out to solve the past mystery of her sister's disappearance, embarking on a quest that dissolves the line between fiction and reality.
  - • **SIMILAR FILMS**
    - ☐ **Berberian Sound Studio** (2012, UK) – Sound designer's psyche collapses while dubbing giallo.
    - ☐ **The Last Matinee** (2020) - A Spanish horror film that also explores a lone cinephile dealing with a bloody massacre in a movie theater.

Meta, Postmodern & Extreme Experiments

- ☐ **Los Sin Nombre (The Nameless)** (1999, Spain) – Meta-cult horror blending surrealism.
  - • **DIRECTOR'S LEGACY:** Jaume Balagueró went on to direct several other acclaimed Spanish horror films, such as *[REC]* and *Sleep Tight*, which were named earlier in the book.
    - ☐ **Venus** (2022) - A supernatural action horror film loosely inspired by the work of H. P. Lovecraft.
- ☐ **The Piano Tuner of Earthquakes** (2005) – Surreal gothic postmodern horror. Dark fairy-tale about a demonic doctor who abducts a beautiful opera singer with designs on transforming her into a mechanical nightingale.
  - • **SIMILAR FILMS**
    - ☐ **The Forbidden Room** (2015) – Surreal dreamlike narrative chaos. In this non-linear amalgamation, submarine crewmen and a woodsman wend their way through a voyage of odd experiences.
    - ☐ **The Hourglass Santorium** (1973) - A Polish film with a labyrinthine narrative and surreal visuals.

Pairing Night: Watching Meta & Surreal Horror

Starter Pack (Accessible & Iconic)
- • *Scream* (1996) – The rules of slashers explained, then shattered.
- • *The Final Girls* (2015) – A grief-driven, clever meta spin that's surprisingly heartfelt.
- • *One Cut of the Dead* (2017) – Start-to-finish delight: begins as cliché, ends as genius.

Intermediate Weirdness (Surreal Turns Up)
- • *Hausu* (1977) – Candy-colored chaos where logic dissolves.
- • *In the Mouth of Madness* (1994) – Carpenter's underrated meta-Lovecraft mind-bender.
- • *Censor* (2021) – Blurs reality and the "video nasties" she edits.

Deep Dive (Brain-Melt Territory)
- • *Persona* (1966) – The identity-breakdown film that influenced half the genre.
- • *Santa Sangre* (1989) – Circus surrealism and trauma, Jodorowsky-style.
- • *Skinamarink* (2022) – A slow, liminal plunge into nightmare atmosphere.

How to Watch
- • Don't multitask. These films thrive on disorientation. You'll miss their tricks if you scroll.
- • Watch with friends if possible; half the fun is debating what the hell just happened.
- • Keep a notepad (or mental one) for images or lines that feel like they don't "fit." Chances are, they're the point.

Quick Facts to Sound Like the Smartest Person in the Room

- *Hausu* was co-conceived with input from director Nobuhiko Obayashi's 10-year-old daughter, explaining its dream-logic absurdity.
- Jodorowsky's *Santa Sangre* was partly based on a real Mexican "religious cult" murder case, blending true crime into surrealism.
- Carpenter's *In the Mouth of Madness* is the closest mainstream cinema has come to a direct Lovecraftian "madness from reading fiction" narrative.
- *One Cut of the Dead* was made for about $25,000 and became a global cult phenomenon, grossing over 1,000x its budget.
- *Skinamarink* (2022) was filmed almost entirely in the director's childhood home for under $15,000 then went viral on TikTok before blowing up in theaters.
- Jordan Peele has called *Get Out* both a horror film and a "social documentary in disguise," showing how meta-horror can engage culture directly.

Self-Aware. Self-Destructive

Zombie Horror

Zombie horror charts one of cinema's most radical transformations. From voodoo slavery in the 1930s to Romero's flesh-eaters in the 1960s, then fast infections, global plagues, and comic self-parody, zombies have always been mirrors of cultural anxiety: colonialism, consumerism, contagion, and collapse.

Why People Are Drawn to It
Because zombie films are collective nightmares. They collapse the barrier between "us" and "them." Neighbors, coworkers, family members, now rendered monstrous yet familiar. Zombies embody pandemics, conformity, and apocalyptic fear, but also the thrill of survival fantasy: Could I make it? With their blend of social allegory and gore, they let audiences watch society fall apart safely, from a theater seat.

Essentials
- **White Zombie** (1932, USA) – Often cited as the first zombie feature: Bela Lugosi and voodoo mind-control. Drawing upon Haiti's colonial history and fears of spiritualism, *White Zombie* is an eerie, dreamlike horror film where a sinister voodoo master creates emotionless human slaves to work in his sugar mill and to fulfill the twisted obsession of a jealous suitor.
- **Night of the Living Dead** (1968, USA) – Romero's reinvention: cannibalistic corpses + social critique. George A. Romero's *Night of the Living Dead* is a landmark horror film that uses a zombie apocalypse as a vehicle for searing social commentary on American society in the 1960s, highlighting the breakdown of order, the failures of humanity, and the tragic consequences of racial prejudice.
- **Dawn of the Dead** (1978, USA/Italy) – Mall-bound satire of consumerism; Tom Savini's gore FX breakthrough. *Fun Fact:* Released in different cuts (Romero's U.S. version vs Argento's European edit).
- **28 Days Later** (2002) – Blending gritty realism with intense, fast-paced horror, *28 Days Later* uses a devastating "Rage" virus as a vehicle to explore the fragility of civilization and the chilling notion that the greatest threat to humanity is humanity itself.
- **Train to Busan** (2016, South Korea) – Global high point for modern zombie horror; speed, emotion, spectacle. Yeon Sang-ho revitalizes the zombie genre by setting its outbreak aboard a speeding train, fusing relentless action with sharp social allegory. Its mix of claustrophobic suspense and emotional sacrifice makes it both a thrill ride and a critique of selfishness in the face of catastrophe.

Deep Cuts
- **The Plague of the Zombies** (1966, UK) – Hammer Films' eerie take, with iconic grave-rising. Transplants voodoo horror to the Cornish countryside, blending gothic atmosphere with social critique of class exploitation. Its eerie makeup and shambling undead predate Romero, making it a crucial bridge between traditional gothic horror and the modern zombie film.
- **The Living Dead at Manchester Morgue** (1974, Spain/Italy) – Eco-horror spin: pesticides awaken the dead. Jorge Grau combines eco-horror with zombie terror, as agricultural machines using ultrasonic waves inadvertently reanimate the dead. Mixing social critique with atmospheric dread, it stands as one of the strongest European precursors to Romero's zombie revolution. *See the Complete List of Video Nasties
- **Burial Ground** (1981, Italy) – Infamous for grotesque zombies. Andrea Bianchi is an Italian exploitation take on the zombie craze, infamous for its graphic gore and unsettling incest subplot. With crumbling estates, relentless undead, and taboo-breaking shocks, it exemplifies Euro-horror's penchant for excess and transgression.
- **Cemetery Man (Dellamorte Dellamore)** (1994, Italy) – Surreal, philosophical spin on cemetery caretaking. Michele Soavi's blends zombie horror with surrealist black comedy, following a cemetery caretaker whose job of killing the reanimated dead spirals into existential absurdity. Mixing gore, romance, and metaphysical musings, it transforms the zombie film into a meditation on love, death, and the futility of meaning itself.
- **The Sadness** (2021, Taiwan) – Grotesque violence reimagines rage zombies as a metaphor for cruelty. Rob Jabbaz pushes the zombie infection narrative into extreme territory, with a rage-inducing virus that unleashes

sadistic violence and sexual brutality across Taiwan. Unflinching in its transgression, the film turns societal collapse into a spectacle of excess, testing the limits of both body horror and audience endurance.

Critical Essay

"Zombies Aren't Just Flesh-Eaters — They're Mirrors."

Myth: Zombies = brainless splatter fodder.

Reality: Every major wave refracts cultural fears. Romero's dead indicted racism, war, and malls-as-morgues. The Italian boom grafted colonial and plague anxieties. Fast-zombie revivals like *28 Days Later* embodied pandemic dread and military overreach. Global hits (*Train to Busan*, *[REC]*) showed the genre mutating into family melodrama, urban collapse, and viral terror. Zombies endure because they evolve with us, always half social allegory, half guts.

Global Spotlight: Beyond the U.S.

- **Italy** – Lucio Fulci's *Zombi 2* (1979) turned splatter excess into pulp poetry.
- **Spain** – *[REC]* (2007) reinvented found-footage with ferocious infection horror.
- **France** – *La Horde* (2009) and *The Night Eats the World* (2018) show two extremes: chaos vs isolation.
- **South Korea** – *Train to Busan* (2016) blended action spectacle with family drama, setting the global bar.
- **Japan** – *Wild Zero* (1999) gave us Guitar Wolf vs alien zombies; *Tokyo Zombie* (2005) went full absurdist.
- **Taiwan** – *The Sadness* (2021) pushed the envelope with sadistic, NC-17-level violence.

Foundations of the Zombie Genre

☐ **White Zombie** (1932) – A young man turns to a witch doctor to lure the woman he loves away from her fiancé, but instead turns her into a zombie slave. Scenes from *White Zombie* have appeared in other films, including *The Hand That Rocks the Cradle* (1992), *Nadja* (1994), and Tim Burton's *Ed Wood* (1994). For a time, the film was

considered lost until it was rediscovered in the 1960s. The screenplay was based on the 1929 book *The Magic Island*, a non-fiction account by William Seabrook of his time exploring voodoo practices in Haiti. Since it was made before the stricter Motion Picture Production Code was enforced, the film was able to show more suggestive and disturbing material. Its independent, low-budget nature also led to a more experimental, dreamlike visual style that some modern critics have compared to director Val Lewton's work. The heavy metal band White Zombie, led by musician and film director Rob Zombie, took their name directly from the film. *White Zombie* was one of the few American horror films approved for release in Nazi Germany.

- **ADAPTIONS**
  - ☐ **Revolt of the Zombies** (1936) – Spiritual successor to *White Zombie*. An international expedition is sent into Cambodia to destroy an ancient formula that turns men into zombies.

☐ **King of the Zombies** (1941) – WWII espionage and voodoo reanimation. On a spooky island, three stranded travelers find an evil doctor working with foreign spies and in control of zombies.

- **ADAPTIONS**
  - ☐ **Revenge of the Zombies** (1943) – Nazi scientists experiment with voodoo. After the death of Max's spouse, Lila, Max holds a funeral for her, but he has also reanimates her as a zombie. He is amazed when Lila show signs of free will and challenges him for control.

☐ **Voodoo Island** (1957) – Boris Karloff and voodoo undead. A scholarly type is asked to investigate the possible island site for a large resort hotel--an island rumored to be infested with zombies.

- **Plan 9 from Outer Space** (1959) – So-bad-it's-good alien-zombie resurrection. Evil aliens attack Earth and set their terrible "Plan 9" into action. As the aliens resurrect the dead of the Earth, the lives of the living are in danger.
  - **ADAPTIONS**
    - **Plan 9** (2015) - An independent science fiction-comedy horror film that serves as a modern homage and partial remake. The story focuses on a small town named Nilbog ("Goblin" spelled backward) being invaded by aliens who resurrect the dead.
- **The Plague of the Zombies** (1966) – Hammer's gothic take on voodoo reanimation. During a mysterious epidemic in a small Cornish village, the local doctor summons his professor friend for help. *The Plague of the Zombies* is noted for its pioneering imagery of zombies rising from the grave, predating George A. Romero's *Night of the Living Dead* by two years.
- **Night of the Living Dead** (1968) – A ragtag group of Pennsylvanians barricade themselves in an old farmhouse to remain safe from a horde of flesh-eating ghouls that are ravaging the Northeast of the United States. Romero lost copyright due to a clerical error, making the film public domain and fueling its cult circulation, countless remakes and riffs.

  - **SEQUELS**
    - **Dawn of the Dead** (1978) – During an escalating zombie epidemic, two Philadelphia SWAT team members, a traffic reporter and his TV executive girlfriend seek refuge in a secluded shopping mall. Different cuts exist (Romero's, Argento's European cut), each with distinct rhythm and score.
      - **ADAPTIONS**
        - **Zombi** (1978, Italy) - The Italian version of George A. Romero's *Dawn of the Dead.*
        - **Zombi 2** (1979, Italy) - The film directed by Lucio Fulci, known in the U.S. simply as *Zombie*. Strangers searching for a young woman's missing father arrive at a tropical island where a doctor desperately seeks the cause and cure of a recent epidemic of the undead.
        - **Zombi 3** (1988, Italy) - A direct sequel to *Zombi 2*, co-directed by Lucio Fulci and Bruno Mattei.
        - **Zombie 4: After Death** (1989, Italy/Philippines) – This film was directed under the pseudonym "Clyde Anderson" and shot in the Philippines using the same studio space as *Zombi 3*. It was later sold to other distributors and re-titled as *Zombie 4* in Japan and *Zombie Flesh Eaters 3* in the UK.
        - **Zombie 5: Killing Birds** (1988, Italy) - Often considered the fifth film in the unofficial series, this was made before *Zombi 3* and *Zombie 4: After Death* but released after them. It was also directed by Claudio Fragasso under a pseudonym.
        - **Zombie Nightmare** (1987, Canada) - This film was released as *Zombie: Nights of Terror* in the US, but it is not an official part of the series.
        - **Burial Ground: The Nights of Terror** (1981, Italy) – Sleazy cult favorite with grotesque zombies. *Burial Ground* was one of several films that were retitled to capitalize on the success of Lucio Fulci's 1979 film *Zombi 2* (released in the US as *Zombie*). It was often marketed as *Zombie 3*, but it has no direct connection to Fulci's film, which received its own official sequel in 1988.
        - **Dawn of the Dead** (2004) - A popular and successful remake directed by Zack Snyder.
    - **Day of the Dead** (1985) – As the world is overrun by zombies, a group of scientists and military personnel sheltering in an underground bunker in Florida must decide on how they should deal

with the undead horde. The character of Bub, the intelligent zombie, had a cameo appearance in the AMC television series, *The Walking Dead*.

- **ADAPTIONS & SEQUELS**
  - ☐ **Day of the Dead 2: Contagium** (2005) – Loosely connected "prequel."
  - ☐ **Day of the Dead** (2008) - This direct-to-video remake is a loose adaptation of the original, with a different plot and faster-moving zombies. It was panned by critics.
  - ☐ **Day of the Dead: Bloodline** (2017) - This remake promised to stay closer to Romero's original vision but received poor reviews.
- ☐ **Land of the Dead** (2005) – Class warfare as zombies evolve.
- ☐ **Diary of the Dead** (2007) – Found-footage style Romero experiment.
- ☐ **Survival of the Dead** (2009) – Romero's final, island-set zombie entry.
- ☐ **Twilight of the Dead** (In Development) - Planned as a capstone to the series, this film's story was conceived by Romero before his death in 2017 and is currently in production.
- **ADAPTIONS**
  - ☐ **The Return of the Living Dead** (1985) - The first movie establishes an alternate universe where *Night of the Living Dead* is a film based on real events. The zombies in this series notably crave brains and can speak. A new film, titled *Return of the Living Dead*, is in development from Living Dead Media LLC, with Steve Wolsh writing and directing.
    - **SEQUELS**
      - ☐ **Return of the Living Dead Part II** (1988) – Sequel with slapstick zombie comedy. Curious kids unearth the barrels that previously helped revive the dead, which proves the second time's an undead charm.
      - ☐ **Return of the Living Dead III** (1993) – Tragic romance with self-mutilation.
      - ☐ **Return of the Living Dead: Rave to the Grave** (2005) – Teen rave zombie outbreak.
  - ☐ **Night of the Living Dead** (1990) - The official color remake directed by Tom Savini with a revised script by George A. Romero. It notably features a more capable version of the character Barbra.
  - ☐ **Children of the Living Dead** (2001) - Produced by Russo as a direct sequel to his 30th Anniversary Edition, though it has little connection to the rest of the series.
- ☐ **Tombs of the Blind Dead** (1972, Spain) – Templar knights return as undead revenants. More than 50 bands have written songs paying tribute to the film series.
  - **THE BLIND DEAD SERIES**
    - ☐ **Return of the Blind Dead** (1973) – Sequel to the Templar revenants. Often considered the best in the series. It features the Templars laying siege to a village during a celebration.
    - ☐ **The Ghost Galleon** (1974) – Blind Dead terrorize stranded models at sea.
    - ☐ **Night of the Seagulls** (1975) – Final Blind Dead entry.
  - **ADAPTIONS**
    - ☐ **Mansion of the Living Dead** (1982) - A spiritual sequel directed by Jesús Franco, an ode to the Blind Dead.
    - ☐ **Graveyard of the Dead** (2009) - A low-budget, shot-on-video, unauthorized follow-up.
    - ☐ **Curse of the Blind Dead** (2021) - An unofficial remake.
    - ☐ **Scream of the Blind Dead** (2021) - An impressionistic variation on the first half-hour of the original film.
- ☐ **Garden of the Dead** (1972) – Prisoners inhale toxic gas and rise as zombies.
  - **SPIRITUAL SIBLINGS**
    - ☐ **Children Shouldn't Play with Dead Things** (1972) - Directed by Bob Clark, features a theatrical troupe digging up a corpse on an island cemetery. The zombies in this film, similar to *Garden of the Dead*, possess a degree of intelligence and dexterity not typical for the era.
    - ☐ **Grave of the Vampire** (1972) - Also directed by John Hayes, was often the top-billed feature when shown with *Garden of the Dead* on double bills. While not a zombie film, it shares a similar low-budget, exploitation aesthetic.

Godfather of the Dead

George A. Romero[32]

George A. Romero (1940–2017), born in the Bronx and raised in Pittsburgh, transformed horror with a single low-budget film. *Night of the Living Dead* (1968) not only invented the modern zombie: flesh-eating, contagious, apocalyptic, but also smuggled social commentary into every bite. Casting Duane Jones, a Black lead, at the height of civil rights unrest was revolutionary; pairing that with the film's nihilistic ending made it a landmark of both genre and politics. From there, Romero returned again and again to the undead, using them less as monsters than as mirrors, reflecting back America's racial strife, consumerist excess, Cold War militarism, and widening class divides.

Romero's style was unmistakable: raw Pittsburgh grit, blue-collar settings, and unglamorous realism that grounded his allegories. He thrived on bleak ambiguity, his survivors rarely "won" so much as endured, and even victory was poisoned by paranoia, cruelty, or irony. His zombie films evolved alongside America's anxieties: the farmhouse claustrophobia of *Night*, the mall satire of *Dawn*, the militarized bunker paranoia of *Day*, the class revolt of *Land*, and the survivalist experiments of *Diary* (2007) and *Survival* (2009). Yet Romero's reach went beyond zombies. *Martin* (1978) reframed the vampire myth as lonely addiction, and *Creepshow* (1982) paid lurid homage to EC Comics with Stephen King, fusing pulp with grotesque humor.

Romero's influence cannot be overstated. Without him, there is no *The Walking Dead*, no *28 Days Later*, no *Resident Evil* games or films, no *Train to Busan*. His zombies gave the world a new myth: not mystical revenants but shambling, flesh-hungry corpses animated by contagion, an image so powerful it became global cultural shorthand for societal collapse. Equally vital was his independent spirit. Making *Night* outside Hollywood with a team of Pittsburgh friends, Romero proved that horror could be self-funded, self-distributed, and world-shaking. His DIY model inspired countless filmmakers to pick up cameras, proving horror was not just a genre but a movement.

Signature Works (Curated)
- **Night of the Living Dead (1968)** — Stranded survivors in a farmhouse face the undead. Broke taboos by killing the heroine's love interest and casting a Black lead at the height of civil rights turmoil.
- **Dawn of the Dead (1978)** — Zombies overrun a mall; satire of consumer culture disguised as splatter. Essential Savini effects.
- **Day of the Dead (1985)** — Military bunker paranoia and Bub the "thinking" zombie. Bleakest entry of the trilogy.
- **Creepshow (1982)** — Team-up with Stephen King; EC Comics-inspired anthology blending pulp and grotesque.
- **Land of the Dead (2005)** — Zombies evolve intelligence, and class divisions mirror the fortress city of the elite.

The Fingerprints
- Social allegory in every outbreak.
- Zombies as blank screens for cultural fears.
- Pittsburgh grit: blue-collar settings, unglamorous realism.
- Bleak, ambiguous endings.

Pairing Night Watchlist
- *Night of the Living Dead* — Watch for the civil rights allegory and claustrophobic pacing.
- *Dawn of the Dead* — Note the mall satire and Savini's practical gore.
- *Day of the Dead* — Observe Bub's performance and the shift to military paranoia.

Quick Facts to Sound Smart
- *Night of the Living Dead* was made for just $114,000 and grossed over $30 million.
- The word "zombie" is never once spoken in the original trilogy.
- *Dawn of the Dead* had two official cuts: Romero's slower, satirical version and Argento's faster, gorier European version.
- Romero's zombies inspired the *Resident Evil* video game franchise, which in turn spawned its own film empire.

[32] "George Romero, 66ème Festival de Venise (Mostra)" Nicolas Genin (https://www.flickr.com/photos/22785954@N08, Creative Commons Attribution-Share Alike 2.0)

80s–90s Zombie Boom

- ☐ **Zombie Holocaust** (1980, Italy) – Hybrid of zombie horror and cannibal gore.
- ☐ **Erotic Nights of the Living Dead** (1980, Italy) – Yes, it's exactly what the title suggests. The film was often released in different versions, with some cuts including more explicit content. It was made to capitalize on the success of other zombie films of the era, particularly George A. Romero's *Dawn of the Dead* and Lucio Fulci's *Zombi 2*.
- ☐ **Nightmare City** (1980, Italy) – Running zombies decades before 28 Days Later.
- ☐ **Kung Fu Zombie** (1981, HK) – Martial arts hero vs hopping zombies.
  - • SPIRITUAL SEQUELS
    - ☐ **Kung Fu from Beyond the Grave** (1982, HK) - Also starring Billy Chong, this film is often cited as a spiritual successor. While not directly connected, it similarly blends kung fu with the supernatural, focusing on ghosts and black magic instead of zombies.
    - ☐ **Shaolin vs. Evil Dead: The Ultimate Power** (2004, HK) - A much later film, this is part of a different series but fits the "kung fu zombies" theme. It stars Gordon Liu and features a Taoist priest fighting a vampire and his legion of undead followers.
  - • SIMILAR FILMS
    - ☐ **Encounter of the Spooky Kind** (1980, HK) - A rickshaw driver's wife and his rich client are secret lovers, and they decide to get rid of him without being implicated, so they hire a powerful sorcerer to kill him, but the sorcerer's colleague intervenes to protect him.
      - • SEQUELS
        - ☐ **Encounter of the Spooky Kind II** (1990, HK) - This stand-alone sequel was released ten years later. It stars Sammo Hung and Lam Ching-ying but has no relation to the plot or characters of the first film. The Chinese title of the film translates as "Ghost Bites Ghost."
    - ☐ **The Dead and the Deadly** (1982, HK) - Another early Hong Kong horror-comedy, this one also focuses on ghosts and Taoist magic, though with a different cast and plot.
    - ☐ **A Chinese Ghost Story** (1987, HK) - This film similarly blends kung fu, horror, and romance within a fantastical, supernatural setting, involving ghosts and demons.
- ☐ **Oasis of the Zombies** (1982) – Nazi zombies rise in the desert. *Oasis of the Zombies* was made to capitalize on the success of George A. Romero's 1978 film *Dawn of the Dead*. It is often considered a low-budget clone, borrowing heavily from established zombie tropes.
  - • SIMILAR FILMS
    - ☐ **Zombie Lake** (1981, France) – Nazi zombies resurface in French countryside.
- ☐ **Mutant** (1984) - Two brothers discover that the residents of a small Southern town are being infected by a form of toxic waste, turning them into blood-ravenous zombies.
  - • SIMILAR PRODUCTIONS
    - ☐ **Nightmare at Noon** (1987) - Some consider this film a "sideways sequel" to *Mutant* because it shares a similar plot, where a contaminated water supply causes people to turn into raving lunatics.
    - ☐ **The Crazies** (1973) - George A. Romero's original film, featuring a military attempt to contain a town infected by a rage-inducing bio-weapon, is a clear influence on *Mutant*.
    - ☐ **The Children** (1980) - A film where children are turned into monsters after a chemical accident echoes the scenes in *Mutant* where mutated children attack survivors.
- ☐ **Zombie High** (1987) – School conformity as pseudo-zombie allegory. A college freshman begins to notice that students at her new school are losing their individuality. She discovers that the faculty are operating on the students' brains to make them docile and productive, but she's having none of it.
  - • SIMILAR FILMS
    - ☐ **I Was a Teenage Zombie** (1987) – Campy teen comedy with zombies. Teenage vigilantes kill a drug pusher only to have him return as a zombie.
    - ☐ **Disturbing Behavior** (1998) - This film features a similar plot of a high school student uncovering a conspiracy to create "perfect" students in a new town. The new kid in Cradle Bay, Washington stumbles across something sinister about the town's method of transforming its unruly teens into upstanding citizen

- [ ] **Stacy: Attack of the Schoolgirl Zombies** (2001, Japan) – Teenage girls become flesh-eaters at 17. Girls surrounding 17 years old are affected by an illness that make her to be 'Stacies': they feel a strange and momentary happiness until they become zombies.
- [ ] **Dead Heat** (1988) – Buddy-cop comedy with reanimated criminals.
  - **HOMAGE & SIMILAR FILMS**
    - [ ] **Zombie Cop** (1991) - This is a standalone film that features a cop who is murdered and comes back as a zombie to track down his killer. It is a very similar plot to *Dead Heat* but is not an official sequel.
    - [ ] **Fido** (2006) – Retro suburban comedy where zombies are pets.
- [ ] **Chopper Chicks in Zombietown** (1989) – A gang of tough women bikers are the only thing that stands between a crowd of zombies, which have been accidentally let out of their secure cave, and those still alive in the town.
  - **CAMPY HUMOR & GENRE-BLENDING FILMS**
    - [ ] **Planet Terror** (2007) – Rodriguez's grindhouse infected-zombie epic.
    - [ ] **Zombieland** (2009) – Road-trip comedy in a zombie wasteland.
      - **SEQUELS:**
        - [ ] **Zombieland: Double Tap** (2019) – Sequel with new characters and laughs.
    - [ ] **Deathgasm** (2015, New Zealand) – Metal band unleashes demonic forces.
      - **SEQUELS:**
        - [ ] **Deathgasm Part 2: Goremageddon** (2025) - The sequel will follow Brodie after he resurrects his former bandmates to win a battle-of-the-bands competition. However, one of the bandmates goes rogue, and Brodie must stop a zombie horde from ruining his chances with his ex-girlfriend.
- [ ] **The Dead Next Door** (1989) – Low-budget gore cult classic. An elite anti-Zombie team is assembled by the Government to cope with an ever-growing undead infection and the religious cult zealots who fanatically protect the festering foes.
  - **SIMILAR FILMS**
    - [ ] **The Dead Pit** (1989) - Another low-budget horror film from the same era.
    - [ ] **FleshEater** (1988) – A group of college students on an overnite hayride come across a group of maneating zombies. They must fight for their lives while trying to escape and warn the authorities.
    - [ ] **Cemetery Man (Dellamorte Dellamore)** (1994, Italy) – A cemetery man must kill the dead a second time when they become zombies.

2000s Zombie Renaissance

- [ ] **Versus** (2000, Japan) – Yakuza vs zombies in dimension-crossing forest. There are 666 portals that connect this world to the other side. These are concealed from all human beings. Somewhere in Japan exists the 444th portal.... The forest of resurrection.
  - **SIMILAR FILMS**
    - [ ] **Junk** (2000, Japan) – Bank robbers in zombie-filled factory.
    - [ ] **Wild Zero** (1999, Japan) – Rock band Guitar Wolf fights alien zombies.
    - [ ] **Bio Zombie** (1998, Hong Kong) – Zombies in a shopping mall, HK style.
- [ ] **28 Days Later** (2002) – Four weeks after a mysterious, incurable virus spreads throughout the United Kingdom, a handful of survivors try to find sanctuary.
  - **SEQUELS**
    - [ ] **28 Weeks Later** (2007) – Sequel escalates military and moral chaos.
    - [ ] **28 Years Later** (2025) - Serving as a direct sequel, the third film in the series was released in June 2025. It marks the return of Boyle as director and Garland as writer. Original star Cillian Murphy is an executive producer.
    - [ ] **28 Years Later: The Bone Temple** (2026) - Shot back-to-back with the 2025 film, this sequel is scheduled for release in January 2026. Directed by Nia DaCosta and written by Alex Garland, it will feature original star Cillian Murphy. A third and final film in the new trilogy has been announced, with Danny Boyle attached to direct.

- ☐ **Resident Evil** (2002) – A special military unit fights a powerful, out-of-control supercomputer and hundreds of scientists who have mutated into flesh-eating creatures after a laboratory accident.
  - • **ADAPTIONS & SEQUELS**
    - ☐ **Resident Evil: Apocalypse** (2004) – Raccoon City collapses.
    - ☐ **Resident Evil: Extinction** (2007) – Post-apocalyptic wastelands.
    - ☐ **Resident Evil: Afterlife** (2010) – Umbrella grows global.
    - ☐ **Resident Evil: Retribution** (2012) – Franchise deepens clones and chaos.
    - ☐ **Resident Evil: The Final Chapter** (2016) – Franchise finale.
    - ☐ **Resident Evil: Welcome to Raccoon City** (2021) – Reboot faithful to games. This reboot of the film franchise disregards the Alice storyline and instead creates a new origin story based more closely on the plot of the first two video games. The film follows classic game characters like Claire and Chris Redfield, Jill Valentine, and Leon S. Kennedy
- ☐ **House of the Dead** (2003) – Uwe Boll's infamous game adaptation.
  - • **SEQUELS**
    - ☐ **House of the Dead 2** (2005) - This direct-to-TV sequel premiered on the Sci Fi Channel in 2006.
    - ☐ **Dead and Deader** (2006) - A "spiritual sequel" in all but name: While a third *House of the Dead* film was announced, it was ultimately released as *Dead and Deader* (2006) with no official tie-in to the video game franchise.
- ☐ **Alone in the Dark** (2005) - The first film adaptation, directed by Uwe Boll. A detective of the paranormal slowly unravels mysterious events with deadly results. Not to be confused with the Slasher Horror movie of the same title.
  - • **SEQUELS**
    - ☐ **Alone in the Dark II** (2008) – Necromantic zombies in sequel.
- ☐ **Tokyo Zombie** (2005, Japan) – Martial arts comedy with apocalyptic zombies.

Modern Global & Indie Zombies

- ☐ **Grindhouse** (2007) - Quentin Tarantino and Robert Rodriguez's homage to exploitation double features in the '60s and '70s with two back-to-back cult films that include previews of coming attractions between them.
  - • **ADAPTIONS**
    - ☐ **Hobo with a Shotgun** (2011) - A homeless vigilante blows away crooked cops, pedophile Santas, and other scumbags with his trusty pump-action shotgun.
    - ☐ **Machete** (2010) - After being set-up and betrayed by the man who hired him to assassinate a Texas Senator, an ex-Federale launches a brutal rampage of revenge against his former boss.
    - ☐ **Machete Kills** (2013) - The U.S. government recruits Machete to battle his way through Mexico in order to take down an arms dealer who looks to launch a weapon into space.
    - ☐ **Thanksgiving** (2023) - After a Black Friday riot ends in tragedy, a mysterious Thanksgiving-inspired killer terrorizes Plymouth, Massachusetts, the birthplace of the infamous holiday.
- ☐ **[REC]** (2007, Spain) – Found-footage infection spreads in apartment.
  - • **SEQUELS**
    - ☐ **[REC] 2** (2009) – SWAT team descends into infection chaos.
    - ☐ **[REC] 3: Genesis** (2012) – Wedding massacre prequel.
    - ☐ **[REC] 4: Apocalypse** (2014) – Naval ship outbreak finale.
  - • **ADAPTIONS**
    - ☐ **Quarantine** (2008) - In this film, a reporter and her cameraman follow two firefighters to an apartment building. After a mutated rabies virus breaks out, the government seals off the building to contain the infection, trapping all inside. The film is a faithful, found-footage remake of the first *[REC]* movie.
    - ☐ **Quarantine 2: Terminal** (2011) – Rabid creatures stalk passengers in an airport.
  - • **SINGLE-TAKE CAMERAWORK**
    - ☐ **Fish & Cat** (2013, Iran) - An Iranian film that uses a single-take structure to create a surreal, looping narrative around a group of students and a pair of cannibals at a lake.

- ☐ **Victoria** (2015, Germany) - A young Spanish woman who has recently moved to Berlin finds her flirtation with a local guy turn potentially deadly as their night out with his friends reveals a dangerous secret. This German thriller was also filmed in a single, continuous take, creating a high-stakes, real-time viewing experience.
- ☐ **One Cut of the Dead** (2017, Japan) – Things go badly for a hack director and film crew shooting a low budget zombie movie in an abandoned WWII Japanese facility, when they are attacked by real zombies.
  - • **ADAPTIONS**
    - ☐ **Final Cut** (2022) - A French remake of the film titled *Final Cut* (*Coupez!*), directed by Michel Hazanavicius, was released in 2022. It re-enacts the plot of the original but with a new cast and in a French setting.
- ☐ **Utaya: July 22** (2018, Norway) - A harrowing Norwegian film that follows a young woman's experience during the real-life terrorist attack in 2011, captured in a single, 72-minute shot.
- ☐ **Let's Scare Julie** (2019) - A real-time, continuous one-take film about a group of teen girls whose prank on their reclusive neighbor goes terribly wrong.
- ☐ **MadS** (2024) - A teenager stops off to see his dealer to test a new drug before heading off for a night of partying. On the way home, he picks up an injured woman and the night takes a surreal turn.
- ☐ **La Horde** (2009, France) – Cops and criminals vs zombie horde in tower.
  - • **FRENCH COUNTERPARTS**
    - ☐ **The Night Eats the World** (2018, France) - This film focuses on a lone survivor in a quiet, eerily empty Paris. It has been noted as a tonal counterpoint to *La Horde*'s frantic action.
    - ☐ **The Returned** (2004, France) - A less conventional, more dramatic take on the reanimated dead, also from France.
- ☐ **The Dead** (2010, UK) – African desert survival against zombies. An American mercenary, the sole survivor of a plane crash, has to run the gauntlet across Africa, battling with the living dead.
  - • **SEQUELS**
    - ☐ **The Dead 2: India** (2013, UK) – Zombie outbreak in India. An infectious epidemic spreads through India as an American turbine engineer learns that his pregnant girlfriend is trapped near the slums of Mumbai. Now he must battle his way across a 300mile wasteland of the ravenous undead.
- ☐ **World War Z** (2013) – Brad Pitt races to stop global outbreak. Former United Nations employee Gerry Lane traverses the world in a race against time to stop a zombie pandemic that is toppling armies and governments and threatens to destroy humanity itself.
- ☐ **Wyrmwood: Road of the Dead** (2014, Australia) – Mad Max with zombies.
  - • **SEQUELS**
    - ☐ **Wyrmwood: Apocalypse** (2021, Australia) – Sequel with bigger action.
- ☐ **Maggie** (2015) - A teenage girl in the Midwest becomes infected by an outbreak of a disease that slowly turns the infected into cannibalistic zombies. During her transformation, her loving father stays by her side.
  - • **CHARACTER-DRIVEN ZOMBIE FILMS**
    - ☐ **The Girl with All the Gifts** (2016, UK) - A scientist and a teacher living in a dystopian future embark on a journey of survival with a special young girl named Melanie. The film is often compared to the video game series *The Last of Us* due to their similar premise of a world ravaged by a fungal pandemic.
    - ☐ **Here Alone** (2016, USA) – Woman's survival in desolate zombie land.
    - ☐ **Cargo** (2017, Australia) – Father protects infant after infection.
- ☐ **Train to Busan** (2016, Korea) – While a zombie virus breaks out in South Korea, passengers struggle to survive on the train from Seoul to Busan.
  - • **ADAPTIONS & SEQUELS**
    - ☐ **Train to Busan Presents: Peninsula** (2020) - A former soldier returns to the quarantined Korean peninsula on a heist mission to retrieve a truck full of money. He finds the land overrun by zombies and a rogue militia, but also encounters a family of survivors.
    - ☐ **Seoul Station** (2016, Korea) – Animated prequel to *Train to Busan*.
- ☐ **Rampant** (2018, Korea) – Court intrigue meets zombie outbreak.

- ☐ **Valley of the Dead (Malnazidos)** (2020, Spain) – Civil War soldiers vs Nazi zombies.
- ☐ **#Alive** (2020, Korea) – Influencer trapped in zombie apocalypse.
  - **ADAPTIONS**
    - ☐ **Alone** (2020) - Both *#Alive* and the American film *Alone* are based on the original script "*#Alone*" by Hollywood writer Matt Naylor. Naylor is credited as a co-writer on the screenplay for *#Alive*. Both films follow a similar premise of a young person trapped in their apartment during a zombie apocalypse. They must find creative ways to survive and eventually make contact with another survivor in a neighboring building.
- ☐ **The Sadness** (2021, Taiwan) – A young couple trying to reunite amid a city ravaged by a plague that turns its victims into deranged, bloodthirsty sadists.
- ☐ **Virus-32** (2022, Argentina) - A rapid spreading virus which transforms people into intelligent, ultra-violent, extra-fast zombies. After each wave of attack by the monsters, they're left incapacitated for 32 seconds while they recover their strength.
- ☐ **Evil Dead Rise** (2023) - A twisted tale of two estranged sisters whose reunion is cut short by the rise of flesh-possessing demons, thrusting them into a primal battle for survival as they face the most nightmarish version of family imaginable. A second follow-up film is also in development, with Francis Galluppi selected by Sam Raimi to write and direct.
  - **SEQUELS**
    - ☐ **Evil Dead Burn** (2026) - A new standalone film titled *Evil Dead Burn* has begun filming and is slated for a theatrical release on July 24, 2026. It is directed by Sébastien Vaniček and will feature a new cast.

Enter the Rotting Realm

Pairing Night: Watchlist

Starter Pack (Genre Basics)
- *Night of the Living Dead* (1968) – Ground zero of the modern zombie.
- *Dawn of the Dead* (1978) – Consumerism with entrails.
- *Train to Busan* (2016) – A fast, emotional ride for newcomers.

Intermediate (Global & Bold)
- *Zombi 2* (1979) – Shark vs zombie; Italian gore classic.
- *[REC]* (2007) – Found-footage panic in a locked apartment.
- *28 Days Later* (2002) – Rage-virus dread rebooting the genre.

Deep Dive (Experimental & Extreme)
- *Cemetery Man* (1994) – Surreal meditation disguised as zombie flick.
- *The Sadness* (2021) – The most violent, shocking mutation yet.
- *Burial Ground* (1981) – Cult sleaze with unforgettable grotesque twists.

How to Watch
- Watch Romero's trilogy together — they chart U.S. anxieties across decades.
- Try pairing one U.S. film with a global counterpoint (*Night* vs *[REC]*; *Dawn* vs *Train to Busan*).
- Compare "slow" vs "fast" zombies to feel the genre's tonal divide.

Quick Facts to Sound Like the Smartest Person in the Room

- *White Zombie* (1932) - Due to its very low budget of around $50,000, much of the movie was filmed on leftover or rented sets on the Universal Studios lot, borrowing scenery and props from classics like *Dracula* and *Frankenstein*.
- *Night of the Living Dead* (1968) - Due to budget constraints, the filmmakers used Bosco chocolate syrup for blood. The zombies are shown eating roasted ham covered in chocolate sauce in one of the most famous scenes.
- *Dawn of the Dead* (1978) was co-financed by Dario Argento, who cut his own version for Europe.
- In Fulci's *Zombi 2* (1979), the infamous shark vs zombie sequence was filmed with a real shark.
- *Day of the Dead's* Bub is widely regarded as the first sympathetic zombie character.
- *28 Days Later* (2002) was shot on DV cameras, allowing London's empty streets to be filmed at dawn.
- *Train to Busan* (2016) grossed nearly $100M worldwide, proving zombie horror's global dominance.
- *The Sadness* (2021) pushed censors to the edge; some countries cut up to 10 minutes of violence.

Folk Horror

Folk horror is rooted in the soil: rural landscapes, pagan rituals, witchcraft, and the clash between old traditions and modern skepticism. From silent witchcraft docudramas to A24's *The Witch* and *Midsommar*, folk horror thrives on the idea that the land itself remembers and punishes.

Why People Are Drawn to It
Because folk horror feels ancient. It taps into fears older than cinema: superstition, curses, rituals, and the sense that isolation breeds terror. These stories pit the individual against communities bound by unseen laws, asking: are the locals mad, or have they glimpsed truths outsiders can't face? The appeal is part ethnography, part nightmare: horror not imported, but inherited.

Essentials
- **Häxan** (1922, Sweden) – The experimental pseudo-documentary *Häxan* explores the historical persecution of alleged witches, combining academic narration with surreal, often grotesque and humorous reenactments of medieval superstition to critique religious paranoia and the hysteria surrounding female autonomy.
- **Witchfinder General** (1968, UK) – Vincent Price as ruthless witch-hunter exploiting paranoia. Based on the historical exploits of Matthew Hopkins during the English Civil War, *Witchfinder General* is a brutal folk horror film that explores the abuse of power, the breakdown of law, and the destructive cycle of violence and revenge.
- **The Wicker Man** (1973, UK) – Pagan rituals vs Christian outsider; folk horror's crown jewel. Robin Hardy fuses mystery and folk ritual, as a devout policeman investigates a pagan island community only to become its ultimate sacrifice. Its sunlit dread, musical eeriness, and shocking finale make it a cornerstone of folk horror, where belief systems clash with devastating consequences.
- **The VVitch: A New-England Folktale** (2015, USA) – Puritan family unravels in wilderness isolation. Blending psychological paranoia and religious fanaticism with folklore, Robert Eggers' *The VVitch* depicts a 17th-century Puritan family's destruction as they are cast out into the wilderness and torn apart by suspicion, fear, and a very real supernatural evil lurking in the woods.
- **Wake in Fright** (1971, Australia) - Based on the novel by Kenneth Cook, *Wake in Fright* is a disturbing psychological drama and Ozploitation film where a cultured schoolteacher's vacation spirals into a nightmarish, booze-fueled bender in a remote mining town, exposing the darker, more savage aspects of Australian masculinity and the corruption within himself.

Deep Cuts
- **The White Reindeer** (1952, Finland) – Sámi vampire-shapeshifter myth brought to icy life. Erik Blomberg blends Finnish folklore with atmospheric horror, telling of a lonely woman cursed to transform into a vampiric reindeer that preys on men. Its stark Arctic landscapes and mythic tone make it an early folk horror classic, where nature, sexuality, and superstition intertwine.
- **Alison's Birthday** (1981, Australia) – Teen girl trapped in a Celtic cult ritual. An Australian folk horror in which a young woman's 19th birthday celebration hides a druidic ritual meant to trap her soul. With its suburban occultism and understated dread, the film reimagines ancient pagan sacrifice within the frame of modern domestic life.
- **Eyes of Fire** (1983, USA) – Pioneer settlers encounter occult forces in the woods. Avery Crounse sets his folk horror in the American frontier, where a group of settlers encounters a haunted wilderness infused with witchcraft and Native folklore. Its dreamlike visuals and eerie atmosphere turn the untamed landscape into both historical backdrop and supernatural menace, embodying the collision of colonization and myth.
- **Dark Waters** (1993, Russia) – A monastery conceals pagan aquatic rituals. A gothic folk horror steeped in religious dread, following a young woman who uncovers occult secrets on a remote convent island. With its crumbling catacombs, apocalyptic imagery, and Eastern European surrealism, the film evokes Lovecraftian terror filtered through Catholic ritual and decay.

- **La Llorona** (2019, Guatemala) – Genocide reframed through folk curse and ghostly vengeance. Jayro Bustamante reframes the Latin American ghost legend as political allegory, blending supernatural horror with the real horrors of Guatemala's civil war and genocide. Through its slow-burn atmosphere and spectral justice, the film turns folklore into a reckoning with historical trauma and collective guilt.

Critical Essay
"Folk Horror Isn't Just British Paganism."

Myth: Folk horror = rural England + wicker baskets.

Reality: The genre is global. Finland's *The White Reindeer* adapts Sámi shapeshifter myths. Mexico's *La Llorona* reframes indigenous folklore as Gothic tragedy. Guatemala's 2019 *La Llorona* uses the same myth for political reckoning. Indonesia's *Satan's Slaves* roots horror in Muslim folk rituals. Folk horror is everywhere land, ritual, and belief shape lives from Appalachian ghost tales to Japanese huldra myths.

Global Spotlight: International Folk Horrors
- **Nordic & Eastern Europe** – *The White Reindeer* (1952, Finland); *Thale* (2012, Norway); *November* (2017, Estonia).
- **Latin America** – *La Llorona* (1933–2019, Mexico & Guatemala); *We Are What We Are* (2010, Mexico).
- **Australia & New Zealand** – *Alison's Birthday* (1981); *Wake in Fright* (1971) as folk-adjacent dread.
- **Asia** – *Nang Nak* (1999, Thailand); *Bakeneko: A Vengeful Spirit* (1968, Japan).
- **Israel** – *The Golem* (2018), revisiting Jewish clay protector myth.

- ☐ **Häxan** (1922, Sweden) – Fictionalized documentary showing the evolution of witchcraft, from its pagan roots to its confusion with hysteria in Eastern Europe. Re-edited in 1968 with a jazz score and narration by William S. Burroughs (*Witchcraft Through the Ages*).

  - **ADAPTIONS & WITCHCRAFT FILMS**
    - ☐ **Witchcraft Through the Ages** (1968) - This is the most significant adaptation of the original film, Häxan. It was re-edited by British director and distributor Anthony Balch, with a new jazz score by Daniel Humair (featuring Jean-Luc Ponty on violin) and narration by author William S. Burroughs. This version, cut to around 75 minutes, became a cult favorite, fitting the counterculture spirit of the late 1960s.
    - ☐ **The VVitch: A New-England Folktale (The Witch)** (2015, UK/Canada) - Distributed by A24, this film uses a historically grounded folk-horror setting to explore similar themes of a family's internal strife and mistrust in the face of an external threat. An isolated Puritan family in 1630s New England comes unraveled by the forces of witchcraft and possession. Director Robert Eggers used authentic 17th-century diaries for dialogue.
    - ☐ **Hagazussa** (2017, Germany) - After the loss of her tormented mother, the erratic behavior of a 15th century woman living in an isolated mountain village becomes a threat to the safety of her infant child.
    - ☐ **November** (2017, Estonia) – In a poor Estonian village, a group of peasants use magic and folk remedies to survive the winter, and a young woman tries to get a young man to love her.

- ☐ **Hellbender** (2022) - A modern folk horror film about a mother and daughter living in isolation in the woods, with the daughter beginning to question her mother's true nature and their shared magical ancestry.
- ☐ **The Devil's Bath** (2024) - A German folk horror film that similarly explores a woman's isolated experience, paranoia, and the grim realities of 18th-century life. Austria in the 18th century. Forests surround villages. Killing a baby gets a woman sentenced to death. Agnes readies for married life with her beloved. But her mind and heart grow heavy. A gloomy path alone, evil thoughts arising.

☐ **La Llorona** (1933, Mexico) - In modern Mexico, a malevolent spirit targets a family, linking tragic past events of abandoned, infanticidal mothers to a possessed intruder's attempt to sacrifice their son. One of the earliest Mexican films to adapt the legend, this version is considered more faithful to the original folklore than the 1963 film.

- • **ADAPTIONS**
  - ☐ **La Llorona** (1960, Mexico) - A film by director René Cardona, released shortly before *The Curse of the Crying Woman*, offered another spin on the folklore.
  - ☐ **The Curse of the Crying Woman** (1963, Mexico) – La Llorona folk myth. After fifteen years of being away, a woman returns with her husband to her aunt's hacienda in the Mexican countryside, without realizing that her relative is a sorceress who wants to use her to bring an evil witch back to life.
  - ☐ **KM 31: Kilometer 31** (2006, Mexico) - Following a horrible car accident on a wooded road near Mexico City, Agata goes into a coma. Her twin sister Catalina must try to solve the mystery of her sister's accident next to the Km. 31 marker and discovers a terrifying local legend. Draws its inspiration from the Mexican folklore legend of *La Llorona* (the Weeping Woman), a ghost who drowns people in a river while searching for her own lost children. The film also includes other legends of ghosts appearing on highways.
    - • **SEQUELS**
      - ☐ **Kilometer 31-2 (KM-31-2: Sin Retorno)** (2016, Mexico) - The story picks up seven years after the events of the first film, focusing on a police officer whose life was impacted by the paranormal events at Kilometer 31. He is drawn into a new mystery involving missing children and a sinister plan linked to the original haunting.
  - ☐ **La leyenda de la Llorona** (2011, Mexico) - This Mexican animated film, part of the *Las Leyendas* franchise, reinterprets the story for a family audience, portraying La Llorona as a more sympathetic character.
  - ☐ **La Llorona** (2019, Guatemala) – Political genocide reframed as folk curse. A highly-regarded Guatemalan art house horror film that uses the legend to explore themes of political corruption and social injustice during the country's civil war.
  - ☐ **The Curse of La Llorona** (2019) - An American-produced supernatural horror film that was a part of *The Conjuring* universe. The film received largely negative reviews for its reliance on jump scares and generic storytelling.
  - ☐ **The Legend of La Llorona** (2022) - Another American-produced horror film that focuses on a family's vacation in Mexico that is terrorized by the legendary figure.

☐ **The White Reindeer** (1952, Finland) – Woman cursed to transform into vampiric reindeer. The film's use of a female shapeshifter who can transform into an animal to lure and feed on her victims evokes classic vampire folklore, particularly in how the protagonist, Pirita, becomes a "bloodthirsty shapeshifter" after a shaman's magic goes wrong. With the resurgence of the folk horror subgenre in the 21st century, *The White Reindeer* has been re-examined and hailed as a classic of the genre. It is often programmed alongside more recent folk horror films at festivals and has been featured in the Severin Films *All the Haunts Be Ours** box set. The film is celebrated for its dreamlike quality, starkly beautiful cinematography of the Lapland region, and reliance on atmosphere rather than explicit dialogue. In this respect, it draws influence from Scandinavian silent horror films of the 1920s.

☐ **Lake of the Dead** (1958, Norway) - A group of friends travel to a cabin in the Norwegian forest. It's a rumor that at night a crazy man can be heard screaming at a lake nearby the cabin.

☐ **The City of the Dead** (1960, UK) - A young college student arrives in a sleepy Massachusetts town to research witchcraft; during her stay at an eerie inn, she discovers a startling secret about the town and its inhabitants.

☐ **Il demonio** (1963, Italy) - A lonely, sexually-uninhibited young peasant is subjected to an exorcism after she hexes a man who rejects her advances.

☐ **Viy** (1967, Soviet Union) - A young priest is ordered to preside over the wake of witch in a small old wooden church of a remote village. This means spending three nights alone with the corpse with only his faith to protect him. Based on Nikolai Gogol's folktales, particularly the ones collected in his book *Evenings on a Farm near Dikanka*.

- **GOGOL'S FOLKTALES:** Nikolai Gogol's folktales, written in the early 19th century, drew heavily on Ukrainian folklore, blending the supernatural with satire, rural life, and gothic atmosphere. Collected in works like *Evenings on a Farm Near Dikanka* (1831–32), they introduced readers to witches, devils, and spirits rooted in Slavic oral tradition. Among these, *Viy* stands out as the first Russian horror story to gain international fame: a tale of a seminarian forced to pray over the corpse of a witch, culminating in the terrifying appearance of Viy, a demonic figure with eyelids so heavy they must be lifted by others. First published in 1835, *Viy* bridged folklore and literature, shaping the foundations of Russian horror and later inspiring stage and film adaptations, including the landmark 1967 Soviet film.
    - ☐ **May Night** (1952, Soviet Union) - A Soviet fantasy film also based on a short story by Gogol.
    - ☐ **The Overcoat** (1959, Soviet Union) - A Soviet drama film based on Gogol's short story of the same name. While not strictly a horror film, the story's supernatural conclusion involves a ghost seeking revenge for his stolen overcoat.
    - ☐ **The Night Before Christmas** (1961, Soviet Union) - This Soviet-era Christmas fantasy movie was based on one of Gogol's short stories.
    - ☐ **A Holy Place** (1990, Yugoslavia) - This Serbian (Yugoslav) horror film is also based on Gogol's story.
    - ☐ **Evil Spirit: Viy** (2008, Korea) - A South Korean horror film with a loose adaptation of the Gogol story.
    - ☐ **Viy** (2014, Russia) - Released internationally as *Forbidden Empire*, this Russian dark fantasy film is loosely based on the myth of the monster Viy.
    - ☐ **Gogol. Origins** (2017, Russia) - This Russian fantasy-horror film is loosely based on several works from Gogol's collection *Evenings on a Farm near Dikanka*
    - ☐ **Gogol. Viy** (2018, Russia) - This Russian film was part of a series based on Gogol's works.

☐ **Witchfinder General** (1968, UK) – During the English Civil War, a young Roundhead seeks vengeance against a vicious witch-hunter and his henchman, who have terrorized the soldier's fiancée and wrongfully executed her uncle. Sometimes grouped with *The Blood on Satan's Claw* and *The Wicker Man* as the "Unholy Trinity" of folk horror.

- **SIMILAR FILMS**
    - ☐ **The Blood of Satan's Claw** (1971) - Produced by Tigon British Film Productions (the same company behind *Witchfinder General*), this film is often grouped with *Witchfinder* and *The Wicker Man* as a definitive work of folk horror.

☐ **Bakeneko: A Vengeful Spirit** (1968, Japan) - A Vassal kills his lord and his wife with her cat commit suicide to avoid marrying him. Will they return and try to get revenge?

☐ **Lokis. Rekopis profesora Wittembacha** (1970, Poland) - Clergy investigates folklore rumor of noblewoman birthing bear-human hybrid after attack. Nobleman's wife bitten, he disappears into woods after creature's origins uncovered.

☐ **Wake in Fright** (1971, Australia) - After a bad gambling bet, a schoolteacher is marooned in a town full of crazy, drunk, violent men who threaten to make him just as crazy, drunk, and violent.

☐ **Season of the Witch (Hungry Wives)** (1972) - A neglected, unhappy suburban housewife gets mixed up in witchcraft with unexpected consequences.

Robert Eggers[33]

Born in New Hampshire in 1983, Robert Eggers emerged from theater and production design before making his feature debut. His horror is rooted in historical authenticity, folklore, and meticulous world-building. Eggers doesn't just tell a story, he resurrects a time and place so vividly that its fears feel lived-in. His work bridges art-house rigor with primal dread, pulling horror back to its folkloric and mythic roots.

Signature Works (Curated)
- *The Witch* (2015) — A Puritan family in 1630s New England is undone by paranoia, isolation, and whispers of a witch in the woods. A new classic of folk horror.
- *The Lighthouse* (2019) — Two lighthouse keepers spiral into madness on a remote island; equal parts nautical myth, cosmic dread, and black comedy.
- *The Northman* (2022) — While more a Viking epic than straight horror, its violence, ritual, and mythological visions push into nightmare territory.

The Fingerprints
- Period-accurate language and settings: archaic dialogue, historical costuming, tactile authenticity.
- Folklore as terror: witches, sea legends, and pagan ritual reimagined as lived horror.
- Obsession with isolation: characters cut off from society descend into paranoia or delirium.
- Stark, painterly visuals: chiaroscuro lighting, symmetrical compositions, harsh landscapes.
- Ambiguous supernatural: the horror often lies in whether the characters are cursed, mad, or both.

Legacy & Influence
Eggers recharged folk horror for the 21st century, following the path laid by Shirley Jackson and *The Wicker Man* but with unmatched historical rigor. *The Witch* became an A24 touchstone, helping brand "elevated horror." He's influenced a wave of folkloric, slow-burn horror (*The Ritual*, *The VVitch* homages, even *The Northman* spinoff discourse in pop culture). His emphasis on authenticity has made him a beacon for filmmakers seeking to marry horror with arthouse prestige.

Pairing Night Watchlist
- *The Witch* (2015) → Look for how the family's faith turns their paranoia into self-destruction; the witch may be less frightening than their own belief system.
- *The Lighthouse* (2019) → Track the shifting power dynamics; every fart, every seagull, every storm is part of its descent into mythic madness.
- *The Northman* (2022) → Note how ritual and vision sequences feel horrific even within an epic—Eggers bends genre lines but keeps dread intact.

Quick Facts to Sound Smart
- *The Witch* was subtitled "A New-England Folktale," and much of its dialogue came directly from 17th-century journals and court records.
- Willem Dafoe and Robert Pattinson stayed in near-freezing conditions during *The Lighthouse*, enhancing the film's sense of misery and delirium.
- Eggers originally worked in theater and production design; his eye for texture and period detail comes from that background.
- He cites Bergman, Tarkovsky, and Murnau as key influences.
- Eggers initially planned *Nosferatu* as his follow-up to *The Witch*; while delayed, it's still in development with Bill Skarsgård and Lily-Rose Depp attached.

- ☐ **The Wicker Man** (1973) – Pagan conspiracy engulfs an outsider's sanity. A puritan police sergeant arrives in a Scottish island village in search of a missing girl, who the pagan locals claim never existed. A third film in Hardy's trilogy, based on Norse mythology, was never completed before his death in 2016. Its original cut was nearly lost, salvaged from a U.S. distributor's vault.
  - • **SEQUELS & ADAPTIONS**
    - ☐ **The Wicker Tree** (2011) - A "spiritual successor" rather than a direct sequel, this film is based on Hardy's 2006 novel, *Cowboys for Christ*.
    - ☐ **The Wicker Man** (2006) – Infamous Nic Cage remake. The film is widely ridiculed for its unintentional comedy, particularly Cage's over-the-top performance.
- ☐ **Leptirica** (1973, Serbia) - The village needs a miller, but the vampire needs a victim.
- ☐ **The Death Wheelers (Psychomania)** (1973, UK) - An amiable, psychopathic leader of a violent teen motorbike gang is spurred by his mother, a Satan-worshiping spiritual medium, into committing suicide and returning to life as an "undead."
- ☐ **Nazareno Cruz and the Wolf** (1975, Argentina) - Nazareno Cruz is the seventh son of a couple living in a high mountain village. According to a myth, a seventh son will become a wolf on nights of the full moon. Everyone in the village is relieved when this doesn't happen. The boy grows up and falls in love with a beautiful girl, Griselda. When he's 20 years old, he is visited by the Devil, who offers him the wealth of the world if he will turn his back on his love for Griselda, and if he fails to do this, he will become a wolf.
- ☐ **The Shout** (1978) - A traveler by the name of Crossley forces himself upon a musician and his wife in a lonely part of Devon, and uses the aboriginal magic he has learned to displace his host.
- ☐ **Beauty and the Beast** (1978, Czechoslovakia) - In this gothic rendition of the classic fairy tale, a merchant's youngest daughter is held prisoner by a mysterious winged beast.
- ☐ **Alison's Birthday** (1981, Australia) – A young girl is subjected to a reign of terror so that her soul can be transferred to the body of an old crone.
  - • **SIMILAR THEMES & DIRECTOR'S PROJECTS:**
    - ☐ **The Sentinel** (1977) – Tenant in NYC discovers sinister psychological conspiracy. Starring Ava Gardner and the film debut of Beverly D'Angelo. Jeff Goldblum was dubbed in all but one scene.
    - ☐ **Kadaicha** (1988) - Coughlan wrote the screenplay for this Australian horror film, which is about a sacred Aboriginal burial ground.
    - ☐ **Cubbyhouse** (2001) - Coughlan directed this film, which is also about devil worship and has a connection to *Alison's Birthday*'s occult themes.
- ☐ **Superstition** (1982) - A witch put to death in 1692 swears vengeance on her persecutors and returns to the present day to punish their descendants.
  - • **SEQUELS**
    - ☐ **Witch Story** (1989) - The 1989 Italian film *Witch Story*, directed by Alessandro Capone, was marketed as *Superstition 2* in the United States. Despite the title, the movie is not a direct sequel, and the plots are unrelated, though both are horror films centered on a vengeful witch.
- ☐ **Eyes of Fire** (1983, USA) – A preacher is accused of adultery, and he and his followers are chased out of town. They become stranded in an isolated forest, which is haunted by the spirits of French colonists controlled by evil. It was a Pioneer of American folk horror. While not a commercial success at the time, *Eyes of Fire* is now recognized as a key work of American folk horror, a subgenre that explores dark and unsettling stories in rural or isolated settings.
- ☐ **The Wolf (Wilczyca)** (1983, Poland) - Ex-guerrilla Kacper, possessed by late wife Maryna's spirit, is pursued by female werewolf. He recognizes werewolf traits in Julia, a countess involved with Austrian officer.
- ☐ **The Enchanted** (1984) - Sailor Royce Hagan returns from the sea and occupies his deserted family ranch in a remote part of backwoods Florida. A strange family is living in the woods on his property. A Florida Folk Mystery hangs over the ranch.

- ☐ **Tilbury** (1987, Iceland) - In the year 1940 when there were British forces in Iceland, a country boy goes to Reykjavik to work for the army. He also wants to know what became of his childhood sweetheart. He soon discovers that she's having an affair with a British soldier. He starts to suspect that the soldier, instead of being an officer and a gentleman, is in fact a very peculiar kind of monster.
- ☐ **The Dreaming** (1988, Australia) - A doctor treats a sick aboriginal person, who had defied a tribal taboo and visited a sacred cave. The doctor soon finds herself having disturbing dreams and finds herself involved in a 200-year-old mystery.
- ☐ **Celia** (1989, Australia) - An imaginative and somewhat disturbed young girl fantasizes about evil creatures and other oddities to mask her insecurities while growing up in rural Australia.
- ☐ **The Witches** (1990) - A young boy on holiday with his grandmother discovers a convention of witches led by the evil Grand High Witch, who plans to turn all of England's children into mice. The film was an adaptation of Roald Dahl's 1983 novel of the same name.
  - • **ADAPTIONS**
    - ☐ **The Witches** (2020) - This film is a remake co-produced by Robert Zemeckis and Guillermo del Toro. While it follows a similar plot, it made several changes, including the time period, setting, and ending.
- ☐ **Clearcut** (1991, Canada) - A white lawyer finds his values shaken when he is paired with an angry Indigenous activist who insists on kidnapping the head of a logging company to teach him the price of his destruction.
- ☐ **Dark Waters** (1993, Russia/UK/Ukraine) – A girl travels to an island, after the death of her father, to find out why the father funded a monastery on the island. The film features a mysterious cult, an ancient aquatic demon, and a remote, storm-battered island. Its focus on unknowable, cosmic evil resonates with the works of horror author H.P. Lovecraft.
- ☐ **Anchoress** (1993, Belgium/UK) - In the 14th-century, a visionary girl is to become an Anchoress, a walled-in recluse, so that she can live in the Virgin's house forever. Over time she awakens to her own sensuality and explores her own female, earth-based spirituality.
- ☐ **The Craft** (1996) - A young girl new to a Catholic school befriends a coven of witches whom the other students either shun or fear. But when a powerful invocation goes wrong, the consequences could endanger their lives.
  - • **SEQUELS**
    - ☐ **The Craft: Legacy** (2020) - This film is a "legacy sequel," following a new group of teenage witches at the same high school as the original coven. The plot includes a family connection to the original film's antagonist, Nancy Downs (played by Fairuza Balk, who makes a cameo appearance). While it pays homage to the original, it focuses on modern themes and features a new story.
- ☐ **Nang Nak** (1999, Thailand) - Mak goes home from war and lives together with his wife and baby happily until a friend decides to reveal a secret.
- ☐ **Little Otik** (2000, Czech) - A childless couple passes off an anthropomorphous tree stump as their baby, but things get out of hand when the monstrosity comes to life and demands to be fed. The film is based on the 19th-century Czech folk tale *Otesánek* by Karel Jaromír Erben.
  - • **OTHER FOLK TALES**
    - ☐ **Alice** (1988, Czech) - A dark and surreal retelling of Lewis Carroll's classic story, blending live-action with disturbing stop-motion animation. It shares *Little Otik's* technique of bringing inanimate objects to life. Included among the *1001 Movies You Must See Before You Die.*
    - ☐ **Lamb** (2021, Iceland) - An Icelandic folk horror film about a couple who discover a human-lamb hybrid creature on their farm. The film explores themes of motherhood and nature in a strange and unsettling way.
- ☐ **Wake Wood** (2009, Ireland) – Pagan ritual resurrects a dead child. The parents of a girl who was killed by a savage dog are granted the opportunity to spend three days with their deceased daughter.
  - • **OTHER THEMES**
    - ☐ **The Other Side of the Door** (2016) - This film also follows a grieving couple who move to an isolated location and attempt to bring their child back from the dead through a ritual.
    - ☐ **The Resurrected** (1991) - A more obscure film that also deals with a resurrection ritual.
- ☐ **Black Death** (2010, UK) - Set during the time of the first outbreak of bubonic plague in England, a young monk is given the task of learning the truth about reports of people being brought back to life in a small village.

Elevating Horror

A24

Origins & Mission
Founded in 2012 by Daniel Katz, David Fenkel, and John Hodges, A24 started as a boutique distribution company before evolving into one of the most influential studios of the 21st century. Their mission wasn't just to make movies, but to curate cultural moments: stylish, daring, and distinctly art-house. A24 horror emerged as a new kind of prestige terror: slow-burn, character-driven, and visually meticulous that blurred the line between independent cinema and mainstream horror.

Signature Style
A24 horror is defined by art-house dread: atmospheric pacing, painterly visuals, and existential themes. These films often use folklore, trauma, or cosmic indifference as the true monster, placing audiences inside characters' spiraling psychology rather than relying on cheap scares. Common fingerprints include naturalistic sound design, stark landscapes, and narratives where grief or isolation feel as threatening as the supernatural.

Essential Titles
- *The Witch* (2015) – Robert Eggers' puritan nightmare; folk horror filtered through historical realism and paranoia.
- *Hereditary* (2018) – Ari Aster's devastating family tragedy that mutates into occult terror; instantly canonized as a modern classic.
- *Midsommar* (2019) – Folk horror in daylight; a breakup movie dressed as a pagan fever dream.
- *The Lighthouse* (2019) – Eggers again, with black-and-white maritime madness and mythic descent into insanity.
- *Talk to Me* (2023) – Viral sensation blending possession horror with Gen Z social media culture.

Cultural Footprint
A24 didn't just release horror, they rebranded it. Their films pulled the genre into the art-house conversation, winning critics and awards attention without losing genre fans. They turned "elevated horror" into both a buzzword and a movement, paving the way for ambitious new filmmakers (Eggers, Aster, Philippou brothers) and reshaping what audiences expect from horror: not just scares, but cinema with depth, aesthetics, and discourse. A24 became a badge of taste, especially among younger viewers, where their branding itself feels cult-like.

Legacy & Influence
A24's approach to horror sparked an industry-wide shift, proving that genre films could thrive on the festival circuit and compete for critical prestige without sacrificing commercial appeal. Their success encouraged rival studios and streamers to greenlight more atmospheric, allegorical horror, while cementing directors like Robert Eggers and Ari Aster as modern auteurs. Beyond box office, A24 rewired audience expectations: horror became a vehicle for exploring grief, identity, and social unease with the same seriousness as drama, ensuring that "prestige horror" is no longer an exception but a permanent part of cinema's landscape.

Watchlist – An A24 Sampler
- *The Witch* (2015) → Watch for how historical authenticity and folklore merge into suffocating dread.
- *Hereditary* (2018) → Study how grief and trauma fuel both the narrative and the scares.
- *Midsommar* (2019) → Note how horror works in broad daylight through ritual, culture, and psychological fracture.

Quick Facts to Sound Smart
- *Hereditary* (2018) made over $80 million worldwide on a $10 million budget, becoming A24's highest-grossing film until *Everything Everywhere All at Once*.
- *The Witch* (2015) won Best Director at Sundance, cementing Robert Eggers as a major auteur on his debut.
- *The Lighthouse* (2019) earned an Oscar nomination for cinematography, rare recognition for a modern horror film.
- The term "elevated horror" wasn't coined by A24, but their marketing savvy made it synonymous with their brand, sparking debates among critics and fans.

- ☐ **Kill List** (2011, UK) – Hitmen stumble into terrifying cult conspiracy. Nearly a year after a botched job, a hitman takes a new assignment with the promise of a big payoff for three killings. What starts off as an easy task soon unravels, sending the killer into the heart of darkness.
  - • **DARK & UNSETTLING SERIES FROM BEN WHEATLEY**
    - ☐ **Sightseers** (2012, UK) - Chris wants to show girlfriend Tina his world, but events soon conspire against the couple and their dream caravan holiday takes a very wrong turn. Tony Way (Crich Tourist) is seen eating a Cornetto. This movie was Executively Produced by Edgar Wright, who directed *Shaun of the Dead* (2004), *Hot Fuzz* (2007), and *The World's End* (2013), a.k.a. "the Cornetto Trilogy."
    - ☐ **A Field in England** (2013, UK) - Amid the Civil War in 17th-century England, a group of deserters flee from battle through an overgrown field. Captured by an alchemist, the men are forced to help him search to find a hidden treasure that he believes is buried in the field. Ben Wheatley's black-and-white folk horror film follows a group of deserters from the English Civil War. They descend into madness and psychological collapse after taking psychedelic mushrooms, with reality becoming increasingly strange and disjointed.
    - ☐ **In the Earth** (2021,UK) - As the world searches for a cure to a disastrous virus, a scientist and park scout venture deep in the forest for a routine equipment run.
- ☐ **The Lords of Salem** (2012) - Radio DJ Heidi is sent a box containing a record--a "gift from the Lords". The sounds within the grooves trigger flashbacks of her town's violent past. Is Heidi going mad, or are the Lords back to take revenge on Salem, Massachusetts?
- ☐ **Bone Tomahawk** (2015) - In the Old West, a small-town sheriff and his rag-tag posse set out to rescue several townspeople from a brutal cave-dwelling, cannibalistic Indian tribe. Starring Kurt Russell, Patrick Wilson and Matthew Fox. At Fantastic Fest, S. Craig Zahler said that he wanted much of the film's mysticism to remain ambiguous and debatable.
- ☐ **Thelma** (2017, Norway) - A confused religious girl tries to deny her feelings for a female friend who's in love with her. This causes her suppressed subconsciously-controlled psychokinetic powers to reemerge with devastating results. The film's moody atmosphere and psychological focus have been compared to the works of Swedish director Ingmar Bergman.
- ☐ **Errementari (The Blacksmith and the Devil)** (2017, Spain) - A quiet village is thrown into turmoil upon disturbing a reclusive and feared blacksmith rumored to be in league with the devil. The film adapts a version of the folktale collected in 1903 by Father Joxemiel Barandiaran and sets the story in the Basque Country in 1843. It is known for its authentic portrayal of Basque folklore, including its use of an almost-extinct Alavese dialect and its depiction of demons inspired by medieval Basque imagery.
  - • **BASQUE FOLKLORE HORROR:** Rooted in the unique mythology of the Basque region, one of Europe's oldest cultural traditions, blending pre-Christian beliefs with later Christian overlays. Its stories often center on beings tied to the mountains and caves of the Pyrenees: the Basajaun, a wild man and forest guardian; the Lamia, seductive, siren-like women with animal features; and Mari, a powerful goddess who controls weather and fate from her mountain dwellings. Witches (*sorginak*) and their sabbaths figure prominently too, tied to the region's history of witch trials in the 16th–17th centuries. Horror inspired by Basque folklore often channels the tension between rural superstition and outside authority, turning landscapes into sites of both protection and menace. Modern films like *Errementari: The Blacksmith and the Devil* (2017) carry this tradition forward, fusing local legend with gothic and supernatural dread.
    - ☐ **Akelarre** (2020, Spain) - Also known as *Coven*, this film vindicates the figure of witches during the real-life witch-hunt conducted in Navarra in 1610, drawing on Basque mythology and a feminist perspective.
    - ☐ **Atarrabi & Mikelats** (2020, France/Belgium) - Adapts the Basque legend of Atarrabi and Mikelats, the story of the sons of the goddess Mari-Mother Earth, who are raised by the devil.
    - ☐ **Irati** (2022, Spain) - Director Paul Urkijo Alijo, who also directed *Errementari*, created this historical fantasy adventure film based on the graphic novel *El ciclo de Irati*. The film features a wealth of Basque mythological figures, including the goddess Mari, the serpent-like god Sugaar, the giants known as *Jentilak*, and the cyclops Tartalo.
- ☐ **Edge of the Knife** (2018, Canada) - When a man accidentally causes the death of the son of his best friend, the man is wracked by grief and runs off into the woods.

☐ **The Field Guide to Evil** (2018, Turkey) – An anthology of international folk horror tales. They are known as myths, lore, and folktales. Created to give logic to mankind's darkest fears, these stories laid the foundation for what we now know as the horror genre.

- **OTHER ANTHOLOGY FILMS**
  - ☐ **Phobia (4Bia)** (2008, Thailand) - Four chilling tales intertwine: a teenager's unsettling text messages, a bullied student's dark revenge, a camping trip gone wrong, and a flight attendant's nightmarish ordeal. Each story explores fear and the supernatural.
    - **SEQUELS**
      - ☐ **Phobia 2** (2009, Thailand) - This is a direct sequel and another horror anthology film featuring a different set of stories. The film includes segments directed by some of the same directors from the first film and features a broader range of horror, including zombies and ghosts.
  - ☐ **The ABCs of Death** (2012) - A horror anthology featuring 26 short films, each representing a letter of the alphabet.
    - **SEQUELS**
      - ☐ **The ABCs of Death 2** (2014) - A sequel to the first film, continuing the theme of alphabetically organized shorts.
  - ☐ **Ghost Stories** (2017) - A British anthology that follows a paranormal investigator who uncovers three supernatural cases.
  - ☐ **Nightmare Cinema** (2018) - This anthology features a theater that shows patrons their fears on screen.
  - ☐ **The Mortuary Collection** (2019) - A mortician tells tales of the dead to a young woman who applies for a job.

☐ **The Witch in the Window** (2018) – Suburban but folk-rooted haunting.

☐ **Caveat** (2020, UK) - A lone drifter suffering from partial memory loss accepts a job to look after a psychologically troubled woman in an abandoned house on an isolated island.

- **SPIRITUAL SUCCESSOR**
  - ☐ **Oddity** (2024, Ireland) - A psychic medium attempts to uncover the truth behind her sister's murder at the site of the crime. Damian McCarthy's next film, also an Irish supernatural horror, is considered a spiritual successor to *Caveat*. It shares a similar style of psychological unease and unsettling visuals.

☐ **You Won't Be Alone** (2022, Australia) - In an isolated mountain village in 19th century Macedonia, a young girl is kidnapped and then transformed into a witch by an ancient spirit.

☐ **Mandrake** (2022) - A probation officer, Cathy Madden, is tasked with rehabilitating a notorious killer named 'Bloody' Mary Laidlaw back into society following a two-decade sentence.

☐ **Frogman** (2023) - Three friends in search of the Loveland Frogman finds out that he is more than just a local legend. The Loveland Frogman is an Ohio cryptid said to be a 4-foot-tall, humanoid frog spotted along the Little Miami River since the 1950s. First reported by police in 1972, it remains a spooky mix of local folklore and campfire legend.

Pairing Night: Watchlist

Starter Pack (Core Folk Horror)
- *Häxan* (1922) – Witchcraft hysteria as early ethnography.
- *The Wicker Man* (1973) – The benchmark of the subgenre.
- *The VVitch* (2015) – Modern revival with Puritan paranoia.

Intermediate (Regional & Global)
- *The White Reindeer* (1952, Finland) – Frozen folklore and shapeshifting terror.
- *Eyes of Fire* (1983, USA) – American pioneer folk horror rediscovered.
- *La Llorona* (2019, Guatemala) – Political ghosts meet folk legend.

Deep Dive (Unsettling & Obscure)
- *Alison's Birthday* (1981, Australia) – Cult ritual down under.
- *Dark Waters* (1993, Russia/UK) – Cosmic folk rituals in monastic halls.
- *Midsommar* (2019) – Bright, brutal ritual horror in the open sun.

How to Watch
- Pair *Häxan* with *The VVitch* — silent ethnography meets Puritan paranoia.
- Compare *The Wicker Man* (1973) with *Midsommar* (2019) — daylight rituals of sacrifice across decades.
- Explore global myth with *The White Reindeer* (Finland) and *La Llorona* (Guatemala).

Quick Facts to Sound Like the Smartest Person in the Room
- *Häxan* (1922) is part horror, part anthropology using stop-motion demons to illustrate medieval hysteria.
- *The Wicker Man* (1973) was originally released as a "B movie" alongside *Don't Look Now*. Critics later reclaimed it as essential.
- *The VVitch* (2015) only used natural light and candlelight for authenticity.
- *The White Reindeer* (1952) is sometimes programmed with *The VVitch* and *Midsommar* as a proto-folk horror.
- *La Llorona* (2019) won multiple international awards, elevating folk horror into political arthouse cinema.
- The Severin Films box set *All the Haunts Be Ours* (2021–2024) restored dozens of rare folk horrors, fueling the subgenre's rediscovery.

Press Play for Pagan Terror

*All the Haunts Be Ours

The Severin Films box set *All the Haunts Be Ours: A Compendium of Folk Horror* is a massive, multi-volume collection of films, documentaries, and supplementary materials exploring the history and breadth of the folk horror genre. Each volume includes restored feature films, special features, and a book of essays and fiction.

VOLUME 1 (2021)

- *Woodlands Dark and Days Bewitched* (2021): The centerpiece documentary on the genre.
- *Eyes of Fire* (1983): An American film about a cursed forest.
- *Leptirica* (1973): A Serbian film based on vampire folklore.
- *Witchhammer* (1970): A Czech film about real-life witch trials.
- *Viy* (1967): A classic Soviet film based on a Gogol story.
- *Lake of the Dead* (1958): A Norwegian film about a haunting.
- *Tilbury* (1987): An Icelandic film about a shape-shifting monster.
- *The Dreaming* (1988): An Australian film about Aboriginal curses.
- *Kadaicha* (1988): Another Australian film involving a sacred burial ground.
- *Celia* (1989): An Australian film about a child's dark imagination.
- *Alison's Birthday* (1981): An Australian film about a sinister family.
- *Wilczyca* (1983): A Polish werewolf film.
- *Lokis: A Manuscript of Professor Wittembach* (1970): A Polish film about a bear-human hybrid.
- *Clearcut* (1991): A Canadian film involving Indigenous folklore and environmentalism.
- *Il demonio* (1963): An Italian film about witchcraft and possession.
- *Dark Waters* (1993): A Russian film about a girl at a dark monastery.
- *A Field in England* (2013): A modern English film about deserters, mushrooms, and occultism.
- *Anchoress* (1993): A 14th-century English story about a visionary anchoress.
- *Penda's Fen* (1974): An iconic BBC television play.
- *Robin Redbreast* (1970): Another BBC television play that influenced *The Wicker Man*.

VOLUME 2 (2024)

- *The White Reindeer* (1952): The classic Finnish film about Sámi folklore.
- *Psychomania* (1973): A British biker film involving the occult.
- *The Enchanted* (1984): An American experimental film.
- *Bakeneko: A Vengeful Spirit* (1968): A Japanese ghost cat film.
- *November* (2017): An Estonian film with black-and-white visuals.
- *City of the Dead* (1960): A foundational British horror film.
- *Nang Nak* (1999): A Thai ghost story.
- *Nazareno Cruz and the Wolf* (1975): An Argentinian film about a man cursed to become a werewolf.
- *Edge of the Knife* (2018): A Canadian film in the Haida language.
- *Beauty and the Beast* (1978): A Czechoslovakian film.

Found Footage Horror

Grainy tapes, handheld chaos, shaky cameras found footage trades polish for "proof." By pretending we're watching raw evidence, it dissolves the barrier between fiction and reality. The horror isn't just what you see, but the illusion that it *really happened*.

Why People Are Drawn to It

Found footage sells the *forbidden look*. It feels illicit, like we're watching something we weren't meant to see. The lo-fi aesthetic makes scares feel spontaneous, while gaps in the footage force our brains to imagine worse than the lens reveals. At its best, the subgenre transforms accidents, glitches, and amateur mistakes into fear.

Essentials

- **Cannibal Holocaust** (1980, Italy) –Ruggero Deodato's *Cannibal Holocaust* (1980) stands as one of the most infamous milestones in horror history, a brutal mirror reflecting both exploitation and self-condemnation. The film's found-footage structure pioneered realism-driven terror, blurring fiction and documentary so convincingly that Deodato was briefly arrested for murder until his actors appeared in court alive. Its unflinching depictions of colonial violence and Western voyeurism transformed it from mere shock cinema into a savage critique of media exploitation itself, making it simultaneously a cultural indictment and a moral scandal that redefined the limits of horror realism
- **The Blair Witch Project** (1999, USA) – Daniel Myrick and Eduardo Sánchez revolutionized horror through its minimalist found-footage realism, turning shaky cameras and unseen terror into tools of psychological dread. Its viral marketing and improvisational performances blurred fact and fiction, igniting a cultural phenomenon that redefined how horror could be made, sold, and experienced.
- **Paranormal Activity** (2007, USA) – Home surveillance fright juggernaut. Oren Peli distilled found-footage horror to its purest form, using domestic space, static cameras, and slow-building tension to evoke primal fear. Made for just $15,000 and grossing over $190 million, it proved that suggestion and silence could terrify more effectively than spectacle, spawning a new wave of minimalist, home-based supernatural horror.
- **Noroi: The Curse** (2005, Japan) – Labyrinthine folk-horror doc that snowballs into cosmic terror. Kōji Shiraishi expands found-footage horror into sprawling documentary realism, weaving news clips, interviews, and occult investigations into a slow-burning web of dread. Its meticulous world-building and cultural specificity make it one of Japan's most unsettling horror films, where the horror emerges not from jump scares but from the quiet accumulation of the inexplicable.
- **Lake Mungo** (2008, Australia) – Joel Anderson's faux-documentary ghost story transforms grief into existential horror, using interviews, found footage, and uncanny images to explore loss and uncertainty. Its restrained realism and emotional depth make it one of the most haunting meditations on death in modern horror, where the supernatural feels indistinguishable from sorrow itself.

Deep Cuts

- **Grave Encounters** (2011, Canada) –The Vicious Brothers turns the found-footage format inward, following a ghost-hunting TV crew who become trapped in a real haunted asylum. Blending reality TV parody with escalating supernatural terror, it captures the early 2010s' fascination with media fakery and the claustrophobic dread of being consumed by one's own performance.
- **Troll Hunter** (2010, Norway) – André Øvredal reimagines found footage through Nordic folklore, following film students who uncover a secret government operation managing real trolls in the Norwegian wilderness. Mixing deadpan humor with mythic spectacle, it grounds the fantastical in documentary realism, turning ancient legend into bureaucratic absurdity.
- **The Bay** (2012, USA) – Ecological collapse captured as a fake doc. Barry Levinson fuses eco-horror with found footage, chronicling a parasitic outbreak through news reports, phone videos, and government archives. Its fragmented narrative and environmental critique turn the format into social commentary, revealing how technological saturation and institutional denial amplify real-world terror.

- **Hell House LLC** (2015, USA) – Haunted house attraction spirals into tragedy. Stephen Cognetti revitalizes found-footage horror by setting its terror inside a haunted house attraction gone wrong. Through its layered mockumentary style and escalating realism, it captures the uncanny blend of staged fear and genuine horror, turning performance itself into the source of dread.
- **Host** (2020, UK) – Rob Savage distilled the found-footage format for the digital age, unfolding entirely over a Zoom call during pandemic lockdown. Shot remotely and running under an hour, it weaponized the isolation and glitches of online communication, proving that horror could evolve—and terrify—within the constraints of real-world crisis.

Critical Essay

"Why Do Found Footage Films Look Bad on Purpose?"

Myth: Bad camerawork = bad movie.

Reality: Shakiness, cut-outs, and distortion *are the point*. They simulate authenticity like real footage discovered, not staged. The style tricks your brain into watching as though it's *evidence*.

Early VHS fuzz (*Cannibal Holocaust*) became digital glitches (*Paranormal Activity*) and later screen-life storytelling (*Host*). What began as accident turned into aesthetic.

Global Spotlight: International Found Footage

- **Asia** – *Noroi* (Japan), *Incantation* (Taiwan), *Gonjiam: Haunted Asylum* (Korea).
- **Australia** – *Lake Mungo* (2008), *The Tunnel* (2011).
- **Europe** – *REC* (2007, Spain), *The Borderlands* (2013, UK).
- **North America** – *The Blair Witch Project* (1999), *Hell House LLC* (2015).

- ☐ **Cannibal Holocaust** (1980, Italy) – An anthropologist ventures into the Amazon rainforest on a rescue mission, where he recovers footage shot by a film crew documenting their disastrous encounters with local cannibal tribes. Due to its controversial nature and success, many Italian cannibal films were released as unofficial sequels in different regions to attract an audience. Its found-footage structure prefigured *The Blair Witch Project* by two decades. So convincing, director Ruggero Deodato was briefly charged with murder until actors appeared in court alive.
  - **ADAPTIONS**
    - ☐ **Cut and Run** (1985, Italy) - Directed by Ruggero Deodato, this film was known as *Inferno in diretta* in Italy and was not a sequel.
    - ☐ **White Slave** (1985, Italy) - Distributed as *Cannibal Holocaust 2: The Catherine Miles Story*, this is another unrelated film released to capitalize on the name.
    - ☐ **Natura Contro** (1988, Italy) - Often referred to as *Cannibal Holocaust II* in certain markets, this film was also not a direct continuation. Four friends head into the jungle to locate a lost professor but instead face off against treasure hunters who are torturing and killing natives.
    - ☐ **The Green Inferno** (2013) – Eli Roth's cannibal homage to Fulci/Deodato. The film is a homage to the Italian cannibal films of the 1970s and '80s, particularly *Cannibal Holocaust*, which had a film-within-a-film also titled "The Green Inferno."
  - **JONESTOWN MASS SUICIDE FILMS:** The Italian exploitation film *Cannibal Holocaust* (1980) drew direct inspiration from the Jonestown Massacre of 1978, when over 900 members of the Peoples Temple died in a mass murder-suicide orchestrated by cult leader Jim Jones in the Guyanese jungle. The tragedy's media coverage: marked by images of isolation, fanaticism, and human depravity deeply influenced director Ruggero Deodato, who sought to explore similar themes of moral collapse and voyeuristic obsession. The film's depiction of a documentary crew descending into savagery within an ungoverned jungle echoed both the physical and psychological landscape of Jonestown, transforming real-world horror into cinematic transgression.
    - ☐ **The Sacrament** (2013) – Found-footage recreation of Jonestown mass suicide.
    - ☐ **Jonestown: The Life and Death of Peoples Temple** (2006) - An Oscar-shortlisted documentary that features never-before-seen footage and interviews with survivors.

- ☐ **Jonestown: Paradise Lost** (2007) - A documentary with dramatic reenactments and eyewitness accounts.
- ☐ **Jonestown: Terror in the Jungle** (2018) - A four-part Sundance TV docuseries that re-examines the tragedy on its 40th anniversary.
- ☐ **Cult Massacre: One Day in Jonestown** (2024) - A three-part Hulu docuseries with firsthand accounts and new audio recordings of Jim Jones.
- ☐ **Guyana: Cult of the Damned** (1979) - A fictionalized, exploitation film based on the events, released just a year after the massacre.
- ☐ **Guyana Tragedy: The Story of Jim Jones** (1980) - A CBS miniseries that was critically praised, with Powers Boothe winning an Emmy for his portrayal of Jim Jones.
- ☐ **The Jonestown Haunting** (2020) - A low-budget horror film where a survivor returns to the site 10 years later and finds it a breeding ground for the supernatural.
- ☐ **The Final Reckoning** (2024) - A horror film on Tubi where a survivor returns to the jungle with her daughter decades later.

- **The Blair Witch Project** (1999) – Three film students vanish after traveling into a Maryland forest to film a documentary on the local Blair Witch legend, leaving only their footage behind. The marketing team posted fake missing person flyers at festivals. Also, early internet chat rooms spread its "true story" myth, changing horror marketing forever. In April 2024, Lionsgate and Blumhouse announced a "reimagining" of The Blair Witch Project is in the works. $60k budget, $250m gross; viral marketing legend.
    - **SEQUELS**
        - ☐ **Book of Shadows: Blair Witch 2** (2000) - A group of tourists arrives in Burkittsville, Maryland after seeing *The Blair Witch Project* (1999) to explore the mythology and phenomenon, only to come face to face with their own neuroses and possibly the witch herself.
        - ☐ **Blair Witch** (2016) - A direct sequel to the 1999 film that ignores the 2000 sequel. It follows the sister of the original protagonist, Heather Donahue, as she searches for answers about her disappearance.
    - **ADAPTIONS**
        - ☐ **Curse of the Blair Witch** (1999) - A mockumentary released before the original film to promote the legend.
        - ☐ **The Massacre of the Burkittsville 7** (2000) - A follow-up mockumentary that delves deeper into the Rustin Parr case.
        - ☐ **Shadow of the Blair Witch** (2000) - Another mockumentary in the franchise.
- ☐ **The Signal** (2007) - A horror film told in three parts, from three perspectives, in which a mysterious transmission that turns people into killers invades every cell phone, radio, and television. The film's mix of gruesome body horror and psychological dread has been compared to the work of David Cronenberg.
- ☐ **Paranormal Activity** (2007) – After moving into a suburban home, a couple becomes increasingly disturbed by a nightly demonic presence. This is the most-profitable film of all-time. It cost $60,000 to make and $400,000 to market and then grossed over $89 million! Steven Spielberg reportedly stopped watching the screener halfway because it spooked him. Even, its test screening had people walking out. Not from boredom, but because they were too scared.
    - **SEQUELS**
        - ☐ **Paranormal Activity 2** (2010) - A prequel and parallel sequel to the original, focusing on the family of Katie's sister and revealing the demonic backstory.
        - ☐ **Paranormal Activity 3** (2011) - A prequel showing the childhood experiences of sisters Katie and Kristi in 1988.
        - ☐ **Paranormal Activity 4** (2012) - A sequel set five years after the first film, as a new family encounters demonic activity linked to Katie and her possessed nephew.
        - ☐ **Paranormal Activity: The Marked Ones** (2014) - A spin-off following a new group of characters who confront a demonic cult in a Latin American community.
        - ☐ **Paranormal Activity: The Ghost Dimension** (2015) - Originally promoted as the finale, this film explores the true nature of the demon, Tobi, using a special camera.
        - ☐ **Paranormal Activity: Next of Kin** (2021) - The most recent installment is a stand-alone sequel and soft reboot. It follows a new story about a woman visiting an Amish community with a documentary crew.

- ☐ **Lake Mungo** (2008, Australia) – Strange things start happening after a girl is found drowned in a lake. An Australian mockumentary about a family grieving a drowning victim who begins experiencing strange phenomena.
  - • **MOCKUMENTARIES**
    - ☐ **The Poughkeepsie Tapes** (2007) – Faux-doc of sadistic killer's recorded crimes. In an abandoned house in Poughkeepsie, New York murder investigators uncover hundreds of tapes showing decades of a serial killer's work.
    - ☐ **The Last Exorcism** (2010) – Documentary on fake preacher turns real. A troubled evangelical minister agrees to let his last exorcism be filmed by a documentary crew.
      - • **SEQUELS**
        - ☐ **The Last Exorcism Part II** (2013) - The sequel picks up with Nell Sweetzer (Ashley Bell) after she is found alone in the woods, terrified and unable to recall the preceding events. As she tries to rebuild her life in New Orleans, the demon Abalam returns with an even more sinister plan.
    - ☐ **Grave Encounters** (2011) – For their ghost hunting reality show, a production crew locks themselves inside an abandoned mental hospital that's supposedly haunted and it might prove to be all too true.
      - • **SEQUELS**
        - ☐ **Grave Encounters 2** (2012) – This follow-up to the original 2011 film is also in the found-footage style. It follows Alex Wright, a film student who is obsessed with the original movie and believes the events were real. In May 2015, the Vicious Brothers announced plans for a third installment, a prequel titled *Grave Encounters 3: The Beginning*. The project never went into production, reportedly due to the poor reception and lack of momentum from the second film.
    - ☐ **The Conspiracy** (2012) - A documentary about conspiracy theories takes a horrific turn after the filmmakers uncover an ancient and dangerous secret society.
    - ☐ **The Taking of Deborah Logan** (2014) - An elderly woman battling Alzheimer's disease agrees to let a film crew document her condition, but what they discover is something far more sinister going on.
    - ☐ **Hell House LLC** (2015, USA) – Five years after an unexplained malfunction causes the death of 15 tour-goers and staff on the opening night of a Halloween haunted house tour, a documentary crew travels back to the scene of the tragedy to find out what really happened.
      - • **SEQUELS**
        - ☐ **Hell House LLC II: The Abaddon Hotel** (2018) - Released exclusively on Shudder, this sequel is set eight years after the events of the original film. It follows a journalist and her team as they investigate the mysterious Abaddon Hotel, uncovering more details about its dark history and the evil that resides there.
        - ☐ **Hell House LLC III: Lake of Fire** (2019) - The third installment again returns to the Abaddon Hotel, which has been purchased by a billionaire for an immersive theater experience. This film provides more backstory and lore regarding the entity behind the hotel's haunting.
        - ☐ **Hell House LLC Origins: The Carmichael Manor** (2023) - This fourth film serves as both a prequel and a sequel, exploring a separate haunting at the Carmichael Manor that connects to the events at the Abaddon Hotel.
        - ☐ **Hell House LLC: Lineage** (2025) - The fifth and potentially final installment in the franchise departs from the found-footage style of the previous films. It follows a new set of characters as they uncover their connection to the Abaddon Hotel and the Carmichael Manor.
- ☐ **Home Movie** (2008) – Found family tapes with unsettling twist. In the remote woods of Upstate New York, David and Clare Poe are attempting to live an idyllic life. However, their twin children's bizarre behavior might just tear the family apart.

- **Troll Hunter** (2010, Norway) – A group of students investigates a series of mysterious bear killings, but learns that there are much more dangerous things going on.
  - **ADAPTIONS**
    - **Troll** (2022, Norway) - This film, directed by Roar Uthaug, features a giant troll awakened in Norway's misty fjords and is not connected to *Trollhunter*. A sequel, *Troll 2*, is scheduled for release in 2025.
- **The Tunnel** (2011, Australia) – An Australian found-footage film where a news crew investigates a story about a government cover-up in abandoned subway tunnels, only to encounter a hostile presence.
  - **CLAUSTROPHOBIC SETTING HORROR**
    - **Creep** (2004, UK) - A woman becomes trapped in the London Underground after a party and is hunted by a deranged killer who lives in the tunnels.
    - **End of the Line** (2007, Canada) - Karen boards a late-night train and fights with several other passengers to survive a murderous night after becoming trapped in a tunnel.
    - **Meandre** (2020, France) - A woman finds herself locked in a series of strange tunnels full of deadly traps.
- **The Bay** (2012) – Chaos breaks out in a small Maryland town after an ecological disaster occurs.
  - **ENVIRONMENTAL THEMES**
    - **Outbreak** (1995) - An older but influential film about a deadly virus outbreak, focusing more on the scientific and military efforts to contain it.
    - **Carriers** (2009) - As a lethal virus spreads globally, four friends seek a reputed plague-free haven. But while avoiding the infected, the travelers turn on one another.
    - **Contagion** (2011) - This film, released just one year before *The Bay*, similarly explores the terrifying reality of a fast-spreading epidemic and a government cover-up.
    - **Gaia** (2021) - An injured forest ranger on a routine mission is saved by two off-the-grid survivalists. What is initially a welcome rescue grows more suspicious as the son and his renegade father reveal a cultish devotion to the forest.
- **Chernobyl Diaries** (2012) – Tourists trapped in Pripyat. Six tourists hire an extreme tour guide who takes them to the abandoned city Pripyat, the former home to the workers of the Chernobyl nuclear reactor. During their exploration, they soon discover they are not alone.
  - **RADIATION HORROR:** The 1986 Chernobyl disaster remains one of history's most haunting real-world horrors, its imagery of radiation, desolation, and human error shaping decades of post-apocalyptic storytelling. The explosion at Reactor No. 4 and the subsequent cover-up exposed the fragility of modern civilization, inspiring countless films and series to blend fact with fear. Whether through found footage, dramatization, or documentary realism, Chernobyl endures as a symbol of invisible terror, where science, politics, and the supernatural collapse into one.
    - **Chernobyl** (2019) - This highly acclaimed HBO miniseries is a historical drama based on the real events of the disaster and is not connected to the plot of *Chernobyl Diaries*.
    - **Chernobyl: Abyss** (2021) - A Russian film about a fictionalized firefighter who becomes a liquidator during the disaster. It was released on Netflix and has no connection to the 2012 horror film.
    - **Chernobyl: The Lost Tapes** (2022) - A British documentary film featuring newly discovered archive footage of the disaster.
- **Devil's Pass** (2013) – Dyatlov Pass expedition goes wrong. The film's source material is one of Russia's most famous unsolved mysteries, which has inspired numerous other non-official adaptations. The real-life incident occurred in 1959, when nine Russian hikers disappeared and were later found dead under unexplained circumstances in the Ural Mountains.
- **The Den** (2013) –While studying the habits of web cam chat users from the apparent safety of her own home, a young woman's life begins to spiral out of control after witnessing a grisly murder online.
  - **SCREEN LIFE HORROR**
    - **Unfriended** (2014) – Entire film via desktop chat. A group of online chatroom friends find themselves haunted by a mysterious, supernatural force using the account of their dead friend.
      - **SEQUEL**
        - **Unfriended: Dark Web** (2018) - A sequel to the 2014 film that further explores the dark side of online anonymity.

- ☐ **Ingrid Goes West** (2017) - Explores themes of social media obsession, identity, and the blurring line between online and real life. After her release from a psychiatric ward, a woman obsessed with social media moves to LA to stalk an Instagram star, but her plan takes a dark turn.
- ☐ **Cam** (2018) – Camgirl's doppelgänger replaces her online. Alice, an ambitious camgirl, wakes up one day to discover she's been replaced on her show with an exact replica of herself.
- ☐ **Host** (2020) – Six friends hire a medium to hold a seance via Zoom during lockdown, but they get far more than they bargained for as things quickly go wrong.
- ☐ **Searching** (2020) - A thriller told entirely through computer screens, starring John Cho. After his teenage daughter goes missing, a desperate father tries to find clues on her laptop.
- ☐ **I Blame Society** (2020) - A struggling filmmaker realizes that the skill set to make a movie is the same to commit the perfect murder.
- ☐ **Untitled Horror Movie** (2021) - A comedy about making a horror movie. When six co-stars learn their hit TV show is about to be canceled, they decide to shoot their own film, unintentionally summoning a spirit with an affinity for violence.
- ☐ **Dashcam** (2021) - This horror film follows a livestreaming musician who gets caught up in a series of nightmarish events. The film is also presented entirely from the perspective of her phone.
- ☐ **Superhost** (2021) - With their follower count dwindling, travel vloggers Teddy and Claire pivot to creating viral content around their most recent "superhost," Rebecca, who wants more from the duo than a great review.
- ☐ **We're All Going to the World's Fair** (2021) - Alone in her attic bedroom, teenager Casey becomes immersed in an online role-playing horror game, wherein she begins to document the changes that may or may not be happening to her.
  - • **THE SCREEN TRILOGY:** The films in Jane Schoenbrun's trilogy are thematically linked rather than narratively connected, exploring themes of gender dysphoria, online loneliness, and the blurred lines between online and offline realities.
    - ☐ **I Saw the TV Glow** (2024) - Explores a friendship forged over a shared love for a supernatural television show. A third installment in the trilogy is in development.
- ☐ **Deadstream** (2022) - A disgraced internet personality attempts to win back his followers by livestreaming one night alone in a haunted house. But when he accidentally upsets a vengeful spirit, his big comeback event becomes a real-time fight for his life.
- ☐ **Influencer** (2022) - While struggling on a solo backpacking trip in Thailand, social media influencer Madison meets CW, who travels with ease and shows her a more uninhibited way of living, but CW's interest in her takes a darker turn.
- ☐ **The Visit** (2015) - Two siblings become increasingly frightened by their grandparents' disturbing behavior while visiting them on vacation. This is film is also part of the psycho-biddy genre.
  - • **SEQUELS**
    - ☐ **The Visit II: The Forgotten Ones** (2025) - The film focuses on a troubled 17-year-old girl who is sent to live with family in the same Pennsylvania farmhouse from the original movie. There, she uncovers the mystery behind the original events and encounters new unsettling horrors.
- ☐ **The Fear Footage** (2018) - On April 19th, 2016, Deputy Leo Cole vanished. The next morning, his body camera was found.
  - • **SEQUELS**
    - ☐ **The Fear Footage 2: Curse of the Tape** (2020) - A direct sequel that picks up where the first film left off. The plot centers on a character from the first film, who realizes his real life has been captured on the mysterious tape, leading him to investigate further.
    - ☐ **The Fear Footage: 3AM** (2021) - The third and final installment of the trilogy follows a YouTuber who travels to the town of Darkbluff to investigate the lore surrounding the tapes.
- ☐ **Late Night with the Devil** (2024) - A desperate 1970s late-night talk show host, determined to boost his plummeting ratings, invites a supposedly possessed girl onto his Halloween special, unwittingly unleashing evil on live television.

The Blumhouse Formula

Blumhouse Productions

Origins & Mission

Founded in 2000 by Jason Blum, Blumhouse cracked the Hollywood code by proving you don't need big budgets to scare audiences worldwide. Their mission was simple but revolutionary: produce low-cost horror with creative freedom for directors, then let box office returns (often massive) do the talking. By keeping budgets lean, Blumhouse could take risks on edgy concepts while ensuring profits even on modest hits.

Signature Style

Blumhouse specializes in micro-budget, high-concept horror: films built around one terrifying idea executed cheaply but effectively. Their hallmarks include found footage, jump scares, and suburban dread that feels uncomfortably close to home. Stylistically, they embrace stripped-down realism, letting terror emerge from the everyday. They also became known for turning small hits into *franchises* stretching stories into cultural events.

Essential Titles

- *Paranormal Activity* (2007) – The $15,000 found-footage phenomenon that earned nearly $200 million, putting Blumhouse on the map.
- *Insidious* (2010) – James Wan's astral-projection haunted-house tale, blending domestic horror with surreal nightmare logic.
- *The Purge* (2013) – High-concept dystopia (all crime legal for one night) that birthed sequels, TV, and political allegories.
- *Get Out* (2017) – Jordan Peele's Oscar-winning satirical horror on race and assimilation; elevated Blumhouse into prestige territory.
- *The Invisible Man* (2020) – Leigh Whannell's reimagining of the Universal monster, blending gaslighting, tech-horror, and social commentary.

Cultural Footprint

Blumhouse didn't just dominate 21st-century horror, it reshaped the industry. They democratized scares, showing studios that horror could be cheap, risky, and wildly profitable. They made horror directors household names (James Wan, Jordan Peele, Leigh Whannell), expanded horror into mainstream awards conversations (*Get Out*), and turned micro-budgets into billion-dollar box office totals. Their strategy also influenced Netflix, Shudder, and the modern streaming horror boom.

Legacy & Influence

Blumhouse reengineered the DNA of modern horror, not through invention, but through *discipline*. Their methodical approach: creative autonomy under strict budgets became a training ground for a new generation of genre auteurs. What Universal once did for monsters, Blumhouse did for ideas: every fear became a franchise, every nightmare a social experiment. Their collaborations gave rise to directors who blurred the line between arthouse and mainstream, from Jordan Peele's satirical realism to Leigh Whannell's technological paranoia. More than a studio, Blumhouse became a cultural barometer, turning low-cost filmmaking into a proving ground for the anxieties of the 21st century: surveillance, privilege, violence, and systemic rot.

Watchlist – A Blumhouse Sampler

- *Paranormal Activity* (2007) → Watch for how pure suggestion and cheap effects built one of horror's most profitable films ever.
- *The Purge* (2013) → See how a simple "what if?" concept expanded into a cultural allegory.
- *Get Out* (2017) → Proof that horror can be Oscar-winning social commentary as well as terrifying.

Quick Facts to Sound Smart

- Jason Blum began his career at Miramax before launching Blumhouse in 2000.
- Blumhouse partners frequently with directors like James Wan, Jordan Peele, and Leigh Whannell.
- Blumhouse's model inspired "elevated micro-budget" trends embraced by A24 and streaming platforms alike.
- Blumhouse holds multiple Guinness World Records for highest profit margins in film history.
- The company's production model is now taught in film schools as the "Blumhouse Formula."

Cursed Media

- ☐ **Ringu** (1998, Japan) – When her niece is found dead along with three friends after viewing a supposedly cursed videotape, reporter Reiko sets out to investigate. She finds the tape, watches it and receives a phone call informing her that she'll die in a week. Nakata used almost no music during Sadako's attacks, amplifying the dread. **Memorable quote:** *"She never sleeps."*
  - **SEQUELS**
    - ☐ **Spiral** (1998, Japan) - A young pathologist seeks answers to the mysterious death of a friend and soon comes into contact with the same cursed videotape that caused the death of the friend's wife and son, which is haunted by the curse of Sadako, a relentless spirit. Based on Kōji Suzuki's second novel in the Ring series, but is more ignored in favor of *Ring 2.*
    - ☐ **Ring 2** (1999, Japan) - Reiko takes Yôichi into hiding when her son begins to display frightening powers. Meanwhile, Mai Takano and the authorities begin a desperate search for them, as the mysterious Ring curse spreads.
    - ☐ **The Ring Virus** (1999, Japan) - After the mysterious death of her niece and other three teenagers on the same hour and with the symptoms of heart attack, the journalist Sun-ju decides to investigate their last moments.
    - ☐ **Ring 0: Birthday** (2000, Japan) - In this prequel to Ring, a young Sadako becomes an actress in hopes of escaping her troubled past. But strange visions and terrifying powers begin to manifest...
    - ☐ **Sadako** (2019, Japan) - A group of people must find out how to stop the newborn deadly curse, which has born and gone viral after a Youtuber accidentally captured a vengeful ghost on camera.
  - **CROSSOVER SERIES**
    - ☐ **Sadako 3D** (2012, Japan) - The spiteful ghost of Sadako, a murdered woman whose body was thrown down a well, reaches the Internet searching for a host in order to live once again.
    - ☐ **Sadako 3D 2** (2013, Japan) - Fuko Ando is a 24-years-old graduate student in psychology. She is tasked to take care of her 4-year-old niece. Soon, mysterious events occur around her niece.
    - ☐ **Sadako vs. Kayako** (2016, Japan) - The vengeful spirits of the Ring and Grudge series face off.
    - ☐ **Sadako DX** (2022, Japan) - People who watch a cursed video suddenly die. These deaths take place all over Japan. Ayaka Ichijo is an extremely smart graduate student with an IQ of 200. Her younger sister happens to watch the cursed video for fun.
  - **ADAPTIONS**
    - ☐ **The Ring** (2002) – A cursed videotape dooms its viewers, reviving the ghost story for the digital age.
    - ☐ **The Ring Two** (2005) - Six months after the incidents involving the lethal videotape, new clues prove that there is a new evil lurking in the darkness.
    - ☐ **Rings** (2017) - A young woman finds herself on the receiving end of a terrifying curse that threatens to take her life in 7 days.
- ☐ **Kairo (Pulse)** (2001, Japan) – Loneliness and suicide epidemic merge into paranoia.
  - **ADAPTIONS**
    - ☐ **Pulse (2006)** – An American remake of *Kairo* was released in 2006. Directed by Jim Sonzero, it stars Kristen Bell and is based on the same premise of ghosts invading the human world through the internet.
    - ☐ **Pulse 2: Afterlife** (2008) - This direct-to-video sequel continues the story of the digital ghosts, exploring the aftermath of the technology-based apocalypse. It is set after the events of the 2006 remake and stars Jamie Bamber. Some sources suggest this and the third film are two halves of the same story.
    - ☐ **Pulse 3: Invasion** (2008) - The third film in the American series, also direct-to-video, concludes the narrative following the apocalypse. It focuses on a character trying to find a safe haven from the invading ghosts.
- ☐ **Phone** (2002, Korea) - Investigative reporter Ji-won begins to receive a series of menacing calls. To escape the terrifying and relentless clanging of the telephone, she changes her number and moves out. But the threatening campaign of terror continues unabated.

- ☐ **One Missed Call** (2003, Japan) – Phone curse kills recipients. Yumi tries to assuage the fears of a friend, Yoko, who has received a disturbing voice mail from herself. In the message, Yoko screams while chatting with Yumi. Three days later, the exact call plays out, and Yoko dies.
  - • **SEQUELS & ADAPTIONS**
    - ☐ **One Missed Call 2** (2005, Japan) - The first sequel expands the scope of the curse, with the deadly phone calls moving beyond Japan to Taiwan.
    - ☐ **One Missed Call: Final** (2006, Japan) - The third and final installment of the original trilogy features a new twist on the curse, in which students on a school trip to Korea can send the fatal call to someone else to save their own life.
    - ☐ **One Missed Call** (2008) - This American remake is a loose adaptation of the original 2003 film. Though it was a moderate box office success, it was critically panned.
- ☐ **Noroi: The Curse** (2005, Japan) – A prominent paranormal journalist Kobayashi goes missing shortly after completing a documentary. What begins as an investigation into strange noises soon evolves into the chilling mystery of a demonic entity named Kagutaba.
- ☐ **White Noise** (2005) – An architect's desire to speak with his wife from beyond the grave becomes an obsession with supernatural repercussions.
  - • **SEQUELS**
    - ☐ **White Noise: The Light** (2007) - Also marketed as *White Noise 2*, this direct-to-video film is a standalone sequel to the 2005 original. It stars Nathan Fillion and Katee Sackhoff and tells the story of a man who, after a near-death experience, can see the auras of people who are about to die.
- ☐ **Incantation** (2022, Taiwan) – Six years ago, Li Ronan was cursed after breaking a religious taboo. Now, she must protect her daughter from the consequences of her actions.
- ☐ **Gonjiam: Haunted Asylum** (2018, South Korea) - A South Korean film where a horror web series crew explores a real-life haunted asylum.
- ☐ **The Canal** (2014, UK) - A film archivist finds his sanity crumbling after he is given an old 16mm film reel with footage from a horrific murder that occurred in the early 1900's.
- ☐ **Antrum: The Deadliest Film Ever Made** (2018, Canada) - A mockumentary that presents a supposedly lost 1970s film that was cursed and caused deaths at every screening. The film includes the alleged cursed footage.
- ☐ **Rent-A-Pal** (2020) - 1990: David, 40, looks after his dementia mom. He uses a video dating service to no avail. He buys a "Rent-A-Pal" video tape and things change.
- ☐ **Sound of Silence** (2023, Italy) - An Italian horror film where a family must uncover the dark secret behind a cursed radio that begins to cause unsettling events.

Pairing Night: Watchlist

Starter Pack (Core Found Footage)
- • *Cannibal Holocaust* (1980) – Origins, banned and infamous.
- • *The Blair Witch Project* (1999) – Modern myth-making.
- • *Paranormal Activity* (2007) – Domestic hauntings captured by home tech.

Intermediate (International & Inventive)
- • *Noroi: The Curse* (2005) – Japan's cosmic slow-burn.
- • *Lake Mungo* (2008) – A ghost story disguised as a grief doc.
- • *Grave Encounters* (2011) – Paranormal TV gone wrong.

Deep Dive (Unsettling Experiments)
- • *Troll Hunter* (2010) – Mythology meets government conspiracy.
- • *The Bay* (2012) – Found-footage as ecological horror.
- • *Host* (2020) – Pure pandemic invention.

How to Watch

- • Pair *Cannibal Holocaust* with *The Green Inferno* (2013) to compare exploitation origins and Roth's homage.
- • Watch *The Blair Witch Project* back-to-back with *REC* (2007). One minimalist, one maximalist, both terrifying.
- • End with *Lake Mungo* and *Host* for found footage as intimate grief and communal digital séance.

Quick Facts to Sound Like the Smartest Person in the Room

- *Cannibal Holocaust* (1980) - Deodato had the actors sign contracts requiring them to disappear from the media for a year after shooting to maintain the illusion of found footage.
- *The Blair Witch Project* (1999) - The actors had no script. Each day, the actors were given notes detailing the plot points for them to improvise. The tension that develops between the characters feels real because the actors were reacting to real-life challenges.
- *Lake Mungo* (2008) fooled many viewers into believing it was a real documentary.
- *Noroi: The Curse* (2005) runs 2+ hours but builds horror through accumulation, not jump scares.
- *Host* (2020) was filmed entirely during COVID lockdowns. Actors shot their own stunts at home.

Horror Filmed Live

International Horror

Horror may thrive on local fears, but its resonance is global. Across Japan, Korea, Spain, Mexico, Argentina, Turkey, and beyond, filmmakers reshape cultural trauma, folklore, and history into nightmare fuel. These films remind us: terror translates.

Why People Are Drawn to It

International horror brings *new monsters and unfamiliar rules*. What terrifies in Tokyo isn't the same as in Madrid or Seoul, but each reframes dread through unique cultural anxieties. Watching them makes you feel unmoored not just because of the supernatural, but because you're outside your cultural comfort zone.

Essentials

- **Kwaidan** (1964, Japan) – Four ghostly folk tales told with painterly beauty. Masaki Kobayashi transforms Japanese ghost stories into painterly tableaux, merging folklore and fine art through hauntingly stylized visuals. Its deliberate pacing and surreal color design elevate traditional kaidan tales into meditations on memory, beauty, and the quiet persistence of the supernatural.
- **Ringu** (1998, Japan) – Cursed videotape modernized the ghost story. Hideo Nakata redefined modern horror with its cursed videotape and atmosphere of creeping dread, replacing jump scares with a sense of inevitable doom. By merging ancient yūrei folklore with late-20th-century technology, it birthed the J-horror wave and reshaped global horror aesthetics for a new digital age.
- **Ju-On: The Grudge** (2002, Japan) – Endless curse that can't be contained. Takashi Shimizu weaponizes repetition and disjointed chronology to create a curse that feels endless and inescapable. Its pale ghosts and domestic hauntings turned everyday spaces into sites of terror, solidifying J-horror's signature blend of tragedy, contagion, and supernatural vengeance.
- **A Tale of Two Sisters** (2003, Korea) – Gothic trauma with devastating twists. Kim Jee-woon blends gothic family drama with psychological and supernatural horror, unraveling trauma through dreamlike imagery and unreliable perception. Its elegant direction and emotional depth made it a cornerstone of Korean horror, where grief and guilt haunt as powerfully as any ghost.
- **The Wailing** (2016, Korea) – Possession, paranoia, and rural dread collide. Na Hong-jin fuses police procedural, shamanic ritual, and cosmic horror into a sprawling study of faith and corruption. Set in a rural village besieged by illness and possession, it blurs superstition and reason until both collapse, creating one of modern horror's most terrifying portraits of doubt.

Deep Cuts

- **Onibaba** (1964, Japan) – Samurai-era desperation becomes demonic. Kaneto Shindō transforms a wartime folktale into erotic and psychological horror, where survival and desire intertwine in the swaying reeds of feudal Japan. Its haunting use of landscape and the demonic mask turn human desperation into mythic terror, blurring the boundary between sin and survival.
- **Thirst** (2009, Korea) – Vampire priest torn between desire and morality. Park Chan-wook reimagines vampirism through the lens of faith, guilt, and forbidden desire, following a priest transformed into a creature of appetite. With lush visuals and dark humor, it merges erotic tragedy with moral decay, turning salvation itself into the ultimate corruption.
- **The Devil's Backbone** (2001, Spain) – Ghost child amid Spanish Civil War. Guillermo del Toro intertwines ghost story and war tragedy, set in a Spanish orphanage during the final days of the Civil War. Through its haunting imagery and melancholic tone, the film redefines the ghost as a symbol of innocence and historical trauma, where the real horror lies in human cruelty rather than the supernatural.
- **Terrified** (2017, Argentina) – Paranormal dread infects a Buenos Aires suburb. Demián Rugna turns suburban Buenos Aires into a nexus of the uncanny, where multiple hauntings unfold with clinical realism and no clear cause. By fragmenting perspective and denying explanation, it transforms domestic horror into cosmic dread, suggesting evil as an uncontainable force woven into everyday life.

- **Under the Shadow** (2016, Iran/UK) – Djinn stalks mother and child in war-torn Tehran. Babak Anvari blends war horror and folklore, following a mother and daughter haunted by a djinn amid the bombings of 1980s Tehran. Its confined setting and political subtext turn the haunting into a metaphor for repression, fear, and the inescapable weight of both patriarchy and war.

Critical Essay
"Why International Horror Hits Harder"
- Different cultures = different fears. Japanese horror thrives on shame and lingering spirits (*Ringu*), while Korean horror often blends grief, religion, and societal collapse (*The Wailing*).
- Spanish and Latin films use political history as horror. Franco-era ghosts (*The Devil's Backbone*), cartel trauma (*Tigers Are Not Afraid*).
- These movies don't always play by Western genre rules. Endings may be unresolved, villains may win, and ambiguity is the point. That unpredictability is why they haunt so deeply.

Asian Horror
HONG KONG
- ☐ **Encounters of the Spooky Kind** (1980) – A rickshaw driver's wife and his rich client are secret lovers, and they decide to get rid of him without being implicated, so they hire a powerful sorcerer to kill him, but the sorcerer's colleague intervenes to protect him.
  - **SEQUELS**
    - ☐ **Encounters of the Spooky Kind II** (1990) - A martial arts student and teahouse worker named Abao fights to protect his fiancée from a wealthy rival. The love triangle quickly turns into an all-out supernatural battle when the rival enlists a wicked sorcerer to attack Abao, who in turn must rely on the help of a benevolent female ghost to survive.
- ☐ **Hex** (1980) - A man who believes that he has murdered his wife, sees her return as a vengeful ghost.
  - **SEQUELS**
    - ☐ **Hex vs. Witchcraft** (1980) - A comedic sequel released in the same year.
    - ☐ **Hex After Hex** (1982) - A second, even more absurd sequel.
- ☐ **The Imp** (1981) - Ging-Keung encounters sinister turns of fate where he works, and he becomes frightened enough to consult with a Taoist priest. The priest informs him that his workplace had been the site of murdering.
- ☐ **Possessed** (1983) - Siu and Ming are two cops. Siu is being bothered by ghosts.
  - **SEQUELS**
    - ☐ **Possessed II** (1984) - The Siu family move into a new flat. There are disturbing signs, for instance the cemetery next door.
- ☐ **Witch from Nepal** (1986) - A Hong Kong man vacations to Nepal where a local tribe imbues him with magical powers which he must use to fight a growing evil.
- ☐ **Peacock King** (1988) - Two magically powerful monks are sent on a quest to fight the King of Hell. an adaptation of the Japanese manga series *Kujaku Ō* by Makoto Ogino. It is part of a larger franchise that includes a sequel film and an anime series.
  - **SEQUELS**
    - ☐ **Saga of the Pheonix** (1990) - The Holy Maiden of Hell, Ashura possesses immense power that can destroy humanity. Buddhist monks trap her in a deep cave to keep her from falling into evil hands. Kindhearted Abbot Jiku grants her wish to enjoy the human world for 7 days.
- ☐ **The Eight Immortals Restaurant: The Untold Story** (1993) - Macau cops begin to suspect a man running a pork buns restaurant of murder, after tracing the origin of a case full of chopped up human remains that washed ashore, which leads them to him. The film is based on the "Eight Immortals Restaurant murders," which occurred in Macau in 1985. The cannibalism aspect, however, was sensationalized for the film.
  - **SEQUELS**
    - ☐ **The Untold Story 2** (1998) - An unhappily married couple invite the wife's cousin, who comes from Mainland China, to live with them. She has a horrible way of overcoming hardship and becomes the master of the barbecue.

☐ **The Untold Story 3** (1999) - An unrelated third film produced by Danny Lee, who also produced the original. Inspector Lee and his team of investigating officers look into the strange disappearance of a respectable loan shark.

- **OTHER HONG KONG CATEGORY III HORROR FILMS:** A Hong Kong Category III horror film is a horror movie that received Hong Kong's most restrictive rating for its extreme content, which can include graphic violence, gore, nudity, and sexual themes. These films often push boundaries and can be highly disturbing, leading them to be censored or banned in other regions.

  ☐ **Devil Fetus** (1983) - A bizarre cult classic featuring a demonic fetus, black magic, and surreal, grotesque special effects.

  ☐ **Men Behind the Sun** (1988) - A controversial and brutal historical exploitation film based on the atrocities committed by the Japanese army's Unit 731 during World War II.

  ☐ **Riki-Oh: The Story of Ricky** (1991) - An over-the-top, hyper-violent adaptation of a Japanese manga, set in a dystopian prison. It is known for its inventive and gory special effects and is often considered a Category III masterpiece.

  ☐ **Dr. Lamb** (1992) - Based on the true story of a serial killer and taxi driver, this film is known for its brutal violence and disturbing psychological aspects. It was produced by Danny Lee, who frequently worked on Category III films.

  ☐ **Ebola Syndrome** (1996) - A Chinese restaurant worker wanted for murder in Hong Kong contracts Ebola in South Africa, becomes immune to it, and unknowingly spreads the virus there, then comes back to Hong Kong and continues to infect people with it.

  ☐ **Intruder** (1997) - A psychological horror film that deals with a home invasion and supernatural elements, with a dark and intense atmosphere.

  ☐ **Voodoo (Gon Tau: An Oriental Black Magic)** (2007) - A policeman travels to Thailand and has an affair. When he has to return to Hong Kong, he promises that he will return. He doesn't, that sends his life into a spiral thanks to the girl's connections in the black magic world.

  ☐ **Dream Home** (2010) - A more recent Category III film that follows a woman's violent and visceral quest to acquire her dream apartment.

  ☐ **In the Room** (2015) - While not strictly horror, it is a Category III film that features themes of exploitation and sexual content.

☐ **Home Sweet Home** (2005) - Haunted high-rise horror with Michelle Yeoh.

☐ **Rule Number One** (2008, Singapore) - An action-thriller that follows the events that occur after a man calls the police to let them know of the mysterious presence in his house.

☐ **Revenge: A Love Story** (2010) - Kit is a young man hunted by the police after a series of murders. A mystery unravels and out comes a story about revenge.

JAPAN

☐ **Kwaidan** (1964, Japan) – A collection of four Japanese folk tales with supernatural themes.

☐ **Onibaba** (1964, Japan) – Two women kill samurai and sell their belongings for a living. While one of them is having an affair with their neighbor, the other woman meets a mysterious samurai wearing a bizarre mask.

- **DIRECTOR'S RELATED WORK**

  ☐ **Kuroneko** (1968, Japan) – Ghostly women avenge samurai violence.

☐ **Whispering Corridors** (1998, Korea) - In a Korean school, students are regularly beaten and mistreated by their teachers. However, the spirit of one pupil, who died ten years ago, periodically returns in the guise of a new girl, thus able to gain a revenge on the culprits.

- **THE WHISPERING CORRIDORS FILM SERIES**

  ☐ **Memento Mori** (1999) - The second installment focuses on a ghostly presence tied to a lesbian relationship at the school.

  ☐ **Wishing Stairs** (2003) - The third movie is about a set of "wishing stairs" that grants wishes with sinister consequences.

  ☐ **Voice** (2005) – The fourth movie in the series. While practicing after hours in her high school, an aspiring singer is mysteriously killed and her body vanishes. Her invisible ghost is trapped in the school, but her best friend is able to hear her voice.

  ☐ **A Blood Pledge** (2009) - The fifth film in the series deals with a student's suicide and the mysterious pact made between four friends.

☐ **The Humming** (2020) - The sixth and most recent film also features a ghost in the school, with a plot involving a missing student.

☐ **Ju-On: The Curse** (2000) – A teacher visits the house of one of his students after the boy goes missing, only to have a horrifying excuse for his absence from school.

- **SEQUELS**

  ☐ **Ju-On: The Curse 2** (2000) - On his request, the sensitive sister of a real estate agent visits a house he intends to sell, only to cross paths with its resident curse.

  ☐ **Ju-On: The Grudge** (2002) – Ghost curse spreads endlessly. A mysterious and vengeful spirit marks and pursues anybody who dares enter the house in which it resides. Toshio's spirit is often heard meowing throughout the film. Not only does this imply that his spirit merged with his deceased cat Mar, but it also relates to an old Japanese legend where the damned spirits of lost children become strays and as a result, produce a cat's meow.

  ☐ **Ju-On: The Grudge 2** (2003) – As their curse spreads on, the ghosts find their chance to live once again through the pregnancy of a cursed woman.

  ☐ **Ju-On: Black Ghost** (2009) - After losing her child at birth, the dark horror of the grudge begins growing within her.

  ☐ **Ju-On: White Ghost** (2009) - Akane begins seeing visions of a female ghost wearing the same yellow hat and red satchel she wore as a school child.

  ☐ **Ju-On: The Beginning of the End** (2014) – A school teacher visits the home of a boy who's been absent from school for a long period of time, unaware of the horrific tragedy which occurred in the boy's household many years ago.

  ☐ **Ju-On: The Final Curse** (2015) – Mai will now uncover the dark secrets of Ju-on and will try to end the curse once and for all.

- **ADAPTIONS**

  ☐ **The Grudge** (2004) - An American nurse living and working in Tokyo is exposed to a mysterious supernatural curse, one that locks a person in a powerful rage before claiming their life and spreading to another victim.

  ☐ **The Grudge 2** (2006) - Three interwoven stories about a terrible curse. A young woman encounters a malevolent supernatural force while searching for her missing sister in Tokyo; a mean high school prank goes horribly wrong; a woman with a deadly secret moves into a Chicago apartment building.

  ☐ **The Grudge 3** (2009) - A young Japanese woman who holds the key to stopping the evil spirit of Kayako, travels to the haunted Chicago apartment from the sequel, to stop the curse of Kayako once and for all.

☐ **A Tale of Two Sisters** (2003, Korea) – After being institutionalized in a mental hospital, Su-mi reunites with her sister, Su-yeon, and they return to live at their country home. But strange events plague the house, leading to surprising revelations and a shocking conclusion.

- **ADAPTIONS**

  ☐ **The Uninvited** (2009) – The most prominent adaptation of the film is the 2009 American remake, *The Uninvited*. The plot follows Anna (Emily Browning) as she returns home from a psychiatric facility after her mother's death. She and her sister, Alex (Arielle Kebbel), become convinced that their new stepmother (Elizabeth Banks) is responsible for their mother's passing. It incorporates the same major plot twists as the original film.

☐ **Into the Mirror** (2003, Korea) - An ex-cop, now working as a security guard in a shopping mall, tries to uncover the secret behind a series of mysterious deaths linked to mirrors.

- **ADAPTIONS**

  ☐ **Mirrors** (2008) – Staring Kiefer Sutherland. Ben guards a partly-destroyed property by night but begins to see strange images in its impeccable mirrors. After his sister is killed, he is convinced that evil forces are out to get him.

  - **SEQUEL**

    ☐ **Mirrors 2** (2010) - When Max, who is recovering from a traumatic accident, takes a job as a nighttime security guard, he begins to see visions of a young mysterious woman in the store's mirror.

- ☐ **Marebito** (2004, Japan) - A fear-obsessed freelance cameraman (Shinya Tsukamoto) investigates an urban legend involving mysterious spirits that haunt the subways of Tokyo.
- ☐ **Infection** (2004, Japan) - Takes place in a dark, isolated hospital, where a doctor's mistake has led to dire consequences for a patient.
  - • **J-HORROR THEATER**
    - ☐ **Premonition** (2004) - From director Norio Tsuruta, this film centers on a schoolteacher who discovers a newspaper that can predict future tragedies, including his own.
    - ☐ **Reincarnation** (2005) - Directed by Takashi Shimizu (*The Grudge*), the film is about an actress who takes on a role in a horror movie filmed at a hotel where a real massacre occurred, leading her to experience the past's terrifying events.
    - ☐ **Retribution** (2006) - Directed by Kiyoshi Kurosawa (*Cure*, *Pulse*), this psychological horror follows a detective who is haunted by the ghost of a woman he believes he murdered.
    - ☐ **Kaidan** (2007) - A period horror film directed by Hideo Nakata (*The Ring*), this movie adapts the classic Japanese folktale of a vengeful ghost seeking justice.
    - ☐ **The Sylvian Experiments** (2010) - The final film in the series, it is also known as *Kyōfu* (Fear). It was directed by Hiroshi Takahashi (*The Ring*, *The Ring 2*).
- ☐ **Hansel and Gretel** (2007, Korea) - After meeting a mysterious girl on an dark stretch of road, a young salesman is invited to a beautiful house with bizarre secrets and no way to escape.
  - • **FOLKLORE**
    - ☐ **The Red Shoes** (2005) - The film is a modern, loose adaptation of the 1845 Hans Christian Andersen fairy tale "The Red Shoes." A woman stumbles upon a pair of pink high heels while walking down a subway platform. She picks them up and takes them home only to find out that they are cursed and can ruin her life.
    - ☐ **The Piper** (2015) - A dark and disturbing folk tale based on the Pied Piper legend. A traveling musician promises to rid a village of its rats but faces horrifying consequences when he is betrayed.
    - ☐ **The Mimic** (2017) - Inspired by a Korean urban legend, this horror film focuses on a family that takes in a mysterious young girl and discovers she can mimic voices. The sense of an unnatural child invading a family home is similar to *Hansel and Gretel*.
- ☐ **Carved: The Slit-Mouthed Woman** (2007) - A suburban town in Japan is the victim of what is supposedly just an urban legend, a woman's spirit with a horribly disfigured face who is intent on kidnapping children for unknown reasons. The film is based on the popular Japanese urban legend of Kuchisake-onna, or the "Slit-Mouthed Woman."
  - • **SEQUELS**
    - ☐ **Carved 2: The Scissors Massacre** (2008) - A prequel to the 2007 film that presents a more grounded and different origin story for the Slit-Mouthed Woman.
    - ☐ **Kuchisake-onna 0: The Beginning** (2008) - This is another prequel to the 2007 film, which focuses on a different set of characters and a different origin story for the Kuchisake-onna.
- ☐ **The Wailing** (2016, Korea) – Soon after a stranger arrives in a little village, a mysterious sickness starts spreading. A policeman, drawn into the incident, is forced to solve the mystery in order to save his daughter.
  - • **KOREAN OCCULT HORRORS**
    - ☐ **The Priests** (2015, Korea) - Two priests have to find out if a young girl was attacked by an evil spirit or human molester in order to save her life.
    - ☐ **Svana** (2019, Korea) - Pastor Park works to expose suspicious religious groups. He's hired to look into the cult group Deer Mount. Meanwhile, Police Captain Hwang investigates a murder case and the main suspect is a member of the Deer Mount cult.
    - ☐ **The 8th Night** (2021, Korea) - With prayer beads in one hand and an ax in the other, a monk hunts down a millennia-old spirit that's possessing humans and unleashing hell on Earth.
    - ☐ **The Medium** (2021, Thailand/Korea) – Thai found-footage about a shaman lineage facing true possession. A horrifying story of a shaman's inheritance in the Isan region of Thailand. What could be possessing a family member might not be the Goddess they make it out to be.
    - ☐ **Exhuma** (2024, Korea) - The process of excavating an ominous grave unleashes dreadful consequences buried underneath.

- **Creepy** (2016, Japan) - Ex-detective Takakura and wife Yasuko face danger as their sinister neighbor Nishino is linked to disappearances and manipulates Yasuko. Themes of trust, trauma, and hidden darkness unfold in this psychological thriller of suburban menace. It is directed by Kiyoshi Kurosawa and is based on the 2012 novel of the same name by Yutaka Maekawa.
- **Howling Village** (2019, Japan) - After her brother goes missing, a young psychologist visits an infamous haunted and cursed location known as 'Howling Village' to investigate his disappearance and uncover her family's dark history.

MALAYSIA / SINGAPORE

- **The Maid** (2005) - In Chinese superstition, the seventh month of the lunar calendar is regarded as the month when the gates of hell open for forsaken spirits to walk the earth for 30 days. Unknown to Rosa, she arrives on the eve and her hell is about to begin.
- **Munafik** (2016) - Adam is a Muslim medical practitioner who is unable to accept the fact that his wife is no longer in this world. Later on, he agrees to treat a depressed woman named Maria but strange and unsettling things start to happen.
  - **SEQUELS**
    - **Munafik 2** (2018) - A direct sequel that continues the story of Ustaz Adam as he confronts a black magic cult leader. A third installment was announced, but production has been delayed due to the COVID-19 pandemic. The director confirmed that he has a plot in mind to complete the trilogy.
- **Soul** (2019) - Set in the past, in which a family gets a visit from a strange little girl with a frightening prediction. The film's unique aesthetic, incorporation of Malay folklore, and minimalistic storytelling earned it critical acclaim internationally.
  - **MALAY FOLKLORE:** Malay folklore originates from the ancient animist beliefs, Hindu-Buddhist mythology, and later Islamic influences that shaped the Malay Archipelago (modern-day Malaysia, Indonesia, Brunei, and Singapore). It is a tapestry of spirits, shapeshifters, and moral parables rooted in village life and the natural world. Central to its mythology are supernatural beings like the *Pontianak*, a vengeful female spirit of a woman who died in childbirth, and the *orang minyak*, an oil-covered man who prowls at night. Folktales often blend horror, morality, and mysticism, warning against greed, betrayal, and disrespect for the unseen. Passed down through oral tradition, Malay folklore reflects the region's deep reverence for nature and its fear of disturbing the delicate balance between the human and spirit realms.

    - **Pontianak** (1957) - This classic film helped launch the *Pontianak* genre in Malaysian cinema. It was followed by two sequels, *Dendam Pontianak* (1957) and *Sumpah Pontianak* (1958).
    - **Pontianak Harum Sundal Malam** (2004) - A more modern and dramatic retelling of the Pontianak legend, exploring themes of betrayal and vengeance.
    - **Revenge of the Pontianak** (2019) - A Singaporean-Malaysian co-production that offers a fresh take on the classic ghost story.
    - **200kg Vampire** (2024) - A horror-comedy that features a heavier-than-average Pontianak who terrorizes a village.
    - **Susuk** (2008) - This film features a young trainee nurse who turns to the forbidden practice of "Susuk," a ritual that uses spiritual items for beauty and power.
    - **Dukun** (2018) - This film was banned for over a decade before its eventual release. It is based on a real-life case involving a shaman who used black magic for power.

- [ ] **Zombi Kampung Pisang** (2007) – The first Malaysian zombie movie, which blends horror and comedy as a peaceful village is struck by a zombie apocalypse.
- [ ] **Hantu Kak Limah** (2018) - A horror-comedy film about a ghost haunting a village, based on local folklore.
- [ ] **Pusaka** (2019) – This film delves into an unexplained haunting and features an abandoned house that holds dark family secrets.
- [ ] **Tiger Stripes** (2023) - This film follows an 11-year-old girl who experiences a horrifying physical transformation.
- [ ] **Pulau** (2023) - A group's dare on a deserted island awakens an ancient and vengeful force.

PHILIPPINES
- [ ] **Patayin mo sa sindak si Barbara** (1974) - Classic tale of jealousy and possession. A Filipino cult classic horror film directed by Celso Ad. Castillo. When a woman's envious sister takes her own life, her spirit returns to torment the living, twisting love and loyalty into a ghostly revenge that consumes the entire family.
  - **ADAPTIONS**
    - [ ] **Patayin sa sindak si Barbara (Kill Barbara with Panic)** (1995) - Remake with modern effects. A woman must fight against the evil will of her selfish sister, even beyond death.
- [ ] **Feng Shui** (2004) - After finding a Feng Shui amulet, Joy starts to see a string of fortunate events come her way. Soon, she realizes it is, in fact, a curse. Now she must break the cycle of good fortune and death in order to save her family.
  - **SEQUELS**
    - [ ] **Feng Shui 2** (2014) - A sequel to the 2004 film was released 10 years later, with actress Kris Aquino reprising her role. The sequel continues the story of the cursed *bagua* mirror, which has now fallen into the hands of a new protagonist.
- [ ] **Sukob** (2006) - A newlywed couple becomes cursed after violating an old Filipino wedding taboo, unleashing a vengeful force that hunts them and their loved ones one by one.
- [ ] **The Entity** (2019) - A family is haunted by what appears to be the ghost of their youngest daughter.

TAIWAN
- [ ] **The Tag-Along** (2015) - Based on true events and long-circulating urban legend in Taiwan, "The Little Girl in Red." The myth began after hikers found footage showing a mysterious girl in a red dress following a man who later went missing. The story quickly spread through news and folklore, turning the girl into a ghost said to lure victims into the mountains or the afterlife. The film adapts that legend into a modern haunting about grief, guilt, and the unseen forces that prey on the living. Wei is nowhere to be found one day before his grandma returns from her own strange missing incident. Wei's girlfriend desperately searches for his whereabouts and finds that it is the horrifying mystery of the little girl in red that has followed and haunted them all along.
  - **SEQUELS**
    - [ ] **The Tag-Along** (2017) - A mother goes in search of her missing teenage daughter after her sudden disappearance. She is told that her daughter was last seen in the company of a girl in red, leading the mother to attempt to unravel the mystery behind the girl.
    - [ ] **The Tag-Along: The Devil Fish** (2018) - A prequel to both films, also directed by David Chuang, that focuses on a different but related urban legend about the "Devil Fish."
- [ ] **The Bride** (2015) - Han and Hao are about to get married soon when Hao picks up a strange red envelope on the street and then all hell breaks loose with a vengeful supernatural bride wreaking havoc on his life.
- [ ] **The Rope Curse** (2018) - Hoping to make a viral video by streaming a mysterious rope ritual, a couple falls into a deadly curse instead that turns their lives upside down. The film is based on a real-life Taiwanese urban legend and a local ritual called the "Rope Ritual."
  - **SEQUELS**
    - [ ] **The Rope Curse 2** (2020) - This sequel focuses on a different story involving a Taoist priest and a woman possessed by a powerful Thai demon. It was also directed by Shih-Han Liao, who directed the first film.
    - [ ] **The Rope Curse 3** (2023) - The third film shifts to a different story about a young exorcist who gets entangled in supernatural events at a hotel.

☐ **Detention** (2019) - In 1962 Taiwan, student Fang and teacher Mr. Chang fall in love amidst the restrictive White Terror period banning sensitive books. Despite this, Mr. Chang secretly organizes a banned book study group with fellow teacher and student. The film is an adaptation of the popular Taiwanese horror game *Detention*. The game's story and themes of psychological horror set against the backdrop of Taiwan's White Terror period (1947–1987) provide the basis for the film's narrative.

THAILAND

☐ **Body sob 19** (2007) - The plot draws parallels to an actual murder case in Thailand involving a physician who was convicted of dismembering his estranged wife. A boy has reoccurring nightmares about a beautiful girl being cruelly murdered, but everyone around him tries to convince him that the girl is only a figment of his imagination.

☐ **Pee Mak** (2013) - After serving in the war, Mak invites his four soldier friends to his home. Upon arrival they witness the village terrified of a ghost. The four friends hear rumors that the ghost is Mak's wife Nak. Based on Thai folklore. Based on the famous Thai folk tale of Mae Nak Phra Khanong.

- **MAE NAK PHRA KHANONG LEGEND:** One of Thailand's most famous ghost stories, the Mae Nak Phra Khanong legend tells of a devoted wife who dies in childbirth while her husband, Mak, is away at war. Unaware of her death, he returns home to live with her ghost and their child until villagers reveal the truth. Enraged, Mae Nak's spirit haunts the community, unable to let go of her love. Blending romance and terror, the tale endures as a symbol of undying devotion turned tragic, retold in countless Thai films, plays, and TV dramas for over a century. Mae Nak's remains are believed to be buried at Wat Mahabut, a shrine where people pray for blessings related to childbirth and avoiding military conscription.

  - ☐ **Mae Nak Phra Khanong** (1959) - This early Thai adaptation is one of the most famous and influential film versions of the story. Directed by Rangsi Thatsanaphayak.
  - ☐ **Ghost of Mae Nak** (2005) - Directed by British filmmaker Mark Duffield, this version brings the legend into a modern Bangkok setting, where a young couple's new home disturbs the ancient spirit.
  - ☐ **Nak** (2008) - This CGI-animated film is a more lighthearted and child-friendly take on the classic ghost story. A group of Thai ghost legends have grown tired of haunting and move to the country to help humanity.
  - ☐ **Mae Nak 3D** (2012) - One of several versions that have been produced with varying degrees of success.
  - ☐ **Make Me Shudder 2: Shudder Me Mae Nak** (2014) - This is a horror-comedy sequel to another film, which involves teenagers investigating the Mae Nak shrine.
  - ☐ **Bayama Irukku** (2017) - This Tamil-language film was an unofficial Indian remake of *Pee Mak*. After a group of friends discovers that one of their friends is facing problems with his wife, who they believe is possessed by a ghost, they try to save him with the help of an exorcist.
  - ☐ **Daeng Phra Khanong** (2022) - This film focuses on the child of Mae Nak, exploring a different part of the legend. The legend of Mae Nak Prakanong, about a female spirit in the era of King Rama V, is well known but not much is known about her unborn son Dang. He is the spirit of a child who wants nothing more than to befriend humans.

OTHER

☐ **Macabre** (2009, Indonesia) – Six friends on a road trip stumble upon a strange girl and her enigmatic mother. The mother invites them for dinner, trapping and hunting them. Her family systematically eliminates the friends one by one through a nefarious ritual.

☐ **May the Devil Take You** (2018, Indonesia) – When her estranged father falls into a mysterious coma, a young woman seeks answers at his old villa, where she and her stepsister uncover dark truths.

- **SEQUELS**
  - ☐ **May the Devil Take You Too** (2020) - Also directed by Tjahjanto, this sequel is also known as *May the Devil Take You: Chapter Two*. It follows Alfie two years after the first film, as she is once again drawn into a terrifying battle against demons when a new group of survivors seeks her help. A third installment is planned to conclude the series.

Bollywood & Indian Horror
THE FOUNDATIONS & GOTHIC ERA

- ☐ **Mahal** (1949) - A young lawyer is involved with a ghostly woman in his new house, where the builder and his fiancée died shortly after it was built.
  - • **REINCARNATION THRILLERS**
    - ☐ **Madhumati** (1958) - Directed by Bimal Roy (the editor for *Mahal*), this is arguably the most famous reincarnation film from Bollywood. The story of two lovers separated by death who find each other again was a direct result of *Mahal*'s success.
    - ☐ **Bees Saal Baad** (1962) - A gothic horror film with a similar tone to *Mahal*, involving a wealthy heir who returns to his family's mansion and is haunted by a ghost.
    - ☐ **Mera Saaya** (1966) - A suspense film where a woman returns claiming to be the deceased wife of a high court lawyer. The lawyer doubts her identity, but she claims to be a reincarnation of his wife.
    - ☐ **Karz** (1980) - A later and more energetic reincarnation thriller that follows a man who, during his second life, begins to remember his brutal murder from his first life. This film was remade multiple times, including as *Om Shanti Om* (2007).
- ☐ **Who Kaun Thi** (1964) - One stormy night, a doctor offers a ride to a ghostly woman he meets on the side of the road. Later, he discovers his intended bride is identical in appearance to the ghost. Who was she and why does she haunt him?

THE RAMSAY BROTHERS ERA (1970s- 90s VHS ROOM)

- ☐ **Darwaza** (1978) - Haunted haveli, secret curses, and a monstrous killer. For generations, a family lives in fear of a dark and terrible curse.
- ☐ **Hotel** (1981) - A haunted hotel run by sinister forces.
- ☐ **Purana Mandir** (1984) - A horror film involving a demonic creature terrorizing a couple. It is also a cult classic from the Ramsays. After a rich young girl learns about a demon and it's terrible curse brought by her family for generations, she decides to go to her paternal village with her lover, and his friend, to find out the truth.
- ☐ **Doosri Shaadi** (1984) - A lesser-known horror film from the Ramsays.
- ☐ **Tahkhama** (1986) - Treasure hunters encounter underground monsters.
- ☐ **Dak Bangla** (1987) - Supernatural terror in a colonial-era mansion. The film borrows from mummy lore, gothic horror, and reincarnation themes, which are prevalent in both Western and Indian cinema. A man moves in with his wife to a Mansion as a caretaker and finds out that not only some thugs have invaded that place but also a mummy walled in the dungeon with a dark past.
- ☐ **Veerana** (1988) - One of the most popular Ramsay Brothers films, featuring a malevolent spirit, reincarnation, and classic horror tropes. A beautiful young girl, unfortunately possessed from her childhood by a vengeful spirit, wanders around lonely places to seduce and kill people, gradually becoming lost into a dark world of revenge and lust.
- ☐ **Saaya** (1989) - A photographer who knows black magic is killed while lusting after a policeman's wife and his ghost haunts the couple.
- ☐ **Bandh Darwaza** (1990) - Another Ramsay Brothers film centered on a vampire and black magic. A wealthy male banishes a demon, but years later his very own daughter resurrects it.
- ☐ **Haveli** (1991) - Another Ramsay spookfest with forbidden romance and curses.

PSYCHOLOGICAL & SUPERNATURAL SHIFTS (1990s-2000s)

- ☐ **Raat** (1992) - Cult possession film, considered India's *Exorcist*.
  - • **ADAPTIONS**
    - ☐ **Bhoot** (2003) - Urmila Matondkar anchors this modern possession tale in a haunted apartment. This film is a remake of *Raat*, although it is a more modern take on the possessed-in-a-haunted-apartment story.
      - • **SEQUELS**
        - ☐ **Bhoot Returns** (2012) - This film serves as a sequel to *Bhoot*, continuing the theme of a family haunted by a demonic presence. Starring Manisha Koirala,

features a different cast and plot but follows a similar supernatural-in-the-home formula.

- ☐ **Kaun?** (1999) - While alone in the house, a woman hears news of serial killer on the loose. And then a stranger rings the doorbell...
- ☐ **Vaastu Shastra** (2004) - Evil forces stalk a young mother and child in their new home.
- ☐ **Phoonk** (2008) - An atheist is forced to consult an exorcist after his daughter shows signs of being possessed.

THE MODERN PRESTIGE WAVE (2010s-Present)

- ☐ **Ragini MMS** (2011) - Found-footage Bollywood spin with supernatural sex appeal. Out to relax and have fun at a farmhouse, a couple experience horror at the hands of an unknown entity.
  - **SEQUELS**
    - ☐ **Ragini MMS 2** (2011) - A sequel to the 2011 film that follows a film crew shooting a movie based on the original scandal in the same haunted house. A third film in the franchise is in development.
    - ☐ **Ragina MMS Returns** (2017) - A web series that premiered on the streaming platform ALT Balaji.
- ☐ **Horror Story** (2013) - Seven youngsters decide to spend a night in an abandoned haunted hotel. What they mistook as merely rumors, dawns on them to be the truth as they realize they are not alone inside.
- ☐ **Ek Thi Daayan** (2013) - When gifted magician Bobo finds himself assailed by hallucinations and seeks professional help, he learns he's being haunted by a sinister spirit.
- ☐ **Pari** (2018) - Supernatural horror with Anushka Sharma as a mysterious woman tied to a cult. Arnab tries to help Ruksahana, who is found under mysterious circumstances in a house. He lets her stay at his home until he discovers something strange about her.
- ☐ **Pizza** (2012, Tamil) - A pizza delivery boy lands in a mysterious circumstance and it works a dramatic change in his life.
  - **SEQUELS & ADAPTIONS**
    - ☐ **Pizza II: Villa** (2013) - A standalone sequel in which a man finds a series of prophetic paintings in an ancient mansion.
    - ☐ **Pizza 3: The Mummy** (2023) - The protagonist on a probe to solve a series of murders that take place exactly where he delivers food. A fourth film has been announced.
    - ☐ **Pizza** (2014, Hindi) - Delivery boy trapped in a haunted house.
- ☐ **Bulbbul** (2020) - A man returns home after years to find his brother's child bride now grown up and abandoned, and his ancestral village plagued by mysterious deaths. The film was inspired by Bengali folklore and the paintings of artist Raja Ravi Varma.
  - **OTHER BENGALI FOLKLORE HORROR:** Bengali folklore, one of the richest oral traditions in South Asia, traces its origins to ancient rural Bengal spanning present-day West Bengal and Bangladesh, where myths, ghost stories, and moral parables were passed down through generations of village storytellers, bards, and poets. Rooted in animism and later shaped by Hindu, Buddhist, and Islamic influences, it blends the mystical with the everyday, populating the landscape with spirits like the *petni* (female ghost), *bhut* (restless soul), and *daini* (witch). These tales, often told through song, dance, and local theatre (*jatra*), reflect deep cultural preoccupations with fate, morality, and the unseen world. Bengali folklore has profoundly influenced literature, cinema, and art, most notably through writers like Rabindranath Tagore and filmmakers like Satyajit Ray, whose works channel the haunting lyricism and supernatural realism of Bengal's collective imagination.
    - ☐ **Monihara** (1961) - Part of Satyajit Ray's anthology film *Teen Kanya*, this psychological ghost story follows a man haunted by the spirit of his jewel-obsessed wife.
    - ☐ **Nishi Trishna** (1989) - This film taps into the vampiric myths of rural West Bengal to tell its horror story.
    - ☐ **Putuler Protisodh** (1998) - This film features an abused daughter-in-law who returns as a *chudail* (a vengeful spirit born from a violent death) to seek revenge on her in-laws.
    - ☐ **Bhooter Bhabishyat** (2012) - This horror-comedy revolves around a group of ghosts who face the prospect of losing their home when a building is slated for demolition.
    - ☐ **Jekhane Bhooter Bhoy** (2012) - This film is an anthology of four ghost stories, some adapted from famous Bengali authors like Rabindranath Tagore and Satyajit Ray.

- [ ] **Bhoot Chaturdashi** (2019) - Four youngsters head to an abandoned mansion to shoot a documentary but end up encountering strange paranormal activities.
- [ ] **Parnashavarir Shaap** (2023) - This web series features an occultist who faces a haunting mystery after an Aghori tantric surfaces.
- [ ] **Bhootpori** (2024) - A more recent horror-fantasy film that features a young boy who befriends the ghost of a deceased woman and helps her uncover the truth about her death.
- [ ] **Bhoot Part One: The Haunted Ship** (2020) - A bereaved shipping officer investigates the mystery behind a ghost ship that washes ashore in Mumbai. The film is based on a real-life incident from 2011 involving an abandoned cargo ship, the MV Wisdom, which ran aground on a Mumbai beach. Although, the title includes "Part One," a sequel has not moved forward. The film is not connected to Ram Gopal Varma's *Bhoot* franchise, which includes *Bhoot* (2003) and the standalone sequel *Bhoot Returns* (2012).
  - **HAUNTED SHIP & CONFINED TERROR**
    - [ ] **Death Ship** (1980, UK) - A low-budget horror film where shipwreck survivors are rescued by a ghost ship.
    - [ ] **Ghost Ship** (2002, US) - A horror film about a salvage crew that discovers a derelict passenger ship on the Bering Sea, only to find that it is haunted by a malevolent entity.
    - [ ] **Blood Vessel** (2019, Australia) - An Australian horror film where a group of survivors from a torpedoed hospital ship is rescued by an abandoned German trawler.

REGIONAL HORROR GEMS (NON-HINDI BUT PAN-INDIAN)
- [ ] **Arundhati** (2009, Telugu) - A warrior queen's spirit battles evil in this fantasy-horror epic.
- [ ] **Yavarum Nalam (13B)** (2009, Tamil/Hindi) - A man experiences a supernatural occurrence at his newly purchased apartment; a soap opera being telecast exclusively on his TV, which shows the future of his family.
- [ ] **Eeram** (2009, Tamil) - Vasu investigates the suicide of Ramya since he's not convinced that she killed herself. The main suspects are her husband and neighbors. As the death toll rises, Vasu deals with his own secret past.
- [ ] **Prema Katha Chitram** (2013, Telugu) - Three friends and a stranger go to a house and plan to commit suicide. But later they realize the house is haunted.
  - **SEQUELS & ADAPTIONS**
    - [ ] **Prema Katha Chitram 2** (2019) - The film was followed by a standalone sequel titled *Prema Katha Chitram 2* (2019), with a new cast and a different director. It was a box office failure.
    - [ ] **Chandralekha** (2024) - Four people who decide to commit suicide in resort but find themselves haunted by vengeful ghost.
- [ ] **Maya** (2015, Tamil) - A woman takes on the challenge of watching a horror film, alone in a theatre.
- [ ] **Lapachhapi** (2017, Marathi) - A new-born Indian baby... An age-old horror practice and the fact how evil are certain human practices.
  - **ADAPTIONS**
    - [ ] **Chhorii** (2021, India) - Eight-month pregnant Sakshi must save herself and her unborn child from the evil within society and from the fear that lies in the paranormal world.
      - **SEQUELS**
        - [ ] **Chhorii 2** (2025) - Sakshi must rescue her seven-year-old daughter from a superstitious cult while fighting societal malpractices and the horror that continues to haunt her and young women around her.
- [ ] **Aval (The House Next Door)** (2017, Tamil/Hindi) - A young married couple begin to encounter several paranormal attacks, when a family moves into a neighboring house, that is being haunted by a vengeful spirit, which leads them to perform an exorcism in order to help save the neighbors.

CONTEMPORARY EXPERIMENTS & HYBRIDS
- [ ] **Raaz** (2002) - Sanjana and Aditya decide to give their marriage one last chance. They plan a holiday in Ooty, but they don't know that a strange figure is waiting for them to come. The 2002 film is an unofficial adaptation of the Hollywood film *What Lies Beneath* (2000).
  - **SEQUELS**
    - [ ] **Raaz: The Mystery Continues** (2009) - An artist comes to realize that the woman he has been been painting is real and is being haunted by a ghost.

- [ ] **Raaz 3: The Third Dimension** (2012) – When an ingénue's sudden popularity threatens to shove her out of the spotlight, a movie star uses black magic in an attempt to derail her career.
- [ ] **Raaz Reboot** (2016) - The fourth installment of a horror series that explores secrets, mysteries and human frailties.
- [ ] **Krishna Cottage** (2004) - An incomplete book containing nine-and-a-half stories is revealed to be cursed and endangers the life of a bunch of college friends after one of them ends up reading it. Reviewers noted similarities to *Scream* and *I Know What You Did Last Summer*.
- [ ] **1920** (2008) - After forsaking his family and religion, a husband finds his wife is demoniacally possessed.
  - **SEQUELS**
    - [ ] **1920: Evil Returns** (2012) - A famous poet, Jaidev, meets a woman who has lost her memories. He brings her to his house and tries to help her, but things take an ugly turn when she gets possessed by an evil spirit.
    - [ ] **1920 London** (2016) - After her husband is possessed by an evil spirit, a woman turns to her former lover to perform an exorcism.
    - [ ] **1921** (2018) - A decade after 1920. When Ayush arrives in England to learn music, he is shocked and scared when the manor he is living in becomes haunted by spirits. To exorcise them, he seeks the help of Rose, a woman who can see and speak with them.
    - [ ] **1920: Horrors of the Heart** (2023) - A young girl walks into a world of darkness is search of revenge but darkness consumes her making her a victim of that very revenge.[34]
- [ ] **Haunted – 3D** (2011) - Disregarding tales that Glen Manor is haunted, Rehan travels to Koti, Shimla, to prepare the house for sale. Realizing the stories are true, he is taken back to year 1936, hoping to rewrite history. Big-budget attempt at India's first 3D horror. *Haunted 3D: Ghosts of the Past*, is scheduled for release in late 2025, with Vikram Bhatt returning to direct and Mimoh Chakraborty reprising his role.
- [ ] **Stree** (2018) - In the small town of Chanderi, the menfolk live in fear of an evil spirit named "Stree" who abducts men in the night. Based on the urban legend of "Nale Ba" that went viral in Karnataka in the 1990s. The location in Bhopal was chosen because of the mysterious stories associated with the place. After reaching the place, the locals informed the production team about the unexplained events that had taken place in the area and the safety precautions that they must follow. Keeping in mind the advice given by the locals, a set of guidelines to be followed by everyone were created and placed in all the rooms inside the fort.
  - **SEQUELS & THE MADDOCK HORROR COMEDY UNIVERSE:** The Maddock Horror Comedy Universe, spearheaded by producer Dinesh Vijan under Maddock Films, is India's first interconnected horror-comedy franchise that redefined how Bollywood approaches the supernatural. Beginning with *Stree* (2018), inspired by the Indian urban legend of a vengeful female spirit, the universe expanded with *Roohi* (2021) and *Bhediya* (2022), blending folklore, humor, and social commentary into a cohesive mythos. Each film explores local legends through a modern, witty lens, using satire and regional color to address deeper cultural anxieties: gender, superstition, and transformation while keeping the scares accessible and entertaining. Together, these films have built a uniquely Indian cinematic universe that fuses folklore with franchise storytelling, proving that horror and laughter can thrive side by side.
    - [ ] **Stree 2: Sarkate Ka Aatank** (2024) - A direct sequel to the original, which continues the story of the menacing spirit and was also a major box office success. A third *Stree* film is planned for 2027.
    - [ ] **Roohi** (2021) - Hired to kidnap a bride, two bumbling pals get into a wacky predicament when one falls for their abductee, and the other falls for the spirit that possesses her.
    - [ ] **Bhediya** (2022) - A film about a werewolf that is also part of the franchise. It features a key character that connects it to the events of *Stree*.
    - [ ] **Munjya** (2024) - A spin-off film featuring a different folk creature, with a post-credits scene that connects it to the *Stree* universe. A young man's visit to his native village unveils a family secret and a vengeful spirit, the Munjya, who wants to get married. Now the young man must fight to protect himself and his love from Munjya's clutches.
    - [ ] **Thama** (2025) - The next announced film in the franchise, described as a vampire movie.
    - [ ] **Mahayudh** (2028) - A two-part crossover event featuring characters from across the universe is planned for 2028.

---

[34] Because you know I have to at this point, this one is absolutely horrible with a disgustingly low 2.7 stars on IMDB.

The First Family of Fear

The Ramsay Brothers[35]

Born into a family of filmmakers in Bombay, the seven Ramsay brothers: Shyam, Tulsi, Kumar, Keshu, Kiran, Gangu, and Arjun became the undisputed pioneers of Indian horror cinema. Beginning in the early 1970s and dominating through the 1980s, they built Bollywood's first true horror production dynasty. Working on shoestring budgets but boundless imagination, they fused Gothic tropes, Indian folklore, and pulp storytelling into a uniquely desi brand of terror, equal parts eerie and campy. Their films embraced graveyards, haunted havelis, seductive spirits, and grotesque monsters, wrapped in melodrama, song, and spectacle. What began as low-budget curiosity evolved into a cult movement that defined horror for an entire generation of Indian audiences.

Signature Works (Curated)
- *Do Gaz Zameen Ke Neeche* (1972) — Their breakout hit, mixing vengeance from beyond the grave with emotional melodrama.
- *Hotel* (1981) — A haunted property, masked killer, and eerie atmosphere set the template for their later works.
- *Purana Mandir* (1984) — Their biggest success; a demon curse and ancient temple setting elevated Indian horror to blockbuster status.
- *Veerana* (1988) — The quintessential Ramsay mix: eroticism, witchcraft, and lurid supernatural horror.
- *Tahkhana* (1986) — A subterranean nightmare filled with monsters and revenge, showcasing their special-effects ingenuity.

The Fingerprints
- Haunted havelis and ancient curses: Gothic castles reimagined through Indian mythology.
- Practical effects and rubber monsters: DIY horror at its most inventive.
- Melodrama and morality: Love, betrayal, and revenge interwoven with the supernatural.
- Soundtrack scares: Echoing screams, thunderclaps, and eerie synths amplifying dread.

Legacy & Influence
The Ramsay Brothers didn't just create horror, they created the *language* of Indian horror. Long before modern studios embraced the genre, they gave Indian audiences permission to scream, laugh, and believe. Their films laid the foundation for everything from *Bhoot* and *Tumbbad* to the *Maddock Horror Comedy Universe*. Today, their legacy lives on in the nostalgia of midnight reruns, cult fan circles, and the DNA of every Bollywood ghost story that followed.

Pairing Night Watchlist
- *Purana Mandir* (1984) → Classic Ramsay: blood, love, and demonic resurrection.
- *Veerana* (1988) → The ultimate haunted seductress tale.
- *Tahkhana* (1986) → Indian monster-movie madness at its peak.

Quick Facts to Sound Smart
- The Ramsays made over 30 horror films between the 1970s and 1990s.
- They popularized horror on Indian television with the cult series *Zee Horror Show* (1993–2001).
- Their practical effects team often worked out of their family bungalow, turning kitchens into creature labs.
- *Purana Mandir* was among the top-grossing films of 1984—proving Indian audiences craved fear as much as romance.
- Their influence still echoes in Bollywood's fusion of horror, humor, and heightened drama.

Eastern European Horror

- ☐ **Mother Joan of the Angels** (1961) - A priest is sent to a small parish in the Polish countryside which is believed to be under demonic possession and there he finds his own temptations awaiting. Adaptation of a 1943 novella of the same name by Jarosław Iwaszkiewicz. The novella itself is loosely based on the real-life 17th-century Loudun possessions in France.
  - • **LOUDUN POSSESSION HORROR**
    - ☐ **Die Teurfel von Loudun** (1969) - This German TV movie is an opera adaptation of the events. It focuses on Urbain Grandier's fight against fanaticism and features elements of the demonic possession of the Ursuline nuns.
    - ☐ **The Devils** (1971, UK) – Ken Russell's infamous story of possession and religious frenzy. The film stems from *The Devils of Loudun* by Aldous Huxley.
- ☐ **Witchhammer (Kladivo na carodejnice)** (1970, Czechoslovakia) - In the 1600s, an overzealous clergy hauls innocent women in front of tribunals, forces them to confess to imaginary witchery, and engages in brutal torture and persecution of their subjects.
- ☐ **Dead Mountaineer's Hotel** (1979, Soviet Union/Estonia) - Police gets a call-out to a lonely hotel in the Alps. When an officer gets to the hotel everything seems to be all right. Suddenly, an avalanche cuts them out from the rest of the world, and strange things are going to happen. The film is based on the 1970 novel by Arkady and Boris Strugatsky, who also wrote the screenplay.
- ☐ **Curse of Snakes Valley** (1988. Poland/Soviet Union) - Pulp adventure horror inspired by Jules Verne's Gothic Carpathian novel *Master of the World.* The trio of adventurous pals, a man who is a scientist, a fine lady and a former military pilot are in the Indochina jungles looking for some mysterious vase that holds a metal container that is of no mundane origin.
- ☐ **Legyen világosság (Let There Be Light)** (1996, Hungary) - A haunting, slow-burn drama where faith, guilt, and superstition collide in a remote Hungarian village, exposing how darkness festers not from the absence of God, but from the people who claim to serve Him.
- ☐ **Hukkle** (2002, Hungary) - The story is loosely based on the "Angel Makers of Nagyrév," a historical serial murder case that took place in Hungary in the early 20th century. It is a dialogue-light mosaic of vignettes that portrays life in a rural village. While the plot is driven by a hidden murder mystery, it is not the main focus.
- ☐ **Trackman** (2007, Russia) - A perfect bank heist turns deadly when the robbers and their hostages flee to the abandoned underground subway station where they encounter the Trackman, a deformed madman that prowls the darkness.

- ☐ **Life and Death of a Porno Gang** (2009, Serbia) - An aspiring film maker turns to porn after little success, then falls into a pursuit of crime with his band of misfits and suffers the repercussions of their unprecedented journey.
- ☐ **Strigoi** (2009, Romania) – When the villagers killed Constantin Tirescu, they thought it was justice. Vlad Cozma thinks it was murder. Now Constantin thinks pickles might go nice with blood. The film is based on Romanian folklore surrounding the *strigoi*, a type of vampire, but is an original screenplay by Faye Jackson.
  - • **FILMS FEATURING STRIGOI & OTHER ROMANIAN MYTHS:** Rooted in ancient Romanian folklore, the Strigoi are restless spirits believed to rise from the grave to torment the living: draining vitality, spreading disease, or preying on loved ones. The myth dates back to pre-Christian Dacian traditions and evolved through centuries of superstition, blending pagan beliefs about the soul with Christian ideas of damnation. Often seen as the prototype of the modern vampire, the Strigoi could be living or undead, capable of shapeshifting, invisibility, and returning home at night. Fear of these beings shaped Romanian burial customs, with rituals

like staking or burning the dead to prevent their return. Beyond the Strigoi, Romanian mythology teems with nocturnal entities: the *moroi* (child spirits), *iele* (seductive forest nymphs), and *pricolici* (werewolf-like creatures) each embodying the tension between nature, faith, and the supernatural. These myths have deeply influenced Romanian culture, from village rituals to global vampire lore, immortalized most famously through Bram Stoker's *Dracula* and the dark mystique of Transylvania itself.

- ☐ **Beyond the Hills** (2012, Romania) - This film, directed by Cristian Mungiu and based on a true story, features an exorcism that is rooted in archaic religious beliefs prevalent in rural Romania.by Cristian Mungiu, this film offers a more grounded, drama-focused account of the events, and it won the Best Screenplay award at the Cannes Film Festival.
- ☐ **Miss Christine** (2013) - A Romanian gothic horror film based on the novella of the same name by Mircea Eliade. It tells the story of a man who falls in love with the spirit of a girl who haunts an old mansion.
- ☐ **The Devil Complex** (2016, UK) - This found-footage horror film is based on the legend of the Hoia Baciu Forest, also known as the "Bermuda Triangle of Romania" due to its association with paranormal activity and missing people. Rachel and her team of film makers travel to Transylvania, Romania, to document the paranormal phenomena within Hoia-Baciu Forest.
- ☐ **Vampir** (2021, UK/Serbia/Germany) - This film, directed by Branko Tomovic, is based on Balkan folklore and centers on a man who moves to a small Serbian village that is haunted by the myth of the *strigoi*. A man from London comes to a small remote village in Serbia to look after the cemetery. He starts to have nightmarish visions and suspects the friendly villagers have a more sinister intention with him.

☐ **The Man in the Orange Jacket** (2014, Latvia/Estonia) - Post-Soviet social horror; isolation, guilt, and identity collapse. A man is fired from his job and begins to stalk his former boss and his wife. After breaking into their home and claiming it for his own, he begins to see ghostly visions.

☐ **Strangled** (2016, Hungary) - Based on the true story of a serial killer who operated in Hungary in the 1960s during the communist era, a period following the 1956 uprising and its subsequent suppression by the regime. The film explores how the political climate influenced the case, with the regime needing to demonstrate its control over law and order, leading to both an unjust conviction and a real tyranny.

☐ **The Noonday Witch** (2016, Czech Republic) - Folkloric ghost terror tied to motherhood. A mother and daughter move to an isolated house, with mom saying dad's away working. Their bond strains when the lie surfaces. As their relationship deteriorates, the Noonday Witch appears, drawing nearer - real threat or delusion?

☐ **The Painted Bird** (2019, Czech/Slovakia/Ukraine) - A young Jewish boy somewhere in Eastern Europe seeks refuge during World War II where he encounters many different characters. The film is based on Jerzy Kosiński's 1965 novel. The book was originally claimed to be autobiographical but has since been largely debunked as fiction based on other survivors' stories.

☐ **Post Mortem** (2020, Hungary) - A post mortem photographer and a little girl confront ghosts in a haunted village after the First World War. Although people are trying to pass this movie off as the first Hungarian horror flick, it's not. That description goes to *Legyen világosság* from 1996. Peter Bergendy's 'Post Mortem' (2020) was Hungary's official entry for the Oscars® in 2022. The film was screened on 50 international film festivals, selected for 24 main official competitions, and won 29 awards.

☐ **The Hater** (2020, Poland) - A young man searches for purpose in a net of hatred and violence that he tries to control. A razor-sharp study of digital manipulation and moral decay, it reveals how online validation and algorithmic hate can twist isolation into extremism, turning social media into a breeding ground for modern monsters.

- • **THEMATIC PREQUEL**
    - ☐ **Suicide Room** (2011, Poland) - After suffering extreme humiliation at school, Dominik holes himself up in his room and begins spending all his time in a virtual reality chat room. Upon its release in cinemas in Poland, it was the number one movie for three weeks. One of the photographs in the golden tree is of Yukio Mishima, the Japanese author who famously committed suicide by seppuku. The names of several real teenagers who had committed suicide are included and easy to find during the Facebook sequences.

☐ **Luzifer** (2021, Austria) A man with the mental faculties of a child must save his mother, thereby becoming god and devil.

The Alchemist of Italian Horror

Mario Bava

Born in 1914 in San Remo, Italy, Mario Bava was the son of a cinematographer and began as a special effects artist before stepping into the director's chair. His painterly eye and mastery of atmosphere made him the "Godfather of Italian Horror." Bava bridged Gothic horror with modern thrillers, pioneering both the *giallo* template and supernatural Italian cinema. His low budgets forced him into creative innovation: colored gels, mirrors, and camera tricks gave his films their dreamlike intensity.

Beyond horror, Bava defined the visual grammar of Italian genre cinema. From peplum epics to sci-fi, training future auteurs in how to make beauty out of limitation. His influence transformed Italy's B-movies into works of baroque artistry and cinematic myth.

Signature Works (Curated)
- *Black Sunday* (1960) — A witch returns from the grave for revenge; Gothic imagery so powerful it was banned in the UK.
- *Black Sabbath* (1963) — Horror anthology (and the band's namesake) with tales of vampires, witches, and spectral terror.
- *Blood and Black Lace* (1964) — Proto-giallo; killers in leather gloves stalk fashion models, setting the blueprint for Argento and slashers alike.
- *Kill, Baby, Kill* (1966) — A cursed village and ghostly child; one of the most visually influential horror films of the 60s.
- *A Bay of Blood* (1971) — A violent inheritance tale with shocking set-pieces that directly inspired *Friday the 13th*.

The Fingerprints
- Gothic lighting: bold reds, greens, purples—color as mood and menace.
- Stylized violence: elegant, sometimes surreal compositions of death.
- Fatalism: characters doomed by greed, lust, or supernatural curses.
- Experimental camerawork: zooms, tracking shots, and visual trickery decades ahead of Hollywood.

Legacy & Influence
Bava is the root system of modern horror: Argento built *giallo* on his foundation; slashers like *Halloween* and *Friday the 13th* trace directly to *A Bay of Blood*; his gothic visuals echoed in Tim Burton, Guillermo del Toro, and Nicolas Winding Refn. Even the horror anthology format popularized by *Creepshow* owes a debt to *Black Sabbath*. Though he never achieved the mainstream fame of Hitchcock or Carpenter, Bava's fingerprints are everywhere in horror's visual DNA.

Pairing Night Watchlist
- *Black Sunday* (1960) → Watch for the iconic mask-of-satan opening scene; Gothic horror distilled to its essence.
- *Blood and Black Lace* (1964) → Observe the fashion-house setting and stylized kills that prefigure slasher tropes.
- *A Bay of Blood* (1971) → Pay attention to the body count and elaborate kills. Slasher DNA begins here.

Quick Facts to Sound Smart
- *Black Sabbath* inspired Ozzy Osbourne's band to rename themselves after it.
- *A Bay of Blood*'s murder set-pieces were lifted almost shot-for-shot in *Friday the 13th Part 2*.
- Bava worked uncredited as cinematographer on *I Vampiri* (1957), Italy's first sound-era horror film.
- His mastery of color gels created an atmosphere directors still copy today (e.g., *Suspiria*, *Mandy*).
- Martin Scorsese and Quentin Tarantino have both cited Bava as an influence on their visual style.

Europe & Elsewhere

☐ **Day of Wrath** (1943, Denmark) - The young wife of an aging priest falls in love with his son amidst the horror of a merciless witch hunt in 17th-century Denmark. The film is an adaptation of the 1909 Norwegian play *Anne Pedersdotter* by Hans Wiers-Jenssen. The original play was based on a real 16th-century Norwegian witchcraft case involving Anne Pedersdotter, who was burned at the stake in 1590.

☐ **Your Vice is a Locked Room and Only I Have the Key** (1972, Italy) - A string of murders are committed near the estate of a degenerate author, whose abusive relationship with his wife is further complicated by the arrival of his manipulative niece.

☐ **Veronika Voss** (1982, Germany) – Fassbinder's psychological horror. The final film in the trilogy, released just before Fassbinder's death. It examines the emotional toll of the Nazi era and the "collective amnesia" of post-war Germany through the tragic fate of its protagonist.

- • **PREQUELS**
  - ☐ **The Marriage of Maria Braun** (1979) - The first film in the trilogy, following a German woman navigating the economic and social changes of post-war Germany.
  - ☐ **Lola** (1981) - The second film, exploring the lives of a saloon singer and a building commissioner in post-war Germany.

☐ **The Devil's Backbone** (2001, Spain) – After Carlos - a 12-year-old whose father has died in the Spanish Civil War - arrives at an ominous boys' orphanage, he discovers the school is haunted and has many dark secrets which he must uncover.

- • **SISTER FILM**
  - ☐ **Pan's Labyrinth** (2006, Spain) – Dark fantasy rooted in fascist trauma.

☐ **The Uninvited** (2004, Spain) - In the dark corridors of Félix's house, an intruder is hiding. Is he real, or is he a manifestation inside the obscure maze of his mind?

☐ **Next Door** (2005, Norway) - John has just been left by his girlfriend Ingrid. That day he allows himself to be seduced into a mystical and scary world, where it is impossible to separate truth from the lies. The first Norwegian-made film to get an 18 rating in 17 years in Norway. The last one to get an 18 rating before this one was Hotel St. Pauli (1988).

☐ **Dabbe** (2006, Turkey) - A cruel suicide wave spreads from the United States to a small Turkish town, where a man kills himself after spending time on the computer. His friends are still getting disturbing emails from him.

- • **SEQUELS**
  - ☐ **Dabbe 2** (2009) – A Turkish family is trying to stay alive at the edge of the apocalypse.
  - ☐ **Dabbe: Demon Possession** (2012) – A family's house in Turkey becomes possessed by evil spirits that want to kill humans.
  - ☐ **Dabbe: The Possession** (2013) – Ahead of her wedding, Kübra is possessed by demons. When an examination reveals more horror, her friend, a psychiatrist, tries to perform an exorcism.
  - ☐ **Dabbe 5: Zehr-I Cin** (2014) - This Turkish horror film follows a housewife who is haunted by a tribe of Jinn. Jinn have become a popular subject in Turkish horror movies since the early 2000s.
  - ☐ **Dabbe 6: The Return** (2015) - Mukadder died suddenly one night. Cause of death was cerebral hemorrhage. According to her sister, the killers are different sizes. There are demons behind everything.

☐ **Sauna** (2008, Finland) – Border settlement haunted by sins. *Sauna* mixes historical drama with supernatural horror, exploring themes of sin, atonement, and post-war trauma in 16th-century Finland.

☐ **Eskalofrío** (2008, Spain) - A lonely adolescent moves with his mother to an isolated village and a series of odd events shock the community.

☐ **Citadel** (2012, UK/Ireland) - An agoraphobic father teams up with a renegade priest to save his daughter from the clutches of a gang of twisted feral children who committed an act of violence against his family years earlier.

- **Witching and Bitching** (2013, Spain) - A gang of armed robbers finds a safe haven in a secluded village crammed with witches--only to encounter the bizarre, the unexpected, and the occult. Can they save themselves, and the rest of the world from the next witch apocalypse?
- **Siccîn** (2014, Turkey) - Öznur loves her cousin Kudret since childhood. Kudret marries Nisa. Jealous Öznur uses black magic to win Kudret. The spell unleashes evil forces. The *Siccîn* film series is known for its prolific output of new installments, all directed by Alper Mestçi and focusing on stories involving black magic and djinn (supernatural beings in Islamic mythology). An official Indonesian adaptation titled *Sijjin* was released in November 2023. This remake was produced by Rapi Films and SkyMedia and features a reimagined story centered on themes of obsession and black magic.
  - **SEQUELS**
    - **Siccîn 2** (2015) - Centers on a woman tormented by a family curse following the mysterious death of her son. Adnan and Hicran are happily married however when their son die as a result of a mysterious accident Adanan becomes distant from his wife. Hicran starts investigating her past to see how it could connect to the death of her son.
    - **Siccîn 3** (2016) - Explores a love story gone wrong, leading to a pact with a djinn. Three infant friends are separated by a terrible accident but are reunited years later.
    - **Siccîn 4** (2017) - Follows a family who moves into an old, haunted house occupied by other-dimensional beings. Due to financial problems, Yilmaz family moves in their grandmother Saadet's house. Saadet's old house, is inhabited by beings from another dimension. And this beings don't want anyone in the house, but Saadet.
    - **Siccîn 5** (2018) - Focuses on a woman with a mysterious connection to a historical house in Nevşehir. Hale attracted attention with its different appearance and strange behavior. She lives in a historical and eerily house in Nevsehir with her mother, a depressed grandmother and her aunt Azra. Hale's father had disappeared before she was born and was never seen again.
    - **Siccîn 6** (2019) - A girl becomes haunted by an evil spirit in her family home. A girl is haunted by an evil spirit in her family home. Several bad things begin to happen around her house and to her family members. An old character rises back and tries to save the family from their doomed fate.
    - **Siccîn 7** (2024) - Follows a woman who moves into a mansion and is tormented by paranormal occurrences. Kemal and family move to uncle's mansion after deal with child panhandling mafia, hiding daughter Rüya's illness. Mother Lale's Alzheimer's triggers paranormal occurrences. Meral infiltrates, plans ritual on Black Moon 2018.
    - **Siccîn 8** (2025) - The most recent entry, about a man and his family haunted by supernatural forces. In this Turkish-language horror sequel, a man and his family are tormented by malevolent supernatural forces after he brings his elderly mother into his home.
- **Lake Bodom** (2016, Finland) – Teen camping trip turns deadly. While marketed as a slasher, the film's execution includes psychological and thriller elements, distinguishing it from more straightforward slasher flicks.
- **The Maus** (2017, Spain) - Alex and Selma are a couple in love on a trip to the heart of Bosnia and Herzegovina to discover more about each other. Lost and seemingly surrounded by land mines a pair of locals offer to guide them home.
- **Verónica** (2017, Spain) – Madrid, 1991. A teen girl finds herself besieged by an evil supernatural force after she played Ouija with two classmates. *Veronica* is based on the 1991 Vallecas case in Madrid, involving a teenager named Estefanía Gutiérrez Lázaro. According to police reports, after Gutiérrez Lázaro died mysteriously following a séance with a Ouija board, her family claimed to experience paranormal phenomena in their home.
  - **SEQUELS**
    - **Sister Death** (2023) - The prequel tells the origin story of Sister Narcisa, the blind nun who tries to help Veronica in the 2017 film. After a childhood marked by a miracle, Narcisa, a novice nun joins a school to teach young girls.
- **Possum** (2018, UK) - After returning to his childhood home, a disgraced children's puppeteer is forced to confront his wicked stepfather and the secrets that have tortured his entire life. *Possum* is an adaptation of a short story of the same name by Matthew Holness, who also wrote and directed the film. The short story was originally published in the 2008 horror anthology *The New Uncanny: Tales of Unease*, which featured stories based on Sigmund Freud's theories on the uncanny.

The Italian Hitchcock

Dario Argento[36]

Born in Rome in 1940, Dario Argento started as a film critic and screenwriter (he co-wrote *Once Upon a Time in the West* with Sergio Leone) before becoming the master of Italian horror. He helped define *giallo* cinema: lurid Italian thrillers blending murder mysteries, baroque violence, and stylized visuals. Argento's work is drenched in nightmare logic, operatic soundtracks (often by prog-rock band Goblin), and painterly cinematography where every murder feels like performance art.

Signature Works (Curated)
- *The Bird with the Crystal Plumage* (1970) — Argento's debut; a stylish murder mystery that ignited the giallo craze of the 70s.
- *Deep Red* (1975) — Often called the definitive giallo; virtuoso set-pieces, shocking kills, and a haunting Goblin score.
- *Suspiria* (1977) — A horror opera of witches at a ballet academy; neon color palettes, dream logic, and one of the most famous horror scores ever recorded.
- *Tenebrae* (1982) — Meta-horror where an author's books inspire a string of murders; blends giallo with postmodern commentary.
- *Opera* (1987) — Infamous for its needle-to-the-eyelids imagery; a slasher staged as high art.

The Fingerprints
- Color as violence: reds, blues, greens used as emotional weapons.
- Elaborate camera movements (tracking shots, POV sequences, impossible angles).
- Murder as choreography: stylized, almost balletic killings.
- Goblin scores that pulse with dread and psychedelic energy.
- Stories that dissolve into dream logic, prioritizing mood over realism.

Legacy & Influence
Argento's bold use of color and sound influenced everyone from John Carpenter to Nicolas Winding Refn. *Suspiria* became a cornerstone of modern horror aesthetics, echoed in films like *Black Swan*, *Mandy*, and Luca Guadagnino's 2018 *Suspiria* remake. His giallo style inspired entire generations of filmmakers. Slashers like *Halloween* owe a debt to his mix of POV stalking, fetishized weapons, and shocking violence. Argento remains a touchstone for anyone interested in horror as visual and sonic art.

Pairing Night Watchlist
- *Suspiria* (1977) → Pay attention to the saturated colors and the sound design. Horror as sensory overload.
- *Deep Red* (1975) → Watch how Argento turns murder into a staged spectacle; the jazz-prog score is as important as the visuals.
- *Tenebrae* (1982) → Notice the meta-narrative: the killer mirrors the artist, blurring creation and destruction.

Quick Facts to Sound Smart
- Argento's *Suspiria* was originally written for children; he kept the dialogue but cast adults, creating its uncanny feel.
- He often cast his daughter, Asia Argento, in later works (*Trauma*, *The Stendhal Syndrome*).
- *Deep Red* contains one of the earliest uses of a Steadicam in Italian cinema.
- Goblin, his frequent collaborators, recorded the *Suspiria* score before filming; Argento blasted it on set to unnerve actors.
- Quentin Tarantino and Guillermo del Toro have both cited Argento as a lifelong influence.

Latin America

ARGENTINA

- ☐ **Cemetery of Terror** (1985) - On Halloween, a group of medical students steal the corpse a serial killer from a morgue and raise him from the dead, inadvertently putting themselves and a group of young neighborhood children in danger.
  - **OTHER GALINDO JR. FILMS**
    - ☐ **Don't Panic** (1987) - On his seventeenth birthday, Michael unwittingly unlocks the evil forces of a Ouija board. Another cult Mexican horror film.
    - ☐ **Grave Robbers** (1989) - Teenagers accidentally resurrect a satanic killer who targets the local police captain's daughter to birth the antichrist.
- ☐ **Cold Sweat** (2010) - Home-invasion with buckets of nitroglycerin terror.
- ☐ **Terrified (Aterrados)** (2017, Argentina) – When strange events occur in a neighborhood in Buenos Aires, a doctor specializing in the paranormal, her colleague, and an ex-police officer decide to investigate further.

BRAZIL

- ☐ **The Secret of the Mummy** (1982) - Laughed at when he announces the discovery of the elixir of life, scientist Professor Expedito Vitus devotes himself to the reconstitution of a map that has been divided into eight parts. The owners of these parts are being mysteriously murdered. Thanks to this map, he ends up making the most important archaeological discovery of the century: the tomb of Runamb, the Mummy, in the sands of Egypt. Back in Brasil, the professor brings the Mummy back to life, who was actually a dangerous psychopathic murderer obsessed with the image of Nadja, the dancer who had rejected him. Heavily draws on classic monster movies from Universal and Hammer horror studios, filtered through a distinct Brazilian lens. The film is considered a cult classic, especially among fans of bizarre and unconventional horror cinema. It has gained some traction in the U.S. through independent distributors and has been re-examined by modern critics for its unique style and humor.
- ☐ **The Black Fables** (2015) - A group of kids embarks in a macabre adventure, full of characters from the Brazilian popular imaginary - the werewolf, a witch, a ghost, monsters and The Saci. With the anthological meeting between four of the most important names in the Brazilian horror: Rodrigo Aragao, Petter Baiestorf, Joel Caetano and Jose Mojica Marins, the eternal Coffin Joe.
  - **BRAZILIAN FOLKLORE & MYTHOLOGY:** Rooted in centuries of cultural fusion, Brazilian folklore is a vibrant tapestry of Indigenous spirit tales, African orixás, and colonial superstition. It emerged during the colonial era as oral storytelling carried across plantations, rainforests, and rivers, blending creation myths, trickster spirits, and moral fables into a shared national mythology. Figures like *Curupira*[37], the forest guardian with backward feet who protects nature from hunters, and *Boitatá*, the fiery serpent of the plains, embody Indigenous reverence for the land. From Afro-Brazilian traditions come *Iemanjá*, the ocean goddess of love and fertility, and *Exu*, the mischievous gatekeeper between worlds. These myths still shape Brazilian identity today, from *festa junina* celebrations and Candomblé rituals to cinema and literature that frame the country's natural beauty as both enchanted and haunted.

  - ☐ **Curupira: O Demônio da Floresta** (2021) - A group of young people on a weekend excursion in the Amazon become lost and are hunted by the macabre figure.

---

[37] "Jardim Botânico Plantarum 11" Sturm (https://commons.wikimedia.org/wiki/User:Sturm) Creative Commons Attribution-Share Alike 4.0

- ☐ **Skull: The Mask** (2020) - A police officer's investigation into a ritualistic murder reveals a terrifying mask connected to a powerful, vengeful entity.
- ☐ **Good Manners** (2019) - A dark fantasy film that reimagines werewolf folklore in a contemporary setting.
- ☐ **The Devil Lives Here** (2015) - A group of teenagers stays with a friend at an old farmhouse and becomes caught in a conflict involving a supernatural entity.
- ☐ **Dark Sea** (2013) - Deals with the consequences of a strange creature from the sea.
- ☐ **Night of the Chupacabras** (2011) - Centered on the titular mythical creature.
- ☐ **Black Swamp** (2008) - Features zombie-like creatures emerging from a contaminated mangrove swamp.
- ☐ **Who is Afraid of the Werewolf** (1975) - This film focuses on the werewolf legend, a popular piece of Brazilian folklore. The story follows two young men who encounter a strange family, and an ancestral curse involving a male child born after seven daughters, who is destined to become a werewolf.
- ☐ **Sin in the Sacristy** (1975) - In this film, a man on the run for murder meets a "lost soul" who tasks him with several missions. He must confront various creatures from Brazilian folklore, including the *Mula sem Cabeça* (the headless mule) and the *Mãe-d'Água* (mother of the waters).
- ☐ **The Nightshifter** (2018) - Stênio, the nightshifter of a morgue, has the ability to communicate with the cadavers that are brought to him every night. Based on the short story *Morto Não Fala* by Brazilian author Marco de Castro.

CHILE

- ☐ **Hidden in the Woods** (2012) - Ater their abusive father is jailed, two sisters being raised in a remote area of Chile find they have to answer to their uncle, a drug kingpin who wants his missing product back.
  - • **ADAPTIONS & SEQUELS**
    - ☐ **Hidden in the Woods II** (2022) - The story picks up ten years after the events of the original film and follows Anny, one of the survivors, as her new life is violently interrupted by gangsters.
    - ☐ **Hidden in the Woods** (2014, US) - An English-language remake of the original film was released in 2014, also directed by Valladares.
- ☐ **La Casa Lobo (The Wolf House)** (2018) - Tells the story of Maria, a young woman who takes refuge in a house in southern Chile after escaping from a German colony. The film was inspired by the real history of Colonia Dignidad, a German colony in Chile that was used as a torture and interrogation center under the Pinochet dictatorship. The film's narrative style is meant to evoke the type of indoctrination and propaganda that was used within the cult.

MEXICO

- ☐ **Even the Wind is Afraid** (1968) – Girls that were punished to sat at a boarding school during Spring Break have no idea the school is haunted by the restless spirit of a former student seeking revenge.
  - • **OTHER TABOADA FILMS**
    - ☐ **The Book of Stone** (1969) - Governess Julia discovers her young charge Sylvia's only friend is Hugo-a stone statue guarding an occult grimoire. As mysterious events escalate from cryptic symbols to voodoo dolls, the line between stone and flesh grows ominously thin.
    - ☐ **Darker than Night** (1975) - Four beautiful women move to an old house, inherited by the aunt of one of them, and witness strange things.
    - ☐ **Poison for the Fairies** (1986) - A 10-year-old girl convinces a lonely classmate that she is a witch, forcing the child to become her assistant. Though their games are initially rather naive, they gradually take a nasty and violent turn.
- ☐ **Here Comes the Devil** (2012, Mexico) – A couple loses their children near some caves in Tijuana. The children return to their parents the next day, unharmed. However, something has happened to them.
  - • **DIRECTOR THEMES**
    - ☐ **Scherzo Diabolico** (2015) - A black comedy thriller also directed by Bogliano. A bored accountant can't win for losing. He is passed over for promotion at work, has a nagging shrew of a wife, and is generally disrespected by all he comes in contact with. He devises a scheme to

get what he feels he is owed. After executing his well thought out plan of kidnap and ransom, things soon go straight to hell.

- ☐ **Black Circle** (2018) - A Swedish-Mexican horror film directed by Bogliano. The lives of two sisters change dramatically, since they were hypnotized by a mystical vinyl record from the 1970s.
- ☐ **The Exorcist (La Exorcista)** (2022, Mexico) - A Mexican horror film also directed by Bogliano. Ofelia, a young nun recently arrived at the town of San Ramon, she is forced to perform an exorcism on a pregnant woman. Just when it looks like the possession has ended, she discovers that the evil presence has not vanished.

- ☐ **The Similars** (2015) - On the rainy night of October 2, 1968, eight characters waiting on a remote bus station for a bus heading to Mexico City start experiencing a strange phenomenon.
- ☐ **Tigers Are Not Afraid** (2017, Mexico) – A dark fairy tale about a gang of five children trying to survive the horrific violence of the cartels and the ghosts created every day by the drug war.

PERU

- ☐ **Maligno** (2016) - A bloodcurdling legend becomes reality when a mysterious hole opens in the main hospital of a city, and a dark presence is released.
  - • **PERUVIAN URBAND LEGENDS & FOLKLORE:** Peruvian folklore is a haunting blend of Incan mythology, colonial superstition, and modern urban legend, where the ancient and the uncanny coexist. Rooted in the Andes and Amazon, these stories date back thousands of years, when oral traditions preserved tales of gods, spirits, and shapeshifters tied to nature's power. Among the most enduring figures are El Tunche, the whistling forest spirit said to punish the wicked; La Jarjacha, a cursed human-llama hybrid born of sin; and Pishtaco, a terrifying fat-sucking creature once used to explain colonial exploitation. Over time, these legends evolved into urban myths told in Lima's streets and jungle towns alike, shaping Peruvian identity through fear, morality, and the lingering tension between the sacred and the modern world.

    - ☐ **Pishtaco** (2003) - This film focuses on the myth of the Pishtaco, a legendary figure in the Peruvian highlands said to murder travelers and extract their body fat for various purposes. The legend gained popularity during the civil war and is often seen as a cautionary tale.
    - ☐ **General Cemetery** (2013) - This found-footage movie is based on urban legends from the main cemetery of Iquitos. It follows a grieving teenager who uses a Ouija board to contact her deceased father, unleashing a series of terrifying paranormal events.
    - ☐ **Face of the Devil** (2014) - This film focuses on the Amazonian legend of the El Tunche, a whistling spirit that preys on travelers lost in the jungle. A group of friends on vacation in the remote Amazon find themselves hunted by the entity.
    - ☐ **The Mystery of Casa Matusita** (2014) - A found-footage film inspired by the well-known Peruvian urban legend of the "House of Matusita," a allegedly haunted mansion in Lima.
    - ☐ **The Demon of the Andes** (2014) - This film features the Jarjacha, a half-human, half-llama demon from Andean mythology that is born from incest. The legend states that the creature preys on its victims to satisfy its hunger.

- ☐ **Sinister Circle** (2016) - After the death of a group of teenagers using the Ouija, the psychologist Fernanda and her son return to Peru, but they will find themselves surrounded by an evil entity as big as its wicked sect.

VENEZUELA

- ☐ **Infection** (2019) - Film about an epidemic outbreak of a new rabies virus in Venezuela and a father trying to save his son from contagion.

Master of the Macabre

Guillermo del Toro[38]

Born in Guadalajara, Mexico in 1964, Guillermo del Toro grew up steeped in Catholic imagery, fairy tales, and monster movies. Trained in makeup and special effects, he combined his love of Gothic tradition with political allegory and deep empathy for monsters. His films live at the intersection of horror and dark fantasy. Where fairy tales are violent, innocence is fragile, and monsters are often the most human characters on screen.

Signature Works (Curated)
- *Cronos* (1993) — Alchemical vampire device in a family pawnshop; his breakout feature, merging folklore with personal drama.
- *The Devil's Backbone* (2001) — A ghost story set during the Spanish Civil War; a template for horror as political memory.
- *Pan's Labyrinth* (2006) — Fairy tale and fascism collide; a modern masterpiece of magical realism and Gothic horror.
- *Crimson Peak* (2015) — A Gothic romance with haunted mansions, dripping with blood-red style and Victorian dread.
- *The Shape of Water* (2017) — Dark fairy tale romance with a fish-god; won the Academy Award for Best Picture.

The Fingerprints
- Monsters as metaphors: the "Other" is treated with sympathy, while humans often embody cruelty.
- Baroque visuals: ornate sets, rich color palettes, and insect/clockwork motifs.
- Catholic and folkloric imagery: saints, devils, fairy tale archetypes woven into political allegory.
- Blending horror with tenderness: even the most grotesque images carry beauty.

Legacy & Influence
Del Toro elevated Gothic horror and fantasy into prestige cinema, proving monsters can win Oscars. He revived interest in Spanish-language horror, influenced directors like Issa López (*Tigers Are Not Afraid*) and J.A. Bayona (*The Orphanage*), and championed genre creators through mentorship and producing (e.g., *Scary Stories to Tell in the Dark*). His *Cabinet of Curiosities* (2022) expanded his Gothic brand into anthology television, shaping the next generation of horror storytellers.

Pairing Night Watchlist
- *The Devil's Backbone* (2001) → Notice how the ghost is less a monster than a wound, embodying war's trauma.
- *Pan's Labyrinth* (2006) → Look for the dual structure: fairy tale fantasy vs brutal fascist reality.
- *Crimson Peak* (2015) → Watch for his homage to Hammer Horror—lush, colorful, and unapologetically Gothic.

Quick Facts to Sound Smart
- Del Toro's *Bleak House* (his Los Angeles home) is a private museum filled with monsters, books, and curiosities.
- He was originally attached to direct *The Hobbit* films but left after years of delays. His designs still shaped the trilogy.
- *Pan's Labyrinth* lost the Best Foreign Film Oscar but won three Academy Awards for its craft (cinematography, art direction, makeup).
- He often sketches his monsters before writing the script—his notebooks are legendary, filled with creature designs and Catholic symbols.
- Del Toro calls monsters "patron saints of imperfection," a philosophy running through all his work.

NOLLYWOOD & AFRICAN HORROR

EGYPT & NORTH AFRICA

- ☐ **The Blue Elephant** (2014) - While trying to help an inmate at the mental hospital, a psychotherapist unravels mysteries he never thought existed. An adaptation of the best-selling 2012 Arabic novel of the same name by Egyptian writer Ahmed Mourad.
  - **SEQUELS**
    - ☐ **The Blue Elephant 2** (2019) - Dr. Yehia Rashed is now married to his old love Lobna. His life is thrown into chaos when a new inmate at the hospital predicts the death of his family within three days, forcing Yehia to take the hallucination-inducing "blue elephant pills" once again to understand what's happening.
- ☐ **122** (2019) - On a blood-soaked night, in the very place meant to save lives, a young man and his beloved aren't fighting to reach the hospital-they're desperate to escape it. Trapped in a nightmare, they must survive until dawn. *122* was one of the first Arab films to be shot in the immersive 4DX format, an effect-based viewing experience. In Egypt, the number 122 is the equivalent of emergency numbers like 911 or 999 in other countries, which adds to the film's tense premise.

NIGERIA (NOLLYWOOD SUPERNATURAL THRILLERS)

- ☐ **Living in Bondage** (1992) - The O.G. Nollywood cult-classic; blood rituals for wealth. This movie marked the beginning of the video movie industry in Nigeria. Down and out businessman uses witchcraft to get ahead.
  - **SEQUELS**
    - ☐ **Living in Bondage: Breaking Free** (2019) - After a 26-year gap, a highly successful legacy sequel was released.
- ☐ **Nneka the Pretty Serpent** (1994) - Femme fatale serpent-spirit classic.
  - **SEQUELS**
    - ☐ **Nneka the Pretty Serpent** (2020) - Reimagined for a modern audience. When her parents are murdered, Nneka encounters the Queen of the Coast who offers to help her in revealing the identities of people who killed her parents. This changes the course of her life as she sets out on a mission of revenge.
- ☐ **Karishika** (1996) - A girl "Karishika" has been sent by Lucifer to the world to come and kill, destroy, and tempt people in order to increase the population in hell. A remake is currently in development by Play Network Studios, a Nigerian production company known for rebooting classic Nollywood films.
  - **SEQUELS**
    - ☐ **Karishika 2** (1998) - A direct sequel to the original film was released two years later. It continued the story of Karishika, the demonic agent of Lucifer, and her quest to lure souls to hell.
- ☐ **Blood Money** (1997) - Occult, ritual killings, and the price of greed.
- ☐ **Diamond Ring** (1998) - Ghostly revenge on a student who steals jewelry from a corpse.
- ☐ **Issakaba** (1999) - Terror has overtaken the locals as hoodlums ceaselessly rob and maim their victims. For solution, the king and his cabinet sought for help in the hands of a vigilante group called the Issakaba boys.
  - **SEQUELS**
    - ☐ **Issakaba 2** (2000) – The story of the vigilante group continues in this direct sequel, which was also released in multiple parts.
    - ☐ **Issakaba 3** (2001) - The third installment in the series continues the story of the Bakassi Boys and their fight against crime.
    - ☐ **Issakaba 4** (2001) - The vigilante group's story concludes in this final installment.
- ☐ **Ojuju** (2014) - Nigerian spin on zombie outbreak, using contaminated water.

SOUTH AFRICA

- ☐ **Dust Devil** (1992) – A woman on the run from her abusive husband encounters a mysterious hitch-hiker.
- ☐ **House on Willow Street** (2016) - After a young woman is kidnapped, her captors soon come to realize that in fact they may be the ones in danger and this young woman has a dark secret inside her.

Pairing Night: Watchlist

Starter Pack (Japan & Korea)

- *Kwaidan* (1964) – Classical folklore on screen.
- *Ringu* (1998) – Modern technological ghost curse.
- *The Wailing* (2016) – Possession, paranoia, and ritual dread.

Intermediate (Spain & Latin America)

- *The Devil's Backbone* (2001) – Haunted Civil War orphanage.
- *Verónica* (2017) – Ouija séance in Madrid.
- *Tigers Are Not Afraid* (2017) – Cartel violence through children's eyes.

Deep Dive (Global & Experimental)

- *Under the Shadow* (2016) – Djinn meets post-revolution Iran.
- *Baskin* (2015, Turkey) – Surreal descent into hell.
- *Satan's Slaves* (2017, Indonesia) – Cult horror reborn.

How to Watch

- Pair *Ringu* with its U.S. remake *The Ring* (2002) to see how atmosphere shifts across cultures.
- Watch *The Devil's Backbone* alongside *Pan's Labyrinth* (2006). One ghostly, one fantastical, both rooted in fascist trauma.
- End with *The Wailing* and *Under the Shadow* for maximal cultural disorientation.

Quick Facts to Sound Like the Smartest Person in the Room

- *Kwaidan* (1964) is so painterly it won the Special Jury Prize at Cannes.
- *Ringu* (1998) was the highest-grossing Japanese horror film until *Ju-On*.
- *Ju-On* (2002) was shot in just nine days but spawned a global franchise.
- *The Wailing* (2016) mixes Korean shamanism, Christianity, and Japanese folklore into one possession story.
- Guillermo del Toro calls *The Devil's Backbone* (2001) his "most personal film."
- *Tigers Are Not Afraid* (2017) was praised by Stephen King and Guillermo del Toro as one of the decade's best horror films.
- Indonesia's *Satan's Slaves* (2017) became the highest-grossing horror film in the country's history.

Horror Without Borders

Documentaries of Horror

- ☐ **Document of the Dead** (1980) - A look at the filming of George A. Romero's *Dawn of the Dead*. It features interviews with Romero and shows behind-the-scenes footage, offering a unique glimpse into the creation of a horror classic.
- ☐ **Hammer: The Studio that Dripped Blood** (1987) - An older but essential documentary about the influential British studio Hammer Film Productions and their signature Gothic horror films.
- ☐ **Vincent Price: My Life and Crimes** (1994) - This documentary features an intimate, extended interview with Vincent Price reflecting on his career, from his time in Universal's classic monsters era to the Roger Corman Edgar Allan Poe films.
- ☐ **Lon Chaney: Behind the Mask** (1996) - An earlier documentary about Lon Chaney that includes clips from his films and interviews with those who knew him.
- ☐ **Universal Horror** (1998) - Kevin Brownlow's look at the classic monster movies of Universal Pictures in the 1930s, featuring rare footage and stories from the era.
- ☐ **Lon Chaney: A Thousand Faces** (2000) - Narrated by Kenneth Branagh, this documentary covers the life and work of the silent film star known as "the Man of a Thousand Faces," whose iconic makeup creations and performances laid the groundwork for horror acting.
- ☐ **Videodrome: Forging the New Flesh** (2004) - A behind-the-scenes look at the film's production, with a specific focus on the groundbreaking and nightmarish practical effects created by Academy Award-winning makeup effects artist Rick Baker.
- ☐ **Lugosi, the Dark Prince** (2006) - A look into the life and tragic career of Bela Lugosi, the Hungarian actor who became a horror sensation for his portrayal of Count Dracula and later faded into obscurity.
- ☐ **Lovecraft: Fear of the Unknown** (2008) - A chronicle of the life, work and mind that created the Cthulhu mythos.
- ☐ **A History of Horror with Mark Gatiss** (2010) - A three-part BBC series where the British writer and actor examines the history of the genre, from classic silent films to modern scares.
- ☐ **Never Sleep Again: The Elm Street Legacy** (2010) - An exhaustive, nearly four-hour documentary on the complete history of the *A Nightmare on Elm Street* franchise.
- ☐ **Ray Harryhausen: Special Effects Titan** (2011) - A tribute to the master of stop-motion animation, Ray Harryhausen, featuring interviews with filmmakers he influenced, such as Steven Spielberg, Peter Jackson, and Guillermo del Toro.
- ☐ **Amicus: House of Horrors** (2012) - This documentary explores the history of Amicus Films, Hammer's main rival in producing Gothic horror and anthology films.
- ☐ **Crystal Lake Memories: the Complete History of Friday the 13ᵗʰ** (2013) - A comprehensive documentary that covers every film in the *Friday the 13th* series, based on the book of the same name.
- ☐ **Smoke and Mirrors: The Story of Tom Savini** (2015) - A retrospective on the life and career of legendary special effects and make-up artist Tom Savini, featuring interviews with many horror creators.
- ☐ **Nightmares in the Makeup Chair** (2018) - A documentary that captures Robert Englund returning to his role as Freddy Krueger for the last time, showing the special effects process and sharing stories from the *Nightmare on Elm Street* series.
- ☐ **Eli Roth's History of Horror** (2018-Present) - A television series on AMC that features interviews with icons like Stephen King, Quentin Tarantino, and Jamie Lee Curtis to explore the biggest themes and subgenres of horror.
- ☐ **Horror Noire: A History of Black Horror** (2019) - This documentary on Shudder explores the history of Black Americans in Hollywood through their connection to the horror genre, featuring interviews with Jordan Peele and Tony Todd.
- ☐ **Leap of Faith: William Friedkin on The Exorcist** (2019) - A cinematic conversation with the director of *The Exorcist*, offering an intimate look into the making of one of the most influential horror films of all time.
- ☐ **In Search of Darkness: A Journey into Iconic '80s Horror** (2019) - An exploration of '80s horror movies through the perspective of the actors, directors, producers and SFX craftspeople who made them, and their impact on contemporary cinema.

- **SEQUELS**
  - ☐ **In Search of Darkness Part II: The Journey into '80s Horror Continues** (2020) - Dives deeper into the practical-effects decade of '80s horror movies with all-new interviews from genre icons and industry experts alongside the original cast.
  - ☐ **In Search of Darkness Part III: The Final Journey Into '80s Horror** (2022) - Conclusion to In Search of Darkness trilogy featuring the straight-to-video horror classics that populated the shelves at the video rental store. Imaginative, gory, experimental and entertaining. These hidden gems are ripe for rediscovery.
  - ☐ **In Search of Darkness: 1990-1994** (2024) - Shifts focus from the '80s to explore the horror movies of the first half of the 1990s. The film aims to re-evaluate the decade, often viewed as a downswing for the genre.
  - ☐ **In Search of Darkness: 1995-1999** (2025) - The upcoming follow-up to the 1990–1994 film will cover the second half of the decade.

☐ **Hail to the Deadites** (2020) - A documentary about the fans of the *Evil Dead* films and explores the classic franchise's undying and ever-growing popularity.

☐ **Cursed Films** (2020-2022) - A Shudder original series that investigates the facts and myths surrounding films rumored to be cursed, including *The Exorcist*, *Poltergeist*, and *The Omen*.

☐ **Woodlands Dark and Days Bewitched: A History of Folk Horror** (2021) - A thorough overview and dissection of the subgenre of 'folk horror, ' with contributions from many of the major creators and clips from cinema all over the world.

☐ **Boris Karloff: The Man Behind the Monster** (2021) - Karloff, examining his illustrious 60-year career in the entertainment industry and his enduring legacy as one of the icons of 20th century popular culture.

☐ **The Found Footage Phenomenon** (2021) - An independent documentary charting the origins of the found footage sub-genre, tracking it through to the technique's current form, and asking what the future is.

☐ **The 101 Scariest Horror Movie Moments of All Time** (2022) - A Shudder series where filmmakers, critics, and actors break down the most terrifying scenes in horror cinema, exploring how they were created and their impact.

☐ **Queer for Fear: the History of Queer Horror** (2022) - A docuseries from Shudder and Bryan Fuller that explores the history of the LGBTQIA+ community's contributions to and relationship with the horror genre.

☐ **Living with Chucky** (2022) - A documentary where filmmaker Kyra Gardner, daughter of special effects artist Tony Gardner, interviews the cast and crew about their experience working on the *Child's Play* movies.

☐ **The Life and Deaths of Christopher Lee** (2024) - Explores the life of the renowned actor, from his early days fighting in World War II to becoming a horror icon with Hammer Film Productions and later a respected character actor in films like *The Lord of the Rings*.

The Future of Horror: Beyond the Shadows We Know

Where We Are Now

Horror has always been a mirror. Sometimes cracked, sometimes blood-smeared, sometimes reflecting back things we'd rather not see. From Gothic ruins to streaming jump-scares, it evolves alongside culture's deepest anxieties. Right now, horror is thriving: art-house prestige (*Hereditary*, *The Witch*), micro-budget hits (*Host*, *Terrifier 2*), global exports (*Train to Busan*, *The Wailing*), and franchise revivals (*Halloween*, *Scream*, *The Conjuring Universe*). But where does it go when every ghost has already haunted and every slasher has already killed?

The answer: it mutates. Horror has never been about novelty of monster, but novelty of *lens*. The future lies in strange mergers, new technologies, and cultural fears that are just beginning to flicker.

Emerging Themes

1. Climate Horror (Eco-Terror Evolved). We've dipped a toe in (*The Bay*, *Gaia*), but as climate collapse accelerates, horror will fully mine ecological dread. Expect "apocalypse slow-burns" where weather itself becomes the monster, or tales of invasive species and mutated landscapes. Imagine *The Thing* but with rising seas and toxic air as the alien.

2. Digital & AI Horror. We've had "killer apps" and haunted Zoom calls, but true AI horror hasn't yet been tapped. Future stories may explore algorithmic possession, where a consciousness seeps into devices across timelines. Expect horror where your digital shadow itself turns predator, or where simulations fracture the line between identity and code. (*Black Mirror* was just the warm-up.)

3. Bio-Horror & Posthuman Dread. Cronenberg opened the door, but CRISPR and biotech are writing new scripts. The next wave may tackle horror of genetic editing gone intimate: families reshaping their children, corporations harvesting organs, AI designing bodies for "optimal" survival. Flesh will mutate not because of aliens, but because *we asked it to*.

4. Cosmic Folk Horror. Folk horror has surged, but its future lies in fusion with cosmic dread. Picture ancient rituals explained through quantum physics, rural cults invoking black holes instead of demons, eldritch myths colliding with modern science. The barn as both altar and portal.

5. Capitalist Surrealism. Satirical horror is moving beyond *Get Out* and *Sorry to Bother You*. Imagine entire corporations as the monster, not metaphorically, but literally. A streaming platform that feeds on viewers. An influencer mansion that consumes its residents. Workplace horror as Kafka meets *The Thing*.

Possible Genre Fusions

- **Rom-Com Horror**: Love stories that unravel into body horror or possession where attraction itself is parasitic.
- **Musical Horror 2.0**: Past attempts (*Repo! The Genetic Opera*) were cult curiosities, but the rise of genre-bending musicals (*Barbie*, *La La Land*) suggests horror-song hybrids could return, with dissonance as terror.
- **Sports Horror**: Untapped territory. Imagine basketball haunted by phantom players, or blood sacrifices on a soccer field. Sports already flirt with ritual, fandom, and violence. Horror is the natural next step.
- **Luxury Horror**: High fashion, fine dining, tech billionaires. Expect more satirical nightmares where wealth itself becomes monstrous (*The Menu*, *Infinity Pool* were only appetizers).

How We'll Watch It

- **Interactive Horror**: VR and AR will make viewers not just audience but victim. Imagine exploring a haunted house where you can't tell if the whisper came from the headset or the room you're in.
- **Algorithm-Driven Horror**: Netflix and AI-powered platforms could generate bespoke scares. A haunted house that knows your phobias, a slasher who calls you by name. Terrifying because the horror is uniquely yours.
- **Global Streaming Collisions**: Horror will no longer be dominated by Hollywood. Expect genre leaders from Korea, Indonesia, Nigeria, and Latin America to redefine scares for the next century.

The Next Monsters

- **The Corpse of Nostalgia**: Revivals and remakes aren't slowing, but the backlash may become the horror itself. Stories where characters are literally trapped in endless reboots.
- **The Invisible Algorithm**: Hauntings framed not by ghosts but by metrics. What if your life's worth is dictated by likes, and the penalty for failure isn't social, but mortal?
- **The AI Child / Partner / Doppelgänger**: Not a killer robot, but the horror of intimacy with something almost human. Expect tenderness laced with revulsion.

Legacy of Fear

Horror thrives because it adapts. The Gothic was about God, the slasher about suburbia, found footage about media, prestige horror about trauma. The next era will be about systems bigger than us: climate, code, capital and the tiny cracks where humanity either survives or dissolves.

As Guillermo del Toro once said: *"Horror is a rehearsal for death."* The future of horror is a rehearsal for futures we don't yet understand. Futures where the monsters are not in castles or closets, but in the data, the air, the body, and the system itself.

The Tour of Terror

There comes a moment, for every devoted acolyte of horror, when the screen no longer suffices. The grain of old film and the flicker of shadow cease to contain the appetite for terror, and one begins to crave the real geography of the macabre: the places where horror was born, filmed, or rumored to breathe still.

This is not a sightseeing tour. It is a pilgrimage. A journey through cinematic ghosts, cursed architecture, and landscapes forever haunted by what they once pretended to be.

To the horror connoisseur, these sites are not mere curiosities, they are sacred texts carved in brick and bone. The creaking staircases of abandoned hotels. The misted lakes that swallowed fictional victims. The corridors where blood once flowed through the veins of story or the rumor of something older.

Each destination carries its own ritual: a photograph at the Psycho house; a quiet pause at Georgetown's exorcist stairs; a night at the Stanley Hotel, where guests still whisper about Room 217. Around the world, castles, graveyards, forests, and motels have transformed from sets into shrines, forming a dark map of cinema's underworld.

The Tour of Horror is that map. It traces the living architecture of fear, where celluloid met the real world and left a scar. What follows is a journey for those who seek immersion over comfort, who understand that true horror never dies; it simply changes its address.

I. America — Haunted Hollywood & Suburban Nightmares
The Psycho House[39] — Universal Studios, California

Legacy & Lore: Perched on a lonely hill of the Universal backlot, the *Psycho* house remains one of horror's most enduring silhouettes. A Victorian skeleton against the Californian sun, looming over the hillside. Built in 1959 for Alfred Hitchcock's masterpiece, it was designed to suggest menace even in daylight. Its angles are wrong, its windows too human. From certain distances, it seems to watch.

Location & Access: The façade still stands at Universal Studios Hollywood and can be visited via the *Studio Tour*, which passes directly by Bates Motel and Norman's infamous house. The site is not open for self-guided exploration, but the tram lingers long enough for photographs.

Best Time to Visit: Go near dusk, when the light fractures into gold and shadow across the motel sign. Autumn weekdays bring thinner crowds, and the park's *Halloween Horror Nights* often resurrect Norman for guests who linger after dark.

Tours & Events: Universal's *Horror Nights* offers themed mazes inspired by Hitchcock, and occasionally a live "Norman Bates" greets trams. Knife in hand, smile too wide.

Haunted Hotel Nearby: Stay at the *Beverly Garland Hotel* in North Hollywood, a mid-century retreat often rumored to harbor residual energy from the era's golden age of thrillers, and just minutes from the Universal gates. Chic, retro, and eerily still at midnight.

---

39 "The set of the 1960 Hitchcock's movie Psycho at the Universal Studios Hollywood, California, USA" Diego Delso (https://www.wikidata.org/wiki/Q28147777, Creative Commons Attribution-Share Alike 4.0)

Camp Crystal Lake — Blairstown, New Jersey

Legacy & Lore: The quiet woods around Blairstown conceal the birthplace of the modern slasher. In 1980, *Friday the 13th* turned Camp No-Be-Bo-Sco, a functioning Boy Scout camp, into the cursed Camp Crystal Lake. The film's low-budget dread became legend; Jason's maskless debut would spawn decades of sequels and pilgrimages.

Location & Access: Camp No-Be-Bo-Sco remains private at 11 Sand Pond Rd, Hardwick Township, NJ 07825, but each year it opens for limited *Crystal Lake Tours*. Tickets sell out within hours, with proceeds supporting the Scouts. Visitors are escorted through original filming sites: the cabins, the docks, the forest paths where cinematic teenagers met their doom.

Best Time to Visit: Spring and fall, when mist coils over the lake and the surrounding Delaware Water Gap bursts with color.

Tours & Events: The *Crystal Lake Tours* team hosts overnight experiences with screenings, photo ops, and campfire Q&As. Hardcore fans can even book the "Final Chapter" package, which ends with a night beside the lake itself. $150–$175, includes memorabilia and a guided walk through filming spots.

Haunted Hotel Nearby: The *Water Gap Country Inn*, just across the state border in Pennsylvania, dates back to the early 1900s and is whispered to have its own ghosts. Footsteps echoing in unused corridors, laughter from the old ballroom. *The Inn at Millrace Pond* — 18th-century inn with creaking floors and colonial ghosts, perfect for fans seeking atmosphere.

The Myers House[40] — South Pasadena, California

Legacy & Lore: A plain white two-story house, yet one of the most feared addresses in American horror. Fans can still visit Laurie Strode's house on Oxley Street and the infamous hedge where Michael lurked. *Halloween* (1978) transformed this modest home into the birthplace of the slasher archetype. What made it terrifying was its ordinariness: evil not in castles, but in cul-de-sacs. Though Michael Myers' hometown is fictional Illinois, nearly all *Halloween* (1978) was shot in South Pasadena.

Location & Access: Located at 1000 Mission Street, South Pasadena, CA, the original structure was moved slightly from its film position but preserved intact. Visitors are welcome to photograph from outside; local ordinances prohibit interior tours.

Best Time to Visit: October, of course. South Pasadena celebrates *Halloween* each year with neighborhood screenings and themed photo stations. Visit early morning or at twilight for the best light and fewest tourists.

Tours & Events: Nearby *SugarMynt Gallery* hosts annual *Haddonfield Halloween* exhibitions with film props, Michael Myers masks, and Q&A nights with cast members. Self-guided *Halloween Movie Map* tours online.

Haunted Hotel Nearby: The *Biltmore Hotel* in downtown Los Angeles used in countless thrillers and rumored to be haunted by the spirit of the "Black Dahlia." It's the perfect base for a citywide horror itinerary. *The Bissell House Bed & Breakfast* — a Victorian property rumored to have its own resident watcher.

The Myers House (North Carolina Replica)

Legacy & Lore: If you are near North Carolina, a life-size replica of the *Halloween* house stands in Hillsborough, North Carolina, built by a fan named Kenny Caperton. It serves as both personal residence and museum, hosting screenings and horror nights.

Location & Access: Private home; limited public events.

Best Time to Visit: Halloween weekend.

Tours & Events: Annual *Halloween Bash* with film screenings and charity raffles.

Haunted Hotel Nearby: *The Colonial Inn* — haunted by 19th-century soldiers, blending Southern Gothic and slasher devotion.

---

[40] "The Century House aka Halloween House, South Pasadena, CA" Jeremy Thompson, Creative Commons Attribution 2.0

The Amityville House[41] — Long Island, New York

Legacy & Lore: At 108 Ocean Avenue, Amityville, New York, on Long Island, stands one of America's most controversial haunted houses. Part crime scene, part cinematic myth. After the 1974 DeFeo murders, the Lutz family's 28-day ordeal inspired *The Amityville Horror* (1979) and a franchise that blurred journalism and possession.

Location & Access: The house remains a private residence, its iconic quarter-moon windows replaced to deter gawkers. Out of respect, visitors should not trespass, but many photograph from the public street. 108 Ocean Avenue, Amityville, New York, on Long Island.

Best Time to Visit: Autumn, when Long Island's leaves burn red and the air carries the chill of coastal fog.

Tours & Events: The *Amityville Historical Society* offers nearby walking tours covering local lore and the broader history of the area, separating film fiction from grim fact.

Haunted Hotel Nearby: The *Oheka Castle* in Huntington, roughly thirty minutes away, has its own ghost stories and grand Gothic air. Once a retreat for the Roaring Twenties elite, now a hotel fit for haunted luxury.

The Texas Chainsaw House[42] — Kingsland, Texas

Legacy & Lore: Built in 1909, this modest Victorian farmhouse became the slaughterhouse of nightmares in *The Texas Chain Saw Massacre* (1974). Director Tobe Hooper's handheld chaos turned rural Texas into an apocalyptic dining room.

Location & Access: The house was relocated from its original La Frontera Road site to Kingsland and restored as part of the *Grand Central Café*. Guests can dine where Leatherface once lived. 1010 King Ct, Kingsland, TX.

Best Time to Visit: Late autumn and winter offer cooler weather for Hill Country travel.

Tours & Events: The restaurant occasionally hosts themed dinners and fan gatherings, especially around Halloween. Staff indulge visitors' curiosity but remind them that no chainsaws are kept on premises.

Haunted Hotel Nearby: Stay at the *Driskill Hotel* in Austin, Texas's most famous haunt, known for phantom children, vanished brides, and corridors that echo with the Old South's aftertaste.

The Exorcist Stairs[43] — Georgetown, Washington, D.C.

Legacy & Lore: Seventy-five stone steps descend between Prospect and M Streets. The path Father Karras tumbled down in *The Exorcist* (1973). Fans and locals alike call it "holy ground."

Location & Access: The stairs are public, located beside the Car Barn building. A commemorative plaque was added in 2019.

Best Time to Visit: Twilight or nightfall, when the lamps ignite a yellow haze over the Potomac.

Tours & Events: The *Georgetown Walking Tour* often ends here, pairing true Washington history with horror lore. Every Halloween, locals host small vigils with film screenings nearby.

Haunted Hotel Nearby: The *Hay-Adams Hotel*, overlooking the White House, harbors the ghost of Clover Adams, who took her life there in 1885. Guests claim she still lingers, opening doors and humming softly.

---

[41] "112 Ocean Avenue in February 2010" Doug Kerr (Creative Commons Attribution-Share Alike 2.0)

[42] "Chain Saw Massacre House3" Austex (https://en.wikipedia.org/wiki/User:Austex) Creative Commons Attribution-Share Alike 3.0

[43] "Exorcist Stairs" Dmitry K (https://www.flickr.com/people/64772693@N00, Creative Commons Attribution 2.0)

Elm Street House — Los Angeles, California

Legacy & Lore: Wes Craven's *A Nightmare on Elm Street* (1984) was filmed at 1428 North Genesee Avenue, West Hollywood, a quiet, leafy street concealing Freddy Krueger's cinematic birthplace.

Location & Access: Private property; respectful viewing only. Nearby, the "Thompson house" from the same film is visible across the street.

Best Time to Visit: Late afternoon for soft light and minimal traffic.

Tours & Events: LA's *Dearly Departed Tours* occasionally includes Elm Street in its "Horror Filming Locations" route.

Haunted Hotel Nearby: The *Hollywood Roosevelt Hotel* opened in 1927, rumored to host the ghost of Marilyn Monroe and other spectral starlets of old Hollywood. *The Cecil Hotel* infamous real-life horror inspiration just blocks away.

The Winchester Mystery House[44] — San Jose, California

Legacy & Lore: A labyrinth built by grief and guilt. Heiress Sarah Winchester believed she was haunted by the spirits of those killed by the Winchester rifle. To appease them, she built endlessly. Stairs to nowhere, doors that open into voids, windows within floors. *Winchester* (2018) dramatized her obsession, but the house's true horror is architectural madness itself.

Location & Access: Open daily for tours. Both daytime historical tours and nighttime candlelight versions are offered. 525 S. Winchester Blvd, San Jose, CA.

Best Time to Visit: Autumn or winter, when the fog lingers over the Santa Clara Valley.

Tours & Events: Halloween brings the *Unhinged* immersive haunted experience. The house also hosts seances and themed dinners throughout the year.

Haunted Hotel Nearby: The *Hotel De Anza* in downtown San Jose. Art Deco beauty with a reputation for spectral residents and vintage glamour.

Sleepy Hollow — Tarrytown, New York

Legacy & Lore: Washington Irving's 1820 tale gave America its first enduring ghost: the Headless Horseman. Centuries later, Tim Burton's *Sleepy Hollow* (1999) transformed the legend into baroque cinema. The town still lives under its mythic shadow.

Location & Access: An hour north of Manhattan in the Hudson Valley. The Old Dutch Church and adjacent burying ground are open for tours.

Best Time to Visit: October. The entire town becomes an autumnal stage set.

Tours & Events: *The Great Jack O'Lantern Blaze* illuminates 7,000 carved pumpkins each fall, and *Horseman's Hollow* offers haunted walking trails through the cemetery.

Haunted Hotel Nearby: *Tarrytown House Estate*, a historic mansion overlooking the Hudson, hosts themed Halloween weekends and is rumored to shelter more than one resident spirit.

Salem — Massachusetts

Legacy & Lore: The witch trials of 1692 were horror before horror had a name. Salem's tragedy gave rise to centuries of storytelling from *The Crucible* to *Hocus Pocus* to Rob Zombie's *The Lords of Salem*. The entire town is a living museum of hysteria and myth. The city has leaned into its image, blending history with humor. The *Ropes Mansion* and Old Burial Hill appear in the film, while actual trial sites still host candlelit memorials.

Location & Access: Easily reachable from Boston by car or commuter rail. The town's historical district is walkable, lined with preserved 17th-century homes.

Best Time to Visit: October, when Salem transforms into an open-air festival of witchcraft and remembrance.

Tours & Events: The *Salem Witch Museum, House of the Seven Gables*, and nightly *Ghosts of Salem Tour* are essential. Each October, the *Salem Horror Fest* brings independent filmmakers and panels on horror, feminism, and folklore. *Haunted Happenings Festival* (October); *Witch City Walking Tours* year-round.

Haunted Hotel Nearby: *The Hawthorne Hotel* (built 1925) considered one of the most haunted in America. Guests report moving furniture, flickering lights, and phantom perfume. Once used as a set for *Bewitched* (1970).

---

44 "Winchester Mystery House 2023-07-17 02" The wub (https://commons.wikimedia.org/wiki/User:The_wub, Creative Commons Attribution-Share Alike 4.0)

The Lizzie Borden House[45] — Fall River, Massachusetts

Legacy & Lore: "Lizzie Borden took an axe…" begins the nursery rhyme born from this brutal 1892 double murder. The house became a true-crime landmark and one of America's most interactive haunts.

Location & Access: Now a fully operational bed-and-breakfast and museum at 230 Second St, Fall River, MA.

Best Time to Visit: Year-round, but the anniversary of the murders (August 4) draws the devoted.

Tours & Events: Guests can stay in Lizzie's room or that of her slain parents. Themed seances, murder reenactments, and midnight ghost hunts are offered weekly.

Haunted Hotel Nearby: Stay put. Breakfast is served where the bodies were found.

The Mütter Museum — Philadelphia, Pennsylvania

Legacy & Lore: A cathedral of the macabre rather than a haunt, this medical museum of anatomical oddities channels the body horror of Cronenberg decades before his birth. Preserved skulls, wax tumors, conjoined twins, a museum of mortality that belongs in every horror pilgrim's itinerary.

Location & Access: Open daily, operated by The College of Physicians of Philadelphia at 19 S. 22nd St, Philadelphia, PA.

Best Time to Visit: Weekdays before noon for quiet reflection.

Tours & Events: Special exhibits rotate frequently; Halloween brings *After Hours* candlelit evenings.

Haunted Hotel Nearby: *The Bellevue Hotel*, a Gilded Age masterpiece two miles away, has its own spectral rumors, mostly of music playing in empty ballrooms.

The LaLaurie Mansion — New Orleans, Louisiana

Legacy & Lore: Perhaps America's most infamous haunted residence. Madame Delphine LaLaurie's atrocities against enslaved people in the 1830s turned this elegant French Quarter mansion into a legend of cruelty and vengeance. It appeared in *American Horror Story: Coven* and countless ghost documentaries.

Location & Access: Private residence at 1140 Royal Street. Exterior viewing only.

Best Time to Visit: Nighttime walking tours capture its atmosphere best, especially in the humid glow of the Quarter.

Tours & Events: Companies like *Haunted History Tours* and *French Quarter Phantoms* include the mansion on their "Ghosts and Legends" circuits.

Haunted Hotel Nearby: *The Hotel Monteleone*, also in the Quarter, is a literary landmark and paranormal hotspot. Guests have witnessed spectral children playing in the halls.

Cinematic Outliers Worth Pilgrimage
- **The House of Usher (set model)** – Universal archives occasionally display Corman's Gothic sets for tours.
- **Monroeville Mall, Pennsylvania** – Site of *Dawn of the Dead (1978)*; hosts annual *Living Dead Weekend*. 200 Mall Cir Dr, Monroeville, PA.
- **Bonaventure Cemetery, Savannah, Georgia** – Featured in *Midnight in the Garden of Good and Evil*, now a Southern Gothic touchstone. 330 Bonaventure Rd, Savannah, GA.
- **The Villisca Axe Murder House, Iowa** – Open for overnight stays; poltergeist activity frequently recorded. 508 E 2nd St, Villisca, IA.

Film Pilgrimage Notes (for the American Leg)
To tour America's horror heritage is to traverse the nation's contradictions: its innocence and brutality, its optimism and decay. Travelers seeking the full cinematic experience should plan their route seasonally: New England for autumn leaves and witch-trial skies, California for year-round access to studios and suburban horror homes, and the Southwest for eerie desolation. Many sites are private; always photograph respectfully. Seek out local ghost tours, they are the oral historians of the genre, keeping legends alive between screenings. Each site blurs the line between fiction and haunting until one wonders which came first, the story or the spirit.

---

[45] "Lizzie Borden House (Bed Breakfast) (3535957840)" dbking (flickr.com/photos/65193799@N00, Creative Commons Attribution 2.0)

II. Europe — Castles, Crypts, and Cult Classics

Europe is the ancestral home of horror, where superstition predates cinema, and every fog-shrouded alley or crumbling keep seems to hum with the memory of something unspeakable. From Transylvania's mountains to London's catacombs, this is not just where horror was filmed, it's where it was born. Each site carries the scent of old stories: candle smoke, damp stone, and the echo of a language no longer spoken by the living.

Bran Castle[46] — Transylvania, Romania

Legacy & Lore: High above the town of Bran, a fortress pierces the Carpathian mist, the so-called "Castle Dracula." Though historically linked only loosely to Vlad the Impaler, its towers and turrets became the iconographic stand-in for Stoker's fictional keep. The walls drip with both myth and marketing, yet the setting remains eerily convincing. Bran Castle was not a direct inspiration but became associated with the novel over time. Its medieval spires and mountain mists made it horror's first global landmark. The castle now embraces its legend with torchlit tours and vampire balls.

Location & Access: Near Braşov, central Romania. Strada General Traian Moşoiu 24, Bran 507025, Romania. Open daily, with guided tours available in multiple languages.

Best Time to Visit: October, when fog curls around the battlements and bats appear at dusk. No other dates compare.

Tours & Events: The castle hosts an annual *Halloween at Dracula's Castle* masquerade, complete with torchlit processions and midnight feasts in the courtyard.

Haunted Hotel Nearby: *Teleferic Grand Hotel* in Poiana Braşov: luxurious mountain retreat, occasionally beset by unexplained whispers in empty corridors after stormy nights. *Count Kalnoky's Guesthouse*, in nearby Micloşoara: run by descendants of Transylvanian nobility.

Whitby Abbey — North Yorkshire, England

Legacy & Lore: Bram Stoker stood here in 1890, staring at the skeletal remains of this 7th-century abbey and imagining Dracula's ship crashing into the nearby shore. Whitby's ruined arches are the very birthplace of Gothic atmosphere.

Location & Access: Overlooking the North Sea on England's northeast coast. Operated by English Heritage; open daily.

Best Time to Visit: Spring and fall, when the wind off the sea howls like the undead.

Tours & Events: Twice yearly, Whitby hosts the *Goth Weekend*, a pilgrimage for black-clad devotees who fill the town's pubs with velvet, lace, and reverent excess.

Haunted Hotel Nearby: *Bagdale Hall Hotel*, a Tudor manor rumored to host a spectral chambermaid forever making beds that were never unmade.

Highgate Cemetery — London, England

Legacy & Lore: No single graveyard has influenced horror cinema more profoundly. Its Victorian angels, choked in ivy, became the visual language of death itself. In the 1970s, it was the site of the so-called *Highgate Vampire* panic. Tabloid hysteria that fed directly into Hammer Horror's final gasp.

Location & Access: Divided into East and West cemeteries; guided tours required for the West. Swain's Ln, London N6 6PJ, UK.

Best Time to Visit: Late afternoon for haunting light through Gothic foliage.

Tours & Events: *Friends of Highgate Cemetery* conduct historical and literary tours. Private photography sessions can be booked for filmmakers and academics.

Haunted Hotel Nearby: *The Langham Hotel*, London, frequently cited as England's most haunted, with room 333 supposedly occupied by a Victorian suicide who still turns up in mirrors.

Château d'Orava[47] — Oravský Podzámok, Slovakia

Legacy & Lore: A jagged miracle of medieval engineering, Orava Castle clings to a 400-foot cliff and to cinematic immortality. F.W. Murnau's *Nosferatu* (1922) used this fortress as Count Orlok's lair, birthing the entire vampire film tradition.

Location & Access: Accessible from the town of Dolný Kubín. Guided tours offered daily April–October. hrad 1, 027 41 Oravský Podzámok, Slovakia.

Best Time to Visit: Summer for ease of travel; autumn for the full Gothic spectacle.

Tours & Events: Annual *Nosferatu Nights* screenings are held within the castle's courtyard, complete with silent-film orchestras.

Haunted Hotel Nearby: *Hotel Hviezdoslav* in nearby Kežmarok, baroque charm with a history of unexplained drafts and spectral piano music in the salon.

The Paris Catacombs — Paris, France

Legacy & Lore: Beneath the City of Light lies a city of bones. The Catacombs hold the remains of six million Parisians, stacked in endless walls of skulls. Films like *As Above, So Below* (2014) turned these ossuaries into literal gateways to Hell, but reality is no less suffocating.

Location & Access: Entrance at Place Denfert-Rochereau; timed tickets required. 1 Av. du Colonel Henri Rol-Tanguy, 75014 Paris, France.

Best Time to Visit: Weekdays before noon. Avoid midsummer when queues stretch for hours.

Tours & Events: Official routes cover 1.5 km of tunnels, but hidden chambers extend far beyond — strictly off limits. The annual *Catacombs by Candlelight* event offers rare nighttime access.

Haunted Hotel Nearby: *Hotel du Vieux Paris* — intimate, candlelit, and often described as having "a presence" that stands beside the bed.

The Wicker Man Locations — Dumfries & Galloway, Scotland

Legacy & Lore: The 1973 cult masterpiece *The Wicker Man* filmed across remote Scottish villages, their windswept isolation essential to its pagan dread. Though the giant effigy was burned, its ashes remain part of cinematic folklore.

Location & Access: Key sites include St. Ninian's Cave, Culzean Castle, and the harbor of Kirkcudbright. Accessible by bridge from the mainland.

Best Time to Visit: Late summer, near Lammas, when locals still honor the harvest with small fires.

Tours & Events: Fan-run *Wicker Man Pilgrimages* retrace the film's shooting locations annually, concluding with a candlelit toast to "the crops." *The Wicker Man Trail* connects filming villages with local folklore stops.

Haunted Hotel Nearby: *Culzean Castle* offers overnight stays; guests report ghostly bagpipes echoing through the coastal wind. *Kinloch Lodge*, Skye — candlelit and ancient, its owner claims the spirits are polite.

Prague's Old Jewish Cemetery — Prague, Czech Republic

Legacy & Lore: Burial ground of legends. Layer upon layer of graves: 12,000 visible, perhaps 100,000 beneath inspired the myth of the Golem. The 1920 silent film *Der Golem* was shot nearby, sealing Prague's status as the cradle of mystical horror.

Location & Access: Located in Josefov, the city's Jewish Quarter. Entry included in the Jewish Museum ticket.

Best Time to Visit: Autumn, under overcast skies.

Tours & Events: The museum occasionally screens *Der Golem* with live accompaniment within the old synagogue, an unforgettable echo chamber.

Haunted Hotel Nearby: *Hotel Paris Prague* — Art Nouveau masterpiece where guests have reported phantom footsteps pacing past locked doors.

Poenari Fortress — Arefu, Romania

Legacy & Lore: If Bran is myth, Poenari is fact. Vlad the Impaler's true stronghold sits in ruins above the Argeş River, reachable only by 1,480 steep stone steps. Few visitors make the climb, those who do swear they feel watched.

Location & Access: Two and a half hours from Bucharest. Transfăgărăşan, Arefu 117040, Romania

Best Time to Visit: Early morning or late afternoon for mountain light and solitude.

Tours & Events: Local guides host the *Vlad Tepes Experience*, a grueling hike culminating in a candlelit picnic within the ruins.

Haunted Hotel Nearby: *Hotel Dracula*, Curtea de Argeş — kitsch meets uncanny, featuring a bar shaped like a crypt.

Castle Frankenstein[48] — Darmstadt, Germany

Legacy & Lore: Yes, there truly is one. Built in the 13th century, the castle near Darmstadt predates Mary Shelley's novel by centuries, yet local legend speaks of an alchemist named Konrad Dippel whose experiments with corpses may have inspired *Frankenstein*.

Location & Access: Open year-round; 40 minutes from Frankfurt.

Best Time to Visit: October, when the annual *Burg Frankenstein Halloween Festival* transforms the ruins into a living Gothic carnival.

Tours & Events: The festival includes costumed processions, fire shows, and theatrical recreations of Dippel's experiments.

Haunted Hotel Nearby: *Hotel-Restaurant Burgschänke* sits at the base of the hill, and staff whisper about phantom clanking echoing down from the battlements after closing.

The Reichenbach Falls — Meiringen, Switzerland

Legacy & Lore: While known as the site of Sherlock Holmes's fictional death, these falls later became shorthand for Gothic fatalism. The cliffs' stark majesty influenced early horror cinematography seen in *Nosferatu*'s mountain imagery and countless Euro-horror finales.

Location & Access: Accessible by funicular from Meiringen village. Reichenbach, 3860 Meiringen, Switzerland.

Best Time to Visit: Spring snowmelt swells the torrent into sublime violence.

Tours & Events: Annual *Reichenbach Reenactment Day* celebrates literature's most famous plunge.

Haunted Hotel Nearby: *Hotel Rebstock*, 18th century, where several guests claim to hear falling water inside their rooms long after the funicular closes.

The Island of Poveglia[49] — Venetian Lagoon, Italy

Legacy & Lore: Known as "the world's most haunted island." Once a quarantine zone, later an asylum, now abandoned, though rumored to be cursed. While rarely depicted on film directly, its aura haunts Italian horror's obsession with decay and madness.

Location & Access: Technically off-limits; reachable only by private boat and permit. Small island between Venice and Lido in the Venetian Lagoon.

Best Time to Visit: Dusk, if you dare, though few captains agree to dock.

Tours & Events: Unofficial night tours can sometimes be arranged through Venice's paranormal guides. Proceed at your own peril.

Haunted Hotel Nearby: *Hotel Danieli* in Venice — its baroque corridors have been linked to whispers and sudden chills; it served as the model for countless haunted palazzos on film.

The Catacombs of Rome — Appian Way, Italy

Legacy & Lore: Long before Paris, Rome's underground labyrinths stored its dead: early Christians, martyrs, and anonymous bones that inspired generations of ecclesiastical horror from *The Church* (1989) to *The Nun* (2018).
Location & Access: Catacombs of San Sebastiano and San Callisto are open to the public via guided tour. Via Appia Antica, 110/126, 00179 Roma RM, Italy.
Best Time to Visit: Mornings before noon; cool, quiet, and reverent.
Tours & Events: Seasonal night tours explore the iconography of death and resurrection.
Haunted Hotel Nearby: *Hotel Aventino*, elegant and eerily tranquil, overlooking the same ancient road that leads underground.

The Black Forest — Baden-Württemberg, Germany

Legacy & Lore: Fairy tales were horror before horror wore fangs. The dense, ancient Black Forest birthed the Brothers Grimm. The genesis of all European dark fantasy. It later served as visual inspiration for *The Company of Wolves* and *Gretel & Hansel*.
Location & Access: Southwest Germany, near Freiburg and Triberg.
Best Time to Visit: Autumn, when the canopy burns gold and the fog thickens.
Tours & Events: Folklore trails like the *Grimm Path* and local storytelling festivals celebrate the forest's macabre heritage.
Haunted Hotel Nearby: *Hotel Schloss Hornberg*, an actual castle with panoramic views and periodic reports of singing heard from the forest below.

Moosham Castle[50] — Salzburg, Austria

Legacy & Lore: Built in the 13th century, Moosham was once infamous for its witch trials. Known as the "Witches' Castle," it later appeared in *The Vampire Lovers* and inspired Hammer's gothic European aesthetic.
Location & Access: About an hour south of Salzburg; open May through October. Moosham 12, 5585 Unternberg, Austria.
Best Time to Visit: Late summer, when its stone halls trap the last heat before winter.
Tours & Events: Guided tours emphasize the witch trials and eerie paintings in the chapel.
Haunted Hotel Nearby: *Hotel Schloss Mönchstein*, also in Salzburg — opulent, yet its mirrors reportedly fog from within.

Leap Castle — Offaly, Ireland

Legacy & Lore: Perhaps Ireland's most haunted home. Built in the 15th century, it witnessed centuries of betrayal, imprisonment, and massacre. Its "Bloody Chapel" houses the remains of those thrown into its oubliette. Featured on *Ghost Hunters International* and *Most Haunted*.
Location & Access: Privately owned; tours available by appointment. EIRCODE ? R421, Leap, Roscrea, Co. Offaly, Ireland.
Best Time to Visit: Overcast winter afternoons, when crows circle the battlements.
Tours & Events: The owner, musician Sean Ryan, conducts personal tours and occasional music sessions among the bones.
Haunted Hotel Nearby: *Kinnitty Castle Hotel* — opulent and genuinely haunted, with numerous reports of disembodied whispers and cold spots.

Predjama Castle[51] — Postojna, Slovenia

Legacy & Lore: Built into a cliff face, half fortress, half cave. Once home to the rebellious knight Erasmus Lueger, who was killed while eating dinner by a cannonball. He's said to still haunt the dining hall. Its otherworldly architecture has appeared in several Eastern European thrillers.

Location & Access: Near Postojna Cave Park; open daily. Predjama 1, 6230 Predjama, Slovenia.

Best Time to Visit: Spring or autumn to avoid summer crowds.

Tours & Events: Combined cave-and-castle tours explore its hidden passageways.

Haunted Hotel Nearby: *Hotel Jama*, adjacent to the caves, claims to have rooms where the temperature drops abruptly, even in midsummer.

Film Pilgrimage Notes (European Leg)

Europe's horror geography rewards patience. Castles often close for restoration; cemeteries demand reverence. Travel off-season for silence. Winter and early spring veil these places in natural gloom. Always dress for stone and weather, and never underestimate the power of solitude: the true haunt of Europe lies not in its ghosts but in the echo of your own footsteps.

III. Asia & the Pacific — Spirits, Legends, and Shadows

Asia's horror is older than religion and more intimate than death. It breathes through ritual, architecture, and urban myth. A ghost in every mirror, a whisper in every tree. To travel through Asia's horror landscape is to enter worlds where the line between the living and the dead was never meant to be clear.

Aokigahara Forest — Mount Fuji, Japan

Legacy & Lore: At the foot of Mount Fuji spreads Aokigahara, the Sea of Trees, one of the quietest places on Earth. Its dense canopy blocks wind and sound, making even footsteps feel blasphemous. Known as a site of both myth and tragedy, it's inspired countless Japanese horror works and Western films like *The Forest* (2016).

Location & Access: Accessible via bus or car from Tokyo; trailheads near the Saiko Lake region.

Best Time to Visit: Winter or early spring, before foliage thickens and compasses lose signal.

Tours & Events: Guided treks by local ecologists focus on geology and preservation; unofficial "ghost tours" are discouraged for ethical reasons.

Haunted Hotel Nearby: *Hotel Mystays Fuji Onsen Resort* — sleek and modern, yet guests often speak of hearing forest wind long after their windows are closed.

Old Changi Hospital[52] — Singapore

Legacy & Lore: Built in 1935 and occupied by Japanese forces during World War II, Old Changi Hospital remains one of Asia's most feared places. Torture, experiments, and death are rumored to echo in its empty wards. It became both set and subject in *Haunted Changi* (2010), a found-footage film that blurred fiction and documentary.

Location & Access: Upper Changi Road North. Officially closed; fenced and guarded. 2 Simei St 3, Singapore 529889

Best Time to Visit: There is no "safe" time. Visits are technically off-limits. View from public roads or join sanctioned heritage walks.

---

[51] "Predjama Castle, Slovenia, 20240502 0831 7409" Jakub Hałun (https://commons.wikimedia.org/wiki/User:Jakubhal, Creative Commons Attribution 4.0)

[52] "Changi Hospital" Lajmmoore (https://commons.wikimedia.org/wiki/User:Lajmmoore, Creative Commons Attribution-Share Alike 4.0)

Tours & Events: *Asia Paranormal Investigators* occasionally host perimeter tours during the Ghost Month (August–September).

Haunted Hotel Nearby: *The Fullerton Hotel*, a colonial-era icon downtown, has its own wartime spirits. Soldiers and nurses seen wandering the mezzanine.

The Quarantine Station — Manly, Sydney, Australia

Legacy & Lore: Overlooking Sydney Harbour, this 19th-century quarantine complex processed thousands of immigrants during smallpox and plague outbreaks. Many never left. *The Quarantine Station* is now both hotel and living museum, and one of Australia's most credible haunting sites.

Location & Access: 30 minutes from Sydney by ferry; within Sydney Harbour National Park. North Head Quarantine Station, Sydney, NSW 2095, Australia.

Best Time to Visit: Autumn (March–May), when the weather cools and the sea mist lingers.

Tours & Events: Daily history tours; nightly *Ghostly Encounters* walks using EMF devices and storytelling.

Haunted Hotel Nearby: You can stay on-site. Rooms converted from old isolation wards. Guests often report the scent of hospital disinfectant at midnight.

Kuchisake-onna's Urban Trail — Tokyo, Japan

Legacy & Lore: The "Slit-Mouthed Woman," Japan's most infamous urban legend, supposedly haunts alleys near Shinjuku and Setagaya. Her story, a vengeful spirit asking, "Am I beautiful?" has inspired films like *Carved: The Slit-Mouthed Woman* (2007).

Location & Access: Urban legend territory, not fixed geography, but small Shinto shrines in Setagaya honor her myth with offerings.

Best Time to Visit: Evening, when lanterns flicker and Tokyo's hum softens.

Tours & Events: Folklore-focused night walks led by scholars of *kaidan* (ghost stories) trace her evolution from myth to media.

Haunted Hotel Nearby: *Hotel Gracery Shinjuku*, topped by a giant Godzilla head, playful yet somehow protective.

Bangkok's Sathorn Unique Tower — Thailand

Legacy & Lore: Abandoned mid-construction after the 1997 financial crash, this 49-story skyscraper became a symbol of urban decay and of Thai ghost belief. Locals say the unfinished tower trapped wandering souls. The horror film *The Promise* (2017) turned that superstition into cinematic tragedy.

Location & Access: Sathorn District, central Bangkok; entry officially prohibited but visible from the river.

Best Time to Visit: Sunset, when the skyline ignites behind its skeletal frame.

Tours & Events: Photography tours from adjacent rooftops; some local guides offer exterior night walks.

Haunted Hotel Nearby: *Mandarin Oriental Bangkok* — elegance haunted by history, not horror; Graham Greene wrote there of "tropical fever dreams."

Oiwa Shrine[53] — Tokyo, Japan

Legacy & Lore: Dedicated to Oiwa, the betrayed wife whose ghost inspired *Yotsuya Kaidan* (1825), Japan's most famous revenge tale. Her story birthed *The Grudge*, *Ringu*, and the archetype of the long-haired spirit woman.

Location & Access: In Yotsuya district; open to the public. 752 Irishikenchō, Hitachi, Ibaraki 311-0402, Japan.

Best Time to Visit: Summer's Obon season, when families honor their dead.

Tours & Events: Visitors bring offerings to seek Oiwa's forgiveness before performing her story on stage. A superstition observed by Japanese filmmakers to this day.

Haunted Hotel Nearby: *Park Hyatt Tokyo* — serene, minimalist, and towering; the kind of place where a ghost could drift unnoticed among the clouds.

---

53 "Oiwa Shrine (51847441284) Raita Futo from Tokyo, Japan (https://www.flickr.com/people/128275472@N07<, Creative Commons Attribution 2.0)

Lawang Sewu — Semarang, Indonesia

Legacy & Lore: Meaning "A Thousand Doors," this Dutch colonial building was used as a Japanese military base during World War II. Its basement, once a torture chamber, is said to house restless souls. The 2007 film *Lawang Sewu: Dendam Kuntilanak* transformed its real darkness into cinematic myth.

Location & Access: Central Semarang, open to the public as a historical landmark. Jl. Pemuda No.160, Semarang 50132 Indonesia.

Best Time to Visit: Twilight, when sunlight fractures through the stained-glass windows into corridors that seem to breathe.

Tours & Events: Daily heritage tours, plus occasional nighttime ghost events hosted by local paranormal researchers.

Haunted Hotel Nearby: *Hotel Ciputra Semarang* — modern comfort near an ancient haunting; several staff members refuse to clean rooms alone after dark.

Tuen Mun Road Ghost Curve — Hong Kong

Legacy & Lore: A seemingly cursed stretch of highway infamous for fatal accidents and apparitions. Local legends claim spirits from nearby cemeteries appear in drivers' lanes, causing crashes. It inspired urban-legend sequences in Hong Kong horror anthologies like *Troublesome Night* and *Tales from the Dark*.

Location & Access: Between Tsuen Wan and Tuen Mun. Public road. Drive with caution, or not at all.

Best Time to Visit: Never alone, and never after midnight.

Tours & Events: *Hong Kong Paranormal Society* sometimes includes this site on their "Roads of the Dead" itinerary.

Haunted Hotel Nearby: *The Peninsula Hong Kong* — world-famous, and said to host the ghost of a World War II general who appears in its mirrors.

Poblacion, Makati — The White Lady of Balete Drive, Philippines

Legacy & Lore: Perhaps the Philippines' most famous ghost story, the *White Lady of Balete Drive* is said to appear to taxi drivers late at night — a woman in white whose face, when seen in the mirror, is bloodless and hollow. She inspired countless TV dramas and horror films, most notably *Shake, Rattle & Roll*.

Location & Access: Balete Drive, Quezon City, Metro Manila. A public road bordered by century-old trees.

Best Time to Visit: Ghost Month (August) or All Saints' Day (November 1), when offerings appear beneath the trees.

Tours & Events: Heritage Manila's *Phantom Metro Tour* includes Balete Drive and other urban legends of the capital.

Haunted Hotel Nearby: *The Manila Hotel* — 1912 colonial grandeur with its own resident specter, a headless soldier said to roam the 3rd floor.

Hue Imperial Citadel[54] — Hue, Vietnam

Legacy & Lore: Once the heart of Vietnam's Nguyen dynasty, Hue witnessed brutal battles during the 1968 Tet Offensive. Thousands died within its walled city, and their spirits are said to linger amid the ruined palaces. The citadel's otherworldly quiet has drawn filmmakers exploring postwar horror and ancestral haunting.

Location & Access: Central Hue; UNESCO World Heritage Site open daily. Phú Hậu, Huế, Hue City, Vietnam.

Best Time to Visit: Dawn or dusk, when the Perfume River fog rises through the ancient gates.

Tours & Events: Guided day tours include historical context; ghost tours are unofficial but locally whispered.

Haunted Hotel Nearby: *La Residence Hue Hotel & Spa* — art deco elegance built in the 1930s; several guests have reported hearing distant drums echoing through the courtyard.

---

[54] "Vietnam, Hue, Imperial City of Hue, Meridian Gate" Vyacheslav Argenberg (https://commons.wikimedia.org/wiki/User:Argenberg, Creative Commons Attribution 4.0)

Sundarbans Mangrove Forest — Bangladesh / India Border

Legacy & Lore: A labyrinth of rivers and mangroves home to the *Dakini*, the forest witch of Bengali legend, and to man-eating tigers said to be her avatars. Horror films like *Patalghar* and *Tigers of the Sundarbans* drew on its mythic dread. Nature itself as supernatural.
Location & Access: Shared between India and Bangladesh; accessible via boat tours from Khulna or Gosaba.
Best Time to Visit: Winter (November–February), when waters calm and mist clings low.
Tours & Events: Government-approved eco-tours only; many guides carry charms against evil spirits.
Haunted Hotel Nearby: *The Tiger Garden International Hotel*, Khulna — its generators often fail without reason on new-moon nights.

The Aokigahara of Korea — Jangsan Mountain, Busan

Legacy & Lore: Locals speak of the *Jangsan Beom*, a fox spirit that lures hikers into the fog with the voice of a crying woman. The legend has fueled Korean horror games, podcasts, and short films.
Location & Access: Jangsan Mountain hiking trails above Busan.
Best Time to Visit: Winter, when mist thickens and daylight dies early.
Tours & Events: None officially — locals advise against ascending alone after dark.
Haunted Hotel Nearby: *The Westin Josun Busan*, overlooking Haeundae Beach; guests occasionally report the sound of weeping carried on the sea wind.

Kawah Ijen Crater — East Java, Indonesia

Legacy & Lore: A volcanic crater lake that glows electric blue at night from burning sulfur. Local miners tell of spirits guarding the sulfur fields, an image that appeared in *Firegate: Piramid Gunung Padang* (2016) and influenced Indonesia's resurgence of elemental horror.
Location & Access: Near Banyuwangi; requires guided trek.
Best Time to Visit: Night hikes begin around 2 a.m. to witness the blue fire.
Tours & Events: Trekking tours with gas masks; spiritual guides tell stories of the "smoke djinn."
Haunted Hotel Nearby: *Ijen Resort & Villas* — serene yet prone to power outages at the exact moment the crater flares.

Mt. Osore — Aomori Prefecture, Japan

Legacy & Lore: Known as "Mount Fear," Mt. Osore is Japan's gateway to the underworld. Buddhist mediums called *itako* still communicate with the dead here. Its volcanic fumes and desolate landscape appear in many Japanese horror sequences depicting liminal realms.
Location & Access: Shimokita Peninsula, northern Japan.
Best Time to Visit: July, during the *Itako Taisai Festival*, when mediums publicly channel spirits.
Tours & Events: Pilgrimage tours only; visitors can stay at the temple's inn and participate in ritual offerings.
Haunted Hotel Nearby: *Osorezan Bodai-ji Temple Inn* — the rooms are plain, the silence eternal.

Film Pilgrimage Notes (Asia & Pacific Leg)
Asia rewards sensitivity over spectacle. Many sites, especially in Japan, India, and Singapore, hold real grief and cultural sanctity. Never trespass or photograph without consent. Move slowly; bow often. Horror here is not confrontation but coexistence. Spirits as witnesses rather than antagonists. Bring incense instead of EMF meters; the dead prefer offerings to evidence. And remember: horror here doesn't hunt you, it notices you.

IV. Latin America — Colonial Phantoms and Cursed Lands

Latin America is where horror lives in daylight. The same streets that host festivals also honor the dead; the same churches that promise salvation house bones that never rested. This is the hemisphere where Catholicism and indigenous mythology merged into something feral. Where miracles can curse, and ghosts wear the faces of saints.

The House of La Llorona — Xochimilco, Mexico City

Legacy & Lore: "La Llorona," the Weeping Woman, is Latin America's most enduring ghost. A mother who drowned her children and wanders forever mourning them. In Xochimilco's canals, locals claim to hear her wails after midnight. Her legend predates Christianity and continues to inspire modern horror films across the world.
Location & Access: Accessible by *trajineras* (flat-bottom boats) from the Xochimilco docks.

Best Time to Visit: October and November, especially during Día de los Muertos.

Tours & Events: Every fall, a live open-water theatrical reenactment called *La Llorona en Xochimilco* takes place on floating stages surrounded by candles and fog.

Haunted Hotel Nearby: *Hotel Geneve*, Zona Rosa — 1907 elegance haunted by faint crying in the stairwell during the rainy season.

The San Ángel Inn[55] — Mexico City, Mexico

Legacy & Lore: Once a 17th-century monastery, now an upscale restaurant, San Ángel Inn was used as a filming site for Guillermo del Toro's *Cronos* (1993), blending Catholic decay with alchemical horror. Its courtyards and candlelit bar are still said to be visited by "monks of the golden blood."

Location & Access: San Ángel neighborhood; open daily for dining.

Best Time to Visit: Evenings after 8 p.m., when live guitar echoes through the cloisters.

Tours & Events: Private dining tours include the hidden wine cellar and its preserved well — rumored to be bottomless.

Haunted Hotel Nearby: *Las Alcobas* — boutique modern luxury near Polanco, occasionally plagued by elevator malfunctions during storms.

Pátzcuaro & Janitzio Island — Michoacán, Mexico

Legacy & Lore: The heart of Mexico's Day of the Dead. At midnight on November 1st, candlelit boats cross Lake Pátzcuaro toward Janitzio Island, where families spend the night communing with their ancestors. Horror filmmakers often draw from this imagery: living cemeteries, glowing altars, the thin line between life and death.

Location & Access: Fly to Morelia, then drive two hours west to Pátzcuaro.

Best Time to Visit: Día de los Muertos (November 1–2).

Tours & Events: Annual *Noche de Muertos* celebration; visitors are welcome but must behave with reverence.

Haunted Hotel Nearby: *Hotel Mansión Iturbe*, a colonial mansion overlooking the main square; guests report candlelight flickering even when rooms are empty.

Cartagena de Indias — Colombia

Legacy & Lore: Behind its pastel facades and Caribbean sunlight lies a city built on slavery, witchcraft trials, and secret catacombs. Local legends of *La Cruz del Diablo* and *El Mohán* shaped Colombian Gothic cinema, and Guillermo del Toro has cited Cartagena's colonial eeriness as inspiration.

Location & Access: Old Town Cartagena; UNESCO World Heritage Site.

Best Time to Visit: Late November to February. Dry season with cooler nights.

Tours & Events: *Cartagena Paranormal Tour* visits the Inquisition Palace, San Pedro Claver Church, and the buried cells beneath.

Haunted Hotel Nearby: *Sofitel Legend Santa Clara* — a 17th-century convent turned hotel, said to house the spirit of a novice nun who still walks the corridors at dawn.

Valparaíso & Cerro Alegre — Chile

Legacy & Lore: The "city of stairs" hides labyrinthine alleys once used by smugglers and sailors. Its decaying port and surreal murals inspired Jodorowsky's *Santa Sangre* (1989), a surreal horror parable of faith and madness.

Location & Access: Two hours from Santiago; UNESCO World Heritage Site.

Best Time to Visit: March–May, after the tourist season.

Tours & Events: Street-art tours and local folklore nights hosted by poets and artists.

Haunted Hotel Nearby: *Fauna Hotel*, perched on the cliffs; guests sometimes feel the bed rock gently though the sea is miles below.

---

55 "Entrada San Angel Inn" Marypaz Musi (https://commons.wikimedia.org/wiki/User:Marypaz_Musi, Creative Commons Attribution-Share Alike 4.0)

Buenos Aires Recoleta Cemetery — Argentina

Legacy & Lore: An architectural marvel and one of the most photographed cemeteries on Earth, Recoleta houses presidents, poets, and ghosts. The most famous: Rufina Cambaceres, a young socialite buried alive after being mistaken for dead. Scratches remain on her coffin.

Location & Access: Recoleta district, Buenos Aires; open daily. Junín 1760, C1113 Cdad. Autónoma de Buenos Aires, Argentina.

Best Time to Visit: Early morning for solitude, or dusk for haunting light.

Tours & Events: Guided tours highlight both architecture and legends.

Haunted Hotel Nearby: *Alvear Palace Hotel* — opulent, timeless, and allegedly home to a tuxedoed phantom who still attends the opera.

Teatro Nacional — San José, Costa Rica

Legacy & Lore: Costa Rica's most prestigious theater is rumored to be cursed by an actress who fell to her death during rehearsals in 1890. Visitors claim to hear applause in empty halls. Featured in local ghost docuseries.

Location & Access: Downtown San José; open daily for performances and tours.

Best Time to Visit: Evening performances under thunderstorm skies.

Tours & Events: Cultural Heritage tours daily; occasional Halloween concerts by candlelight.

Haunted Hotel Nearby: *Hotel Grano de Oro* — boutique colonial property with phantom piano notes reported at midnight.

Real de Catorce — San Luis Potosí, Mexico

Legacy & Lore: A silver-mining ghost town reborn as a mystic hub. Its cobbled streets appeared in *The Mexican* (2001) and *The Day of the Dead* sequences in travel documentaries. Locals speak of *El Charro Negro*, a demonic horseman who offers gold for souls.

Location & Access: Northern Mexico; reachable through a one-lane tunnel through the mountains.

Best Time to Visit: October–February, for cool weather and sparse tourists.

Tours & Events: Jeep tours, peyote pilgrimages, and annual festivals honoring St. Francis, where miracles and hauntings overlap.

Haunted Hotel Nearby: *Hotel El Real*, an adobe relic with flickering lights and soft guitar music when no one is playing.

The Island of the Dolls (*Isla de las Muñecas*)[56] — Xochimilco, Mexico City

Legacy & Lore: If *La Llorona* is Mexico's maternal ghost, *Isla de las Muñecas* is her child's nightmare. Located within the same canal system as her legend, this island is covered with hundreds of decaying dolls strung from trees placed by a recluse named Don Julián Santana, who believed the dolls warded off an angry spirit. It appeared in *Destination Truth*, *Ghost Adventures*, and multiple Mexican horror shorts.

Location & Access: Accessible only by boat from the Embarcadero Cuemanco in Xochimilco.

Best Time to Visit: Early morning or late afternoon; avoid weekends when the canals are crowded.

Tours & Events: Small-boat tours (about $40–$60 USD) include the island and surrounding haunted waterways.

Haunted Hotel Nearby: *Hotel Círculo Mexicano* — contemporary, minimalist, but locals say guests sometimes bring a doll from the island and regret it.

The Teatro Colón — Bogotá, Colombia

Legacy & Lore: Opened in 1892 and patterned after Italian opera houses, Teatro Colón is one of South America's most beautiful and allegedly cursed theaters. Electricians have reported lights turning on in empty balconies. Its ornate gloom was used in the film *Satanás* (2007).

Location & Access: Historic downtown Bogotá. Cerrito 628, C1010 Cdad. Autónoma de Buenos Aires, Argentina.

Best Time to Visit: Evening performances, especially symphonies.

Tours & Events: Daily guided tours and night concerts.

Haunted Hotel Nearby: *Hotel de la Ópera* — directly across the street; staff have heard phantom applause when the theater is dark.

The Jesuit Ruins of Trinidad — Itapúa, Paraguay

Legacy & Lore: Haunting red sandstone ruins of 17th-century Jesuit missions stand silent under tropical skies. By night, locals claim to see "the walking fathers," spectral priests still performing mass.

Location & Access: Near Encarnación; UNESCO World Heritage Site. rinidad 072201, Paraguay.

Best Time to Visit: April–June, during mild weather.

Tours & Events: Evening sound-and-light show called *Imagen y Sonido de la Reducción*, a spectral retelling projected across the ruins.

Haunted Hotel Nearby: *Hotel Tirol del Paraguay* — serene forest lodge where guests report hearing distant bells at midnight.

Valle de los Ingenios — Trinidad, Cuba

Legacy & Lore: A once-prosperous valley of sugar mills where enslaved people toiled and died. The crumbling towers and mansions of the 18th century still radiate sorrow. The valley inspired visual motifs for *Juan of the Dead* (2011), Cuba's cult zombie satire.

Location & Access: Near Trinidad, Cuba; accessible via guided taxi or train. V57P+99W, Trinidad, Cuba.

Best Time to Visit: December–April (dry season).

Tours & Events: Historical tours ($15 USD) include the Manaca Iznaga Tower. Climb it, and you can still hear the wind wailing like chains.

Haunted Hotel Nearby: *Iberostar Grand Trinidad* — colonial elegance in a city of echoes.

Estadio Centenario — Montevideo, Uruguay

Legacy & Lore: Yes, even a stadium can be haunted. Built in 1930 for the first FIFA World Cup, the Estadio Centenario has a lesser-known reputation: several construction workers died during its rushed building phase, and night watchmen claim to see their silhouettes on the bleachers.

Location & Access: Montevideo city center; open for tours. Av. Dr. Américo Ricaldoni, 11400 Montevideo, Departamento de Montevideo, Uruguay.

Best Time to Visit: Twilight, when stadium lights hum but no match is scheduled.

Tours & Events: Sports museum by day; occasional paranormal night tours.

Haunted Hotel Nearby: *Radisson Montevideo Victoria Plaza* — the elevator doors sometimes open to unlit floors.

The Poveglia of Brazil: Ilha das Cobras — Rio de Janeiro

Legacy & Lore: A small forbidden island off Rio's port, once used as a leper colony and later a prison. Rumors persist of human experiments during the 1930s. While access is restricted, fishermen claim to hear screams at night.
Location & Access: Visible from Praça XV pier, Rio de Janeiro; no official tours.
Best Time to Visit: From a distance, at dusk.
Tours & Events: Local sailors may offer boat rides around the perimeter for $20–$30 USD.
Haunted Hotel Nearby: *Hotel Santa Teresa MGallery* — a 19th-century coffee mansion turned luxury retreat, beautiful by day, breathless by night.

Pátio del Diablo — Arequipa, Peru

Legacy & Lore: A hidden courtyard said to have been the site of secret Inquisition punishments. Locals call it *The Devil's Patio* because of strange burn marks that appear on its stones after storms. The site influenced Peruvian horror novels and indie films of the 2000s.
Location & Access: Historic Arequipa; open sporadically for heritage tours.
Best Time to Visit: Cloudy afternoons, when the white volcanic stone glows gray.
Tours & Events: Cultural night tours and festivals in nearby plazas.
Haunted Hotel Nearby: *Casa Andina Premium Arequipa* — built on an old colonial mansion, its corridors are known for sudden drops in temperature.

Film Pilgrimage Notes (Latin America Expanded)

Latin America is not just haunted, it's alive. Its ghosts don't perform; they participate. They are never silent they sing, dance, and mourn. To walk through these sites is to realize that horror here isn't entertainment, it's ancestry. Every site here is sacred in its own way; photography should be reverent, not voyeuristic. The candles of Xochimilco, the bones beneath Lima, the songs of Janitzio, all belong to the same language of remembrance. The best time to travel is late October through early November, when the veil between the living and the dead is culturally, and cosmically, thinnest. Travel light, carry flowers, and never mock the dead. They are the only ones who truly know where the story ends. To understand Latin American horror, don't chase screams, chase songs. You'll find them in the candles, the drums, and the bones that learned to celebrate eternity.

V. The Real & the Mythic — Pilgrimages of Fear

Cinema invented its own cartography of terror. Its streets, motels, and basements became as sacred as any cathedral. Fans still search for them, not to be scared, but to stand where a story once breathed. This is the realm of the impossible pilgrimage: towns that never existed, houses rebuilt for sequels, castles that live forever on celluloid. These are the places that turned geography into mythology.

The Addams Family Mansion — Los Angeles, California

Legacy & Lore: The original *Addams Family* house (from the 1960s TV series) stood at 21 Chester Place, Los Angeles — a Romanesque mansion later absorbed by Mount St. Mary's University. Though long demolished, fans can visit the location and nearby Victorian neighborhoods that inspired its macabre charm. The cinematic version (1991) was filmed on sets at Hollywood Center Studios, but the façade design borrowed from this real mansion's profile. The look of the house in the show was also influenced by a Victorian home on Elm Street in Westfield, New Jersey, which Charles Addams, the creator of the cartoons, passed regularly.
Look-Alike Houses
- **Waterville, NY Home**: A 6,000-square-foot, historical building known as "Star Manor" is frequently noted for its strong resemblance to the Addams Family mansion.
- **Brooklyn, NY Replica**: A townhouse in the Clinton Hill neighborhood of Brooklyn was decorated with gothic, Morticia-approved décor for a promotional campaign in 2019.

Location & Access: Former site near downtown L.A.; nearby Carroll Avenue offers similar preserved Victorian homes.
Best Time to Visit: Late afternoon, when the sky over Los Angeles looks theatrical and gray.
Tours & Events: *Haunted Los Angeles Walking Tour* includes Chester Place and surrounding "movie ghost" locations.
Haunted Hotel Nearby: *Hollywood Roosevelt Hotel* — the mirror in Suite 1200 is said to show Marilyn Monroe's reflection, but many guests swear they've seen Cousin Itt.

Derry, Maine — (Bangor, Maine)

Legacy & Lore: Stephen King's fictional Derry is modeled after his hometown of Bangor. Fans flock to its Victorian neighborhoods and storm drains in homage to *It*. A red balloon placed at the corner of Jackson and Union Streets has become an unofficial landmark.

Location & Access: Bangor, Maine.

Best Time to Visit: September, to echo the novel's timeline.

Tours & Events: *Stephen King's Bangor Tour* ($50 USD) visits real inspirations for *It*, *Pet Sematary*, and *Salem's Lot*.

Haunted Hotel Nearby: *Hollywood Casino Hotel Bangor* — not haunted, but the slot machines occasionally glitch with clown laughter.

The Hill House[57] — Bishop's Stortford, England

Legacy & Lore: Shirley Jackson's *The Haunting of Hill House* (1959) may be fictional, but its 1963 film adaptation used Ettington Park Hotel in Warwickshire as its stand-in, a Gothic Revival mansion so photogenic it feels sentient.

Location & Access: Alderminster, Stratford-upon-Avon, Warwickshire, CV37 8BU, England.

Best Time to Visit: Foggy winter mornings.

Tours & Events: Hotel guests can explore the original filming areas.

Haunted Hotel Nearby: Ettington Park itself — haunted by a monk said to walk the cloisters by candlelight.

The Blair Witch Woods — Seneca Creek State Park, Maryland

Legacy & Lore: The haunting forests of *The Blair Witch Project* (1999) remain eerily untouched. Fans hike the *Blair Witch Trail* to find the film's locations. Stick figures, ruins, and all.

Location & Access: Near Burkittsville, Maryland. 11950 Clopper Rd, Gaithersburg, MD.

Best Time to Visit: October for fog; early spring for isolation.

Tours & Events: Guided "Witch Walks" by local horror historians.

Haunted Hotel Nearby: *Historic Inns of Frederick* — cozy, colonial, and allegedly haunted by a Civil War nurse.

The Red Room House — Pasadena, California

Legacy & Lore: Featured in Mike Flanagan's *The Haunting of Hill House* (Netflix, 2018), this sprawling Pasadena mansion doubles as the "Red Room." It remains a symbol of modern gothic rebirth.

Location & Access: Private residence; visible from the street only.

Best Time to Visit: Twilight, when its windows flare crimson in the sun.

Tours & Events: None official; horror bus tours sometimes stop nearby.

Haunted Hotel Nearby: *The Langham Huntington Pasadena* — long-standing haunt of Hollywood royalty and rumored echoes.

Twin Peaks' Great Northern — Snoqualmie Falls, Washington

Legacy & Lore: Technically more surreal than horror, but *Twin Peaks'* Pacific Northwest atmosphere influenced countless psychological horror films. The *Salish Lodge & Spa* doubled as The Great Northern.

Location & Access: Snoqualmie, Washington; overlooks a 268-foot waterfall.

Best Time to Visit: Rainy season (November–March).

Tours & Events: "Twin Peaks Experience" packages and guided filming site maps.

Haunted Hotel Nearby: You're sleeping in it; the falls sing lullabies.

---

[57] "Ettington Park - geograph.org.uk – 1230695" Richard Croft (https://www.geograph.org.uk/profile/1904, Creative Commons Attribution-Share Alike 2.0)

Quick Horror Sites

The Evil Dead Cabin — Morristown, Tennessee (USA)
The original 1981 cabin burned down, but its foundation and chimney remain hidden in the woods, a secret Mecca for horror fans.
Tip: The site is on private land; only respectful, guided visits are tolerated.
Nearby: *Shady Grove Campground* offers "Evil Dead" nights with screenings and forest hikes.

The Fog Town — Point Reyes Lighthouse, California (USA)
Used in John Carpenter's *The Fog* (1980). The isolated lighthouse and drifting mists remain unchanged.
Best time: Winter mornings, when the Pacific rolls in like smoke.

The Midsommar Village — Hårga, Hälsingland, Sweden
The real location that inspired *Midsommar* (2019). While the film built sets, the surrounding villages host actual solstice festivals of haunting beauty.
Tip: Go for the summer solstice — bring respect, not flower crowns.

The Wailing House — Gokseong, South Korea
The rural village setting of *The Wailing* (2016) can be toured; locals now host ghost festivals every August.
Best time: Rainy season, when mist sits low over the fields.

Pripyat, Ukraine — Chernobyl Zone of Alienation
Not horror fiction, but the inspiration for countless apocalyptic films (*Chernobyl Diaries*, *S.T.A.L.K.E.R.*).
Tip: Government-sanctioned day tours only. Silence here feels supernatural.

The Suspiria School — Freiburg, Germany (Tanzakademie Joos-Hall)
The façade of Argento's 1977 *Suspiria*. Bright red stucco and baroque windows radiate uncanny beauty.
Tip: Visit at twilight for that *giallo* glow; interior tours are rare but available on heritage days.

The Hereditary House — Utah, USA
A private residence used for Ari Aster's modern masterpiece *Hereditary* (2018). Not open for tours, but fans visit the nearby canyons used for exterior shots.
Tip: Combine with a drive through Salt Lake City's historic avenues, the landscape itself carries the film's unease.

The Witch Cottage — Essex County, Massachusetts (USA)
Near the real woods where *The Witch* (2015) was filmed. Local farms now host "Colonial Horror" experiences featuring lantern walks and folklore reenactments.

The Pan's Labyrinth Forest — Navarre, Spain
Guillermo del Toro's dreamscape was filmed in the beech woods of the *Sierra de Urbasa*. The twisted trees and natural caves remain untouched. Nature as Gothic cathedral.

The Nosferatu City — Lübeck, Germany
Used as the stand-in for Wisborg in Murnau's *Nosferatu* (1922). Its medieval lanes still cast jagged shadows at dusk.
Tip: Visit during the *Nordic Film Days* festival for screenings among the spires.

The Conjuring Farmhouse — Harrisville, Rhode Island (USA)
The real 1736 farmhouse that inspired *The Conjuring* (2013). Right now, it is in legal dispute and up for auction. Comedian Matt Rife and YouTuber Elton Castee, who are paranormal enthusiasts and already own the Warrens' former home in Connecticut, have publicly expressed interest in purchasing the property.
Best time: Fall; the surrounding woods feel alive.

To complete the Tour of Horror is to realize that cinema never left its birthplace. Every house, castle, and forest still breathes its role; every shadow still holds a reel of film. Horror isn't confined to the screen, it's an atlas of emotion, built brick by brick, frame by frame, on the world itself. Walk gently, take nothing, and remember: these places watched you long before you arrived.

VI. Haunted by Words: Literary Houses of Horror

Edgar Allan Poe House — Baltimore, Maryland, USA

Legacy & Lore: A narrow brick row home where Poe lived from 1833 to 1835, now a museum filled with first editions, period furnishings, and an unmistakable heaviness in the air. Visitors often describe a quiet sense of being watched.

Known For: Birthplace of *The Tell-Tale Heart* and *MS. Found in a Bottle.*

Best Time to Visit: October, during the annual Poe Festival and cemetery tours.

Tour Notes: The Poe House is small, hauntingly intimate, and often described as "too quiet for comfort."

H. P. Lovecraft House — Providence, Rhode Island, USA

Legacy & Lore: Lovecraft's former home on College Hill still gazes down on the streets that inspired Arkham and the Miskatonic tales. The surrounding architecture feels uncannily like his fiction: austere and intellectual, as though reality's veneer is too thin here.

Known For: *The Call of Cthulhu, The Shadow over Innsmouth,* and the invention of cosmic dread.

Best Time to Visit: Autumn, when the city feels like it's holding its breath.

Tour Notes: The *Lovecraft Walking Tour* (offered by the Providence Athenaeum) visits his home, grave, and favorite writing haunts.

Bram Stoker's House — Dublin, Ireland

Legacy & Lore: The Georgian townhouse where Stoker lived before writing *Dracula.* His window overlooked Dublin Bay — a view many believe inspired the Gothic coastal settings of his novel.

Known For: The birth of the world's most enduring vampire myth.

Best Time to Visit: Around Halloween, when Dublin hosts its *Bram Stoker Festival.*

Tour Notes: The exterior remains residential, but the festival hosts guided tours tracing Stoker's Dublin life.

Mary Shelley's House (Shelley Memorial) — Bath & Marlow, England

Legacy & Lore: Shelley conceived *Frankenstein* in Geneva, but her English homes at Bath and later Marlow retain her presence. The Bath townhouse, where she edited her manuscript, radiates a quiet melancholy.

Known For: *Frankenstein; or, The Modern Prometheus,* arguably the first science fiction novel.

Best Time to Visit: November through winter, echoing the cold isolation that birthed her creature.

Tour Notes: *Mary Shelley's House of Frankenstein* in Bath is now a museum blending biography, science, and horror set design.

Robert Louis Stevenson's House — Edinburgh, Scotland

Legacy & Lore: The author of *Strange Case of Dr. Jekyll and Mr. Hyde* grew up here, in a city that itself feels divided between light and dark. The house remains a private residence, but the mood of duality still clings to the surrounding streets.

Known For: *Dr. Jekyll and Mr. Hyde* and *The Body Snatcher.*

Best Time to Visit: Winter, when Edinburgh's fog wraps the city like conscience itself.

Tour Notes: The *Literary Edinburgh Tour* passes by his home, university, and the dark closes that shaped his imagination.

Sir Arthur Conan Doyle's Undershaw — Surrey, England

Legacy & Lore: The country home Doyle built in 1897, where he wrote *The Hound of the Baskervilles.* Gothic moors, fog, and mystery all seem to emanate from the property.

Known For: Blending rationality and supernatural dread through Sherlock Holmes.

Best Time to Visit: Late autumn, when the Surrey hills are fog-drenched.

Tour Notes: Now restored as a school; exterior visits and photography permitted.

Daphne du Maurier's Ferryside — Fowey, Cornwall

Legacy & Lore: Overlooking the Cornish coast, this home inspired *Rebecca* and *Jamaica Inn.* Sea mist and gulls mirror her tone of beauty laced with menace.

Known For: The romantic Gothic tradition; her influence on *Suspicion* and *The Birds.*

Best Time to Visit: Spring or early summer, when the cliffs bloom.

Tour Notes: Private residence; exterior viewing and du Maurier walking tours available.

Henry James' Lamb House — Rye, England

Legacy & Lore: James wrote *The Turn of the Screw* here in 1897. The Georgian garden house became a symbol of repression and spiritual unease. Its small rooms reportedly echo with typewriter keys when empty.
Known For: *The Turn of the Screw* and *The Aspern Papers.*
Best Time to Visit: September or October, when Rye's cobblestones and harbor fog seem to replay the novella's atmosphere.
Tour Notes: Now a National Trust property with literary exhibits and garden readings.

Junji Ito's Studio (Tomie's Town) — Gifu Prefecture, Japan

Legacy & Lore: Though not open to the public, fans often make pilgrimages to Gifu, where Ito based many of his twisted suburban nightmares. The quiet streets and abandoned lots look eerily like panels from *Uzumaki*. Locals accept their fame with wry amusement "We're all spirals here."
Known For: *Uzumaki*, *Tomie*, and redefining horror manga as existential art.
Best Time to Visit: Overcast winter days, when the landscape feels like black ink.
Tour Notes: No official tours; independent fans host informal "Ito pilgrimages" to recognizable landmarks.

Lafcadio Hearn's Residence — Matsue, Japan

Legacy & Lore: The Greek-Irish writer who introduced Japanese ghost stories to the West lived in this traditional house, still intact with tatami mats and paper doors. Hearn's *Kwaidan* remains one of the most beautiful ghost collections ever written.
Known For: Bridging East and West through the aesthetics of haunting.
Best Time to Visit: Early spring for cherry blossoms — and stillness.
Tour Notes: The *Lafcadio Hearn Memorial Museum* next door offers bilingual ghost-story readings.

Alejandro Jodorowsky's Family House — Tocopilla, Chile

Legacy & Lore: The surrealist filmmaker and mystic spent his childhood in this coastal town, which later became the backdrop of his film *The Dance of Reality.* The reconstructed house serves as both memorial and portal. A place where cinema, memory, and magic converge.
Known For: *Santa Sangre*, *The Holy Mountain*, and psychomagic philosophy.
Best Time to Visit: Chilean autumn (March–May), when the desert light softens.
Tour Notes: Tours available through the *Museo de Tocopilla* and film heritage programs.

Global Pilgrimage Note:
For literary devotees, these houses form an invisible network of energy — sites where words condensed into worlds. Some echo with despair, others with creation; all share a single truth: *haunting and genius are often the same condition.*

VII. Haunted Hotels of the World
"Every hotel holds its ghosts; only some make the reservation permanent."

The Americas
The Stanley Hotel — Estes Park, Colorado
- **Legacy & Lore:** The Stanley is more than inspiration, it is possession. Stephen King's stay in Room 217 birthed *The Shining*, and its long corridors still whisper with orchestral echoes and phantom laughter.
- **Location & Access:** The hotel operates year-round, offering standard lodging as well as *Night Spirit Tours* through the basement and concert hall.
- **Best Time to Visit:** October through early winter, when fog rolls down from the Rockies and the wind turns every hallway into a living soundtrack.
- **Tours & Events:** Ghost tours run nightly; *The Shining Ball* in late October invites guests in 1920s attire for a candlelit masquerade.

Timberline Lodge, Oregon
- **Legacy & Lore:** While Stephen King based *The Shining* on Colorado's Stanley Hotel, Kubrick shot the film's exterior at Timberline Lodge on Mount Hood. The hotel embraces its cinematic haunting, a masterpiece of isolation and symmetry. A monument of isolation perched 6,000 feet above sea level. Inside, every hallway feels like a memory loop.
- **Location & Access:** Located within Mount Hood National Forest, about 90 minutes from Portland. The lodge is open year-round for both day visitors and overnight stays.

- **Best Time to Visit:** Winter, when snow drapes the roofline exactly as it does in the film. The isolation becomes sublime.
- **Tours & Events:** Film-themed weekends and Halloween parties; visitors can request "Room 237" (actually 217 at the Stanley). No official *Shining* tours, but staff acknowledge its fame with trivia nights and occasional screenings. Guests sometimes leave small toy axes at doorways, offerings to the cinematic gods.

The Crescent Hotel — Eureka Springs, Arkansas
- **Legacy & Lore:** Marketed as "America's Most Haunted Hotel," the Crescent's beauty hides a ghastly past. Once a fraudulent cancer hospital run by Norman Baker, it later became the backdrop for paranormal investigations and a feature of *Ghost Hunters*.
- **Location & Access:** Open year-round as a functioning hotel in the Ozarks.
- **Best Time to Visit:** Late fall, when fog settles on the hills.
- **Tours & Events:** Nightly ghost tours descend into the old morgue. *Eureka Springs Paranormal Weekend* each January invites guests to conduct real investigations.

The Queen Mary — Long Beach, California
- **Legacy & Lore:** Launched in 1936, retired in 1967, and now eternally docked, the *Queen Mary* may be the most haunted ship in the world. Used in multiple horror productions and known for its chilling "Door 13," it's a floating museum of maritime dread.
- **Location & Access:** Open daily for tours and overnight stays. 1126 Queens Hwy, Long Beach, CA.
- **Best Time to Visit:** October for the *Dark Harbor* event, the ship transforms into a multi-level haunted attraction.
- **Tours & Events:** Beyond *Dark Harbor*, regular paranormal tours are led by investigators who have logged thousands of EVP recordings.
- **Haunted Hotel Nearby:** None required. Book a cabin and listen for footsteps pacing above your bed.

The Queen Anne Hotel — San Francisco, California
- **Legacy & Lore:** Built in 1890 as a finishing school for girls, now an opulent Victorian hotel haunted by the kindly ghost of Miss Mary Lake, its original headmistress. Featured in *Haunted Hotels* (2001) and countless travel specials.
- **Location & Access:** Open to guests year-round in Pacific Heights. 1590 Sutter St, San Francisco, CA.
- **Best Time to Visit:** Winter for fog-drenched mornings.
- **Tours & Events:** Ask the concierge for the "Haunted History" pamphlet, they keep it behind the desk.

The Bourbon Orleans Hotel — New Orleans, Louisiana
- **Legacy & Lore:** Once a grand ballroom and later a convent, this French Quarter landmark carries centuries of layered hauntings. Guests report ghostly dancers gliding beneath chandeliers and a spectral nun patrolling the upper floors. Known for both elegance and its friendly phantoms, it's considered one of New Orleans' most spiritually active hotels.
- **Location & Access:** 717 Orleans St, in the heart of the French Quarter. Walking distance to Jackson Square.
- **Best Time to Visit:** Late fall, when the Quarter's humidity lifts and All Saints' Day fills the city with candles.
- **Tours & Events:** The hotel offers its own evening "Ghosts of the Bourbon Orleans" tour for guests, complete with historical storytelling in the courtyard.

The Hotel del Coronado — San Diego, California
- **Legacy & Lore:** Opened in 1888, this seaside Victorian masterpiece is haunted by Kate Morgan, a young woman who died mysteriously on the beach in 1892. Her spirit, elegant and melancholy, is said to wander the hallways of the fourth floor. Featured in *Some Like It Hot* (1959), it remains a Hollywood-meets-haunting classic.

- **Location & Access:** 1500 Orange Ave, Coronado Island, accessible via the San Diego–Coronado Bridge.
- **Best Time to Visit:** Winter for dramatic Pacific storms and fewer crowds.
- **Tours & Events:** "Haunted Happenings" guided tours offered year-round; Halloween season features twilight ghost walks along the shore.

The Omni Parker House — Boston, Massachusetts
- **Legacy & Lore:** Founded in 1855, the Parker House is America's longest continuously operating hotel and allegedly one of its most haunted. Guests have reported knocks, flickering lights, and the scent of whiskey and cigars said to herald the ghost of Charles Dickens, who once resided here.
- **Location & Access:** 60 School St, downtown Boston, steps from the Freedom Trail.
- **Best Time to Visit:** Autumn, when Boston's cobblestones glow with fallen leaves and literary ghosts feel closest.
- **Tours & Events:** The hotel occasionally features in Boston's *Haunted Footsteps Ghost Tour*; ask the front desk for access to the "Dickens Suite."

The Sagamore — Bolton Landing, New York
- **Legacy & Lore:** Built in 1883 on a private island in Lake George, the Sagamore is both Gilded Age glamour and spectral legend. Ghosts of elegant guests, children playing on the golf course, and a mysterious couple in 1920s attire are frequently reported. Its isolation makes it a perfect lakeside haunting.
- **Location & Access:** 110 Sagamore Rd, Bolton Landing, NY, accessible via Route 9N, about 4 hours from NYC.
- **Best Time to Visit:** October, when the Adirondack foliage reflects in the lake like stained glass.
- **Tours & Events:** "Ghost Tours at the Sagamore" are offered to guests on select weekends, combining local lore with moonlit walks.

The Fairmont Banff Springs — Alberta, Canada
- **Legacy & Lore:** The "Castle in the Rockies," opened in 1888, is home to the "Ghost Bride," a young woman who fell down the grand staircase before her wedding. Staff also report a ghostly bellhop who assists guests with luggage — then vanishes. Its mix of luxury and legend makes it Canada's most famous haunted hotel.
- **Location & Access:** 405 Spray Ave, Banff, Alberta, inside Banff National Park.
- **Best Time to Visit:** Winter for snowbound ambience and frozen silence.
- **Tours & Events:** The Fairmont offers seasonal "Ghosts of the Castle" tours and a lavish Halloween gala in the ballroom.

The Fairmont Empress — Victoria, British Columbia
- **Legacy & Lore:** One of Canada's grandest hotels, the Empress (1908) exudes Edwardian luxury and ghostly charm. The apparition of its original architect, Francis Rattenbury, is often seen wandering the lobby, still inspecting his masterpiece. Guests also report phantom footsteps and echoes of music in the Palm Court.
- **Location & Access:** 721 Government St, Victoria, BC, overlooking the Inner Harbour.
- **Best Time to Visit:** Late autumn, when fog drifts over the harbor and the fireplaces are lit.
- **Tours & Events:** Afternoon "Ghostly Tea" events each October, combining hauntings with classic high tea.

The Gran Hotel Bolívar — Lima, Peru
- **Legacy & Lore:** Once the jewel of Lima's postcolonial elegance (est. 1924), the Gran Hotel Bolívar is rumored to host ghostly guests from its golden age — including soldiers, socialites, and even Hollywood stars. Frequent paranormal reports include mirrored apparitions and sudden temperature drops in the hallways.
- **Location & Access:** Plaza San Martín, central Lima.
- **Best Time to Visit:** Winter (June–August), for atmospheric fog rolling through the city.
- **Tours & Events:** Private paranormal tours can be arranged through local guides; bartenders at the Pisco Bar happily share ghost stories with your cocktail.

Europe
Dragsholm Slot — Zealand, Denmark
- **Legacy & Lore:** Built in the 12th century, now a luxury hotel, Dragsholm houses at least three ghosts: the White Lady (walled alive by her father), the Grey Lady (a maid still doing her rounds), and a tormented nobleman who died in chains. It's been featured in Danish horror documentaries and folklore for centuries.
- **Location & Access:** An hour west of Copenhagen; open year-round. Dragsholm Allé 1, 4534 Hørve, Denmark.
- **Best Time to Visit:** Late fall, when the mist from Lake Lammefjord creeps to the gates.
- **Tours & Events:** Guided ghost walks, gourmet dinners, and overnight stays in "haunted suites."

Ballygally Castle[58] — County Antrim, Northern Ireland

- **Legacy & Lore:** Overlooking the North Channel since 1625, Ballygally Castle is as famous for its views as its ghosts. The most beloved is Lady Isobel Shaw, who allegedly fell or was pushed from the tower. She now gently knocks on guests' doors before vanishing. It's Northern Ireland's oldest inhabited castle still functioning as a hotel.
- **Location & Access:** Coast Road, Ballygally, about 40 minutes north of Belfast.
- **Best Time to Visit:** Spring through early autumn, when the sea mist rolls across the Causeway Coast.
- **Tours & Events:** Ask to see "The Ghost Room" in the turret, preserved as a small museum dedicated to Lady Shaw's story.

The Langham Hotel — London, England

- **Legacy & Lore:** Opened in 1865, the Langham is London's grand dame of haunted hotels. Charles Dickens, Mark Twain, and Arthur Conan Doyle all stayed here and may have left more than luggage. Room 333 is infamous: guests report a Victorian gentleman in gray standing by the bed during storms.
- **Location & Access:** 1C Portland Place, near Regent's Park.
- **Best Time to Visit:** Late autumn or December. Fog season in London, when the city itself feels spectral.
- **Tours & Events:** No official ghost tours, but staff at the Palm Court Bar are known to recount its paranormal history between cocktails.

Château de Brissac — Loire Valley, France

- **Legacy & Lore:** Known as "The Giant of the Loire," this seven-story château is haunted by *La Dame Verte* (The Green Lady), the ghost of Charlotte de Brézé, murdered by her husband after an affair. Her sorrowful wails echo in the chapel at dawn. The castle inspired several European Gothic tales of betrayal and haunting.
- **Location & Access:** Near Angers, Loire Valley; 3 hours from Paris by train.
- **Best Time to Visit:** Late summer or harvest season, when the vineyards burn gold.
- **Tours & Events:** Guided tours year-round; occasionally hosts candlelight concerts and "Nights of the Green Lady."

Parador de Jaén[59] — Andalusia, Spain

- **Legacy & Lore:** Perched high above the city in a 13th-century Moorish fortress, the Parador de Jaén offers panoramic views and a resident ghost known as *La Terrible Moorish Princess*. She is said to haunt Room 22, weeping for a forbidden love. In 1984, staff witnessed inexplicable lights and whispering in the stone corridors.
- **Location & Access:** Castillo de Santa Catalina, Jaén, Spain.
- **Best Time to Visit:** Early spring, when Andalusian hills turn green and the fortress glows at sunset.
- **Tours & Events:** Guests can request Room 22 (if available); local folklore tours depart nightly from the old town.

Hotel Burchianti — Florence, Italy

- **Legacy & Lore:** Once a noble family home, this pink marble gem near the Duomo is one of Italy's most haunted hotels. Guests have reported ghostly children skipping down halls, icy cold spots, and a spectral maid still tending rooms. Mussolini allegedly stayed here during WWII though the ghosts predate him.
- **Location & Access:** Via del Giglio 8, Florence, Italy.

- **Best Time to Visit:** Winter, when Florence's fog and quiet streets amplify the Gothic atmosphere.
- **Tours & Events:** No formal tours, but the owners welcome ghost hunters and historians by appointment.

Schloss Cecilienhof — Potsdam, Germany
- **Legacy & Lore:** Built in 1917 and famous as the site of the 1945 Potsdam Conference, Cecilienhof is a Tudor-style palace with royal hauntings. Staff report phantom footsteps, flickering lamps, and the scent of roses where Crown Princess Cecilie once walked. It stands as a haunting reminder of Europe's turbulent 20th century.
- **Location & Access:** Im Neuen Garten, Potsdam, 45 minutes from Berlin.
- **Best Time to Visit:** Autumn, when the leaves mirror the castle's red brick façade.

- **Tours & Events:** Open to the public; guided tours include the historic rooms where Churchill, Truman, and Stalin met.

Hotel Palácio Estoril — Estoril, Portugal
- **Legacy & Lore:** During World War II, the Palácio Estoril was a playground for spies, diplomats, and exiled royals, inspiring Ian Fleming's creation of *James Bond*. Guests have seen shadowy figures pacing balconies at night, said to be "the men who never checked out." The hotel blends espionage, elegance, and eerie calm.
- **Location & Access:** Rua Particular, Estoril, about 25 minutes from Lisbon.
- **Best Time to Visit:** Late September, after the summer crowds but before the Atlantic winds rise.
- **Tours & Events:** Book the "Spy Trail Experience," a guided walk tracing Estoril's wartime intrigue.

Asia & the Pacific
The Banff of the East: Fairmont Peace Hotel — Shanghai, China
- **Legacy & Lore**: Opened in 1929, this Art Deco landmark weathered war, revolution, and countless ghost rumors. The *Peace Hotel* inspired scenes in *Empire of the Sun* and remains Shanghai's most atmospheric haunt.
- **Location & Access**: The Bund, central Shanghai; open year-round. 20 Nanjing Rd (E), Waitan, Huangpu, Shanghai, China, 200002.
- **Best Time to Visit**: Rainy season (April–June), when neon reflections ripple like spirits across the river.
- **Tours & Events**: Heritage tours recount its wartime guests and mysterious deaths

The Taj Mahal Palace — Mumbai, India
- **Legacy & Lore:** Opened in 1903, this architectural jewel has hosted kings, presidents, and ghosts alike. During the 2008 attacks, parts of the hotel were devastated and many claim the spirits of staff and guests still linger in silent tribute. The ghost of the architect, who allegedly died before its completion, is said to patrol the grand staircase.
- **Location & Access:** Apollo Bunder Rd, Colaba, facing the Gateway of India. 30 minutes from Mumbai airport.
- **Best Time to Visit:** November to February, when the monsoon air clears and the sea breeze carries the scent of salt and sandalwood.
- **Tours & Events:** Heritage Tours offered daily; inquire about the "Architect's Walk" through historic wings and the original ballroom.

The Grand Hyatt — Taipei, Taiwan
- **Legacy & Lore:** Sleek and modern on the surface, this five-star tower was allegedly built over a World War II execution ground. Guests describe wailing in the night and restless energy in corner suites. Buddhist monks were invited to bless the building, the wooden talismans in the lobby remain.
- **Location & Access:** 2 Songshou Rd, Xinyi District, Taipei, beside Taipei 101.
- **Best Time to Visit:** March to May for mild weather and empty corridors.
- **Tours & Events:** No official ghost tours, but the concierge will discreetly acknowledge its legend; rooms #1201 and #1202 are favorites for thrill-seekers.

The Savoy Mussoorie — Uttarakhand, India
- **Legacy & Lore:** Inspiration for Agatha Christie's *The Mysterious Affair at Styles* and cited by Stephen King as an influence for *The Shining*, the Savoy (1902) epitomizes colonial-era Gothic. The spirit of Lady Garnet Orme, found poisoned in her room, is said to wander the hallways whispering for justice.
- **Location & Access:** Library Bazaar, Mussoorie Hill Station, Uttarakhand.
- **Best Time to Visit:** April to June for mist-filled mornings and cool mountain air.
- **Tours & Events:** The hotel offers heritage walks through the old ballroom and gardens; staff recount the Lady Orme story upon request.

The Q Station (Manly Quarantine Station) — Sydney, Australia
- **Legacy & Lore:** Once a quarantine site for ships entering Sydney Harbour, this 19th-century complex processed thousands during epidemics. Some never left. Today, the Q Station doubles as a heritage hotel and one of the Southern Hemisphere's premier paranormal destinations.
- **Location & Access:** 1 North Head Scenic Dr, Manly, NSW, within Sydney Harbour National Park.
- **Best Time to Visit:** Autumn (March–May), when fog drapes the cliffs.
- **Tours & Events:** Nightly *Ghostly Encounters* tours with EMF equipment; guests can sleep in restored hospital quarters overlooking the sea.

Middle East & Africa
La Mamounia — Marrakech, Morocco
- **Legacy & Lore:** Opened in 1923, La Mamounia has hosted Winston Churchill, Alfred Hitchcock, and generations of royalty, yet beneath its opulent tiles lies a deep mystique. Built on an 18th-century royal garden said to house a jinn portal, guests report shadow figures gliding through the orange groves at dawn. The hotel inspired parts of Hitchcock's *The Man Who Knew Too Much* (1956).
- **Location & Access:** Avenue Bab Jdid, Marrakech, Morocco; ten minutes from Jemaa el-Fnaa square.
- **Best Time to Visit:** October to March, when desert nights carry a chill and the garden's silence feels infinite.
- **Tours & Events:** Book the "La Mamounia Experience" for a historical tour of its Moorish architecture; locals whisper that the hammam's steam rooms are older and holier than the hotel itself.

The King David Hotel — Jerusalem, Israel
- **Legacy & Lore:** Opened in 1931, the King David stands as one of the Middle East's most symbolic landmarks. In 1946, a bombing in its southern wing claimed 91 lives; visitors report ghostly soldiers and muffled explosions echoing through marble halls. It remains both a national monument and a site of uneasy reverence.
- **Location & Access:** 23 King David St, Jerusalem, Israel; overlooking the Old City walls.
- **Best Time to Visit:** Late autumn, when Jerusalem's nights cool and the air feels ancient.
- **Tours & Events:** Private historical tours can be arranged through the concierge; the "King's Wing" remains a quiet memorial space.

The Mount Nelson Hotel[60] — Cape Town, South Africa
- **Legacy & Lore:** A colonial-era grand hotel (1899) painted soft pink to celebrate peace after the Boer War, the "Mount Nellie" hides gentler ghosts than most. Guests have seen a woman in 1940s dress gliding through the Palm Court and phantom piano music rising from empty rooms. During WWII, it housed Allied officers; some are said to still walk the verandas.
- **Location & Access:** 76 Orange Street, Gardens, Cape Town; nestled beneath Table Mountain.
- **Best Time to Visit:** Late summer (February–April) when evening winds carry the scent of jasmine through open corridors.
- **Tours & Events:** Heritage high teas, historical garden tours, and ghost-story evenings hosted by local historians.

The Palace of the Lost City — Sun City, South Africa

- **Legacy & Lore:** Completed in 1992, this opulent fantasy resort was designed to resemble a mythical African kingdom, and according to staff, the myth came true. Guests report phantom drumming, whispers in uninhabited suites, and visions of "the Lost King" watching from the mosaicked atrium. Built atop tribal lands, it's said to rest on a ley line of ancestral energy.
- **Location & Access:** Sun City Resort, North West Province, about two hours from Johannesburg.
- **Best Time to Visit:** May–September, during South Africa's dry season when the surrounding savanna glows gold.
- **Tours & Events:** Safari and cultural tours available daily; spiritual cleansing ceremonies can be booked with local Sangomas upon request.

The Stanley Hotel — Nairobi, Kenya

- **Legacy & Lore:** Established in 1902, this was the first luxury hotel in East Africa, a watering hole for explorers, hunters, and the ghosts they brought with them. Ernest Hemingway and Karen Blixen were regulars. Guests claim to see phantom porters carrying luggage up the grand staircase, and some swear the bar echoes with laughter from long-gone colonials.
- **Location & Access:** Kimathi Street, Nairobi, Kenya; central business district.
- **Best Time to Visit:** July–October, during Kenya's cool dry season when Nairobi's nights feel still and electric.
- **Tours & Events:** The hotel hosts colonial-history dinners and storytelling evenings about the early adventurers of East Africa; its "Thorn Tree Café" is said to hum after midnight.

Epilogue: The Eternal Check-Out

A final, cinematic reflection that ties the idea of haunted hospitality back into the soul of horror. Every hotel as a liminal space between the living and the lost.

Ghost Twins: Around the World

Bodie, California — Kolmanskop, Namibia — Doel, Belgium

Three ghost towns separated by oceans but united by stillness. Bodie's wooden saloons and decayed pianos crumble under Sierra Nevada snow; Kolmanskop's German villas sink into dunes of amber sand; Doel's brick houses are tagged with the faces of saints and skeletons. Each stands as a cinematic graveyard of industry: the American West, African colonialism, and European urbanization all ending the same way: in silence.

The Stanley Hotel, USA — The Savoy Mussoorie, India

Both mountaintop sanctuaries built for elites, later turned into sanctuaries for ghosts. King wrote *The Shining* at the Stanley; Indian novelist Ruskin Bond set hauntings at the Savoy. Their ballrooms echo the same tune, isolation as invitation.

Salem, Massachusetts — Pendle Hill, England

Two witch-trial landscapes divided by centuries. Salem commercialized its trauma; Pendle preserved it in stone and silence. Every October, both towns honor women once condemned for the same unspeakable gift: intuition.

Bran Castle, Romania — Hunyad Castle, Transylvania — Whitby Abbey, England

Three Gothic siblings in the Dracula family tree. Bran gave the silhouette, Hunyad the legend of Vlad, Whitby the English introduction. Visit all three, and you trace the vampire's full migration.

Poveglia Island, Italy — Hashima Island, Japan

Two forsaken islands once teeming with the condemned. One a plague pit, the other an industrial hive. Now both are quarantined by time, their concrete veins empty but humming with aftershocks of suffering.

The Catacombs of Paris, France — The Capuchin Crypt, Rome, Italy

Cathedrals of bone: one sprawling and democratic, the other ornate and devotional. Paris organized its dead; Rome arranged them into art. Together, they embody Europe's holy relationship with death as architecture.

The Overlook Hotel, USA — Fairmont Banff Springs, Canada — Dragsholm Slot, Denmark

Three hotels that define the haunted luxury archetype. The Overlook's madness is fictional; Banff's bride is eternal; Dragsholm's noble skeleton remains in its wall. Each proves wealth doesn't buy safety, only more beautiful ghosts.

Salem's Lot, USA — Sleepy Hollow, New York — Glamis Castle, Scotland
Three places that remind us horror loves heritage. Sleepy Hollow turns fear into folklore; Glamis hides centuries of royal skeletons. The deeper the roots, the darker the rot.

Crystal Lake, New Jersey — Loch Ness, Scotland — Lake Tōya, Japan
The world's haunted waters. Jason, Nessie, and the drowned spirits of Ainu myth all rise from reflection, monsters made of still water and human projection.

The Queen Mary, California — RMS Queen Elizabeth, Hong Kong
Sister ships in spirit. One moored as a museum, the other lost to fire. The Queen Mary's ballroom still sways; her twin burned at sea, forever dancing in the dark.

Passport to Paranormal

Trivia of Terror

Haunted: Core Edition
The original nightmare that started it all. Blends trivia, dares, and chaos for those who think they've survived every scare.
1. Which 1973 film made audiences vomit in theaters worldwide?
   → *The Exorcist*
2. What Stephen King story trapped an author under the care of his "number one fan?"
   → *Misery*
3. Which director redefined possession with "The Power of Christ compels you?"
   → *William Friedkin*
4. What horror movie begins with a babysitter and a phone call upstairs?
   → *When a Stranger Calls*
5. In what film did a cursed videotape mark you for death in seven days?
   → *The Ring*

Slasher Edition
Blood, blades, and bad decisions. The Slasher Edition celebrates the killers who never die and the teens who never learn.
1. What holiday does Michael Myers prefer for his work?
   → *Halloween*
2. Who is Camp Crystal Lake's most infamous employee?
   → *Jason Voorhees*
3. Which horror icon hunts in your dreams?
   → *Freddy Krueger*
4. What small town fears a man in a William Shatner mask?
   → *Haddonfield, Illinois*
5. Which 1996 meta-horror film asked, "What's your favorite scary movie?"
   → *Scream*

Occult Edition
Cross the threshold. The Occult Edition conjures witches, rituals, and demonic bargains best left unspoken.
1. What 2015 film gave us the phrase "Wouldst thou like to live deliciously?"
   → *The Witch*
2. Which horror classic features a coven hiding in a ballet academy?
   → *Suspiria*
3. Who directed *The Ninth Gate* starring Johnny Depp?
   → *Roman Polanski*
4. What demon torments the Warrens in *The Conjuring* universe?
   → *Valak*
5. Which 1968 film made Satanic panic fashionable?
   → *Rosemary's Baby*

Found Footage Edition
Every scream caught on camera. The Found Footage deck drags you through shaky cams, lost tapes, and doomed explorers who never stop filming.
1. Which 1999 indie film made forests and stick figures terrifying?
   → *The Blair Witch Project*
2. What franchise documents demonic activity through home security cameras?
   → *Paranormal Activity*
3. What Spanish horror follows a news crew trapped in an infected apartment?
   → *[REC]*
4. Which 2007 monster film is shot entirely on a handheld camera in New York?
   → *Cloverfield*
5. What film warned "Don't look in the basement" through found VHS tapes?
   → *V/H/S*

Psychological & Paranoia Edition

It's all in your head or is it? This edition toys with sanity, obsession, and the fine line between victim and villain.

1. In *Black Swan*, what art form becomes a descent into madness?
   → *Ballet*
2. Which Kubrick masterpiece asks, "All work and no play…?"
   → *The Shining*
3. What 2019 film explores class warfare under one roof with hidden tunnels?
   → *Us*
4. Which 2017 horror made hypnosis its deadliest weapon?
   → *Get Out*
5. What Polanski classic keeps you questioning a pregnant woman's reality?
   → *Rosemary's Baby*

Possessed Edition

Unholy spirits and cursed souls take center stage. The Possessed Edition channels everything that should've stayed buried and dares you to exorcise it.

1. What film features a young girl's demonic voice saying, "Your mother sucks in hell?"
   → *The Exorcist*
2. Which 2013 movie brought us the cursed book *Naturom Demonto*?
   → *Evil Dead*
3. What 2005 remake stars Ryan Reynolds as a possessed stepfather?
   → *The Amityville Horror*
4. In *The Conjuring 2*, what elderly ghost torments the Hodgson family?
   → *Bill Wilkins*
5. Which 2022 film begins with a séance gone wrong and a talking embalmed hand?
   → *Talk to Me*

Monster Edition

From creatures of the deep to beasts of the night, this edition is pure creature-feature chaos.

1. Which 1931 film gave us, "It's alive!?"
   → *Frankenstein*
2. What 1954 monster rose from nuclear fear in Japan?
   → *Godzilla*
3. Who directed *The Shape of Water*, the romance with a sea god?
   → *Guillermo del Toro*
4. Which Antarctic parasite imitates its victims perfectly?
   → *The Thing*
5. What 1986 film remade a scientist into an insect nightmare?
   → *The Fly*

8. Gore & Grindhouse Edition

Bloody, brutal, and unapologetic. The Gore & Grindhouse deck is pure exploitation: chainsaws, scream queens, and gallons of fake blood.

1. What 1974 Texas film redefined low-budget terror?
   → *The Texas Chain Saw Massacre*
2. Which 2004 movie introduced the sadistic "games" of Jigsaw?
   → *Saw*
3. Who directed *Hostel*, ushering in the torture-porn era?
   → *Eli Roth*
4. What Italian director made *Suspiria* a neon nightmare?
   → *Dario Argento*
5. What film's tagline promised, "The last house on the left?"
   → *The Last House on the Left*

9. Gothic Edition
Decadence meets decay. The Gothic Edition drips with candlelight, cathedrals, and doomed romance.
1. Who wrote the novel *Dracula*?
   → *Bram Stoker*
2. What 1994 film turned a vampire's confession into art?
   → *Interview with the Vampire*
3. Which 1961 film haunted viewers with ghostly children and fog?
   → *The Innocents*
4. What Guillermo del Toro film features a crimson-bleeding mansion?
   → *Crimson Peak*
5. Which 1935 sequel gave us the Bride with the scream heard round the world?
   → *Bride of Frankenstein*

10. Serial Killer Edition
Real monsters walk among us. This edition dives into true crime, inspired horror, and the twisted minds behind the mask.
1. What Wisconsin killer inspired *Psycho* and *The Texas Chain Saw Massacre*?
   → *Ed Gein*
2. Which 2007 film follows detectives chasing the Zodiac Killer?
   → *Zodiac*
3. What Netflix series dramatizes Jeffrey Dahmer's murders?
   → *Dahmer – Monster: The Jeffrey Dahmer Story*
4. What 1991 film gave us a cannibal and a fava-bean pairing?
   → *The Silence of the Lambs*
5. Which 2002 film starred Christian Bale as a blood-obsessed yuppie?
   → *American Psycho*

11. Vampire Edition
Eternal night, eternal hunger. The Vampire Edition bleeds through centuries of cinematic seduction and gothic dread.
1. Who played the original *Nosferatu* in 1922?
   → *Max Schreck*
2. What 1987 film gave us "Sleep all day, party all night?"
   → *The Lost Boys*
3. Which franchise brought us the Volturi and sparkling immortals?
   → *Twilight*
4. What 1994 film paired Tom Cruise and Brad Pitt as undead lovers?
   → *Interview with the Vampire*
5. Who directed *Let the Right One In*?
   → *Tomas Alfredson*

SCAN TO SUMMON THE DECKS

Soundtrack of Scary

THE SACRED SHADOWS:
PRE-CINEMA & CLASSICAL FOUNDATIONS
(The birth of dread through symphony and superstition.)

Before horror had cameras, it had orchestras. Long before fangs and fog, composers conjured the uncanny through dissonance, ritual rhythm, and melodies that flirted with the abyss. These pieces became horror's DNA resurrected across a century of film scores.

- **Johann Sebastian Bach – "Toccata and Fugue in D Minor" (1704)** - The unofficial anthem of Gothic horror. The organ's thunderclap of terror. Immortalized in *Phantom of the Opera* (1925) and *Dr. Jekyll and Mr. Hyde* (1931), this became the cathedral of Gothic sound. The piece never won an award, but it won eternity. Nominated in spirit for every Halloween ever.

- **Hector Berlioz – "Symphonie Fantastique: Dream of a Witches' Sabbath" (1830)** - One of horror's earliest hallucinations. A descent into opium-fueled delirium and infernal marriage rites. Later inspired Herrmann, Goldsmith, and Elfman's orchestrations of obsession.

- **Franz Liszt – "Totentanz (Dance of Death)" (1849)** - Virtuoso piano meets infernal ceremony. Referenced across early Gothic films and modern horrors like *The Ninth Gate* (1999). The original virtuoso's duel with Death himself.

- **Richard Wagner – "Ride of the Valkyries" (1851)** - Though warlike rather than sinister, its use in *Bride of Frankenstein* and *Apocalypse Now* transformed it into an operatic symbol of doom: glory, madness, and annihilation.

- **Johann Strauss II – "The Blue Danube Waltz" (1866)** - Used with eerie irony in *2001: A Space Odyssey*. A reminder that even beauty can become horror's mask when paired with silence and void.

- **Modest Mussorgsky – "Night on Bald Mountain" (1867)** - Demons gather on the mountaintop, the first cinematic Sabbath in symphonic form. Disney's *Fantasia* turned it into nightmare made motion.

- **Camille Saint-Saëns – "Danse Macabre" (1874)** - Death conducts the dance. Violins mimic bones rattling in joyless rhythm as skeletons waltz through the night. Used in *Fantasia* (1940) and every haunted attraction since.

- **Giuseppe Verdi – "Dies Irae" from *Requiem* (1874)** - The day of wrath immortalized in Latin fire. Its echo haunts Kubrick's *The Shining* (1980) and *The Exorcist* (1973). A requiem for the damned.

- **Claude Debussy – "Prelude to the Afternoon of a Faun" (1894)** - Not horror, but seduction of the uncanny. The dreamlike sensuality later influenced Gothic eroticism in films like *Crimson Peak* and *The Hunger*.

- **Carl Orff – "O Fortuna" from *Carmina Burana* (1935)** - No score in history has shouted damnation louder. Used in *The Omen*, *Excalibur*, *The Doors*, *Final Destination 2*, and countless trailers. A choral apocalypse that feels like prophecy.

CLASSIC MONSTERS & UNIVERSAL SHADOWS
(The birth of cinematic fear: fog, operas, and orchestras.)

Universal Studios turned horror into mythology. The monsters walked and the music wept, roared, and stalked with them. Every note from this era became a heartbeat for the genre.

- **Tchaikovsky – "Swan Lake: Overture" (1931, used in *Dracula*)-** Bela Lugosi's entrance rode on borrowed beauty. Tchaikovsky's romantic overture framed the Count's immortality as tragic elegance, setting horror's sonic archetype.
- **"Ave Maria" – Traditional / Used in *Frankenstein* (1931) -** Played over the village mourning sequence, this sacred melody brought grace to monstrosity. Horror as tragedy, not punishment.
- **Heinz Roemheld – "The Black Cat" (1934) -** One of cinema's first horror soundscapes influenced by modernism and war trauma used dissonance long before Bernard Herrmann.
- **Franz Waxman – "Bride of Frankenstein Main Title" (1935) -** Waxman built a Gothic opera: tragic, thunderous, divine. The brass chords almost chant her name. Set the standard for monster scoring, emotion before fear.
- **Charles Previn – "Son of Frankenstein" (1939) -** Sweeping, storm-born strings. Science meets sorrow. Became the template for every "mad laboratory" cue to follow.
- **Clifford Vaughan – "The Invisible Man Returns" (1940) -** Playful but menacing orchestration, horror's early dance with irony.
- **Charles Previn – "The Wolf Man Theme" (1941) -** Lush, lyrical, and doomed. The tragedy of Lon Chaney Jr. in strings and brass. One of cinema's first sympathetic monster motifs.
- **Hans J. Salter – "The Mummy's Hand / Ghost of Frankenstein Themes" (1940–42) -** Salter's eerie tonal shifts defined mummy and ghost tropes for decades, echoed later in *The Creature from the Black Lagoon*.
- **Roy Webb – "Cat People Theme" (1942) -** Silence, restraint, and psychological tension. Webb used empty space as music, influencing modern sound design from *The Haunting* to *Hereditary*.
- **Roy Webb – "I Walked with a Zombie" (1943) -** A Caribbean Gothic built on rhythm and restraint. Voodoo ritual turned hypnotic lullaby.

THE AGE OF PARANOIA, POSSESSION & PASSION
(1950s–1970s)
"Science made monsters. Faith made demons."

As the Cold War hummed and color film bloomed, horror music fractured — half laboratory, half cathedral. The atomic age gave us metallic fear; the European revival gave it religion, sex, and poetry. Between the two, modern horror was born.

- **Alfred Hitchcock Presents Theme – Charles Gounod's *Funeral March of a Marionette* (19th c.) -** Television's weekly requiem. The macabre became domestic ritual.
- **Bernard Herrmann – "The Day the Earth Stood Still" (1951) -** The first electronic apocalypse. Two theremins, organ, and tape echo turned sci-fi into sermon. Invented the "alien" sound that still defines the genre.
- **Dimitri Tiomkin – "The Thing from Another World" (1951) -** Cold-war terror wrapped in orchestral shockwaves. Influenced John Carpenter's minimalist re-score three decades later.
- **Herman Stein & Henry Mancini – "This Island Earth / It Came from Outer Space" (1953–54) -** Universal's atomic duets: swirling theremins, choral dread, and scientific hubris set to sound.
- **Akira Ifukube – "Godzilla Theme" (1954) -** The growl that mourned Hiroshima. Brass marches meet percussive roars, a requiem for radiation. Won Japan's Mainichi Film Music Award and became the national sound of catastrophe.

- **Henry Mancini – "Creature from the Black Lagoon" (1954)** - Lurking brass and jazzy syncopation. Fear turned to exotic adventure. Horror's bridge to Hollywood elegance.
- **Miklós Rózsa – "The Power" (1958)** - Mind-control paranoia with proto-psychedelic strings. Paved the path to *Village of the Damned* and *Scanners*.
- **Van Cleave – "The Blob Theme (Beware the Blob)" (1958)** - Rock-and-roll novelty meets monster panic. Burt Bacharach's lyrics made terror danceable.
- **Ronald Stein – "Attack of the 50 Foot Woman" (1958)** - Sci-fi feminism scored in swing-time. Satire meets subversion.
- **James Bernard – "Dracula (Hammer Theme)" (1958)** - The Hammer resurrection. Bernard's brass literally spells *DRA-CU-LA!* thunderous, erotic, unmistakable.
- **Franz Reizenstein – "The Mummy" (1959)** - Ancient dread through lush symphony. Hammer's orchestral grandeur replaced shrieks with seduction.
- **Les Baxter – "The Fall of the House of Usher Suite" (1960)** - Corman's Poe series begins. Orchestral fever-dreams drenched in Technicolor melancholy. Gothic horror becomes pop-opera.
- **Bernard Herrmann – "Psycho: The Murder" (1960)** - Shrieked violins, stabbed into history. Every scream since owes it blood.
- **Krzysztof Penderecki – "Threnody for the Victims of Hiroshima" (1960)** - Used in *The Shining*, *The Exorcist*, *The Thing*. Pure avant-garde despair, terror without melody.
- **Ronald Stein – "Dementia 13" (1963)** - Coppola's early horror. Chamber strings twist into proto-psychoid anxiety.
- **Delia Derbyshire – "Doctor Who Theme" (1963)** - BBC radiophonic pioneer. Tape-loop horror disguised as television jingle. Birthplace of electronic dread.
- **Roberto Nicolosi – "Black Sabbath" (1963)** - Mario Bava's anthology theme: dark jazz meets cathedral bells. The birth of Italian Gothic cinema's mood.
- **Carlo Rustichelli – "Castle of Blood" (1964)** - Gothic elegance through harpsichord and echo. Barbara Steele's tragedy given sonic perfume.
  Vic Mizzy – "The Addams Family" (1964) - The iconic and instantly recognizable tune, which features finger-snaps and a harpsichord melody.
- **Piero Piccioni – "The 10th Victim" (1965)** - Italian futurism meets pop murder. Lounge horror, precursor to *Suspiria's* playful menace.
- **Krzysztof Komeda – "Rosemary's Baby Lullaby" (1968)** - Innocence weaponized. Mia Farrow's voice turns cradle song into curse. Golden Globe–nominated, spiritually haunting.
- **Jerry Goldsmith – "Planet of the Apes Main Title" (1968)** - Percussive chaos that redefined film scoring. Influenced *Alien*, *The Omen*, and every existential horror thereafter.
- **Bernard Herrmann – "Twisted Nerve Whistle" (1968)** - A childlike motif later whistled by *Kill Bill's* assassin, proof that innocence terrifies most.
- **James Bernard – "Taste the Blood of Dracula" (1970)** - Hammer's decadence apex. Gothic thunder scored like opera. No subtlety, all power.
- **Jerry Goldsmith – "The Mephisto Waltz" (1971)** - Piano meets pact. A symphonic love letter to evil, pre-Omen rehearsal.
- **Jerry Fielding – "Straw Dogs Suite" (1971)** - Moral decay underscored in atonal tension. Horror without monsters, just men.
- **Billy Goldenberg – "Duel" (1971)** - Spielberg's first predator. Motor and metal turned into minimal percussion symphony.
- **Ennio Morricone – "The Bird with the Crystal Plumage" (1970)** - Jazz, whispers, heartbeat percussion. Giallo's sonic DNA. Erotic fear in 12/8 time.

- **Bruno Nicolai – "The Red Queen Kills Seven Times" (1972) -** Strings, whispers, and heartbeat percussion, feminine vengeance becomes music.
- **Mike Oldfield – "Tubular Bells" (1973) -** Minimalist hypnosis turned blockbuster terror. Charted Top 10 worldwide, won a Grammy, and birthed *The Exorcist's* possession.
- **Paul Giovanni – "Willow's Song" (1973) –** *The Wicker Man* **-** Pagan seduction rendered in folk melody. Haunting, erotic, and entirely human. Folk horror's siren call.
- **Michael Small – "The Stepford Wives Theme" (1975) -** Domestic bliss scored like hypnosis. Horror as consumer lullaby.
- **Goblin – "Profondo Rosso (Deep Red)" (1975) -** Progressive-rock nightmare. Harpsichord and heartbeat bassline birthed the modern slasher rhythm.
- **John Williams – "Jaws Theme" (1975) -** Two notes. One Oscar. Infinite nightmares. Won Academy Award; became the heartbeat of primal fear.
- **Alan Howarth & Carpenter – "Assault on Precinct 13 Theme" (1976) -** Proto-slasher pulse. Carpenter's synth revolution begins here.
- **Jerry Goldsmith – "Ave Satani" (1976) -**Latin Black Mass for boys' choir. Won Academy Award for Best Original Score (*The Omen*, 1977). The devil finally had an anthem.
- **John Barry – "King Kong 1976 Theme" -** Romantic tragedy for the giant heart. Oscar-nominated; redefined monster empathy.
- **Ennio Morricone – "The Exorcist II: The Heretic" (1977) -** Flute choirs and African rhythm. A heresy of sound after *Tubular Bells*. Critically panned, now revered.
- **John Barry – "The Quiller Memorandum / The Deep" (1977) -** Underwater dread transformed into erotic spy-wave. Precursor to aquatic horror scores.
- **Goblin – "Suspiria Theme" (1977) -** Whispers, bells, and synth hallucinations. Nominated for Nastro d'Argento; still unbeaten in sheer witchcraft.
- **Fabio Frizzi – "City of the Living Dead / The Beyond" (1979–81) -** Lucio Fulci's apocalypse in synth and organ. Italian horror's baroque afterlife.
- **Lalo Schifrin – "Amityville Horror Theme" (1979) -** Children's chorus meets hell-house tension. Nominated for Academy Award; banned from early screenings for "too scary."
- **Riz Ortolani – "Cannibal Holocaust Theme" (1980, recorded 1979) -** Pastoral melody disguising atrocity. The most beautiful horror ever written for the most banned film ever made.

By the time *The Omen's* choir shouted in Latin and Goblin's witches whispered in Italian, horror's music had completed its metamorphosis from orchestral damnation to electric delirium. Every heartbeat that followed in the 1980s slasher boom pulsed from these notes.

THE AGE OF SLASHERS, TEEN ANGST & NIGHTMARE GLAM (1978–2000s)

"Fear found its rhythm, and horror learned to dance."

From Carpenter's heartbeat synths to Marilyn Manson's industrial scream, this was horror's pop revolution when the genre stopped whispering and started thrashing. These weren't just scores, they were spells, parties, dirges, and revenge fantasies, all wrapped in eyeliner and VHS static.

- **Stevie Wonder – "Superstition" (1972) – The Thing / Jeepers Creepers -** Blues funk turned horror omen. The soundtrack of bad timing.
- **Pino Donaggio – "Carrie (The Prom Scene)" (1976) -** Sweet orchestration collapses into psychic rage. A masterclass in tonal inversion.

- **Blue Öyster Cult – "(Don't Fear) The Reaper" (1976)** - Romantic death anthem. From *Halloween* to *The Stand*, mortality never sounded so cool.
- **The Damned – "Neat Neat Neat" (1977)** – **Baby Driver / Halloween Kills** - Punk energy weaponized for cinematic chaos. *Legacy:* the sound of teenage rampage and ritual murder montages.
- **John Carpenter – "Halloween Theme" (1978)** - Composed in 5/4 time on a cheap synthesizer. No orchestra, no budget, just dread. The heartbeat of the slasher era. *Legacy:* Spawned sequels, imitators, and the modern horror sound.
- **Goblin – "Dawn of the Dead" (1978)** - A score that's both feral and hypnotic. A sonic apocalypse of pounding basslines, tribal percussion, and eerie synth refrains. Their music transforms the zombie mall siege into an operatic descent into consumerist hell.
- **Harry Manfredini – "Ki Ki Ki Ma Ma Ma" (1980)** – **Friday the 13ᵗʰ** - A whisper turned into fear itself. Recorded voice samples of "kill her, mommy" became slasher symphony.
- **Wendy Carlos & Rachel Elkind – "Main Title (The Shining)" (1980)** - The "Dies Irae" rewritten in synth, Kubrick's descent into madness scored like a cathedral collapsing.
- **Ennio Morricone – "Humanity Part II" (1982)** – **The Thing** - Minimal, pulsing, tragic, Carpenter's collaborator gives paranoia a heartbeat colder than Antarctica. *Nominated for* Saturn Award for Best Music.
- **John Carpenter – "Chariots of Pumpkins" (1982)** – **Halloween III: Season of the Witch** - Synth apocalypse. Equal parts haunted carousel and digital nightmare. *Legacy:* Became one of Carpenter's most sampled tracks.
- **John Harrison – "Prologue / Welcome to the Creepshow" (1982)** – **Creepshow** - John Harrison's synth-and-organ overture opens Creepshow with pure comic-book horror flair. Part EC Comics nostalgia, part midnight movie menace. The track's eerie laughter, theremin-like tones, and thunderclap drums set the mood for the film's anthology of terror, embodying the perfect balance of camp and creep.
- **Goblin – "Tenebrae" (1982)** - Argento's giallo fever turned into disco nightmare. Harpsichords, choirs, and paranoia. *Nominated for* Nastro d'Argento; still DJ-sampled worldwide.
- **Michael Jackson – "Thriller" (1982)** - Grammy-winning, MTV-defining, Vincent Price–narrated masterpiece. *Won* 8 Grammys; eternal king of pop horror.
- **Jerry Goldsmith – "Poltergeist" (1982)** - A masterclass in deceptive beauty, opening with the ethereal "Carol Anne's Theme," a lullaby so sweet it masks the terror to come. As the film descends into spectral chaos, the music erupts into shrieking brass and atonal dread, blending classical orchestration with avant-garde experimentation. Nominated for the Academy Award for Best Original Score, it remains one of Goldsmith's most haunting and influential works, defining suburban supernatural horror for decades to follow.
- **Jerry Goldsmith – "Gremlins" (1984)** A mischievous masterpiece of dark whimsy, walks the line between Christmas cheer and chaotic horror.
- **Charles Bernstein – "A Nightmare on Elm Street Theme" (1984)** - Dreamlike yet metallic, this score made Freddy Krueger immortal. The synths sound like they're bleeding.
- **Rockwell – "Somebody's Watching Me" (1984)** - Pop paranoia in 4/4. The unofficial theme for suburban dread.
- **Screamin' Jay Hawkins – "I Put a Spell on You" (1956, reissued 1984)** - The birth of rock horror. Used in countless films. The original possession ballad.
- **Ray Parker Jr. – "Ghostbusters" (1984)** - Paranormal funk. *Oscar-nominated* for Best Original Song; pure 80s immortality.
- **Oingo Boingo – "Dead Man's Party" (1985)** - Danny Elfman's Halloween anthem. The song you dance to while something watches.
- **The Cramps – "Surfin' Dead" (1985)** – **Return of the Living Dead** - Rockabilly necromania. Zombies go punk.
- **45 Grave – "Partytime (1985)** – **Return of the Living Dead** - A deliriously punk celebration of decay, fuses camp, chaos, and corpse humor into one undead anthem.

- **Alice Cooper – "He's Back (The Man Behind the Mask)" (1986) – Jason Lives -** Camp, blood, and glam. Horror becomes music video mythology.
- **Huey Lewis and the News – "Hip to Be Square" (1986) – American Psycho -** Yuppie horror's soundtrack to sociopathy. Blood never grooved so hard.
- **Iron Butterfly - "In-A-Gadda-Da-Vida" (1968) – Manhunter (1986) -** The sound of transformation, madness, and descent. That droning organ and tribal drum solo embody everything 80s psychological horror stood for: ritual, power, and delirium.
- **Harry Manfredini – "Friday the 13th Part VI: Jason Lives – Main Titles" (1986) -** Gothic grandeur and 80s power-synth. Horror's rock opera moment.
- **Christopher Young – "Hellraiser Main Title" (1987) -** Gothic sensuality meets industrial horror. Organs, choirs, and desire braided into a lament for the damned.
- **Alan Silvestri – "Predator Theme" (1987) -** Technically action, spiritually horror, percussion and brass sculpting jungle paranoia.
- **Dokken – "Dream Warriors" (1987) – A Nightmare on Elm Street 3 -** Hair metal meets Freddy. MTV horror perfection.
- **Harry Belafonte – "Day-O (The Banana Boat Song)" – Beetlejuice (1988) -** Possession has never been so fun. Calypso meets chaos as ghosts crash a dinner party in one of cinema's greatest musical moments.
- **The Dickies – "Killer Klowns from Outer Space" (1988) -** Carnival punk at its wildest. A cult classic theme song for cosmic absurdity.
- **The Ramones – "Pet Sematary" (1989) -** Written for Stephen King's film. Campy, macabre, iconic. *Nominated for* a Razzie, loved by fans forever.
- **Screaming Mad George – "Society Suite (The Shunting)" (1989) -** Body horror's most grotesque symphony. Surreal, satirical, and unforgettable.
- **Angelo Badalamenti – "Twin Peaks Theme" (1990)-** Dream-pop dread. Not strictly horror, but its influence haunts everything from *It Follows* to *Hereditary. Won* Grammy for Best Pop Instrumental Performance.
- **MC Hammer – "Addams Groove" (1991) – The Addams Family -** The creepiest, kookiest hip-hop crossover in history. MC Hammer turned gothic chic into dance-floor gold with this Grammy-nominated hit.
- **Goo Goo Dolls – "I'm Awake Now" (1991) – Freddy's Dead: The Final Nightmare -** Channels insomnia, fear, and defiance, a perfect fit for Freddy's dream-haunting mythology. Its grunge-punk energy captured early '90s horror's shift from camp to angst, making it one of the standout songs in the franchise's soundtrack legacy.
- **Philip Glass – "It Was Always You, Helen" (1992) – Candyman -** With its cathedral-like organ and echoing soprano, the theme mourns as much as it terrifies. A requiem for obsession, myth, and doomed romance. Though never nominated for an Oscar, it's revered as one of horror's most artful and unforgettable scores.
- **Korn – "Kidnap the Sandy Claws" (1993 / 2008 Remix) -** Nightmare Before Christmas gets nu-metal. Halloween becomes rebellion.
- **Danny Elfman – "This Is Halloween" – The Nightmare Before Christmas (1993) -** Whimsical macabre perfection. *Grammy-nominated;* the blueprint for gothic musical cinema.
- **The Cure – "Burn" (1994) – The Crow -** Gothic grief and beauty incarnate. *The Crow* soundtrack became the holy scripture of 90s darkness.
- **Nick Cave & The Bad Seeds – "Red Right Hand" (1994) – Scream, Hellboy, Peaky Blinders -** Ominous, sexy, biblical menace. The ultimate "villain walking" track.
- **Nine Inch Nails – "Closer (Precursor Mix)" (1995) – Se7en -** Mechanical lust meets serial killer aesthetics. Defined the sound of psychological horror for a decade.
- **Marilyn Manson – "Sweet Dreams (Are Made of This)" (1995) -** Eurythmics reborn in purgatory. Used in *House on Haunted Hill* remake; pure industrial seduction.

- **Bonnie Tyler – "Total Eclipse of the Heart" (1983) – Urban Legend (1998) -** Romantic hysteria turned to slasher poetry. Reclaimed as ironic perfection.
- **Rob Dougan – "Clubbed to Death (Kurayamino Mix)" – The Matrix (1999) -** Neo-noir electronica fused with horror aesthetics; became trailer staple for dystopian thrillers.
- **Harvey Danger – "Flagpole Sitta" (1997) – Disturbing Behavior (1998) -** Paranoid pop anthem. Teen fear disguised as sarcasm.
- **Rob Zombie – "Dragula" (1998) -** From *The Matrix* to *Bride of Chucky*, industrial dominance defined the late 90s. The mosh pit became the haunted house.
- **Rob Zombie – "Living Dead Girl" (1998) -** Industrial burlesque anthem. Horror's first self-aware superstar director sings his own myth.
- **Class of '99 – "Another Brick in the Wall Part 2" (1998) –** *The Faculty* - Late-'90s alt-rock supergroup turns Pink Floyd's anti-authority anthem into a body-snatcher battle cry. Snarling guitars, zombified school choir, pure teen-uprising energy.
- **Korn feat. Amy Lee – "Freak on a Leash (Gothic Remix)" (1998–2007) -** Bridged horror's dark femininity and nu-metal rage; frequent fan edit in *Resident Evil* fan culture.
- **Gary Jules – "Mad World" (2001) – Donnie Darko -** A soft apocalypse in song form. Minimalism meets existential despair. *Won* Rolling Stone's "Best Movie Song of the Decade."
- **Drowning Pool – "Bodies" (2001) – Dracula 2000, Saw trailers -** Metal rage meets cinematic montage. Became a staple of early-2000s horror marketing.
- **Charles McDonald – "You Are My Sunshine" (2001) – Jeepers Creepers -** A deceptively gentle classic turned nightmare fuel, this rendition of "You Are My Sunshine" underscores *Jeepers Creepers* with chilling irony. It is also featured in the movie *Annabelle: Creation*.
- **John Murphy – "In the House – In a Heartbeat" (2002) –** *28 Days Later* - Post-apocalyptic adrenaline; used in horror trailers ever since.
- **The Vogues – "Turn Around, Look at Me" – Final Destination 3 (2006) -** Retro fatalism; every lyric foreshadows death. 60s sunshine becomes morgue light.
- **The Carpenters – "We've Only Just Begun" – 1408 (2007) -** Creepy optimism; the calmest descent into madness ever scored.
- **Nick Cave & Warren Ellis – "Song for Bob" (2007) -** Elegiac horror. The quiet grief that ends the apocalypse. Used in *The Road* and *The Mist*, sorrow as survival.
- **Tiny Tim – "Tiptoe Through the Tulips" (1968) – Insidious (2010) -** Whimsical nightmare. The scariest falsetto ever recorded. *Legacy:* Revived an entire subgenre of ironic terror.
- **Patience & Prudence – "Tonight You Belong to Me" – American Horror Story: Murder House (2011) -** Vintage innocence turned ghostly. A 1950s love song twisted into dread.

THE NEW AGE OF ELEVATED HORROR (2010–Present)

"Fear slowed down, dressed in ritual, and whispered instead of screamed."

The 2010s didn't invent horror's sophistication, it remembered it. Minimalism became sacred again. Every synth, scream, and silence served the story. Horror became *beautiful*, terrifying, and critically adored.

- **Le Castle Vania – "John Wick Mode" (used in horror trailers) -** Neo-noir dread meets club pulse. Influenced *The Menu*, *Infinity Pool*, and *The Perfection*.
- **Arcadia – "Goodbye Horses" (1988) – Silence of the Lambs (recurrent) -** Used across decades, chilling perfection of character psychosis. Timeless queer-coded menace.
- **Charlie Clouser – "Hello Zepp" (2004–2021) – Saw Franchise -** Operatic industrial suspense. The reveal anthem of an entire generation. Expanded through *Spiral*; *Grammy-nominated*.

- **Joseph Bishara – "Insidious Theme" (2010) -** Screeching violins, childlike waltz, demonic lullaby. Reinvented mainstream supernatural sound design.
- **Joseph Bishara – "The Conjuring Theme" (2013) -** Relentless, sparse, and diabolical. A return to practical horror music: creaks, strings, whispers, breath.
- **Disasterpeace – "Heels" (2014) – It Follows -** Retro synths pulse like guilt. Carpenter's spiritual descendant. *Independent Spirit Award* nominee for score.
- **Abel Korzeniowski – "Theme from Penny Dreadful" (2014) -** Victorian sorrow in full symphonic bloom. Haunting, romantic, tragic. Gothic television at its most elegant.
- **Mica Levi – "Love" (2014) – Under the Skin -** Alien seduction rendered in strings. *BAFTA-nominated, Academy shortlisted.*
- **Daniel Hart – "What We Do in the Shadows Main Theme" (2014) -** Playful mock-gothic anthem. Horror comedy's most stylish entrance.
- **Mark Korven – "The Witch Main Theme" (2015) -** Strings, breath, and ritual percussion. Primitive, pure, and holy. Korven also built the "Apprehension Engine" an instrument made to scare you.
- **Sam Raimi & Joseph LoDuca – "Ash vs Evil Dead Theme" (2015) -** Guitar and gore, horror's rock revival. Campy, loud, perfect.
- **Glen Campbell – "Rhinestone Cowboy" (2015) -** A bittersweet country-pop classic turned sinister through cinematic irony. In multiple horror films.
- **Abel Korzeniowski – "A Cure for Wellness" (2016) -** Psychological luxury and illness made operatic. A modern nod to *Vertigo* and *The Omen*.
- **Benjamin Wallfisch – "Every 27 Years" (2017) – IT -** Piano and childlike motifs become cosmic dread. *Saturn Award* nominee; *Grammy* for "Best Score Soundtrack."
- **Michael Abels – "Sikiliza Kwa Wahenga" (2017) – Get Out -** Swahili for "Listen to your ancestors." A warning disguised as melody. *Won* World Soundtrack Award for Discovery Composer; *nominated* for multiple critic honors.
- **Ben Salisbury & Geoff Barrow – "The Alien" (2018) – Annihilation -** Synth landscapes unravel into Lovecraftian beauty. Cited by critics as "the sound of consciousness breaking apart."
- **Colin Stetson – "Reborn" (2018) – Hereditary -** Avant-garde saxophones and human breathing as score. Terror through dissonance; grief through sound. *Won* several critic awards.
- **Thom Yorke – "Suspirium" (2018) –** Melancholy piano spell. *Oscar-shortlisted;* hypnotic, mournful, transcendent.
- **The Newton Brothers – "Hill House / Bly Manor Themes" (2018–2020) -** Ghost stories scored like requiems. Each theme mourns, rather than screams.
- **Billie Eilish – "bury a friend" (2019) -** Modern pop's descent into nightmare. Grammy-winning; the new face of psychological pop horror.
- **Michael Abels – "I Got 5 on It (Tethered Mix)" (2019) – Us -** Luniz's 1995 hip-hop anthem twisted into orchestral dread. Turned pop culture into nightmare. *Nominated* for Saturn Award.
- **Bobby Krlic (The Haxan Cloak) – "Fire Temple" (2019) – Midsommar -** Folk horror euphoria, the sound of grief dissolving into ritual. *BAFTA-nominated;* an anthem for pagan rebirth.
- **Mark Korven – "The Lighthouse" (2019) -** Sea shanty meets madness. Foghorns turned symphonic. *Won* multiple critic awards; psychological soundscape masterpiece.
- **Brian Tyler – "Ready or Not" (2019) -** Baroque action-horror elegance. Bridal vengeance scored like a bloody ballet.
- **Lana Del Rey – "Season of the Witch" (2019) – Scary Stories to Tell in the Dark -** Melancholy incantation. Folk-horror aesthetic wrapped in dream pop. *Critic's Choice nominee.*

- **Phoebe Bridgers – "I Know the End" (2020)** - Apocalyptic crescendo; screams and horns meet quiet doom. Used in multiple horror fan edits; internet folk horror icon.
- **The Weeknd – "After Hours / Heartless / Blinding Lights Trilogy" (2020)** - Neon dread. Synth horror meets fame decay. Influence spans *The Idol*, *Talk to Me*, and *Smile*'s aesthetic lineage.
- **Nick Cave & Warren Ellis – "All Things Move Toward Their End" (2021)** - The final words of modern horror. The music of quiet apocalypse: grief, beauty, and acceptance.
- **Florence + The Machine – "Call Me Cruella" (2021)** - Gothic glam revival. Disney villainy reborn as punk opera.
- **Mark Korven – "The Black Phone Theme" (2022)** - Retro dread, analog texture. A love letter to 70s horror sound. Captured the spirit of childhood fear in sound design form.
- **Cristobal Tapia de Veer – "Smile" (2022)** - Discordant choir horror. Distorted beauty meets panic attack energy. Composer also scored *The White Lotus*, proving true horror wears masks.
- **Disasterpeace – "Birth" (2022) – Bodies Bodies Bodies** - Satirical dread and danceable doom. For the TikTok generation of horror lovers.
- **Rob Simonsen – "Smile (Reprise)" (2022)** - Emotional horror's full circle. Sadness and sickness intertwined.
- **Lady Gaga – "Bloody Mary (Wednesday Mix)" (2022)** - Netflix's gothic revival anthem. Revived on TikTok via Wednesday's dance scene; *charted globally again 10 years later.*
- **Yeah Yeah Yeahs – "Heads Will Roll" (2009, resurgent 2022)** - *Jennifer's Body* cult classic turned internet ritual. The anthem of feminine rage.
- **Doja Cat – "Demons" (2023)** - Mainstream horror-rap fusion; music video homages *The Shining* and *Hereditary.*
- **Olivia Rodrigo – "Vampire" (2023)** - Heartbreak reframed as bloodletting. The teenage scream reborn as chart-topping confession.
- **Mitski – "Bug Like an Angel" (2023)** - Existential horror through serenity. Modern melancholy cinematic enough for *The Witch 2.*

In the digital age, horror music isn't just a score, it's possession through headphones. From *Carpenter's synthesizer* to *Eilish's whisper*, we've come full circle: the ritual of fear reborn as art, pop, and prophecy.

THE FINAL HORROR SOUNDTRACK ADDENDUM: "THE ICONS WE ALMOST SUMMONED"

FROM SCREEN TO LEGEND

- **The Rolling Stones – "Paint It Black" (1966)** - A Vietnam-era dirge that became horror shorthand for despair and doom (*The Devil's Advocate*, *The Witcher*, *Westworld*).
- **The Rolling Stones – "Sympathy for the Devil" (1968)** - Used in countless horrors and thrillers (*Interview with the Vampire*, *The Devil's Advocate*). Evil's most elegant theme song.
- **Blue Öyster Cult – "Godzilla" (1977)** - Yes, a novelty track, but also the most joyful monster anthem ever made.
- **Talking Heads – "Psycho Killer" (1977)** - Predates the slasher boom and yet it *is* the slasher boom in sound. *Legacy:* Sampled and quoted in a hundred films and trailers.
- **Warren Zevon – "Werewolves of London" (1978)** - Iconic piano riff and howl. Equal parts camp and cool.
- **AC/DC – "Highway to Hell" (1979)** - Used in *Final Destination 2*, *Supernatural*, and dozens more. Hell's official road trip song.
- **Creedence Clearwater Revival – "Bad Moon Rising" – An American Werewolf in London (1981)** - Playful prophecy of doom; the full moon's folk anthem.

- **AC/DC – "Who Made Who" –** *Maximum Overdrive (1986)* - Stephen King directed chaos to this; it's horror's headbanging moment.
- **The Cranberries – "Zombie" (1994)** - Grief and protest turned horror metaphor.
- **Rob Zombie – "Superbeast" (1999)** - The late-90s horror identity. Pure adrenaline and fire.
- **Marilyn Manson – "This Is Halloween" (2008)** - His cover made the original even darker. Perfect Halloween reboot.
- **Queen – "Don't Stop Me Now" –** *Shaun of the Dead (2004)* - The zombie apocalypse disco classic.
- **Bonnie Tyler – "Holding Out for a Hero" –** *Shrek 2 / Bandits / horror trailers galore* - Overused? Yes. Iconic? Eternally.

PSYCHOLOGICAL, CHILLS & ATMOSPHERE

- **Roy Orbison – "In Dreams" –** *Blue Velvet (1986)* - The most unnerving lip-sync in cinema. Lynchian horror given lullaby form.
- **Angela Badalamenti – "Mysteries of Love" –** *Blue Velvet (1986)* - Dream pop turned dread.
- **Johnny Cash – "The Mercy Seat" (1988)** - Biblical death row song, covered by Nick Cave, used in multiple horror soundtracks.
- **Nine Inch Nails – "Something I Can Never Have" –** *Natural Born Killers (1994)* - Beautiful nihilism. Played like a murder confession.

CULT, CAMP & CHAOS

- **Rocky Horror Picture Show – "Science Fiction/Double Feature" (1975)** - Meta-horror meets musical longing. The hymn of every midnight moviegoer.
- **The Ramones – "Chainsaw" (1977)** - A two-minute horror movie about *Texas Chainsaw Massacre.*
- **Weird Al Yankovic – "Nature Trail to Hell" (1984)** - A parody that's better than most real slashers.
- **Jonathan Coulton - "Skullcrusher Mountain" (2003)** - Villain love song turned internet cult classic.

BONUS DEEP CUTS (FOR TRUE HORROR SCHOLARS)

- **Harry Belafonte – "Jump in the Line" (1961)** - Because every horror story should end with a dance on the ceiling.
- **Peter Gabriel – "Intruder" (1980)** - The first song ever recorded with gated drums. Sounds like someone breaking in.
- **Bauhaus – "Dark Entries" (1980)** - Post-punk descent used in *The Hunger.*
- **Shriekback – "This Big Hush" –** *Manhunter (1986)* - Dreamlike menace; the true soul of Michael Mann's horror.
- **The Smiths – "How Soon Is Now?" –** *The Craft (1996)* - Witchcore perfection. The anthem of misunderstood power.
- **Marilyn Manson – "Tainted Love" (2001) –** *Not Another Teen Movie / Resident Evil* - Camp goth meets nostalgia.

THE LOST ICONS: FINAL ADDITIONS TO THE ANTHOLOGY OF HORROR SOUNDTRACK

CINEMATIC & CULT ESSENTIALS

- **Shirley Bassey – "Where Do I Begin (Love Story)" /** *American Horror Story* **reuse** - Tragic melodrama elevated to murder-ballad status in modern horror TV.
- **Joy Division – "Atmosphere" (1980)** - The funeral march of post-punk; featured in *Donnie Darko* and countless fan requiems.
- **The Smiths – "Asleep" (1986) –** *The Perks of Being a Wallflower* **/ horror trailers** - A suicide lullaby whispered through decades of melancholic cinema.

- **New Order – "True Faith" (1987)** - Used in *American Psycho 2* and horror montages. Neon dread disguised as dance.
- **Annie Lennox – "Love Song for a Vampire" (1992)** – *Bram Stoker's Dracula* - A baroque ballad dripping with gothic tragedy. *Golden Globe nominated;* the definitive vampire elegy.
- **Massive Attack – "Angel" (1998)** - Used in *The Matrix, Constantine, House on Haunted Hill;* the ultimate stalker bassline.

THE HORROR-ADJACENT LEGENDS

- **Garbage – "#1 Crush" (1996)** – *Romeo + Juliet / The Craft trailers* - Obsession, witchcraft, desire, the 90s in one breath.
- **Placebo – "Running Up That Hill" (2003 Cover)** – *Bones / Haunted trailers* - Dark-wave perfection; the goth resurrection of Kate Bush.
- **Fever Ray – "If I Had a Heart" (2009)** – *Vikings / The Northman trailers* - The sound of pagan horror: slow, primal, and genderless.

FROM THE SHADOWS OF CINEMA

- **Dead Can Dance – "The Host of Seraphim" (1988)** – *The Mist (2007), Baraka (1992)* - Apocalyptic sorrow incarnate. *The Mist*'s ending owes everything to this track.
- **Radiohead – "Climbing Up the Walls" (1997)** - A true horror song hiding in plain sight. Used in *The Last Exorcism* trailer; clinically terrifying.
- **Cocteau Twins – "Lorelei" (1984)** - Otherworldly angelic dread; soundtrack to countless horror dream sequences.
- **Lisa Gerrard & Hans Zimmer – "Now We Are Free" (2000)** – *Gladiator / horror trailers* - Ethereal transcendence often reused for supernatural finales.
- **Peter Gabriel – "Darkness" (2002)** - Used in multiple horror fan films. Existential dread in symphonic form.
- **Thom Yorke – "Hearing Damage" (2009)** – *The Twilight Saga: New Moon* - Vampire depression rendered electronic.
- **Clint Mansell & Kronos Quartet – "Welcome to Lunar Industries" (2009)** – *Moon* - Cold isolation; psychological sci-fi horror's modern sound.

HORROR TV & GAMING ANTHEMS

- **Akira Yamaoka – "Theme of Laura" (2001)** – *Silent Hill 2* - Melancholy, industrial, unforgettable, defines survival-horror sound.
- **Akira Yamaoka – "Promise (Reprise)" (2001)** - Sorrow as soundtrack; often used in fan edits and horror compilations.
- **Bear McCreary – "The Walking Dead Main Title" (2010)** - Rust, fear, humanity. Instantly recognizable.
- **Gustavo Santaolalla – "The Last of Us Theme" (2013)** - Fragile guitar strings that could break your heart or summon apocalypse.
- **Mick Gordon – "Rip & Tear" – DOOM** *(2016)* - Metal horror reborn. demons never sounded so alive.

SEASONAL, PARTY, AND DARK-POP ESSENTIALS

- **My Chemical Romance – "Mama" (2006)** - A war-torn horror musical in three minutes.
- **Florence + The Machine – "Seven Devils" (2011)** – *Revenge trailers / horror TV* - Arguably *the* most cinematic witch song of the century.
- **Hozier – "Arsonist's Lullabye" (2014)** - Modern gothic hymn. Rage and repentance intertwined.
- **Halsey – "Control" (2015)** - Possession in first person. A supernatural manifesto for Gen Z.
- **Melanie Martinez – "Tag, You're It / Milk and Cookies" (2015)** - Childhood twisted into nightmare pop.
- **Ruelle – "Monsters" (2015)** - Soft menace turned empowerment; staple of horror show endings.
- **Sam Smith – "Writing's on the Wall" (2015)** – *Spectre* - Bond ballad turned existential horror theme; cinematic death wish.

- **Kaleo – "Way Down We Go" (2016)** - Trailer staple for sin, revenge, and descent.
- **Bishop Briggs – "River" (2016)** - Used in *The Hunger Games*, *Resident Evil* trailers; baptism by fury.
- **Labrinth & Zendaya – "All For Us" (2019)** - Euphoria turned to cult ritual.

THE HALLOWED EXTRAS:
HALLOWEEN HONORABLE MENTIONS

"When October hits, these songs wake up on their own."

VINTAGE & NOVELTY CLASSICS

- **Screamin' Jay Hawkins – "Little Demon" (1956)** - The lesser-known sibling to "Spell on You." Raw, unhinged brilliance.
- **Bobby "Boris" Pickett – "Monster Mash" (1962)** - The original Halloween novelty hit. A graveyard smash that never died.
- **Rocky Horror Picture Show Cast – "Time Warp" (1975)** - The ultimate audience-participation anthem. "It's just a jump to the left…"
- **Little Nell & Richard O'Brien – "Sweet Transvestite" –** *Rocky Horror Picture Show* - Glam-horror masterpiece; equal parts camp and chaos.
- **Elvira, Mistress of the Dark – "Trick or Treat" (1983)** - Camp queen anthem; pure VHS-era kitsch.
- **Ellen Greene & Rick Moranis – "Suddenly Seymour" (1986) -** Tenderness amid terror; the only duet that makes a carnivorous plant cry. A cult classic of sincerity in a nightmare.
- **Bette Midler – "I Put a Spell on You" (1993) –** *Hocus Pocus* - Halloween karaoke royalty.

GOTH, PUNK & ALTERNATIVE ESSENTIALS

- **Bauhaus – "Bela Lugosi's Dead" (1979)** - The gothic national anthem.
- **The Misfits – "Halloween I & II" (1981)** - Punk horror distilled to its black-and-orange core.
- **The Cramps – "Goo Goo Muck" (1981)** - Psychobilly sleaze recently resurrected by *Wednesday*.
- **The Cure – "Lullaby" (1989)** - *Arachnophobia* made sensual.
- **Echo & the Bunnymen – "People Are Strange" –** *The Lost Boys* **(1987)** - The definitive vampire club vibe.
- **Type O Negative – "Black No. 1 (Little Miss Scare-All)" (1993)** - Doom metal romance at its most theatrical.
- **The Horrors – "Sea Within a Sea" (2009)** - Neo-goth grandeur. Post-apocalyptic ballroom music.

CINEMATIC DEEP CUTS & TV HAUNTS

- **Harry Manfredini – "Jason's Theme (Part III 3-D Mix)" (1982)** - Disco slash, literally.
- **Danny Elfman – "Beetlejuice Main Title" (1988)** - Whimsical chaos incarnate.
- **Danny Elfman – "Edward Scissorhands – Ice Dance" (1990)** - The sound of bittersweet magic under snow.
- **Graeme Revell – "The Craft Main Title" (1996)** - Witchy perfection.

HIDDEN MODERN GEMS

- **The Killers – "Bones" (2006)** - Desert-goth romance directed by Tim Burton.
- **Aurora – "Running with the Wolves" (2015)** - Modern fairy-tale ferocity.
- **Lovecraft (Chicago Collective) – "Beyond the Void" (2020)** - Synth-wave horror revival perfection.
- **Creeper – "Annabelle" (2020)** - Modern horror-punk resurrection.
- **Boy Harsher – "Machina" (2022)** - Eerie synth intimacy; featured in *Halloween Ends*.
- **Florence + The Machine – "Haunted House (Unreleased live version, 2022) -** For when the party ends and the spirits linger. Because the night always wants an encore.

MISSING, BUT ESSENTIAL

- **The Animals – "House of the Rising Sun" (1964)** – Brooding, haunted-house standard. The Original.
- **Sam the Sham & The Pharaohs – "Lil' Red Riding Hood" (1966)** – Fairy-tale creep with a wink.

- **Eagles – "Witchy Woman" (1972)** – Classic-rock witch anthem
- **Alice Cooper – "Welcome to My Nightmare" (1975)** – Shock-rock Halloween DNA.
- **DJ Jazzy Jeff & The Fresh Prince – "A Nightmare on My Street" (1988)** – Beloved Elm Street-era novelty/rap.
- **Jace Everett – "Bad Things" (2008)** – *True Blood* theme; sultry Southern-gothic.
- **The Prodigy – "Firestarter" (1996)** – Menacing rave energy; '90s Halloween floors.
- **OutKast feat. Kelis – "Dracula's Wedding" (2003)** - A funk-goth fantasy turns vampirism into a metaphor for love and fear of intimacy. André 3000 and Kelis croon over harpsichords, synths, and undead seduction, blending humor and horror with effortless cool.
- **Ghost – "Square Hammer" (2016)** – Modern arena-goth banger tailor-made for October.
- **MGMT – "Little Dark Age" (2017; viral 2021-22)** – Synth-noir that soundtracks modern spooky edits.

DISNEY / SPOOKY-FAMILY CANON

- **Disney's Haunted Mansion – "Grim Grinning Ghosts" (1969)** – The theme every Halloween Park plays.
- **Hocus Pocus – "Come Little Children (Sarah's Theme)" (1993)** – Ultra-recognizable, chills-inducing.

Paranormal Playlist

Index of Film

H

M

Q

Bibliography

"'10 Best Mockumentary Horror Movies.'" *CBR (Comic Book Resources).* Accessed October 5, 2025. https://www.cbr.com/best-mockumentary-horror-movies/.

"'10 Facts About *Night of the Living Dead.*'" *Mental Floss.* Accessed October 5, 2025. https://www.mentalfloss.com/article/91635/10-facts-about-night-living-dead#:~:text=4,.crew's%20leftover%20lunch%20was%20employed.

"'10 Movies to Watch If You Liked *Hereditary.*'" *Business Insider.* Last modified April 2020. https://www.businessinsider.com/movies-similar-to-hereditary-horror-2020-4#:~:text=Films%20like%20%22The%20Witch%2C%22,unusually%20large%20sum%20of%20money.

"'13 Horror Movie Musicals to Add to Your Watchlist.'" *HorrorFam.* Accessed October 5, 2025. https://horrorfam.com/horror-movie-musicals/#:~:text=13%20Horror%20Movie%20Musicals%20to%20Add%20to,*%20The%20Horror%20of%20Party%20Beach%20(1964).

"'30 Fun Facts About *Misery.*'" *Halloween Year Round.* Last modified November 30, 2020. https://halloweenyearround.wordpress.com/2020/11/30/30-fun-facts-about-misery/#:~:text=In%20the%20original%20novel%2C%20Annie,a%20fan%20of%20choreographing%20fights.

"'60 Things You Didn't Know About Alfred Hitchcock's *Psycho.*'" *Film Companion.* Accessed October 5, 2025. https://www.filmcompanion.in/features/60-things-you-didnt-know-about-alfred-hitchcocks-psycho#:~:text=11,.those%20seen%20in%20this%20movie.

"'Abbott and Costello Meet Frankenstein: Making a Monster Comedy.'" *Antonia Carlotta.* Accessed October 5, 2025. https://www.antoniacarlotta.com/home/abbott-and-costello-meet-frankenstein-making-a-monster-comedy#:~:text=to%20be%20buffoons.-,He%20said%20he%20loved%20the%20horror%20films%20when%20he%20felt,Monsters%20and%20ruining%20their%20legacy.

"About: *Hammer House of Horror (1980).*" *Hammer House of Horror TV Series (Official Website).* Accessed October 5, 2025. https://www.hammerhouseofhorrortvseries.co.uk/about/#:~:text=Welcome.%20In%201980%2C%20Hammer%20Films%2C%20the%20renowned,for%20television%20titled%20Hammer%20House%20of%20Horror.

"'Abraham Lincoln: Vampire Hunter' NBC Series Announced." *Variety.* Last modified October 2018. https://variety.com/2018/tv/news/abraham-lincoln-vampire-hunter-nbc-series-1202976374/.

"Absolute Horror Wiki: *And Now the Screaming Starts!*" *Absolute Horror Wiki.* Fandom. Accessed October 5, 2025. https://absolutehorror.fandom.com/wiki/And_Now_the_Screaming_Starts!#:~:text=And%20Now%20the%20Screaming%20Starts!%20is%20a%201973%20British%20gothic,now%20a%20four%2Dstar%20hotel.

"Absolute Horror Wiki: *Asylum (1972).*" *Absolute Horror Wiki.* Fandom. Accessed October 5, 2025. https://absolutehorror.fandom.com/wiki/Asylum_(1972)#:~:text=Asylum%20(also%20known%20as%20House,debut%20on%20November%2017%2C%201972.

"'Adaptations.'" In *The Cambridge Companion to Frankenstein*, edited by Andrew Smith, Cambridge University Press. Accessed October 5, 2025. https://cambridge.org/core/books/abs/cambridge-companion-to-frankenstein/adaptations/17F0524D1F4490EB16B681148DBF5F36#:~:text=In%201958%2C%20the%20year%20after%20its%20success,the%20programme%20in%20a%20very%20specific%20way.

"American Gothic." *Headhunter's Horror House Wiki.* Fandom. Accessed October 5, 2025. https://headhuntershorrorhouse.fandom.com/wiki/American_Gothic#:~:text=American%20Gothic%20is%20an%20independent,Studios%20on%20October%202025th%2C%202005.

"'*Angst* (1983).'" *Film at Lincoln Center.* Accessed October 5, 2025. https://www.filmlinc.org/films/angst/.

"'Anthony Hopkins.'" *Turner Classic Movies (TCM).* Accessed October 5, 2025. https://www.tcm.com/tcmdb/person/88825%7C14307/Anthony-Hopkins.

"'Basque Mythology on Screen.'" *BasqueCulture.eus.* Accessed October 5, 2025. https://basqueculture.eus/en/stories/audiovisual/basque-mythology-on-screen.

"'Berserk' (1967) Review." *Alt Film Guide (AltFG).* Accessed October 5, 2025. https://www.altfg.com/berserk-movie-1967/#:~:text=Danny%20Fortune%20Published:%2017%20years,Hollywood%20vet%20v%20British%20sexpot.

"'Best Dracula Adaptations, According to Rotten Tomatoes.'" *MovieWeb.* Accessed October 5, 2025. https://movieweb.com/best-dracula-adaptations-according-to-rotten-tomatoes/#:~:text=It%20is%20not%20a%20perfect,94%25%20based%20on%2051%20reviews.

"'Best Horror Films Based on African Folklore.'" *MovieWeb.* Accessed October 5, 2025. https://movieweb.com/best-horror-based-on-african-folklore/#:~:text=Juju%20Stories%20is%20a%20Nigerian,college%20woman%20attracts%20her%20crush.

"Best Horror Movies of All Time." *Rotten Tomatoes Editorial.* Last modified 2025. https://editorial.rottentomatoes.com/guide/best-horror-movies-of-all-time/#:~:text=Dead%20of%20Night%20(1945)%20Tomatometer%20icon%2095%25,classic%20horror%20anthology%20that%20remains%20highly%20influential.

"'Best Johnny Depp and Tim Burton Movie Collaborations.'" *Collider.* Accessed October 5, 2025. https://collider.com/best-johnny-depp-and-tim-burton-movie-collaborations/#:~:text=Tim%20Burton%20has%20delighted%20audiences,animated%20and%20live%2Daction%20projects.

"'Best Krampus Movies to Watch This Holiday Season.'" *Creepy Catalog.* Accessed October 5, 2025. https://creepycatalog.com/krampus-movies/#:~:text=out%20of%20you.-,Best%20Krampus%20Movies,Devil%20Returns%20(see%20below).

"'Best One-Off Slasher Movies with No Sequels.'" *MovieWeb.* Accessed October 5, 2025. https://movieweb.com/best-one-off-slasher-movies-no-sequel/.

"'Best Time-Loop Horror Movies.'" *Collider.* Accessed October 5, 2025. https://collider.com/best-time-loop-horror-movies/.

"'Best Vampire Adaptations.'" *Book Riot.* Accessed October 5, 2025. https://bookriot.com/best-vampire-adaptations/#:~:text=In%201963%2C%20an%20Italian%20film,I%20love%20this.

"'Best Vampire Movies of All Time.'" *TheWrap.* Accessed October 5, 2025. https://www.thewrap.com/best-vampire-movies-of-all-time/.

"'Best Vampire Movies.'" *IGN.* Accessed October 5, 2025. https://www.ign.com/articles/best-vampire-movies.

"'Bigelow's *Near Dark* Becomes A24 Series.'" *Dark Horizons.* Accessed October 5, 2025. https://www.darkhorizons.com/bigelows-near-dark-becomes-a24-series/#:~:text=By,the%20group%20often%20singled%20out.

"'Black Friday' (1940)." *J.B. Kaufman's Movie of the Month.* Accessed October 5, 2025. https://www.jbkaufman.com/movie-of-the-month/black-friday-1940#:~:text=What%20one%20finds%2C%20instead%2C%20is,whom%20recognize%20him%20any%20more!.

"'The Black Sleep' (1956) Review." *Mana Pop.* Accessed October 5, 2025. https://manapop.com/film/the-black-sleep-1956-review/#:~:text=While%20The%20Black%20Sleep%20may,fans%20of%20vintage%20horror%20cinema.

"'The Blair Witch Project: Movie Facts.'" *Creepy Catalog.* Accessed October 5, 2025. https://creepycatalog.com/the-blair-witch-project-movie-facts/#:~:text=1.,%E2%80%94Heather%20Donahue%2C%20Michael%20C.

"Blaxploitation Horror Films." *Wikipedia: The Free Encyclopedia.* Last modified 2025. https://en.wikipedia.org/wiki/Blaxploitation_horror_films#:~:text=Blacula%20(1972)%2D%20directed%20by,has%20sex%20with%20a%20puppet.

"'Blood Bath' (1966)." *House of Mortal Cinema* (blog by John L. Probert). Last modified May 2016. https://johnlprobert.blogspot.com/2016/05/blood-bath-1966.html#:~:text=%E2%80%9CA%20box%20set%20of%20four,different%20to%20warrant%20individual%20releases.

"'Blood Bath' (1966) Review." *FlickFeast.* Accessed October 5, 2025. https://www.flickfeast.co.uk/reviews/film-reviews/31-days-horror-6-blood-bath-1966/.

"'Blood for Dracula (1974).'" *Enzian Theater.* Accessed October 5, 2025. https://enzian.org/film/blood-for-dracula/#:~:text=4K%20Restoration,for%20the%20first%20time%20ever.&text=%E2%80%9COutrageous%2C%20hilarious%20and%20shocking%2C,art%20at%20its%20very%20best.%E2%80%9D&text=%E2%80%9CUdo%20Kier's%20Idiosyncratic%20Dracula%20and,bad%20search%20for%20virgin%20blood.%E2%80%9D&text=%E2%80%9CPaul%20Morrissey's%20loose%20cin%C3%A9ma%2Dv%C3%A9rit%C3%A9,amateur%20actors%20into%20underground%20stars.%22.

"'Blood for Dracula.'" *Film at Lincoln Center.* Accessed October 5, 2025. https://www.filmlinc.org/films/blood-for-dracula/.

"'Blood for Dracula: Udo Kier and Paul Morrissey's Return to Excess.'" *Wasteland Arts.* Accessed October 5, 2025. https://www.wastelandarts.com/post/blood-for-dracula#:~:text=Like%20its%20precursor%20Flesh%20for,return%20to%20heights%20of%20wealth.

"'Bloodsucking Bastards (2015).'" *Rotten Tomatoes.* Accessed October 5, 2025. https://www.rottentomatoes.com/m/bloodsucking_bastards#:~:text=This%20film%20reminded%20me%20a,plus%20the%20office%20Content%20collapsed.

"'The Boogeyman and Other Monsters in Modern Horror.'" *Collider.* Accessed October 5, 2025. https://collider.com/the-boogeyman-horror-movies/#:~:text=Still%2C%20with%20Boogeyman%20being%20an,and%20Tim%20Burton's%20singing%20entity.

"'Bordello of Blood (1996).'" *The Bedlam Files.* Accessed October 5, 2025. https://thebedlamfiles.com/film/bordello-of-blood/#:~:text=The%20resulting%20film%2C%20directed%20by,added%20for%20its%20DVD%20release).

"'Book Series in Order: *Night Watch.*'" *Books on Board.* Accessed October 5, 2025. https://www.booksonboard.com/book-series-in-order/night-watch/.

"'Buffy the Vampire Slayer: Every Change from the 1992 Movie to the TV Show.'" *Screen Rant.* Accessed October 5, 2025. https://screenrant.com/buffy-vampire-slayer-tv-show-every-change-1992-movie/#:~:text=The%201992%20Buffy%20the%20Vampire,is%20set%20in%20Los%20Angeles.

"'Captain Kronos: Vampire Hunter (1974).'" *The Horror Syndicate.* Accessed October 5, 2025. https://thehorrorsyndicate.com/captain-kronos-vampire-hunter-1974-deep-cuts/#:~:text=Synopsis:,films)%20round%20out%20the%20cast.

"'Captive Wild Woman (1943) Review.'" *Mana Pop.* Accessed October 5, 2025. https://manapop.com/film/captive-wild-woman-1943-review/#:~:text=In%20conclusion%2C%20Captive%20Wild%20Woman,creative%20ingenuity%20of%20its%20time.

"'Carl Theodor Dreyer's Vampyr (1932).'" *366 Weird Movies.* Accessed October 5, 2025. https://366weirdmovies.com/carl-theodor-dreyers-vampyr-1932/#:~:text=But%20it%20turned%20out%20Dreyer,often%20find%20the%20film%20provocative.

"'Castle Freak (1995): A Bonkers Lovecraftian Remake.'" *Brian Fanelli Blog.* Last modified December 8, 2020. https://brianfanelli.com/2020/12/08/castle-freak-a-bonkers-lovecraftian-remake/#:~:text=Here's%20a%20piece%20of%20advice,)%2C%20are%20the%20film's%20leads.

"'CBS Late Movie Month: *Kingdom of the Spiders* (1977).'" *Bands About Movies.* Last modified July 3, 2023. https://bandsaboutmovies.com/2023/07/03/cbs-late-movie-month-kingdom-of-the-spiders-1977/.

"'The Class of Nuke 'Em High: 30 Years of Readin', Writin', and Radiation.'" *Daily Dead.* Accessed October 5, 2025. https://dailydead.com/class-of-nuke-em-high-30-years-of-readin-writin-radiation/#:~:text=Alongside%20The%20Toxic%20Avenger%2C%20Class,of%20siding%20with%20The%20Cretins.

"'Clive Barker's *Books of Blood*: Every Movie Adaptation Ranked.'" *Screen Rant*. Accessed October 5, 2025. https://screenrant.com/clive-barker-books-blood-every-movie-adaptation/#:~:text=Lord%20of%20Illusions%2C%20released%20in,horror%20movies%20of%20the%201990s.

"'Collaborators: Tim Burton and Johnny Depp.'" *Yahoo Entertainment*. Accessed October 5, 2025. https://www.yahoo.com/entertainment/collaborators-tim-burton-johnny-depp-230000371.html?guccounter=1&guce_referrer=aHR0cHM6Ly93d3cuZ29vZ2xlLmNvbS8&guce_referrer_sig=AQAAAJ6SsYF7gb07qKVzkRNg1DKtvToDsZynx6eSM-aAm-P5zyhxrgDAdrWi1TWIQI6qy_88ui-PfkbXaqkFM9Djjq4qNP2X6NaIOy2JWrF3kKNbWHUD_1nJ2wSlwNVwETNbe_euflbEfU-Fy2QnaFjTF6bo9TXjKWkYc5z6u_aYc8-U.

"'The Complete List No. 4.'" *TheCompleti.st*. Accessed October 5, 2025. http://thecompleti.st/no4.

"'Contemporary Rape-Revenge Films (2013–2019): Trauma, Gender, and the Female Gaze.'" Master's thesis, Chapman University, 2019. *Digital Commons @ Chapman University*. https://digitalcommons.chapman.edu/cgi/viewcontent.cgi?article=1025&context=film_studies_theses#:~:text=Contemporary%20rape%2Drevenge%20films%20(2013,I%20found%20it.

"'The Conjuring Universe Movies in Order.'" *Good Housekeeping*. Accessed October 5, 2025. https://www.goodhousekeeping.com/entertainment/movies/g36730886/the-conjuring-movies-in-order/.

"'Corman, Lovecraft, and American International Pictures.'" *The Solute*. Accessed October 5, 2025. https://www.the-solute.com/corman-lovecraft-and-american-international-pictures/#:~:text=While%20the%20AIP%20films%20are,Case%20of%20Charles%20Dexter%20Ward.

"'Count Dracula: 13 Alternate Versions.'" *Monster Complex*. Accessed October 5, 2025. https://www.monstercomplex.com/blog/count-dracula-13-alternate-versions#:~:text=Although%20not%20the%20first%20horror,historically%2C%20or%20aesthetically%20significant.%E2%80%9D.

"'The Creeper: Universal's Forgotten Monster.'" *Herald-Mail Media*. Last modified July 10, 2022. https://www.heraldmailmedia.com/story/lifestyle/columns/2022/07/10/universals-the-creeper-was-hagerstown-native-rondo-hatton/65365369007/#:~:text=But%20toward%20the%20end%20of,Creeper%2C%20were%20released%20posthumously.

"'The Creeping Flesh (1973).'" *Monster Kid Classic Horror Forum (Tapatalk)*. Accessed October 5, 2025. https://tapatalk.com/groups/monsterkidclassichorrorforum/the-creeping-flesh-1973-t53180.html#:~:text=Quite%20frankly%2C%20this%20is%20a,any%20criticisms%20of%20plot%20absurdities.

"'The Crime of Doctor Crespi (1935).'" *The Last Drive-In*. Accessed October 5, 2025. https://thelastdrivein.com/category/classic-horror-2/the-crime-of-doctor-crespi-1935/.

"'Criminally Insane' (1975)." *Moria: Science-Fiction, Horror and Fantasy Film Review*. Accessed October 5, 2025. https://www.moriareviews.com/horror/criminally-insane-1975.htm#:~:text=Criminally%20Insane%202%20(1987)%20was,Gers%20in%20the%20title%20role.

"'Daily Dig: *Mutant* (1984).'" *Morbidly Beautiful*. Accessed October 5, 2025. https://morbidlybeautiful.com/daily-dig-mutant-1984/.

"'Ded Movies Blog: *Night Monster* (1942).'" *DED Movies Blog*. Last modified October 10, 2020. https://dedmoviesblog.wordpress.com/2020/10/10/31-nights-night-monster/#:~:text=As%20I%20discussed%20with%20The%20Wolf%20Man,better%20half%20of%20its%20original%20double%20bill.

"'Def by Temptation (1990) — A Hidden Gem of Early-'90s Horror.'" *Cinapse*. Last modified November 2018. https://cinapse.co/2018/11/def-by-temptation-a-hidden-gem-of-early-90s-horror/#:~:text=Def%20by%20Temptation%20lives%20somewhere,character%20development%20coming%20into%20this.

"'Die, Monster, Die! (1965).'" *Surgeons of Horror*. Last modified September 28, 2024. https://surgeonsofhorror.com/2024/09/28/die-monster-die-1965/#:~:text=Even%20in%20his%20later%20years,story%20meanders%20through%20its%20setup.

"'Dirk Manning Resurrects Lost Silent Film *London After Midnight* as a Graphic Novel.'" *Current Magazine (eCurrent)*. Accessed October 5, 2025. https://www.ecurrent.com/film/dirk-manning-resurrects-lost-silent-film-london-after-midnight-as-a-graphic-novel/#:~:text=Novel%20%2D%20Current%20Magazine-,Dirk%20Manning%20Resurrects%20Lost%20Silent%20Film%20%E2%80%9CLondon%20After%20Midnight%E2%80%9D%20as,Photo%20courtesy%20of%20Manning.

"'Donovan's Brain' (1953)." *Sci-Fi History Haven*. Last modified February 15, 2016. https://scifist.wordpress.com/2016/02/15/donovans-brain/#:~:text=This%20wasn't%20even%20the,in%2Da%2Dvat%20trope.

"'Dracula, Prince of Darkness.'" *We Are Cursed to Live in Interesting Times* (blog). Last modified December 2016. https://wearecursedtoliveininterestingtimes.blogspot.com/2016/12/dracula-prince-of-darkness.html#:~:text=HAMMER'S%20DRACULA%20SERIES:%20*%20THE%20HORROR%20OF,LEGEND%20OF%20THE%207%20GOLDEN%20VAMPIRES%20(1974).

"'*Eden Lake* and the British Hoodie Horror Genre: How They Reinforced Policies to Demonise the Working Class.'" *The Conversation*. Accessed October 5, 2025. https://theconversation.com/eden-lake-and-the-british-hoodie-horror-genre-how-they-reinforced-policies-to-demonise-the-working-class-168701#:~:text=Other%20%E2%80%9Choodie%20horrors%E2%80%9D%20followed%2C,class%20system%20to%20frighten%20audiences.

"'The Evil Bong Collection.'" *The Movie Database (TMDb)*. Accessed October 5, 2025. https://www.themoviedb.org/collection/467577-evil-bong-collection.

"'Every Movie in Godzilla's Showa Era Ranked.'" *MovieWeb*. Accessed October 5, 2025. https://movieweb.com/every-movie-in-godzilla-shwa-era-ranked/.

"'Explaining the Meaning Behind David Lynch's *Eraserhead*.'" *Far Out Magazine.* Accessed October 5, 2025. https://faroutmagazine.co.uk/explaining-the-meaning-behind-david-lynchs-eraserhead/#:~:text=Put%20simply%2C%20Eraserhead%20is%20an,triumphs%20within%20his%20own%20subconscious.

"'Films: *Spirits of the Dead* (1968).'" *Weegie Midget Reviews.* Last modified October 28, 2024. https://weegiemidget.wordpress.com/2024/10/28/films-spirits-of-the-dead-tales-of-mystery-and-imagination-tales-of-mystery-1968/#:~:text=Spirits%20of%20the%20Dead%20%E2%80%A2,by%20an%20acclaimed%20European%20director.

"'A Flower in the Mud: Val Lewton's *Isle of the Dead*.'" *The Criterion Collection.* Accessed October 5, 2025. https://www.criterion.com/current/posts/5998-a-flower-in-the-mud-val-lewton-s-isle-of-the-dead#:~:text=Producer%20Val%20Lewton%20was%20inspired,less%20sinister%20look%20than%20usual.

"'Frankenstein and the Monster from Hell' (1974)." *Moria: Science-Fiction, Horror and Fantasy Film Review.* Accessed October 5, 2025. https://www.moriareviews.com/horror/frankenstein-and-the-monster-from-hell-1974.htm#:~:text=During%20this%20time%2C%20they%20remade%20Curse%20with,effort%2C%20Frankenstein%20and%20the%20Monster%20from%20Hell

"'Fright Night (Franchise).'" *Wikiwand.* Accessed October 5, 2025. https://www.wikiwand.com/en/articles/Fright_Night_(franchise).

"'From Beyond and the Legacy of Body Horror.'" *Game Rant.* Accessed October 5, 2025. https://gamerant.com/lovecraft-from-beyond-body-horror/#:~:text=From%20Beyond%20is%20based%20on,Beyond%22%20is%20a%20short%20story.

"'*Ganja & Hess* (1973).'" *Film Freedonia.* Last modified September 3, 2015. https://filmfreedonia.com/2015/09/03/ganja-hess-1973/#:~:text=Ganja%20&%20Hess's%20revival%20owes%20much,curation%20as%20well%20as%20narrative.

"'The Ghost Breakers (1940) Review.'" *Cinema Retro.* Accessed October 5, 2025. https://www.cinemaretro.com/index.php?/archives/11715-REVIEW-THE-GHOST-BREAKERS-1940-STARRING-BOB-HOPE-AND-PAULETTE-GODDARD;-KINO-LORBER-BLU-RAY-RELEASE.html#:~:text=Based%20on%20the%201909%20stage,Says%2C%20which%20starred%20Fred%20MacMurray.

"'Godzilla vs. Hedorah 2: The Lost Sequel.'" *Toho Kingdom.* Accessed October 5, 2025. https://www.tohokingdom.com/cutting_room/godzilla_vs_hedorah_2.html#:~:text=This%20is%20the%20result%20of,director's%20chair%20for%20the%20movie.

"'The Gorgon (1964).'" *Pete Worrall Film Blog.* Accessed October 5, 2025. https://www.peteworrall.com/the-gorgon-19642495582d#:~:text=May%20contain%20spoilers,nice%20move%2C%20in%20my%20opinion.

"'Guilty Pleasures: *Sssssss* (1973).'" *Thrilling Days of Yesteryear.* Last modified August 1, 2017. https://thrillingdaysofyesteryear.wordpress.com/2017/08/01/guilty-pleasures-sssssss-1973/#:~:text=The%20special%20make%2Dup%20effects,movie%20is%20particularly%20memorable!).

"'Hammers' *Frankenstein* Films Ranked.'" *We've Got Back Issues.* Last modified October 29, 2024. https://wevegotbackissues.com/2024/10/29/hammers-frankenstein-films-ranked/.

"'The Hammer Legacy.'" *Hammer Films Official Website.* Accessed October 5, 2025. https://hammerfilms.com/pages/the-hammer-legacy#:~:text=Hammer%20(%20Hammer%20Films%20)%20's%20undoubted,of%20both%20Peter%20Cushing%20and%20Christopher%20Lee.

"'He Never Died (2015) Review.'" *The Screen Slut.* Accessed October 5, 2025. https://thescreenslut.com/he-never-died-review/#:~:text=Unfortunately%20for%20fans%20of%20He,unfortunately%20it%20has%20been%20scrapped.

"'Head of the Family (1996).'" *Film Nerd.* Accessed October 5, 2025. https://www.film-nerd.com/head-of-the-family-1996/#:~:text=Synopsis,store%20for%20him%20and%20Loretta.

"'The House of Fear (1939).'" *Classic Monsters of the Movies.* Accessed October 5, 2025. https://www.classic-monsters.com/the-house-fear-universal-1939/#:~:text=Universal's%20often%2Doverlooked%20The%20House,William%20Gargan%20and%20Irene%20Hervey).

"'The Howling Movies: Correct Viewing Order.'" *SlashFilm.* Accessed October 5, 2025. https://www.slashfilm.com/1583739/correct-order-to-watch-the-howling-movies/.

"IMDB News: *The New Film Is a Set in a Metropolitan City Post-Coronavirus Pandemic.*" *IMDb.com.* Accessed October 5, 2025. https://imdb.com/title/tt0070656/news/#:~:text=Variety%20details%2C%20%20"The%20new%20film%20is%20a,set%20in%20a%20metropolitan%20city%20post-coronavirus%20pandemic."

"'In *Vampire's Kiss*, We're Laughing with Nicolas Cage, Not at Him.'" *Flood Magazine.* Accessed October 5, 2025. https://floodmagazine.com/62164/in-vampires-kiss-were-laughing-with-nicolas-cage-not-at-him/#:~:text=called%20Vampire's%20Kiss..comic%20tragedy%20of%20yuppie%20culture.

"'The Incredible Shrinking Man (1957).'" *Moria: Science-Fiction, Horror and Fantasy Film Review.* Accessed October 5, 2025. https://www.moriareviews.com/sciencefiction/incredible-shrinking-man-1957.htm#:~:text=For%20a%20time%20afterwards%2C%20writer,Thompson%20as%20a%20miniaturised%20spy.

"'The Incomprehensible Horror of Lovecraft.'" *Josh Link Substack.* Accessed October 5, 2025. https://joshlink.substack.com/p/the-incomprehensible-horror-of-lovecraft.

"'The Incubus (1982).'" *Diary of a Movie Maniac.* Last modified March 18, 2015. https://diaryofamoviemaniac.wordpress.com/2015/03/18/the-incubus-1982/.

"'Innocent Blood (1992).'" *Midnight Only.* Last modified December 10, 2016. https://www.midnightonly.com/2016/12/10/innocent-blood-1992/#:~:text=The%20film%20was%20a%20hit,few%20degrees%20in%20different%20directions.

"'Inside David Cronenberg's *Videodrome*.'" *No Film School*. Last modified October 2013. https://nofilmschool.com/2013/10/behind-the-scenes-of-david-cronenbergs-videodrome#:~:text=As%20I%20mentioned%20before%2C%20Cronenberg's,%5Bvia%20TheSheik1976%20YouTube%20Channel%5D.

"'The Invisible Ray (1936).'" *This Island Rod*. Last modified October 2021. https://thisislandrod.blogspot.com/2021/10/the-invisible-ray-1936.html#:~:text=Accepting%20the%20judgement%2C%20Janos%20turns%20about%20and,power.%204D%20Man%20(1959)%20is%20a%20semi%2Dremake.

"'Island of Terror (1966).'" *We Are Cursed to Live in Interesting Times* (blog). Last modified September 2016. https://wearecursedtoliveininterestingtimes.blogspot.com/2016/09/island-of-terror.html.

"'It Came from Outer Space (1953) 3D Blu-ray Review.'" *Aurora's Gin Joint*. Last modified October 2, 2016. https://aurorasginjoint.com/2016/10/02/new-3-d-bluray-of-it-came-from-outer-space-1953-is-outstanding/.

"'John Carpenter's Apocalypse Trilogy: Why You Should Skip *Halloween* and Watch These Instead.'" *IGN*. Accessed October 5, 2025. https://www.ign.com/articles/skip-halloween-and-watch-john-carpenters-apocalypse-trilogy-instead.

"'John Carpenter's *Vampires* Franchise Order.'" *It's a Stampede!* Last modified August 16, 2025. https://itsastampede.com/2025/08/16/what-is-the-order-of-the-john-carpenter-vampires-movies/#:~:text=The%20Vampires%20movies%20in%20order&text=To%20date%20there%20are%20three,Vampires:%20The%20Turning%20(2005).

"'Larry Fessenden Announces *Trauma*, a Sequel to *Habit*.'" *Variety*. Last modified August 5, 2025. https://variety.com/2025/film/news/trauma-larry-fessenden-film-monsters-habit-sequel-1236478682/#:~:text=Trauma':%20Larry%20Fessenden's%20New,5%2C%202025%2011:00am%20PT.

"'LesardSic's *Son of Svengoolie* Film List.'" *Letterboxd*. Accessed October 5, 2025. https://letterboxd.com/lesardsic/list/every-film-featured-in-son-of-svengoolie/detail/page/5/.

"'Let the Right One In vs. Let Me In.'" *The Film Magazine*. Accessed October 5, 2025. https://www.thefilmagazine.com/let-the-right-one-in-vs-let-me-in/#:~:text=Two%20years%20later%2C%20Cloverfield%20director,and%20unease%20it%20maintains%20throughout.

"'London After Midnight and Mark of the Vampire.'" *Movies Silently*. Last modified February 20, 2015. https://moviessilently.com/2015/02/20/missing-silents-london-midnight-mark-vampire/#:~:text=Fake%20blood%2C%20wax%20teeth%20and,surprised%2C%20I%20suggest%20stopping%20here

"'The Man Who Could Cheat Death' (1959) Review." *ZekeFilm*. Last modified March 10, 2017. https://www.zekefilm.org/2017/03/10/blu-ray-review-the-man-who-could-cheat-death/#:~:text=Though%20those%20centered%20around%20Dr.%20Frankenstein%2C%20starring,Lee%2C%20play%20the%20hero%20for%20a%20change.

"'M (1931).'" *RogerEbert.com*. Accessed October 5, 2025. https://www.rogerebert.com/reviews/great-movie-m-1931#:~:text=Certainly%20%E2%80%9CM%E2%80%9D%20is%20a%20portrait,monster%20others%20see%20in%20him.

"'The Mad Ghoul (1943).'" *Classic Monsters of the Movies*. Accessed October 5, 2025. https://www.classic-monsters.com/the-mad-ghoul-universal-1943/.

"'The Magnetic Monster (1953).'" *Monster Movie Kid*. Last modified June 21, 2017. https://monstermoviekid.wordpress.com/2017/06/21/sci-fi-horrorfest-the-magnetic-monster-1953/.

"'The Man with the X-Ray Eyes: Roger Corman's Visionary Descent.'" *Nik Dirga*. Last modified March 27, 2025. https://nikdirga.com/2025/03/27/my-favourite-roger-corman-x-the-man-with-x-ray-eyes/#:~:text=But%20my%20favourite%20film%20Corman,but%20then%20things%20get%20%E2%80%A6%20darker.

"'Mario Bava's *Planet of the Vampires* (1965) Is a Clunky Yet Stylish Precursor to *Alien*.'" *Musings of a Middle-Aged Geek Blog*. Last modified April 23, 2024. https://musingsofamiddleagedgeek.blog/2024/04/23/retro-musings-mario-bavas-planet-of-the-vampires-1965-is-a-clunky-yet-stylish-precursor-to-alien/#:~:text=In%201965%2C%20famed%20gothic%20horror,directly%20influential%20as%20this%20film

"'Mark of the Vampire (1935).'" *Bela Dracula Lugosi Blog*. Accessed October 5, 2025. https://beladraculalugosi.wordpress.com/1935-mark-of-the-vampire/.

"'Mark of the Vampire (MGM, 1935).'" *Classic Monsters of the Movies*. Accessed October 5, 2025. https://www.classic-monsters.com/mark-of-the-vampire-mgm-1935/#:~:text=Mark%20of%20the%20Vampire%20(also,police%20to%20catch%20a%20murderer.

"Mark of the Vampire." *Wikipedia: The Free Encyclopedia*. Last modified 2025. https://en.wikipedia.org/wiki/Mark_of_the_Vampire#:~:text=Mark%20of%20the%20Vampire%20is,undead%20now%20plaguing%20the%20area.

"'The Meaning of "The New Flesh": Revisiting *Videodrome* and Its Remake.'" *Reactor Magazine*. Accessed October 5, 2025. https://reactormag.com/the-new-flesh-the-second-lemgvideodromelemg-remake/#:~:text=Which%20is%20why%20Cronenberg%20did,control%20of%20your%20own%20body.

"'Meatball Machine (2005).'" *Film Threat*. Accessed October 5, 2025. https://filmthreat.com/reviews/meatball-machine/#:~:text=Share,so%20they%20can%20do%20battle%E2%80%A6%E2%80%9D.\

"'The Midnight Meat Train.'" *TV Tropes*. Accessed October 5, 2025. https://tvtropes.org/pmwiki/pmwiki.php/Literature/TheMidnightMeatTrain#:~:text=Literature%20/%20The%20Midnight%20Meat%20Train&text=A%20horror%20short%20story%20by,of%20New%20York%20City...

"'Mill Creek Thrillers from the Vault: *The Return of the Vampire* (1943).'" *Bands About Movies*. Last modified March 2, 2023. https://bandsaboutmovies.com/2023/03/02/mill-creek-thrillers-from-the-vault-the-return-of-the-vampire-1943/#:~:text=EDITOR'S%20NOTE:%20This%20was%20originally,there%20can%20be%20a%20vampire.

"'The Monolith Monsters (1957).'" *Mana Pop*. Accessed October 5, 2025. https://manapop.com/film/the-monolith-monsters-1957-review/#:~:text=In%20the%201950s%20threats%20from%20outer%20space,and%20start%20the%20whole%20process%20over%20again.

"'The Mummy' (1959) Screening Description." *Agile Ticketing*. Accessed October 5, 2025. https://prod5.agileticketing.net/websales/pages/info.aspx?evtinfo=164934~d9433c7f-6460-4bb3-8c24-1659bd316930&epguid=f0ec0aed-4fbb-448d-8dcc-85035e7071ee&#:~:text=Description,British%20Hammer%20film%20The%20Mummy.

"'Murders in the Zoo (1933).'" *Contains Moderate Peril*. Last modified October 21, 2023. https://www.containsmoderateperil.com/blog/2023/10/21/murders-in-the-zoo-1933.

"'My Favourite Roger Corman Film: *The Man with the X-Ray Eyes*.'" *Nik Dirga*. Last modified March 27, 2025. https://nikdirga.com/2025/03/27/my-favourite-roger-corman-x-the-man-with-x-ray-eyes/#:~:text=But%20my%20favourite%20film%20Corman,but%20then%20things%20get%20%E2%80%A6%20darker.

"'Near Dark: Underrated Vampire Remake Finds New Life on TV.'" *MovieWeb*. Accessed October 5, 2025. https://movieweb.com/underrated-vampire-near-dark-tv-remake/#:~:text=Near%20Dark%2C%20one%20of%20the,plot%20synopsis%20goes%20as%20follows:.

"'Nosferatu: The Haunting History Behind the Unauthorized Classic.'" *SYFY Wire*. Accessed October 5, 2025. https://www.syfy.com/syfy-wire/the-haunting-history-behind-nosferatu#:~:text=Murnau's%20Nosferatu%20is%20an%20unauthorized,were%20ordered%20to%20be%20destroyed.

"Obscure British Horror Recommendations." *Reddit: r/horror*. Accessed October 5, 2025. https://www.reddit.com/r/horror/comments/gzd806/any_recommendations_for_obscure_british_horror/#:~:text=Other%20recommendations%20include:%20*%20**The%20Frighteners**%201972%2D1973,and%20Imagination**%20Classic%20Brit%20horror/thriller%20anthology%20programme.

"'Park Chan-wook's *Thirst* (2009).'" *Collider*. Accessed October 5, 2025. https://collider.com/park-chan-wook-thirst-movie/#:~:text=Why%20Park%20Chan%2Dwook%20Added,forced%20to%20kill%20to%20survive.

"'Persona' (1966)." *Ingmar Bergman Foundation*. Accessed October 5, 2025. https://www.ingmarbergman.se/en/production/persona.

"'Phantom of the Rue Morgue.'" *Warner Bros. Wiki (Fandom)*. Accessed October 5, 2025. https://warnerbros.fandom.com/wiki/Phantom_of_the_Rue_Morgue.

"'Planet of the Vampires.'" *Movies Films and Flix*. Accessed October 5, 2025. https://moviesfilmsandflix.com/tag/planet-of-the-vampires/#:~:text=Some%20concepts%20found%20here%2C%20and,that%2C%20it%20should%20be%20commended!.

"'Queen of Blood (1966): Retro Musings.'" *Musings of a Middle-Aged Geek Blog*. Last modified November 18, 2018. https://musingsofamiddleagedgeek.blog/2018/11/18/retro-musings-1966s-queen-of-blood-shares-plenty-of-hemoglobin-with-alien/#:~:text=%E2%80%9CQueen%20of%20Blood%2C%E2%80%9D%20directed,%E2%80%9CEasy%20Rider%E2%80%9D%20Dennis%20Hopper.

"'Ranking Every Johnny Depp / Tim Burton Role.'" *Halloween Year Round*. Last modified June 9, 2020. https://halloweenyearround.wordpress.com/2020/06/09/ranking-every-johnny-depp-tim-burton-role/#:~:text=Many%20directors%20are%20known%20for,very%20interesting%20or%20memorable%20one.

"'A Return to *Salem's Lot* (1987).'" *Obsessive Movie Nerd*. Last modified March 2, 2013. https://obsessivemovienerd.com/2013/03/02/the-cohen-case-files-a-return-to-salems-lot-1987/#:~:text=Before%20I%20can%20get%20into,the%20titular%20New%20England%20town.

"'A Return to *Salem's Lot* Streams on Max.'" *CBR (Comic Book Resources)*. Accessed October 5, 2025. https://www.cbr.com/a-return-salems-lot-stream-max/#:~:text=Salem's%20Lot%20Appears%20in%20Various,the%20events%20of%20Salem's%20Lot.

"'Review: *The Transfiguration* (2016) Is an Overlooked Vampire Drama That Cuts Like a Knife.'" *Horror Press*. Accessed October 5, 2025. https://horrorpress.com/reviews/8788/review-the-transfiguration-2016-is-an-overlooked-vampire-drama-that-cuts-like-a-knife/#:~:text=Reviews-,%5BReview%5D%20'The%20Transfiguration'%20(2016)%20Is%20an,Near%20Dark%2C%20Nosferatu%2C%20etc.

"Robert Bloch." *Fantastic Fiction*. Accessed October 5, 2025. https://www.fantasticfiction.com/b/robert-bloch/.

"Robert Bloch." *Letterboxd*. Accessed October 5, 2025. https://letterboxd.com/writer/robert-bloch/#:~:text=Strait%2DJacket%20(1964),Journey%20to%20Midnight%20(1968).

"'Ryan Coogler's *Sinners* Sequel Not Likely — No Planned Franchise.'" *MovieWeb*. Accessed October 5, 2025. https://movieweb.com/ryan-coogler-sinners-sequel-not-likely-no-planned-franchise/#:~:text=If%20you%20found%20yourself%20compelled,from%20multi%2Dpicture%20cinematic%20universes:.

"'Ryan Coogler's *Sinners* Sequel Moves Forward.'" *Deadline*. Last modified June 2025. https://deadline.com/2025/06/ryan-coogler-sinners-sequel-1236420856/#:~:text=Ryan%20Coogler%20(L);%20Michael,that%20was%20original%20and%20unique.%E2%80%9D.

"'The Saga of the Swamp Thing and the Horror of Humanity.'" *Medium (by N. Brehmer)*. Accessed October 5, 2025. https://nbrehmer.medium.com/saga-of-the-swamp-thing-and-the-horror-of-humanity-4d1b79db995e.

"'Scream, Pretty Peggy (1973).'" *Classic Horrors Club*. Last modified April 26, 2024. https://classichorrors.club/2024/04/26/scream-pretty-peggy-1973/#:~:text=Peggy%2C%20familiar%20with%20the%20house's,bed%20while%20her%20leg%20heals.

"'Shadow of the Vampire (2000).'" *Rotten Tomatoes*. Accessed October 5, 2025. https://www.rottentomatoes.com/m/shadow_of_the_vampire#:~:text=Movie%20Info,character%20and%20only%20at%20night.

"'She-Wolf of London and Similar Films.'" *Letterboxd*. Accessed October 5, 2025. https://letterboxd.com/film/she-wolf-of-london/similar/#:~:text=The%20Undying%20Monster%20(1942),You're%20Next%20(2011).

"'Stake Land II (*The Stakelander*) Announced.'" *Entertainment Weekly (EW)*. Last modified June 21, 2016. https://ew.com/article/2016/06/21/stake-land-sequel-stakelander/#:~:text=It%20was%20announced%20Tuesday%20that,Kristina%20Hughes%2C%20and%20Steven%20Williams.

"'The Strange Door (1951).'" *Alex on Film*. Last modified November 4, 2016. https://alexonfilm.com/2016/11/04/the-strange-door-1951/#:~:text=delivered%20anything%20less.-,*.,her%20father%20is%20long%20dead.

"'The Story of Krampus.'" *Fear Columbus.* Accessed October 5, 2025. https://fearcolumbus.com/krampus/the-story-of-krampus/#:~:text=The%20roots%20of%20the%20Krampus,children%20receive%20gifts%20and%20sweets.

"'Subspecies (Film Series).'" *Wikiwand.* Accessed October 5, 2025. https://www.wikiwand.com/en/articles/Subspecies_(film_series).

"'Summer of Fear (1978).'" *Last Movie Outpost.* Last modified October 2024. https://lastmovieoutpost.com/retro-review-summer-of-fear-1978/#:~:text=Wrenage,Let's%20find%20out!.

"'Sundown: The Vampire in Retreat (1989).'" *Musings from a Cursed World* (blog). Last modified December 2014. https://wearecursedtoliveininterestingtimes.blogspot.com/2014/12/sundown-vampire-in-retreat.html#:~:text=Sundown-%20Vampire%20in%20Retreat%20(technically,he%20was%20talking%20about%20there.

"'Sundown: The Vampire in Retreat' Blu-ray Review." *Psychotronic Cinema.* Last modified November 19, 2021. https://psychotroniccinema.com/2021/11/19/sundown-the-vampire-in-retreat-blu-ray-review/#:~:text=Sundown:%20The%20Vampire%20In%20Retreat%20is%20a%20film%20directed%20by,distributor's%20legal%20and%20financial%20issues.

"'This Israeli Film's Theatrical Premiere Was a First for the Nation's Horror Scene.'" *Ynet News.* Last modified 2025. https://www.ynetnews.com/culture/article/rysfmugfh#:~:text=The%20first%20theatrical%20show%20premiered,at%20the%20Tribeca%20Film%20Festival.

"'Tropedia: Troma.'" *Fandom.* Accessed October 5, 2025. https://tropedia.fandom.com/wiki/Troma.

"'Twenty Circus and Carnival Horror Movies.'" *Creepy Catalog.* Accessed October 5, 2025. https://creepycatalog.com/20-circus-and-carnival-horror-movies/.

"'Twenty Essential Psycho-Biddy Films.'" *Creepy Catalog.* Accessed October 5, 2025. https://creepycatalog.com/20-essential-psycho-biddy-films/#:~:text=More%20psycho%2Dbiddy%20films%E2%80%A6,attic%20of%20her%20decaying%20mansion.

"'The Uncanny' Blu-ray Review: A Purrfect Cat-Centric Horror Anthology." *Bloody Disgusting.* Accessed October 5, 2025. https://bloody-disgusting.com/reviews/3572116/blu-ray-review-uncanny-purrfect-cat-centric-horror-anthology/#:~:text=%5BBlu%2Dray%20Review%5D%20The%20Uncanny%20is%20a%20Purrfect,about%20the%20old%20grindhouse%20trailers%20is%20present.

"'Universal's Kharis Mummy Movies.'" *Black Gate.* Last modified June 10, 2017. https://www.blackgate.com/2017/06/10/universals-kharis-mummy-movies/.

"'Vamp (1986).'" *Moria: Science-Fiction, Horror and Fantasy Film Review.* Accessed October 5, 2025. https://www.moriareviews.com/horror/vamp-1986.htm#:~:text=Vamp%20was%20one%20of%20a,how%20dated%20it%20has%20become.

"'The Vampire's Ghost (1945).'" *Horror and Sons.* Last modified April 8, 2024. https://horrorandsons.com/2024/04/08/the-vampires-ghost-1945-movie-review/#:~:text=The%20Vampire's%20Ghost%20is%20an,as%201951's%20Flight%20To%20Mars.

"'The Vampire's Ghost.'" *DanDayJr35 Blog.* Last modified December 2017. https://dandayjr35.blogspot.com/2017/12/the-vampires-ghost.html#:~:text=The%20rest%20of%20the%20cast,had%20never%20seen%20it%20before.

"'Vampyr (1932).'" *Cody's Film and TV Blog.* Last modified October 2022. https://codysfilmandtvblog.blogspot.com/2022/10/vampire-flicks-vampyr-1932.html#:~:text=There%2C%20he%20and%20writer%20Christen,be%20his%20final%20film%2C%20Gertrud.

"'Van Helsing Movie Franchise.'" *MovieWeb.* Accessed October 5, 2025. https://movieweb.com/van-helsing-movie-franchise/#:~:text=Universal%20Pictures%20was%20so%20confident,have%20been%20an%20exciting%20sequel.

"'Vincent Price: *The Last Man on Earth.*'" *Vault of Thoughts.* Last modified September 23, 2020. https://www.vaultofthoughts.com/2020/09/23/vincent-price-last-man-on-earth/#:~:text=Richard%20Matheson's%20seminal%20post%2Dapocalyptic,the%20spirit%20of%20the%20novel.

"'War-Gods of the Deep (1965) a.k.a. *City Under the Sea.*'" *Cinema Retro.* Accessed October 5, 2025. https://www.cinemaretro.com/index.php?/archives/12720-STREAMING-REVIEW-WAR-GODS-OF-THE-DEEP-AKA-CITY-UNDER-THE-SEA1965-STARRING-VINCENT-PRICE,-TAB-HUNTER-AND-SUSAN-HART-AMAZON-PRIME.html#:~:text=Nicholson%20and%20Arkoff%20kept%20mining,%22Out%20of%20the%20Past%22.

"'War-Gods of the Deep (1965).'" *Cinema Retro.* Accessed October 5, 2025. https://www.cinemaretro.com/index.php?/archives/12720-STREAMING-REVIEW-WAR-GODS-OF-THE-DEEP-AKA-CITY-UNDER-THE-SEA1965-STARRING-VINCENT-PRICE,-TAB-HUNTER-AND-SUSAN-HART-AMAZON-PRIME.html#:~:text=Nicholson%20and%20Arkoff%20kept%20mining,%22Out%20of%20the%20Past%22.

"'The Wasp Woman (1959).'" *Forgotten Filmcast.* Last modified October 28, 2012. https://forgottenfilmcast.wordpress.com/2012/10/28/the-wasp-woman/#:~:text=In%201958%20the%20world%20first,of%20%E2%80%9CThe%20Wasp%20Woman?%E2%80%9D.

"'The Wasp Woman (1959).'" *Forgotten Filmcast.* Accessed October 5, 2025. https://forgottenfilmcast.wordpress.com/2012/10/28/the-wasp-woman/#:~:text=In%201958%20the%20world%20first,of%20%E2%80%9CThe%20Wasp%20Woman?%E2%80%9D.

"'Week in American Gothic: Revisiting the Forgotten TV Horror.'" *Kinemalogue.* Last modified July 2024. https://www.kinemalogue.net/2024/07/american-gothic-week-in-case-any-of-you.html.

"'Wendigo: Scariest Films Featuring the Mythical Beast, Ranked.'" *Screen Rant.* Accessed October 5, 2025. https://screenrant.com/scariest-movies-featuring-wendigo-ranked/#:~:text=1%20Dark%20Was%20The%20Night,attempts%20at%20finding%20the%20beast.

"'White Zombie (1932).'" *Classic Monsters of the Movies.* Accessed October 5, 2025. https://www.classic-monsters.com/white-zombie-halperin-1932/#:~:text=White%20Zombie%20was%20shot%20in,presentation%20and%20appallingly%20hissy%20soundtrack.

"'Wikipedia: List of Vampire Films.'" *Wikipedia: The Free Encyclopedia.* Last modified 2025. https://en.wikipedia.org/wiki/List_of_vampire_films..

About the Author

Sarah M. Melland

Raised in Altoona, Wisconsin, Sarah Melland was the kid who won every writing award her schools could invent. She went on to study Film Production at the University of Wisconsin–Milwaukee before graduating Summa Cum Laude in Mass Communications from Arizona State University. Her talent earned her creative writing scholarships across multiple states, but it was her lifelong obsession with storytelling that shaped her into the force she is today.

Her work spans every medium capable of making you feel something: books, films, blogs, and empires. She's the author of *The Breakup Band-Aid*, *Practicing Love*, *A Single Girl's Guide to IVF*, *Jane Austen: Unabridged*, *A Single Girl's Ultimate Bucket List*, *The Anthology of Cinema* series, *The Red Flag Translator*, and the groundbreaking true-crime dissection *Pattern Interrupted: How the Karen Read Trial Broke the Narrative Machine*. Each project reflects her signature fusion of intellect, emotional truth, and dark humor.

As Founder & CEO of Ripe Melland Media, Melland turned betrayal into blueprint. After co-writing a raw, award-buzzed breakup film that drew attention from Oscar-nominated producers, only for her writing credit to be nearly stolen, she did what every underestimated woman should: she built her own studio. That moment of reinvention became the origin story of Ripe Melland Media, a white-label script and content house revolutionizing how screenplays are sold, credited, and produced.

Since then, Melland has been contracted to write courtroom thrillers, biographical dramas, and adaptations, including the upcoming true story of a UFC fighter's escape from abuse and rise to the American dream. Each script is built with the precision of *Save the Cat*, the depth of the 8x8 story grid, and the narrative control of Robert McKee's *Story*, but always filtered through her own instinct for emotional truth and audience psychology.

Before launching her media company, Melland served as the Director of Marketing for the largest boat-lift manufacturer in the world, where she somehow made industrial steel look sexy. Prior to that, she honed her voice at a leading Florida advertising agency, crafting brand campaigns that turned small clients into household names. Those experiences forged her rare ability to merge art with commerce. A skill that now fuels her expanding creative empire.

Through YourDatingUnExpert.com, Melland became the unapologetic voice of women burned out by modern dating. The platform fuses therapy and entertainment through savage humor, viral video series (*TrashTV+*), and her upcoming book *The Dating Survival Bible*. She's not here to coach you, she's here to dissect the psychology behind your worst romantic decisions and make you laugh until you accidentally spit wine on your phone.

At her core, Melland is a film historian and futurist, as fluent in German Expressionism and Hammer Gothic as she is in streaming-era horror and AI-generated cinema. Her *Anthology of Cinema* series spanning *Horror, Romance, Comedy, and Beyond* is both a love letter to the evolution of film and a blueprint for the next generation of storytellers. Her voice blends academic precision with poetic grit, bridging the language of criticism and creation.

In every project, from screenplays to cultural analysis, Melland's goal remains the same: to build worlds that outlast her and rewrite the systems that once tried to silence her.

Be the first to know when the next volume drops:

www.ingramcontent.com/pod-product-compliance
Lightning Source LLC
Chambersburg PA
CBHW081651120626
46550CB00010B/2862